FAMILIES at Risk

*A guide to understanding and protecting
children and care providers involved
in out-of-home or adoptive care.*

By Jodee Kulp

*To laugh
   is to risk
appearing the fool.*

*To weep
   is to risk
appearing sentimental.*

*To reach out for another
   is to risk
involvement.*

*To expose feelings
   is to risk
exposing your true self.*

*To love
   is to risk
not being loved
in return.*

*To hope
   is to risk
despair.*

*To try
   is to risk
failure.*

Charles Swindoll

BETTER ENDINGS NEW BEGINNINGS BOOKS
BY JODEE KULP

JOURNEY TO LIFE

FAMILIES AT RISK

Families at Risk
Copyright ©1993 by Jodee Kulp

Printing History
First published July 1993
Second published January 1994

94 95 96 97   10 9 8 7 6 5 4 3 2

Published by:
Better Endings New Beginnings
119 North Fourth Street, Suite 401
Minneapolis, Minnesota 55401
(612) 341-9870   Facsimile: 337-5104

Printed in United States of America

Library of Congress Catalog Card Number: 93-73076

ISBN 0-9637072-0-5

For Love of Joseph
and all the
special children who have
filled our collective hearts.

This book is dedicated to all surrogate and foster families who strive to provide safe and loving services to children who need care.

That task requires us to understand not only our children, but also an immensely complicated, often contradictory, and at times hostile, social welfare system. The rewards and difficulties are many. We learn to expect both.

*If and when **you** face allegations of abuse or neglect, understand that your association and/or support group will neither believe nor disbelieve your case.*

It's your own battle.

This book will provide tools, knowledge, and access to the system. You'll need all three to continue your lives in a positive, healthy direction.

Preface

*The Chinese symbol for the word **crisis** has two meanings—*
danger and opportunity.
In English, crisis means "turning point."

A crisis can be a turning point in life. Confronted by danger adults can usually seek opportunity. On the other hand, children who are overpunished, abused, or neglected are in crisis regardless of the adult's situation. For these children there is little opportunity in crisis—they must survive the danger.

—Protecting children is the heart of Families at Risk—
Maltreatment of a child is wrong.

What maltreatment is and how it is defined varies. Throughout this book I hope to add clarity to this vital issue and insight into the complex and often conflicting realities of children and families dealing with loss, previous experiences with maltreatment, and out-of-home care. I hope to provide tools to protect children and keep families healthy if faced with allegations of child maltreatment and tools that promote honest communication and effective investigation.

I begin with *"Who's Watching The Children?"* This section is significant and sets the stage for the reader to understand the reality of being a child living in out-of-home care. Sections 4 and 5 add insight:

Section 4—Sometimes Reality Hurts
— Chapter 9—*"Evacuation . . . for Safety or Protocol?"*
— Chapter 10—*"Who's Kidding? It's OK for Our Kids to be Different."*

Section 5—The Fine Line . . .Discipline, Punishment, Maltreatment, or Abuse
— Chapter 11—*"Discipline or Punishment"*
— Chapter 12—*"Defining Child Maltreatment"*
— Chapter 13—*"Guidelines for Care Providers"*

Professional parenting and child welfare system issues run throughout the text. It may appear at times I advocate for adults or system rights. Neither receives my true advocacy. As adults, we may want to excuse our behavior or blame the child when the real solution lies in our understanding and dealing with the child's crisis. The power of control is with the adult; not with the child. In most cases, adults have the capacity to make a choice.

In a licensed professional parenting family, an allegation of child maltreatment is tragic.
***If true**, the parents have failed the children.*
***If false**, the ensuing investigation is extremely traumatic for everyone.*

Thousands of families operate unaware of the potential for allegations against them. *Families At Risk* is written for them, their children, and the professionals with whom they interact. I have met scores of families who have received allegations, have listened to their questions, and sought the answers—answers to questions not previously asked because of the inevitable trauma that results when wounds are opened and examined.

Families at Risk *is based on these premises:*

— Children must be safe—emotionally, physically, and psychologically—while in surrogate, foster, and adoptive care.

— Children and families are traumatized by being moved *abruptly* in response to abuse allegations.

— *All* families—guilty or innocent—are at risk of allegations.

— *All* family members—guilty or innocent—suffer during investigation.

— Agencies may make decisions to remove children without all pertinent and objective information regarding the child's or care provider family's needs.

— Care providers lack understandable up-to-date information regarding agency and government procedure, the system of child welfare, a child's background and the way the system works during an investigation.

— Few support services are available to providers under investigation.

It is my hope that the present child welfare system can change positively to provide safety for both the children and the parents caring for these children.

Many foster parents pay a high price for a license to love. Caring for other people's children is a high risk profession. Every year 30,000 foster families give up and close their doors to kids who need love, hope, and homes. The complexity of children and a puzzling, bureaucratic, sometimes arbitrary, but generally well-meaning, foster care system contribute to the loss. But fear of or actual abuse allegations probably tops the list.

In fact, over the past four years (1988 - 1991), the Minnesota Department of Human Services has received 542 reports of suspected maltreatment in Minnesota's foster homes. Of the 117 cases (22%) substantiated, less than 5% resulted in license revocation.

In substantiated cases, children are saved. But in unsubstantiated cases, families are still traumatized, marriages and jobs still threatened, tax money still wasted. And worst of all children are still hurt. A high risk profession, indeed.

The Minneapolis Star Tribune's timely series, Licensed to Abuse, presented a riveting and disturbing picture of a child welfare system in desperate need of reform. *The victims aren't statistics. They are our children.* Protecting them—as well as the great majority of the 100,000 foster families in America who share a deep commitment to making the system work—requires us to understand two often underemphasized points.

1. Foster children and families find themselves in the uncharted territory of new experiences and old secrets.

Not all children enter foster care as victims of abuse and neglect. Some come from loving families in the midst of medical or financial hardship. Many others have physical or emotional problems that simply can't be handled at home. But in every case, foster children and older adopted children carry their past—often including deep feelings of grief, loss, lack of trust, and confusion—into their new family situations.

Foster and surrogate care providers are in the unique position of professionally parenting other people's children.

What is appropriate behavior in the primary families may fall under scrutiny when you are raising children who belong to another set of parents.

Allegation and investigation is an appropriate way to uncover maltreatment of children; however, what is seen from outside the family as appropriate intervention may appear from the inside as inappropriate.

Professional parents must understand that an allegation of maltreatment of children is very real and to be expected.

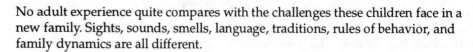

No adult experience quite compares with the challenges these children face in a new family. Sights, sounds, smells, language, traditions, rules of behavior, and family dynamics are all different.

The resulting problems—many predictable and natural enough—are all the tougher for parents to diagnose and solve because rules of confidentiality often prohibit social services from offering straightforward explanations about a child's past life experiences.

2. *Allegations of abuse in foster and adoptive families can be expected. Even the best and most experienced parents are vulnerable to reports of suspected maltreatment.*

Recognizing child abuse and neglect is an important first step in preventing it. However, discriminating child behavior resulting from a history of maltreatment and actual present maltreatment is difficult. Allegations are common because of the behaviors and complicated histories of surrogate, foster, and adoptive children. Society often does not understand the reality of raising children with compounded losses who are coping with previous experiences of abuse and neglect.

Allegations against surrogate, foster, and adoptive parents come in two forms—*"with merit"* and *"without merit."* An allegation with merit simply means that there is reason to believe that some kind of dysfunction or incident has occurred in the family which could be maltreatment to children. Allegations without merit can come from a variety of sources. In some cases, false allegations are made by a child who is angry over a particular incident; by a birth parent who wants the child returned; by a vindictive person from the foster/adoptive parents' past; or another concerned individual who doesn't understand the child's behavior.

The task of separating the real from perceived child abuse is tricky and confusing. Some common examples include:

— A grieving child will often appear withdrawn—not from abuse, but from sadness.

— A previously neglected child who has learned to beg, steal, or forage for food in neighborhood trash cans may continue that behavior in foster and adoptive care.

— A previously sexually abused or exploited child—hungry for attention or affection—may behave provocatively in public, abuse other children at home or at school, or inappropriately touch others.

— A previously physically abused child may believe that attention comes only from hurting others. Bullying, arson, vandalism, and cruelty to animals are common among these children—and sometimes defeat even the most patient of surrogate parents—while the root cause remains a deeply repressed secret.

— A previously maltreated child may have repressed memories of past maltreatment and experience flashbacks. Although the actual maltreatment involved previous caregivers, these flashback memories may be misdirected against new, safe care providers.

Confidentiality laws and respect for the child often prohibit providing concerned outsiders with a true explanation. Even care providers may lack information because of confidentiality and legal requirements. Make no mistake: confidentiality has its place in the child welfare system. The point is that these regulations sometimes hurt rather than help. Without adequate knowlege of a child's past, misinterpretation, miscommunication, and harm can be done to both children and families.

In any search for truth, no stone can remain unturned. I decided to stand in the middle of the child welfare system and overturn stones.

I found the bigger the stones were, the more they needed to be moved.
Author

Even when allegations are proved false, family trauma still occurs. The point, of course, is that neither the allegation nor the investigation should be abusive in itself.

A complete professional investigation is the
most important component of the outcome of the allegation.
An abusive investigation is never warranted.

The fact is American children continue to be abused and children can suffer cycle after cycle of maltreatment as they are moved from family to family. Professionals, along with surrogate parents across the nation, want to prevent abusive parents from caring for these children.

— Our Story—

Our family has cared for children living away from their homes since 1979. Some were foster children. Others came as exchange students. Initially we worked with teenagers. In 1986, a five-month-old baby girl whose mother had died arrived. Through adoption April became a permanent member of our family. Additional children sprinkled into our lives through respite care. Then in the fall of 1989, our social worker called to ask if we would consider caring for another child. Joseph (not his real name) arrived shortly after. This tiny refugee, whisked suddenly into our lives, grew happy, strong, and healthy. Then, as suddenly as he had arrived— he was gone. As a foster child, it was expected that Joseph would be leaving our home. Reunification between birth children and their families is our foster parenting goal. It was not expected that he would leave with three hours notice and remain in foster care for three additional years.

An allegation was made against our home. An investigation ensued and Joseph was removed. The allegation had nothing to do with Joseph or how we cared for him. Joseph, through no fault of his own, was again losing a family he loved. He was being forced to start over, without warning or preparation—with another family, in another home. This move for Joseph was significant. He would never again be the same little boy we had worked so hard to reach. New breakages were added to an already fragile child.

The child welfare system is complex. Laws vary from state to state. Procedures vary from county to county and agency to agency. Individual departments may interpret the same law differently.

The process of writing this book has been amazing. When I went searching for information about allegations and investigations, I naively thought it would be an easy task. It wasn't. After our own investigation was completed and our license was revoked, I wanted answers. I attended the University of Minnesota foster parenting program in demonstrated competency and chose *"Understanding Allegations and the Procedures Involved"* as my final paper.

My goal was to create a working tool for other foster parents facing similar situations. I thought a brochure would be adequate. But, after meeting with the executives of the Minnesota Foster Care Association and discussing the effects that abuse allegations and investigative procedures have on surrogate, foster, and adoptive homes, I decided that a brochure would hardly be a start. Together we built an outline for this book. Together we called and met with professionals in the adoptive and foster care system. We accumulated and assessed mountains of information. In the acknowledgments section you will meet the many people who have contributed their expertise and knowledge to the process and contents of this book. I am very grateful to them.

The phone rang several times that day in the spring of 1990:

> *"In 1984, you received counseling that we would like to research. I'll be right over to get the releases to check it out. It's just routine."*
> **Licensing Worker**

> *"Someone named *** is causing you big trouble— I'd be careful."*
> **Counselor**

The most devastating call came days later:

> *"It looks like it's substantiated and going under investigation. We can assume that Joseph will be moving shortly. You can appeal it when it gets to the state level. You'll receive a certified letter after they have investigated and made their decisions."*
> **Licensing Worker**

—Parenting Terms Interchange—

Because I am directing this book to surrogate, foster, and adoptive parents, some of the terms used will differ from the medical and psychological words you may be used to. I do not do this out of disrespect to the people who have laid the foundations; I have simply adjusted language to more clearly convey the challenge of parenting surrogate, foster, or adoptive children.

Personalities, family dynamics, and developmental age all vary with the surrogate children we care for. The physical age of a child may have nothing to do with the child's emotional, intellectual, or developmental age. This book does not deal with specific developmental issues. Additional research by the reader will be necessary to choose appropriate responses for individual situations.

I have tried to be impartial to the gender of individuals and in most cases I have used *"kid, kids, child, children"* when referring to the young people involved. In some cases, these pronouns do not accurately work in the context of the paragraph. When this happens, you will find female or male pronouns used randomly and either gender reference would be appropriate.

Children in care have a number of significant adults in their lives who can be referred to as parents. I have chosen to use the term *"parent"* when referring to birth, natural, or original parent. To the child, these people will always be *"their parents,"* and I believe it is appropriate to maintain that focus for the reader. In some cases, where clarity is necessary, I have used the term birth, primary, natural, or custodial parents.

The other significant adults caring for a child most often will be referred to as *"care providers."* This is a generic term used to reflect the wide range of adults providing care—relatives, foster parents, adoptive parents. I also use professional parents, foster parents, surrogate parents, and kinship caregivers when those terms apply more directly to the specific parenting group.

The word *"family"* also becomes very significant because it may not be the caregiver's concept of family. A broader view of family is needed for the child in care and may include gang members, friends, or neighbors. Therefore one must look at what a family provides versus how it looks. The functions of a family are to provide security, support, and continuity of relationships. In addition, the family empowers individuals within it by providing nurturing, social values, education, self-esteem, belonging, and vision.

The term foster family *"home"* has been avoided as often as possible. The definition of the word home includes "the place where one likes to be or feels safe" and "the place of one's origin." These two definitions do not always apply in foster family life. The word home many not represent the same thing to the professional and the child. *To the child—home is where the heart is.*

—Laws and Policies Get Complicated—

Throughout this book I have used Minnesota statutes and rules as examples of laws, public laws, and interpretation that are written to protect children and families. The federal laws and Minnesota state statutes and rules are current as of May 10, 1992. Laws constantly change and differ from state to state. *It is crucial to read and understand your own laws, as well as the proposed legislation affecting your family. Ignorance is not an excuse.*

In addition, it is important to understand that Minnesota has a state-regulated, county-administered system. This is significantly different from a state-

---

More calls:

"What about April, our adopted daughter?"

"She's already adopted. We can't do anything about her. You sound upset. Are you going to be all right? Maybe I should have seen you in person instead of calling you at the office."
Licensing Worker

I cancelled my meetings for the rest of the day, went for a walk around the block, called both my mother and mother-in-law, fell apart in my husband's arms. Not knowing how long we would be able to stay together as a family, I went home to play with the kids.

administered and regulated system. Additional research will be needed to understand how your own state operates. Any information contained within the following pages is not to be construed as legal advice or guidance on specific cases. Caring for children in out-of-home care is highly personal and varied.

I looked for the *"commissioner"* and found hundreds of people working on behalf of the commissioner and no "person" with the authority or responsibility to help care providers after allegations are made. The commissioner emerged as a bureaucratic abstraction which could share and access information with a significant number of other commissioners, but not with the individuals directly involved.

The authority and power available to *"one"* and many times *"each"* commissioner was incredible. Data privacy and confidentiality laws emerged as a legal channel to share gossip and perpetuate rumors among individuals deemed appropriate by a *"commissioner"*—any, each, and all commissioners involved. Yet, when data were requested by individuals directly involved, the data shared so freely inside was suddenly off-limits, hiding behind the veil of confidentiality. What became apparent early on in my research was the very controlling position a *"commissioner"* held and what a vulnerable and potentially dangerous position an accused individual was in, especially if professional and thorough investigation procedures were not followed.

I discovered agency policy is often very well written and interpreted with concern for both children and the families who care for them. The problem with policy, however, lies in practice. In law as in life, our morals and ideals generally outperform our behaviors.

I discovered files and case documentation that appeared both readable and valid. But the perspective changed when I interviewed the individuals facing maltreatment allegations, along with the psychologists, attorneys, friends, medical, professional, clergy, or other social workers involved in the case. These discussions with supporting individuals changed my original conclusions drawn from the file data.

The testimonies and stories of individuals and families have had names changed to protect individuals and families, and to respect the Data Privacy Act. If a particular testimony contains the names of people you know who have actually had such an experience it is solely by coincidence, unless permission from parties involved has been granted.

I discovered licensing discrepancies in child welfare roles. Foster parents were required to be licensed to care for another person's child. Yet licensing requirements were not always required for caseworkers, licensing workers, or investigators working with children and families in the foster care system.

This book has been designed and written on four levels; qualified and researched data; testimonial histories of actual situations; graphs, tables and charts; and visual graphic illustrations. In places you may find technical information in conflict with real life family situations. These paradoxes uncover pieces of the truth. The sidebars may seem confusing or conflicting with the text. Read the sidebars separately from the body copy to soften the conflict. Researched material has been documented in references. Many illustrations are contributions from my seven-year-old daughter.

—*The Cause is Change*—

Data privacy protects the innocent. It also protects a system from change. Enough was enough. I moved from passive communication to active communicator. Welcome to **Families at Risk.**

There is something very different about the removal of a child because of allegation and the "bon voyage" you give to a child reaching legal age or going home to primary parents. I'm sure the experience I felt as a foster parent is similar to the feelings a birth parent feels when children are removed and placed in protective custody.

Acknowledgments

This project could not be accomplished alone. I am sincerely grateful for the hundreds of cumulative hours put in by the following people:

MY FAMILY: My husband and daughter, who put up with the mounds of research and the time I had to dedicate to writing this book. My parents, who were very supportive offering dinners, weekend child care and manuscript review. My eighty-seven-year old grandmother who read and commented on the book as it progressed. My mother-in-law, the late Dr. Carrie Kulp, who challenged me to seek the truth and uncover problems needing to be revealed.

CHILDREN: My daughter, April, who contributed antics, dialogue, and illustrations. Joseph, whose name has been changed to protect his innocence, but who was the catalyst to begin this project. All the other children whose life experiences are found in the stories of this book.

MINNESOTA FOSTER CARE ASSOCIATION: Greg Olson, Executive Director; Dorothy Bodlovik, Editor MFPA *News and Views* and previous editor of *NAFP National Advocate*; Judy Howell, Secretary and SOS for PEA founder and foster and adoptive parents who challenged me to write *Families at Risk* and formed my task force, meeting with me every two weeks for a year, fielding questions, gathering information, and encouraging completion of this project.

FRIENDS AND EDITORS: Linda Kusserow, whose logic and conciseness continuously refined this manuscript. Steve Johnson, whose eloquence and vocabulary added the highlights and detail I missed. Jenni Schoppers, whose directness and practicality added needed refinements, Kathy Haley, Mary Jo Kelly and Frances Johnson, who proofed the manuscript and added consistency.

NATIONAL FOSTER PARENT ASSOCIATION: Gordon Evans, the *"father of foster care,"* who provided data and information as I requested it and a review of the manuscript.

UNITED STATES CHILDREN'S BUREAU: Jake Terpstra, Foster Care Specialist, who provided support, wisdom, and content editing.

CHILD WELFARE LEAGUE OF AMERICA: Eileen Mayers Pasztor, DSW; Program Director for Kinship, Family Foster Care and Adoption.

NATIONAL FOSTER RESOURCE CENTER, EASTERN MICHIGAN UNIVERSITY: for permission to reprint materials developed under funding from the National Center on Child Abuse and Neglect, and the Children's Bureau, especially Emily Jean McFadden for *Preventing Abuse in Foster Care.*

PRIVATE AGENCIES: Nancy Anderson, social worker, PATH; Lynda Bennett, social worker, Wilder Foundation; Joan Riebel, MSW, Executive Director, Family Alternatives, National Foster Parent Association Social Service Agency of the Year 1993; and Randy Ruth, social worker, PATH, foster parent and president of the Minnesota Foster Parent Association for their support, wealth of information, and personal sharing of their lives and profession.

PUBLIC AGENCIES: Becky Richardson, Hennepin County Foster Care; Bonnie Prokosh, National Foster Parent Association Social Worker of the Year 1993, Ramsey County Foster Care; Cathy Bruer-Thompson, adoption social worker, Hennepin County Adoption; and Fern Carlson, social worker, Isanti County for their support, wealth of information, and personal sharing of their lives and profession.

Five months later with no further govenment contact:

The certified letter lay on the kitchen table next to the acceptance letter to the university. One stated revocation of our foster care license, the other acceptance into an advanced parenting program for foster parents. I called my sister-in-law, my emotions torn between disbelief and excitement to begin a new training program.

"Where is your heart, Jodee?" my wise sister-in-law asked?

***"Always with the children."** I answered.*

"Then go to the university. The state can take your licenses. They cannot take your heart."

And so begin my journey from naivete and ignorance in the workings of the system to the beginning of wisdom.

*The results, **Families at Risk,** has been accomplished only by the support and help of many caring others.*

MINNESOTA ADOPTION RESOURCE NETWORK: Judith Anderson for manuscript review and advocacy for children with special needs.

DEPARTMENT OF HUMAN SERVICES: James Loving, Licensing Divisions, who reviewed and added insight into the needs, responsibilities, and concerns of government officials for children in licensing foster parents.

AUTHORS:
Jean Insley-Clarke, author of *Self Esteem a Family Affair* and *Growing Up Again*, who reviewed affirmations and self-esteem sections in this book and added some wonderful final touches.
Mary Martin Mason, speaker and trainer on infertility and adoption issues and author of *The Miracle Seekers* and her forthcoming book, *The Renaissance of Adoption.*
Mike Robin, social worker and author of *Assessing Child Maltreatment Reports: The Problem of False Allegations,* for review of sections of this book.
Robert Wilhite, MSW, counselor and author of *The Family Game of Anger*, for manuscript review.

THE NORTH AMERICAN COUNCIL FOR ADOPTABLE CHILDREN: Joe Kroll, Executive Director for serving on the initial project task force and contributing volumes of resource materials from the council.

CULTURAL DIVERSITY: Sonja Carbonal, MA, LICSW, LP, whose background in social services, psychology, and minority cultures was exceedingly appreciated.

BIRTH PARENTS: Greg and Linda Johnson, Porter and Debbie Thomas, Rick Cotter and Debbie Burdett and unnamed others . . . who were willing to share their lives and experiences in order to help other families.

ADOPTIVE PARENTS: David and Lauren Runnion-Bareford, Renae

FOSTER PARENTS: Sue Magnuson, Larry and Liz Chevalier, Jeanette Howard, Judy and Lee Howell, Dorothy Bodlovik, Greg and Dianne Olson, Susan O'Neill and many, many unnamed others.

PEDIATRICIAN: The late Dr. Jeff Alexander who provided insight into the world of abuse and child pediatrics.

LAW ENFORCEMENT: Jill Behnke, 911 and dispatch; Scott Gudmunson, Police officer; Scott Mattsen, Data Privacy Information.

UNIVERSITY OF WISCONSIN—MADISON SCHOOL OF SOCIAL WORK: Rosemarie Carbino, Clinical Professor who has studied the dynamics of social service agency reactions to reports of child maltreatment. A very special thank you to her research and permission to use her work

UNIVERSITY OF MINNESOTA: Mary Lou Gilstad, Early Childhood Development Program Coordinator for the University of Minnesota, who developed the training program Demonstrated Competency in Foster Parenting and Training for Trainers programs which gave me the courage to begin this book.

And to her qualified trainers: Deb Jones, Argo and Associates, Inc. and PACER (Parents Advocacy Coalition for Educational Rights), Dr. Wayne Caron, University of Minnesota, and Dr. Lane Fischer.

LEGAL COUNSEL: Robert Roby, Robert Levy and Marc Kurzman, attorneys at law, whose time, advice, and help was exceedingly appreciated, and whose work is valued by the clients they serve.

GROWN FOSTER CHILDREN: Rebekha Larson, Michael Benoit and others whose rich writing and memories blessed this book with a dose of reality.

I rolled up my sleeves and entered the task as a researcher. As a researcher, I could live for the truth and the present, not regretting the past or fretting about the future.

In its own way **Families at Risk** *became a refuge, a healing retreat for me to search for answers to questions I was confused and frustrated by.*

It is my hope **Families at Risk** *can be such a retreat and a place of new beginning for thousands of others.*

Join me on my journey into the realities of out-of-home care for children and the risk to caring families.

Table of Contents

---

*The most important
part of our culture is
our particular family.*

*"The most basic
culture in which we
develop is the culture
of our family, and our
parents are 'culture
leaders.' Moreover, the
most significant aspect
of that culture is not
what our parents tell
us but rather what
they do—how they
behave toward each
other, toward our
siblings and above all,
toward us. In other
words, what we learn
about the nature of the
world when we are
growing up is
determined by the
nature of our
experience in the
microcosm of the
family. It is not so
much what our parents
say that determines
our world view as it is
the unique world they
create for us by their
behavior."*

M. Scott Peck, M.D.
The Road Less Traveled

*There can be no new beginning
without an ending!*

SECTION I

Who's Watching the Children?

*Keeping children physically,
emotionally, and psychologically secure
while on a child welfare journey*

Cripple him, and you have Sir Walter Scott.

Lock him in a prison cell and you have John Bunyan.

Bury him in the snows of Valley Forge and you have George Washington.

Raise him in abject poverty and you have Abraham Lincoln.

Strike him down with infantile paralysis, and he becomes Franklin Roosevelt.

Burn him so severely that the doctors say he'll never walk again and you have Glenn Cunningham—who set the world's one-mile record in 1934.

Deafen him and you have Ludwig van Beethoven or Thomas Edison.

Have him or her born black in a society filled with racial discriminations, and you have Booker T. Washington, Marian Anderson, George Washington Carver.

Call him a slow learner, "retarded" and write him off as uneducable and you have Albert Einstein.

Ted Engstrom

Figure 1.1   Foster child in foster care system

Chapter 1

Brown Bag Consignment Kids

America's children in out-of-home care are
set adrift in a sea of systems and procedures.
Awash in protocols, laws, and codes.
Floating from home-to-home, sometimes
finding safe harbors, sometimes stormy seas.
Setting their sail in life with a crooked mast and cracked vessel.
Moving along with a broken rudder and very sporatic wind.

Children arrive daily on doorsteps in America with brown paper bags, plastic garbage bags, or a broken clothes basket. Joseph arrived with a brown paper bag, big crossed chocolate brown eyes, and a limp left side. As with other children we have cared for, a five to ten minute conversation with the social worker summed up the history we received regarding Joseph. Yet, this tiny 10-month-old bundle contained more life experiences than any of us knew—or that Joseph could explain.

Joseph snuggled his little flat head in my arms. Remarkable, I thought, that a child's head could be so flat. I carried him in to the house. April had already prepared her old crib with a new blanket, a teddy bear, and her mommy's antique little pillow. She had her own program to help love and care for her new baby brother and made sure his life included all the important objects a baby needs. I put up the baby gate, shut all the doors, and put Joseph on the floor to crawl. April provided all her favorite baby toys. Joseph looked up and dragged himself with his functional side to the toy pile. His brown eyes looked quiet and unexpressive. He seemed pleasant.

Days passed and Joseph remained quiet and aloof. His favorite activity was snuggling in my husband's lap. He became as astute as our three dogs, knowing the sound of my husband's car and when he would be coming through the door.

Joseph took to water like a little fish. We spent hours in the hot tub holding his functional side as he swam around and around using his unused little arm and leg. Two weeks after the introduction to the hot tub, he announced his first words, *"Hot tub!"* In those two weeks he had not cried once. We encouraged him to climb stairs, and for weeks Joseph crawled up the stairs, always starting with his limp arm and leg. We supported him to stand, and he began to pull himself

"Mrs. Kulp, we'll be by to move Joseph today. You understand we can't set a precedent."

"Do you have to come today? Can't we have a little time to say goodbye? Where is he going?"

"Don't worry, we've found a good home. He'll be fine. We'll—let's see—it's 4:00 now, I guess we can give you until 7:00 pm before we pick him up."

I hung up the phone and left the office for home. In less than three hours I would be saying goodbye to Joseph. How do you say goodbye to an 18-month-old who thinks you're his mother? How do you prepare someone to move in three hours? The 13-minute drive home was the longest 13 minutes I had ever spent. I prayed, **"Why? Why? I don't understand. Please help me during these next three hours in saying goodbye. Help me do what's right for this little boy."**

The driveway loomed ahead.

up using his weak little arm. The bunkbeds became our favorite place of play, up and down, over and over.

After two months of living with us, Joseph trembled when we changed his diaper. We had been given no history of his past and Joseph was too little to explain the fear. Once the fear had subsided, he proceeded to display raging temper tantrums. Each time the temper tantrums subsided, we had a new little boy. By 15 months, Joseph was smiling and happy. It was as though once all the bad feelings had been safely expressed, Joseph felt free.

He surprised everyone when he took off and ran. Eyes twinkling, laughing with delight, he darted across a warm sand beach. From that point on he ran—he had too much lost time to make up for by simply walking! No limping, no disability— just two strong little legs. The hours spent swimming and climbing had worked!

Just before he was removed from our home, at 17 months, his vocabulary contained more than 25 words. He could discern different motor sounds and he could match colors in his wooden puzzles. He was not afraid to have a good temper tantrum or run into arms for hugs and kisses. He refused to be left with strangers and would cry until one of our family members had returned. He had melded into our life and in his toddler mind he was home.

Joseph sailed into our lives in a day, harbored and mended for eight months, and then blew out on a different course as alone as when he came in. He set out for uncharted territory, with no directions, no maps, and no permanent program. His life and ours were changed because of an allegation and the investigation procedures that followed. Joseph was adrift again in the system. Although the allegation had nothing to do with our relationship or parenting of Joseph, Joseph was the victim, losing again the people he knew and loved.

Luckily for Joseph, we were able to secure permission from child protection to call and visit. Initially, I phoned his new foster mother daily. Our family visited, bringing the favorite red wagon harnessed to our three large dogs for walks in the park. Sometimes we included our babysitter, whom Joseph dearly loved. When Grandma came from California, we made sure he got her hugs. We always drove Joseph's favorite big yellow four-wheel-drive truck. When Joseph went to his first respite home to give his new foster mother a break, we visited. He knew we knew where he was. When Joseph had surgery on his eyes, April and I stayed at the hospital with his foster mother, and we all snuggled him when he woke up.

As Joseph has grown older, it has been remarkable how much he remembers. I liken it to good friends you see only once in many years and yet the years don't matter once you see them again. Joseph has always refused to say "goodbye"— he says an emphatic NO! We can say "see ya later," to which he smiles, waves and says OK. One day I called and talked with Joseph. Considering this 30-month-old had spoken only 25 words when he left and had not seen or spoken to us for the last eight months, the conversation was loving and caring. *"Joeee, where you go? You fall off your bike and go to hospital? When you come home? You OK Joeee?"* — *Yes, Joseph, I'm OK.*

During his third year Joseph announced he had a daddy and he knew who he was. When asked, he closed his eyes and said it was a secret. He kept his secret for a whole year. Finally, on his fourth birthday he announced, *"My daddy used to rub my legs with oil."*

"Who's your daddy?" asked the foster mother.

Joseph proudly proclaimed, *"Karl who lives with Jodee."* It was true. Three years earlier when Joseph was a year old, my husband would rub his legs with oil. In four-year-old Joseph's mind he had decided this was "his" father.

The amount of time our family had spent holding, teaching, laughing, and playing with this little boy will hopefully impact his future development. Joseph knows what it is to be loved. The trust and attachment he had achieved was damaged, but he had developed a male and maternal attachment and could possibly attach again in a new home. In his favor, his new foster mother recently had a little boy in foster care reunited with his birth mother, so Joseph and his new mother, both grieving, needed each other.

In June 1993, it will be three years since he left our home, almost four years since he left his birth mother. He has lived in four different homes and countless respite stays. I often wonder, knowing the pain of separation and loss I felt, how birth mothers ever survive the loss of a child. I also know I will never truly understand the pain and fear Joseph felt. One can only imagine. His recent psychological testing discovered attachment disorder due to multiple placements. His physical testing discovered uneven gross motor skills possibly due to a stroke in infancy. Recommendations have been made for both occupational and attachment therapy, but no permanent home is in sight. Joseph's life is still adrift in the sea of child welfare. No one knows where or when he will get a permanent home.

His older twin sisters have now been in foster care for five years. His baby sister, Ruth, was removed promptly from the hospital while the mother was still recovering from Caesarean birth, and is now two. To Ruth, her mother is the only daily mothering figure she has known—the foster mother. After three years. Joseph and his twin sisters were told who their tummy mommy is. It was quite a shock that Ruth's tummy mommy is also theirs. His older brother has been reunited, after much effort, with his (not Joseph's) father.

Joseph's mother has since married a pleasant man and begun to put her life in order. The likelihood of permanent custody remains unknown, although there is talk of reunification. They visit Ruth and dream of custody, but presently are too poor to manage caring for all the children. For Joseph and his sisters, life continues together in a very loving foster home. Joseph has two foster brothers he loves, but there will come a day when they also will be separated.

Moving children from home to home is always chaotic. For some children, it's permanently damaging. The system designed to protect them cannot quiet their uncertainty of who their next provider will be. For Joseph, one thing is certain: he will face at least one additional move in his life and need to cope. Someday, someone may be able to pick up the pieces and help him start over.

Attachment - The anchor for healthy development

Dr. Ken Magid and Carole A. McKelvey, in their excellent book, *High Risk, Children Without A Conscience*, study the need for attachment in depth. They state, "*What happens, right or wrong, in the critical first two years of a baby's life will affect that child as an adult. A complex set of events must occur in infancy to assure a future of trust and love. If the proper bonding and subsequent attachment does not occur—usually between the child and mother—the child will develop mistrust and have a deep-seated rage. He becomes a child without a conscience.*"

"*Somehow, the normal process that causes attachment to occur—the very process that develops a social conscience—was short-circuited in Ted Bundy or Charles Manson. Not all unattached children grow up to be criminals, but most suffer some form of psychological damage. It may be that such children simply are never able to develop a true loving relationship, or they can end up conning others for their own benefit. These, too, can be considered tragedies, for no child should have to grow up without this trust bond and loving beginning.*" (Magid 1987, p3)

Promptly at 7:00, the People Mover drove into the driveway. We strapped Joseph into a car seat, hugged, kissed him, waved goodbye, and walked into the house. There would be no words spoken for quite some time, until April's little voice piped up.

"Don't cry, Mommy. He's gone. You know what the problem with babies is? They can't make choices. If he could make choices, he'd still be here."

Children who are attached . . .
. . . have less jealousy and clinging behaviors.
. . . are able to handle stress and frustration.
. . . can express themselves openly.

In the attached child's heart and mind he/she are secure that at least one other person cares about them and feels they are valuable.

How will this new place ever be home?

"Did he talk when he left your home six months ago? Was he really quiet? He only says two words—Mammom and Apple."
Joseph's new foster care mother

"Mommy, he's not saying Apple. He's saying April. If somebody gave me an apple for April, I'd throw it on the floor."
April

Attachment—*The psychological tie between two people, such as parent and child, that allows them to have emotional importance to each other.*

Attachment Disorder—*Difficulty with the ability to make genuine, meaningful attachments with another, usually because of poor or negative early parenting. There is a range of severity, but Bourgigonon and Watson describe three forms: traumatized, inadequately attached, and non-attached.*
(McNamara 1990)

Depending on what the social worker says up front, young foster children usually arrive knowing little about where they are, what is expected, and how kindly these new people will be. This is where the love, sweat, and tears of foster and adoptive parenting combine to develop the beginnings of attachment.

It's not easy building trust in a child who may feel betrayed, kidnapped, or abandoned. Months and years may go into replacing the damage done by an unprepared move. Whatever attachments can be formed, and whatever bridge of trust can be built, will determine if this placement will be productive for the child in developing loving relationships with others in the future.

Vera Fahlberg, M.D., pediatrician and director of the world-renowned Forest Heights Lodge, a treatment center for emotionally disturbed children, says, *"The bond that a child develops to the person who cares for him in his early years is the foundation for his future psychological development and for his future relationships with others. A primary person to whom the child can become attached, who responds to the child's needs and who initiates positive activities with the child seems to be indispensable."*

"In human societies the initial bonding occurs between the infant and his primary caregiver, who is usually his mother figure. This primary caregiver can be the birth mother, a foster mother or an adoptive mother. In some cases the primary caregiver is the father or siblings. It is important that all parents realize that physical care is not enough to lead to the development of a physically and psychologically healthy child." (Falhberg 1979, p 5,7)

Figure 1.3
Vera Falhberg (1979)
Arousal Reaction Cycle

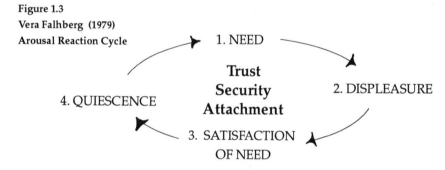

Figure 1.3 above illustrates Vera Fahlberg's model for building trust, security, and attachment. This can be illustrated by the infant feeling a NEED and physically showing DISPLEASURE of not getting the need taken care of. Depending on the response of the caregiver the cycle will be completed with the SATISFACTION OF NEED and QUIESCENCE or quieting of the child. The way in which the need is taken care of will determine the outcome. Care unconditionally given to the child will build trust, security, and attachment to the caregiver. If the need is not taken care of or if it is handled with anger or disrespect, the child although quieted, withdraws and begins to lose trust in the caregiver. The cycle continues with each interaction between the child and caregiver.

Attachment plays an important part in all our relationships, starting from the moment of birth and continuing through old age. Without attachment in our important relationships, we remain insecure and untrusting.

We can illustrate this same scenario in the adult world. If employees have a NEED and voice DISPLEASURE and the NEED IS TAKEN CARE OF there is a period of CONTENTMENT and a building of trust, security, and attachment to the company. If the need is ignored or mishandled employees will feel powerless and unappreciated. Distrust and disloyalty may begin to emerge.

> *Attachment is the anchor a child begins to set life on.*
> *Commitment from the adult is the bedrock for attachment*

SOCIAL	SPIRITUAL	INTELLECTUAL	PERSONALITY
Accepting affection from others	Understands logical consequences for actions	Is confident enough to try new things	Expresses needs and wants
Giving affection to others	Handle fear and worry	Can think logically about a problem or situation	Can feel feelings and sort out what feeling is
Physically and emotionally can take care of oneself	Cope with stress and frustration	Sort out what one perceives	Maintain good self-esteem and self-concept
Develop healthy future relationships	Develop a conscience	Draw on perceived data for new ideas or solutions	Become responsible, self-reliant, and handle criticism
Can unconditionally take care of another person	Develop satisfying spiritual relationship	Attain full intelligence potential	Attain full personality potential

Figure 1.4   Attachment Model

The development of attachments is the anchor that secures the beginning of meeting basic social, spiritual, intellectual, and personality needs. For example, in Figure 1.4, attachment is the anchor for the child to be confident to try new things, think logically about a problem or situation, sort out the problem, invent new approaches or solutions, and begin to reach intellectual potential. These attachments begin very early in life and are built one upon another. Therefore one attachment will bridge the next and so on. A child will have more difficulty attaching to new relationships if early attachments are not made or the child has had major or recurrent losses in attached relationships.

Children in out-of-home care often have attachment problems. They may never have attached to any adult. Or they may have suffered repeated losses and fear the pain of losing the people they love. They may refuse to try to attach. Dr. Foster Cline, who has spent years working with children in out-of-home care, states, *"More than half of all troubled children we see in practice have a history of being shuffled and bounced about."* According to Dr. Cline, the unattached child displays the following characteristics: (Cline 1979, p 128)

- *Lack of ability to give and receive affection.*
- *Cruelty to others.*
- *Speech pathology.*
- *Lack of long-term friends.*
- *Parents appear angry or hostile.*
- *Preoccupation with fire, blood, gore.*
- *Superficial attentiveness or friendliness with strangers.*
- *Self-destructive behavior.*
- *Phoniness.*
- *Marked control problems.*
- *Abnormalities in eye contact.*
- *Various types of learning disorders.*
- *Severe problems with stealing, hoarding, and gorging on food.*
- *A particular type of pathological type of lying—"primary process lying."*

Attachment traumatized child—A child severely traumatized in an earlier relationship usually reluctant to trust or hope again.

Inadequately attached child—A child whose primary attachments usually were interrupted, unhealthy, or sporadic in nature, and now has difficulty re-establishing new attachments.

Non-attached child—The most serious. Generally occus when a child has been deprived of early opportunities to make a primary attachment.
(Bourgignon/Watson)

Parents must not jump to conclusions or label a child unattached. If a child displays characteristics of an unattached child, the provider needs to carefully document these behaviors: when the behavior occurs and how it manifests itself. At certain developmental times in childhood some of these behaviors are considered normal. Consult a professional if there are a significant number of unattached behaviors displayed or the behavior is disrupting the family unit. The care provider can be extremely strategic in providing the data necessary for a professional psychologist to work with a child in an efficient and healthy way. Professional psychologists are trained in assessing children and helping parents understand the child's behavior and how to work toward correcting it. A psychologist can help an unattached child develop skills to begin to trust others.

Social researchers have made a sobering discovery. *An unattached child, even at the young age of three or four, cannot easily attach himself despite being provided with the most favorable conditions. Most expert clinical workers and adoptive and foster parents can testify that to win such a child, become important to the child, be needed by the child and finally to be loved by the child, may take months and years.* (Magid 1979 p 66) A surprise move to another home can destroy all that work and do further harm.

Adopted children or children who have spent some of their childhood in foster care, account for a disproportionate number of unattached children. This isn't surprising to those who know that the proper bonding cycle is not fostered in children who have had significant breaks early in their lives. These are children who have been put at particularly high risk. (Magid 1987, p 148)

The future of non-attached children is bleak if those working with them cannot bring them into human relationship. They become the unattached men and women of the next generation. They may lack normal human emotion and fail to find love and happiness. Whether that means they'll become criminals depends upon the extent of their rage and other variables. (Magid 1987, p 66)

The most priceless thing you can give a child is your time.

Unattached children take time. Integrate the child into family living. Comfort the child and be aware of the child's emotional needs. Show interest in the child and the child's development, ideas, likes and friends. Demonstrate gentleness and patience. Set and enforce limits, making sure enforcement is consistent, kind, and caring. Set realistic expectations of performance and accomplishment. Encourage the child. Have the courage to believe in the child so the child can begin to believe in himself. Seek pleasurable time together and have fun.

Separation and loss

In our adult world, a support network initially forms around the grieving person to listen and provide sympathy. If a spouse dies, adults are comforted by friends and the community. If the family pet dies, the family pulls together to support and love each other. If a natural disaster occurs, neighbors and the community rally and work together to rebuild and restore. In each case, adult loss usually encompasses significant others who reach out and care. Adults are affirmed it's OK to grieve.

When a child is removed unprepared from a home—who and where is the support system? The life support network found in the adult world does not often exist for these children. It is part-time (overworked social workers), brand new (new foster or adoptive family), or appears nonexistent to the child who is in intense pain with losses that hurt too much to risk feeling.

Joseph had been gone three months and I felt fairly secure in how I was handling the loss and grieving process. I had graduated from calling Joseph's new foster mother every day to every three days and finally to Saturday morning to hear how he was doing. I had given the car seat to a friend. The walker and the crib were now packed and put away in the garage. We had visited Joseph and knew his new home was loving, clean, and well parented. Regardless of what I knew, a bag of no-hull yellow puff popcorn in a shopping cart pushed by a grandfatherly old man triggered fond memories of Joseph and April sharing popcorn and laughing with my 86-year-old grandfather.

I crumbled again with the sadness of the loss.

Chapter 1 - Brown Bag Consignment Kids

Comparison of severity of stresses on people of different ages

Stress Level	Adult	Child/Adolescent
1. None	No apparent psychological stressor	No apparent psychological stressor
2. Minimal	Minor violation of the law; small bank loan	Vacation with family
3. Mild	Argument with neighbor; change in work hours	Change in school-teacher; new school year
4. Moderate	New career; death of a close friend; pregnancy	Chronic parental fighting; change to new school; illness of close relative; sibling birth
5. Severe	Serious illness in self or family; major financial loss; marital separation; birth of child	Death of peer; divorce of parents; arrest; hospitalization; persistent and harsh parental discipline
6. Extreme	Death of close relative; divorce	Death of parent or sibling; repeated physical or sexual abuse
7. Catastrophic	Concentration camp experience; devastating natural disaster	Multiple family deaths

Figure 1.5 DSM III-R Comparison of stress levels

"In my foster home we took a Reader's Digest stress test with our foster teenagers— the results revealed they had all died ."

PRIMARY CHILDREN:

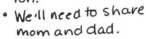

- OK, now what are we in for.
- Do you think this kid will be nice, fun?
- We'll need to share mom and dad.
- What if this kid messes with my stuff?

FOSTER PARENTS:

- How is this child going to fit in?
- What don't we know that we should?
- What can we do to help the child?
- How will this child change my life?

FOSTER CHILD:

- I've lost my home and everything I know.
- My parents are gone.
- Who are these new strangers?
- What are they "really" like?

Most normal human losses occur one at a time. For the foster or adopted child losses often occur immediately and multiply.

Losses for out-of-home care children are repetitive and compounded.

A past ungrieved loss remains forever alive in the unconscious, which has no sense of time. Thus past losses or even a reminder of the loss, will evoke fear of further loss in the future. (Simos 1979) The new losses and separation with its resulting grief bring up prior ungrieved losses stored previously in the unconscious of the child. The complexity of losses these children face often are not recognized by the people who are responsible for their care. In addition, children facing multiple losses have difficulty expressing what is bothering them.

Loss? Let me tell you about loss. My whole life is being "run" by strangers!

"Mommy? Why didn't we adopt Joseph like me? If we had adopted him he'd be a keeper right?"
April

Because, Honey, the government is Joseph's parent.

"What's government?"

It's a lot of people who get to make decisions for other people.

"Do they live with them?"

No.

"Do they tuck them in at night and say prayers?"

No.

"Do they feed them breakfast?"

No.

"Well, what do they do then?"

Honey, they get to make the choices.

"That's stupid. Joseph can make better choices than that. He just can't talk."

Loss of Self

The child's whole life changes very suddenly and unexpectedly. The compounded losses experienced by children in out-of-home care are vast. These are children, not adults, children without the support systems or coping skills psychologically healthy adults have had time to develop.

PERSONHOOD—who we are and our positions in life
The child faces unknown changes and does not know if needs will be met. These changes bring about culture shock and loss of self-esteem, independence, ego, expectations, and lifestyle. Children lose their family position (i.e., the oldest, youngest, middle child), family role (i.e., scapegoat, hero, mascot), family identity (i.e., tribe, blue collar, single parent), and possibly even their names. Children with special needs or disabilities also may be faced with badly perceived body image, and loss of body function or control. Minority children may face the loss of contact with their culture or language. Regardless of whether or not their differences were accepted in their last home, they were known, and the unknown is frightening to children.

CHILDHOOD—freedom to play and explore
Children who grow up in troubled families lose the joy of childhood. They lack the liberty to play freely or express themselves. Threat of abuse, loss, separation, conflict, or divorce may have been a common occurrence. Normal emotional, psychological, and physical development may have been interrupted or skipped due to the family situation. Transitional objects such as a blanket or soft toy may not have accompanied these children to their new homes. To the normal teenager, leaving childhood behind is a natural loss. For the child who has had few positive experiences, this is a difficult time to reprocess earlier losses, compounded by physical changes and peer pressure. Healthy parenting, liberty to play, and freedom from want may be new experiences.

Loss of Relationships

IMPORTANT LIVING RELATIONSHIPS—people or pets
Due to the dynamics of the child welfare system, all close or meaningful relationships may be lost. The present situation may appear to the child as desertion, abandonment, or kidnapping. Lost people include: birth parents, stepparents, grandparents, stepgrandparents, sisters, brothers, stepsisters, stepbrothers, aunts, uncles, cousins, neighbors, classmates, friends, family friends, teachers, clergy, postal carrier, doctors, dentists, nurses, and the neighborhood store clerk—basically any person having a significant relationship with the child. In addition, foster/adoptive children gain new siblings and/or lose siblings each time they move. Pets cannot be overlooked. To a child, a relationship with a pet is precious. Children faced with the loss of a pet may express the same degree of concern they feel toward the loss of a person. The unconditional love shared by the animal with the child may be the only positive love experience a child has had.

In addition, the child's life history may include abandonment, separation, rejection, or divorce. With each move, they start over.

IMPORTANT EXTERNAL OBJECTS—geographics and objects

The geographic move displaces all of the child's relationships with external objects. The neighborhood and community may be significantly different. The church, school, stores, and medical buildings are no more familiar than the people in them. The favorite hideout, whether it be a tree or under a table, is no longer available. The pillow, blanket, and bed don't feel or smell the same. In addition, sentimental objects may have been forgotten, destroyed, or lost in the process of crisis intervention and emergency placement.

ENVIRONMENTAL LOSSES—experiences of five senses

Not enough emphasis is placed on the environmental losses a child experiences. For the foster/adoptive child everything changes: smells, sounds, foods, language, vocabulary, style of touches, expectations, perceptions, and style of relationships. The smell of coffee brewing in the morning or dinner cooking on the stove. The dog coming in from outside. The smell and touch of the hug from a birth parent. The burning wood or oil from the stove. The sounds of the family members brushing their teeth, walking across the room, or blow drying their hair. The bark of the dog when the mail carrier brings the mail. The nicknames and special family words children grow up with. The sound of the wind in the trees or a branch against a window. The train as it passes. The noon whistle. The nighttime shadows in the bedroom or the rays of morning sunlight. The favorite mud puddle or running water place. The touch from past relationships, regardless if the touch was good or bad.

The trauma for these children cannot be denied.
Children need security and nurturing to begin to process losses.

When faced with sudden loss, the child reacts by creating a set of cushions to allow reality to slowly settle in. The experience of *emotional trauma* has lasting psychological effects, just as the experience of physical trauma has lasting physical effects. We can understand trauma better if we think of a physical wound inflicted suddenly and violently—it is felt deeply and because it is easy to see the damage we seek care.

In the case of a large gash, if it is treated properly, cleaned, and dressed, it will begin to heal with no infection. Although it hurts as it heals, it continues to grow stronger. Eventually the pain lessens or goes away and the body is restored to health. But scar tissue remains and makes a permanent change.

In the case of a broken bone, if it is treated and well set, the mended place may actually be stronger than it was before, but the bone is changed forever.

In the case of a broken home . . .

Grief—Healing for pain and suffering

Separation and loss are natural human experiences. As we grow up, we learn to handle our fears of both temporary and permanent separation from important people, experiences or objects.

Every member of a family is important and has a different role to play.

Good family relationships require sensitivity—neither expecting too much nor too little. All members contribute to the good of the whole.

Harmonious family living is based on respect. We must be sure to demonstrate respect for the child and his rights, as well as to the parents and grandparents for their rights.

All family members must be respected in their roles, whether they are infants, children, adolescents, young adults, parents, or grandparents.

A child's feelings upon separation from home are often compared to a death in the family. A child experiences not just the loss of family, but an entire world. In order to work through the pain of separation and loss, it is important for children to experience feelings as they occur, without trying to change them. Once a feeling is expressed, no matter how negative, it isn't nearly as powerful as it was while unexpressed and formless. When feelings are out in the open, talked out, and looked at from a realistic perspective, they often lose their negative powers. As we listen to children, it is important that we hear exactly what they are saying, not what **we** want to hear or **think** they **should** be saying. In other words, we must listen with our eyes and ears as well as our minds and hearts.

The only way out of the pain of a loss is to process each stage of grief.

Losses are always painful—both because of their immediate impact and because they stir up feelings and memories of earlier losses. When we suffer a loss, we grieve. The feelings of grief are strong, painful, and hard to sort out. Although they never come one at a time or in perfect order, generally we go through these feelings in stages.

No two human beings or family systems grieve the same way. Grieving for every person is exhausting. *Most children take a minimum of from nine months to a year to go through all the stages of grieving.* (Hennepin County Adoption 1990) If a child is moved during one stage of grief, he may be stuck there and may require professional therapy. The stages often overlap and the child may move back and forth between stages.

There are many good ways to organize and list stages of grief to help understand and assist grieving children. Many additional models are available in books on grieving, and I respect each. But in this book I have chosen a vocabulary and model I believe reflect the issues grieving children in out-of-home care experience, especially children with a history of past maltreatment.

The five stages are: preservation, protest, sorrow, hope, and faith.

1. Preservation: Honeymoon for the parents or survival of the fittest?

The word *preservation* means to keep from harm and damage, to protect, or to save. It also means to prepare for future use, to keep up, or maintain. The foster or adoptive child often arrives in emotional shock. In some models of grieving this is referred to as denial, shock, or alarm. I prefer preservation.

I believe the grieving child is striving for personal emotional and psychological preservation. Just as our physical bodies go into shock to protect our vital organs (the heart and brain), emotional shock shuts down internal systems to protect our emotional vital organs (the spirit and the mind). The shock can be more of a problem than the problem itself. In both cases, it can threaten life (physical or emotional) even though the injuries and conditions causing the shock may not be fatal. The degree of shock can be increased by illness, poor resistance to stress, pain, rough handling, and delay in treatment. Treatment and healing must be directed at the cause and cannot come solely from the injured person.

The first one to three weeks in a new home may be considered a honeymoon for the parents, but it's not fun for the child. There is no childlike freedom in the false happiness, uncontrollable silliness, remote quietness, or robot-like actions these children exhibit to please the new parents.

Social service workers often say, *"He's adjusting just fine—he just loves his new home."* The child may be agreeable to have around, do everything asked, and never mention his family. But in reality this child may be running on emotional remote control. In the daytime hours the child appears to be adjusting just fine, but be unable to eat. Colds, infections, and upset stomachs are common. In the nighttime when the emotional fortress is left unguarded, the child begins to experience nightmares, nightterrors, roaming, or bedwetting.

"Adjusting just fine" may be accurate if we are willing to accept preservation as a viable beginning to sort out life.

Children in out-of-home care often feel they have no one to *"really"* talk to. Isolated, they draw their own conclusions regarding being removed from their family. They develop their own strategies to cope with these feelings.

The experience of separation and loss can be so painful that a child may avoid grieving altogether, stuff feelings deep inside, and appear to have no reaction at all. In clinical terms this is called Post Traumatic Stress Disorder or PTSD. (Refer to the DSM III-R for more information.) The child's feelings and reactions may be set aside for years—until sparked by a crisis or a feeling of complete safety.

No matter how well the child disassociates from painful feelings, they can never get rid of them. The child is no longer consciously aware of the original trauma or feelings, but those feelings exist, deep in the subconscious. When the child is stressed, when a crisis occurs, when life is threatened, or things seem out of control these unconscious feelings snap into action. The event or crisis sets off a natural survival instinct imbedded in the unconscious that the conscious mind cannot overrule.

PTSD does not heal easily, nor does it gradually disappear over time. Until an active process of healing takes place, children continue to experience a constriction of feelings, a decreased ability to recognize which feelings are present, and a persistent sense of being cut off from surroundings. The child may remain on constant alert for any additional recurrences, or may feel guilt/shame for having abandoned or betrayed others by being removed from one traumatic situation and put into another. Some become *"model children"* with no outward reactions at all, keeping *"the secret"* carefully hidden.

Some experts believe that PTSD is more damaging and more difficult to treat if:

1. The traumas occur over a prolonged period of time (longer than six months).

2. The traumas are human rather than environmental in origin.

3. Those around the affected person tend to deny the existence of the stressor or the stress.

4. The traumas and/or events of the loss are repeated.

Children in out-of-home care often face all four situations with each move they make. The honeymoon or adjustment period experienced with children in out-of-home care can be PTSD-related. The child's struggle to figure out all the new details and absorb the compounded losses consumes an incredible amount of energy. And it is often impossible for children to risk admitting the losses and/or the feelings of these losses to strangers.

It is helpful to have a *"feeling"* vocabulary when working with children who have experienced losses. Following is a list of some feelings children in care may be experiencing, but are not be able to understand or express.

At four, Joseph shuts down to ward off emotional pain. A word of correction even done quietly and lovingly can result in feelings of rejection and retreat into his inner world. On the other hand, with no notice he can react enraged.

Joseph no longer behaves with the unleashed freedom he had when he left our home.

A Spec of Sand

You cannot hurt me,
*   no you can't*
For I have made myself
*   into a spec*
*   of sand*

I can't absorb
*   your hurtful words*

for they cannot enter
*   no abuse can*
*   damage me*

for I am strong
*   and small*

*   no feelings*
*   can I feel*

for sand has no feeling
*   no pain*
*   no understanding*
*   no living*
*   no loving*
*   no giving*

Author
Journey to Life, 1986

Children in the Preservation Stage may feel:

Abandoned	Doubtful	Miserable	Shocked
Afraid	Embarrassed	Nervous	Silly (Giddy)
Ambivalent	Empty	Numb	Skeptical
Angry	Exhausted	Odd	Small
Annoyed	Fearful	Out of Control	Solemn
Astounded	Frightened	Overwhelmed	Strange
Bad	Grieving	(In) Pain	Stupid
Betrayed	Helpless	Panicked	Stunned
Concerned	Homesick	Petrified	Surprised
Confused	Hurt	Powerless	Tense
Crushed	Ignored	Pressured	Terrible
Defeated	Insignificant	Puzzled	Terrified
Depersonalized	Isolated	Queer	Ticked Off
Depressed	Left out	Rejected	Tired
Deserted	Lonely	Reluctant	Trapped
Devastated	Longing	Resigned	Uncomfortable
Disturbed	Lost	Restless	Uneasy
Dominated	Low	Sad	Weak
Divided	Melancholy	Scared	Worried

Just as a chameleon alters its color to blend into the environment, these children alter their external behavior for protective purposes. They can laugh, smile, look surprised or serious in an instant. The exterior display—the public performance—hides the hurt, anger, shame, and loneliness within. If the child appears constantly happy or content, you may want to use the table below to discover how real these feelings are. Sometimes, negative feelings are so scary that to express them seems prohibitive. So the child puts on a facade appearing:

Brave	Eager	Kind	Satisfied
Calm	Glad	Nice	Unafraid
Cheerful	Helpful	Pleased	Wonderful

But during the Preservation Stage the child may actually go through something like this:

Actions	Feelings	Thoughts
Pretends the loss doesn't exist or doesn't matter	Can't acknowledge the pain or experience	Doesn't want to believe the loss
Withdraws, becomes very quiet and sleeps a lot, is slow motion	Can't express feelings or is afraid to feel	Thinks he is cause of and responsible for loss
Gets sick—infections, colds, stomachaches	Stuffs feelings until safe to feel	Decides to behave well to go home
Gets so busy he can't experience the pain	Appears accepting of situation	Thinks he will soon be back home

During the Preservation Stage the child needs continuity of relationships.

— Some contact with his previous family and other persons important to the child, unless the child has been seriously harmed by them. A phone call, note, or letter. Visits if possible and as soon as possible.

— A picture of family members or significant others now separated.

— *Affirmations of Trust-Building*—*"Knowing it's OK just to be." The child needs to decide to live, thrive, trust and reach out to have his needs met.* (Clarke 1989)

— A case plan that is accurate and has small visible steps for measured progress. This plan needs to be explained to the older child and a written copy given to the care provider. For the younger child, an explanation needs to be given by the social worker to the child with the new care provider present along with a written copy. It is important that vocabulary used by social workers and care providers is similar and the same message is understood by the child.

During the Preservation Stage the care provider can help by . . .

— Quietly accepting the child's losses and being available to listen. Avoid making judgments about the child's situation or other people involved in the child's life. Refrain from interrupting when the child is speaking.

— Sharing feelings with the child, so he knows how you are feeling and how you react to those feelings.

— Encouraging and supporting contact with previous family if possible.

— Permitting the child to show affection at his own pace. Providing loving and consistent care. Hold and look at the child when you are speaking. Read stories, sing songs, or write notes to the child. Make sure the child knows you care about him, whether he is quiet or active.

— Being reliable and trustworthy. Set up a schedule and stick to it, or explain why the schedule is going to change. Do not surprise the child in the beginning with a lot of new and different experiences.

— Providing a healthy physical environment and protecting the child from additional abuse.

— Doing something to make your house comfortable for the child. Provide a secure place that is "only theirs."

— Realizing your home may represent security for the child. Carefully explain what will happen when you go to the store, go outside to work in the yard, go to church, visit friends, go on vacation, etc.

— Finding things the child is good at or likes. After the child begins to become secure in the home, begin to provide a variety of experiences. Encourage family participation and interaction. Let the child plan some activities.

— Providing learning experiences for the child using all his senses as the child begins to step out and trust the family. The child needs to know that how he sees, hears, tastes, smells, and touches are OK with you. Limits and boundaries will need to be established. *(See Chapter 13)*

— Letting the child know it's OK to ask for help, and that you will help. But that you will also allow the opportunity for reasonable independence.

In order to establish trust during the Preservation Stage, the child needs to hear these messages:

— *I will do my best to keep you safe and protect you.*

— *You belong here now.*

— *I am glad you are alive.*

— *I am glad you are here and I want you here.*

— *You can get to know me and I will be honest with you.*

Chapter 1 - Brown Bag Consignment Kids 15

A Chance at Life and Love
For all those who give of themselves to those without

All this to make a change, to give the innocent a chance. The freedom to love, to cry, to laugh, to dance.

No, it doesn't happen overnight, though we may wish with all our might.

But in the end . . . which is for the child a beginning . . . it is all worthwhile.

For a good self-image a chance at life, love and a smile.

Rebekha Larson
Former child in care

"That really bugs you
doesn't it? I'm glad
you tell me when
things bug you."
Foster Father

— *I care about you and what happens to you.*

— *What you need is important to me.*

— *You can grow at your own pace.*

— *All your feelings are important to me.*

Children in the Preservation Stage need active professional parenting. It is important for care providers to continuously reach out to the child with unconditional love. For some children, this process may take days or weeks. For others it may be months, years, or a lifetime. Care providers must prepare to be extremely sensitive to the needs of these fragile children in the Preservation Stage. Their young lives and futures depend on it.

2. Protest: Finally. . . Time for a New Beginning

The day of protest has come. It's been anticipated for quite some time. The child in care is beginning to react and is challenging the parental role. The question haunts his mind—*"If I was so bad, so unlovable that nobody wanted me, why do you have me?"* As feelings begin to surface, a raging battle boils inside, and the whole force of his being is directed at an effort to recapture what has been lost. In some ways this behavior is not unlike the temper tantrums of a two-year-old. The difference, however, is that the child may be an eight-, ten-, or fifteen-year-old, harboring years of rage and life experiences.

Children in battle with themselves during the Protest Stage often feel they are drowning, and just as a drowning person flails and thrashes and is difficult to save, so is this child. Like lifeguards, parents and professionals need training and knowledge in dealing with the child in protest. Otherwise the child may be stuck in this stage or lost.

Protest is often where we see the child's most destructive behaviors. Yet it is during this stage that most of the healing work is accomplished. The Protest Stage of the grieving process is painful, but crucial to the development of the child. These children's behavior can be baffling if you have never experienced it before. *It is during this time that many abuse allegations are made against surrogate parents*. Professional parents need to recognize the Protest Stage of the grief cycle and refocus on the growth of the child instead of the protest experiences. This reframing of attitudes can provide a safety net for both the child and the parent.

Focusing on the positive side of protest allows care providers to think clearly even when their emotions are ready to explode. *(See also Chapter 13)*

During the Protest Stage it is important to remember:

1. The child is finally willing to begin to trust by taking risks in negative behavior and experiencing reactions. The child will try to push all kinds of emotional buttons to discover the level of support and candidness care providers will provide.

2. The child needs to feel something better is being offered to replace his carefully constructed defenses.

3. The beginning sense of loss felt by the child may serve as a point of emotional contact between parent and child.

4. The child is feeling out of control in most areas of his life.

5. Only by removing anger, rage, or hatred can the child find room for happiness, joy, and love.

In addition to the emotions experienced during the Preservation Stage, the child begins feeling the pain of the losses. This new growth is expressed through feelings and actions most adults want to avoid. Avoidance is dangerous to the relationship and mental health of all involved. The child needs to understand where his anger is coming from, know how the care provider is feeling, and also how the care provider is handling those feelings.

During the Protest Stage the child may feel:

Afraid	Disenchanted	Imposed upon	Sad
Aggressive	Disgusted	Indignant	Serious
Anxious	Distressed	Infuriated	Small
Annoyed	Disturbed	Irritated	Sneaky
Assertive	Enraged	Jealous	Spiteful
Bad	Evil	Mad	Stingy
Bitter	Exasperated	Mean	Tempted
Bold	Exploited	Miserable	Tense
Brave	Fearful	Naughty	Terrible
Challenged	Flustered	Obnoxious	Threatened
Cheated	Frantic	Outraged	Thwarted
Clever	Frustrated	Persecuted	Troubled
Condemned	Frightened	Powerful	Unafraid
Contemptuous	Furious	Powerless	Uncertainty
Cruel	Guilt/shame	Quarrelsome	Wicked
Defensive	Hateful	Rageful	Worthless

Uncertainty about the situation and fear of the unknown can be strong forces in provoking anger. The child may feel overwhelmed with unexpressible feelings. These multiple misunderstood primary feelings often are expressed with a secondary feeling—anger. For example, *"hurt," "unfairness,"* and *"fear"* may be the primary feelings, yet anger is the *"expressed or repressed"* feeling. Children may feel they are worthless and a burden on the new family. The child may misperceive that the new care provider is the source of all the problems. *"If this stupid foster parent hadn't gotten involved, I'd still be with my parents."*

In order to risk expressing anger, a child needs to feel it is safe to do so. Children with repressed anger need outlets. Care providers may become the safe individuals to whom a child can transfer unexpressed angry feelings. Regardless of how difficult and uncomfortable this stage feels, the relationship has made progress. This stage is extremely frustrating, yet for these children anger is a healthy expression. The child needs assurance that it is normal and human to feel. Every human being feels anger—yesterday, today, and in the future. The adult needs to guide and model appropriate and effective methods of safe venting for the child. Both adults and children can get angry in a responsible manner and work out conflicts that are not abusive to others. *(See sidebar page 19.)*

It's OK to feel anger—feel the heart beat faster, allow the tears, trembling, and change in voice. The feeling anger does not victimize people, places, or things. Lorraine Bilodeau, MS, is author of *The Anger Workbook,* an excellent tool for parents living with a child experiencing the Protest Stage. Bilodeau explains, *"Anger is an internal reaction, which an individual learns to name, to an external event. Anger has many functions. Modern life would be very different and much more difficult today if anger had been omitted or eliminated from the human experience.* (Bilodeau p17, 1992).

Anger is a vehicle for communication that always carries a message. The person who expresses anger is trying to present information. Often it is information that, without the anger, he wouldn't have the courage to express. Communicating anger reduces the use of physical attack when used as the first response to a threatening or frustrating situation verbally

When children really hurt, it may feel good to strike out and hurt someone or something. For a brief period the child can feel control and power in a world that is hurting him. A care provider must not give up when the going gets toughest. This is when the child needs the care provider the most!

Timing is important in working with hurting and fragile children. An appropriate word or action at the correct time moves mountains and begins releasing the child from pain.

Adults can have incredible impact on the future psychological health of each child they care for or influence.

Probably 80-90 percent of our interaction with other people is controlled by our response to old hurts from our childhood.
Henslin 1991

It is estimated that the life of one individual directly influences more than 300 other people over a period of four generations.

Ideas to help a child safely express anger:

Communicate:

- Write angry words on paper or with chalk
- Write a furious letter
- Journal your feelings
- Talk into a tape recorder

Creative Work:

- Make angry pictures
- Mold clay
- Make angry music
- Do an angry dance

Relax:

- Take a hot shower
- Breathing exercises
- Foot massage, temple/face massage
- See stress reduction ideas in Chapter 15
- Read
- Lie down and listen to mellow music

Helpful Work:

- Knead bread, roll out dough
- Pick up sticks, pull weeds, rake yard
- Shovel snow
- Put all toys away
- Stack wood
- Throw dirty laundry down stairs or into washer
- Build a tree house or hammer nails into an old piece of wood

Recycling:

- Crumple up newspapers for the wood stove or crumple up newspapers and throw them in a bag
- Stomp on aluminum cans and throw them in a recycling can.
- Rip up some old sheets for the rag bag

Anger protects personal dignity, identity, and self-esteem. When a person feels put down, ignored, ridiculed or victimized, anger is likely to occur. This feeling encourages the individual to stand up for self and defend against being cheated, belittled, or emotionally attacked. It is the piece of self that says, "You don't have a right to treat me this way."

Anger functions in any culture as a social regulator. It defines social behavior and protects societal values. Each culture determines when an angry response is appropriate and how that response is to be expressed. Anger is considered appropriate when the norms, mores, and laws of the culture are violated. The intensity of the response depends on the importance of the violations. Thus anger defines the boundaries of acceptable behavior for social situations.

Anger functions as a social bond. When a group of people focus anger collectively on an outside group, individual, or situation, the anger ties individuals of the group together. They have a common enemy. The lines of the "we vs. they" are drawn. To be a member of the "we" you have to be angry at the "they" group. Anger over social injustice is an example of this type of anger.

In some cases the response to anger is instinctive. Anger's most basic function is survival. It is necessary in hands-on fighting. It provides the incentive to struggle against the elements and accomplish what would have been physically impossible without the additional strength that comes from anger. Adrenaline, the chemical involved in anger arousal, produces a numbing effect on the body which allows the person to continue to fight when hurt. The dampening of pain makes the person stronger. Without pain, the body comes closer to reaching its absolute strength potential. It also creates tunnel vision and concentration is focused on the opposing force. The individual does not defeat the self—self-doubt and fear of failure do not impinge on the combatant's ability to struggle. The individual does not experience pain until after the struggle, when the adrenaline level drops. (Bilodeau p18 1991) It is appropriate to feel anger when you or a loved one is endangered—real or perceived.

When a person uses anger constructively, it acts as a motivating force for change, for meeting personal needs, and for gaining a desired goal.
These circumstances are often accompanied by the thoughts,
"That's it. I've had enough. I deserve better."

For anger to be useful, people must do more than merely experience the feeling of anger. Those whom anger motivates productively undergo a four-step process.
1. They feel the anger.
2. They recognize the situation that provoked it.
3. They identify a healthy, productive goal that would alleviate the situation.
4. They maintain the anger until they can take the first steps toward the goal. (Bilodeau 1991, p18)

The child needs freedom to describe the anger producing event, tell why he is angry, what he wishes done, how he is frustrated because he can't do anything about it, and why he wishes he could *"punch their lights out."* As long as the child hides these negative feelings, he will remain separated from his caregivers. The child needs to be assured that appropriate expression of anger to a *"true"* friend is acceptable, safe, and often provides an opening for greater understanding.

The Protest Stage is "no picnic." Some adoptive and foster families never make it through this important battleground. Just hanging in there is exhausting. *Outside empathetic adult support is crucial; without it the results can be disastrous.*

This volatile period is not only difficult to handle, but also may be devastasting if a child uses his feelings of anger against a provider family by making false abuse, neglect, or sexual allegations. The provider family then faces the trauma of an investigation, the child faces a potential move, and social services may be put through hoops not knowing if the child has made up the data.

It is important to note the damage done to the child if an allegation is made during the Protest Stage and the child is removed. By outward appearances, all is well and the problem solved. Immediately, both the care provider family and child in care may feel relief to be rid of a difficult situation. Social services, seeing the resulting honeymoon in the next home, may disbelieve what the care provider family shared regarding the behavior of the child. In truth, the devastating result is that another incompleted grieving cycle has begun and the child will need to begin dealing with another compounded loss—separation from a family he has just begun to trust and attach to.

During the Protest Stage the child needs . . .

— Parents to maintain outer control while the child is learning inner control.
   — Firm boundaries regarding appropriate and inappropriate behavior and consistent natural and logical consequences for behaviors.
   — Clear explanation of effects caused by behavior.
   — Immediate and consistent discipline, not long term.
   — Rules that are simple, direct, and kept to a minimum.

— Firmness without dominance. Standing firm makes it clear you are willing to see the conflict through to resolution. It creates an atmosphere of hope. Firmness does not escalate the situation, but it makes it clear to the other person that change is needed. Firmness does not yield easily under pressure. It is stable and consistent. Respect for the child's needs and wishes is essential and it allows the child time to voice his or her side. Domination places our will, superiority, and influence on the child without respect for child's need.

— A sport or activity to help reroute negative energy. Be the biggest fan. Encourage the child.

— An outside support person to help develop additional perspectives, develop problem-solving techniques, and provide the child with another safe adult to talk to and begin to trust.

— Help increase self-esteem, self-awareness, and self-confidence. Continue to find concrete ways to build these. Arrange personal time with the child by finding unique things the child likes to do and enjoy them together—stargazing, rock climbing, water skiing, mountain biking, whitewater rafting, in-line skating, etc.

— Acceptable ways of expressing anger. Make sure you are clear about what is permissible to do when angry. *(See sidebars on pages 18-19.)*

Tell/Talk	Journal	Yell	Special breathing
Fuss box	Draw	Punching bag	Dance/Workout
Walk	Sports	Sad chair	Shoot baskets
Jog or run	Tantrum mat	Centering	Ask for help

— Good examples shown in honesty—truth telling. Make sure it is safe to tell the truth. Don't try to trap the child in a lie. Continue to build trust.

— To hear "*I*" messages from parents—I feel, I see, I think, I hear—avoid "*You*" messages to the child *(You did, You are, etc.)*

— To learn to work with their emotional thermometer. What does the child do when he/she is getting angry? Find the subtle clues of erupting anger and help the child understand and manage these before the explosion.

Exercise/workout:

— Run, walk fast
— Jump rope
— Ride bike
— Shoot baskets
— Swim
— Swing

There are some safe negative actions that may help a child safely express rage. These actions, however, should be modified to more constructive outlets of anger as the rage is released.

Safe screaming gives release:

— Scream in your own room or in the shower
— Say "I'm gonna scream for X minutes," set a timer and then do it
— Get out the family tantrum mat and enjoy a tantrum within the boundaries of the mat
— With a young child go for a ride in the car and let the child scream while contained in a child safety seat
— Use the anger exercise on page 330.

Even safe hitting endorses hitting, use these anger release ideas with caution:

— Hit a punching bag
— Hit a thick stick on a tree
— Hit snowballs or baseballs
— Hit a pillow or mattress
— Throw snowballs at a tree
— Throw rocks into the water
— Slam/drop telephone book on the floor
— Rip up an old telephone book
— Twist a wire
— Wring wet towels
— Blow into a paper bag or balloon and pop
— Fill balloons with water and throw on sidewalk

ANGER

CONSTRUCTIVE	DEPRESSIVE	AGGRESSIVE
Sense of personal adequacy *Positive self-concept* *Positive self-talk*	**Sense of personal inadequacy** *Deny self-concept* *Negative self-talk*	

PRECEIVED THREAT — EVENT
Adrenaline flows

UNCOMFORTABLE FEELINGS OCCUR
Fear —Anxiety
frustration, confusion, hurt, misunderstood, put down,
out of control—etc.

ANGER
Adrenelin flow continues

Productive	Internalized	Externalized
Assertive Response	*Depressive Response*	*Aggressive Response*
Fear and anger are OK and real	**Fear is better than anger**	**Anger is better than fear**
Actions not destructive to self or others	*Suicide*	*Homicide*

Do you hear yourself thinking?

"Ladies don't get angry." "Men don't feel afraid." "Fear is wrong."
"The other person is responsible." "I wouldn't act like this if - - - -"
"Anger is bad or a sin." (read "The Way Out of the Wilderness" *by Earl R. Henslin)*
"He/She is angry because I am a bad person. If I was better ---"
"Fear is OK but anger is not." or "Anger is OK but fear is not."
"I can't talk about it." or "I won't talk about it."

The diagram above is adapted from the work of Lorraine Bilodeau, MS and research has been taken from *The Anger Workbook* (1992). Inquiries regarding Bilodeau's work and a wide variety of helpful other materials can be obtained by requesting a catalog and writing: CompCare Publishers, 3850 Annapolis Lane #100, Minneapolis, MN 55447 or call 1-800-328-3330 or (612)559-4800.

When a child seems not to need you, want you, or care how you feel about him—that's the moment he needs you most.

A rejecting child needs you to be the adult. Reach out to the child more than halfway. Listen to meanings—not just words.

"Mom? What's a word of the state?"
April

It means that a child is in the state's care and they are called a 'ward' not a 'word.'

"You mean a state like Minnesota takes care of them."
April

People in the state, Honey. The state is just land.

"You're wrong, Mom. Joseph is not a ward. To the people in the state, Joseph is just a 'word' like you put on paper."
April

This chart helps explain the actions, feelings and thoughts of children in the Protest Stage.

Actions	Feelings	Thoughts
Actively or passively acts out * Roaming	Rageful and angry about loss	Thinks he is being unjustly treated
Bedwetting Nightmares Nightterrors	Unconscious release; embarrassed	Release of tensions and anxiety
Refuses to be comforted * Runs away * Avoidance	Desires help but refuses it when offered	Thinks he should be in control
Complains about tiny injuries and small emotional upsets	Lonely and needs attention	Needs closeness and attention, but does not know how to ask
Ignores major injuries (broken bones)	Brave and tough exterior; afraid and unsure interior	Pretends he is someone he isn't, i.e., Rambo, Ninja, etc.
May turn anger inward to himself * Suicide * Self mutilation	Overwhelmed by situation No one cares	Proves that maybe someone cares
Medicates self * Substance abuse * Eating disorders	Afraid of self-control	Thinks he needs short term high or false courage
May turn anger outward to others: * Pets * Other children * Parents	Persecuted by people who have power; powerlessness	Thinks others deserve to feel their pain.
May turn anger outward on things: * Set fires * Vandalize * Graffiti	Frustrated; lonely; needs attention; jealous of others' property; angry	Thinks he will feel better if he returns some indirect injury; gets daily high from destruction
Tries to take control * Hoarding food * Lying	Fearful; angry; out-of-control; powerless	Thinks he has been cheated out of material things
Stealing Cheating Manipulate others to child's advantage	Feels worthwhile by possessing things; deserving of objects	Thinks things represent caring; wants to get fair share
Impulsive behavior; lacks good judgment	Apathetic about future	Doesn't think before acting—cause and effect
Sexual acting out	Not emotionally satisfied	Needs to feel loved by someone

See also Chapter 13 for additional understanding of anger reaction vs. response.

There is one medicine for a broken heart—Love.

If somehow in the midst of our deepest sorrow, we find hope in our tomorrow, then we have won a greater battle indeed, a stronger will, so that with confidence we may succeed.

Rebekha Larson
Former foster child

A healthy expression of anger means that we own it, we admit to it, and we work through it as it surfaces:

I am angry because. . .
. . . it isn't the way I thought it would be.
. . . I want to be with my real Mom and Dad.
. . . My parents aren't there for me.
. . . I've been abused.

During the Protest Stage the care providers can help themselves by . . .

— Seeking out supportive and trusting friends who will lend a listening ear, empathy, and ideas while working with the child. The local or state foster/adoptive agency may know of another family with similar interests. Get therapy for yourself and the child if you need it. Attend support groups. Take classes. Take time out. Have fun. Find time to play and relax.

— Documenting the child's daily behaviors. A pattern may emerge that would be easy to miss if it isn't written down. Include behavior, food ingested, what you felt was cause of behavior. *(See Chapter 14.)*

— Communicating—making sure key people involved in the child's life have enough information to understand peculiar behavior patterns. Develop a plan for key people that includes: who to contact and when, what behaviors may be expected, and what behavior modification techniques are approved and appropriate. Check confidentiality laws with your social worker and together inform—in writing—medical and school personnel working with the child. *(See Chapter 14.)*

— Making sure you know medical/educational status of the child. Alert the child's medical/educational team to the behaviors you are observing.

During the Protest Stage care providers can help the child by . . .

— Helping the child avoid the most difficult situations.

— Talking to the child about the behavior you want stopped. Go after the real problems, not the manifestations of the symptoms. Ask for ideas you can work on together to help him change.

— Finding opportunities to encourage, praise, and hug the child. If it is difficult to do this, write notes, put little trinkets in the child's lunch bag, or make a cassette tape to explain your thoughts.

— Use the Kidz Care Notebook. Draw and write with the child to open communication beyond active anger. *(See Chapter 14)*

— Use the *"Two Places Called Home"* workbook by Deb Jones and Lane Fischer. *(Instructions for ordering can be found in Chapter 9.)*

The child needs to hear these messages during the Protest Stage:

— *I will not make you put these new feelings of anger away. I will help you understand them or find someone who can help you.*

— *I will continue to provide care, safety, and protection.*

— *When you are angry, I will help you solve the problem.*

— *It's OK for you to be angry. I won't let you hurt yourself or others.*

— *It's OK for you to ask to get your needs met, and I will help you learn to ask.*

— *I will help you get control of your life and the feelings you have.*

— *You can think and feel at the same time. Your angry feelings are important to me.*

— *Behavior that is inappropriate will have consequences that are approved in writing by you and your social worker.*

— *You can be powerful and ask for help.*

— *It's OK to be angry and I will express the anger I feel.*

— *You can learn to think for yourself, and I will think for myself. It's OK to be different from me.*

3. Sorrow: Working through the pain to a new beginning

The Sorrow Stage is similar to the Preservation Stage, but in sorrow the child has no urge to care for himself. In place of plans and desires is a sense of helplessness and apathy. He may go to bed, get sick, hide in the garage, or go into a fetal position. He will not start anything new and may regress to thumbsucking, bedwetting, and playing with toys. Even teenagers display some infantile behavior during this stage. Depending on how well adjusted the child is and his capacity to handle extreme stress, this stage may last several months.

Eventually the child realizes the loss can't be controlled or repaired. The child has an intense awareness of how much the lost experiences, objects, and people are missed—particularly at moments shared and treasured (mealtimes, bedtime, holidays, etc.) or on anniversary dates when the loss occurred. This is the time of intense hurting and suffering that I refer to as sorrow. If a foster or pre-adoptive child has reached this stage when an allegation is made, a move becomes proof again that they are unlovable and worthless.

During the initial phase of sorrow the child often plea bargains with God.
Usually the pleas and bargains are impossible and unrealistic such as:
"If God will let me return home, I'll be good, do well in school, and never be angry or bad again." In reality this is the calm before the storm. The child cannot achieve the unattainable goal of always being good and the social system or legal situation may not allow a return home. In time, the tightly controlled energy of being good wears out and the child is left desolate. The child may now feel additional guilt and shame. His perception is now final abandonment, this time from God.

If a child has moved away from protest and conflict and life is beginning to relax a bit, it may be time to sit down with the child and talk about what other kids do when they are dealing with the kinds of losses your child has experienced.
A discussion of a story or movie that deals with sorrow, pain, mourning, tears, and suffering may open a way to talk about or express the feelings we all have when we are suffering. It is important for the future spiritual development of the child to address this issue.

A sense of isolation and loneliness again creeps in on the child. This time however, there is not the hope that existed in the Preservation Stage. Children in this stage wonder: *"Why is life so hard?"* or *"Am I the only kid in the world this is happening to?"* Adults do not like to see children hurting. Sometimes it is easier to discourage the child's feelings. We tell children, *"Don't worry about the past,"* or *"Everything is going to be all right now,"* rather than quietly allowing the child to accept and work through the pain. When this happens to a child, the child is denied support services which help cope with losses.

During the Sorrow Stage children may feel:

Apathetic	Distracted	Hurt	Pitiful
Betrayed	Distressed	Insulted	Powerless
Burdened	Disturbed	Intimidated	Rejected
Cheated	Doubtful	Isolated	Remorseful
Condemned	Empty	Jealous	Sad
Crushed	Exasperated	Lonely	Scared
Defeated	Exhausted	Longing	Serious
Depressed	Fearful	Lost	Sorrowful
Desolate	Frightened	Melancholy	Threatened
Despairing	Grief	Miserable	Troubled
Devastated	Guilty	Nervous	Unfortunate
Disappointed	Helpless	Overwhelmed	Weak
Disgusted	Homesick	(In) Pain	Worried

Children need an unchanging anchor in their lives, something to hold on to, even when everything around them is moving.

It is important to remember that all of the feelings associated with grief ebb and flow, and that you and your child will inevitably go back over these emotions time and time again.
We love to neatly compartmentalize things, to finish one, then go on to the next. But it doesn't work that way with emotions like grief.
(Schaefer/Lyons, 1986)

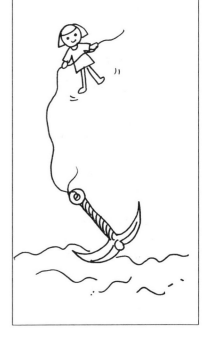

This chart helps to explain the actions, thoughts, and feelings children experience in the Sorrow Stage.

Actions	Feelings	Thoughts
Has sad face, poor posture, poor hygiene	Feels defeated and confused	Thinks he may give up
Plea bargains for return of what was lost	Feels pity for self— "poor me"	Thinks life is unfair
Clings to objects, pets, not people	Withdrawn and desolate	Thinks objects are safe and won't add to loss
Reacts excessively to small hurts, whiny	Emotional hurts, shame	Assigns guilt to others
Wants to be left alone	Feels worthless	Thinks he's unacceptable and no good
Potential suicide	Emptiness, unfulfilment	Thinks, " why continue on?"
Very "me" centered	Needy	Thinks situation is hopeless

During the Sorrow Stage the child needs . . .

— To hear sympathy, not pity. Feeling sorry for the **"it"** *which happened* is sympathy. Feeling sorry for the **"you"** *to whom it happened* is pity. Pity is damaging, even when justifiable and understandable. Pity is condescending. Adults tend to underestimate children and regulate them to retreat in sad passivity, full of complaints and demands.

> *"I understand how you feel, how much it hurts, or how difficult it is for you. I am sorry about **it** and I will help you overcome the hardships of your situation."*
> NOT
> *"I look down on **you**. I am better than **you**. I have all the answers. I will rescue, fix, or control **you** to help **you**. You poor thing. I feel so sorry for **you**. I'll do all I can to make up for what **you** suffer."*

— To hear affirmations used during the Preservation Stage, to feel secure because you are there.

— To learn and understand acceptable expressions of feelings during times of suffering.

— To lean on a solid support system and understand that all people suffer during certain times in their lives.

During the Sorrow Stage the foster/adoptive parents can help by . . .

— Listening. Listening. Listening.

Listening is hard to do. When a parent just sits and does not say much it can be tremendously beneficial. The child needs to know he is not alone, that you accept him as he is, bad feelings and all. And that you're available to help and are trying to empathize.
(To really listen and understand a part of the pain.)

— Accepting the child as a separate and important human being.

- Realizing that all people, including children, must ultimately solve their own problems and deal with their own feelings. Telling a child not to feel a certain way is an automatic turn-off.

- Remembering that as the new care provider you are not responsible for what the child is feeling. The past is a memory. A child who does not cope with memories and feelings may act and feel as if past events are in the present. *The child's present can gain control over the past.* Memories need to be shared with feelings to be resolved. Once shared, reality can begin to take the place of the memory.

- Setting limits that do not attach guilt or shame. Avoid all shaming statements. *(See Chapter 12 for shaming statements.)* Setting no conditions for care and love.

Messages a child needs to hear during the Sorrow Stage include:

- *All of your feelings are OK with me.*

- *You can learn to differentiate between past and present.*

- *When you feel sad you can come to me.*

- *I care about you.*

- *You can come to me if you are not trusting your feelings.*

- *You can think for yourself.*

- *You can get help instead of staying in distress.*

- *You are entitled to sincere compliments, encouragement, and appropriate praise for even the littlest improvements.*

On bad days, when the child cannot be comforted, don't try to do more than say, *"I know this is a rotten day. Tomorrow may be better. I'm here if you need me. I care about you."*

Extreme patience is needed. It is not unusual to feel you have given everything, gotten nowhere and are further behind now than in the beginning of the relationship. *Hang on!*

4. Hope: A sense of mastery over the past

In the Hope Stage, the struggle with reality is over and the child begins to find peace in the present. The child realizes that no matter how much the past is loved and missed, life goes on. Good days outnumber the bad days and suddenly the future has possibilities and options. It is the time of forgiving and reaching for the future, but not forgetting or burying the past. The child begins to reorganize life and finds feelings of hope.

During the Hope Stage, children begin to feel:

Affectionate	Helpful	Pleased	Strong
Assertive	Hopeful	Proud	Supported
Calm	Inspired	Reassured	Sympathetic
Cheerful	Kind	Relaxed	Trusting
Curious	Loving	Relieved	Unafraid
Glad	Nice	Resigned	
Good	Peaceful	Responsive	
Grateful	Pleasant	Satisfied	

Charlie Chaplin's mother was poor. She even had to put her child in an orphanage, but she visited him and gave him the assurance he was loved, that he was valuable and important.

The experience of being loved can be sensed in all the Chaplin films. In spite of hunger, misery, and calamity, there is always room for feelings, for tears, for tenderness, for life.
(Miller 1990)

"There should really be a law that a foster or adoptive kid's first piece of clothing is a life preserver to their past and a suitcase to store their stuff in."
Joseph's new foster mom

The Hope Stage, although not always a happy time, is the time of acceptance. It is the beginning of peace with the loss and present situation—the beginning of open acknowledgment of reality and the more positive side of grief.

Children experiencing the loss of their primary family will continue to rework losses at different stages of their development. Grief issues probably will resurface during adolescence, parenthood, and during significant events such as the death of a family member. If a child has moved beyond the Sorrow Stage and into the Hope Stage, these significant life experiences will allow for greater understanding and open the door for grief work that still needs to be done.

During the Hope Stage the child ...

Actions	Feelings	Thoughts
Becomes more involved with people	Reassured that everyone is not out to get him	Begins to thinks beyond needs of self
Becomes more involved in activities	Unafraid to try something new	Believes in self again; self-confidence
Takes care of appearance; posture improves	Reassured that life will continue	Begins to like self again; increased self-esteem
Responds positively to affection and offers affection	Responsive and accepting of positive interaction	Begins to thinks beyond self
Behavior more balanced and stable	Relaxes and takes life easier	Begins to think about feelings, ideas
Shows emotions and begins to ask for help	Relieved to find he's not alone	Begins to think about new relationships

During the Hope Stage the child needs ...

— A time and a place for talking, sharing, and listening.

— Tasks that will boost self-esteem.

— Encouragement to try new things. Specific examples need to be praised and encouraged. *(See Chapter 11.)*

— Options and choices for today and tomorrow.

During the Hope Stage care providers can help by ...

— Being available when the child asks for time or help. Offer problem-solving tools. Be a reliable source the child can come to for information about the world, people, and relationships.

— Giving lots of positive strokes to reward and encourage the learning of new skills, trying new things, and interacting with people.

— Continuing to offer safety, love, and protection.

Messages children need to hear during the Hope Stage are ...

— *You have a lot of courage and are a strong person.*

— *You can find a way of doing things that works for you.*

— *You can learn rules to help you live with others.*

— *You can learn when and how to disagree.*

— *You are lovable even when you differ from others.*

— *I care about you even when we differ.*

— *I like growing with you.*

— *It's OK to hope that life (things) will get better.*

5. Faith: Walking out on future paths

When a child has successfully completed the grieving cycle, a renewed and restored faith in life emerges. With this acceptance the child acquires a new ability—being able to find pleasure in the growth that emerges from the experience. The loss can now be remembered with poignancy, compassion, and caring instead of pain.

This chart explains the actions, feelings, and thoughts children experience in the Faith Stage.

Actions	Feelings	Thoughts
Has healthy relationships with others	Cares for other people	Knows that relationships with others are valuable
Takes care of himself as he is capable	Is happy about his life and who he is	Knows that he is stronger from his experiences
Unconditionally can help or care for others	Respects others' needs	Finds value in others less fortunate
Supportive of others in loss situations	Has clarity in feelings of his personal losses	Has a sense of strength from process
Can play and celebrate life	Joy and spontaneity	Values joy and love; is capable of feeling fulfilled

Faith is not an ending, but another beginning for the child. It is here the child becomes capable of stepping off into more natural physical, emotional, and psychological development. The child has a future.

During the Faith Stage the child needs . . .

— To know that negative experiences can be used in positive ways and someone will help.

— To know that you are glad the grief cycle is over and understand how difficult it was to make the transition.

— To know that some things in the future may trigger expressions of protest or sorrow. To try to predict some of those instances so the child can work through them with understanding and not be surprised by an unusual reaction.

— To know that you care, and will continue to offer care, safety, and protection.

Preparation for anniversary dates

Significant changes in feelings or behaviors may occur on the anniversary of the loss or during times significant to the child's past, even though the child may seem to have resolved grief.

> *Problems do not go away. They must be worked through or else they remain forever a barrier to the growth and development of the spirit.*
> M. Scott Peck

Young children who cannot remember the date of the event may react to the season in which the event occurred. One of the common triggers for the anniversary reaction is the sense of smell— the scent of pine or cinnamon, a turkey roasting in the oven, fall leaves, spring rain. Holidays and birthdays are not the only events that trigger reactions—the date the child lost the birth family, the date the child left a significant foster home, and the date the child was separated from other siblings—also are major anniversary days and may be hard to figure out. Reactions may occur when packing for a trip, changing classrooms, or upon the illness or death of a significant other person. A child may also have an intense reaction to seeing another child facing a similar loss or experience. Flashbacks of maltreatment may occur when a sequence of events occurs such as vacuuming on Saturdays, family photos, or coaching a child in a softball game. Unusual reactions to seemingly normal events may provide clues to a child's history. Knowledge of triggers and anniversary dates in the child's past allows a care provider to prepare for unusual behaviors and to intervene to diminish the child's reactions.

Helpful ideas to work through anniversary dates:

— Acknowledge the timing and situation. Keep a journal of reactions so you can refer back to experiences from previous years.

— Discuss the reactions with the child — use "I" messages.
"*I see that you are really quiet these last days.*
I think that you are experiencing some feelings from some of the things that have happened in your life.
I feel sad when I see you so quiet, I really care about what's going on in your life. Can I share some of my own feelings about how I handle anniversary dates?"

— Look through *The Life Book* or *Two Places Called Home Workbook* , talk about the past and the people the child remembers. *(See Chapter 9)*

Summary

In order to maintain healthy physical, emotional, and psychological development children must feel secure. The relationships they form with care providers, whether birth parents, foster parents, or adoptive parents, must be valued. Previous relationships must be honored and not judged by the new caregivers.

When children are moved, adults must remember that:

— *Attachment is the foundation for building future relationships and healthy psychological development. Attachments a child makes must be valued, respected, and supported.*

— *Unattached children become emotionally and psychologically disabled adults.*

— *Loss is not as traumatic if a child is prepared and provided with support through the grieving process.*

— *Years later, even when the grieving process appears complete, anniversary dates, smells, sounds, and seemingly normal events can trigger unusual responses or flashbacks which result in additional grieving.*

In order to ensure emotional and psychological well-being, children must not be removed from homes, except in absolute emergencies, without full and adequate preparation for the move. *(See Chapter 9.)*

References

Al-Aidy, Deb Contag, Haines, Judy, and Studaker, Peg. 1990. *Family Preservation the Second Time Around*. Minnesota: The North American Council on Adoptable Children.

Bilodeau, Lorraine. 1992. *The Anger Book*. Minnesota: CompCare.

Bourguingnon, Jean-Pierre, and Watson, Kenneth W. 1987. *After Adoption: A Manual for Professionals Working with Adoptive Families*. Illinois Department of Children and Family Services.

Cermak, Timmen L. 1991. *Adult Children of Alcoholics, Vol. 1 and 2*. Minnesota: Johnson Institute.

Clarke, Jean Illsley and Dawson, Connie. 1989. *Parenting Ourselves, Parenting Our Children*. Minnesota: Hazelden.

Clarke, Jean Illsley. 1978. *Self Esteem: A Family Affair*. New York: Harper/Collins.

Cline, Foster. 1979. *Understanding and Treating the Severly Disturbed Child*. Evergreen, Co: Evergreen Consultants in Human Behavior.

Dean, Amy E. 1988. *Making Changes*. Minnesota: Hazelden.

Dorris, Michael. 1989. *The Broken Cord*. New York: Harper Perennial.

Falhberg, Vera. 1990. *Attachment and Separation. Putting the Pieces Together Series*. Michigan Department of Social Services.

Falhberg, Vera. 1987. *Child Development. Putting the Pieces Together Series*. Michigan Department of Social Services.

Falhberg, Vera. 1980. *The Child in Placement. Common Behavioral Problems. Putting the Pieces Together Series*. Michigan Department of Social Services.

Falhberg, Vera. 1990. *Helping Children When They Must Move. Putting the Pieces Together Series*. Michigan Department of Social Services.
For Falhberg books: National Resource Center for Special Needs Adoption of Spaulding, P.O. Box 337, Chelsea, MI 48118.

Farmer, Steven. 1989. *Adult Children of Abusive Parents. A Healing Program for Those Who Have Been Physically, Sexually or Emotionally Abused*. New York: Ballantine.

Jewett, Claudia L. 1979. *Adopting The Older Child*. Massachusetts: The Harvard Common Press.

Jones, E. P. 1990. *Where is Home? Living Through Foster Care*. New York: Four Walls Eight Windows

Kaye, Yvonne. 1991. *The Child That Never Was. Grieving Your Past to Grow Into the Future*. Florida: Health Communications.

Larsen, Earnie. 1988. *Old Patterns. New Truths*. Minnesota: Hazelden

Lerner, Harriet Goldhur. 1985. *The Dance of Anger*. New York: Harper/Collins.

Magid, Ken and McKelvey, Carole A. 1989. *High Risk, Children Without a Conscience*. New York: Bantam Books.

McNamara, Joan and McNamara, Bernard. 1990. *Adoption and the Sexually Abused Child*. Maine: University of Southern Maine.

Middelton-Moz, Jane and Dwinnell, L. 1986. *After the Tears: Reclaiming the Personal Losses of Childhood*. Florida: Health Communications.

Middelton-Moz, Jane and Dwinnell, L. 1986. *Children of Trauma*. Florida: Health Communications.

Miller, Alice. 1983. *For Your Own Good: Hidden Cruelty in Child-Rearing and the Roots of Violence*. New York: Farrar, Straus, Giroux. (Translation from German)

Miller, Alice. 1990. *Banished Knowledge. Facing Childhood Injuries*. New York: Double Day. (Translation from German)

Miller, Alice. 1991. *The Untouched Key. Tracing Childhood Trauma in Creativity and Destructiveness*. New York: Double Day. (Translation from German)

Peck, M. Scott. 1978. *The Road Less Traveled*. New York: Touchstone Books

Rainbolt, Beverly and Greene, Michael. 1990. *Behind the Veil of Silence. Family Violence and*

Joseph's life—and the life of our family—did not end with the revocation of our license. In a way, the revocation may have been the ending preceding a new beginning.

For me. . .
It encouraged my search for the tools families need when working with children in care. And it clarified how detrimental quick and traumatic moves are to children in care, and the lasting impact those moves have on individual lives and society's future.

It spawned a yearning to discover the formula to develop teamwork and cooperation between all individuals involved in the child's life.

And it solidified my commitment to provide information to advocate for change in a very powerful system.

Alcohol Abuse. Minnesota: Hazelden.

Ray, Veronica. 1991. *Choosing Happiness. The Art of Living Unconditionally.* Minnesota: Hazelden.

Ray, Veronica. 1988. *Design for Growth. Twelve Steps for Adult Children.* Minnesota : Hazelden

Schaefer, Dan and Lyons, Christin. 1986. *How Do We Tell The Children, A Parents' Guide To Helping Children Understand and Cope When Someone Dies.* New York: Newmarket Press.

Simos, Bertha G. 1979. *A Time to Grieve: Loss as a Universal Experience.* New York: Family Services Association of America,

Spencer, Marietta. *Different Roles of Parenting.* Children's Home Society of Minnesota.

Turecki, Stanley and Tonner, Leslie. 1989. *The Difficult Child.* New York: Bantam.

Wegscheider-Cruse, Sharon. 1985. *Choice-Making for Co-depdendents, Adult Children and Spirituality Seekers.* Florida: Health Communications.

Whitfield, Charles L. 1987. *Healing the Child Within.* Florida: Health Communications.

Children's materials

Anderson, Deborah. 1986. *Jason's Story: Going To A Foster Home.* Minneapolis: Dillon

Bunin, Catherine and Sherry. 1976. *Is That Your Sister? A True Story About Adoption.* New York: Pantheon Books

Freeman, Lory. 1982. *It's My Body: A Book to Teach Young Children How to Resist Uncomfortable Touch.* Seattle: Parenting Press.

Freeman, Lory. 1986. *Loving Touches: A Book For Children About Positive, Caring Kinds of Touching.* Seattle: Parenting Press.

Gesme, Carole. 1985. *The Ups and Downs With Feelings Games.* Daisy Press, 16535 9th Avenue North, Plymouth, MN 55447.

Harambee: The Book Club for African-American Families and Friends, P.O. Box 603, Wilton, CT 06897. (203) 834-0669.

Holz, Loretta. 1984. *Foster Child.* New York: Julian Messner

One day April summarized surrogate parenting very well.

"You know what Mom?
There are two kinds of mommies—
Heart mommies and tummy mommies.
I got to grow inside of both mommies.
They both love me in the same place!"

And from Joseph . . .

"I was your baby, right?"
Yes, Joseph, you were our foster baby.
"You love me forever?"
Yes, we love you forever.
We don't have to be together to love each other.
"Love you, Joeeeee. See you later."

See you later, too, Joseph.

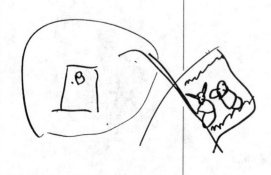

For Joseph . . .
The system moves
around and about him.
He waits. His heart
knows a family loves
him regardless of
whether we're together.
And as he says . . .

"No bye!
See ya later!"

Chapter 2

Professional Public Parenting 101

*Adults caring for other people's children
need to understand the
legal and personal dynamics
of parenting children in out-of-home care.*

My husband and I became licensed foster parents in 1979. We were idealistic and excited over the prospect of helping children. And the situation seemed ideal. Our active outdoor lifestyle seemed the perfect fit for teenage boys—scuba diving, hiking, white water kayaking, skiing, snowmobiling, and camping. I was self-employed, working out of our home, and we had three very large, affectionate dogs.

Our first *"quiet, shy"* (as described by our social worker) 13-year-old foster son sent shock waves through our home. Over a decade later, the neighbors still shake their heads as they recall their experiences with him. Neither our family nor social services could possibly have foreseen what we were about to experience.

This quiet, shy child rubbed the dogs' noses on sand paper and the screen door to hear them yelp, ripped frogs in half for the thrill of seeing them suffer, killed baby birds, stole our kitchen butcher knives, and used the bathroom towels for toilet paper. He mixed concoctions of miscellaneous goop for gaining super-natural power, and began a collection of harmful vaporous materials. Yet we kept believing that with a little more attention and love, we could help this child. We could change him. Finally, we began to question whether this child was more troubled than most. We asked the social worker if all foster children behaved similarly. She immediately arranged for psychiatric support and we enrolled in additional behavior modification classes.

In psychiatric counseling, he charmed the therapist and shared the horrors of his young life. After months of weekly counseling, I had the opportunity to sit in on a session. I related a number of experiences from my perspective. The therapist was shocked at how badly he'd been snowed. I had assumed the therapist would see through the stories, but in an attempt to reach deeper problems, he had permitted our foster son to vent his frustrations with a generous dose of falsehood and fabrication. We immediately agreed that changes were necessary.

Becoming a professional public parent means your family will now include: social services, the new foster child, birth family, and pre-existing life experiences of the child. All of these are important and all of them become part of your family!
Foster parent for 12 years

It is pretty hard to be objective about something as painfully personal as losing custody of your children and having them placed in foster homes.
Birth parent

It is surprising how many legitimate excuses you can come up with to avoid visiting your children in foster homes. Sometimes a failure to visit frequently on the part of the natural parents is not an indication that they don't care, but that they care too much.
(McAdams 1973)

Handout from Child Welfare League 1973

The remaining sessions proved more positive and we saw improvement as we became part of the child's treatment team.

Then, one morning, I woke up to find the dog peacefully sleeping at the foot of my bed. The pictures on the walls had been removed and a missing butcher knife was left on my blanket. Was this a joke? A threat? I called the emergency helpline and our quiet, shy child was removed and sent back to his mother.

Our social worker spent hours explaining that although unfortunate, our experience was unusual for a first time placement. She would keep her eyes out for a child who would be a better fit. A short time later a 15-year-old boy arrived. This child was challenging, but sensitive and caring. He faced the complexities of being an abused and neglected child, a chemically experimenting teen, and a very angry young man. His life was complicated by living in out-of-home care with strangers, a new school system, an all new neighborhood, separation from his siblings, and his first experience in living with a strong, nurturing adult male. For two and a half years he lived in our home as a part of our family. Today, he is 26 and self-sufficient. He still keeps in touch.

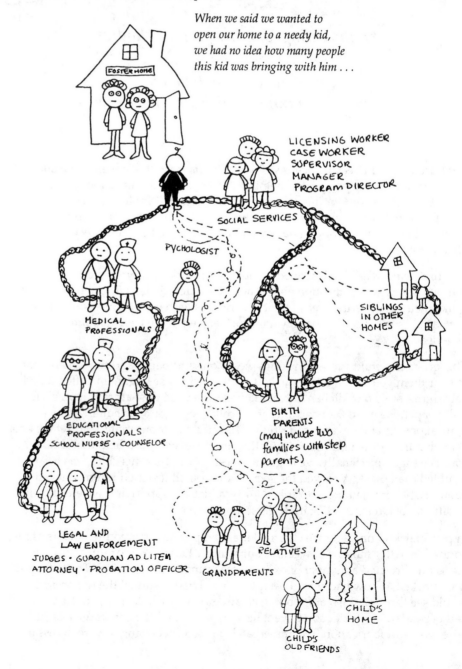

When we said we wanted to open our home to a needy kid, we had no idea how many people this kid was bringing with him . . .

Sensitivity and patience are required to nurture, understand, and parent any child. Additional doses of care are needed to allow children living in out-of-home care to develop a sense of safety for healing. Complicating day-to-day parenting is the necessity of the care providers to become a parallel member or co-parent of the child's natural family and a team member in the social welfare system.

Nurturing and parenting skills are challenged 24 hours a day by both the children and the system. When the social worker hangs up the phone, the care provider still has the life of a *"real"* child to nurture. When the weekend begins for the worker, the care provider has Friday night, Saturday, and Sunday to complete without a break. Yet, when legal or vital decisions need to be made for the child, social services and/or the birth parent is responsible for making the right decision, with limited direct contact with the child in care. Indeed, a carefully balanced juggling performance is necessary to be effective professional public parents.

What is foster care?

Successful family foster care is a team effort. The Child Welfare League and the National Foster Parent Association collaborated during 1990 as the National Commission on Family Foster Care (NCFFC) to develop the book *Blueprint for Fostering Infants, Children, and Youths in the 1990s.*

The *Blueprint* (1991) defines family foster care as:

> *An essential child welfare service option for children and parents who must live apart while maintaining legal, and usually, affectional ties. When children and parents must be separated because of the tragedy of physical abuse, sexual abuse, neglect, maltreatment, or special circumstances, foster family care provides a planned, goal directed service in which the care of children and youths takes place in the home of an agency-approved family. The value of family foster care is that it can respond to the unique, individual needs of infants, children, youths, and their families through the strength of family living, and through family and community supports. The goal of family foster care is to provide opportunities for healing, growth and development leading to healthier infants, children, youths, and families, with safe and nurturing relationships intended to be permanent. (NCFFC 1991)*

Foster care is intended to be a temporary, short-term solution for providing relief to families. In the best cases the child is provided a surrogate family or group setting while an intensive effort is made to correct or improve the condition which precipitated out-of-home care. Out-of-home care is provided only after in-home family preservation services have been considered, provided, or refused by the child's family.

— *And . . .* Foster care providers have been carefully selected and trained to provide the level of care necessary for children with special needs.

— *And . . .* Social services workers have the time and the resources to screen and monitor families caring for surrogate children.

Relatives are often called upon to help care for these children. Although relatives should be considered first, a careful assessment must be made in deciding if relative care is appropriate, and if services can be provided to help the relative meet the needs of the child. If relative care can't meet the needs of the child, a non-relative, same culture, foster family home is considered the least restrictive and most normal setting for children needing out-of-home care. When reunification is not possible, another permanency plan, such as long term foster care or adoption, is activated.

*The foster father
continues ...*

*The court recessed
and I could see this
immense man looming
toward me and his
children. I could feel
the cold, calculation of
his untrusting eyes.*

*"Let's go outside so
you and your children
can be together,"
I ventured.*

*He nodded his head
and looked at his wife.
Her eyes registered the
look of a lost puppy
wanting to jump in her
master's lap, pleading
hope, mixed with pain
and confusion.*

**And from the birth
mother ...**

*The fact that you are
visiting your child
in a foster home is a
reminder that you are,
at least for the time
being, a failure as a
parent. You are very
sensitive, during the
first visits. It would
have been easier to
talk to my children if
I had been kept
up-to-date on what
they had been doing.
I understand frequent
phone calls can be very
disruptive, but a brief
note once a week
would have made
communication
between my child and
me less strained.*
(McAdams 1973)

What do foster parents provide for children?

A licensed foster family has an important part to play as a child attempts to recover from the effects of difficult life experiences. But the legal dynamics of children in care, the child's original family system, and social services prohibit parenting the child in care in the same way you would parent your own child.

In her book, *Helping Children When They Must Move* (1989), Vera Falhberg outlines what foster care providers can and cannot provide, while working within the confines of the foster care system.

FOSTER PARENT CAN	FOSTER PARENT CAN'T
Provide safety.	*Solve family problems.*
Provide shelter.	*Provide security.*
Provide respite for families.	*Provide stability and continuity.*
Provide family while awaiting legal release or termination following abandonment.	*Provide continuity in terms of medical care.**
Provide an opportunity to assess child without the family and visa versa.	*Help natural parents deal with special needs of the child who is not home.*
Provide positive parenting experiences.	*Provide continuity in terms of schooling.**
Provide more adequate stimulation in cases of neglect.	*Increase bonding to birth family.*

*NOTE TO CURRENT CARE PROVIDERS: The Social Security Act issued on May 31, 1990 provides for continuity of medical and educational services for children in out-of-home care. Section 475 (1) of this act was amended to include in the definition "case plan" the requirement that a foster child's case plan must include certain specific information regarding his/her educational status. The amendment requires (mandates) inclusion but is not limited to the following information: (1) The names and addresses of the child's health and educational providers. (2) The child's school record. (3) The child's medical problems. (4) Any other relevant health and educational information concerning the child determined to be appropriate by the state agency. Names and addresses of previous educational and medical providers allows care providers better continuity of care. Care providers who do not have this information on the children they are caring for can request this information under the authority of this act.

Why is professional parenting a partnership in caring for out-of-home children?

Care providers are better equipped to deal with difficult situations when they understand the scope of the job. Training is crucial to help foster parents handle challenging emotional, behavior, and medical problems in children. Each child in care requires different parenting and legal requirements. Foster parent role and boundary requirements vary with each parent-child-agency relationship.

Foster families and agencies are interdependent partners. The relationship between the foster family and the agency must be one of mutual trust and respect. A relationship established with the birth family allows the child to know that the role of the foster parent is temporary, and that the foster parent is supportive of the birth family. Foster care services must promote family preservation, ethnic and cultural diversity. Co-parenting or parallel parent programs that encourage unity in parenting speed up reconciliation for children and birth parents.

When providers are involved in the development of a case plan, they join the social worker and birth parent in a team effort, working toward the same objectives. Foster parents then can work together with social workers, birth parents, and other service providers, participating in case planning, administrative reviews, and juvenile court proceedings. They keep information about the child's progress and development and make daily decisions for the child in their care. Without this participation, foster care providers can knowingly or unknowingly sabotage even the best laid plans of social workers by losing focus on the professional role they play. Separating day-to-day care from the global perspective of the child's natural and cultural family system may be difficult for care providers. They can forget that they are only a small piece in the total family treatment program.

Foster parents can assist the agency, parents, family, and child in reaching long term goals. The foster parent(s) must be committed to supporting the child's relationship with the family of origin. If family reunification is not warranted, foster parents still have the essential role in helping children manage their feelings about their parents and places of origin.

The responsibility of initiating this team effort cannot be placed solely on social services. Indeed, foster care providers are often in the best position to know immediately when to initiate a team effort. They can promote economic, social, health care, and mental health supports. They can prepare children, youths, and families for responsible relationships. They can strengthen linkages among formal and informal networks and support services needed to meet the complex needs of the child in care. It is stated in *Establishing Parent Involvement in Foster Care Agencies* (Blumenthal, Weinberg 1984) that:

> *Foster parents are in a position to play a significant part in maintaining ties between children and their parents, rebuilding the parent-child relationship, and reestablishing the family unit. (Felker 1981) Moreover, they have an important role in helping parents resolve the problems that led to placement. Thus foster parents become invaluable resources to agencies and parents. And the two most important roles they need to assume are team member and "parallel" parent.*

> *As **team members**, foster parents are partners with the worker, parents, child, and other service providers. They must be provided with essential information as the reasons why the child is placed in care, the goals for the family, and the plan for working with the child and parents. Foster parents are collaborators who participate in the continuing planning and decision-making process. Because they are likely to observe parent-child visits and work directly with parents, they are in a position to make invaluable contributions. In accordance with the case plan, foster parents may be responsible for monitoring and documenting parent-child contacts. Foster parents may also be advocates for parents during case conferences . . .*

> *. . . As **"parallel parents,"** foster parents are family aides. They do not assume parenting responsibility, they share it. Parents continue to help with the care of their children and to make decisions concerning them.*

Foster parents serve as

1. **SUPPORTERS**—*they listen and encourage; are accepting and respectful.*

2. **TEACHERS**—*they discuss with parents what they know about child development, child care, community resources, and agency policies.*

From the foster father . . .

Together we walked the sterile halls of the courthouse. The birth parents—volatile and violated—and the foster parents—questioning and questioned. Most importantly, in front of us skipped their children.

And the birth mother . . .

No matter how courteous a foster parent is, I felt I had very little to say in the decisions made for my child. Why can't the natural parent be consulted on decisions regarding the child, even if they are only small ones, such as the color of a coat or choice of a haircut? Being asked your opinion on matters concerning your child is a step toward making decisions yourself, and would help restore confidence in the ability to do so. Both the social worker and foster parent need to involve the natural parent even if she or he doesn't show too much interest in being involved.

(McAdams 1973)

Handout from Child Welfare League 1973

---

3. **MODELS**—*they demonstrate loving and caring, sharing and giving, structure and limits, discipline, daily problem solving, mutual respect, a value on individual separation and growth, values such as patience, tolerance of difference and fair play, dealing with feelings that are both painful and positive, communication, and household management, and child management techniques.*

4. **ADVOCATES**—*they use their knowledge of agency policy and practice, community resources, and legal processes to assert the needs of parents on behalf of their children.*

Professional foster parents' responsibilities may be more difficult, challenging, and time-consuming than in the past, but their experiences are also likely to be far more rewarding and satisfying. Cooperation between parents and foster parents can result in the provision of concrete assistance needed by parents to bring about a return to home, a more consistent emotional environment for foster children, and a reduction of the demands placed on caseworkers to be all things to all people. (Blumenthal, Weinberg 1984)

*The role of foster parents may no longer be attractive to or appropriate for the volunteer. Professional foster parenting is increasingly more difficult involving treatment of seriously disturbed children. Professional foster parents must have a clear understanding and active role involving work with the primary family, the courts, and others. **It is not just a matter of loving a child anymore.*** (Stehno 1990, p556)

How do children find themselves in foster care?

Basically it involves a balancing act of rights and obligations.

— Parents have the right to raise their own children in their own homes, to protect them, and care for them.

— Children have the right to be raised by their own families.

When there is clear evidence of abuse, neglect, or exploitation, child protection workers have the legal responsibility to investigate. Family members have all the rights guaranteed them under the United States laws and the laws of the state in which they live. Social workers are not permitted to intrude unnecessarily. Any intervention into family life on behalf of children must be guided by laws and policies which define the rights, powers, and responsibilities of the intervening authorities. Family intervention should be directed toward creating a safe atmosphere in the child's home and be as unobtrusive as possible.

The best child welfare is good family welfare.

Jamie, a single mother with four children, suffered from mental illness and was hospitalized. Prior to hospitalization and placement of her children, their care had been categorized as neglectful. Since she had no relatives to provide kinship or relative care, her children were placed in foster homes until she was well enough to begin providing for them. Her journey took many years and gradually each child was reunited with her in her own home. Today, Jamie recognizes, and is grateful for, the quality of care her children received. The foster families who cared for her children provided support and learning experiences when she herself could not provide them.

Jamie's children needed out-of-home care to give Jamie time to heal and to provide them with the warmth of a family. Jamie's children were temporarily placed in protective custody. The agency working with Jamie had legal responsibility to find and supervise care for her children.

From the foster father . . .

We looked at each other. He a tall, hard-muscled oil rigger, who had experienced sides of this world I had only glimpsed at in documentary materials. I, a slight middle class scholar. Our worlds had kept us separated. His children now brought us together.

And a birth mother . . .

I believe one of the most damaging things a surrogate parent may do to a child, without meaning to, is to undermine that child's opinion of the natural parent. It must be very difficult for a surrogate parent to refrain from passing moral judgment on a natural parent whose offenses have been particularly unpleasant or even criminal, but that person is still the child's parent and the more the foster parent knocks him, the more the child is obligated to defend him . . .
(McAdams 1973)

Family services are provided by government to strengthen families so children may remain home without risk.

Social workers must respect cultural differences and pay careful attention to individual and family dynamics. Family preservation services consider variations in communication, life view, family roles, structure, customs, and traditions among different kinds of people. A family situation cannot be judged on a social worker's personal experiences, culture, or biases. Moreover, too many *"new, improved, better"* services can put additional stress on an already strained family and escalate a difficult situation. Conflict may arise due to such factors as service locations, unavailable transportation, and affordable babysitting.

Good social work policy does not permit children to be removed unless frontline support services have been provided, assessed, and failed. Standard criteria that must be met to provide services include:

1. *Parenting behavior falls below minimum standards such that a child is likely to be harmed. Or the conditions of the home are such that a child is in danger.*

2. *The family needs child welfare services to keep the family together or to help them through a crisis that threatens family stability.*

3. *It is probable that the provision of the department's services will alleviate the conditions or change what has led to harm or what threatens harm.* (Stein, Rzepnicki 1983)

Possible services available for birth parents prior to removal of children:

- Homemaker services
- Kinship families
- Legal aid
- Job training, education
- Crisis nursery
- Emergency utilities
- Emergency caretakers
- Public health programs
- Support groups
- Chemical abuse treatment
- Parent aide
- Medical services
- Employment services
- Drop-in day care or day care
- Emergency food, shelter
- Financial assistance/budgeting
- Parenting classes
- Infant stimulation programs
- Educational programs
- Counseling/therapy

Possible services for the children:

- Day care
- School counselors
- Play groups
- Big sister/big brother program
- YMCA
- Therapy
- Pre-school
- Special school programs
- Foster grandparents
- Scouting
- Boy's and Girl's Club
- Professional counseling

Services for the parent and child:

- Supervised parent-child modeling programs
- Crisis nursery/respite care
- Residential programs for abusive and neglectful families
- In-home therapists

Support services which fail need assessment as to why they did not work.

Sometimes out-of-home care may be the most effective alternative. In some cases children are removed temporarily when risk is imminent. Children cannot be removed, however, without parental or guardian consent, Juvenile Court order, or by a law enforcement officer. In Minnesota a CHIPS (Child in Need of Protective Services) Petition may be served to protect a child from a dangerous situation.

The birth parent adds insight . . .

The foster parent who gives you orders or instructions in front of your child undermines your authority with your child. You are told to have the child back by 5:00 and scolded not to be late, or told not to send your child out without a sweater as he's just recovering from a cold. These instructions may be necessary, but no matter how young your child is, the child is aware that you presently have little authority and this increases the child's concern regarding your responsibility. If it is necessary to give instructions about taking the child away from the foster home on an outing, it would be better to do so out of the child's presence.

At a time in our history when paperwork and budgets can determine actions for a family . . . I wonder . . . Does the time it takes to fill out the paperwork and follow protocol eliminate application in a necessary program?
Author

Children may be placed in out-of-home care due to:

- Parents who for good cause, desire temporarily relief of child's care.
  - Parent confined to prison
  - Parental hospitalization
  - Chemical dependency of parent
  - Child or parent participating in in-patient treatment program
  - Physical illness or mental illness which renders parent incapable of direct parenting
- Maltreatment, abuse, or neglect while the perpetrator(s) or family situation is rehabilitated
- Has been illegally placed for adoption or care

- Need for additional supervision in a family setting
  - disabilities or complicated medical problems (into homes trained to handle their special situations)
  - juvenile delinquency
  - running away
  - juvenile chemical abuse
  - habitual truancy from school
  - a delinquent act prior to age 10
- Abandonment or homelessness

Children may be placed out-of-home by the following decision-makers:

- Birth parents
- Social services
- Juvenile officers
- Juvenile court judge

- Relatives with guardianship
- Counselors
- Probation officers
- Department of corrections

What kinds of surrogate homes and parents are available to children who need care when a birth parent cannot provide?

If a child must be removed from the parent and taken under protective custody, current child welfare practices look for the least restrictive safe place. In an emergency, a child may be placed in a shelter home while the family situation is being assessed. If out-of-home care is deemed necessary, the following out-of-home options are presently being used.

Children may be placed in these current out-of-home settings:

- Relatives/kinship homes
- Emergency/temporary shelter
- Respite family foster home
- Family foster home
- Group family foster home
- Independent living skills home
- Residential facility

- Residential treatment–behavior
- Hospital psychiatric ward
- Residential treatment–chemical
- Halfway house–behavior
- Halfway house–chemical
- State correction facility

The role of government should be temporary in custody of children. A timely and executable permanency plan is essential when children are out of the care of their parents. Family living situations offer the least restrictive of all out-of-home care for children in need of surrogate care.

Depending on the situation, any of the following types of unlicensed and licensed surrogate family homes may be used:

Relative care: Placement with relatives is considered first whenever out-of-home care is necessary. This alternative offers a natural and permanent relationship, which, when healthy, lasts a lifetime and extends to future generations.

MINNESOTA STATUTE 245A.02 Subd, 13. Individual who is related means a spouse, a parent, a natural or adopted child or stepchild, a stepparent, a stepbrother, a stepsister, a niece, a nephew, an adoptive parent, a grandparent, a sibling, an aunt, an uncle, or a legal guardian.

Since a child is generally most familiar with relatives, the separation trauma is lessened. The child and the birth parents may be able to visit frequently. The relatives may be aware of the child's experiences and able to help the child accept the past and feel a worthwhile part of the family.

Formalized kinship care: This formal relative (kinship) caregiver status is linked to state and federal child welfare laws that provide for the care of a child in a licensed or approved home. In some states relatives may receive financial assistance to care for these children. In turn, these relatives are expected to meet foster home licensing requirements and cooperate with child protection agencies in developing and implementing case plans, including permanency goals. *(Minnesota State Licensing Act presently prohibits the state from licensing individuals who are "related." Some counties, however, may approve related individuals so dollars can be paid to allow a child to remain in an extended family or community.)*

"With all the advantages of using relatives for family foster care, it is not necessarily without problems. Individual family problems are caused or sometimes affected by problems with the extended family. One needs to know something of the inter-family relationship to determine whether a relative home is the most appropriate place for a child." says Jake Terpstra, U.S. Foster Care Specialist of the U.S. Children's Bureau.

Tribal care: In 1978, a federal law *(PL 95-608)* was passed to protect Native American children and tribes by establishing national standards which state courts must follow before and after Native American children are removed from their parents or guardians. The law provides for notice to the tribe of hearings involving child custody matters. The law outlines the following order of placement preferences:

(1) The child's extended family.
(2) Other members of the tribe or a tribe-approved foster home.
(3) A state-approved Native American foster home, including single parents.
(4) A Native American operated or approved institution.
(5) A non-Native American foster home.

It is hoped this type of legislation will preserve the tribal culture and heritage in the lives of Native American children.

Kith (and kin) care: Kith are friends, church members, acquaintances, or neighbors of the child who are not related but are considered by the child to be a part of an extended family or cultural community. For example, the godparents in a Hispanic community or barrio may not be related, but may have pledged to serve as surrogate parents for another family's child. To care for a specific child, these individuals must obtain a restricted care provider license.

Family foster care: A family home is licensed to provide one or more of the following types of full-time care for unrelated children. Family foster care supplements what the parents of origin or relatives cannot provide. *The word "supplement" is used since there can be no substitute for the family of origin. All foster parents must be able to support the cultural and ethnic heritage of children in their care.* (CWLA 1991, pp 39-40)

*Foster parents are **service providers** not recipients. They are part of the treatment team for the child—to protect, nurture, and strengthen the child in out-of-home care. Some of the types of foster family homes are:*

Emergency shelter home is a foster family home designated primarily to time-limited emergency care, usually lasting not longer than 30 days for any child.

From the foster father . . .

The court decided the children would remain with us for the next six months. The birth family was allowed to maintain contact with their children during this time.

Court adjourned and we parted. I, the foster father with their children, heading home. They, the parents, with hope, to a cheap motel.

Later, they would drive their home—a van— the 1,500 miles from where they had come with hopes of reuniting their family.

From the birth mother . . .

You see your child in a home situation where everything is apparently orderly and calm, and quite often materially superior to anything you are going to be able to offer them, and you wonder, why the hell you are trying to rock the boat . . . maybe it would be better to leave your child there, it would be a lot less upsetting for everyone involved if you would just drop out of the picture . . . Yes, sometimes staying away is the easiest for everyone.

Interim home is a foster family home caring for children expected to return home within one year or to be placed for adoption within two years.
Permanent home is a foster family home caring for children (whether state wards or not) under written agreement for planned care until the child reaches majority.
Restricted home is a family home licensed for a specific child. These families may not accept other children than what is specified.
Special services home is a foster family home able to provide extraordinary care or services by virtue of training, experience, or special skills.
Group family foster home is a family foster home providing care for no more than ten children, including the family's own children. These homes are often very effective with teenagers.

Pre-adoptive care: When the rights of the natural parents have been terminated—by voluntary or involuntary means—a licensed agency may place children in an unlicensed pre-adoptive home before final adoption. The agency first completes a pre-adoptive home study. In Minnesota, adoption must then occur within two years.

How are foster care providers licensed?

The states rightfully take a cautious approach in licensing families and individuals to provide care for children who are separated from their biological parent, relatives, or legal guardians. Licensing standards are developed to protect children needing out-of-home care. These, however, are minimum standards and are not necessarily *"best practice"* or *"state of the art standards."* These minimum standards must be maintained by all licensed provider homes. Failure to maintain such standards will result in negative licensing actions or what is called sanctions.

Agencies charged with the responsibility of recruiting, selecting, and training foster parents perform complete licensing studies. This includes a background study of the applicant and others who will be involved with children in care. A written record of a home study includes an on-site inspection of residence; three letters of reference; reports from the fire marshal, building officials, and health officials governing the program; plus any other reports necessary to evaluate the applicants' qualifications.

The home study also includes interviews with all family members and adults living in the household and personal references. The evaluation of individuals must meet specific qualifications. If a family has been previously licensed, references from agencies the applicant has previously been licensed with are also included. When requirements are met, a license must be issued. Issuance of a license, however, does not mean immediate placements of children. It is not uncommon to find a licensed provider with no individuals in care. Once licensed, the care provider is expected to meet all the legal requirements of that license. Even an excellent foster home in violation (sanctions) of licensing laws is not tolerated and the license holder can face:

- Correction order
- Probation
- Fines
- Suspension
- Revocation
- Immediate suspension

A sanction does not mean removal of children from out-of-home care. Immediate suspension is the only situation requiring children to be removed. A social worker, however, may remove a child anytime—sanction or not.

It may be easier to understand licensing if a person thinks in terms of a driver's license and driving. An excellent driver who drives a car and breaks the highway laws may face a fine or license suspension. With the privilege of driving comes the responsibility to obey the law. If the law changes the license holder is still responsible.

How do laws and rules affect the out-of-home care system?

In this book I have used federal law and state statutes and rules from the State of Minnesota. The federal laws and Minnesota state statute law *(MS)* and rule *(MR)* information are current as of May 10, 1992. In all cases, laws supersede rules. Variances are possible from rule requirements, but laws cannot be changed without legislative action.

```
┌─────────────────────────────────────────────────┐
│            FEDERAL LEGISLATION                    │
│         TITLE IV- SOCIAL SECURITY ACT             │
│ CHILD ABUSE PREVENTION, ADOPTION, AND FAMILY      │
│              SERVICES ACT                         │
│       INDIVIDUALS WITH DISABILITY ACT             │
│              CIVIL RIGHTS ACT                     │
│             NATIVE AMERICAN ACT                   │
└─────────────────────────────────────────────────┘
        ┌─────────────────────────────────────────┐
        │              STATE                       │
        │      State Statutes - Laws               │
        │      State Rules - Interpret Statutes    │
        │ Data Privacy Act, licensing, children,   │
        │ foster care, family preservation,        │
        │ minority heritage, adoption, juvenile    │
        └─────────────────────────────────────────┘
          ┌───────────────────────────────────────┐
          │        STATE LICENSING AGENCY         │
          │      Department of Human Services      │
          │ Interpretation of state licensing      │
          │ statutes, rules                        │
          │ Implementation of law and rules        │
          │ Certify licensing agencies and issue   │
          │ licensing sanctions                    │
          └───────────────────────────────────────┘
           ┌──────────────────────────────────────┐
           │      DELEGATED LICENSING AGENCY       │
           │        (County or Private)            │
           │ Interpretation of state licensing      │
           │ statutes, rules                        │
           │ Agency procedures and protocols        │
           │ formal and informal                    │
           │ Implementation of law and rules        │
           └──────────────────────────────────────┘
            ┌─────────────────────────────────────┐
            │              CLIENT                  │
            │ Needs and requirements of child in   │
            │ out-of-home care who is being         │
            │ provided with services from           │
            │ licensed agency                       │
            └─────────────────────────────────────┘
            ┌─────────────────────────────────────┐
            │         AGENCY CASEWORKER            │
            │ Execution of interpretation of       │
            │ statutes, rules, procedures, and      │
            │ protocols made on case-by-case basis  │
            └─────────────────────────────────────┘
            ┌─────────────────────────────────────┐
            │       FOSTER CARE PROVIDER           │
            │ Licensed service provider to child   │
            │ in care                               │
            │ Responsible to comply with all        │
            │ law and rules.                        │
            └─────────────────────────────────────┘
```

Figure 2.1—*Hierarchy example of law, rule, procedure, protocol, needs, and requirements a Minnesota foster parent must work within. Minnesota is a state-supervised/county agency-administered system. Each state system is slightly different and licensed care providers need accurate knowledge of requirements necessary to do their job.*

Laws, statutes, and rules are constantly changing.
What is current and accurate today may not be current 30 days from now.
Always consult with an attorney for answers to your legal questions.

A foster mother states . . .

We have learned during the past nineteen years of fostering children that listening carefully to the birth parents' frustrations allows us insight into the frustrations we are about to experience.

Often parents tell us horrendous stories about their children and in the beginning we doubt their sincerity. Humbly, six months later, we share our parenting experiences.

In other cases, the difference in family lifestyles may allow a child to behave very differently in each home. The same volatile behavior reappears immediately when birth family reunification occurs.

A social worker . . .

Many parents stress that recreation would temporarily relieve the pressures on their family and allow them access to the others in their community.

Federal legislation supersedes state legislation, and individual states must follow the federal laws to obtain federal funding for their programs. According to federal law PL96-272, states cannot collect Title IV E funding for out-of-home child care unless the home is licensed. Interpretation of federal law varies from state to state. Each state has its own statutes and rules. Individuals taking care of other people's children need to be familiar with these laws and rules.

Changes in legislation can directly affect anyone.
Ignorance is not an excuse.
Updates on rules and statutes are available
from elected representatives.

Federal legislation affects state licensed out-of-home programs for minors. The Social Security Act - Title IV attaches requirements of compliance on States in order to receive federal funding in caring for out-of-home placed children. Section 504 of the Civil Rights Act for Handicapped Persons, 1973 prohibits discrimination based on disability including the mental health of disturbed children. Federal legislation information can be obtained from your US Senator or Congressperson.

The Data Privacy Act requires state compliance in confidentiality, record keeping, and release of personal information. Licensing laws and rules require minimum standards which must be met to care for children in out-of-home care. State statutes and rules regarding licensing responsibilities can be obtained from state representatives, licensing agencies, the state law library, a law school library, the State Department of Public Welfare, or from a major public library in the Government Documentation section.

In Minnesota, foster home licenses are issued by the commissioner of the Minnesota Department of Human Services based on a licensing agency recommendation. The license authorizes a family to provide foster care for a determined period of time, in accordance with all the terms of the license. Once a license is issued, the licensee is responsible for following federal laws, state statutes, state rules, and agency procedures.

Accepting a license to parent other people's children transforms a person into a "political parent." It is the personal responsibility of a care provider family and the professionals working in social services to keep updated on current law. If statutes and laws are not easy to interpret or place the citizens in jeopardy, it is the right of the individual to challenge that specific legislation. Elected representatives, state and local agency representatives, and lobbying associations can be contacted in writing, by phone, or by personal interview to begin to make changes. Individuals must have courage to question legislation which causes double binds or is confusing. Legislation which may hinder caring for children needs to be carefully reviewed.

Here's a sampling of the laws and rule parts governing Minnesota foster care licensing. Each state license carries different expectations, procedures, and qualifications. Know the statutes and rules that apply to your situation.

*MINNESOTA STATUTE MS 245A.04 Subd. 3. **Study of Applicant.***
(a)   Before the commissioner issues a license, the commissioner shall conduct a study of the individuals specified in clauses (1) to (4) according to the rules of the commissioner. The applicant, license holder, the bureau of criminal apprehension, and county agencies, after written notice to the individual who is the subject of the study, shall help with the study by giving the commissioner criminal conviction data and reports about abuse or neglect of adults in licensed programs substantiated under section 626.557 and the maltreatment of

minors in licensed programs substantiated under section 626.556. The individuals to be studied shall include:

    (1) the applicant;

    (2) persons over the age of 13 living in the household where the licensed program will be provided;

    (3) current employees or contractors of the applicant who will have direct contact with persons served by the program; and

    (4) volunteers, who have direct contact with persons served by the program to provide program services, if the contract is not directly supervised by the individuals listed in clause (1) or (3).

    MINNESOTA RULE MR 9543.3030 (D)

    volunteers who provide program services to persons served if:

    (1) the volunteer has direct contact with persons served; and

    (2) the volunteer is not directly supervised.

Minnesota State Statute 245A.04 Subd. 3a(4) and Minnesota Rule 9543.3030(D)(2) are examples of how state legislation can place both social service workers and foster care providers in a double bind. Both legislation (statute/law) and rule were passed to protect children in care, yet if misinterpreted could actually compromise the care of a child. Professionals and care providers questioned the interpretation of this law and rule.

> *Will this law and rule prevent children in care from participating in activities with other children? Does "volunteer" include piano teacher, next door neighbor, Sunday school teacher, scout leader, or soccer coach? Can the child go to the zoo with her best friend without a review of the friend's family? If the child does go and something happens, is the foster care provider non-compliant or failing to provide adequate supervision?*

These questions, raised by Minnesota professionals and foster parent association members, initiated additional review of this law and rule. The Department of Human Services then issued an Informational Bulletin #91-50C (June 7, 1991). Parts of that bulletin follow.

***Licensed family day care** requires background studies on all substitute caregivers.*

***Licensed foster care programs** requires that babysitters and other substitute caregivers for the licensed care provider receive background studies if the services are provided at the licensed site.*

    A study is required:

    1. *When a substitute is providing services at the licensed site and the service provided is identified in any of the client's contracts or individual plans for services.*

    2. *When the license holder is absent for 24 hours or longer.*

    A study is not required:

    1. *When the substitute caregiver is providing substitute care away from the licensed site.*

    2. *When the license holder is absent for less than 24 hours, and the substitute caregiver is providing a minimal level of supervision that is not considered individualized care (i.e., the service is not identified in a client's plan or contract.)*

I have added this example of a statute (law), rule (which interprets the law), and the additional informational bulletin (which additionally interprets the rule) to illustrate how a good law passed with excellent intentions can be confusing and

---

Foster parents can help foster children stay active in their natural families by:

    Making birthday presents or cake for parents or siblings.

    Making or buying gifts for parents or siblings.

    Maintaining contact with siblings in other homes.

    Keeping a Lifestory Book.

    Participating in child's cultural community celebrations.

    Remembering Mother's and Father's Day.

    Giving praise and compliments to natural parents.

    Helping to send cards or notes of daily activities.

    Keeping good documentation of events, situations, and behaviors.

Love for one set of parents does not imply disloyalty to the other.

*The foster father
continues his story . . .*

*Our foster children's
parents kept up their
part of the deal. For six
months the children
received phone calls.
From job to job and
state to state, the
parents never forgot
to call. Two weeks on
this job, three weeks
on that—the kids
anticipated eagerly
each phone call.*

*During the next six
months, they—the
parents—maintained
contact and when our
eyes again met in the
courtroom, there was a
mutual respect
between us. The kids
awaited the return of
their family.*

**The Child Welfare League
in Blueprint for Fostering
1991 states on page 31 . . .**

*"Most parents,
including those who
abuse and neglect,
do care about their
children, and many
could be much more
effective parents with
appropriate supports."
The National
Commission on Family
Foster Care believes it
is time to "make some
essential decisions
about the role of family
foster care and how it
can serve America's
most vulnerable
citizens in the last
decade of this century."*

contradicting in practice. *If you work under specialized laws and rules you do not understand, write or call to get further clarification. Additional interpretation can be added and worked through immediately if necessary, or during the next revision or legislative session.*

Here's more good reading:

MINNESOTA STATUTE MS 245A.04 Subd4.

The juvenile courts shall also help with the study by giving the commissioner existing juvenile court records on individuals described in clause (2) relating to delinquency proceedings held within either the five years immediately preceding the application or the five years immediately preceding the individual's 18th birthday, whichever time period is longer. The commissioner shall destroy juvenile records obtained pursuant to this subdivision when the subject of record reaches age 23.

For purposes of this subdivision, "direct contact" means providing face-to-face care, training, supervision, counseling, consultation, or medication assistance to persons served by the program. For purposes of this subdivision, "directly supervised" means an individual listed in clause (1) or (3) is within sight or hearing of a volunteer to the extent that the individual listed in clause (1) or (3) is capable at all times of intervening to protect the health and safety of the persons served by the program who have direct contact with the volunteer.

MINNESOTA RULE MR 9543.3030
"Directly supervised" means an individual listed in items A or C is within sight or hearing of a volunteer to the extent that the individual listed in item A or C is capable at all times of intervening to protect the health and safety of the persons served by the program who have direct contact with the volunteer. (See also MR 9543.3040)

MINNESOTA STATUTE MS 245A.04 Subd4

A study of an individual in clauses (1) to (4) shall be conducted on at least an annual basis. No applicant, license holder, or individual who is the subject of the study shall pay any fees required to conduct the study.
(b)   The individual who is the subject of the study must provide the applicant or license holder with sufficient information to ensure an accurate study including the individual's first, middle and last name; home address, city, county, and state of residence; zip code; sex; date of birth; and driver's license number. The applicant or license holder shall provide this information about an individual in paragraph (a), clause (1) to (4), on forms prescribed by the commissioner. The commissioner may request additional information of the individual, which shall be optional for the individual to provide, such as the individual's social security number or race. (See also MR 9543.3050)
(c)   A study must include information from the county agency's record of substantiated abuse or neglect of adults in licensed programs, and the maltreatment of minors in licensed programs, and information from the bureau of apprehension.
The commissioner may also review arrest and investigative information from the bureau of criminal apprehension, a county attorney, county sheriff, county agency, local chief of police, other states, the courts, the national criminal record repository if the commissioner has reasonable cause to believe the information is pertinent to the disqualification of an individual listed in paragraph (a), clauses (1) to (4).
(d)   An applicant's or license holder's failure or refusal to cooperate with the commissioner is reasonable cause to deny an application or immediately suspend, suspend or revoke a license. Failure or refusal of an individual to cooperate with the study is just cause for denying or terminating employment of the individual if the individual's failure or refusal to cooperate could cause the applicant's application to be denied or the license holder's license to be immediately suspended, suspended or revoked.
(e-i)   Additional information regarding study of applicant

MINNESOTA STATUTE MS 245A.04 Sub4. Inspections; waiver.
(a)   Before issuing a license, the commissioner shall conduct an inspection of the program. The inspection must include, but is not limited to:
(1)   an inspection of the physical plant;

(2) *an inspection of records and documents;*

(3) *an evaluation of the program by consumers of the program; and*

(4) *observation of the program in operation*

For the purposes of this subdivision, "consumer" means a person who receives the services of a licensed program, the person's legal guardian, or the parent or individual having legal custody of a child who receives the services of a licensed program.

(b) *The evaluation required in paragraph (a), clause (3) or the observation in paragraph (a), clause (4) is not required prior to issuing a provisional license under subdivision 7, these requirements must be completed within one year after the issuance of a provisional license. The observation in pargraph (a), clause (4) is not required if the commissioner determines that the observation would hinder the persons receiving services in benefiting from the program.*

> **MINNESOTA RULE MR 9545.0020 Subp.5. Orientation and compliance of home before placements.** *No child shall be placed by an agency in an unlicensed home until their home has begun the required orientation, and until that home has been evaluated for compliance with parts 9545.0090, item A; 9545.0180, subparts 3 and 5, items A to E (agency requirement).*

> **MINNESOTA STATUTE MS 245A.04. Subd. 7. Issuance of a license; provisional license.**
> **(a)** *If the commissioner determines that the program complies with all applicable rules and laws, the commissioner shall issue a license. At minimum the license shall state: (1) the name of license holder; (2) the address of program; (3) the effective date and expiration date of the license; (4) the type of license; (5) the maximum number and ages of persons that may receive services from the program; (6) any special conditions of licensure.*

Did you skip over the preceeding material in small, italic print assuming it uninteresting or not applicable? Most people probably would and that attitude presents significant problems. Public ignorance of laws and rules hinders the process of protecting children in care. So for your own good and the welfare of the children you care for—read the small print. The benefits can be priceless!

What kinds of adults make good foster parents?

Foster parenting requires love, understanding, and assuming a lot of responsibility. Here's the Minnesota rule:

> **MINNESOTA RULE MR 9545.0090 Personal qualities of foster family home applicants.** *Foster family home applicants shall be kind, mature, and responsible people with a genuine liking for children. They shall possess consistent and healthy methods of handling the life-style unique to their own families. Evaluation of applicants shall consider cultural differences.*

> *Reason: Children who must live apart from their own homes are uniquely in need of stable, understanding families. Many children needing placement are emotionally, mentally or physically handicapped. These children need extra understanding and parenting to cope with their problems.*

> *A. Satisfactory compliance: A foster family home license shall not be issued or renewed where any person (except foster children) living in the household has any of the following characteristics:*
> *(1) a disqualification under part 9543.3070;*

Minnesota Rule 9543.3070 Disqualification Standards is a list of 60 crimes or anticipatory crimes for which a family will be disqualified. These specific 60 crimes have been selected as having a direct relationship in providing foster care for children. A complete description and specifics can be found in Minnesota Statutes and Rules, listed above.

> *(2) chemical dependency, unless the individual(s) identified as chemically dependent has*

A promising outcome to the foster father's story . . .

Tension filled the air as we walked into the courtroom. The social worker's report was unfavorable.

Ours, carefully documented, showed the concern and faithfulness of these two parents.

The room was silent as the judge spoke. "Take good care of your children."

"When?" asked the father.

"Now," answered the judge.

1993 Minnesota Legislation for Foster Care Providers (Senate File 190)

— *Applicant background studies are now public information.*

— *Strict limits are put on "setting aside" of disqualifications, with lists of specific convictions which disqualify the applicant for 7 years, 10 years, or forever.*

— *Information on convictions from Bureau of Criminal Apprehension is now public for 15 years.*

been chemically free for at least 12 months;

*(3) residence of the family's own children in foster care, correctional facility, or
residential treatment for emotional disturbance within the previous 12 months if, in the
judgment of the agency, the functioning of the family has been impaired.*

The rule goes on:

*B. Satisfactory compliance: In order to protect children in foster care and assure
them the maximum opportunities for growth and development, each family caring for
children shall be evaluated on the following essential elements:*

*(1) have established and are comfortable with their own identity to the degree that
meeting their own needs does not interfere with their meeting the needs of foster
children;*

(2) have optimism, a sense of humor, resiliency, and ability to enjoy life;

*(3) be in touch with their own feelings, be able to express these feelings, and have a
capacity to look at themselves realistically as to the kinds of children they can accept and
work with;*

(4) have health and vigor to meet the needs of children placed with them;

(5) have meaningful extended family, neighborhood, cultural, and community ties;

*(6) have the ability to deal with anger, sorrow, frustration, conflict, and other emotions
in a manner which will build positive interpersonal relationships rather than in a way
that could be emotionally or physically destructive to other persons;*

*(7) have the ability to give positive guidance, care, and training to a child according to
his stage of growth, special abilities, and limitations;*

(8) have the ability to use discipline in a constructive rather than a destructive way;

*(9) understand, accept, and seek to nurture cultural, spiritual, racial, and affectional ties
with the child;*

*(10) have the ability and flexibility to accept a child in placement who has special needs,
treat a foster child as a member of their family, recognizing that a foster child has other
family ties;*

*(11) have the ability to accept the foster child's own family and maintain an
understanding relationship with them;*

(12) have the ability to work with the agency and other community resources;

*(13) have a capacity and willingness to involve themselves in ongoing educational
opportunities, as well as other learning experiences;*

(14) be able to constructively resolve problems when difficulties arise;

*(15) be comfortable in relating to professional treatment personnel of all kinds, including
the ability to discuss differences of viewpoint, and to be an advocate for the foster child
when indicated; and*

*(16) have an ability to openly discuss their attitudes about persons with differing
life-styles and philosophies and a capacity to accept people who are different from
themselves.*

This rule may seem like a long and impossible laundry list for any family.
Families caring for out-of-home children are *"evaluated on"* these criteria and the
rule often includes the phrase *"have the ability to."* Would we want anything less
than these standards for children? The rule can be very subjective—easily
subject to misinterpretation with or without all the pertinent data. Caseworkers,
like children, are different. Parenting methods which may be acceptable to one
caseworker may be inappropriate to another.

What types of expectations are placed on agencies?

The state places high expectations on agencies and workers. Agencies are
required to monitor licensed homes and work together with providers. Both
social workers and licensed families can be held liable if children in care are
mishandled. The agency has overall responsibility for planning with the child.
Foster care is an integral part of that plan. The relationship between the foster

family home and the agency must be one of mutual trust and respect.

— Both the foster family and the agency must sign and abide by the terms of the Foster Parent Agreement.

— The agency must provide information to the foster family regarding the policy, procedure, and intentions of the agency toward placement of children in that foster family home.

— The agency must provide training opportunities to all applicants, foster family home providers, and substitute caregivers.

— An agency representative must visit the foster family home to provide support and information and to assess the quality of care.

It is pertinent that the foster family works in partnership—cooperatively and interdependently—with the agency and birth family.

What are the licensing limitations and why do they exist?

Limitations are placed on foster home licenses to protect the physical, emotional, and psychological health of children.

The state recognizes that care providers must have sufficient time and stamina to provide individual attention for each child. The abilities of parent(s) to provide care to foster children differ greatly. The maximum number of children allowed in foster homes must allow foster parents to devote sufficient time to each child, including their own children. The needs and requirements of individual children vary greatly. In some cases, one special needs child, even with a very qualified and loving family, may be the limit.

In Minnesota, five children total are allowed in interim, special services, and permanent homes, and seven children in emergency shelter homes. The state also stipulates that no more than two children two-years of age or younger who are unrelated to the foster family be in the home at the same time. Variances can be made when sibling groups are involved.

Licensed foster family group homes allow for additional children. The group home license also demands additional responsibilities of the adults involved in the care of children. Information regarding qualifications and restrictions for group homes, halfway houses, treatment centers, and juvenile correctional facilities can be found in state statutes and rules or by requesting the information from the agency that licenses them.

—The importance of saying no!—

Sometimes, for the benefit of everyone involved—the foster family must say no to caring for a child, even if they have not reached their license quota. If the family does not have the skills to handle a particular child it is vital for them to take a step back and say no. If a family's stress level, time commitment, or energy is at its maximum, then no is the correct answer. It is very difficult to say no to a social worker who calls at 4:30 on a Friday afternoon desperate for a home for a child. But in these instances, the care provider must be strong enough to say no and the social worker must be mature enough to accept this answer and continue a frustrating search.

We celebrated that evening together in the place their children had called home for the last 18 months.

That night, we walked together as two fathers. He had many questions regarding his children. He was gracious and complimentary. Toward the end of our walk he shared a confession.

"You know," he said, "when I met you we had already hired the people to kidnap our kids if court didn't work out that day. Anyone that got in the way of the kidnapping would just disappear. After I met you, my wife and I talked and decided your family could keep the children while we worked on what we needed to work on to bring them home. We're glad we did."

Our eyes met and I understood as another father, the love he had for his children.

When children receive care from an unlicensed provider . . .

Unless licensed, an individual, corporation, partnership, voluntary association, other organization, or controlling individual is not allowed to operate a residential or non-residential program or receive a child or adult for care, supervision, or placement in foster care or adoption. This means a family home in Minnesota is required to be licensed prior to accepting an unrelated child. Failure to do so qualifies as a misdemeanor and is subject to a fine of $300.

These Minnesota family homes are exempt from licensure:

— A home providing care and supervision only to child(ren) placed there by an agency for the purpose of legal adoption. (The adoption must be completed within two years of placement.)

— A home providing care and supervision only to children related to the family. *(See page 37 for definition of related.)*

In other states the following exemptions may also apply:

— A home providing care and supervision for a total period of less than 30 days in any 12-month period.

— A home providing care and supervision only for one unrelated child of 16 or 17 years who has been independently placed by himself or his relative for purposes of education or work. For example: foreign exchange students, summer girls for child care and/or housekeeping, farm, resort, outpost workers.

If you need a license, begin the application process immediately.

How do I get a license?

An individual or family interested in providing licensed foster parenting first contacts their county child welfare agency, or a private placement agency, or adoption agency. The agency will provide the proper application for licensing, as developed by the Department of Public Welfare. In Minnesota, you must be at least 21 years old. *(MR 9545.0050)* Age, other than minimum age, and physical handicap are considerations only as they affect a person's ability to provide adequate care or if they will affect a child's adjustment to the family. *(MR 9545.0110)*

> *MINNESOTA RULE MR 9545.0010 Handicap means a condition of mental retardation, mental illness, physical handicap, sight or hearing deficiency, or chemical dependency.*

The mental and physical health of persons living in the foster family home must not constitute a hazard to the children, and the agency may require a physical examination or mental evaluation. The agency may also request consultation from specialists. Each applicant is evaluated on an individual basis. *(MR 9545.0120 agency requirement)* If all adults in the foster family home are employed or otherwise occupied for substantial amounts of time away from home, the plans for care and supervision of the foster children must be approved in advance by the agency. *(MR 9545.0140)*

Basic foster family compliance with licensing means:

— No child in the foster family home shall be subjected to physical or psychological abuse.

— All information about the child and his family shall be kept private.

— The health, developmental, and safety requirements of the state continue to be met when working with children in care.

What is the role of a surrogate care provider?

When a person accepts the responsibility to provide surrogate care for children, the role of parent will be different from the role assumed for children who join the family through marriage, adoption, or birth. For many children, one set of parents are simultaneously the birth, legal, and daily parents.

For children in surrogate care, these different kinds of roles are split. I have adapted a model developed by Marietta Spencer from the Children's Home Society of Minnesota to simplify the differences in role responsibilities when caring for children.

The three different realistic types of parenting roles are: birth parent, legal parent, and daily parent.

Birth Parent: Every child has a birth mother and birth father. In most cases, the birth parent is also the legal and daily parent.

Legal Parent: All children in our society also have legal parents. The legal parent is responsible for making the major decisions in a child's life—where the child will live, go to school, receive health care, if and when the child gets a driver's license, or gets pierced ears.
— For surrogate parents and relatives without guardianship rights, the legal parent is still the birth parent.
— In kinship care, the relative the child is living with may have additional legal rights if the child is in protective custody.
— If the child is placed in foster care voluntarily, the birth parent retains legal rights to the child.

We packed kids, boxes, suitcases, and snacks into their dilapidated vehicle and waved good-bye.

We remained in contact with this family for many years. Life wasn't always perfect for them. Is it ever really perfect for any of us?

But they were a family and they did OK.

Different Realistic Roles of Parenting

Birth Parent
THE PERSON WHO GIVES YOU LIFE

Genetic make-up, determination of gender, physical appearance, intellectual potential, predisposition for certain diseases, basic personality or temperament type (such as shy, stubborn, active), special talents.

Legal Parent
THE PERSON WHO CONTROLS YOUR LIFE

Financial responsibility, safety and security, where you live, where you go to school. Authorize: psychiatric treatment, medical treatment, surgery, pierced ears, permission to travel out-of-state, driver's license, marriage, baptism, autopsy, giving the body or parts of body to science after death, military service if under age, permanent placement agreement, petition for name change, request for tuition waiver.
(abortion legal option differs per state law)

Daily Parent
THE PERSON WHO MAKES A DAILY IMPRESSION ON YOU.

Provide care, food, toys, clothes, give hugs and kisses, discipline, takes care of you when sick, offers praise and encouragement.

Figure 2.2

Adapted from Marietta Spencer Model Roles of Parenting

— In temporary custody or terminated parental rights, the agency or court is the legal parent and makes all of the financial, safety, and security decisions for the child.

Daily Parent: The daily parent meets the needs of the child by providing love, food, clothing, nurturing, and discipline. Daily parents wipe the runny nose, provide the chicken soup, or hold the child when she is sick. Yet they cannot choose what major medical care the child will receive without approval from the legal parent. They provide comfort when there is no date to the prom, reassurance when the final exam was a failure, and understanding when promises are broken. To the child, the daily parent's role seems most like a "real" parent. It is often difficult for the daily parent and the child to understand the different parenting rights belonging to birth, legal, and/or daily parents. But daily parents cannot prevent a child from moving to another home if the legal parent perceives it to be in the child's best interest.

A clear understanding of parenting relationships is important when you are responsible for children in out-of-home care. It is easy to become confused about your legal rights when you are the child or only the daily parent.

The idealization of the parents with the aid of fantasy and repression helps the child survive, thus to attribute bad things to one's nearest and dearest would run counter to natural defenses and the law of life. (Miller 1990)

In addition, the child in care may have *perceived parents*. These parents exist in the child's mind and are very real to the child. To the daily parent the perceived parent can be hard to discover and understand.

Possible perceived parental roles for the child—the fantasy and psuedo-parent.

The fantasy parent. A child's perception of birth parents often does not match reality. Children growing up in abusive homes often focus on the short-lived, infrequent warm and loving experiences and magnify those experiences until they eventually become the memory. In imagination and memory, the child may have a fairytale family. It may be difficult to understand a child's undying love and commitment to a person who has been less than loving. Yet, to acuse the beloved parent any atrocity would mean betrayal. A child who is attached to the perpetrator may feel safer in the unsafe environment than in out-of-home care. When the fantasy parent becomes the child's perceived reality, new care providers may be placed in the position of becoming the perceived perpetrator. Even years later flashbacks may be triggered and a safe, loving care provider may face untrue allegations.

The psuedo-parent. Many times, young children from troubled families assume the role of parenting siblings. Children who have become parents for siblings or who have parented their parents have difficulty letting go of their role and learning to play. These children are often overachievers, overly responsible, and need approval from everyone. They are often not much fun. While appearing strong, they have poor self-esteems. They often provided self-worth to the primary family system, and for the good of all members, maintain their role as someone to be proud of. Inside they are often hurt, confused, and fearful. The 13-year-old who has raised a two-year-old sibling will be devastated when separated from a child she felt was hers. Learning to be a child and let go of adult responsibilities may be impossible.

How do the children fit in?

When the primary family is disrupted and children are moved into other family living situations, parents face changes in legal responsiblities and liabilities. Rights and responsibilities vary with each specific child.

Birth children. These are children born into your family. A birth parent is responsible for a child's genetics, legal parenting, and daily parenting.
LEGALLY : Birth parents are responsible for the basic care, safety, and well-being of the child under the age of majority.

Related children. These are children related by marriage (stepchildren), blood (nieces, nephews, grandchildren), or finalized adoption.
LEGALLY: The birth parent or finalized adoptive parent retains all legal rights to the child, unless the relative is designated as legal guardian.

Children in Tribal care. These include Native American children who are members of a specific tribe or nation, or any other tribe in which the child is eligible for membership.
LEGALLY: Federal law requires Native American children to remain in Native American homes if at all possible. These children are the legal responsibility of the Tribal Court, a court with federally recognized jurisdiction over child custody proceedings. This can be a court of Native American offences, a court established and operated under the code or custom of a Native American tribe, or the administrative body of a tribe vested with authority over child custody proceedings.

Children in Kinship care. These children are related to the surrogate parents through marriage, blood, or adoption. They have been removed from parental custody by child protection authorities because of abuse, neglect, maltreatment, or dependency. They need an alternative family setting.
LEGALLY: The state has temporary legal custody for these children, has assumed statuatory responsibility to protect and provide for them, and is asking members of the child's extended family to provide care.

Children in voluntary foster care. The child's birth parent or legal guardian, for whatever reason, has made a decision to place the child in the temporary care of social services. These placements are time-limited and can occur when a parent is without a support system of relatives and / or is obtaining medical, psychological, or chemical treatment. It may also occur while a parent is securing another living situation, or when a child is "out of control." The foster family is licensed, and the loss of a license would mean the loss of a home for the child.
LEGALLY: The parents retain all legal rights during a voluntary placement but may authorize the agency to carry out certain responsibilities such as providing for routine medical and dental care. A voluntary written placement agreement specifies the legal status of the child, and the rights and responsibilities of the parent or legal guardian, the child, and the agency. Most agreements require the parents to give reasonable notice in order to prepare for a child to return home in the smoothest possible transition. The daily parenting responsibility switches to the new care provider.

The temporary legal custody of children in foster care. Birth parents or legal guardians who have placed their children voluntarily and who are unwilling or unable to quickly re-establish their family may risk involuntary removal of their child by court order. Delinquent or

---

Foster parents serve the nation's most needy citizens—among them are abused and neglected children.

Changing the life for just one child can change the lives of many children for generations to come.

The quality of available workers and services provided varies drastically with each agency, county, and state.

Without proper time to perform a job even the best will fail.

Emancipated and independent adult foster children often look to the foster family for advice and support when parenting their own children.

"When you are a foster parent - you remain a foster parent in the memories of that child forever. Just because the child leaves your home doesn't mean you have left the child's memories."
Foster father

incorrigible children may also be removed from the family. When a child has been removed from the birth or adoptive home, temporary protective legal custody is awarded to social services.

LEGALLY: Agencies with legal custody have the authority to place the child, but the parents still retain rights and responsibilities as guardians. *Parental consent must be obtained for major decisions affecting the child, including :*

—the right to consent to non-emergency surgery;

—admission to hospital for diagnosis or treatment;

—enrollment in a special school or special classes;

—participation in body contact sports;

—notice of any publicity regarding the child.

Unless the agency has been appointed guardian in addition to custodian, parents retain the right to consent to adoption, marriage, or enlistment in the armed services. All legal decisions are made in partnership between the birth parent and the agency. Parents need to be encouraged to act as guardians to the limit of their capacity when the goal is unification.

During the time the agency has legal custody, it is responsible for:

—avoiding precipitous movement of the child;

—informing the foster parents of court hearings concerning the child in their home;

—keeping current court documents in the agency case record; providing evaluations, written reports, and recommendations to the court as appropriate or before expiration of a court order; and—complying with court orders that relate to the agency.

Except by court order only a local agency or licensed child-placing agency may place a child in foster care—with one exception—a Native American tribe with the authority to do so. In most states, agency legal custody is for a specified length of time and must be renewed annually by court order until the child reaches maturity.

The child in permanent foster care. Some children live with foster families long term, even though their parents' rights are not terminated. Children in permanent foster care often remain in a specific home until they reach legal age. Permanent foster care may offer adolescent children a sense of permanency when reunification or adoption are not possible. This often takes the form of a negotiated contract between the child, the birth parents, the foster parents, and social services. It may or may not be written into the case plan. Some children remain with a family indefinitely. No verbal statement has been made discussing permanent placement. This *"social contract"* agreement leaves the child, the family, and the agency vulnerable. Permanent foster care represents pseudo-permanence because social services, the child, or the foster parent can terminate placement without court involvement.

LEGALLY: As with temporary foster care, the legal parental rights may be held jointly by the agency and birth parent, or possibly just the birth parent. In some cases, and in some states, permanent foster children's foster parents may attain additional legal rights through guardianship. If the foster parent accepts guardianship Title IV E funds cannot be paid. If the child remains in permanent foster care there is no guarantee the home will continue to meet licensing requirements. Again, the loss of a license would mean the loss of this home for the child.

The terminated parental rights/pre-adoptive placement/ward of state. When a child has been in out-of-home care and cannot be reunited with the primary family, parental rights are terminated and social services becomes the temporary legal parent. The goal of social services then changes from reunification to finding a permanent home for the child through adoption.

LEGALLY: Parental rights can't be removed unless a Petition for Termination of Parental Rights has been served on the parents or legal guardian, a full hearing has been held and it has been legally proven that the child is and will continue to be dependent (in need of care) or neglected in the future. Only a court can change parental rights or custody of a child. When the court removes the right and custody of a child from a parent, those rights are transferred to a licensed agency. This is generally done for a specific purpose such as adoption. Unfortunately, some children may remain indefinite wards of the state. If a dispute arises, a judge would make a decision regarding who the legal and who the daily parent should be. The family the child is living with may or may not be licensed to care for the child. If the family is licensed a suspected licensing violation could mean the child moves.

The finalized adopted child. Children whose adoptions have been finalized are the legal children of their adoptive parents. They also become legal members of the extended family of the adopting parents. Relatives of the adoptive family become the first alternative placement source for children who need out-of-home care.

Foster parents need to take on a new role of responsibility and professionalism if they are to continue to care for society's children in the 1990's.

As the role of the professional foster parent expands, advanced training will be needed to meet these responsibilities.

CHILD'S LIVING SITUATION	KIND OF PARENT	WHOSE RESPONSIBILITY
Birth **Child**	Birth Parent ⟶	Birth Parent
	Legal Parent ⟶	Birth Parent
	Daily Parent ⟶	Birth Parent
Relative **Care** **(Non-Guardian)**	Birth Parent ⟶	Birth Parent
	Legal Parent ⟶	Birth Parent
	Daily Parent ⟶	Relative of Child
Tribal **Care** *(Licensing may apply)*	Birth Parent ⟶	Birth Parent
	Legal Parent ⟶	Birth, Relative, Tribe or/and Agency
	Daily Parent ⟶	Member of tribe
Kinship **Foster Care** *(Licensing may apply)*	Birth Parent ⟶	Birth Parent
	Legal Parent ⟶	Birth, Relative or/ and Agency
	Daily Parent ⟶	Relative of Child
Voluntary **Foster Care** *(Licensing applies)*	Birth Parent ⟶	Birth Parent
	Legal Parent ⟶	Birth Parent and Agency
	Daily Parent ⟶	Foster and Birth Parent
Temporary Legal Custody **Foster Care** *(Licensing applies)*	Birth Parent ⟶	Birth Parent
	Legal Parent ⟶	Birth Parent and Agency
	Daily Parent ⟶	Foster Parent
Terminated Parental Rights **Foster Care/Pre-Adoptive** **Ward of State** *(Licensing applies)*	Birth Parent ⟶	Birth Parent
	Legal Parent ⟶	Agency/Court
	Daily Parent ⟶	Foster or Adoptive Parent
Terminated Parental Rights **Permanent Foster Care** **Ward of State** *(Licensing applies)*	Birth Parent ⟶	Birth Parent
	Legal Parent ⟶	Foster Parent/Agency
	Daily Parent ⟶	Foster Parent
Adoption **Finalized**	Birth Parent ⟶	Birth Parent
	Legal Parent ⟶	Adoptive Parent
	Daily Parent ⟶	Adoptive Parent

My husband and I work hard with the birth parent(s) during transition time—inviting them to share in preparation and eating of family meals, good night rituals that have been effective, and neutral, fun, co-family outings. Respite care and additional co-parenting are offered once the "fixed child"—huh? — is returned home. As foster parents we try very hard not to lose sight of whose child this really is!

Foster mother

LEGALLY: Adoptive parents have the same rights and responsibilities as birth parents.

Summary

Professional foster parents are assuming greater responsibility for arranging and delivering services and making decisions affecting children in care. The caseworker consults with and monitors, rather than directs, the foster parent. The foster parent may help arrange services and therapy for the child, work with the parents, and be part of the case planning process. (Horowitz 1989)

Foster parents are assuming more responsibilities for a variety of reasons.

— Heavy caseloads carried by caseworkers may render them unable to become deeply involved in each case. Caseworkers are less acquainted with the children assigned to them and the child's need because of high case load. Children entering the child welfare system may exhibit emotional or behavioral disturbances demanding extensive attention; such demands may exceed the caseworker's limited time. *(When this happens, foster parents may step in as surrogate parents under the Education for All Handicapped Children Act)* .

— The large amount of paperwork and documentation for each case. Administrative duties keep caseworkers from frequent direct contact with children assigned to them.

— Insufficient professional education and in-service training.

Professional foster parents need to be part of the permanency plan for the child and can play a big role in helping to carry it through. Training and support service systems need to be available. As foster parents take on functions traditionally reserved for the agency, accommodations must be made to facilitate their expanded role. Agencies and communities must assist and support foster parents as they meet enormous challenges in regard to family living with foster children. Without attention to this issue, children are at risk for inappropriate and multiple placements, insufficient care, more rejection, and further harm.

References

Armstrong, Louise. 1989. *Solomon Says, A Speakout on Foster Care.* New York: Pocket Books

Blumenthal, Karen, Weinberg, Anita.1984. *Establishing Parent Involvement in Foster Care Agencies.* Washington D.C., Child Welfare League

Falhberg, Vera. 1989. *Helping Children When They Must Move.* MI: Dept. Social Sciences

Felker, Evelyn, 1981. *Raising Other People's Kids: Successful Child-Rearing in the Restructured Family.* Michigan: William B. Eerdmanns

Foster Care Task Force and Department of Public Welfare. 1982. *A Practice Guide on Foster Care Services for Workers and Supervisors.* Minnesota: Department of Public Welfare

Hennepin County. 1990. *Child Protection Services Decision Point Policies.* Minnesota: Hennepin County.

Horowitz, Robert, Hardin, Mark, and Bulkley, Josephine. 1989. *The Rights of Foster Care.* Washington, D.C.: American Bar Association

National Commission of Family Foster Care, 1991. *A Blueprint for Fostering Infants, Children and Youth in the 1990s.* The NCFFC was convened by Child Welfare League of America in collaboration with the National Foster Parent Association. Washington, D.C., CWLA.

Stein, Theodore J. and Rzepnicki, Tina. (1982) *Decision Making at Child Welfare Intake. A Handbook for Practitioners.* New York: Child Welfare League.

Stehno, S. Nov-Dec. 1990, p 551-562. *Differential Treatment of Minority Children in Service Systems.* Child Welfare LXIX, 6.

Chapter 3

Knowing Yourself, Knowing Your Family

Caring for other people's children can be stressful. Care providers must be able to recognize stress and know when to ask for support and help.

As a regional and national family advocate, Dorothy has devoted much of her life to improving care provider services in the United States.

> *"Every Sunday the newspaper ads announced 'Kids waiting for homes!' Sunday after Sunday I read those ads and thought, 'I have the time and energy to do that, I could take care of some of those needy kids.' The ads never went away—babies, toddlers, kids, teens—they proclaimed. I thought, why not?*
>
> *My husband wasn't so sure. Was ours the kind of home they needed? How much stress would it put on our existing lifestyle? We needed more information. Then one Sunday a long article explained the urgent need for foster homes. The decision was made.*
>
> *We called the number and three months later we accepted our first child. That was 25 years ago!"*

Minnesota child care statutes begin by stating that licensed foster parents must be kind, mature, and responsible, with a genuine liking for children. They shall possess consistent and healthy methods of handling the lifestyle unique to their own families—considerate of cultural differences—stable and understanding of the unique needs of children living apart from their own homes—and able to cope with the emotional, mental, or physical handicaps these children bring.

Each family has a unique culture and lifestyle. Foster families must identify their own internal and cultural dynamics, then blend them with the additional demands of professional public parenting.

The Early Childhood Studies Program at the University of Minnesota has produced a brochure called the *Quality Care Checklist for Foster Home Care.* The checklist was designed to help parents examine the quality of care they provide and prevent child maltreatment. Care providers are encouraged to periodically review the checklist. Birth parents in general can use the checklist to see how they measure up to the requirements care providers must meet. *(The author has added some culturally sensitive questions to the original list.)*

A Quality Care Checklist for Foster Families

Kris was eight months old when she arrived in foster care. "She's a quiet little girl, you'll hardly even know she's there," said the social worker.

Amy, Kris's new foster mother, put a blanket on the floor. Abby, Kris's new foster sister, went to pick out baby toys. Kris lay motionless on the blanket.

The social worker left feeling confident this quiet little girl would survive, thrive, and blossom in this loving, single-parent home.

Buster, Abby's German Shepherd, let out a large bark.

"Woof!" Kris didn't move. "Woof, Woof!" Kris didn't blink.

Before the social worker had reached his office, Amy knew her new foster daughter was deaf!

About me:

1.	I am a cheerful, friendly person.	Usually	Sometimes	Seldom
2.	I am personally clean and neat.	Usually	Sometimes	Seldom
3.	My home is clean and neat.	Usually	Sometimes	Seldom
4.	When I have problems, I handle them well.	Usually	Sometimes	Seldom
5.	I am a flexible person, not rigid and demanding.	Usually	Sometimes	Seldom
6.	I have a positive attitude about my work with children.	Usually	Sometimes	Seldom
7.	I am in good health, mentally and physically.	Usually	Sometimes	Seldom
8.	I feel good about myself.	Usually	Sometimes	Seldom
9.	I can handle a crisis, an emergency, or unexpected things that happen in a positive way.	Usually	Sometimes	Seldom
10.	I have friends I see often, and I know how to have wholesome fun.	Usually	Sometimes	Seldom
11.	I know how to identify abused children and how to report to the authorities.	Usually	Sometimes	Seldom
12.	I understand why there are corporal punishment regulations, and others designed to keep children safe.	Usually	Sometimes	Seldom
13.	I am pleased that I have training opportunities and I go to workshops whenever I can.	Usually	Sometimes	Seldom
14.	Training has changed my way of thinking about things and doing things. I use what I learn.	Usually	Sometimes	Seldom
15.	I share new things I learn in training with members of my family and with others who care about children in my home.	Usually	Sometimes	Seldom
16.	I ask for help especially when I have a "difficult" child. I know whom to ask.	Usually	Sometimes	Seldom
17.	I know that being with other providers is important because they give me advice and support. I try to talk to other providers frequently.	Usually	Sometimes	Seldom
18.	I am interested in other cultures and do not judge them based on my own world-view.	Usually	Sometimes	Seldom
19.	I research the historic heritage and culture of children living in my home.	Usually	Sometimes	Seldom

Chapter 3-Knowing Yourself

About my family:

20. Other family members support our decision to provide care for children.   Usually   Sometimes   Seldom

21. Other adults in my family share the child care responsibilities.   Usually   Sometimes   Seldom

22. My children accept the foster care children as part of the family.   Usually   Sometimes   Seldom

23. All family members help with daily household tasks.   Usually   Sometimes   Seldom

24. We do fun things together as a family.   Usually   Sometimes   Seldom

25. We do things together that support the cultural heritage of children in our care.   Usually   Sometimes   Seldom

26. Members of my family and additional caregivers understand the foster care regulations in our community and follow them.   Usually   Sometimes   Seldom

27. I am not concerned about any members of my family being alone with the children in care.   Usually   Sometimes   Seldom

28. I am aware of the risk of allegations of abuse against me and my family when we are not careful about the well-being of children placed in care in our home.   Usually   Sometimes   Seldom

About the children in my care:

29. The children in care feel comfortable with our family.   Usually   Sometimes   Seldom

30. The children enjoy being with the members of my family.   Usually   Sometimes   Seldom

31. I know how to handle misbehavior in positive ways.   Usually   Sometimes   Seldom

32. I never spank, hit, shake, or humiliate the children in my care.   Usually   Sometimes   Seldom

33. I try to make all the children feel good about themselves.   Usually   Sometimes   Seldom

34. We often do interesting things that help children to grow and develop positively.   Usually   Sometimes   Seldom

35. I do not yell at children or threaten them when they misbehave.   Usually   Sometimes   Seldom

36. I provide meals and snacks that are good for my children.   Usually   Sometimes   Seldom

37. I provide careful supervision, both indoors and outdoors.   Usually   Sometimes   Seldom

38. All rooms in my home and my yard are safe places for children to be.   Usually   Sometimes   Seldom

39. I am careful about friends or strangers who come to my home.   Usually   Sometimes   Seldom

Day after day, Amy and Abby held, rocked, and cuddled Kris. Day after day, Buster would snuggle up to Kris and nuzzle her.

They became a team, mother, five-year-old daughter Abby, and the attentive canine Buster.

Still, Kris couldn't hold a bottle or pick up a cracker. But tiny triumph by tiny triumph the family provided the love, sweat, and tears little Kris needed.

Finally—the eyes! Finally the eyes made contact! There was a little person inside!

They would reach her. Whatever it took they would love her and help her love herself!

it just takes one adult to put the sunshine into a child's life.

40.	I treat birth parents with respect and encourage contact with their children when permitted.	Usually	Sometimes	Seldom

40. I treat birth parents with respect and encourage contact with their children when permitted. Usually Sometimes Seldom

41. Members of my family treat birth parents with respect and refer to them positively within the hearing range of children in care. Usually Sometimes Seldom

42. I keep myself informed about the case plan and I work within it. Usually Sometimes Seldom

43. I feel comfortable with professionals who are helping children in out-of-home care and I cooperate with them as needed. Usually Sometimes Seldom

44. I feel comfortable about asking social workers to help meet my family's needs and those of children in care. Usually Sometimes Seldom

45. I keep adequate records and communicate appropriately with agency personnel. Usually Sometimes Seldom

Now evaluate yourself!

A parent answering all 45 questions with "usually" serves as a model surrogate care provider. Most likely, however, being human, everyone will have some "sometimes" and "seldoms."

3-5 Seldoms or Sometimes	*Families or individuals providing quality care services. Think about what needs to be done to change a seldom to usually. Awareness may be all that's necessary.*
6-10 Seldoms or Sometimes	*Think carefully about improvements needed. Use this checklist as a reminder of the changes to make. Get some training in the seldom areas. Talk to other providers to see what they do.*
10+ Seldoms or Sometimes	*Concern is needed regarding the quality of your services. Newly licensed and inexperienced providers may score here, and will improve with experience. If the care provider scores in this area, serious reevaluation is necessary. Training and advice from other providers is important. Ask yourself:* *—Am I being stretched in too many directions?* *—Is there personal stress in my life that is hard to manage?*

The above checklist is designed to help keep everyone in the provider home safe and content, including the provider. Risk of actual abuse or unfair accusations decrease when the quality of care improves.

How do I know my own limits and my family's limits?

Typically, foster care provider families are strong. They have been specially screened and selected because of the strengths and qualities they can give to children in need. These families have often experienced their share of troubles and problems, uniting to meet challenges. They are effective problem solvers.

Once Kris had made eye contact she had begun to communicate. Her brightness began to shine, and a stubborn, dynamic personality emerged!

Her balance and walking were unstable. But that didn't seem to matter much to Kris. Away she would run—helter skelter—knocking over everything that got in her way.

A silent little tornado, she left a mass of destruction in her wake. She took on a look of alertness and brightness as, in her silence, she challenged every obstacle.

They feel good about the family unit. No member gets smothered or lost. Each member is encouraged to achieve full potential. Most importantly, they emerge from each crisis wiser and ready to continue living.

In spite of cultural, political, and language differences, strong families share six major qualities:

1. **COMMITMENT.** Members of strong families are dedicated to promoting each other's welfare and happiness. They value the unity of family.

2. **APPRECIATION.** Strong families frequently show appreciation for each other.

3. **COMMUNICATION.** Members of strong families have good communication skills and spend a lot of time talking and listening to one another.

4. **TIME.** Strong families spend time—quality time in large quantities—with each other.

5. **SPIRITUAL WELLNESS.** Regardless of their specific faith or if they attend formal religious services, strong family members have a sense of a greater power in life, and that belief gives them strength and purpose. Hope, love, family, an elevation of the spirit, a reverence for life, and a sense of the sacred are consistent themes carried through in strong families.

6. **COPING ABILITY.** Members of strong families are able to view crisis and stress as an opportunity to grow.

Strong families are made. Step by step. People in strong families work at it constantly.
(Stinnett & DeFrain 1985)

A strong family is a treasure.
Family is the heart and center of each member's thoughts.
Family members pitch in to help because
if one is in pain, then all hurt.
Strong families don't let a problem defeat them.

Whenever a new piece is added to our lives, all or many of our old pieces need to shift to accommodate. In her book, *"Preventing Abuse in Foster Care,"* Emily Jean McFadden lists questions social workers need to ask to help assess a foster parenting home and help match kids to parents. I have included in that list questions families need to answer as a team before beginning to provide care for other people's children. (McFadden 1984)

1. Which do you prefer, the child who is a handful, or the child who clings and needs you?

2. How much affection do you display in your family? How much affection do you expect back from a foster child?

3. How would you describe your family—active or quiet?

4. What things do kids do to get you really mad?

5. What was your worst personal problem and how did you solve it?

6. What would you change about yourself if you could?

7. Besides your immediate family, who else do you go to for personal support?

After a year in care, Amy, Abby, and Buster all needed a break. Our family provided that much needed respite.

Amy and Abby sent Kris to our home for weekend time-out.

Kris and my daughter, April, loved each other. At 18 months they communicated with some sort of baby sign language that brought a stream of giggles from April and smiles from Kris.

Our three large poodles provided transportation. Our house became a circus!

When the weekend was over, I understood much more clearly the incredible love and care Amy and Abby were giving this little girl.

Without personal one-on-one experience with Kris, it would have been easy to judge Amy's mild and patient personality as neglectful, and Kris's spontaneous and stubborn personality as out-of-control and unmanaged.

8. What is a typical day like in your family?

9. How does your family handle problems and crises? Can you describe the way you solved your most recent family problem?

10. How do you handle children who misbehave?

11. How do you handle toilet training?

12. What kind of activities do you do as a family? As a couple?

13. What do you do that brings about a cheerful and happy atmosphere?

14. What do you feel is the most stressful part of care for other people's children? Of parenting in general? Of the foster care system?

15. What changes are coming up in the next few months?

16. How have you handled separations from other children?

17. Have you ever experienced the loss of one of your own biological children or a child very close to you? How did you handle it? How does it affect you today?

18. Do you like to solve problems? How do you ask for help when needed?

19. What do you do for yourself when you need to relax from stress?

Questions the family needs to think through are:

1. Who is the main family authority figure?
    Who is in charge of the children?
    Do these roles conflict?

2. Is there anyone who is spending less time at home, or more time at home lately?

3. Is anyone leaving soon? Permanently?

4. Which kids are closest to each other?
    What do they do for each other?

5. Is anyone fighting with anyone else? Why?

6. As a parent, which kid(s) are you closest to?
    Who needs you the most?
    What happens if you pull back?

7. How are the children going to adjust to sharing parents, their home, and attention?

Good family policy on placement requirements:

Every foster family is different. Blending family systems and children is difficult. Social services refer to this as matching. For example, a deaf elementary child may fit very well in one family, whereas another family may want only infants or teenagers. One child may grow well in a working, single parent home, while another needs a stay-at-home parent. Family members have to agree on types of children they are willing to work with and areas of concern to help social services select children appropriate for their home. So ask yourself:

1. What types of children can the family handle well?
    Previous experience?

2. What are family preferences on mixed ages, sibling groups, genders, cultural background of children?

3. What are family preferences on disability conditions?

    A. Physical (deaf, blind, cerebral palsy, heart disorder, diabetes, HIV, AIDS)

    B. Emotional (separation, grief, attachment issues)

    C. Mental (depression, schizophrenia)

    D. Intellectual (ADD, FAE, FAS, learning disabled)

    E. Previous abuse (neglect, physical, sexual, ritual)

These questions need more than just an immediate response to the social worker. They are questions families contemplating foster care need to ask each other and think through carefully. If differences of opinion arise, a mutual consensus on differences through respectful compromise is crucial *before* children arrive.

Providing care to other people's children can affect a marriage by:

— Solidifing a relationship and making a couple a stronger parenting unit, more loving and supportive.

— Breaking up marriages due to stress, differences of viewpoint, and other pre-existing conditions.

— Forcing parents to quit providing care altogether.

The stresses of surrogate parenting and knowing when you've been stretched

Foster parents, while carefully screened and selected, are still human. They are vulnerable to family life cycle stresses, which are compounded by the placement of the child and child welfare system. Stress becomes a way of life for care providing families.

Stress and burnout are such awesome words—"stretching" seems like a more appropriate word to describe what care providers experience. Each stretch, although painful, exhausting, and stressful, eventually brings new knowledge and release. Most people providing foster care services have been stretched repeatedly, and with each stretch they become slightly more skilled and adaptable to new situations. Learning to cope with stresses of foster care reduces the emotional strains caused by children, social services, and life in general.

Everyone reacts to stress differently. Care providers who are in tune with their bodies can use stress warning signals as an opportunity to manage stress before it gets out of hand.

Stress affects the body. You may experience:

- Muscle tightness, stiff neck, lower back pain
- Upset stomach (tied in knots or butterflies)
- Migraine headaches
- Trembling, twitching, excessive blinking, jumpiness
- Pounding heart or increased perspiration
- Urinary and digestive tract problems - frequent urination, constipation, diarrhea, queasiness
- Fatigue, insomnia, changes in sleep patterns
- Illness, allergies, or colds
- Skin rashes, acne eruption
- High blood pressure, increased heart rate
- Numb extremities
- Speech changes— stuttering, unusual voice volume, laryngitis
- Dry mouth, excessive throat clearing
- Inability to concentrate, inattentiveness, easily distracted, forgetful
- Loss of appetite or increased appetite
- Dizziness or weakness

Hug Therapy Can Be A Stress Reducer!

When you become a skilled hug therapist, the hugs you share are thoughtful, respectful, and care-filled.

1. *Hug therapy is non-sexual. Hug accordingly. Be sure the hugs you dispense are compassionate, not passionate.*

2. *Be certain you have permission before you give a hug.*

3. *Respect the other person's verbal and non-verbal messages.*

4. *Ask permission when you need a hug. Hug dispensers are also hug recipients.*

5. *Be responsible for expressing what you need the way you need it.*

Say, "I really could use a hug right now."
(Keating 1983)

Potential stresses for care providers and children they care for.

Family Issues (Situational)

- **Financial difficulties:** inflation, bills, unplanned expenses, layoff, unemployment
- **Relationship conflicts:** parent-child, spouse, in-laws, friends, neighbors
- **Equipment failure:** car, washing machine, furnace, etc.
- **Illness or death:** spouse, child, grandparents, close friend
- **Child adjustment problem:** school, peer groups, family chores and rules, experimentation with sex, substances

(Developmental)

- Pregnancy, birth, adolescence, leaving home

Resources Lacking

- Training
- Respite care
- Support groups

Community Stress

- Stereotypes of fostering, adverse media coverage
- Neighbors critical of child in care
- Doctors, dentists won't take medicaid
- School unresponsive to needs of child in care

Natural Parent Stress

- Critical of foster care providers. Lifestyle in conflict with care provider values
- Visit disruptive to foster family schedule or routine
- Visits "upset" child

Stressful Child-in-Care Characteristics

- Child has had multiple families and workers, not much consistency
- Doesn't respond to normal discipline
- Health problems requiring special medical attention, multiple professionals, and many appointments
- Withdrawn or hostile behavior
- Child has had exceptionally traumatic background
- Developmental delay
- Bedwetting
- Learning difficulties and school behavior problems
- Provocative behavior, "asks for it"
- Lying
- Stealing
- Fecal smearing, urinating on walls
- Firesetting
- Violent attacks on siblings or animals
- Rocking/head banging
- Excessive crying
- "Tunes out," withdraws, won't listen
- Running away
- Seductive or sexual behaviors

Birth Parent Stress To Child

- Birth parent misses visit
- Birth parent late to pick child up
- Birth parent never calls child or checks in
- Child goes on overnight or weekend visits
- Birth parent makes promises they can't keep
- Child uncertain about future

System Stresses

- Foster care payments don't cover actual expense of child
- Payment late
- Medicaid card late or not yet issued
- Worker too busy to return call promptly
- Policies and procedures change with different caseworkers and supervisors
- Turnover of social workers
- Change in regulations and different interpretations by different agencies
- Care providers not involved in case planning
- Care provider does not know short term or long term plans for child
- Adequate information not given to foster care provider about children in their care
- Expectations and role responsibilities not clear
- No reimbursement for damage done by child in care
- Caseworker and care provider do not agree

Resources Lacking

- Due to cutbacks in Human Services funding, many foster care providers no longer have adequate access to support such as:
  — Foster care provider training programs
  — Mental health and child guidance counseling programs
  — Casework services

Adapted from Emily Jean McFadden (1984) — Preventing Abuse in Foster Care

---

System Stressors On Foster Care Providers

As families, foster care providers are subject to all the normal stressors of contemporary family life. Additionally, they must accommodate the sometimes unclear role expectations unique to fostering. According to Pasztor and Burgess in Finding and Keeping More Foster Families *(1982), "The tendency is for foster care providers to be caught in a trap of conflicting expectations and agency practices."*

The trend seems to be to expect foster care providers to perform as professionals. They must:

- Handle a wide range of emotional/behavioral problems.
- Be accepting and kind toward neglectful and/or abusive parents of children in their care.
- Incorporate a new child into their home on short notice and for an indeterminite period of time.
- Love and let go.
- Work with several different caseworkers simultaneously and with a number of changing workers over a period of time.
- Often perform all of these functions with little or no pre-service training.

Despite these expectations, foster families are simultaneously subjected to such practices as:

- Not receiving complete information about the child in their care, i.e., receiving a sexually active child or sexually abused child.
- Not knowing the child is involved with drugs/alcohol.
- Not knowing the child is a member of a gang or is committing crimes.
- Not being allowed input in case decisions affecting children who have been living in their home.
- Not being allowed to meet adoptive parents.
- Having the child in their care 'interviewed' outside the home by a worker who does not explain the purpose to them.
- Not being encouraged or allowed to meet other care providers.
- Not being thanked for a job well done.

Economic Stressors On Foster Families

- In most foster care programs, the payment rate is substantially lower than the actual cost of caring for the child. Foster care providers are not reimbursed for the time spent for caring for the child unless the child has needs that qualify for a special subsidy.
- During times of inflation and unemployment, family finances are often stretched to the breaking point.

It is not uncommon to find that:

- Pre-placement visits are not reimbursed.
- Funds are not available for the expensive extras, such as school pictures, graduation or yearbooks, which are vital to the child's self-esteem.
- Funds are not available for participation in sports programs, for the equipment and practices.
- Funds are not available for music, art, and dance programs.
- Foster mothers may be discouraged or prohibited from working outside the home to supplement family income.
- Travel expenses related to fostering are not reimbursed promptly.
- Damages done to the foster home by the child are not reimbursed by the agency, and foster care providers have difficulty claiming it on their homeowner's insurance.
- Care providers may have to take extra jobs to make ends meet.
- Care providers may not be able to afford babysitters in order to get away from the children for an evening or weekend of relaxation.
- Paid respite care is minimal and additional respite care may be paid out of foster parents' personal funds.

Stress affects emotions:

You may become at times,

- Impulsive (do things without thinking)
- Irritable (everything bothers you)
- Lethargic (don't care what happens)
- Tense and fearful (self-conscious) though you don't know why

And experience:

- Rapid change in emotions—mood swings
- Hyper excitation (over excitement about situation)
- Feeling disconnected to problem, unable to cope

Stress affects behavior. You may experience:

- Nervous laughter, giggles
- Regression to old behaviors —get your own way —old abuse/neglect behaviors
- Increased smoking, alcohol consumption, or use of medication

- A pattern of lateness
- Sarcasm, exaggeration, combative, or hostile language, blow ups
- Binge eating, cravings, or not eating

Symptoms of stress are signals of an overloaded system. Don't ignore them. Assess what can be done and plan a strategy to reorganize, retreat, relax, or regroup.

Ideas to help relax when stretched!

1. **Care for yourself**. To care for others, you need to care for yourself. Maintaining a strong and healthy body, mind, and spirit is crucial in keeping stress levels manageable. This means good food, rest, and exercise. Please review Chapter 15 for some creative ideas.

2. **Set realistic goals**. Small, measurable goals are easier to accomplish than long-term goals. Successful people work toward long-term goals one step at a time.

3. **Do the same thing differently**. Instead of saying, *"It's time for bed,"* to a pre-schooler and expecting an argument, try, *"The putting-to-bed person is going up the stairs and you'd better follow if you want the story, jammies, drink, potty, brushing teeth, tuck-me-in, prayers, because the putting-to-bed person is putting herself to bed first unless the little feet are scrambling."* Luckily for me, this has always brought attention, action, and giggles from pre-schoolers; just what I need on a stretched day. It may, however, bring on an exclamation of, *"Great, I'll just watch TV for a couple of more hours."* In that case, I've packed up the little tyke, brushed the teeth, helped with potty, and placed the child in bed with a, *"Sure hope the putting-to-bed person gets response tomorrow night. I like the stories and tuck-me-in times and I miss them when you don't cooperate."*

4. **Break away.** Go to a movie, get together with friends, listen to music, play cards, jog, read a book, take a bath. Develop a support or respite system for breaks away from the children.

5. **Take things less personally.** Putting a band-aid on your child isn't going to take pain away. Care providers can't change the past or fix the world. It is easy to get caught into the trap—their pain is my pain. *The reality is "their pain is their pain." The job of the care provider is to be ready with patience, understanding, love, care, support, and listening ears.*

6. **Accentuate the positive**. Pay attention to small accomplishments. Even one tiny positive step a child makes is progress. With foster and adoptive children, sometimes even negatives are significant forward steps if they allow a child to become unstuck from an issue or behavior.

7. **Know yourself.** Self-understanding begins with self-observation. What am I feeling? When? Where? What am I doing in response to these feelings? Keep a journal of feelings to monitor stress. Talk feelings through with a significant other. Find a private place and discuss out loud to yourself how you can work things out. *What can I do differently? What if I respond with the opposite reaction?*

8. **Rest and relaxation.** Ten to fifteen minutes of quiet time. Silence. Time out for peace. Do not rush to relax, and by doing so, learn to control the symptoms, but not fix the stress.

9. **Time off. Time out.** Social service workers can decompress. That means they can leave it at the office, hang up the phone, shut the file folder on the case, even slam the file draw shut, and go home! Foster parenting is 24 hours a day, with no relief. The transition time—personal time for the provider—must be planned. Hire a babysitter for an afternoon to get personal things done—haircut, doctor's appointment, shopping, lunch with a friend. Take up a hobby, attend a Bible study or spiritual enrichment program, play tennis, enjoy gourmet cooking, tend a garden, or work in the garage. Set boundaries around this time—it is restorative.

If the parents are being stretched, the children will also feel the stress and begin acting out— misbehaving, losing concentration, doing poorly in school, and developing sleeping disturbances. All of these manifestations compound the stress in the adult. The book, *Stress in Children, Common Sense Advice on How To Spot and Deal With Stress in Children of All Ages,* by Dr. Bettie B. Youngs (1985) is a valuable resource in helping children cope with stress.

It is general knowledge that children are good barometers of what is taking place in the home. Children in out-of-home care, however, are better compared to a thermostat—they set the stress level to where they feel comfortable. When things are beginning to heal and get healthy, they turn up the temperature and begin to release past pressure.

How care providers can get help when they need it

Some foster parents are reluctant to contact their agency, fearing they will be considered inadequate or be blamed for the child's difficulty. Communicating with other foster parents may be the most valuable resource available to foster parents. In July of 1961, the Univeristy of Indiana published an article titled, *Teacher's Handling of Children in Conflict,* by N. Long and R. Newman. It states:

> *A teacher can't function adequately for long without an informed shoulder to lean on, without an on-the-spot human wailing wall at which to gripe, to rage, to express fears and confess mistakes, to ask questions and wonder aloud . . . Where the human wailing wall is carefully conceived and consistently offered, where the people are provided are . . . informed, sensitive, sympathetic, and understanding, the turnover among teachers, even under the most incredibly difficult conditions, is remarkably lowered.*

If teachers need this service, obviously so do foster parents. Other foster parents can provide that one-to-one empathetic support.

Other foster parents can offer:

Comfort: They can provide a shoulder to cry on, a sympathetic ear, and a nurturing hug. *"I know what you're going through. I understand what you're feeling. I've been there myself."*

A Lesson from the Workshop
The coping saw in my husband's workshop displays all the characteristics a human needs to cope with stress and life in general.

1. It's flexible.

2. It's designed to turn corners and even come full circle.

3. It comes undone at one end so it can fit through a hole.

4. It's very resilient and cannot be broken easily.
(Vineland 1988)

A foster father takes a five minute vacation . . .

"Step back and look at the beauty of life in the midst of chaos . . . watch a bee collecting pollen, notice the bee's sound, its movements. Watch your child. Notice how the child has changed. Notice the color of a green pepper. Step back. Take a five minute vacation, then regroup and get on with the chaos.

By age four, Kris was competent in American sign language and enjoyed playing with deaf and non-deaf children.

Her lack of balance and inability to verbally communicate sometimes got her into trouble. But her optimism and stubbornness always pulled her through.

Susan, Kris's hearing friend, could roller skate. You could almost see the wheels turn inside of Kris's head. Nothing was going to stop her from skating!

Kris spent the weekend in Susan's basement practicing. She would learn how to rollerskate if it took a lifetime!

Comparison. They can be a measure for someone who is unsure of how appropriate or typical a reaction is. *"Is this normal to feel this way? Am I the only one who feels like this? Am I overreacting?"*

Escape. Other foster parents can offer to take you away from it all. They can get you interested in something for a short period of time to give you that necessary break.

Help: They may offer direct assistance or an idea for a solution.

Humor: Jokes and laughter can reduce emotional strain by making things seem less serious, less frightening, and less overwhelming. Humor injects a positive element into a dim situation. Other foster parents can laugh with each other because they understand situations from personal experience.

Insight: They can help you see things differently. They may be able to express thoughts and feelings uncomfortable for the foster parents to say themselves. They can help analyze feelings and give insight into reactions.

Rewards: The best and sometimes only, source of praise, compliments, and recognition for a job well done comes from people who wear the same shoes. Not only are they in a good position to evaluate, but they are in the best position to give feedback that is immediate and meaningful. Foster care providers sometimes need to ask other care providers— *"How am I doing?"* (Maslach 1982)

Agencies are normally well aware of how difficult some children are and the effect a child with problems can have on the entire family. In all cases, honest communication and requests for assistance need to be seen as signs of strength and team cooperation. The provider has the responsibility and right to contact the worker for assistance.

Reaching out for help is very difficult for many people.
A request for help must be interpreted for what is is—
a sign of strength, not weakness.

Guidelines for asking for help

There are many valid reasons to ask for consultation. The agency can assist in helping to handle the child's behavior. In addition, the agency can put the provider family in contact with community resources to help reduce family stress. Here are some guidelines developed by foster parents and social workers. These guidelines are based on situations care providers routinely encounter and request help in solving. (McFadden 1984)

Common problems families face:

- *Family's own children are upset or developing problems as a result of conflict with child in care.*
- *Foster parents or children are experiencing increasing anxiety or conflict about the child in care.*
- *Family cannot afford to maintain the usual lifestyle because of financial expense for child in care.*
- *Needs or problems of the child in care are so encompassing that parents have no time for recreation, privacy, or enjoyment of each other.*

- *It is becoming more difficult for members of the foster family to see the child in a positive light.*
- *Foster child gets "too close" to a parent and tries to shut the other out of the relationship.*
- *Things that go wrong in the foster family are being blamed on the child in care.*
- *Foster child's problems begin to preoccupy another family member. Trouble eating, sleeping, or being able to get a way from the child for a few hours.*

The agency and community can add to or help solve these problems:

- *Medicaid card or foster care payment is late, and there is an immediate need that must be met.*
- *Provider denied access or put on a long waiting list of a community resource and needs help.*
- *Provider needs relevant information about the child's family.*
- *Provider is concerned the child is being hurt in some way by the relationship with the natural family or by the agency plan.*
- *Provider needs training or reading materials relating to a certain problem the child is having.*
- *Provider believes he/she is not receiving adequate compensation or reimbursement for the expenses of the child and the costs incurred.*

- *Assistance in locating community resource to help the child. (Doctor, dentist, team, scout troop, tutoring, etc.)*
- *Provider feeling isolated or unsupported by the agency or staff.*
- *Provider needs to understand the role in the case plan for the child.*
- *Provider is feeling stressed or experiencing value conflicts from involvement with the child's family.*
- *Provider needs the worker's support or advocacy to deal with the school.*
- *Provider is having difficulty coping with the pressure or criticism from the neighbors about the child in out-of-home care.*

These behaviors may precipitate a request for help:

- *Child's behavior is dangerous to self and others.*
- *Child's behavior is getting child into trouble at school or in the neighborhood.*
- *Child does not respond to normal discipline. Provider finds it difficult to stick to discipline techniques approved in the discipline policy.*
- *Child appears to be attempting to provoke provider into more serious physical discipline. Child taunts, "Go ahead and hit me," or physically lashes out.*
- *Child consistently tests limits or breaks rules without seeming to learn from the experience.*
- *Child's behavior does not make sense.*

- *Child's behavior is bizarre, exaggerated, or inappropriate for age.*
- *Child's behavior is causing a great deal of extra expense or work for the provider family.*
- *Child does not respond to normal discipline and provider needs to escalate the level of discipline approved by the agency.*
- *Provider wants to use discipline techniques which are not allowed because the child doesn't respond to his/her best efforts.*
- *Provider feeling frustrated or losing hope of managing the child's behavior productively.*

Why foster care providers fail to request help

Asking for help can be risky. Misinterpreted "red flags" can lead to removal of foster children, allegations against the care provider, or a formal investigation. Foster parents hearing the horror stories of those who have asked for help have begun to feel anxious about speaking to the very worker who is provided to help them cope with the difficulties of caring for foster children.

Foster care provider associations may be able to help foster parents assess the situation and communicate with the agency. Provider associations know of other families who may be experiencing or have experienced similar situations and learned creative and appropriate solutions in dealing with them. Association support team members may be able to advocate for a foster parent's position to social services when a provider family is insecure about communicating sensitive information.

In the spring of 1990, just prior to our allegation, April, Joseph, and I packed the car with presents for a surprise birthday party with four-year-old Kris.

We arrived at the correct time and place and found no one there.

We waited.

Disappointed, April, Joseph, and I went home.

Children With Special Needs Need Special People

Do Respite Foster Care

Give parents of children with special emotional, behavioral or developmental needs a chance to recharge their batteries. It's only one or two weekends a month.

Respite care is a great way to find out what foster care is like. It's also a way of helping if you find yourself too busy to do regular foster care.

CALL ___ -KIDS

HOME FOREVER

After our allegation hit, I didn't contact Amy to see what had happened. Our home was closed to foster care. Joseph was removed. I didn't know what to say. I didn't know what she had been told. I no longer had any support services I could offer her.

Two years later—while writing this book—I called Amy to see how Kris was doing.

"I don't know how Kris is doing," she said.

Kris had been adopted by a professional family just after her fourth birthday, and Amy had only accidently seen her once since.

"How is April? How is Joseph? How are you doing?" she asked on top of my questions.

"April is fine. Joseph's in another foster home. We no longer provide respite, we lost our foster home license, and I'm writing a book on allegations."

Amy's floodgates opened . . .

Some reasons why care providers do not ask for help directly:

- Unsure of how or when to ask for help.
- Unaware that the problem is severe, or that it exists.
- Avoidance of a painful loss or self-esteem.
- Unable to discuss "personal" or "family" matters.
- Confused about the situation.
- Not wanting to "bother" the worker.
- Unresponsivness of worker in the past.
- Fear of social worker's authority.
- Fear of being judged not capable by a social worker.
- Anxiety concerning raising red flags

If you do not have access to an association, call the National Foster Parent Association, U.S. Children's Bureau, or the Child Welfare League—addresses and phone numbers are provided in Appendix.

What if a call for help raises a "red flag"—initiating an assessment and investigation?

The first step in solving a problem is knowledge of its existence. It takes strength to admit something may be wrong. If a foster care provider asks a question or reports a situation which signals a "red flag" it is **not** the end of the world. It **does not** mean there is inappropriate care, the provider has failed, or the home is bad. It does not mean the provider is guilty of something. *A "red flag" means there is a possibility of a potential problem that needs to be reviewed.*

> *Examples of "red flags":*
> *Child unfavorably compared with other children in the home.*
> *Child clings to worker.*
> *Child wants to move, but won't say why.*
> *Foster care provider feels need to escalate discipline.*
> *Foster care provider in training says, "I have a friend who."*

If a "red flag" is signaled, the care provider family should remain open and honest with their worker. It is helpful for the family to call the local or national care provider association for support. *(See list of potential red flags listed in Appendix)*

What kind of services are available to help foster care providers?

In a time of shrinking programs, funds, and an increasing need for extra resources, the effort of finding support services for care providers can be considered heroic. (McFadden 1989, p175-180)

"We've done so much for so long with so little, we're expected to do almost anything with nothing."

Social worker

In addition to training and education programs, more resources are needed to assist foster care providers. It is unrealistic to expect already swamped social workers to devote time to supporting foster parents. Therefore, other foster care providers become one of the best support resources for foster parents. The following ideas have been provided by Emily Jean McFadden and foster care associations across the United States.

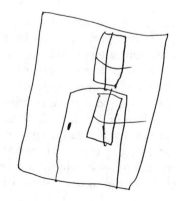

Utilize Other Care Providers:

Buddy care: A licensed foster home on furlough can be used as an emergency respite home for four or five other care provider families in need of support. This buddy family would be a part of the support team for selected children in care and their foster families.

Buddy parent: After licensing or immediately after a child is placed, the foster parent can be matched with an experienced foster parent "buddy" who can provide advice and support.

Crisis hot line: Experienced crisis foster parents trained through provider associations can accept emergency calls at home. Call forwarding can be used to allow one emergency number to access a variety of provider homes 24 hours a day.

Master foster parent: A highly skilled and experienced foster parent can be selected to work with new foster parents, individually or in groups. This role can be especially useful in keeping experienced foster parents on furlough involved in the system. The master foster parent can introduce pre-planned educational material or respond to needs of new foster parents. The master foster parent and social service agency would work as a team in supporting families.

Neighborhood support groups: Regularly scheduled potluck dinner meetings can provide fun and learning activities for children while parents discuss present home situations. These local groups may meet in school rooms, homes, or a church. Siblings who are living separately but nearby can take the opportunity to visit brothers and sisters. College social work students can participate or provide supervision or entertainment for the children. Hands-on experience with foster children and families can provide positive realistic interactions with children in care and the families who care for them.

Ombuds service: An ombuds foster parent is an adult leader who will troubleshoot and advise parents of problems with the child welfare and foster care system. An ombuds can help clear up problems or help bring problems to the attention of the agency staff.

Respite home: Newly licensed foster families can provide respite and gain experience while waiting for placements. Respite homes can be available when a foster family needs a break, is in crisis, or has to leave the state and can't secure permission to take the foster child on a trip. Respite care may also be good for the child who does not have a natural family to visit. Foster children should get to know the respite family ahead of time, through visits between families and shared activities.

Economic Support Systems:

Businesses supporting families: Local businesses can contribute seconds, old packaged, or outdated products to foster families. Cases of trash bags, roller skates, sweaters, coats, and tennis shoes are among some items I've seen contributed to state associations. The local chamber of commerce may agree to help pinpoint businesses interested such a program. Service companies can offer internships for children in care.

Emergency loan fund: Care provider associations or family support groups can hold neighborhood carnivals, car washes, bake sales, and garage sales to raise money for an emergency loan fund. Foster parents can then tap into this fund to cover unusual expenses for foster children, such as clothing for the child who arrives with nothing or an emergency medical visit that demands cash. The loan can be repaid on receipt of the agency check.

"Kris spent the weekend roller skating and came home with bruised buns on Sunday night. On Monday her teacher noticed the bruises. I was accused of child abuse and by the end of the week Kris was gone and placed in her adoptive home."

"You know, my dream for Kris was a good adoptive home. I just thought I would be able to say good-bye."

"How could anyone explain this to Kris. Her world is silent."

"I don't know."

"The new adoptive mother won't have anything to do with me. She wants Kris's past forgotten."

"Once in a park we accidently saw Kris."

"How did she react?"

Foster parent barter group: Foster parents are skilled in many areas—flower arranging, woodworking, plumbing, painting, cooking, tailoring, wallpapering, auto repair, tutoring, dog grooming, arts and crafts, knitting—you name it. A directory can be developed by state associations to promote foster parents supporting other foster parents. Credits can be earned by foster parent "A" who repairs a car for foster parent "B" — Foster parent "A" earns -x- credit points which he can trade in for bathroom plumbing repairs from foster parent "C". This program takes coordination, but it offers connections for foster parents to meet others who work with foster children and stretch limited dollars.

Library: Local libraries provide free programs for children, such as story times, videos, and puppets. Reference material on child development can be checked out with your library card at at no charge. State statutes and rules can be photocopied at nominal fees. The accessible data can save thousands of dollars in attorney research fees.

Video and tape library: Foster parent associations can establish libraries for training. Family and training videotapes or conference and training audio tapes can be made available through a catalog in the association monthly newsletter.

Clothing, toys, and equipment exchange: Major equipment such as a bike for a child who will be in the home for a very short time is an expensive investment for foster parents. The local agency, support group, or association can develop a card file of families with equipment they are willing to trade or swap. Newsletters can list needs and offers to encourage exchanges and connections to other families. The local community support group can also be used as a place to store and trade toys, books, baby things, or sports equipment.

Supportive and Fun Activities:

Circus or show tickets: Sometimes civic groups provide passes or free tickets to shows for deserving children. A block of tickets allows large families to attend these events together instead of allowing only select individuals to attend.

Foster family camp out: An outing for foster families and social service workers can add a relaxed atmosphere to the "team" relationship. County camp sites, 4-H or YMCA camps may be available to foster family groups at a reduced cost. A foster family with a farm or large home may also offer their land area for overnight tenting.

Foster fathers Saturday or night out: It can be especially difficult for working foster fathers to get together and share time with other dads and foster kids. A special interest activity or project along with potluck or picnic can enable communication between foster fathers and begin developing male-to-male support; i.e., fishing contest, softball game, etc.

Foster parents share: The talents and special skills of foster parents can be exciting and interesting for other families to learn and participate in. Interested families could put small classifieds into the association newsletter. Special interests can include:
— Astronomers viewing stars through telescopes
— Hobbyists who build model airplanes, rockets, kites, cars, or boats
— Airplane pilots who offer rides
— Spinners, weavers, and knitters who are willing to demonstrate
— Fishermen with a pontoon boat or a free Saturday
— Farmers with available time to demonstrate caring for animals
— Business owners can offer tours of their companies

Foster family trip: Group discounts may be available for airfare, hotels, and amusement parks. Groups of foster families can get together and obtain discounts for vacations.

Newsletter: A newsletter can publicize forthcoming training, clarify new policies, advise foster parents of new resources, and provide recognition of foster family accomplishments. It can provide a hot line number, comments on books and articles of special interest to foster parents, publicize activities and support systems, list projects and activities families can do together, promote foster parent idea exchanges, and offer classifieds for sharing equipment and resources.

Speakers bureau: Some foster parents may be interesting and exciting speakers who offer insight and ideas to other foster parents, professionals, or social services concerning raising foster and adoptive children.

The agency can also provide some extended services with their limited time and funding.

Professional Support Services include:

Clinics: A regular block of time set aside by foster care social work staff to meet with foster parents. Foster parents, for example, may know that between 9 and 11 a.m. on Wednesdays, they can drop in at the agency and a staff member will be available to discuss their concerns. Although their worker may not always be available at that time, someone from the staff can respond to their immediate concerns and relay their concerns to the worker.

Consultants: A knowledgeable person from the agency or from another agency who agrees to set aside an hour or two a week to consult with foster parents on difficulties they are experiencing with a foster child. Sources of consultation include Public Health, Mental Health, Universities, and Special Education agencies. Often they will provide the service free or at reduced rates. Consultation can be linked to training hours. When a foster parent is unsure whether or not to seek professional help for the child, consultation can help.

Specialists: If several foster parents are experiencing the same problems, it may be useful to identify one staff member as a specialist for that problem and set aside time for the problem to be resolved. Some common problems which are stressful to foster parents include locating practitioners who will accept medicaid, dealing with the school system, working with birth parents, etc.

Worker's office hours: Foster parents need to know when the worker is available and who to contact if the worker cannot be reached. Workers can schedule certain hours each week to receive calls from foster parents or return calls left on voice mail or by messages.

How can the care provider find someone to talk to?

Talking something through with another caring and experienced adult may be all that is needed for a foster parent to work creatively through a seemingly impossible situation. Foster care provider associations or social workers can help foster parents deal with the stresses of foster care. Associations or agencies may know of training programs or an experienced mentor available for the family.

"Do you think the teacher did the right thing by calling and reporting suspected abuse?"

"Of course she did the right thing! If someone did abuse Kris or any child it must be discovered and stopped. The problem wasn't the allegation, it was the way the situation was handled once the allegation was made."

"How was that?"

"Well, Kris was removed from the only home she could remember and the only family she knew. You know how hard it was for her at your house and to sleep away from home."

"Yes, I remember. I hope the new family was prepared for Kris." Kris and April always slept together when Kris spent respite. Bed time was always a struggle. Kris would miss her family, sign, and mouth, 'Mama,' and thrash and kick before going to bed. Sensitive to her loneliness, I would often sleep on the floor beside the bed and hold her hand. Still, she would wake in the night questioning her whereabouts, and need comfort and reassurance.

What about culturally sensitive issues?

In most states, social service agencies are required to preserve children's religious, cultural, and ethnic heritage by placing them with families of similar background. With foster homes in short supply, this is not always possible and cultural difficulties may arise. Care provider families need to understand differences in culture, and values. Educational training programs and sensitivity training prior to placement of a child are very helpful. The child in out-of-home care needs support and acceptance—not only their individual identity, but also of their cultural, religious, and ethnic identity. If a cultural difference is confusing, the care provider needs access to knowledgeable support people —social services, minority councils or organizations, religious institutions, etc.— who understand and respect diversity.

Providers who have difficulty accepting a child's religion, race, color, or national origin potentially will be phased out of providing care. New applicants showing signs of bigotry, racism, or biases face denial of licensure.

What can foster care providers do to prevent allegations of maltreatment or neglect in foster care provider homes?

Foster care providers are vulnerable to charges from both the children they care for and the birth parents who have been denied custody.

Here are some steps foster care providers can take to protect themselves from allegations and the resulting bureaucratic nightmare. The first step to preventing allegations is to prevent maltreatment from happening.

Steps a provider family can take to prevent maltreatment:

— **Understand and follow all licensing regulations.** When a provider is accused of neglect or abuse and has not been in compliance with regulations, the likelihood of a negative licensing action is increased.

— **Maintain a positive relationship with the licensing worker.** Make sure any predetermined variance from regulation is approved IN WRITING beforehand.

— **Pay careful attention to supervision and safety issues**, especially for younger children. Make sure family members understand safety issues, not leaving curling irons unplugged, seat belts fastened, medicine cabinets locked, and routinely do checks to assure the well-being of ALL members of the household.
  — Closely supervise children at all times.
    It is unwise to allow children to play unattended at any time.
  — Do not have too many places where children can hide.
  — Leave nap room doors open and periodically check on children during these times.

— **Develop family policies and follow them** concerning: discipline, children's developing sexuality, toileting, napping routines, and how substitutes will be hired. File a copy of these with licensing agency. *(See Chapter 14)*

— **Conduct daily safety checks** and make sure all hazardous materials are put away. Safety guidelines cannot be compromised.

— **Never use, or threaten to use, corporal punishment** as a means of discipline. This form of discipline cannot be delegated to non-parent guardians, and is prohibited by licensing regulations. Do not use discipline prohibited by licensing. (See chapter 13) A foster parent is a model of appropriate behavior and a teacher of problem-solving and communication skills to the children

---

"I understand the adoptive parents wish to wipe the slate clean, remove the child from the temporary insecurity of foster care, and provide a loving and safe permanent home. I know this professional family can provide for Kris in many ways I, as a single parent, could never hope to provide. I'm really happy for Kris, but I think they left a big part of Kris behind when they kept us completely out of the picture."

My mind wandered. As an adoptive parent and a previous care provider for fragile children, I questioned the sense in not allowing contact with the only family Kris had known. A special part of April's life has been knowing that her tummy mommy had contributed important pieces to her life. It has been important for April to know her birth mother held her and kissed her and cared for her even though she couldn't be her forever mommy.

"Will you take foster children again, Amy?"

Chapter 3-Knowing Yourself

they care for. If methods of discipline vary between birth children and foster children, discuss the variances with the social worker.

— **Carefully screen all helpers/substitutes** including relatives and friends; make sure they understand licensing regulations, house rules, and any specific restrictions about individual children because of court orders, etc.

Other steps designed to prevent false allegations against provider families by parents or older children who may be angry or unhappy:

— **Always report suspected child abuse** to local child protection authorities or the social worker assigned to the case, especially after parental visits. *(See Chapter 4)*

— **Document any changes in behavior in children** including severity and length of these changes, especially after visitation or any changes at school. Include any action taken to deal with inappropriate behavior. *(See Chapter 14)*

— **Keep logs/notebooks on each child** to document visitation, school progress/problems, medical needs, behavioral patterns, or changes and efforts to teach acceptable behavior.

— **Always document any serious conflicts** with parents, children, social workers, licensors, teachers, etc., and keep these records in a file. Request copies of these to be kept with the licensing agency.

— **Keep parents informed of positive progress their child** is making and any interesting things they might like to know about their child's activities. View yourself as a part of a co-parenting team that is attempting to reunify a family, not as a competitor for their children's loyalty.

— **Identify conflicts that arise** with parents, children, teachers, social workers, etc., because of value differences. Be respectful of individual rights to their own point of view. Negotiate and work toward a compromise.

— **Seek outside resources and assistance immediately** if behaviors or issues arise beyond abilities or desires to deal with. Avoid blaming others if possible, and actively seek a solution to resolve the problem to the benefit of all concerned.

Summary:

No one can be a perfect parent every day and under every circumstance. There is no way to completely avoid allegations. Understanding your own personal needs and the needs of family members is crucial in being able to develop a supportive and strong foster family.

— **Be the best parent you can be.**

— **Avoid being stretched.** Know and respect limits. Don't overload your home. Establish appropriate boundaries. If the child is not a good family fit, ask for help before any negative situation can develop.

— **Take breaks from the children and the situation.** Make sure to get away alone with your support team or significant other.

— **Say no to an inappropriate placement.** Children need as much continuity of care as possible, and saying yes to a potentially unhealthy placement could damage your family and harm the child.

— **Be a team member.** Work for the best interest of the child in your care. Build a support system. Foster parenting cannot be done in isolation.

— **Get involved with the child's professional support team** — therapist, counselor, teachers, and medical professionals.

"I don't know. It's really hard to be accused of something you never did."

"Amy, you and Abby did a great job. I know it wasn't just the schooling and therapy Kris was given that moved her from a non-responsive baby to an alert and responsive preschooler. That's a 24-hour-a-day treatment program you, the foster parent, provided. I lived with Kris long enough to understand all the goodness you put into her. You know, Amy, you could do that again for another child."

"Maybe I will. Thanks for understanding. This isn't something I really ever talk about. Good luck on your book."

"You're good with kids, Amy. Good luck."

I hung up the phone. Another allegation. Another story.

Did I dare call any others to say hello?

— **Get all the education and training you can.** Share the information with the support team.

— **Don't use kids to meet your own needs for affection.** Foster kids usually can't give affection for a long time or possibly forever.

— **Become an active member in your local, state, or national care provider association.** Read the information they send you.

— **Understand normal child development.** Avoid questionable situations with children.

— **DOCUMENT!** Don't trust your memory. Keep a journal of situations, reactions, behaviors.

— **Know and follow all state and agency regulations** as they apply to foster care providers. A foster care provider needs to have and understand current regulation.

— **Call your local, state, or national care provider association if you have a question you do not dare ask your worker.** Even if you are not a member of the organization it is more important to get help than to worry about non-membership. Once you have made contact with the association, you can decide to join and become active. The association is available to help you!

Because of the complex, isolated, and personal nature of foster care, it is important that providers develop strong communication and documentation skills to protect themselves, their families, and the children for whom they are caring.

References

Fein, Edith, Maluccio, Anthony, Hamilton, V. Jane, Ward, Darryl. 1983. *Child Welfare After Foster Care: Outcomes of Permanency Planning for Children*. Washington D.C.: Child Welfare League.

Jasinek, Doris & Bell Ryan, Pamela. 1988. *How to Build a House of Hearts*. Minneapolis: Comp Care.

Keating, Kathleen. 1983. *The Hug Therapy Book*. Minneapolis: Comp Care.

Maslach, Christina. 1982. *Burnout the Cost of Caring*. New Jersey: Spectrum Books

McFadden, Emily Jean. 1984. *Preventing Abuse in Foster Care*. Michigan: Eastern Michigan University.

Paztor, Eileen Mayers & Burgess, Elyce. 1982. *"Finding and Keeping More Foster Families*. Children Today, March/April, p.3.

Vineyard, Sue. 1988. *How to Take Care of You...So You Can Take Care of Others. A Survival Guide For Human Service Workers and Volunteers.* Illinois: Heritage Arts Publishing

Youngs, Bettie. 1985. *Stress in Children, Common Sense Advice on How to Spot and Deal with Stress in Children of All Ages*. New York: Avon Books

SECTION II

Families at Risk

Give us the child . . .

. . .the hungry child, who needs more than food and shelter, but yearns for love and attention.

. . .the fearful child who is afraid of the commitment to family life.

. . .the withdrawn child, who spends hours sucking her thumb, rocking or lying down.

. . .the haunted child, who relives the memories of her past in the middle of the night.

. . .the invisible child, who tries to be as inconspicuous as possible.

. . .the worthless child, who cannot even accept a small gift, thanks, or appreciation.

. . .the grieving child, who mourns the loss of her last family.

The child we care for cannot be compared to the attached and healthy children raised from their conception in a secure home. Yet, try to explain to those who see only by reading and hear only the reported news.
(Author)

Readers respond to mom afraid of abuse charges

Dear Abby

Dear Abby: This is in regard to ''Colorado Mother,'' who kept her child home from school because of a black eye and bruised cheek sustained from a fall against a coffee table, which could have looked suspicious to a day-care operator. I would have kept my child home, too, because this is what happened to me:

My 4-year-old son was fooling around at the Laundromat, climbing up and down when he'd been told not to. He fell and got a nasty bruise on his cheek, but since he felt no discomfort, we let him go to preschool and thought nothing of it.

Later, I responded to a knock on my door from a county child abuse investigator! I was appalled. The investigators questioned me, my son and my daughter (who witnessed her brother's fall) and concluded that we were telling the truth, but I learned that once the report was made, I had a record and was on their ''suspicion'' list for a year.

It got to the point where I examined my son's body daily in the bath for any bruises sustained in play. Apparently, one day I missed one, because the investigator called me! However, he did say that the teacher who had made the report was ''overly ambitious,'' constantly reporting on other parents as well. Still, I began to live in fear, worried that the system had gone crazy and might take my child from me. Perhaps I overreacted, but I was terrified.

Abby, anybody can report a neighbor for ''child abuse,'' and it doesn't matter if you're guilty or innocent, the investigation is made, and the record remains!
— **California mother**

Abby says: The same day I received your letter, I also heard from the president of the National Coalition for Child Protective Reform. Read on:

Dear Abby: ''Colorado Mother'' kept her child home from day care because the child had hit her face against the coffee table and got a terrible bruise on her cheek, plus a black eye. The mother feared being accused of child abuse. Abby, you told her she should have sent the child to school, since she had nothing to hide.

As a former assistant commissioner of public welfare in Massachusetts, and a member of the National Board of Directors of the American Civil Liberties Union, I can tell you ''Colorado Mother'' acted wisely, and you are mistaken.

Schoolteachers are instructed to report a child's ''black eye'' or bruise on the chance that the child has been physically abused at home. Yes, children have been pulled out of class and interrogated, and even strip-searched (for more bruises) — a terrifying experience for any child. Children have been placed in foster homes temporarily while social workers try to get to the bottom of suspected child abuse. False allegations traumatize thousands of children every year.

The National Coalition for Child Protective Reform was organized after a conference at Harvard Law School in an attempt to change this system. We believe that the laws allowing nearly unlimited coercive intervention into families need to be narrowed, and child-protective hot lines must be required to carefully screen allegations before launching investigations..
— **Elizabeth Vorenberg, president, National Coalition for Child Protective Reform, Cambridge, Mass.**

Abby says: It is good to know that the witch-hunt of false accusations has not gone unnoticed. Our children should be protected, but parents must also be protected against false accusations.

Abigail Van Buren is a columnist for Universal Press Syndicate. Letters should be addressed to Dear Abby, P.O. 69440, Los Angeles, CA 90069. For a personal reply, enclose a self-addressed, stamped envelope.

Chapter 4

The Hurricane of Allegations

*Regardless of the amount of
care or preparation a parent has taken,
a false allegation of child abuse or neglect
uproots the family and causes
critical damage to the family structure.*

In his book, *"Assessing Child Maltreatment Reports: The Problem of False Allegations,"* Michael Robin, ACSW MPH (1991) writes:

> *The high level of attention and anxiety about child abuse has led, in recent years, to increased reporting to child protection services. The mandatory reporting campaigns, the broadened definitions of child abuse and neglect, and the decline of voluntary, community-based family services have greatly enlarged the pool of children referred to local child welfare authorities as potentially in need of protective services. The reporting net that has been established has included large numbers of maltreated children.*
>
> *But inevitably, it includes a certain portion of cases where no abuse occurred. Some of these cases involve questionable parenting practices rather than actual or potential maltreatment (Daro 1988); the reporting of conditions such as inadequate food, clothing, housing, supervision, etc., that have more to do with conditions of poverty than adequate parenting (Pelton 1989); the reporting of child behavior problems that do not involve parental abuse (Besharov 1991); and the reporting of altogether innocent persons. Many of these persons experience the report as "false" regardless of the motivation of the reporter or disposition of the case.*
>
> *While many believe false allegations are becoming more common, no one knows for sure how extensive the problem is truly. It is unfortunate that there has been so many exaggerated claims and counter-claims about the problem. Many child protection professionals argue that "false allegations" are rare, while advocates for those who claim to be "falsely accused" say the problem is widespread and has reached epidemic proportions. The truth is likely to be somewhere in between.* (Robin 1991)

It is impossible to truly determine whether or not incidents of child maltreatment are increasing or decreasing. Annual reports nationwide of suspected maltreatment have continued to climb to between 2.5 and 2.7 million. Of these reports, however, 60% are now eventually determined to be unsubstantiated or unfounded, compared with only 35% in 1976. Many factors contribute to these statistics, which can be very misleading because every state defines neglect and abuse differently. Simple lack of evidence does not necessarily mean absence of

---

We're in real trouble from Friday night until Sunday morning in getting these kids into safe places after social services has gone home for the weekend.
Police officer

If someone you know has been reported for suspected child abuse or neglect, do not immediately assume the worst. You can help the child, the family, and yourself by thinking logically and not getting emotional.
Author

When you're a foster kid you feel like you're walking on eggs in the new foster home and jello in the system. Neither gives you much security.
Previous child in care

Regardless of the ruckus I know it will create, child abuse is child abuse. It is my job to report it.
Mandated reporter

abuse or neglect—it may mean that sufficient evidence was not identified or that the incident which caused the pain, injury, or trauma did not meet evidence standards. For example, the child may have been too young to give a credible account or the perpetrator may have been able to cover up the evidence or could not be identified. In other cases the investigator may have lacked experience, skill, and adequate resources. (Faller 1985, Besharov 1985)

No individual is immune from allegations of maltreatment. Certain situations and careers are especially vulnerable to maltreatment reports. Individuals involved in any of the following life situations need to use particular caution.

— A profession that requires daily interaction with children, such as foster care providers, day care workers, teachers, nurses, doctors.

— A divorce, separation, or custody dispute.

— Ongoing disputes with relatives or neighbors.

— A stormy marriage or unsettled live-in arrangement with natural, foster, or adoptive children living in the home

— Frequent eruption of discipline problems between parent and child.

Experiencing any of these situations does not mean a report for child maltreatment will occur. However, these situations have shown increased risk and individuals would be wise to prepare themselves. (Spiegel 1986)

When false allegations are made, the lives of at least two individuals—the child and the alleged perpetrator—are affected. Moreover, law enforcement and social services are required to take every complaint of child maltreatment seriously—to screen it and decide whether or not to investigate. The process from allegation to completed investigation may take months. Meanwhile, the accused individual's and family's life is in limbo and children may wait in out-of-home care. All who are concerned about protecting children—medical professionals, educators, clergy, foster parents, foster care provider associations, day care provider associations, national centers for abuse and neglect, child welfare agency staff — are still in the process of discovering how an allegation can best be handled.

Abuse and neglect guidelines vary. This chapter defines and discusses allegations and complaints. Case studies are included that describe the differences in experiences between custodial/birth family and licensed foster family. You will learn about the journey a child experiences in the custody of child protection.

What is an allegation of child abuse or neglect?

An allegation is an accusation of suspected child maltreatment against an individual, family, or facility. An allegation does not mean that child abuse or neglect has occurred. It means that someone **believes** child abuse or neglect may have occurred. The details are not always clear. Allegations are screened to determine if a family assessment or investigation is warranted.

Children may create confusion by:

— Being too young to describe or accurately recall a situation.

— Using vocabulary out of context, such as, *"Daddy did——,"* without clarification of which *"Daddy"* or what exactly *"Daddy"* did.

— Misunderstanding normal and healthy hygiene procedures, or describing them in vocabulary that is misinterpreted by adults.

— Exhibiting separation, grief, or stress-related behaviors which are misdiagnosed as reactions to maltreatment.

If we are to protect children and get help for parents who are hurting children, WE MUST REPORT!

If we are to limit our own liability and that of the organizations we represent, we must educate ourselves about the dynamics of child abuse and neglect.
(Mead 1989)

Professionals who care for children need to watch for the "RED FLAGS" that signal something is amiss. (See Appendix 2.) *These flags alert professionals to examine the situation more carefully. The existence of a red flag does not indicate there is abuse or neglect. It may simply signal that the family is experiencing stress, or that the child is experiencing difficulty, but no danger.*
(McFadden)

When I need to report maltreatment of a child, I go with the parent to child protection and support them through the reporting process.
Psychologist

— Saying something merely to see what the reaction and consequences will be.

— Making irritating, yet seemingly harmless, statements at the wrong time and in the wrong place that can be blown out of proportion as more people get involved.

— Having an undiagnosed physical ailment which presents symptoms or causes conditions appearing to be the result of physical abuse: leukemia, hemophilia or other bleeding disorders, failure to thrive, cerebral palsy, epilepsy, osteogenesis imperfecta, liver diseases causing a vitamin K deficiency, vasculitis, Ehlers-Danlos syndrome, hearing loss or equilibrium complications, vision impairment, or other disabilities.

— Having an undiagnosed physical ailment which presents symptoms or causes conditions which appear to be the result of sexual abuse; bladder infection; yeast infection; colitis; chronic skin conditions such as eczema, seborrhea, lichen sclerosis (Altcheck 1984); vaginal discharge due to respiratory or gastrointestinal infection caused by wiping from the anus to the vaginal area (Adams 1991); blood on panties or diapers due to allergy, injury, early menstural bleeding, or physical ailment.

— Exhibiting unusual behavior due to separation, loss, attachment problems, or previous maltreatment.

— Flashbacks of previous maltreatment trigger misplaced allegations against new safe care providers.

Regardless of whether the allegations are true or false, accusations of child abuse or neglect cause one of the most stressful situations an individual or family can encounter.

Who reports child abuse and neglect?

Anyone can report child maltreatment. In most states any person who reports in "good faith" is immune from civil or criminal liability. The reporter's name is almost always kept confidential. Almost all professionals working with children are mandated (required) by law to report *suspected* abuse or neglect. Reporting requirements vary from state to state. Some states require reports of suspected maltreatment up to three years after the alleged incident. According to Minnesota Rule, the local agency shall accept and screen every report of child maltreatment received from *any* source. Proper screening is crucial and many calls are screened out and not investigated.

The legal aspects of confidentiality are problematic. Almost all helping professionals are required to disclose client information in some circumstances established by statutes, judicial decisions, and public service health needs. Contrary to popular belief, physicians' rights to confidentiality are the same as other professionals' rights. *Only attorneys, and in some cases clergy, have complete or partial immunity from disclosing client information.*

> *The current approach in training sessions is to tell potential reporters to "take no chances" and to report any child for whom they have the slightest concern. This ensures that child abuse hotlines will be innundated with inappropriate and un-founded reports. An important first step must be taken in es-tablishing practical guidelines about what should and should not be reported. Laws and educational materials should be modified to require reporting only when there is credible evidence that the child has been abused or neglected or is in substantial danger of being abused or neglected. (Besharov 1986)*

Clergy	Educators*	Guardian	Pharmacists
Day care staff	Foster parents	ad litem	Social workers
Dentists	Hospital staff	Law	Therapists
Doctors	Group home staff	enforcement	

*A school district in Minnesota classifies the following employees as mandated to report suspected abuse or neglect of a child:

Administrators	Supervisors	Dean	Interpreters
Service staff	Coaches	Food service	Paraprofessionals
Teachers	Counselors	Nurses	Psychologists
Water safety	Secretaries	Clericals	Print shop
Janitors	Community school staff		

In addition to mandated reporters, the following are likely to report abuse or neglect of children:

Concerned individuals. Sometimes neighbors or support groups sense by a child's behavior that something is wrong with a family. When maltreatment is discovered, children's very lives may be saved. Families found maltreating children are forced to change their parenting styles or forfeit their children. When allegations are disproved, families face unnecessary procedures and trauma. Concerned individuals must use caution in judging another family. Social, economic, and cultural differences can easily be misinterpreted. For example, a financially stable person may misinterpret poverty as neglect or abuse, when in reality the family is providing love and care for the children at a level beyond their means.

"Allegators" are those individuals who make allegations maliciously. Even one allegator can cause untold amounts of emotional and financial damage to the accused family. Investigating these types of allegations is difficult because the person making the allegation is deceitful. Time is taken away from legitimate cases. Taxpayers' money is wasted. Reporters in almost all cases face no liability for unsubstantiated or unfounded allegations. In most states the person accused does not have the right to hold the person making false allegations liable for undue suffering or trauma. Examples of allegators include: the angry child who believes an allegation against foster parents is the best way to get home; the natural parent wanting to prove the foster home inadequate; the social service agency misrepresenting a situation with the *"good"* intentions of accessing funding or services for a child; the angry social worker who wants a family out of the system; the vindictive person wishing to cause suffering against a family member.

When should a report be made?

In Minnesota, mandated reporters have the legal obligation to make a report if there is reason to believe a child has been maltreated during the past three years. A mandated reporter is personally responsible and cannot shift the responsibility to a supervisor or another person. (DHS-2917 1990.)

If you are uncertain if a situation should be reported, the child protection staff will help decide.

Karen was is shock.

Why had the police taken her away? Who did something bad? Who were these strangers? When could she go home?

All the smiles and the nice teddy bear the lady gave her did not help her feel better.

Sandy, Karen's mother, was met at preschool by an intake worker who gently explained they had placed Karen under protective custody until they could assess the care Sandy was providing.

If the child is in immediate danger or abandoned, call the local police or sheriff's department. Law enforcement officers have the authority to place a child on a temporary protection hold while the situation is assessed.

If the child is not in immediate danger, and the alleged perpetrator is a parent, guardian, foster care provider, day care provider, or staff member of a licensed facility, contact the local social service agency's child protection unit or the local law enforcement agency.

If the child is not in immediate danger, and the alleged perpetrator is someone outside the family unit and not a licensed staff person, contact the local law enforcement agency. In non-familial, non-facility situations, law enforcement has the responsibility for investigating the report and social services has the responsibility to offer appropriate social services for the purpose of safeguarding and enhancing the welfare of the maltreated child. *Examples of non-familial perpetrators are: teachers, clergy, coaches, school administrators, babysitters, neighbors, etc.*

What happens if a mandated reporter does not report?

If you are a mandated reporter and you fail to report suspected child maltreatment, you may be guilty of a misdemeanor and legally liable. (Mead 1987)

The three potential areas of liability for failing to report suspected abuse are:

Criminal liability: Most states have criminal penalties for failing to report child abuse. These penalties, although misdemeanors, can include up to six months in jail and/or a $1000 fine. An employee or supervisor who instructs any person not to report suspected abuse may be charged with *"obstruction of justice"* — a felony in most states. Communication about the report and the investigation must remain limited to persons and agencies who need to know. Release of information to unauthorized persons, rumors, or gossip can lead to *"defamation of character"* lawsuits. If a county worker or police officer conducting an investigation intentionally discloses the identity of a reporter prior to the completion of an investigation, he/she may be guilty of a misdemeanor.

Civil liability: Civil lawsuits on behalf of re-injured children are not uncommon. Consider this situation based on a California case decision, Landeros vs. Flood (1976). An infant was hospitalized with injuries, treated and released back to the mother. The attending physician failed to file a "suspected child abuse report." Subsequently, the child was treated for new and more serious injuries. The second physician reported the injuries as suspected child abuse. The child was later made a ward of the court and a guardian ad litem was appointed. The guardian then filed suit on behalf of the child against the first doctor for failure to report as required by law. Regardless of the outcome of that specific case, the California State Supreme Court held that any mandated person who fails to perform the statutory imposed duty of reporting raises a presumption that the individual failed to exercise due care and may be held civilly as well as criminally liable. Civil litigation results from failure to protect, false accusations, breaches of confidentiality, and case mismanagement.

Professional liability: Professional review boards have a professional responsibility to take abuse reporting requirements seriously. Possible license suspension or revocation are both considerations for a professional who does not comply with reporting laws. Professional liability is not limited to "not reporting"child abuse. All persons working with children may incur liability for not making a decision or not making the right decision.

"Assess my care! Where is Karen? Why do you have her? What do you think I've done?" Sandy was afraid and hurt.

The social worker continued, "Karen says you rub her vagina and we have no reason to believe she is not telling the truth!"

"Rub her vagina! How could she say such a thing? I don't do that. She's lying. You can't believe a four-year-old against her mother, can you?" Sandy was getting agitated.

"Karen is in emergency shelter. She is safe. We will do an assessment on Tuesday when we get back to the office. Meanwhile you will have to wait."

This is incredible, Sandy thought. Wait until my husband Mark gets home. He'll know what to do.

Who is responsible for complaint review?

Depending on the nature of the complaint and the type of family, individual, or facility involved, different agencies or combinations of agencies will be responsible for screening, reviewing, assessing, or investigating the allegation.

Child Protection Assessment is initiated if a complaint is made on behalf of a child and the alleged perpetrator is within the family unit. The family unit consists of individuals related by blood, marriage or adoption. It would also include a child's guardian and perhaps other individuals living within the same household.

Child Protection and Law Enforcement Investigation is initiated if the complaint is lodged against licensed providers, families, or facilities. Licenses from the following types of departments usually are included: Departments of Public Welfare, Social Services, Human Services, Health, Family Services, or Corrections. In some states a designated and qualified investigative team handles these specialized investigations.

Law Enforcement Investigation is initiated when a complaint is made against an individual who is not within the family or a member of a licensed facility—teachers, clergy, babysitters, friends, and neighbors.

What happens after an incident is reported?

Reports of suspected child maltreatment can come from any source.

If the report is received by a law enforcement agency, a uniformed officer usually will respond within a short period of time. Some police and sheriff's departments send a detective out on this type of call, but very few departments have trained investigators.

If the report is directed to a child protective services agency, it is usually a division of the Department of Public Welfare. Most child protection agencies are busy. When a report is received, the local agency will screen the report to see if it meets the criteria for investigation. In other words, not all calls are investigated. Priority is given to serious injury and molestation cases. Reports of less threatening situations are screened later.

What is included in a report for suspected maltreatment?

When a child protection agency receives a call about suspected child maltreatment, it will request information to help identify the child and family, evaluate the problem, and respond quickly and appropriately.

The reporter will be asked: His or her name, address, and phone number. What happened to the child and when. Where the child is now. The names and addresses of the parents or caretakers. Any firsthand knowledge the reporter has about the child or family.

The reporter should document: Time and date the agency or department was called. Telephone number dialed and name of person taking call. Name of contact person for future calls. Notes on conversation. Address and name of person to send written report to.

A mandated reporter must follow a verbal report with a written report within 72 hours (exclusive of weekends and holidays) in Minnesota. The time limit varies from state to state. The written report should be sent by certified return receipt mail.

The written report to the agency must include: Date and time the child was observed by the mandated reporter. Name(s) of person(s) who accompanied the child. Informant (parent, child, both). Date, time, and place of the injury incident (if known). How the injury occurred. Who allegedly abused/injured the child. Any history of past abuse or injury.

Child abuse laws are different in every state. ***To obtain pertinent reporting law, write or call your state's department of social services or a local licensed social services agency. For Kids Sake, Inc., 753 W. Lambert Rd., Brea, CA 92621, (714) 529-8358 will provide this information to you.***

Who is involved in the follow-through and investigation of a report?

There are significant responses to an allegation by government departments, agencies, and key people.

Department of Public Welfare, Health, Human, or Social Services: This is the department in the state which regulates social welfare programs. Different states have different names and provide varying services within these departments. (Minnesota has a state-supervised/ county-administered system headed by the Department of Human Services.)

Law enforcement: Law enforcement departments are legally required to investigate allegations of abuse or neglect which could be classified or judged as criminal.

County commissioners: Commissioners are elected representatives and may be able to provide names of qualified individuals who will be of assistance in working through the issue of allegation.

County attorney: Provides advice and legal counsel to public agencies, i.e., social services.

Social services: Agency responsible for protecting children. Agencies can be held liable for abuse and neglect to children legally in their custody. Therefore, caution is used when working with foster and pre-adoptive parents. Social workers watch for "red flags" which warn that something may be amiss. These red flags alert them to the necessity for further screening, assessment, or investigation of a family. *(See Appendix for red flag list.)*

Child protection: Child protection has a specialized role in working with children and families. The primary focus is protection of children. *(See Chapter 7 for more role details.)*

Protective services investigator: The protective services investigator determines whether or not maltreatment has occurred. An investigator attempts to remain as objective as possible while gathering all available information. The rights of the alleged victim must be balanced with the rights of the family.

It is important for the investigator to
follow complete investigative procedures
while not permittingthe investigation itself to be abusive.
No investigation should become unreasonably
threatening or intrusive.
The investigator has the right to interview—not conduct an inquisition.

Nothing happened over the weekend. On Tuesday they called work saying they had a family emergency. They didn't know when they would be back, couldn't explain what it was, but said they would keep in touch.

Meanwhile, Karen faced—without her family—a medical examination by a doctor she had never met, psychological testing, and talking, talking, talking. She wanted her mommy and daddy. She wanted her own bed and toys.

Sandy was interviewed to decide if what Karen had said was the truth. If Sandy was a perpetrator, should she leave the home and could Mark parent Karen alone? Did Mark also have problems? Mark was interviewed to find out how much he knew and if the family needed help.

Karen's new foster mother liked and felt sorry for Karen. It was noticeable that Karen missed her mommy and daddy. She tried to comfort Karen and paid special attention to Karen's needs.

"Help me in the bathroom please," Karen asked.

Child's caseworker: The child's agency caseworker is responsible for the case plan for placement of the child and supervision of the child's care.

Reports of suspected maltreatment against licensed care providers also include investigation by the licensing agency to determine if a licensing violation has occurred. Even if maltreatment is unfounded, the license holder may have violated a licensing rule.

Licensing worker: This worker often has had the most direct contact with the foster family, and is also the person who decides to license and relicense the home. When an allegation is made, the licensing worker's position is to protect the child and cooperate with other service providers in the screening, assessment, and determination if licensing rules have been violated, and if the license holder is eligible to continue to care for other people's children.

Once the decision is made to investigate or assess, what new questions arise?

In order for an assessment/investigation to continue, important decisions must be made. How quickly must it begin? Who must be interviewed? Where will the interview be conducted? What risk factors need to be examined? Who needs to be notified—law enforcement, other professionals? Does the county attorney's staff need to be involved? What is the timing of case disposition?

Why are licensed care providers treated differently than primary families?

Foster and pre-adoptive care providers are in a significantly different position than custodial parents. Care providers are service providers; their qualifications differ significantly from those of legal guardians. When an agency approves a family as safe and competent to care for other people's children, it becomes liable for the quality of care the children receive. The agency must now investigate their own team for what appears to be a failure to provide appropriate care.

Allegations against care providers are different than allegations against custodial families; the licensed care provider faces revocation of license and immediate removal of a child.

What are the complaint review, risk assessment, and screening processes?

Each report of maltreatment is screened (reviewed) to determine if an assessment is necessary. If the report does not meet the criteria, the local agency does not conduct an assessment.

A screening must determine three things before an assessment is made:

1.   The allegation must constitute maltreatment—sexual or physical abuse, physical or emotional neglect, infant medical neglect.

2.   There must be sufficient identifying information to permit an assessment.

3.   The report must contain information not previously received by the agency.

What are the criteria of a risk assessment?

Knowledge about child abuse and neglect is a must for the protection of children. Clear definitions must be available to all citizens. Quality and consistent training programs must exist for law enforcement personnel, district attorneys, nurses, doctors, teachers, youth leaders, protective service workers, clergy, day care providers, and foster parents.

Families or individuals facing allegations of maltreatment of children are assessed as *high risk*, *moderate risk*, or *low risk* based on risk assessment factors:

Both "positives" and "negatives" are considered:

— *Vulnerability of child.* Child is unable to protect self or care for self without adult assistance. Child's age under 5, 5-9, or 10+. Child is handicapped, overactive, or has impaired development.

— *Location, severity, frequency, and recency of neglect or abuse.* Medical treatment required or visible injury; pattern or history of abuse or neglect in family; inappropriate sexual touching, exposure, or activities; unreasonable restraint; confinement; dangerous or unhealthy conditions; caretaker unable or unwilling to provide minimum medical, food, shelter, clothing needs; lack of supervision; abandonment.

— *Physical, intellectual, and emotional capacities and control of the person(s) responsible for child's care.* Caretaker is handicapped or impaired intellectually, psychologically, or physically. Caretaker has unrealistic expectations of child. Lack of impulse control. Past violent or criminal behavior. Incapacity due to intoxication by drugs or alcohol.

— *Degree of cooperation of the person(s) responsible for the child's care.* Doesn't believe there is a problem, refuses to cooperate or accept responsibility. Upset with assessment. Uninterested or evasive. Level of chemical dependency interferes with person's ability to follow through. Cooperates and actively works to resolve issue. Demonstrates genuine caring, concern, and awareness. Willing to learn alternative methods of handling issues. Is overly compliant to the point of covering up abuse.

— *Parenting skills and knowledge of person(s) responsible for child's care.* Parent(s) is unwilling or unable to provide. Parent has minimal knowledge of needs of a child. Level and amount of affection expressed—limited, negative, inconsistent, appropriate.

— *Alleged offender's access to child.* In home and has complete access versus out of home and minimal risk to child. Child is supervised and safe versus not supervised.

— *Presence of parent substitute or other adult in home.* Person is alleged perpetrator. Frequency of person in home. Chemical dependency problem. Person is viewed as supportive or stablizing influence.

— *Previous history of child maltreatment.* No previous maltreatment indicated. Pending investigation or assessment. Maltreatment previously determined. Protective services previously provided. Family worked cooperatively with protective services previously and worked through issues.

— *Strength of family support system.* Caretaker has no relatives, friends, or support system. Geographically isolated, no phone and means of transportation. Perceived support system is problematic and contributes to family difficulties. Limited access to support services.

Once a family has been investigated, deep emotional scars may remain for years.

Medical care for children may be delayed because parents fear additional allegation.

Parents may restrain from appropriately disciplining their children. Then as the misbehavior escalates, these parents may overreact and abuse.

Children may use the threat of allegation to exert control over the family.

"When a kid is in an emergency situation and I have a choice between foster care and the group home, I opt for the foster home because I've seen the positive impact and changes in the kids."
Police officer

JOURNEY OF A CUSTODIAL FAMILY REPORTED FOR SUSPECTED CHILD MALTREATMENT

Regardless of the quality of parenting— any family can be at risk for a report of "suspected" maltreatment. A report of "suspected" maltreatment has very different results for children, custodial families, and licensed families.

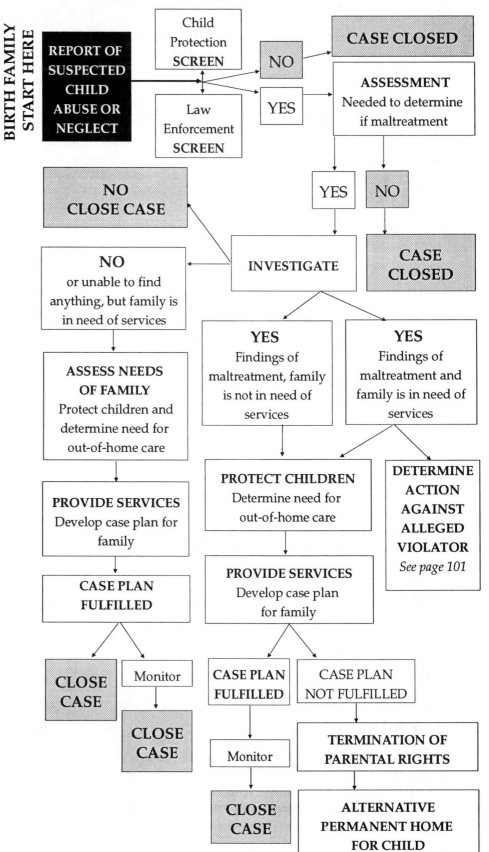

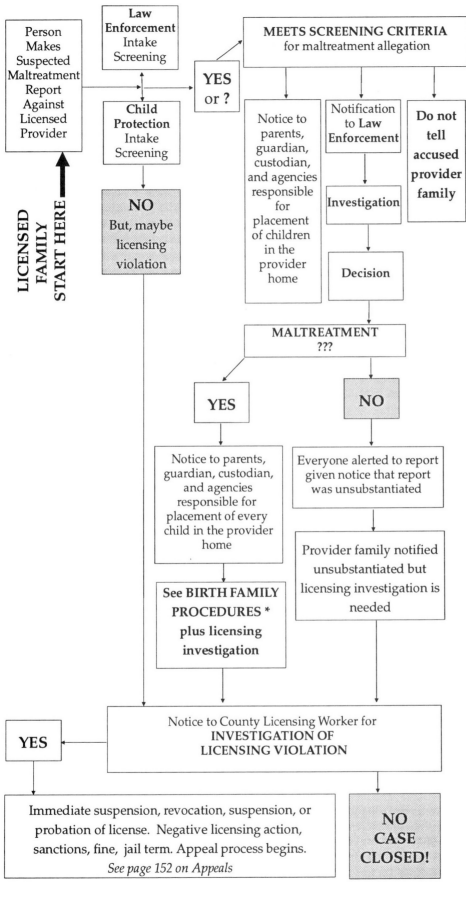

LICENSED FAMILY START HERE

Person Makes Suspected Maltreatment Report Against Licensed Provider

Law Enforcement Intake Screening

Child Protection Intake Screening

YES or ?

NO But, maybe licensing violation

MEETS SCREENING CRITERIA for maltreatment allegation

Notice to parents, guardian, custodian, and agencies responsible for placement of children in the provider home

Notification to **Law Enforcement**

Investigation

Decision

Do not tell accused provider family

MALTREATMENT ???

YES

NO

Notice to parents, guardian, custodian, and agencies responsible for placement of every child in the provider home

Everyone alerted to report given notice that report was unsubstantiated

See BIRTH FAMILY PROCEDURES * **plus licensing investigation**

Provider family notified unsubstantiated but licensing investigation is needed

YES

Notice to County Licensing Worker for **INVESTIGATION OF LICENSING VIOLATION**

Immediate suspension, revocation, suspension, or probation of license. Negative licensing action, sanctions, fine, jail term. Appeal process begins. *See page 152 on Appeals*

NO CASE CLOSED!

INVESTIGATION OF REPORT IN LICENSED FAMILY

The immediate response of the guilty perpetrator and the innocent individual may be the same. The innocent person, however, will shortly begin to focus on the needs of the family and the child. The guilty person will often continue to protect his own interests.

If the allegation is sexual, the accused may withdraw appropriate warm and loving affection from the children.

Proper genital hygiene may be left up to a child who is too young to take responsibility for personal care.

Families may be forced to move and can lose standing in their communities. Some families isolate themselves and hide their emotional wounds.

— *Stress on the family.* Recent death, divorce, pregnancy, or birth. Unemployment, eviction, chemical dependent family member. Inadequate home management skills. Natural disaster. Insufficient income and/or food.

Credibility of the reporter also must be considered in the risk assessment. Is the person reporting a professional, non-professional, relative, friend, or the child? Is the reporter anonymous? Is the reporter involved in any dispute with the family?

How does the screening process differ between birth families and licensed families?

Once a *custodial family* has been screened and *meets the criteria* of potential maltreatment, *an assessment is ordered*. The assessment will determine whether or not a child has been maltreated and whether protective services are needed. The assessment, conducted by a child protection worker, includes gathering facts, assessing the risk to the child, and formulating a plan of services. The child protection worker has the authority to interview the child, any person responsible for the child's care, the alleged offender, and any other person with knowledge of the maltreatment.

Licensed families are subject to licensing laws and rules in addition to the laws and rules governing the maltreatment of children. Licensed families are not assessed; the agency screens the report of maltreatment to determine the *need for investigation. Not just one investigation may result, but two—one for maltreatment and one for licensing violation.*

What are investigators looking for?

Law Enforcement is seeking (investigating) enough evidence to press criminal charges, which must eventually be able to stand up in a criminal court as evidence *"beyond a reasonable doubt."*

Social Services (child protection) is seeking (assessing) credible evidence that a child has been abused or neglected.

Social Services (licensing) is seeking (assessing) licensing violations which may have occurred even if neglect or maltreatment is not determined.

How are interviews with children handled ?

Children have the right to be treated courteously—with respect and dignity. Investigators who threaten—"I know this happened, if you want to see your mommy again, you need to tell me" . . . or embarass—by undressing or examining a child in front of the opposite sex or strangers . . . or humiliate—by discussing assumptions of family situation within hearing distance of child, are acting inappropriately and violating professional boundaries. If you are a parent and do not understand or like what is happening—ask questions. And when necessary, object! (Besharov 1991)

Children are vulnerable in the hands of an interviewer. We would like to believe that each child is treated respectfully and honestly. But, this is not always the case. The Tennessen Warning which was written to tell people their rights, is often waived for children under 10. Interviewers may or may not be qualified in interviewing children. Biases and prejudgments may exist. Questions may be leading or misunderstood. Parents are notified after interviews have occurred or after completion of the assessment. Parental consent may not be necessary to interview the alleged victim, minors in the household, or other minors who have ever lived with the alleged perpetrator. If a parent prevents access to a child for interview, child protection may request a court order. The records of children's interviews are audio, video, or transcribed, and contain the date, time, place, duration of interview, and identity of all persons present. Parents should request a copy of the interview, or request its review by another professional.

What occurs during an investigation?

An investigation is conducted through interviews, reports and observation of the child by a representative of the agency or law enforcement. The investigation examines the child and the living environment. Health care professionals are sometimes involved.

Persons "served" by the program (foster children) have the right to refuse to be interviewed, photographed, or audio or videotaped. However, failure or refusal by a license holder (foster parent) to comply completely is reasonable cause for immediate suspension or revocation of a license.

Social services agencies have virtually 24-hour-a-day access to a foster home. Licensing law allows an agency representative to photocopy, photograph, and make audio and videotape recordings during the inspection. The foster parents may also choose to audio or videotape interviews or request copies from the agency representative.

The investigation might last two hours, six months, or even longer. Moreover, the care provider may not even know the investigation has been initiated. Once the investigation is concluded, the county or investigating agency makes two determinations—whether or not maltreatment occured AND whether or not protective services are needed.

— **A determination that maltreatment did occur** means either . . .
  (a) protective services are needed—protective intervention initiated
                                  or
  (b) child is not in need of protective services—needed services offered.

— **A determination that maltreatment did not occur** means either . . .
  (a) protective services are needed—protective intervention or other services offered
                                  or
  (b) child is not in need of protective services—no service provided.

Although a case may be officially closed and no findings of maltreatment or licensing violation found, the case may not be finished in the minds of some of the individuals involved. A closed case does not necessarily relieve the vulnerability of the provider to social services gossip and mistrust. The same issue may resurface in the future. Additional evidence may be sought and a watchful and wary eye kept over the family whenever they provide care for children.

What is a protective intervention procedure?

Prior to initiating a protective intervention, social services evaluates the risk of permitting the child to remain at home. Keeping the children in the home is preferred, and a request is often made for removal of the alleged perpetrator. If services are refused or the family is uncooperative, the county attorney can be asked to file a CHIPS (child in need of protective services petition). If the risk is great, social services can ask law enforcement to remove and place the child in safe custody (a hold) while further assessment is made.

Most people are familiar with the terms guilty and innocent and assume this is the same vocabulary used in child maltreatment allegations. This is not the case. The following terms are used in allegation findings.

Maltreatment
*   occurred*
Maltreatment
*   did not occur*
Maltreatment
*   cannot be*
*   determined*

Founded
Unfounded

Proved
Unproved

Determined
Non-determined

Validated
Invalidated

Substantiated
Unsubstantiated
Unable to Substantiate

They do not use
Guilty
Innocent

However, children may be removed from their homes regardless of the findings or the standards of evidence. If a preponderance of evidence exists—i.e., a better than fifty percent chance something happened—the case may be considered substantiated and the children placed in out-of-home care. If a family disagrees with the findings, they may ask for a change in determination of maltreatment. The agency head can make a change or an administrative hearing can challege the accuracy and completeness of the data, investigation, and/or determination of maltreatment.

Problems also arise when investigations prove the abuse allegations unfounded. When there is not enough evidence to substantiate child abuse, it may be inappropriate to abruptly remove the child from a provider home.

These factors must be considered:

— The child's level of attachment and security with the family

— The length of time the child has lived in the family.

— The age and development of the child.

— Previous history of grief and attachment issues.

— The number of previous moves the child has experienced.

The possibility of psychological trauma increases when a child is moved unnecessaily from one home to another.

What are the qualifications of investigators?

Qualifications of investigators vary from state to state. The State of Arkansas has developed special agencies or departments with the sole responsibility of investigating allegations of child maltreatment in licensed facilities. These investigators are educated, skilled, and hold degrees in investigation. When a report is investigated by a trained investigative professional, social services, the child, and the alleged perpetrator have a better chance of having the truth uncovered and appropriate action taken. If the investigation function is separate from the licensing function, then the licensing workers who have worked and represented the family previously will still be able to lend support services to the license holder during the investigation.

But the Arkansas process is unique. In many states, the investigators are overburdened, and social services workers are untrained in investigative procedures. They may have a personal agenda. This situation puts the child in danger of losing a good home and the family in danger of losing their license and a child. If a family is facing this type of situation, they need to factually (non-emotionally) document the situation and make an appointment with the investigator's supervisor.

When investigating licensed families, the local agency is in quite a different position:

Coordination of the investigation of a licensed home is handled by three separate and different systems: Child Protection, Law Enforcement and Licensing Agencies. Legal guardians of children in care are also notified that an allegation has been made against someone in the provider home.

Coordination with Law Enforcement

Social services coordinates its investigation with the law enforcement agency to avoid duplication. Each agency, however, prepares an independent report. A law enforcement representative is asked to accompany the child protection worker to interview the child when (1) a report of maltreatment indicates imminent danger to a child or danger to the child protection worker, or (2) the alleged violation involves a criminal statute of sexual abuse or physical abuse.

Coordination with State Licensing Agencies

The local agency coordinates the investigation with the agency responsible for licensing the facility. In Minnesota, the local agency notifies the responsible state licensing agencies within 48 hours, excluding weekends and holidays, of receiving a report of maltreatment . This notification includes:
— The date and time the local agency received the report;
— Identification of the facility, the child or children alleged to be maltreated, and the alleged offender;
— The nature of the maltreatment and extent of injuries to children;
— Immediate treatment and protection measures being provided by the local agency;
— The name of the child protection worker responsible for investigating.

Notice to parents, guardians, or legal custodians

Natural families, legal guardians, and other agencies responsible for placement of child in care. This notice that an allegation has been made may include the following information:
— The name of the facility or provider home;
— That a report of maltreatment of their child has been received;
— The nature of the alleged maltreatment;
— That an investigation is being conducted;
— The protective or corrective measures currently being provided;
— Confirmation that a written report will be furnished when the investigation is completed.

This notice may be required before the agency interviews any child reported to be maltreated unless the interview is necessary to protect children within the facility; and/or the local agency is unable to locate the parents. In addition, the local agency may provide notice to the parents, guardians, or custodians of the other children within the facility *who are not the subjects* of the report. Consideration to notify is based on:
— Whether there are reasonable grounds to believe maltreatment has occurred;
— The seriousness of the maltreatment;
— The number of children reported to be maltreated;
— The length of time it may take to complete the investigation.

There is no requirement (in Minnesota) to immediately notify the licensed family that they are being investigated, or about the nature of the allegation. Sometimes foster children are interviewed in school before the family is informed. Minnesota foster families are often shocked when a law officer or social worker knocks at their door to interview them or visit their foster child.

Interviewing children and persons outside of the family places the family in a difficult situation. Caught off-guard, providers face an uncertain future plagued by isolation, trauma, and misunderstanding. It is difficult for a provider to explain to others that you know nothing of the investigation when previous foster children or the foster child's parent already knows about it.

For thorough investigations to be accomplished, all interdependent units must be cooperative:

1. **Foster parents** *must be available to respond in a non-emotional and logical manner, even under the trauma of allegation.*

2. **Social workers** *must not let their feelings or experiences get in the way of complete investigative procedures.*

3. **Intra-agency** *rivalry must not get in the way of case management.*

4. **Police departments** *and* **social workers** *must trust and respect positions and each other's knowledge and responsibilities in job roles.*

The licensing investigation—non-compliance?

Once the investigation for suspected maltreatment is complete, the care provider faces a second investigation—the licensing investigation. Before suspending, revoking, or making a license probationary, the investigator considers facts, conditions, or circumstances concerning the program's operation, the well-being of persons served by the program, consumer evaluations of the program, and information about the character and qualifications of employees of the license holder. The initial investigation is reviewed to determine whether a risk of harm to the persons served by the program exists and if any disqualification factors apply to the situation.

> *Of interest to Minnesota care providers: Read Minnesota Statute 245A.04 Subd. 6 regarding Commissioner's evaluation.*

What is a licensing investigation?

A licensing investigation, often referred to as a study, compares findings of the initial investigation with all applicable licensing laws, rules, and agency protocol. Licensing laws are much more refined and subjective than laws governing custodial parents. When a licensed family faces an allegation, the licensing agency must investigate to determine compliance. In some cases, the licensing investigation is more devastating than the initial investigation. The family that has already been scrutinized is now placed under a microscope.

What follows a licensing investigation?

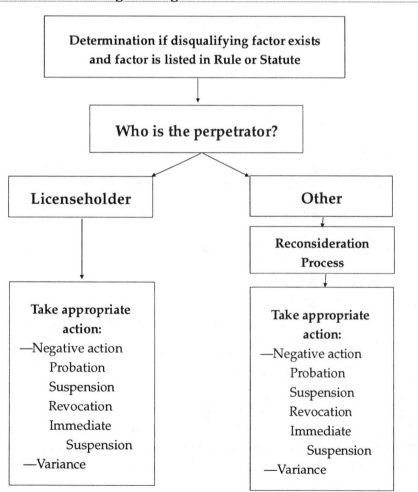

The license may be immediately suspended, suspended, revoked, or made probationary depending on licensing review findings. A license holder whose license is suspended, revoked, or made probationary must be given notice of the action by certified mail. The notice states the reasons for the negative licensing action. All letters of immediate suspension, revocation, suspensions and fines contain information on how to appeal and rights to a contested hearing. Licensing determinations in most cases can be appealed.

The licensing agency and/or state department notifies in writing the license holder and the accused individual of the results of the study. The agency also notifies the child's custodian in writing of the agency's determinations. If the individual accused of maltreatment or violation of license is not allowed to have direct contact with persons served by the program, the agency will explain why. A license holder who is not the subject of study is informed by the agency that information has been found disqualifying the subject (i.e., volunteer, employee, spouse, etc.) from direct contact with persons served by the program. However, the license holder cannot be told what that information is unless the data practices act provides for release of the information and the individual studied authorizes this release.

A notice that the study was undertaken and completed is maintained in the files of the program. What happens to these records varies from state to state and agency to agency. If there were findings to warrant negative licensing action, the certified letter sent to the accused may immediately become public data. This means that the media or others may obtain access to the data prior to the time the certified letter is signed be the inteded recipient. In this letter, the alleged offender may be notified of his/her rights to have the records destroyed, notified of the data classification of the records and provided a contact person's phone number to call with questions.

If the individuals working on behalf of the commissioner of human services find that the license holder has failed to comply with an applicable licensing law or rule, but this failure does not warrant a license sanction, the commissioner may issue a correction order or a fine.

If the license holder's failure to comply with applicable law or rule has placed the health, safety, or rights of children in imminent danger, the commissioner is required to act *immediately to suspend the license.* The notice of immediate suspension is hand-delivered and a certified letter follows. The program must discontinue operation upon receipt of the commissioner's order. All monies paid by government to the care provider stop.

If the license is *made probationary,* the notice informs the license holder of the right to request a reconsideration by the commissioner. The license holder may submit written argument or evidence in support of the request for reconsideration. *In Minnesota, the commissioner's disposition of a request for reconsideration is final and is not subject to appeal.*

To begin an appeal process simply request in writing you would like to appeal.

How long does the agency keep records of allegations relating to reports of maltreatment?

If an individual has been falsely accused and the investigation has been proved unsubstantiated, the accused has the right to have the records destroyed. When determination is made that **maltreatment has not occurred** and child protection services are not needed, the local agency can still retain records for a designated period of time, unless a written request is made to destroy them.

Determination must be made:

— *If the abuse or neglect is likely to occur in the future.*

— *If the situation is chronic or situational.*

— *Of the level of seriousness of the incident.*

— *If it is likely to have occurred at all in the first place.*

Is this a false allegation?

Other family or individual characteristics may come into play:

— *Chemical dependency*
— *Mental illness*
— *Mental handicap*
— *Physical handicap*
— *Custody dispute*
— *Ritualistic abuse*
— *Spousal abuse*
— *Criminal activity*
— *Suicidal child*
— *Homelessness*
— *AIDS related issues*
— *Compulsive gambling*
— *Handicapped child*
— *Adolescent parents*

*Questions regarding the form
provided to biological parent
during an assessment.*

— *What information do you need?*
— *What was the accusation?*
— *What is suspected?*
— *What will happen if I do or do not give information?*
— *How can I be assured the truth will not be twisted?*
— *When and how do we get more information?*
  If we refuse to answer do you assume we are hiding information and are guilty?
— *What kind of services are offered?*
— *Do you have a list of services offered I can see?*
— *If I don't answer any of the questions will I be labeled uncooperative, noncompliant, neglectful, uninterested in the welfare of my children, or abandoning?*
— *Do you have any documented information on how problems such as this have been solved before?*
— *Does the Miranda warning apply here? (You have the right to remain silent...) what will happen if I get an attorney, do I have the right to free legal counsel?*
— *Could you please list the names of these specific people and let me know their credentials and job descriptions?*
— *Which people in the county or state are included in this, could I have more clarification?*
— *Who in the office has access?*
— *With whom do you share information?*
— *Will I have access to these people if they are planning to help me?*
— *Can I have someone represent me?*
— *If they find the report unfounded, is there another investigation with another department?*

(This is a sample form given to Minnesota legal guardian families during protective services assessment entitled "For Your Protection.")

Why do we ask for information?

We are asking you for information on your family because we received a report that your children might be abused or neglected. The law says we have to check out every report that we get.

We will use this information to determine if your children are being abused or neglected and if there are services needed to prevent abuse or neglect to your children.

Do you have to provide any information?

You do not have to answer any of the questions.

What will happen if you give or do not give information?

If you answer the questions, we will be able to make our decisions more quickly and be able to work together with you to solve any problems.

If you do not answer our questions, it will take us longer to determine if your children are abused or neglected and if any services could help your family. We can also go to court, if we need to, to get an order to make you give us the information.

Who we will share the information with?

There are other people who can get some of the information we have about you. They are:

Other social workers, the social services supervisor, the director from our office, and the State Department of Human Services when they need to know to make decisions about services and to supervise work.

We may also give the information to another county or state if you move during or after we talk to you.

The professionals on the case consultation committee of the child protection team, if we go to them for help in making our determinations or planning services for you.

The county attorney's office, if we go to court.

The city police department or county sheriff's department. We must let them know about the report received. They may work with us if the report says your children could be sexually abused or severely physically abused.

Family court services, if they have an active case involving your family and if they need information to do their work.

Do you have any additional rights?

Right to see data—You have a right to see information about you and your children at our office unless your children have asked us not to show it to you. You may not know the name of the person who reported the possible abuse or neglect to us. You may only get that name by going to court. To see information about you, please contact:

Name_____

Address_____

Most of the time we will be able to show you the data within 5 working days. If we are not able to let you see it within 5 working days, we will let you know, and we must show it to you within 10 working days.

Right to get copies—If you want a copy of any information, we may charge you what it costs us to make a copy.

Right to challenge accuracy—If you think some of the information in your file is not correct or some important information is not included, you may ask us to change the information. To do this please put the request in writing to:

Name:_____

Address:_____

Within 30 days of receiving your written request, we will either:

a. Change the data, as you requested; or

b. Let you know we think the file is correct as it is. If we do this, we will attach your written concerns about the information not being correct when we give the information to anyone else.

Right to appeal—You have the right to appeal our decision not to change the data. In order to appeal this decision, you must write a summary of what information you feel is not correct or not accurate and whether you want the information taken out or changed and if you want it changed, what you want it to say. You must send your letter to:

Department of Administration, Address of place to send

If you need help preparing this written summary, we will help you. We will also send the information to the Department of Administration. You may hire an attorney to represent you at this hearing but it is not required.

Signatures_____Date_____
Signatures_____Date_____

Copies of this notice were provided to:

_____

_____

— *What does active mean?*
— *When can I see my records?*
— *Is there a document that tells me how to go to court to find out who made the report?*
— *Between what hours and on what days, what if they don't return calls?*
— *Must I get in contact by writing?*
— *Do I need to send a certified letter?*
— *How will you notify me?*
— *What happens if you don't show it to me within 10 days?*
— *How much are copies?*
— *How do I pay: cash, check, money order?*
— *Can I send you some money in advance so there will be no hassle in getting the copies?*
— *What if I cannot afford to pay for it?*
— *Do I send by certified letter and keep a copy for myself?*
— *Should I get a statement from other professionals i.e., medical, clergy, psychologist?*
— *What do you do with old data?*
— *What do I do next?*
— *How can I be sure you follow through?*
— *Who is the Department of Administration and how do they fit in?*
— *Is there a time frame we can ask for changes in our records?*
— *If we miss the time frame, then what happens?*
— *Does a written summary cost money?*
— *If so, what and how should I pay you?*
— *How will you help me? Is there a specific person I can talk to?*
— *Is it advisable to hire an attorney?*
— *What has happened to people who hire attorneys vs. those who have not?*

An exonerated individual should request complete copies of the investigation file before asking that it be destroyed. This ensures that if a future allegation occurs, data that have already been investigated do not need to be reconstructed.

How can protective service agencies be abusive?

Courts and public agencies are granted power to protect injured children. Protective service agencies have the right to petition civil courts for the removal of children when it is deemed in the child's best interest. In most cases, social services act justly and decisions are well-based. Great care and judgment are used to determine realistic needs of a child and family. Preservation, healing, and reunification lie at the forefront of social service goals.

In a very small percentage of cases, however, unregulated power is wielded in inappropriate ways against innocent people who don't understand how to defend themselves. In these cases it is important for the alleged perpetrator and social services administration to communicate.

In some cases, investigations become persecution instead of prosecution.

> *From the child's perspective, this system has the power to move and remove you arbitrarily, to shift you from place to place and label to label with no input from you, and most often with no explanation or accountability.*
>
> *To be **angry at a parent** for failings, for injustices, allows for eventual confrontation or resolution—either by coming to understand the parent-as-human, or by rejection of that particular human being—painful as all that may be. To be **angry at a system** that will afford you little information about its real motives (and whose real motive may have little to do with the case), and that is entirely uninterested in how you may feel about it, is utterly futile. That the system converts your experience of its confusions and shortcomings into evidence of your problems, your failings, is insidious. (Armstrong 1989)*

Most social service workers are healthy individuals with a high regard for the rights of individuals. However, within any system a dysfunctional minority can wield improper power over co-workers, primary families, or license holders. These individuals cause untold damage in the lives of others when allowed to exercise responsibilities inappropriately.

The foster care provider's confidants and support system—the social worker and social welfare system—become adversaries of the provider. The provider is guilty until proven innocent. The provider's life turns upside down. No independent agency reviews or verifies the paper trail left by agency workers. Records no longer resemble the truth, and yet are perfectly appropriate and convincing at a meeting the care provider or representative is prohibited from attending. If allegations are unfounded and the alleged does not request that records be destroyed, a change in agency staff can reopen closed issues.

Protective service agencies are not obligated to provide *criminal due process*—to read an individual his or her rights, to offer the opportunity to confront accusers, or to allow a trial by jury. But they are obligated to provide *administrative due process*—to provide an appeal process through an administrative hearing or through the head of an agency. A hearing for licensing action must be provided for the license holder upon request. If the license holder does not attend that hearing, he or she automatically loses the appeal.

Caught in the Act or in a Web?

When an allegation is made against a birth family, accused individuals are screened to determine if an assessment is necessary. Depending on the findings of the assessment or screening, the family may or may not be investigated. Child protection staff working with a team of others determine if the report constitutes real neglect or abuse. Proper social work requires communication between families and the system. The communication requires each party to listen without forming a definite conclusion until all the information is on the table. Factual information can be influenced by personal value systems, beliefs, and assumptions. The following example illustrates the dangers of assuming too much.

> *Juan's family is Hispanic. Carlos and Maria, Juan's parents, crossed the Mexican border illegally and later obtained papers for U.S. citizenship. Both have very little education. They came to the United States with the hope of making a better life and are very proud of their progress. Carlos is a sturdy Catholic man with high regard for hard work and honesty. He works long hours in a factory. Maria also works to provide for the family. By American standards they are very poor. By Mexican peasant standards they are wealthy. The parents are very proud of their children and wish success for them as adults in America. Juan is 10 years old, overweight, and as the kids say at school, "gross." He began stealing money from his family to buy junk food. After repeated attempts to punish Juan, Carlos threatened physical punishment: "The next time that you steal something, I will burn your hands."*

This type of threat, although irrational and inappropriate, is familiar to many people. These types of punishment *are practiced today* in some areas of the world. It is not surprising that they are used by individuals who have been shown no alternatives.

> *Carlos kept his word and punished Juan. Juan arrived at school with his hands dressed and bandaged. The school nurse reported the incident to child protection. Carlos spoke broken English, taking a great deal of effort and appearing agitated. He spoke loudly and with great gesture. His frustration at not being able to communicate was interpreted as anger.*

The report was screened and a need for assessment was determined. A child protection *intake worker* was assigned to the family. It was the intake worker's job to assess the family situation and decide if the family needed additional services. Child protection is legally responsible for responding promptly to reports of alleged maltreatment or exploitation of children. They are required to respond immediately to reports of infant medical neglect or if a child is in imminent danger. If a child is not in imminent danger or if a more serious report takes precedence, initiating an assessment can be delayed up to 72 hours. An assessment, however, will be made.

Child protection is required by law to try to prevent out-of-home placement whenever possible and to provide safety for children in their own homes. If reported abuse occurs in a biological family to the natural children in that family, child protection's primary goals are to protect the child and preserve the family unit. Proper social work practice tries to maintain the integrity of the family and provide support services. If necessary, they provide the least restrictive

---

A report of maltreatment begins the child's journey into the social service system. There is no guarantee . . .

. . . the "best interests" of the child will be served . . .

. . . the "best interests" of the family will be served or . . .

. . . that "best interests" will mean anything.

"At first I was really scared. Who were these strangers? Were they monsters? Did they hurt kids? Why were they trying to be so nice to me? Why was everyone always smiling? I sure didn't feel like smiling!"

Child in care

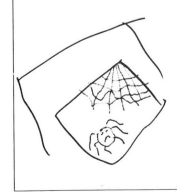

---

out-of-home safe living situation for the child, often with relatives or kin. The family and the social worker then work to develop a case plan to reunite the family with the child as soon as possible.

> *The assessment substantiated the report of maltreatment of Juan by Carlos. In others words, there was physical evidence and there was a conclusion that maltreatment had occurred. The family also was seen as disturbed, and other concerns were raised in addition to the incident of physical abuse. Juan was described as having poor socialization skills. Carlos was described as volatile, Maria as compliant. The other children were described as apprehensive, shy, and withdrawn.*

Once maltreatment has occurred, the county has the legal right to intervene in the family's life. Intervention can be voluntary or involuntary. After the initial screening and assessment, a caseworker is assigned and may request an interview with the child and/or a home visit. During this time the child and the relationship with the parent are scrutinized.

Child protection *has the authority to interview* the child, person, or persons responsible for the child's care, the alleged perpetrator, and any other person with knowledge of abuse or neglect for the purpose of gathering the facts, assessing the risk to the child, and formulating a plan. The job of the case worker is *to assess any physical or emotional harm* to children resulting from maltreatment, *identify the family problems* which contributed to or resulted in maltreatment, and *evaluate the risk of further injury* and the need for emergency intervention.

> *In Carlos's case, voluntary intervention was accepted. Lucia, a culturally sensitive Hispanic social worker, was assigned to work with the family. Lucia had only eight cases. She was part of a family-based program to keep minority families together and provide appropriate services to maintain the family unit.*

For biological non-licensed families in Minnesota, the local agency notifies the law enforcement agency orally and in writing within 24 hours of receiving a report. If an assessment is determined to be necessary from screening the report, the child is personally interviewed. If the situation looks potentially abusive or neglectful for the child, the social worker may ask for a physical examination of child and do an additional check with medical personnel. At this point, an investigation may be requested. If there is an investigation and no finding of abuse, the agency staff (protective services or/and licensing) confirms the investigation results in writing to the accused.

When interviewing biological non-licensed families, the local agency:

Tells the person/family about assessment or investigation policies and procedures, and explains data privacy and the rights of the people involved.
Each person is told:
(1)   Why the information is being requested;
(2)   How the information will be used;
(3)   That the person may refuse to answer the questions;
(4)   The consequences of either answering or refusing to answer questions;
(5)   The other persons or agencies authorized to receive the information being requested; and

Provides in writing:
(1)   The information just discussed;
(2)   How and when the person can access information;
(3)   A description of the procedure for contesting the accuracy and completeness of the agency's records and information.

Birth families in Minnesota are provided the form *"For Your Protection."* This form, which appears on pages 94-95, gives parents some idea of their rights and why they are being asked for information. ***Minnesota licensed care provider families presently receive no such information.***

During the assessment of the family, Lucia grew worried—not because of the problems, but because her perception of the family was so different from that of the professionals who had interacted with them previously. The parents appeared to Lucia to be basically good people with a great deal of love for each other and their children. They seemed mature, and there was no evidence of severe psychological problems. Their values and morals seemed consistent with their culture, and she observed no deviation or severe pathology. There was no drinking, no chemical abuse, no reported violence beyond the burned hands. In the home, Juan appeared to be a normal Hispanic child.

Lucia went to the school to discover what was meant by "poor socialization skills." She found that Juan's eating habits "grossed out" his classmates. Juan would take bread and eat parts of his food with the bread. He would try to eat his soup using bread instead of a spoon. Juan's family is traditional in their eating habits, and at home, Juan would eat his meals using a tortilla instead of a fork or a spoon. Trying to adapt, he used his bread the same way he used a tortilla.

Cross-cultural incompetence occurs when conclusions are drawn with no understanding of the background of the individual. Without a solid foundation of truth a situation can easily be misinterpreted.

Because Lucia's perception of the family was so different from the perceptions of those who were providing services, she decided to get a second opinion. She wanted Juan evaluated by a psychologist who was a leading expert in child protection issues. Juan's family had private insurance and a referral was made. The family would pay the 20% deductible, which was a considerable amount of their income. Carlos and Maria willingly cooperated and brought Juan to the evaluation. Carlos took the day off work without pay, dressed up, and drove 20 miles to the psychologist's office. When he arrived he learned that the psychologist had left a message at his home cancelling the appointment. He was very disappointed. He was given a second appointment.

When he returned to the psychologist's office he found he was not on the schedule. He was very angry. He said the psychologist had given him a card with the date and the time, but that he did not have it with him. Speaking in broken English, with extravagant gestures, he tried to communicate. He was told to leave.

The psychologist called Lucia and described the temper tantrum Carlos had displayed in her office. The psychologist was concerned about the inappropriate and excessive anger this father had displayed. She explained that his behavior could be an illustration of a volatile nature and an inability to handle frustration. She considered the children to be at high risk for abuse and suggested an out-of-home placement to assess the family and protect the children.

If, for the child's safety, it is necessary to separate family members, child protection attempts to place the child with relatives to help maintain family identity, and then ethnic culture. Whenever possible, the alleged perpetrator leaves the home.

I grew tough and strong. By 12 I could take "good" care of myself. I didn't need anyone. I became very good at getting whatever I needed— food, smokes— you know, everything at the corner store was free.

I didn't want to be hurt so I kept my distance from people, and running was the fastest way I knew to stay free of the danger of being hurt. I ran whenever I felt someone was trying to get too close to me. I ran when I was afraid I'd be criticized, rejected, or disciplined! When I ran I forgot about my problems!

Some people cared enough to rescue me. I kept walking, and they kept following me. I didn't want help. It was too scary to trust again. What if I trusted and they shit on me?

The police eventually caught up with me. No school, neglectful home, my ma was fit to be tied. I got put into the children's home and finally got involved in the Child Destruction System otherwise known as CPS. (Child Protection System)

Lucia went and spent time with the family. She wanted to buy time to prevent an unnecessary out-of-home placement. Luckily, the time was available. She worked with the family on issues, helping them to feel comfortable with her and begin to trust. While they were talking, Maria and Carlos kept looking for the missing appointment card. Finally they found it.

Armed with the appointment card, Lucia made a visit to the psychologist. "Is this your handwriting?" she asked. The psychologist immediately remembered and realized she had given Carlos an appointment. She had made a mistake and not written the appointment down on her schedule.

This story illustrates a predicament social workers may find themselves in—caught between the word of a reputable and respected psychologist and the word of a client who has maltreated a child.

The psychologist was apologetic and made an offer to perform the evaluation at no charge to the family. She called Carlos to apologize and offer the new arrangements. Carlos would have none of it. He said, "No, I don't want my child evaluated by you. I have lost two days of work, and you have implied that I lied about the second appointment. I don't trust you." The psychologist, getting nowhere with Carlos, decided to call Maria, apologize and offer to see the child for free. Upon hearing the request, Maria said, "I am sorry, my husband does not want my child to be seen by you. I will not bring him."

The psychologist's concern increased. Obviously, this was an abuse case. The mother was terrified of the father and perhaps a battered wife. The psychologist again requested out-of-home placement for the children. Lucia went back to talk with Carlos and Maria. Maria relayed word-for-word what she had said to the psychologist. The stories matched. Puzzled by these new concerns of wife abuse, Lucia asked Maria, "What do you think? Would you allow your child to be evaluated by this psychologist?"

"Hell, no!" replied Maria. "Even if my husband changed his mind I would not let her evaluate Juan. We cannot trust her. She called us liars. She has not been respectful to us."

"Maria, why didn't you say those things to the psychologist?" Lucia asked.

Maria answered,"She was apologizing. She was feeling so bad. I didn't want her to feel worse by knowing I agree with my husband."

Maria was trying to follow a value of her culture—the value of many cultures—that being considerate is more important than being assertive. By being considerate, which is a nice way of relating to people, this family was facing the risk of having their children removed from their care, perhaps for a small period of time, but at any rate, unnecessarily.

Lucia evaluated the family from a cultural perspective. She evaluated the family's potential for treatment and decided parenting classes were appropriate. Carlos and Maria needed loving, but firm and effective, discipline methods. The plan met the needs of the family and they accepted the services, relieved to have the case closed.

Had Carlos abused Juan? The answer, technically, is yes. The abuse was serious. However, the abuse was determined to be isolated—a one-time occurrence. Carlos did not feel righteous in burning his son's hands. He felt shame and remorse. But once he made the threat, Carlos could not go back on his promise. Carlos's heart ached with love for his son. Carlos and Maria were receptive to help and interested in parenting their children in more effective ways.

When Lucia closed the case there was little doubt that neither the parents nor the children would benefit from moving the children to out-of-home care. There was no one to protect. The family, although poor, undereducated, and lacking good English, was hardworking, loving, and supportive of their children. Their agricultural, peasant background had not prepared them for child protection or the expectations of American society.

This family needed parenting skills —not punishment.

What happens after an assessment or investigation of a birth family?

Birth families under assessment or investigation can expect one of the following outcomes:

Possible decisions:
1. No problem— unfounded report.
2. Not very serious — suggest counseling and/or provide services.

Report filed for future reference:
3. Problem — child taken into protective custody.
4. Serious problem — child taken into protective custody, parent arrested.

If the child is taken into custody or a parent is arrested, the courts intervene to protect the rights of both the child and the parent. If the child is in protective custody, a court hearing determines the best interests of the child. Choices include:

Court decision on child in custody:
1. Return child — close case.
2. Return child as ward of court or in the court's protection.
3. Keep child in protective custody. Order parent into counseling and set date for rehearing.

Criminal court decisions on parent in custody.:
1. Release parent — close case.
2. Release parent on person's recognizance without bail.
3. Set bail for parent.
4. Keep parent in custody, without bail, as dangerous to society.

If the case is not closed or invalidated, then an evaluation of the situation takes place. The child protection services evaluation determines what is needed to protect the child and to help the parent improve his or her parenting. It may recommend to the court anything from releasing the child back to the parent without further action, up to and including termination of parental rights.

If it appears that a crime has been committed, the district attorney evaluates the evidence, including photographs and medical records.

The district attorney may decide to:
1. File no charges.
2. File charges —
   Allow parents to get help, and drop the charges if they complete counseling.

One thing I learned being a system kid is that you could hide an elephant if you put enough distraction up so people would look the other way.

And I liked hiding elephants.
Reflections from an angry system kid, age 25

Word to the wise . . .

If your child is injured at home, send a note of explanation along with the child to school or day care. The child's version of a story may be very different from what truly happened. Between the parent's note and the child's story the person in charge at school or day care can determine what appropriate action is necessary, without jeopardizing their status as a mandated reporter.
School nurse

The best gift one mother could have received was transportation to wash her clothes.

3. File charges —
Plea-bargain admission to a charge related to the offense.
4. File charges —
Prosecute to the full extent of the law.

The effort in the majority of cases is to ensure the safety of the child and help the family get well. Getting well involves some kind of counseling for the offending parent and, in some cases, the injured child. Treatment can be voluntary or court-ordered. The quality or effectiveness of counseling is hard to measure. In most cases, if the parent coorperates and follows recommended treatment, the child is returned.

It is wrong to treat one family member and then send that person back into an unhealthy family situation. The most successful programs treat the family as a unit. Most parents who physically abuse their child were physically abused themselves. If for no other reason than to prevent the abuse from moving into the next generation, the need is great to concentrate on treating the complete family unit and the child.

Ultimately, the courts are faced with balancing society's legal penalties for criminal behavior with the family's need to get well and the child's needs for safety. The courts have great discretionary powers which allow them to send parents to jail or treatment, or to provide support services.

One judge may allow the parent to have the child back under some type of supervision or, in extreme cases, to terminate parental rights and declare the child eligible for adoption. *Another judge handling the same case may send a person to jail.*

If a parent is convicted, he or she may be placed on probation. The county or state probation officer supervises the convicted offender to ensure compliance with the rules of probation. If the rules of probation are violated, and the child is abused again, the parent will likely go to jail and serve out whatever original jail term was waived for probation.

The rules for probation vary, but may include:
1. Break no laws.
2. Do not purchase or consume alcohol or drugs.
3. Attend all required counseling.
4. Report regularly to probation officer.
5. Attend all required educational programs (i.e., parenting training).
6. Do not use physical force/corporal punishment to discipline child.

If a parent is convicted and sent to prison, parole may be possible. Parole is an early release from prison, and the prisoner signs an agreement which outlines specific requirements that must be met. The conditions of parole are very similar to probation. If the rules are violated, the parolee can be returned to prison.

What happens to the child?

Children involved in the process of reported maltreatment are in a shaky position concerning their future. Some children obtain relief from an oppressive lifestyle. For others, the reporting process signals the beginning of a very real nightmare—years in limbo in the child welfare system.

For the child, a report of maltreatment carries the possibility of a move to out-of-home care. A child's journey through child protection services is confusing and at best uncertain. There are six stages a child passes through from

---

"We've had two allegations against our home already, and sadly, we still don't believe it could ever happen to us again. Yet, I'm sure there will someday be a third allegation, and again, I won't be prepared, just more knowledgeable."

Foster father with 19 years of experience professionally parenting high risk and sexually abused teens

You must not assume that just because you are continually asked to handle the most difficult children, that the agency sees you as a highly capable family.

Know the strengths and weaknesses of your family as seen through the eyes of the agency. Be prepared and willing to accept the negatives of an evaluation and work to make the necessary changes as needed.
(Carbino 1990)

initial contact to finalized adoption. The number of children passing through the system decreases with each stage.

The six stages victimized children pass through are:

1. Report of suspected maltreatment.
2. Short term out-of-home care.
3. Long term out-of-home care.
4. Termination of parental rights.
5. Becoming a ward of the state.
6. Adoption.

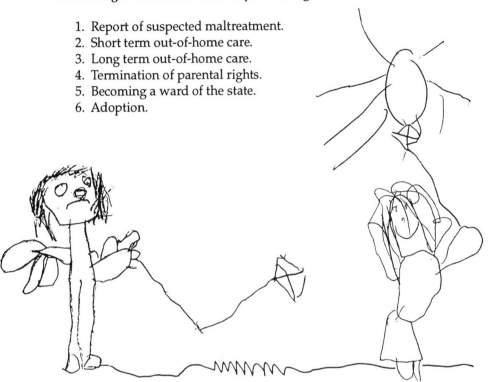

Most children who enter the child protection system remain in stage one, where it is uncertain whether the child will be removed from the home. In reports of suspected sexual abuse, and some neglect and other abuse reports, children are immediately pulled from their homes. These children wait in hospitals, emergency shelters, group homes, or receiving homes while child protection works to assess the family. In some cases the children stay with relatives.

STAGE ONE REPORT OF SUSPECTED MALTREATMENT	What can happen?	Who Investigates Report?
	1. Police have the authority to order a **temporary removal of children** for up to 72 hours, while child protection assesses the child's situation. The child may be placed in an emergency shelter during this time.	—County child protection worker —Intake worker —Culturally sensitive social worker
1. **SCREEN** if this is a valid report.	2. Report **substantiated / child unsafe.** Child is removed from family and placed in out-of-home care.	**Who else is possibly involved?** —Law enforcement —County attorney —Public defender
2. **ASSESS** the child's need for services	3. Report **substantiated / child not in danger**. Child allowed to remain in home and family services are provided.	
3. **INVESTIGATE** the family situation.	4. Report **unsubstantiated/ services needed** for child.	
	5. Report **unsubstantiated/ services not needed**, case closed.	

The same story from the foster parent's perspective:

"We took our foster son to a therapist to help him through some of his anger. My husband and I both went with him and sat him closely between us.

The therapist interpreted that this foster child was holding our family together.

My husband and I sat him between us because we wanted him to feel our support and protection."
Another foster mother

"We joined a family therapy program with our foster son. The families involved in the program had a lot of troubles and we were the only foster family who had ever attended. At first we didn't think we'd benefit from a family program, but looking back it was one of the best time investments we made with our foster son."
Foster father

Child protection officials move a child to safety when they are uncetain that maltreatment has occurred or when a report has been substantiated and the child is in danger. The child is removed from the accused family and placed in what social services deems the least restrictive out-of-home care.

Interviews with children are conducted in person—face-to-face—and must be appropriate to the child's age, development, ability to understand and ability to verbalize. Because these interviews often take place in isolation with a person they may never have met—insecurity, fear, and confusion are normal feelings for children to experience. Both questions and answers can be misunderstood without a trusting relationship and a working knowledge of the child.

Children also are examined for physcial or sexual abuse. These physical examinations are not always conducted in a way that minimizes emotional trauma to the child. The authority to look for signs of maltreatment on a child is not a license to embarass, harm, or humiliate the child. Caution must be maintained while examining a child for potential sexual maltreatment—the examination may be more invasive and sexually abusive than the initial experience. Or it may be the only sexual abuse the child has experienced.

Once child protection is confident the child is safe, they continue to assess the family and provide services which will help preserve the family and reunite the child with the family as soon as possible. The duration of short term care is 72 hours to 30 days. However, treatment plans are often crisis oriented and based upon services readily available or familiar to agency personnel. In addition, policies often do not insure that a family can maintain contact during the foster care placement to give the parent(s) and child(ren) a reasonable chance of reunification.

STAGE TWO **PROVIDE SHORT TERM SAFETY FOR CHILD**	Ensures the child's short-term safety by providing family services and/or sub-stitute care. When the juvenile court becomes in-volved in a child protection case, all parties, including the child, are entitled to legal repre-sentation. Maltreated children also receive a guar-dian ad litem— this person is *not* a legal representative, but a representative of the child's "best interests." Guardians ad litem are not always avail-able, and the case may delayed.	**Who is directly involved?** —Foster care social worker —County agency worker and/or —Private agency worker —Foster parents —Licensing worker —Child's parents **Who else is possibly involved?** —Juvenile court referee and/or judge —County attorney —Public defender —Attorney for child —Guardian ad litem
1. Other family member's home.		
2. Licensed family foster care home or emergency shelter.		
3. Licensed treatment family foster home.		
4. Residential treatment center.		

Many children are returned to their families after a case plan has been developed, and there is evidence that the parents and family are working toward change. Children may return home fearful of law enforcement, medical personnel, social workers and their parents. This short-term out-of-home care often results in behavior changes, which are not necessarily positive.

For other children reunification may not be possible. In some cases it is due to parental negligence, in other cases it is due to negligence by social services. High social service employee turnover leads to frequent transfer of cases and periods of service inactivity. During these times of transition permanancy and family tratment goals become unclear and valuable information is lost.

The angry kid continues . . .

My brother and I got placed in the same foster home. Boy, we sure didn't want to be there. We had to stay clean, no swearing and no smoking.

They had these two little brats—six and four years old. Me and John figured out ways to torture those little brats and then scare them from telling on us. We had them so scared they'd do whatever we asked.

Finally the foster dad found out. I'll bet we chopped enough wood to heat six houses. Once the wood was chopped, it was time to go on to a new placement. They weren't about to keep us around with what he called our shenanigans.

Good riddance and back to behavior modification!

STAGE THREE
PROVIDE
LONG TERM
SAFETY FOR CHILD

A case plan is developed for reunification of the family. Social services enable the family to fulfill the case plan.

See appendix Pages 395-400

Who is directly involved?
—Child's caseworker
—Foster family
—Professional treatment providers
—Psychologists, medical and/or education professionals

Who else is possibly involved?
—Juvenile court referee and/or judge
—Public defender
—Attorney for child
—Guardian ad litem

Most children in care experience at least two moves. Some children experience 20-45 different placements. First the child faces an emergency placement––the first space available (under 30-days)—then on to a more permanent foster home. If a relative, same race, or sibling home opens—another move. Although legal, these moves may not always be in the best interest of the child. An allegation against a provider home—regardless of validity—may immediately disrupt the placement. Foster families caring for these children may request that they be moved or abandon foster parenting altogether. Children in long-term foster care repeatedly lose significant attachments. Licensed families and social services cannot guarantee security or continuity of care to these children.

TOTAL PLACEMENTS PER CHILD

No. of Placements	No. of Children	Percentage %
1	159	11.3%
2	210	15.0%
3	183	13.1%
4	153	10.8%
5	113	8.1%
6	106	7.6%
7	81	5.8%
8	62	4.4%
9	54	3.9%
10	57	4.1%
11-15	128	9.1%
16-20	60	4.3%
21-25	18	1.3%
25-45	17	1.2%
	1,401 Children	**100%**

Source "Looking Out For the Children" Eighth Annual Report of the Nebraska State Foster Care Review Board, 12/31/90

Most children exit the system and are reunited with their families after a case plan is fulfilled by their primary caregivers. To fulfill a caseplan, however, may not be that easy. Families in crisis are often faced with a service system that is bewildering, difficult to navigate in, fragmented and indifferent to their concerns—at a time when they are least equipped to handle more stress and badly need help. Too often, children and parents don't receive the services they need (even if those services are ordered by a court), cannot find transportation to services, encounter poor quality services, or are placed on a long waiting list.

I couldn't believe how stupid they were in my behavoir mod program. When we messed up we got the hot seat and everyone would scream at everyone else. The reality was no one listened, no one cared except the counselors who sat and acted like gods. What did they know?

Ok, ok, I'll scrub the kitchen floor with a toothbrush. Don't you see it's not putting back the love I've missed? The childhood I lost? This floor scrubbing and face screaming is not doing what you think. I kept my mouth shut. I even learned to smile. Two could play at this game.

"How 'bout another foster home, Buddy?" the counselor asked

By now I was 15. I still had all my anger, but I was better at hiding it.

Like I said, I enjoy hiding elephants.

The new foster parents seemed nice. We did stuff together. We went places—fishing, camping, flying in small planes—I even got my scuba license.

It wasn't perfect. They also made me work. They seemed to be always working or doing something. I wasn't very used to that. On top of the work, my foster father worked hard at getting into the little crevices in my life. If there was an elephant, he was an elephant hunter. I hated him trying to dig out things I'd hidden even to myself. He kept harping on me about principles. How stupid were principles, I hadn't needed them so far. He'd put his arm around me—that felt strange. Sometimes the attention made me crazy.

I picked up a six pack of beer and shared it with a friend. My foster parents called my worker and told her and guess what? Into another program I went. For a few beers, I couldn't believe that could really happen to someone.

STAGE FOUR
TERMINATION OF PARENTAL RIGHTS

If family preservation is not possible and reasonable efforts have not succeeded, the county attorney may go to court and move to have parental rights terminated. Termination does not occur very often because it is a difficult, expensive legal procedure. The court must be satisfied that termination is in the best interest of the child. In most states, the child's parents must be proved unable to parent satisfactorily in the future. That standard of proof is very difficult to meet.

Who is directly involved?
—Foster care social worker
—County agency worker and/or
—Private agency worker
—Foster parents
—Licensing worker
—Child's parents

Who else is involved?
—Juvenile court referee and/or judge
—County attorney
—Public defender
—Attorney for child
—Guardian ad litem

STAGE FIVE
BECOMING A WARD OF THE STATE

Time children wait for adoption:

38.8%   < 1 year
15.3%   1-2 years
34.4%   > 2 years
11.5%   unknown
MN 1988 figures

Children whose parents lose parental rights become wards of the state, eligible for adoption.

In Minnesota, children 14 years and older have the option of being assigned to permanent foster care and can "age out" at 18. Children who "age out" may be eligible for additional state support for higher education and health care after they reach majority.

Who is directly involved?
—Department of Human Services representative
—Adoption agency social worker

Who else is possibly involved?
—Juvenile court referee and/or judge
—County Attorney
—Public Defender
—Attorney for Child
—Guardian ad litem
—Foster care social worker
—Foster parents

STAGE SIX
ADOPTION

In Minnesota, about 50% of all waiting children are adopted within two years.

Minority children may wait longer due to difficulty finding same-race homes.

Children of mixed heritage may have even more difficulty because they qualify as the race of minority and some minorities prefer not to adopt mixed-race children.

Wards of the state who wish to be adopted enter the adoption system. Finding adoptive homes for these children is difficult. Most children are older—between 5 and 12 years old, white, and not mentally retarded. Their past may include severe neglect, emotional, physical, sexual, and/or ritualistic abuse. They have lived in a number of different homes, lost people they have loved, and have difficulty attaching to new people. They bring with them pain and pathology. They need special attention and have special needs.

Who is directly involved?
—Department of Human Services representative
—Adoption agency social worker
—Adoptive parents
—Attorney
—Judge for finalization

See page 396-397

What happens to the children when an allegation is made against a licensee?

The birth child or (finalized) adopted child: The goal of child welfare services is to carefully assess the family and offer counseling and support services to keep children in their original or custodial home for as long as possible. If outside placement is necessary, children are placed in the least restrictive setting, preferably with extended family members on a temporary basis. A case plan is established, and depending on the progress of the plan, children are reunited with custodial parents.

The related or kinship care child: The goal of child welfare services is to asssess the relative's home situation carefully and provide services to keep the child in a relative's home. If additional outside placement is necessary, children are again placed in the least restrictive setting on a temporary basis, possibly with another relative or back with a birth parent. A case plan is established, and depending on progress of the case plan, children are reunited with parents or relatives as soon as possible.

The tribal care child: Action would defer to specific tribal law.

The voluntarily placed foster child: The child's parents are notified, and action is decided between social services and parents. The child faces a potential move.

The temporary legal-custody foster child care: For the protection of the agency from legal liabilty if alleged abuse or neglect is proved, children under legal custody of the state are likely to be placed in another facility or foster home.

The permanent foster child: For the protection of the agency from legal liabilty if alleged abuse or neglect is proved, children under legal custody of the state are likely to be placed in another facility or foster home. Children in long-term foster placement, however, face significant separation issues. In the heart and mind of the child, the care provider family is no longer a temporary placement—but is considered home. Careful consideration must be given regarding the personal needs of each child while balancing legal responsibilities.

The terminated parental rights child or a pre-adoptive child: The rights of the pre-adoptive parent are limited. It is likely the child would be removed from the home and placed in another facility or foster home.

FOSTER FAMILY CASE STUDY

Trapped in Protocol,License Violation, or Child Maltreatment?

Even if a foster family provides exceptionally high quality care for children, preventing a report of maltreatment is impossible. A person caring for other people's children cannot assume, *"an allegation will not happen to me, because I would never abuse or neglect a child!"*

When reported abuse occurs in a licensed care provider home, the procedures, liabilities, and responsibilities differ from those of primary families. It is vitally important that a negligent or abusive care provider is not allowed to continue practices detrimental to healthy child development. When it is not known if the

This time the program was different. I didn't go alone. These stupid foster parents followed me and went to counseling with me. Not only that but they went to family counseling with me as their family, and I wasn't even a real part of them.

Finally I was someplace where people did seem to care, where people shared information and judgment wasn't quite so harsh, and where there was space to say what I thought.

I lived with this family two and a half years. I was almost 18, a senior in high school. My grades were OK and I was managing. My foster parents hadn't even met with a vice principal yet that year.

I had proven myself. My foster family trusted me and I was almost beginning to trust them.

One weekend, they allowed me to stay home alone while they went camping. . .

*. . .Two and a half years of surveillance . . . They were letting me free.
. . . Party time!*

As luck would have it—it rained and my foster parents came home the next night. The kids had to jump out the windows and we all ran!

They called SOS and reported what had happened. The next week was total chaos. They had found grass and beer in the house. My foster father volunteered to stick up for me if I'd take a drug test. I told him he'd been teaching me principles and one of my principles was not taking tests. I ran again.

This time the county didn't let me return to their house. One night I broke in to get some of my stuff—tennis shoes, clothes, etc. They put me back in behavior mod. I ran again. I had had enough of them and they had had enough of me. They gave me back to my birth mom.

It was only two months after the party.

I was almost 18.

I had quit school.

I was pissed.

allegation is true or false, the immediate solution—to close the home and remove the children—may seem the simplest.

It would be helpful during an assessment if the agency and the social worker would decide whom they are protecting—the agency, the family, or the child. The mandate of the agency is always to protect the child.

Foster or pre-adoptive children who are already dealing with issues of separation, loss, and grief are constantly alerted to a potential move. Like the warning sirens prior to a hurricane, an allegation sounds the alarm of uncertainty. The investigative procedure disrupts any sense of safety, attachment, and security the child has achieved.

When a report of child maltreatment alleges facility-related sexual or physical abuse, the local law enforcement and social services agencies must coordinate their investigation and assessment activities. Child protection, licensing, and law enforcement officials must, upon the receipt of a report, notify one another and work cooperatively on the assessment and investigation of the report. In some states a separate investigative agency or team is involved. They have the responsibility to determine whether abuse or neglect of a child has occurred and whether a child needs to be placed elsewhere.

Determinations must be made concerning the children at risk, violation of criminal statutes, violations of licensing law, and continuation of the license.

A social worker, often joined by a law enforcement officer, comes to the foster care home or the foster child's school to talk to the child. If the child is at school, the social worker and the officer proceed to the foster care provider's home to meet with providers and discuss the issue. The child's primary family may also be interviewed along with children who were previously cared for by the facility, persons responsible for the child's care, alleged perpetrator(s), and any other person(s) who have knowledge of the alleged maltreatment.

> *John and Mary led eventful professional lives before becoming foster parents. John was a law enforcement officer and Mary was a social worker, working with abused and neglected children. Their inside knowledge of the system and their understanding of the needs of children led them to a unified decision to quit their careers, add on to their home, and provide day-to-day care for the kinds of children who had captured their hearts. They determined they would provide the type of home they often had found lacking in the foster care system.*
>
> *In four years, more than 100 children passed through their home. Experiences and memories of each child ran deep with warmth and caring. Some of them stayed a few days, some stayed more than four years.*
>
> *It was a very unexpected phone call: "We have an allegation against your home. We cannot tell you what it is. We will be coming to pick up the children in two and a half hours."*

Why are children in care provider homes sometimes removed on receipt of a report?

Workers act in terms of what *appears* must be done in any given situation. In some cases, removal of the child may be standard agency practice. Immediate removal of a child may protect the case from being tainted. Removal eliminates some risk of care providers encouraging children to change reports or manipulate investigative procedures. In addition, some children may refuse to remain in a home after an allegation has been made against it.

"Social services called at 2:00 and by 4:30, the children were gone. They were all gone. I couldn't believe it—they just came and took all seven of our foster children. Worse yet, we didn't know what the allegation was, and when we asked, our social worker just said she wasn't allowed to discuss it! I felt like I was living in a nightmare and I couldn't wake up. No one would tell us what the allegation was. They removed all seven children and placed them in new homes," Mary said.

The first afternoon the school didn't have permission to release the children to their new foster parents so the kids had to wait for social services to arrive before they could leave. By the second day, the kids were beginning to withdraw and act out. The teachers were concerned, especially since we had been making progress with these kids. Weeks passed and no one would tell us what the allegation was. We determined by the secrecy it must be a sexual abuse allegation, but who? Why?

Finally, we had an interview. From the questions they asked, John and I were sure it must be sexual. It also appeared the police may be involved. The little girl who had lived with us for four years continued to regress, Day after day she stared blankly into the television set at her new foster home.

What are common strategies interviewers follow?

In her book, *Preventing Abuse in Foster Care* (1989), Emily Jean McFadden recommends that social workers clarify the situation by making the following responses when talking with foster parents.

Action	Example of statement to clarify:
CLARIFICATION:	*"I'm not sure what you are asking, could you explain that again."*
EXPLORATION:	*"Could you tell me more about that?"*
PERSONAL STATEMENT	*"That would upset me, too."* *"I can understand how you must feel."*
REFLECTION OF FEELING:	*"You sound concerned about that."* *"You're having a rough time and feel frustrated."*
PROBE:	*"You know how your husband reacts when he's angry."* *"What do you mean your wife is too involved with your foster son?"* *"Tell me what it's like to spend a day with Johnny."*
REFOCUS:	*"You were telling me about your son's temper tantrums."* *"You were telling me about your husband's activities with your foster daughter."*
OFFER ASSISTANCE:	*"How can I help?"* *"Would it help to talk to another foster parent about what worked?"* *"Can we develop a plan together for her behavior?"*

A child cannot successfully mourn the past and integrate it into the present if he or she is preoccupied with emotional survival. It is crucial for children in out-of-home care to develop a sense of safety and security. The complete treatment team needs to make every effort to help the child through this traumatic time. For foster or pre-adoptive children, there is no guarantee that the outcome of a report will allow them to remain in their current placement or return to their previous family.

Oh, April ! ! !

After a year of study at the University of Minnesota Foster Care Program, April, my husband and I headed off for graduation at the Government Center. The Government Center where April had been adopted, and from which child protection had removed Joseph.

April insisted on wearing a pair of shoes a size too small— nothing was going to budge our determined child. After walking to the Government Center building, her shoes had produced the expected blister. She pleaded to remove her tights and shoes so she could see the blister. The shoes came off. The tights stayed on.

After graduation ceremonies, with sparkling eyes, a smile on her face, punch in one hand and a piece of cake in the other, April loudly and buoyantly proclaimed, "My vagina hurts!"

I don't think the Olympic athletes could have beaten the time it took me to move my body from five feet seven to three feet, and face-to-face contact with this little monkeyshine.

"April, do you need to go potty? Where does it hurt? What's the matter?"

"Oh, Mom," April said. "It really doesn't hurt, I just wanted your attention so I could go in the bathroom and take my tights off!"

I may not have been so startled if I was in my own home—but at a graduation ceremony at the family services building of the Government Center?

Eventually someone disclosed it was a sexual abuse allegation. We ransacked our minds looking for incidents with our children which could have produced this allegation. I had taught Good Touch, Bad Touch in the public school system. Did one of us touch someone inappropriately? When? Who? We couldn't come up with the answers.

We questioned our worker. Can't someone tell us what it is? How can it be so bad? What could have caused a sexual abuse allegation against our home? Could it be the diary incident with our 13-year-old foster daughter, Theresa?

Two years previously, social services had located Theresa's mother, who had been missing for 11 years. The plan was already underway to reunite Theresa and her mother. Theresa was torn between a mother she didn't know and a family that had cared for her for the last four years. Confused and frustrated, Theresa felt John and Mary were rejecting her, and social services was forcing her to reunite with an unfamiliar mother. The relationship between Theresa and the foster family declined as more visits occurred with Theresa's mother. It is not unusual for children facing a potential move to begin a separation process and feel torn between both families.

Mary encouraged Theresa to keep a journal. The diary was a safe, private place to vent anger and confusion and to say things she didn't dare voice aloud. The diary was written in words Theresa had used often in their home, and Mary wasn't concerned about what or how it was written. The diary held Theresa's private feelings and ideas—she could choose to share them or keep them secret.

One night after supper, Theresa was sweeping the kitchen floor. The kitchen is connected to the dining room. Food was flying from the kitchen into the dining room. John came by and said, "Theresa, when you've finished sweeping, you can vacuum the dining room."

"Why? I didn't do anything," Theresa answered.

"You know what you're doing, just vacuum it up, okay?" John said. He put his hand on the broom. Theresa grabbed the broom and tried to tug it away. John held on. Exasperated, Theresa fled to her room and slammed the door.

"What's wrong with Theresa?" asked another child in care. "Why did she act like that? She should apologize."

Meanwhile, Theresa was busy writing in her diary: "Apologize, apologize, everyone wants me to apologize. Mary emotionally abuses me and John sexually abused me. No wonder my life is such a mess. I wish I were dead."

John and Mary had hired two young women to help with the children. One of the women read Theresa's diary and told Mary what she had found. More concerned with the breaching of Theresa's privacy than with the content of the diary, Mary reprimanded the child care helper. Mary and John had not shared Theresa's past with the workers, partially out of respect for Theresa's privacy and partially due to confidentiality and data privacy protocol. Distraught by the information found in the diary, one of the workers shared it with her therapist.

"The investigation is for sexual abuse. John had intercourse with your 13-year-old foster daughter," said the social worker.

John and Mary looked at each other. Never in their wildest dreams had they imagined that allegation. *Now what should they do?*

Some information was missing from the diary. Theresa's birth father's name is also John and he did sexually abuse Theresa when she was four. Theresa has spent years in therapy, and knows all about abuse and randomly uses those terms when she is angry. Theresa has a hard time telling the truth about even small things. She was very angry when she wrote in the diary and was feeling rejected by John and Mary. Theresa is apprehensive and fearful about reunification with her birth mother. She hardly knows her.

Fortunately for John and Mary, when child protection interviewed Theresa, she explained that the *"John"* in the diary was her **birth father**, not her **foster father**. The allegation against John and Mary was unfounded. Two months had passed. Two months of anguish and isolation. Seven children had been moved from a home in which they were doing well. Hundreds of agency hours had been spent proving this allegation unsubstantiated.

This licensed family now went under a licensing investigation.
Did they violate any rules?
Were all procedures being followed?
Has the agency made a mistake in licensing this family?

Two of the seven children were returned. The two babies had adjusted to their new homes and so remained with them. Two elementary-age children also stayed with other care providers. The caseworker for those children *"just could not trust a home that had had an allegation."* Theresa, confused, hurt, and angry, went to another home with possibilities for future reunification with her birth mother. She lost the family she had known and loved for four years.

John and Mary have begun to rebuild their lives and clean up the emotional rubble. The two children who did return are beginning to readjust. Their own adopted children are settling back into security. They were forced to sell their home and live in an apartment until they had a better idea of their future—during the investigation of their group home all income was stopped. On their licensing record is a violation of failing to disclose information—no further action taken.

John and Mary wonder . . .

What if the investigation had not been qualified and complete?
What if Theresa would have been so hurt and angry she maintained the lie?
What if John and Mary had not had previous experience in social work and police investigation? Would they have reacted differently?
How will the next licensing worker feel about working with a family who according to the record "fails to disclose information?"
Can they and their agency rebuild a trusting relationship?
How will this additional move affect the children who were under their care?

Personal feelings of discomfort continue to be felt by both the agency and the foster parents. It becomes a cautious and long road back to the trusting relationship that existed prior to the allegation. Foster families may be relieved to discover the allegation was unsubstantiated and the case closed in child protection, only to be twisted back into the maze of allegations when licensing finds them in violation of a rule and revokes their license. This means that in addition to the initial investigation and trauma experienced, the foster family may experience a licensing investigation.

From age nine months to four-and-a-half years old Maria had watched over Alicia. Maria had stood beside Alicia's mother as she battled mental illness and alcoholism. She had written letters to Alicia's father while he had served his time in the federal prison.

Maria was just the neighbor next door, reaching out to offer help—ready with a cup of tea or hugs for tears for a poor single mother and her young infant.

"Will you care for Alicia?" asked the mother. Maria couldn't say no. Here was a baby girl who needed her and a mother who had willingly reached out for help. Alicia became part of Maria's multi-colored family.

For the next four years, Maria and her husband raised Alicia as their own. They followed state law and became licensed foster parents for Alicia. The county tried to place Alicia with relatives, but none wanted the responsibility of this robust little girl.

So in Alicia's mind, Maria became her permanent caregiver. Her "berry special numma."

What happens if the investigation determines no maltreatment occurred in a licensed family?

The agency faces a number of questions, regardless of whether or not maltreatment or license violation occurred.

1. How can the agency now work with the child, the foster family, and the natural family?

2. Should the children remain in or return to the foster home, or should they be replaced? What is the new case plan? Why is this plan appropriate? How can it be fulfilled?

3. How can the agency work with all interdependent relationships?

Everyone involved is told in writing that there have been no findings of maltreatment in the facility under investigation. This includes notices to parents, guardians, or legal custodians. It also includes state licensing agencies and any ombudsman or professional involved in the program.

Maintainance of data records varies from state to state and county to county. Classification of these records also varies. Inquire about where records are, how they are classified and what remnants of the allegation will remain available for others (and who the others are) to review.

The records of false allegations, incomplete or inaccurate data in files can be damaging to the future of the families if the files mislead future readers. A written statement by the accused of explanation can often be attached to these files if they cannot be changed or destroyed.

False allegations are costly—
to children, to families, to agencies, and to all taxpayers!

The Crisis Hot Lines across the country ring daily from people experiencing allegations. Over and over the crisis line workers hear:

"My reputation. It's ruined!" Susan sobbed. "How do I go on? I've dedicated my life to children. What can I do now?"

Sally had worked on the SOS for Persons Experiencing Allegations Hotline for a long time. Susan's statement and trauma weren't new. She had heard the same pleas before. "How are you doing Susan? Why don't you tell me about it? I'm hear to listen." Sally offered.

"I feel so cheated. I feel used and left out in the cold. No one will talk to me. We have no money to fight this thing. We don't even know what it's all about. The agency said they are sending out a police investigator. Why?"

"Why do you think?"

"I don't know. I really don't know. I can't figure it out."

"Have you been having trouble with any of the children? Any of the neighbors? Your relatives?" Sally asked. Piece by piece Sally dug out answers from Susan. "What is the worst that can happen? Let's talk about it. Let's face it now, Susan. What if you lose your license? What were your future plans? How will your life be affected?" Within Susan

lay answers to her future— with or without her child care license. Together she and Sally brainstormed possibilities. Armed with a vision for either outcome the upcoming investigation was not as haunting.

Sally, age 54, made it through. She lost her license. She lost the twenty acre farm she and her husband had built to retire and parent troubled minority children in. She changed her vision. She is now attending the university to become a psychologist and plans on helping the same children she was previously providing care for. She invested in education, instead of a legal battle.

Someday, young sexually abused Native American women will benefit from her wisdom.

Summary

Reports of suspected maltreatment of children have risen to 2.5 to 2.7 million annually. Foster and adoptive families receive allegations more often than custodial families. These statistics are misleading because of the types of children these famililes care for and the additional classifications of neglect or maltreatment. Surrogate care providers are particularly vulnerable to charges from both the children they care for and the parents who have been denied custody or access to their children. Sometimes a child or even a parent, dealing with loss, anger, and helplessness, aims hostility toward the care provider and alleges maltreatment in an effort to get revenge or attempt to reunify the family.

Being responsible for the care of other people's children is not easy. The structure of the system itself sets the stage for feelings of jealousy and competitiveness. Well-meaning individuals can misinterpret children's reactions or behaviors which may have been established in previous homes, copied from peers, or seen on television. Social workers, medical professionals, or clergy fearing legal actions can draw conclusions without substantial evidence. Care providers may be providing care for extremely difficult children without the proper training in dealing with hard-to-handle behaviors. An approved behavior/discipline plan may not be in place and the care provider may be stretched. Additionally, the Data Privacy Act forbids disclosure to others of why a child may be behaving in a bizarre way. The final reality is that the care provided may be abusive or neglectful, and the child needs to be removed from the provider home.

Social service agencies and provider associations are concerned about the devastating effects allegations have on the children and the providers who care for them. If a child is abused or neglected while under agency legal custody, the agency and child welfare workers face considerable legal liability. Careful selection, training, supervision, and support of foster and pre-adoptive care providers is necessary to provide additional security for children in need of professional public parenting.

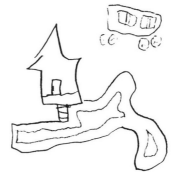

Foster care providers or adoptive parents need to understand their role in parenting foster or adoptive children. Since each child in their care may have a different combination of legal custody realities, legal responsibilities will vary from child to child when an allegation is made. *(See Chapter 2)*

Child welfare practitioners, agencies, foster care providers, and foster care provider organizations need to find ways to ease the effects of child maltreatment report response and still protect children.

After four years of serving time, Alicia's father was free and available to take over the responsibility of parenting Alicia.

Acting responsibly, the county required parenting classes and visitations prior to immediate return.

Understandably, Alicia's father wanted Alicia, now. She was a little girl he had dreamed of parenting. He was a stranger to his own daughter.

Mysteriously, Alicia's father's sister called the county and offered to care for Alicia and get her out of the foster care system—the same sister who had refused contact with the small child for the past four years.

Child protection determined it best to begin visitation with Alicia's aunt.

"Have fun, Honey. See you in two days," Maria shouted as she waved goodbye to Alicia on her first visit to her aunt's house.

Two weeks later Alicia had still not returned. Foster care placement was cancelled. The case closed. Maria's job as "numma" was over.

She called Alicia to see how she was.

"Numma, you said I would only be here two days. I want to come back home. I want to come back home now," Alicia said.

"Honey, a decision has been made and you will be living with your auntie until you can live forever with your very own daddy."

"But, Numma, aren't you even gonna fight for me?" begged Alicia.

"I'm too old to fight with my fists, Honey."

"No Numma, you are always fighting for people. You are always fighting for poor people. Can't you go to a meeting for me like you do for them, Numma?" Alicia pleaded.

Silence.

"Numma, is something wrong? Are you okay?" asked Alicia.

"Oh yeah, Honey, I'm okay. Numma's going to go find a meeting."

"Oh Numma, I knew you really love me."

Are we protecting the children we serve or are we protecting the system and harming the children to whom we have pledged do no harm?

—author—

References

Armstrong, Louise. 1989. *Solomon Says, A Speakout on Foster Care.* New York: Pocket Books.

Besharov, Douglas. 1991. *Child Abuse and Neglect Reporting and Investigation: Policy Guidelines for Decision Making. Assessing Child Maltreatment Reports The Problem of False Allegations.* New York: Haworth Press.

Besharov, Douglas. 1991. *Recognizing Child Abuse: A Guide for the Concerned.* New York: The Free Press.

Burch, G. and Mohr, V. 1979. *Positive Parenting: A Solution for Potential Abusing Parents.* Nebraska: University of Nebraska, Series MSS.

Carbino, Rose Marie. 1991. *Child Abuse and Neglect Reports in Foster Care. The Issue for Foster Families of False Allegations.* In M. Robin (Ed.) Assessing Childr Maltreatment Reports. The Problem of False Allegations. 1991. New York: Haworth Press.

Daro, D. 1988. *Confronting Child Abuse.* New York: Free Press.

Herbruck, Christin Comstock. 1979. *Breaking the Cycle of Child Abuse.* Minnesota: Winston Press, Inc.

Kempe, C.H. and Helfer, R.C. 1980. *The Battered Child, 3rd Edition.* Chicago: University of Chicago Press.

Mantell, David M. October 1988. *Clarifying Erroneous Child Sexual Abuse Allegations.* Connecticut: American Orthopsychiatric Association, Inc. For reprints: David M. Mantell, PhD., 16 Russell St., New Britain, CT. 06052.

McAdams, Phyllis. 1975. *The Parent In The Shadows, Our Foster Child's Natural Parents.* New York: Child Welfare League of America.

McFadden, Emily Jean. 1984. *Preventing Abuse in Foster Care.* Michigan: Eastern Michigan University.

Mead, James. J. and Balch, Glenn M. 1987. *Child Abuse and the Church A New Mission.* California: HDL Publishing Company.

Pelton, L. 1989. *For Reasons of Poverty.* New York: Praeger.

Robin, Michael. 1991. *Assessing Child Maltreatment Reports. The Problem of False Allegations.* New York: Haworth Press.

Wakefield, Hollida and Underwager, Ralph. 1988. *Accusations of Child Sexual Abuse.* Charles C. Thomas Publisher .

Young, Mary de. October 1986. *A Conceptual Model for Judging the Truthfulness of a Young Child's Allegation of Sexual Abuse.* Michigan: American Orthopsychiatric Association, Inc. For reprints: Mary de Young, 2226 Saginaw Road. S.E., Grand Rapids, Michigan 49506.

Chapter 5

You Couldn't Mean Me?

*Families and the foster care system both suffer
from false allegations and the investigation
process that follows.*

Two years ago, I didn't believe allegations happened. Perhaps most other Americans who care for children still don't believe it. In writing this book, I have been astounded at the number of people who have responded to an allegation with the incredulous *"You couldn't mean me?"* I thank Judy and Lee for sharing their story in this chapter.

> *The evening began with laughter and pats on the back from our director and other foster parents we had known and with whom we had shared classes, tears, and experiences for years. In front of our peers we received the annual award, "For Years of Caring," a beautiful crystal box. Jokingly, the director said the box was probably a good place to store belly button fuzz. It was a wonderful banquet and we went home smiling.*
>
> *Of course, the kids immediately rallied around us to see what we had received. Relaxing in his favorite recliner with his dress shirt unbuttoned, Lee announced we'd received a beautiful "belly button fuzz box." The kids were amazed that there might be such a thing, but Lee assured them it was true. He looked down at his belly button and said, "See!" A young adult female, who had been in our care for many years, pulled the piece of lint from Lee's belly button and placed it in the beautiful crystal box, proving that it was ex-actly what Lee had said, a belly button fuzz box.*
>
> *Several days later our worker called. She needed to talk to us and also with our foster daughter. It was an allegation. Someone had called the county about the belly button lint. Could we tell her about it?*
>
> *Our agency called DHS. No action was taken. The danger of a traumatic in-vestigation had passed. So we thought.*
>
> ***And then began the "gift" that keeps on giving—allegations, rumors, and agency gossip.***

In the past, families unfairly hit with allegations simply hid the trouble. Embarrassed and isolated, they buried their experience and went on with their lives, leaving foster parenting and the children they cared for behind them. But as more and more families found themselves in the dark and on the defensive, support organizations brought these families together.

None of us expects our house to burn down, and we cross our fingers we won't be burglarized. But we don't trust luck or providence in these matters—however limited we think these risks are. Sensible people take precautions against even the most unlikely possibilities. While not expecting allegations of abuse to children to be made against them, it is vitally important that foster parents acknowledge the possibility.

Only then may they build safeguards into their fostering practice which will help minimize the inevitable trauma which accompanies such accusations.

Gordon Evans, National Foster Parent Association

How can they believe we could hurt a child? We've been caring for children for years without an incident.

Twelve-year veteran foster parent

Families began to realize that they could depend on one another for support and empathy. They saw that their feelings and experiences had been repeated in family after family, sometimes with fatal results. In one Minnesota case, an allegation was such a shock that it triggered an asthma attack which led to death.

Who cares for the care providers?

Social service agencies that provide support to care providers reduce stress and allow care providers to support and nurture fragile children. When an allegation occurs, however, these very agencies are suddenly caught between legal requirements and emotional relationships.

Care providers facing allegations feel shocked, isolated, and stigmatized. The agency feels a sense of urgency—a need to jump start a seemingly lethargic system. This sense of urgency comes as a surprise to the family, and to refocus under the pressure is difficult.

For years, many child abuse cases went unnoticed and unreported. In 1972, there were 610,000 cases of child abuse reported in the United States. In 1985, that number had mushroomed to 1.7 million, and by 1990, 2.5 million reports were lodged. Yet, more than 65 percent of all reports were unsubstantiated. In other words, each year more than one million families may face investigations of false reports. Reputations are tarnished and privacy is invaded while tens of thousands of children are removed from caring homes. Unsubstantiated reports are deeply unfair to innocent parents and harmful to children.

*Some child protective specialists defend the current high rates of unsubstantiated reports on the grounds that over-reporting is necessary to identify children in danger. To an extent, of course, they are correct. But the current magnitude of reports goes beyond anything reasonably needed. These reports have created a flood that threatens to innundate the limited resources of child protection. Forced to allocate a substantial portion of their limited resources to unfounded reports, child protection agencies are increasingly unable to respond promptly and effectively when children **are** in serious danger. Caseloads per social worker across the nation have increased greatly in size during the last decade. Only the most severely affected children may make it into out-of-home care, in other cases children are wrongly pulled due to inadequate time and training in investigative work. Sometimes child protection workers wrongly determine a report is unfounded, and sometimes they even declare a report unfounded as a means of casework control. However, the great bulk of today's reports involve situations that do not amount to child maltreatment, or for which there is "no credible evidence"—the legal test for determining the validity of a report.* (Spiegel and Besharov 1986)

When care providers face allegation, they stand alone. A report against a licensed home means crisis, and crisis requires immediate attention. In the overloaded system of child welfare, that reaction is often quarantine of the licensed home.

Licensed providers suspected of child maltreatment are considered guilty until proven innocent. The provider is responsible for proving his or her own innocence, often without adequate knowledge or tools, and isolated from the professions who can help. Even when innocence is proved, the community often thinks the foster parents must be guilty or the social service agency would not have taken the child/children away. Many times social services has only a partial perspective of the situation. And most times the community hears only the gossip or the media's painted picture.

If ever a situation arises in which concerns of the foster child differ from the foster family, the child's concerns will prevail. This is a very difficult concept for many foster families to accept. It is also a great source of pain when an allegation takes place. (O'Neill 1991)

Judy and Lee's nightmare had only just begun . . .

How could belly button lint cause such a chain reaction and years of false rumors?

Not long after the first allegation, we received a call and another visit from our worker with more questions.

Rumors were flying. One was I have severe headaches and Lee carries me to bed. Lee could not carry me to our room. I am no small woman, and our bedroom is up two flights of stairs.

Another was that Lee's children were in prison in California. Lee's children live in Minnesota and are not in jail. Their status could be easily verified, and in fact, they could be easily interviewed. We did, however, have a previous foster daughter who is presently in prison in California.

I wanted someone to say, "Hey wait a minute! I've known these people for a long time. I've seen the work they've done with tough kids. I can't believe this is true. Something is not right here."

Judy

Why is the agency in such a difficult position?
How are care providers affected?

Rosemarie Carbino has studied the dynamics of social service agency reactions to reports of child maltreatment. She states that agencies who provide child protective services are mandated by law to assess and investigate child abuse/neglect reports and may be overloaded by the demands of difficult cases. She notes there is a lack of state level policy on how to respond to the unique situation of abuse reports in family foster care and that agencies often lack policy on how to handle abuse reports involving their own foster families. All child-placing agencies, public and voluntary, are concerned about potential legal liability for maltreatment of children in their care. (Carbino 1989)

Care providers and the system respond to allegations differently

The agency's response is different from the care provider family's. The system responds to a combination of legal requirements, agency policies, and agency concern for all four systems directly involved in foster care services: child(ren), agency, foster family, natural family.

The Agency Must be Concerned for All Four Systems Directly Involved in Foster Care Services

CHILDREN	NATURAL FAMILY	AGENCY	FOSTER FAMILY

Social workers often are not trained to look at the big picture, but to think compartmentally as issues arise.

Foster families are *providers of service* and not viewed as **families in need of services.** When a service provider is reported for abuse or neglect, some staff may feel that the family deserves whatever trauma it faces. Workers may be unaware of the trauma the report causes the family and feel incapable of easing it because of the requirements of child protection service law, potential criminal investigation procedures, agency policies, data privacy, and concern for risk of legal liability.

When a provider family receives an allegation, it is common for social workers to feel:

— Caught between anger toward the family for potential harm to a child and compassion for the family as stressed and troubled.

— Embarrassed about community perception of their foster homes.

— Guilty about their selection, training, and support services or about overloading the foster home beyond its capacity to deal with additional foster children.

— Ambivalence to the needs of the reported foster family.

Providers, on the other hand, see allegations as a very personal assault. Foster parents provide their homes and hearts as a service to vulnerable adults and children. Their office is their home. Their family is their business. Many pieces of the care provider's life are directly affected. There is no file folder to shut or office door to lock. *They are home. They are the files.*

And the rumors continued to fly . . .

"Two pregnant foster daughters lived in our home. These two suspicious pregnancies "red flagged" our already allegated home and put my husband under scrutiny. It didn't matter that one arrived pregnant and the other had a serious relationship with her boyfriend."

"How did this happen? Didn't you supervise?"

"Each issue could logically be explained if we were only given a real chance to explain. This was incredible. I wanted to deny the experiences. I wanted to believe it wasn't truly happening. Maybe this would go away if I chose not to deal with it!"

MSW = Master Social Work

Because of differences in perspective, both sides are set up to miscommunicate.

Requirements	Social Services' Requirements and Knowledge	Care Provider's Perception of Situation
Mandate to investigate every report.	*Objective and trained investigator, often from a neighboring county. Agency staff may not know the person conducting the investigative interviews— may not always monitor progress.*	*Report is taken seriously, and they will be dealt with by strangers who know nothing about them. They feel they are being judged without being given a chance. Foster parent questions training and bias of investigators.*
Mandate to protect the confidentiality of the reporter.	*Agency staff know this is required by law to help ensure that child abuse will be reported; they must refuse to tell foster care providers who made the report. Inter-agency communication and gossip is allowed.*	*Foster parents are shocked that they cannot face their accuser and may not be told specifically of what they are accused. They feel powerless. They are frustrated that agency staff know more about the situation and what is being investigated than they do.*
Need to involve community services.	*Agency staff must decide reasonably quickly about the safety of the foster child and others; they may or may not feel guided by agency policy. There may be a perceived need and/or agency requirement to contact the school system and hold immediate interviews without the care provider's knowledge.*	*The foster care providers experience this as an abrupt action by the agency which results in lasting embarrassment and stigma. They feel betrayed by the social workers in whom they have been taught to confide.*
Agency workers may be prohibited from communicating with the foster family.	*Agency staff may not be directly involved in investigation and thus unaware of what is going on. Concerned social workers may be prohibited from speaking with the family.*	*Foster parents want to tell their side. It is uncomfortable to be prohibited from working with the agency. Foster parents begin to distrust the social worker. They want the case acted upon and over with immediately. Once they experience the loss of the working relationships with staff, they lose trust and self-esteem.*
Delay or lack of notification of results.	*Multiple demands require workers to set priorities on their activities and delay action in non-urgent situations.*	*A few hours, not to mention weeks, of "not knowing" seems like forever to foster families. Friends and family are aware the children are gone and ask why.*

The above chart has been adapted from Carbino, Rosemarie (1989). *Child Welfare Issues and How Social Services System Responds to Allegations of Foster Home Abuse/Neglect. Putting Child Welfare Back into Child Protection* in J. Sprouse (Ed.) *Allegations of Abuse in Family Foster Care. An Examination of the Impact on Foster Families* King George, Virginia: American Foster Care Resources, Inc, 27-42.

Write to: *American Foster Care Resources, Inc. PO Box 271, King George, VA 22485 for more information on the Defensive Parenting Training Program.*

What are common feelings of care providers facing allegations?

The foster family is unprepared for the report. Foster care providers generally see themselves as child advocates. Whatever knowledge they have of child abuse laws and procedures has always seemed applicable to "someone else," notably the abusive adults from whom the child was originally removed.

Licensed care providers initially feel that the agency will not treat them as potential child abusers because:

— They have had long years of experience with the agency and many foster children;

— They are doing a good job with the kids they have in their home;

— Their patterns of handling children have continued for a long time with little or no previous feedback from social workers that these might be inappropriate;

— Staff communications to them over time have indicated their value as a foster family.

"Survivor" care providers who have been through an allegation and investigation process share the same feelings:

Alienation	Disbelief	Humiliation	Shock
Anger	Doubt	Indignation	Sorrow
Anxiety	Embarrassment	Isolation	Stigma
Betrayal	Frustration	Overwhelmed	Trauma
Bitterness	Fear	Powerlessness	Tenseness
Confusion	Grief	Rejection	Vulnerability
Defensiveness	Helplessness	Sadness	Victimization
Denial	Hopelessness	Shame	Worry

A common circular pattern of emotions begins for foster care providers. These feelings continue to circulate as the investigation process continues. Once the investigation and resolution are over, the feelings dissipate into acceptance or bitterness.

The diagram below illustrates an emotional cycle of an individual facing allegation and investigation.

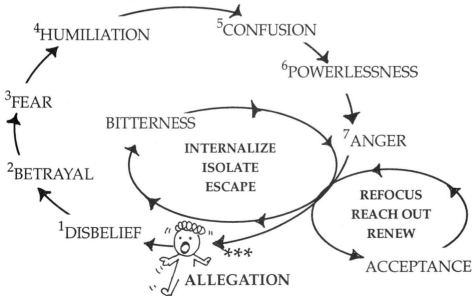

The falsely accused not only face the "law," they also face a powerful social attitude that casts them as "guilty" before the facts are even known.
(Spiegel 1986)

If the parents are supported after the allegation is made and throughout the investigation process, they will be better able to look after children in their care.

The typical pattern of emotions a care provider accused of maltreatment experiences:

1. **DISBELIEF.** Care providers ask, *"How could this really be happening to me?"* The optimistic outlook on life needed to be a good care provider hardly prepares them for an allegation of child maltreatment. Even professional care providers who have had multiple allegations still believe an allegation will never happen again and are shocked when another call comes and children are removed.

2. **BETRAYAL.** Care providers have good reason to feel betrayed. If the allegation is false, the care provider may have been misrepresented to the agency. The children in their care may have been unnecessarily removed , and neighbors may be questioning what is happening. The provider's major support, the social worker, changed role fromadvocate to adversary. Worse yet, the provider may not know what the allegation is.

3. **FEAR.** The unknown is frightening. Providers begin to think the worst when they don't know what the accusation is or what procedures are to be followed. If it wasn't *"something really bad,"* they wouldn't be experiencing this. What is the worst thing that can happen? How does social services handle allegations?

4. **HUMILIATION.** Being accused of child maltreatment causes feelings of inadequacy, shame, loss of self-respect, and loss of self-esteem, even if the report is false. The isolated nature of foster parenting compounds these feelings. In addition, the community may be forming its own opinions, regardless of the realities, and this may have long-lasting effects on the life of the accused.

5. **CONFUSION.** Providers facing allegations are immediately and without warning thrown into an outcast situation. They ask themselves,*"Why are things like they are? Why did it happen? What did the social worker mean when he said ——? Does this happen to other people? What happens next?"* It is hard to find safe caring others with whom the care provider can freely discuss the situation. Knowing what to say and when to share information and with whom can be tricky.

6. **POWERLESSNESS.** Feelings of impotence, anxiety, and uncertainty clutch at the care provider family during this time. The reactions of social services are unpredictable, and from hour to hour the situation may change. Decisions are made without input from the care provider. The children may be removed suddenly without the family being told why. The investigative process may take weeks, months, and sometimes years to resolve. Everything seems to move quickly and slowly all at the same time. The foster parent is on an out-of-control merry-go-round and can't get off.

7. **ANGER.** Anger is normal. *The word anger comes from a Middle English word meaning grief. This seems appropriate; think of how unhappy we feel before, during and after an argument. Rather than deal appropriately with our angry feelings, we often choke them off or stuff them. Anger is (almost) universal. Everyone gets angry; at least, everyone who's normal. (Wilhite 1993)*

An allegation is overwhelming. Many emotions flood the care provider. Like a seacoast battered by waves, the accused person and individuals directly involved with the allegation are weathered down.

One of the most helpful training classes my husband and I have taken is *Understanding and Dealing with Anger* by Robert Wilhite, author of *"The Family Game of Anger."* This workshop looks at the reality of anger, society's acceptance of anger, our personal responses, and how they vary from person-to-person and between family systems.

Wilhite takes the following positions:

1. **Anger is (almost) universal.** *Everyone feels anger and gets angry; at least, everyone who's normal.*

2. **Anger is an appropriate emotion.** *There is nothing wrong with angry feelings. It's how we display those feelings and deal with them that often becomes a problem.*

3. **Anger does not exist in an emotional vacuun.** *Behind the anger is another emotion such as hurt, sadness, or disappointment.*

4. **Anger is expressed in many ways and for many purposes.** *Anger feels different to you than it feels to someone else.*

5. **Anger responses are learned.** *Anger may be a primary emotion, but the way we handle it is modeled on someone else's behavior.*

6. **Anger responses can be altered.** *We may not believe it at first, but we can change the way we respond to our anger.*

Expressions of anger vary greatly among individuals and run the gamut from:
> **Aggressive** *"letting it out"*—fist pounding, yelling, and screaming
> **Productive** *"not taking it any more and respectfully doing something about it"*
> **Depressive** *"keeping it in"*—silence, avoidance, and standoff.

The anger you feel is real when you are involved in an allegation. Your responses to this normal feeling, however, can wreak havoc with the future of your life and the lives of family members. This allegation can negatively or positively affect generations of children.

The initial seven feelings will continue to recycle for some time and will differ for each person. Once the anger stage is reached, three options are available:

1. **BITTERNESS over the experience.** Most care providers go through a couple of cycles of bitterness before choosing a path of acceptance. Bitterness happens when providers refuse to deal effectively with a situation. By internalizing and isolating themselves, providers repress feelings. If feelings are internalized, they can be expanded and magnified. The problem with repressed feelings is that they usually cannot stay repressed forever. Eventually they seep out. For most care providers who remain in the bitterness cycle, personal escape means getting out of the system and getting on with their lives.

2. **RECYCLE the experience of feelings again.** People who remain in the recycling phase continue to go around in circles, feeling the same feelings over again at the same or greater intensity as they first experienced them. There is no growth, only reliving and reprocessing.

3. **ACCEPTANCE of the experience.** Eventually two things become apparent:
   (1) *Recycling the situation does not allow additional resolution or growth; and*
   (2) *bitterness increases negative feelings, which can become dangerous to health and well-being.*
   Neither option provides the tools necessary to stimulate healthy growth. Acceptance is different— it feels good. There is a peace in acceptance. The first cycle of acceptance begins to heal hurtful feelings. Acceptance encourages a person to reach out for help from others. It allows for refocusing on life and gaining a new perspective on the situation. *Acceptance fosters renewal, the courage to pick up the pieces and go on. It allows for a new beginning.*

"Months passed and finally all of the children's workers, all of the adoption workers, their supervisor, our licensing worker and her supervisor, plus a representative from our state foster parent association arrived at our agency for a meeting. Maybe this would end!

It was decided that a person from another county doing our adoption home study would investigate the allegations.

Who suffers from a foster home allegation?

Foster and adoptive parents are involved in a remarkably complex system. Many people are directly and indirectly affected when an allegation is lodged against a provider family.

The pertinent child suffers. It doesn't matter if the allegation is true. This child has already experienced compounded losses and probably abuse or neglect in the past. Regardless of the allegation, this child will experience a variety of feelings and a lot of uncertainty about the future. The potential for separation from the present foster family can cause unresolved past life experiences to resurface.

The other foster children in the home suffer. All foster children are in the insecure position of having no permanent residence. Depending on the legal status of the child, the child may face an unprepared move. In addition, the child may be questioning the allegation.

The preadoptive placement child suffers. Children in preadoptive care are legally wards of the state. Although additional discretion may be used in immediately removing these children, they are likely to be removed from their prospective adoptive homes upon receipt of allegation or initiation of investigation. The preadoptive child, finally feeling secure with a permanent home again, faces the uncertainty of a potential move.

Adopted children suffer. Adopted children, especially children who have been adopted at older ages, may worry about losing their adoptive family. Legally adopted children are considered permanent children in the foster home and are removed only in extreme cases.

Biological children suffer. Biological children may mirror the feelings of parents during an allegation. Feelings of betrayal, anger, confusion, bitterness, and disbelief are all common. Biological children are normally not removed when children in out-of-home care are, since their care is not directly linked to licensing laws and they are not the responsibility of agencies or the state.

The accused care provider suffers. Providers who have been wrongfully accused of maltreating a child suffer the stigma of being a suspected child molester. To a kind and caring adult, this is a tragedy.

The significant other suffers. The significant other may be torn by the dynamics of the investigation and by contradictions in the testimony of social services and the accused. Choosing to believe one side or the other can be very stressful and confusing. Information is often conflicting, emotions run high, and the outcome of the investigation appears to be in the hands of people who, until the allegation, were virtual strangers.

The care provider family system suffers. Care providers wonder why superhuman efforts are made to avoid removal of children from their primary homes, while the removal of children from a provider home remains standard practice. They wonder why foster children don't remain in the foster home pending the outcome of the investigation because continuity of care is so vital to a child's mental health.

Social services systems and programs suffer. Foster care is an underfunded, unappreciated, and misunderstood government function. Yet, it is highly visible in the community. In the absence of professional public relations, foster care is often judged exclusively on its "reported" performance. The tragic fact is that press reports generally overlook the fact that social services functions admirably considering such constraints as funding, the complexity of problems, and the availability of staff.

What are special issues co-parenting foster care providers face?

The investigation places enormous stress on the best of relationships. In high stress situations, emotions run high and partners feel the need to unload on each other. Maintaining respect and honesty is crucial.

When a report is filed and the investigation started, the non-accused spouse may mistrust or be angry with the alleged perpetrator. These feelings can lead to resentment, criticism, sarcasm, withdrawal, and anger. Open communication is crucial. No one is a perfect parent all the time. Both quality and quantity communication is important. Planning additional time with family members, especially a significant other, is helpful in conveying support. Sharing a bowl of popcorn, a good book, a walk, or a video with each other can provide personal relaxation time together at very little cost.

Our love remains constant through good times and bad. Each night before we sleep we tell each other, "I love you." We say it and we mean it. We settle our differences or lay them aside to discuss when we have more accurate information or time. My husband and I don't bury our love by burying our feelings.

Teamwork vs. taking sides:

A good team is not made up of identical players. It utilizes differences to achieve success. Becoming a team versus taking sides is an important issue when dealing with allegation. Many times care providers don't agree on how to handle an allegation. One person may want to quit, and one may want to fight. They disagree because each thinks, "I'm right and you're wrong." Disagreement is more likely because of different perspectives. Utilization of differences builds strong marriages and strong families.

More can be accomplished faster operating as a team. Each team member has pieces the others may need. During an allegation, differences can become strengths because they allow review of alternative approaches to solving difficult issues. *"Please Understand Me, Character and Temperament Types"* by David Keirsey and Marilyn Bates (1978) is an excellent reference book in developing marriage strengths out of differences. This easy-to-read book helps to understand personality and style differences in male/female relationships.

Addressing the issue without escalating conflict:

Here's a typical example:

> *For Alice this had been a very bad day. Everything had gone wrong. The report back from the social worker didn't match what her husband had shared with her. Nothing seemed to make sense. Should she choose sides or become a team member? Which team? Would she be on her husband's or the investigator's?*
>
> *Alice needed truth. Alice tried to write ten things she found important about Allen. She was so frustrated only five ideas came to mind. "Oh well," she thought, "Five will have to do." Apprehensively she went to discuss the report with Allen. Alice began by saying, "Social services came by today and said some things I don't under-stand. I need to ask you about them, but before I do, I want to share with you why you are so important to me." Alice then shared the five things she felt made her relationship with Allen important. By hearing the value Alice placed on their relationship, Allen was more receptive in dealing with the investigation report. Alice and Allen didn't have an easy evening, but Allen knew Alice valued their relationship.*

People make mistakes.

I haven't met a perfect person yet, and I've met a lot of people!

Time continued to pass and the children got older and were not adopted. I became angry! This isn't fair to us or the children.

This time I wrote a letter asking for a meeting of all involved professionals. I believed there had to be more to this than just a questionable allegation against our family to hold up the adoption process.

What had we done to encounter such treatment from the people we had been taught to trust?

By now we had the following entourage of rumors and allegations following us:
1. *Allowing a child-in-care access to my husband's belly button*
2. *Incapacitating headaches*
3. *Potential sexual abuse against two teenage girls*

The letter activated a meeting. In our meeting we discovered there were a number of additional hidden agenda items we weren't aware of.

Everything was on the table. Maybe there would be closure!

Old issues—dealing with historical baggage:

Periods of extreme stress can unlease unresolved issues and old behavior patterns. These reactions may cause additional conflict. For example, if your family of origin employed criticism, evaluating, or dominating behavior, you may see yourself once again pulling those old ghosts out of the closet. Trained care providers know communicating in any of these ways blocks communication, creates bad feelings, and escalates problems. Utilize and appreciate the new tools you have as an adult—tools which were not available to you when you were younger, less knowledgeable, and more vulnerable. These new tools are very helpful when dealing with difficult situations and confronting those old ghosts. ***Don't collect old injuries, grievances, and injustices.***

Individuals who have very close relationships have extreme power to edify or to injure. A significant other is vulnerable to unsolicited expressions of unresolved feelings. Support means each person tempers his or her behavior with care, honesty, and kindness. ***Don't hit below the belt by bringing up past mistakes or throwing around personal information shared in trust.***

What are special issues for single foster care providers?

Children seem to have a sixth sense about knowing when parents are under stress. Most children test the limits of the adult in authority, and many children increase the testing when times get tough. The care provider may wonder why, when so much is happening, children aren't cooperating and making life easier. Children need to know just how far their boundaries can be extended, or just how strong the adult in authority is. Children need continuity during these stressful times and it is crucial for the single parent to decide how to react to various child behaviors and then follow through. Clear rules and expectations, along with open and honest communication, help children cope and work with, rather than against, their parent. ***Make a list of rules and expectations, post it, and stick with the program.***

Single foster parents are immediately and completely isolated when an allegation is made against them. Potentially shut off from the agency, with no significant other in the program to talk to, single care providers are in a very difficult position. Data privacy laws may prohibit discussing details with supportive others. ***Single care providers do not need to "do it all alone."*** They have a right to know what information can be shared and to seek out supportive adults from family, friends, or church. Associations and government agencies may be available to provide information and support. Single care providers should reach out and ask for help. An allegation and investigation are stressful. They don't have to go through these experiences alone.

When children in care are removed because of an allegation, unresolved issues of grief or anger may resurface for the single parent. If the allegation is made by a past significant other, feelings of bitterness, resentment, and anger may compound unresolved feelings left from divorce, loss, or separation.

Single care providers may be financially devastated because of immediate loss of income that often occurs when an allegation is made. Some single adults' only profession is licensed out-of-home care for children or vulnerable adults. These individuals may rely exclusively on foster care monies to live. In one day they may lose the people they care about and for, their job, their reputation, and their income. Initially they may have no other means of support and may not be emotionally equipped to go out and secure new employment. Their level of housing often depends on the number of people they care for. In a short time, they can lose that, too.

Several months passed, and we thought we had seen the end of the absurdity of rumors and allegations.

The next call came from one of our foster children's social workers.

Our teenage mother of two children (ages one year and three weeks) had just turned eighteen. We were told that she had seven days to find a new place to live on her own. She was no longer considered a foster child. We were no longer her foster parents. The case was closed.

The journey of independence is traumatic for most teens. To expect a single mother with a three-week-old baby to make that transition is unfair.

How to deal with an allegation

Immediate reactions may be to flee, fight, or freeze.

— **FLEE** includes isolation and attempted escape from the feelings you cannot express or don't dare to feel. It also includes using mood-altering chemicals to escape intense feelings. This issue is not going away by ignoring it. Flight is not healthy unless you are using it as temporary respite and reprieve—without the use of drugs or alcohol.

— **FIGHT** often results in passive-aggressive acts, externally directed aggression, and a series of constant power struggles. You can easily dig yourself into a hole by attempting to protect yourself immediately and your rights. Don't volunteer information without understanding the rules of the game you are playing. Statements made under the shock of an allegation or during a time of high emotions may be extremely harmful.

— **FREEZE** is characterized by the lack of problem-solving skills. Fear becomes the motivating factor, and the problem gets pushed inward and ignored. Often negative self-talk accompanies a freeze and keeps you immobile. Unreasonable fears surface and you feel helpless. Call your local provider association. Get support immediately.

Although you need to understand the immediate reactions of flight, fight, or freeze, you do not need to use these unhelpful responses. Handling an allegation in any of these ways does not work.

Positive steps a care provider accused of maltreatment can take: (Turner 1992)

1. **DOCUMENT**

    Start a notebook immediately and write everything you are told about the process. Set up a special place for all the information to accumulate. Multi-colored pocket folders cost only thirty cents each and can be labeled to help you quickly file and find information. Documentation is never rude or out of place. Ask to have names, dates, and facts repeated and spelled so you can write them down. Collect and document evidence. Reconstruct a summary as best you can from memory. Use your checkbook, appointment calendar, travel log, menus, telephone notes, and school data to build your data source. Does a pattern emerge?

    Use only evidence that applies to the case. Make this evidence available to investigators, but do not allow your written papers to be taken from you without keeping a copy. Have the investigators accompany you to a copy machine if necessary. Keep anything given to you by officials. Do not trust anything to memory during this stressful process. Make lists to help you remember what you need to do.

    Keep a notebook by the phone to record the exact time a call is made. Secure the name of every person you talk to and write down quotes of key sentences. Follow up on all required phone calls or written notices in a timely manner. Ask for written information from investigators and officials whenever possible. Do not be afraid to take notes or tape record interviews. Write a brief report immediately after each interview. It may help to send a copy of your report to the investigative team.

2. **APPROPRIATE BEHAVIOR**

    Assume you can work your way through this if you just keep taking one step at a time. Don't let yourself be overwhelmed. Develop a very short outline of the situation. Use nonemotional words. Write down points you need covered. Cooperate in giving required information to inves-

---

We have not been lulled into the reality that allegations will never, ever happen again. They probably will. We have no idea what they will be for or when they will occur.

Our teenage foster daughter is now living in her own apartment with her two small children. Recently, another sibling also began requiring her care. She is struggling. She is strong, and we believe she will make it.

Meanwhile, Lee and I care for our rainbow family. Grandpa lives with us and enjoys the commotion. The three children we are hoping to adopt are still waiting.

Our belly button lint box sits in the sunshine on the shelf casting dancing colors on the wall. Its gold plaque glistens as it proclaims,

"For Years Of Caring."

tigators, or be prepared to forfeit your license. The role of the investigator is to determine if maltreatment occurred in your facility, not to measure overall quality of your program. Keep cool—speak calmly and firmly. Be honest and factual with investigators and officials. Be assertive, courageous, stubborn, and curious without being argumentative.

If you don't know, ask what questions are appropriate to ask. Avoid trying to "educate" and antagonize social services or law enforcement officials. Make your point and then STOP TALKING. Don't ramble or volunteer information. If your listener doesn't seem to get the point, back up and state it in a different way. Be confident that you know what you are talking about. Be assertive when asking for information regarding the process and procedures as the investigation progresses. It is your right to know.

Be respectful and deal with business in a businesslike way. Foster parenting is your profession, and you are a professional. When investigators and social service workers come into your home unannounced, try to reframe your thinking from invasion of the very personal space of your home toward being audited as a business. This refocus may allow you to understand that social services is doing its job—business to business.

Find support resources, both personal and professional, to help you acknowledge and deal with the stress of this process. Peer support is possible even with the most controversial problem—find another provider. Vent anger, frustration, and fear to those support persons—not to the investigator or social services. Tell your side of the story without vindictiveness. Do not berate your tormentors. Resist the urge to gossip. With different people there will be different parts of the situation that foster understanding. Some people may be willing to take sides with you in a concrete way—but do not push someone to do this. Some will offer you personal and emotional support without getting deeply involved in the issue. Others may offer ethical and intellecual support without even knowing or liking you. Take each kind of support with appreciation. Keep a card file of these individuals—a brief thank you note at a later date is always courteous.

Be honest with birth parents and professionals about the nature of the allegation; give your side of the story without breaching confidentiality or interfering with the investigation. Respect the birth parents' natural curiosity. They need to know that your environment is safe, reliable, and nurturing. Never tell birth parents about other children in care—only about yourself and your program. Be consistent. Don't tell different bits to different people. If the birth parents don't know, make a plan to tell them. Even if you don't have to use it, it is better to be prepared. Inform birth parents that they have a right to talk to you and each other during the investigation. The birth parents can request information from the agency regarding protocols and timetables. They can require their presence or the presence of another trusted adult or a videotape when their children are interviewed.

Be patient. Have faith in the system. If you are innocent, this fact will eventually surface. It is critical not to make careless and emotional statements during the investigation process. The process may take a minimum of six months to one year if there is a finding of maltreatment and a resulting licensing action. If there is no finding, it may still take a minimum of six weeks to two months, and possibly more than a year.

Do not fear calling investigators to ask about the standing of your case.

3. RESEARCH

You can educate yourself by searching out information. You can maintain your privacy when seeking help through reading materials or confidential services. The rules of the process are not the same as the rules of the judicial or criminal justice systems. Research agency and state information and stay in touch with the system. The state or county law library can provide copies of the current state statutes and rules at nominal copying costs.

Meet with people—association members, law enforcement, social workers, professionals—to learn more about how your particular system operates. Your agency can provide a list of its procedures. Become aware of data privacy laws which affect what information you can obtain from your file with child protection. Request copies of all obtainable information and continue to request information as your case progresses. Keep this data organized for quick reference.

Attend classes with other care providers to exchange information. Ask other providers who they use for legal information, mental health information, and social service information.

4. FIGHT, IF YOU'RE RIGHT

Hire legal counsel. Hiring qualified legal counsel is costly, but having no legal representation may cost more. You may want to invest a minimum amount in legal counsel just to get a better handle on your rights, what has happened to others, and how others have handled allegations. *(See Chapter 7.)*

Don't be afraid to appeal. A license is a privilege, not an automatic right. Call the local care provider association and find out what strategies for appeal have worked best in your county or state. Check liability insurance to see if legal fees are covered. If there is a finding of maltreatment or neglect against you or anyone in your facility, seek legal counsel right away (if not before). Provide your attorney with all the available documentation, ask to have both the child protection and licensing appeal processes double-checked to verify information. *(See Chapter 7.)*

Request a waiver. If you experience a negative licensing action, you may write to your appropriate state licensing department and ask for a review of the case and a waiver of the licensing action. The time limitations for an appeal can be as little as ten days, and depending on your situation, this may be too little time to make an appeal.

What can foster families expect to happen?

Licensed care providers are in a unique position when they are reported for child maltreatment. If the agency policy is to prohibit workers from contact with families, phone calls may not be returned and letters may not be answered. Families feel powerless and vulnerable. Vocabulary and system procedures for dealing with allegations are unfamiliar. Common child protection vocabulary, written to be legally neutral and clinically objective, can be easily misinterpreted. *"I can't talk to you until the investigation is completed"* may seem perfectly appropriate to social services. But the foster family may view this as a violation of personal rights. Unclear statements and mixed messages lead to wrong interpretation and miscommunication by accused families.

Unclear messages often can be cleared up by stating,
"This is my understanding of what you mean . . . Is that correct?" or
"I'm not sure I know what you mean by . . . ."

"Why was I so late? It's only a ten minute drive. Did you brainwash Lisa? Her testimony will no longer be valid." Questions. More questions. "How is our sex life? Have I ever noticed anything peculiar about my husband's behavior with the children?"

Mrs. Smith, you can go now. We will be taking your husband into our custody. I walked out the door and faced Mark and baby Nathan. The tears poured freely. Concerned for my welfare, Mark reached me quickly with his loving, strong arms.

"Darling, what's wrong?" he asked. I choked out the words, "They think you've had sex with the children and you are under arrest."

It was the last statement we said to each other. An officer arrived, Mark, now handcuffed was led down the same long hall Lisa had disappeared into. I was alone, holding baby Nathan.

"The children are safe, Mrs. Smith. They will be placed in an emergency shelter. You can go home now with your baby."

Families going through an investigation see the situation as a private problem. The paradox is that many employees in the agency may know what's happening but are prohibited from sharing. It is not uncommon for a family to hear, *"We discussed your situation in our staff meeting and determined we can't discuss the details with you."* Families are astounded that private and personal information can be shared with others—but they aren't allowed to know what was shared.

> *Feelings of unfair exposure and isolation are normal.*
> *These feelings may take years to heal.*

What do care providers need when they are reported for child abuse?

Foster care providers need to get the facts quickly when they are reported for child abuse. They need to understand agency procedures and gain access to their legal rights and the resources. Most importantly, they need access to support people who have experienced allegations and survived. Foster care providers need social services support, especially during the process of an allegation.

Foster parents need to know:

— The nature of the allegation.

— Whether or not the agency is conducting a review or an investigation.

— The agency role and responsibilities.

Foster parents need social services to:

— Return their phone calls promptly.

— Respect their knowledge and expertise.

— Be honest and follow through on promised services.

— Be appropriately concerned for the welfare of children in care.

— Support, listen, and monitor investigative procedures.

What kind of help can care providers expect from the agency?

Agencies differ greatly in the amount of help they can and will provide a family experiencing allegations. There are, however, a number of services an agency can provide to help care providers through this painful process.

The agency can obtain for the care provider:

— Copies of state laws on child abuse reports/investigations and implications.

— Written copies of agency policy and procedures used when abuse is reported.

— Differences in procedures between child protection services and the U.S. justice system.

— Copy of care providers' legal and procedural rights.

— Legal assistance policy for care providers.

— Copy of Data Privacy Act and agency staff policies.

The foster care provider must understand that written policy and actual practice are not always the same. What looks great on paper may never make it into application of the policy.

If agency policy permits, the agency can:

— Keep the care provider updated on the process and progress of the investigation.

— Allow the family to continue foster care services without disruption to the children relating to school, natural parent visits, etc.

— Provide additional family services to help the provider family cope with increased family stress.

— Keep the care provider home open with children closely monitored.

— Allow foster care providers contact with children who have been removed to allow for some continuity of care and to lessen feelings of abandonment for children.

— Provide legal representation and information throughout process and particularily for appeals of child removals, revocations of license, and court hearings. Legal representation is often too expensive for many foster families.

Why do some agencies prohibit communication between the agency and the care provider family?

Upon receipt of a report of suspected maltreatment in a licensed home, interaction between the social worker and the licensed family changes. The worker is now required by law to act on the complaint and follow formal procedures, regardless of the previous relationship with the family. This doesn't mean a worker remains blind to information gleaned from the *"normal relationship."* It does mean that the worker is not free to minimize the investigation based on personal feelings for the people involved in the allegation.

Agencies want investigators to be as objective as possible, and so they may sever communication between the family facing allegations and the internal staff. Some reasons agencies or departments don't allow foster families and social workers to continue close relationships:

— Obtain objective evidence.
— Protect staff from being emotionally torn.
— Conduct investigations in a timely manner.
— Prohibit agency staff from disclosing information that could harm the investigation.

Can't providers straighten this whole mess out by consulting with their social worker and simply talking it out?

It would seem to make sense, when the relationship between the family and the worker has been established for a long period of time for the provider to just call, sit down over a cup of coffee, and discuss the allegation. **It's not that easy!** *One of the worst things a provider can do is to have an elaborate discussion with the social worker as if the old relationship existed.* Unlike a police officer, the social worker is under no obligation to read Miranda rights. The relationship is no longer cordial, regardless of old warm feelings between each other the situations has place the relationship in an adversarial conflict position.

At the same time, because the social worker is an agent of the state, anything said to the worker pertaining to the allegations is legal evidence and can be used against the accused family. What makes an open discussion so doubly dangerous is that statements are often made out of context, or parents express fears rather than facts. When related to another agency employee by the worker, these statements may come across as a form of confession.

Another family, another story . . .

Jerry was pleased. She had found a solid and structured home for the dynamic teenage girls she was responsible for. This treatment foster home appeared able to provide the firmness and control the girls needed, while still maintaining a caring and nurturing atmosphere. Unluckily for the foster family, Jerry was transferred to another department.

The new social worker was not at all happy with the structure provided by the foster family. She felt the teenagers in care needed more freedom and were being overly controlled. The teenagers agreed. As the social worker intervened, the girls rebelled.

Allegations were made against the family and their drama began . . . same kids, same home, same structure for nine months had been appropriate . . . with the new social worker the tables were turned upside down.
Foster father 19 years

Placement breakdown can occur when surrogate parents wait too long to ask for help working with children in care. It is important when surrogate parent/ child relationships become challenging that the parent reaches out and requests:

— *Further assessment or treatment for the child.*

— *Additional support or direction for managing the child.*

— *Time off or respite care.*

— *Additional training or reading material to help work through issues.*

If you are called to a social worker's office to discuss potential abuse, there are two approaches to take.

1. If the matter is unexpected, simply state that you do not understand the allegation, ask for more information, and get out of the office without making any further statements.

2. If you have some knowledge of what happened, for example if your foster child ran away screaming, "I'm going to get you," it would not hurt you strongly to deny the matter on record and give indication why someone is setting you up.

If you are uncertain what to do, your best bet is to say nothing, according to SAFY in its Policy and Procedures Manual on Abuse Allegations. (1992)

The matter, of course, will not go away if you say nothing. It's already a problem, but you will at least avoid making statements which can be construed as admission by a worker. Your immediate next step should be to contact counsel trained in allegations and licensing procedures. Your provider association should be able to make referrals. The right legal counsel may be your safest confidant. The law provides that all statements between you and your attorney are considered confidential and cannot be revealed to anyone.

What kind of help can the provider expect from provider associations or a private agency?

Most associations have established a support system for those experiencing an investigation. Associations are limited in time and resources, but most can:

— Provide a sympathetic ear.
— Remain neutral about the validity or invalidity of the allegation.
— Provide information about the investigation process.
— Suggest possible resources for foster care providers:
  – published materials and agency policies;
  – referral to the legal system;
  – referral of legal or personal counselors.
— Provide names of "survivors" of the allegation process who can provide emotional support to care providers.

Some associations and private agencies have trained support teams that can work with families dealing with allegations. The Minnesota Foster Care Association has the Volunteer Crisis Support Team. These trained individuals are available 24 hours a day, 365 days a year to counsel and advise foster care providers experiencing crisis situations. Specialized Alternatives For Youth of America in Ohio has recently spent two years developing a policy and procedures manual for abuse allegations. Their extensive work can be used as a model for other agencies and associations. *(Addresses and phone numbers are listed in Appendix.)*

What are confidentiality laws and how do they affect foster care families?

Information about foster children is considered "private" and may be provided to an agent of the welfare system, including appropriate law enforcement personnel who are acting in investigation, prosecution, criminal or civil proceedings related to the administration of the program. Data are given also to personnel of the welfare system who require information to determine eligibility, amount of assistance, the need to provide services of additional programs, or between personnel of the welfare system working in the same program. In addition, data can be shared to administer federal funds or programs. The term "program" means all programs for which authority is vested in a component of the welfare system pursuant to statute or federal law. People potentially working in the same program may include:

- Social Workers
- Medical Personnel
- Foster Care Providers
- Judges
- Psychologists/Therapists

- Agency Employees
- Law Enforcement Personnel
- Attorneys
- Department of Human Services
- Educational Staff

Sensitive and private information regarding children in foster care should be held in confidence by all concerned. Sharing of information should be done only to benefit the child. Care providers build trust in the working partnership by maintaining confidentiality. This presumably means the care provider can communicate with medical/dental personnel who must work with a child in out-of-home care or with the personnel of the school district. In some cases other agencies and community services also may be informed. This means data cannot be divulged to neighbors, families, or others who do not provide services to the child in care. Before sharing data regarding a child in care or his/her family get authorization in writing from the child's worker. Agencies help care providers best when all information necessary is shared immediately as known with the provider. The more information care providers receive, the better they are prepared for an unexpected event.

What is a grievance procedure?

Most state agency licensing laws require agencies to develop a grievance mechanism for resolving differences between the agency and the foster family. They also require that a written statement of procedures be given to licensed families so that they know the proper grievance protocol.

An example of a grievance procedure strategy. Care providers should initially discuss disagreements with either the **caseworker** concerned or the **licensing worker**. If a solution is not found, the foster parent or agency staff may request a meeting with the **supervisor**. Supervisors are responsible for setting a time frame for action and review once a resolution has been reached. If a course of action cannot be agreed upon or if the actions taken have not led to a resolution, any of the involved individuals may request a joint meeting with the **manager of the program**. The request should address the disagreement, the actions taken, and any other pertinent information. The manager may request assistance from **other managers** in the social service division to help facilitate the meeting. If there continues to be no resolution of the disagreement, an **agency grievance panel** will be used to arrive at a final solution.

Grievance panel members include no less than five people—two members from social services (a social worker and a supervisor), two members from foster care provided through the foster care association, and one person who is neither a staff person nor a foster care provider.

— Written statements must be submitted to the panel for adequate review time.

— Data privacy questions are reviewed by the **county attorney's office** which comments on how to handle the issues of confidentiality.

— The panel must abide by current data practices and keep the material confidential. Participants presenting information will be asked to sign a release of information form so that all parties may speak openly.

— The panel must submit a written recommendation for action to the **social services director** within 30 days of the panel meeting.

One day I overheard April telling her six-year-old girlfriend. . .

"When I sleep at my grandma's house, I get to play with her boob. It's warm and soft and when you poke it, it wiggles. My mom's aren't like hers."

Great, I thought. How do I explain this? My mom has had a breast removed because of breast cancer, and she puts her prosthesis on the dresser when she goes to bed. I held my tongue. I would speak to the child's mother.

This widget could get grandma in trouble! Author

Care providers take heed:

As soon as you become aware that a child in care is making, or thinking about making, an allegation against you or a member of your family, document the facts. Then consider calling your provider association or agency to head off trouble before it starts.

But remember, anything you say can be used against you.

Are you caught between the proverbial rock and hard place?

You bet you are!

— The social services director must review the recommendations within five working days of receipt and either approve the recommendations or issue an alternative decision on the matter.

— All parties shall receive written notice on the director's decision.

— The file must be maintained for future grievance panel reference material.

Grievance procedures do not replace the appeal process for licensing action. The appeal process can be found in state statutes.

How can a care provider select a qualified counselor?

The care provider association in each state will know counselors who have worked with families in distress. Referrals from the association or from providers who have experienced allegations are valuable. If a counselor's name comes up more than once by reputable referrals, it is a good indication the individual is worth interviewing. Initial interview with a proposed counselor is helpful in determining if this person will become a member of the support team.

Here are some good questions to ask in choosing a counselor to help the care provider during the investigation:

1. Is the counselor familiar with the dynamics of raising foster and surrogate children?

2. Has the counselor ever worked with families accused of child maltreatment?

3. Is there anything in the provider's past that needs to be addressed— alcoholic parents, personal sexual abuse issues? Does the counselor have personal experience in working with these specific issues?

4. Does the provider feel comfortable with the counselor? With the counselor's support staff? Are they happy on their jobs and present a positive attitude?

5. Does the counselor have children?

6. Does the counselor understand what the provider says and answer questions?

7. Is the counselor available in a crisis or able to provide access to support services if they are needed?

8. Is the counselor connected with other helping professionals?

9. Does the provider's insurance cover the services, or is this counselor affordable?

Foster care providers may look to psychologists, psychiatrists, clergy, social workers, or other professionals who work in support professions. Some of the best-trained, field-experienced, sensitive, and skilled therapists may be social workers who remain in salaried positions rather than moving off into private practice. These individuals have the experience of dealing personally with the sensitive issues surrounding allegations and the investigative procedures. In most states, however, master of social work (MSW) psychotherapy is not recognized by insurance companies. In addition, biases may be present because of internal relationships. In sexual abuse allegations, a board certified child psychologist is warranted because he or she can carry out independent examinations and is less likely to misuse child psychology testing tools.

Stanley's ebony skin stood out in the neighborhood, although in his rainbow family he blended in beautifully. He was loving, kind, and the desire of most parents. Adopted at two he had always had the propensity for misrepresenting the truth and by eleven was a proficient storyteller.

Chris, age eight, was the blond foster girl next door. Sexually abused from two to six years, she also was a wonderful storyteller.

"Mom," said Chris, "Stanley touched my private parts in the woods."

Determining the truth from these two children was difficult. Chris's elaboration grew and included others. Stanley was cleared. The ending results were mostly positive.

— *Stanley has quit lying and understands the necessity for truth.*

— *Chris's therapist has been able to work with her previous sexual abuse issues and some healing has occurred.*

— *The families have remained supportive and friends.*

What is expected of *"professional"* parents?

Foster parents or parents who adopt difficult children are neither saints nor money-grabbing people. They are individuals committed to providing a service others will not. Their success is not measured by whether a child becomes *"normal,"* but by whether or not that child makes small but recognizable steps. Professionals may not notice the progress, but as *"frontline"* parents, they know when they've made a difference. There's not always enough time or energy to wipe all the tears, understand all the pain, or help build a vision for the future. The lives of children in care are filled with uncertainty. The children may or may not stay in homes very long. Success for a foster or high risk adoptive parent is when they can say at the end of a placement—*"I did my best."*

Troubled children continue to enter foster care, and many of these children previously would have been cared for in residential treatment centers. They carry complex histories and behaviors that are hard to understand. Information, training, and support services must be made available to the foster or adoptive family to equip them to handle these children. In addition, the community and educational and medical professionals who interact with these children need to be more aware of expected behaviors. Concerned citizens in both the states of Nebraska and New York have created position statements on allegations against foster/adoptive families in regard to abuse and neglect. *(See Appendix)* These position statements may serve as a catalyst for other states to develop position statements of their own.

Every year, approximately thirty thousand foster families in the United States leave foster parenting. This means the system must recruit thirty thousand new, inexperienced people just to stay even. The loss of experienced foster care families puts additional stress on the system and the children it serves.

Changes in attitude and procedure must occur if we are to keep foster parenting a viable option for children in need of temporary or pre-adoptive care. Losing thirty percent of your staff on an annual basis is devastating to any system. The average time in service of a provider is less than three years. Many providers drop out after their first placement, while some care for hundreds of children over decades.

Allegations, substantiated and unsubstantiated, against foster/adoptive parents have continued to rise. Issues of child abuse, neglect, allegations, and investigation are complex, and will likely only get worse before they get better. *Large scale solutions which take a long time to accomplish will only prolong the complexity of this issue. The sore that is becoming an ulcer. If agencies and foster care providers work together to provide preventive education and to encourage a viable support network, they can buy the time needed to treat the problem systematically. Then, and only then, will the "trauma" of abuse allegations to foster and adoptive families be eliminated.* (O'Neill, Carbino 1991)

Statistics and interviews do not accurately reflect the positive results surrogate, foster, and adoptive care providers have had on many American children. These parents in many cases have been the catalyst to change and have helped children become healthy adults. It is wrong for media and society to point fingers at surrogate parents for the failings in society because of the number of adults in prison, the number of homeless on American streets, or the rise in teenage pregnancy and prostitution.

Summary

Care providers are placed in a high risk position for allegation of child maltreatment when providing care for other people's children. Foster and adoptive homes have continued to receive more allegations than the national

It will always be necessary for the caseworker to support the "old" foster family as well as the child, so that the foster family can help the child move from the home in the least traumatic way possible. Usually foster families have strong feelings when a child needs to be removed from their home. Sometimes the family feels guilty about not being able to meet the needs of a child; other times the family may be angry at the agency for not really preparing them for this particular child's behavior. The foster family should be encouraged to express their feelings to the caseworker; they may need much support in dealing with these feelings. If this is not done, the feelings are apt to be expressed inappropriately and to the child's detriment.
(Falhberg 1979)

norms. There is currently a lack of services and resources for foster families who find themselves in this situation.

Agencies may be unaware of the extent of trauma experienced by families as a result of a child abuse report, investigations, and agency reponses. If there is an absence of coherent child welfare based policy at the national or state levels for this unique situation, a vacuum is created into which all child placement agencies are drawn. Lacking uniform guidelines soundly based on good child welfare practice principles, agencies will develop whatever guidelines appear feasible, resulting in not only a wide range of approaches to the situation, but also some approaches which may be destructive. There is risk that the concern for agency protection from legal liability may at times take precedence over the child welfare practice intended in child protection service.

I see a need for the child welfare field to reclaim responsibility for practice, especially in defining for the legal system what is good practice in child protection, so that harmful practice, such as blanket removals of children from reported foster homes and isolation of foster families, will not be presumed to constitute positive child protection. (Carbino 1991)

References

Besharov, Douglas. 1986. *The Vulnerable Social Worker: Liability for Serving Children and Families.*

Bustanoby, Andre. 1987. *Being a Single Parent.* New York: Ballatine.

Carbino, Rosemarie. 1989. *Child Welfare Issues in How Social Service Systems Respond to Allegations of Foster Home Abuse/Neglect. Putting Child Welfare Back Into Child Protection.* In J. Sprouse (Ed.) *Allegations of Abuse in Family Foster Care, An Examination of the Impact on Foster Families.* King George, Va: American Foster Care Resources, Inc.

Carbino, Rosemarie. 1991. *Consequences of Child Abuse Allegations for Foster Families.* Madison, Wisconsin: Health and Human Issues, University of Wisconsin-Madison.

Dodson, Fitzhugh. 1986. *How to Single Parent.* New York: Harper & Row.

Kaye, Kenneth. 1984. *Family Rules. Raising Responsible Children Without Yelling.* New York: St. Martins Press.

O'Neill, Susan. 1991. *Observations of a Foster Parent and Trainer.* In R. Carbino, Ed., *Consequences of Child Abuse Allegations for Foster Families.* Madison, Wisconsin:: Health and Human Issues, University of Wisconsin-Madison, 21-23.

Richmond, Gary. 1990. *Successful Single Parenting. Going It Alone.* Oregon: Harvest House.

Schaeffer, Brenda. 1991. *Loving Me. Loving You. Balancing Love and Power in a Co-dependent World.* Minnesota: Hazelden.

Specialized Alternatives For Youth of America. 1992. *SAFY Policy/Procedures Manual on Abuse Allegations.* Ohio: SAFY

Spiegel, Lawrence. 1986. *A Question of Innocense.* New York: The Unicorn Publishing Company.

Sprouse, Jacob. 1989. *Allegations of Abuse in Family Foster Care, An Examination of the Impact on Foster Families.* Edited by Jacob Sprouse. American Foster Care Resources, Inc. Post Office Box 271, King George, Virginia 22485.

Stinnett, Nick and DeFrain, John. 1989. *Secrets of Strong Families.* New York: Berkley

Turner, Marian. 1992. *Living with Crisis and Hiring an Attorney* (Brochure) Minnesota: Minneapolis, Minnesota Coalition of Provider Vulnerability.

Wilhite, Robert. 1993. *The Family Game of Anger.* Arizona: Self Care Books.

Each individual circumstance is different and may warrant variances from general guidelines established for the benefit of all. Cases in dispute need additional review by an unbiased group. An elected citizen review board may be a very appropriate vehicle to allow for this assessment. The review board could consist of a small number of individuals, each representing a separate vocational discipline —social worker, attorney, foster parent, birth parent, medical doctor, psychologist. This review board could be used to develop checks and balances in a difficult-to-regulate department. It would allow a place for citizens to go and be heard prior to having to hire legal counsel.
Birth father

The issue is not going to go away.

SECTION III

Communication Goes Both Ways

*Understanding and clarity only come
from good communication
between care providers
and social services.*

*The task force for this
book wanted more
information.*

***All right,* I said
*I'll rent a post office
box, and we'll run
ads looking for
people willing to
share information.***

*I didn't expect
anything . . .
        We Care,
        P.O. Box ---
the newspaper ads
announced.*

*. . . A two-inch thick
package containing the
story of a family's
journey through child
protection lay on my
desk. This family
wanted me to remain
unbiased and draw my
own conclusions. They
gave me no clues
regarding their file.*

*Please open and
read it carefully . . .*

Dear We Care,

We saw your ad in the paper looking for individuals willing to share their stories. If we told you what has happened to us you would not believe us, so we are sending you our file and you can use your own discernment and decide for yourself. We have also enclosed two taped telephone conversations. Please listen to these after you read our file. Since this information has private information, please use consideration when sharing this data, we do not want additional damage to our son.

Thank you for having the courage to do something.

Good luck,
The Smiths

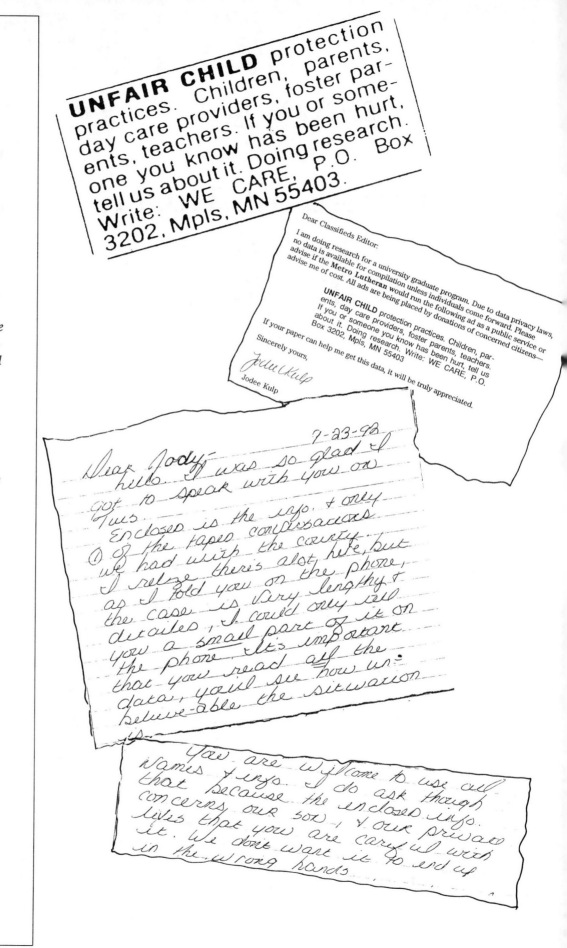

UNFAIR CHILD protection practices. Children, parents, day care providers, foster parents, teachers. If you or someone you know has been hurt, tell us about it. Doing research. Write: WE CARE, P.O. Box 3202, Mpls, MN 55403.

Dear Classifieds Editor:

I am doing research for a university graduate program. Due to data privacy laws, no data is available for compilation unless individuals come forward. Please advise if the **Metro Lutheran** would run the following ad as a public service or advise me of cost. All ads are being placed by donations of concerned citizens—

UNFAIR CHILD protection practices. Children, parents, day care providers, foster parents, teachers. If you or someone you know has been hurt, tell us about it. Doing research. Write: WE CARE, P.O. Box 3202, Mpls, MN 55403

If your paper can help me get this data, it will be truly appreciated.

Sincerely yours,

Jodee Kulp

Jodee Kulp

7-23-92

Dear Jody—
hi Hi. I was so glad I got to speak with you on Tues. Enclosed is the info. + only 1 of the tapes conversations we had with the county, but I relize there's alot here, but as I told you on the phone, the case is very lengthy + detailes, I could only tell you a small part of it on the phone. It's important that you read all the data, you'll see how un-believe-able the situation is.

You are wjlcome to use all Names + info. I do ask though that because the enclosed info. concerns, our son, + our private lives that you are careful with it. We don't want it to end up in the wrong hands.

Chapter 6

Getting The Facts, Fast?

Making sure your viewpoint
is understood is important
to the final outcome of the allegation.
If the investigation is to be complete and the result
fair for your family and the child,
the truth must come out.

When the allegation was made in 1990, I called an attorney to obtain copies of the state statutes and rules. The attorney charged $500, and we received 25 pages of Minnesota state rules. These pages contained very little of the information we actually needed. The counsel we received was hardly a beginning. We faced the next problem — we were out of money.

Two years later, without the emotions of facing an allegation, I decided to find out how to access the information myself. This time I used my public library card, three hours of time, and $25 in cash to copy 767 pages of statutes and rules. I put two pages together, reduced them to fit on an 8-1/2 x 11 sheet of paper and was charged 15 cents per sheet. I also accessed the Federal Information Computer at no cost and printed out 50 feet of reference material I could review at a later date.

I wish I had gone to the public library before I sought an attorney. In less than an hour I had a much clearer picture of the rules and statutes governing foster parents and licensing agencies. It was clear that the statutes and rules dictated procedures which affected foster children and the care providers. Information that had seemed to affect others only glared at me with personal importance. How could I communicate clearly to other foster parents the need for understanding?

I grew up as an American citizen, saying the pledge of allegiance and attending public school in the sixties and seventies. Independence, freedom, and civil rights were the songs of the times. Growing up during that era of idealism, I was ill-prepared for what my family was about to encounter from the child welfare system as we faced allegation and the investigation process.

I believed that if I had something important to say, I would be listened to. *I quickly learned that my questions and concerns were not heard.*

I believed that if I needed information, I could easily access the resources I needed to get the answers. *I learned that my personal files were confidential and closed until the investigation was completed.*

I was curious . . .

The doors of the main public library in Minneapolis stood in front of me. I wondered what information I could access.

Laws are public. They are written for the people. As a citizen, I should be able to get information regarding state and federal laws.

"I need to get some references on state statutes," I said at the information desk.

"No problem," said the gentleman. "Down the hall, take a right at the Government Documents Center. Someone will help you if you ask."

I headed down the hall.

I believed that an attorney could easily help me get the information I needed. *After spending five hundred dollars, all I had was a few state statutes. I still had no idea what they meant, how to access the system, or whom to access to help me.*

I believed that child welfare protected children and worked in their best interests. *I learned that sometimes child welfare works in the system's best interests—to protect itself instead of the children it represents.*

I believed that following correct procedures would insure the health and stability of the child. *I learned that following correct procedures may actually damage the children they were designed to serve.*

I believed that each person must be held accountable for his or her own actions, and if you always told the truth you could work through any situation. *I learned that each person's interpretation of your truth is different.*

I believed that a person was innocent until proven guilty. *I learned I was guilty unless I could prove my innocence, but I did not have the knowledge or the access to the system to do so.*

I believed that I would be notified about my "case" progress. *I learned that notification meant a certified letter from the Department of Human Services four months later, informing me that our license was revoked.*

I believed that I would receive an explanation concerning the next steps to take if we didn't agree with the revocation of our license. *I learned that because we did not know how to appeal and did not appeal within ten days of notification (I was still in shock), that we did not have access to the system for another five years, nor could we reapply for licensure until that time was over.*

I learned something else. Without access to social workers, the system, or information about my case, I remained isolated and defenseless. I came to a new, poignant understanding of the plight of a poor, undereducated birth mother whose children had been placed in foster care. Enervated by my own grief, I wondered how such a mother could pull herself together to get a job, clean her house, and maintain the program set up for her by the social service system to get her children back. Where does she find her inner strength—and resist medicating herself with drugs or alcohol? How can she value services provided when those services include the removal of her children . . . and when does *"services provided"* become harassment?

Here I was—a successful professional with a supportive husband, a warm and loving extended family, lots of friends, and a supportive church. With all of these support systems in place, I still had days when I had difficulty maintaining a healthy lifestyle for myself and my family. I made a personal commitment to find the information I had so desperately needed and couldn't access. I now found myself facing an opportunity instead of a crisis—my experience could be used to help others.

What information do care providers need to properly communicate the truth if an allegation is made against them?

Often there is no written notification. Your life simply changes without knowledge of exactly what the allegation is, who made the allegation, or what will happen next.

In order to proceed logically in acquiring facts, a care provider needs:

— Copy of the allegation in writing. This allows the care provider to access and choose an effective support network. This document can state:

What allegation is:	Date allegation was made:
Actions to be taken by agency:	Investigation to begin on date:
	Name and credentials of investigator:
Agency contact:	(Name, address, phone)

— Complete list of legal rights tailored to the relationship of the care provider and the child. foster child, kinship child, birth child, etc.) This information can be provided by the agency. If the agency cannot provide this information, it can be found in the state law library, county legal library, or main public library.

— Agency procedures regarding accepted social worker contact with the care provider family—what information can be shared and why or why not. The agency should supply this data. (Licensing worker and child's worker are often instructed not to have contact until investigation is complete, in order not to taint evidence.)

— Copy of laws/rules that are alleged to be violated. You may call your association or the Department of Human Services if your social worker or agency cannot communicate with you. The areas of interest to search for are:

Licensing	Children	Juveniles	Maltreatment
Foster Care	Adoption	Neglect	Abuse

— Copy of current state licensing regulations that govern the service you provide.

— Copy of agency or state foster parent agreement.

— List of professionals who have handled similar cases (attorneys, peers, crisis support team, associations, psychiatrists, accessible social workers, etc.) Recommendation may be available from the agency, social worker, or provider association.

— Agency policy on handling allegations and investigations and contact person at the agency. This should be available from the agency.

— Access to any support system within the state or local foster care association.

With this information in hand, the care provider can proceed to develop a network and a support system and begin communicating.

How can providers best communicate?

Whenever two people communicate, messages are transmitted three ways: through body language, tone of voice, and words. Sometimes tone of voice and body language are louder than words. When this happens, what is said may have very little meaning to the listener. When the listener perceives that there is a difference among messages sent by body language, voice, and words, the listener receives the messages in the following way:

When discussion is face to face:
55% of the message is received from body language
38% of the message is received from the tone of voice
7% of the message is received from words.

I began to question . . .

In whose best interest?
— *The social worker's?*
— *The birth parent's?*
— *The legal system's?*

or
— *The child's?*

"Best interests" easily conflict when so many interests are involved.

When discussion is via the telephone:
84% of the message is received from the tone of voice
16% of the message is received from our words. (ProSource 1992)

When body language and voice are out of harmony with words, the total message becomes distorted.

The listener has additional problems to deal with. She may be distracted by her own thoughts while others are still talking. The listener may also place a personal interpretation on the information being received. Some listeners may not be proficiently trained in accepting the communication being sent, and at other times distractions—noise, smells, actions, touch, and interruptions—may interfere with complete transference.

Parents who are alleged to have abused can serve themselves and their children best by remaining calm, respectful, and brief. The professionals who are involved will normally maintain a formal politeness. This same behavior can prove very effective for parents facing allegations. They can help themselves by getting organized. They should plan beforehand what they need to express and write down the points they want to cover. They should speak calmly and firmly. They should listen to what is being said and take notes to develop a paper trail of dates, times, context, attempted contacts, etc.

The accused may prefer to communicate by phone, but letters are more effective because the words the accused wants expressed *are* expressed. Information can easily be dated, duplicated, and filed. It is hard for anyone to change what is written, especially when it has been photocopied and sent to a number of individuals. Certified mail ensures the sender that the recipient received the information because the sender gets a receipt.

When writing to the agency, accused providers should remain concise and logical. They should stick to the facts. If they feel they need to write an emotional letter, they should write it but not send it. It can be filed away to be read or rewritten later in a professional and appropriate tone. Passive and aggressive methods of communication should be avoided. When emotions get in the way of good communication, factual information can easily be misinterpreted and labeled. If communication senders act defensive, receivers may assume that they have something to hide. Shame may become a barrier regardless of whether or not the shame is approriate. How does one answer the questions, *"When did you quit beating your wife?"* or *"When did you last have sex with your foster daughter?"* How does one disprove such statements without feeling and acting defensive?

Assertive or aggressive behavior may be misinterpreted as abusive, aggressive, bitter, defensive, disturbed, domineering, explosive, fanatic, hostile, non-compliant, obnoxious, out-of-control, rageful, reactive, troubled, unreasonable, unstable, or violent.

The final data may be distorted, generalized, or missing important details.

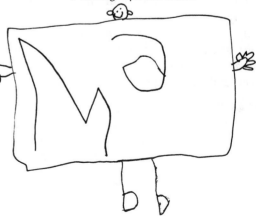

ASSERTIVE PEOPLE	PASSIVE PEOPLE	AGGRESSIVE PEOPLE
Attack the problem	Avoid the problem	Attack the person
Claim rights	Relinquish rights	Claim rights
Recognize the rights of others as equal to their rights	View the rights of others as superior	View their rights as superior to others' rights
Establish a pattern of respect for future interactions	Establish a pattern of allowing others to take advantage	Provoke a reaction in others of fear and avoidance
Let others know how they think and feel	Let others guess how they think and feel	Let others know how they think and feel
Work toward goals	Hope goals will be achieved	Work toward goals
Choose for themselves	Let others choose for them	Choose for themselves and others
Deal with anger	Build anger and resentment	Act out anger
Are confident	Lack confidence	Are cocky, hostile
Request (favors, etc.)	Hope (for favors, etc.)	Demand (favors, etc.)

If biases concerning the family or individual were pre-existing it seemed that regardless of what was said or how it was said, it didn't matter.

The voices and the words resounded, "Who are you to challenge me? I am trained in child welfare, you are only the parents. We know what's right for your child. Trust us. Our people don't make mistakes. You must be wrong."

Passive behavior may be misinterpreted as abandoning, depressed, fearful, guilty, incompetent, insecure, intimidated, isolated, neglectful, nervous, non-responsive, submissive, threatened, uneasy, unfeeling, untrustworthy, and weak.

> *Troung and Lee are Asian parents who are facing an allegation and being interviewed. Troung feels troubled and upset. He is frustrated and bewildered by the situation and how it is being handled. His direct and verbal expressions come across as aggressive. Lee is a thoughtful person who needs to think things through fully before speaking. Her cultural background places her in a position of respect for her husband when she is in public. Her quietness is nothing more than the time she needs to pull her thoughts together and listen to the conversations going on around her. There are many appropriate reasons for people to remain cautious and quiet, even though these may be misinterpreted.*

I continued to read.

In Lee and Troung's situation, a worker might conclude that the husband is abusive, and the wife is an abuse victim herself, or that she may not protect the children from her husband's outbursts. Differences in culture, class, language, and personalities can create roadblocks to good investigative practice. For families facing allegations or investigations, immediate feedback is necessary so all parties can be assured of clear communication.

What kinds of differences can affect communication?

The accused family will meet many different types of individuals as they journey through the allegation experience. The way they react can directly influence their case outcome. Knowing the different roles being played by individuals is helpful in developing appropriate relationships.

A child abuse allegation opens the door to new people entering the lives of the accused. There are curious individuals—neighbors, general public—people who peek in from the outside and never get involved beyond being a spectactor. There are individuals who respond as researchers—investigators, psychologists, doctors—gathering the facts and details objectively but remaining distant. There are judges who set out to provide justice—innocent or guilty—regardless if that's their job. There are helpers—people who offer help, sincerely and unconditionally—some may offer help, however, bound with conditions. Sometimes those closest to the care provider—friends and family—feel so intensely that they become ineffective in helping.

Culturally, each person's background is different. Differences can make communities rich and pleasant places to live. Differences also can cause anxiety, miscommunication, and distrust. Appreciating diversity allows people to live in harmony. Expecting everyone to be the same causes prejudice and discord. Communicating effectively is important. *(See Chapter 10)*

Personalities and job roles play a very important part in hearing clearly what each person is saying. Regardless of their community and family experience, people live in their own individual world, with their own thoughts, perceptions and feelings. The people involved with families under investigation will understand the situation through their own experiences, based on their own histories and education.

Lifestyle differences can cause mixed messages and barriers to effective communication. When a working class family of color communicates with a caseworker who was raised in an upper middle class European family, regardless of intentions, miscommunication can occur.

Economic differences often pose more difficulty in communication than racial differences. Even in the same ethnic group, a wealthy person may have very little understanding of a person from an impoverished background. Educational differences pose similar problems.

What is a mixed message?

A mixed message simply means that the communication sent is not the communication received. Both the sender and the receiver have responsibility for keeping messages clear and understood. Mixed messages are especially distressing during the investigative process because neither the care provider nor the child realizes the true meaning of the question until it is too late for clarification. Care providers need to ask questions and get clarification before answering an investigator's question. When knowledge is unbalanced between two individuals, messages easily get crossed.

How can the way questions are perceived affect answers?

In a training class for providers, we were discussing foster parenting models. Dr. Wayne Carron, a family therapist, was directing the group, and questions were being asked of 39 experienced care providers. Although very diverse (race, culture, education, sex, age, etc.), the group had a common thread—a love of children and parenting. Dr. Carron's questions dealt with our work with children, and he asked us to move from one side of the room to the other, creating a visual living graphic of our responses. He wanted to know if participants were authoritarian or equalitarian. Did we favor structure or autonomy? Did we place more importance on freedom of expression or control?

Brian came into the world out of wedlock and Sharon did not want to raise him or give him up, so as an infant, Brian lived with his grandparents. Sharon moved out of the state.

When Brian was two, Sharon remarried and her new husband adopted Brian. She was ready to settle down and Brian moved in with his own "real" mother.

The problem existed, it seemed, in Brian's head—his grandmother had been his "real" mother. Brian faced separation and loss, and was very angry. Sharon and her new husband loved Brian and worked hard to reunite the family, but Brian would not attach.

By four he was abusive, violent, and very angry. The family sought counseling.

The group had been asked to come to the front of the room and stand in a cluster. As the questions were asked each group member was to move away from the center toward either end of the room. The result was a visual graphic of differences in parenting styles. On most questions, all the parents remained near the center. After years of parenting complex and out-of-home children, our parenting styles had changed and responses were adjusted to the needs of the child in care. We had learned to restructure our instinctive parenting to be more adaptive to the child we were required to parent.

One mature, experienced foster mother moved continuously from one side of the room to the other. It was clear she knew her parenting program. Upon completion of the exercise, she spoke up. The foster children she cared for were emergency, short term placements. For these specific children, she maintained control, kindness, order, stability, and a focus on the present. For emergency shelter care, this was quite appropriate. A different parenting style emerged, however, when she discussed her parenting approach with long-term foster and biological children, whom she parented with flexibility and affection. She encouraged autonomy and freedom of expression. If she had chosen to answer the questions from her parenting style for these children, she would have stood with the group. She displayed two distinct parenting styles in the same family. Yet, when the questions were asked, her mind was on the shelter children and so were her answers.

When Dr. Carron asked whether we preferred allowing children to express rage and anger or maintain control, I felt very strongly that children in care needed to express their emotions and feelings of anger. I moved from the safe and secure middle to the outskirts of expression. Another care provider felt children should control their emotions—she stood against the other wall. Dr. Carron was interested in why there was such a difference. The care provider who believed in control said, *"I believe a child needs to have a trusting relationship with me before I let them have expressions of anger or rage. The child needs to know that I will only let certain expressions happen. I am not against expression, I just believe that control is necessary to allow anger to come out safely."* My parenting position was the same position as hers. I, also, would not allow a child to express volatile feelings until we had worked through safe ways of expression and begun a trusting relationship. Our answers were very different, but our parenting approach was very similar. As you can see, how one perceives the question will dictate the answer. Active listening and further clarification are crucial.

How to listen effectively

Effective listening is a skill developed over time. Listening requires focus, attention, participation, and involvement. Communication requires two distinct roles: receiver and sender. The receiver (listener) role is to listen, gather facts, and process information received. The sender (speaker) role is to send information. The sender also must clarify information received and gather additional information. Active listening means the listener gathers and processes information, makes sure the message sent is clear, and lets the sender know the message sent has been heard and understood. The active listener is also careful not to let his or her mind wander to other subjects, but to concentrate on the sender's message. By processing the information received and letting the sender know the message has been heard and understood, the receiver begins to create an atmosphere of comfort, trust, and additional communication. When the receiver actively listens to the sender, it encourages the sender also to listen actively. Effective listening is done with the whole body and is concerned with content as well as feelings. Feelings are often more important than the words themselves—they are the real meaning. Eye contact and body language can facilitate effective listening. Any communication that is not clear needs to be restated and clarified. The use of notes and a tape recorder may be extremely helpful.

Forty pages into the file . . .

Brian's anger seemed primarily directed at his mother, and most of his violent outbursts included her.

He created major disturbances when asked to comply with any reasonable request.

He was very sneaky and practiced cruel deeds on his little sister. He professed that it was always "an accident."

He lied profusely even when it made no difference.

He threatened his mother with knives and other weapons to inflict pain.

Finally, he began self-mutilating and contemplating suicide.

Fearing for the safety of their son and their family, the family sought additional professional help—an inpatient treatment program for preadolescents.

Care providers may be hearing any of these possible mixed messages:

AGENCY SAYS	CARE PROVIDER'S POINT OF VIEW	POSSIBLE AGENCY REALITY	CARE PROVIDER NEEDS
"Our agency does not remove children unless there is proof of abuse or neglect."	*Foster care providers believe they are innocent until proven guilty and will be treated accordingly. They do not understand the agency conducting an investigation unless they are informed of the charges against them. They also do not understand why the social service agency would remove foster children in their care when they have not been given an adequate chance to state their innocence, or been kept informed of the investigative process.* **Care providers are shocked by this.**	*Because of the internal politics in the foster care system the foster children may be removed before an investigation is completed and/or before guilt can be established or endangerment determined.*	**Foster parents need to ask:** — *How often has your agency removed children before an investigation is complete?* — *Do you have a new written caseplan for the children in our care?* — *How and when will we know the results of the investigation?* — *Is the caseplan based on a thorough case assessment?*
"We respect your wishes and will only place with you the types of children you are comfortable with."	*Few foster care providers turn a child down, especially if the agency indicates that no other home is available. They believe they can also handle this child. These placements that are meant for temporary care (until a permanent home can be found) can extend for weeks or even months. Time and again, licensing rules are ignored. It is true that foster families have the right to deny caring for any child, but they must also abide by civil rights laws, and may have signed statements that they will not reject a child because of culture or race. These signed statements may have nothing to do with the current situation, but because of race, disability, or culture of a child, the care provider fears affirmative action.*	*When a family says they would rather not parent a child, and the agency "begs" them to take the child anyway, the stage has been set. Because of the shortage of homes, age restrictions, behaviors, and numbers of children needing care, child history may be omitted or altered in a phone conversation to accommodate the "emergency placement." The luxury of matching children to families may work well in the books, but it is not always possible in reality.*	**Foster parents need to ask:** — *For a permanency caseplan and complete history of the child.* — *Has the child made previous allegations against care providers?* — *What type of abuse or neglect has the child experienced?* — *Does social services know of any behavior or discipline problems?* — *Names of other professionals who have worked with the child.* — *Additional training requirements.* — *The type of contact with the birth family that is anticipated.* **If the child is not fitting in your family, let the social worker know. Don't try to tough it out. The results may not be effective for the child or your family**

AGENCY SAYS:	CARE PROVIDER'S POINT OF VIEW	POSSIBLE AGENCY REALITY	CARE PROVIDER NEEDS
"If you ever have a problem and you need me, I'll be here. Just call."	When things are going well, it's easy for a care provider to not keep in touch with the agency. However, if a problem suddenly does crop up and the policies have changed, the provider may have trouble understanding and accessing the system.	More often than not, the foster care coordinator or new licensing worker will give this message to new foster care providers. It is sincere, but it is not uncommon for agency personnel to change, or for a whole agency to restructure without notifying its foster care providers. If providers only call when they have a problem and never on a positive note, the view of the agency toward the provider may be skewed.	*Providers must take personal responsibility to:* — Request notification of changes in team members or their supervisors and phone numbers. — Request written notification of all policy changes that could affect their family, then date and file policy changes. — Meet with complete team when a team member changes to clarify caseplan goals and history.
"Along with our agency's written policy, we encourage our care providers to use common sense and good judgment."	Common sense and good judgment cannot be the only answer. There must be written policies on discipline. Common sense and good judgment vary from person to person. Both are affected by community mores and ethnic traditions. Ideas of what is discipline and what is abuse also differ.	If a written policy on discipline and abuse is available, it should be the sole guideline. If there is a not a written policy, one should be written. It is unfair to care providers and agency personnel when disciplinary policies are not written and readily available. Clarity in policies is essential to eliminate the potential for liability on everyone's part.	*What can a care provider do?* — Get a copy of agency guidelines for abuse and neglect. — If a policy does not exist, call your provider association for a copy of their guidelines. — Get approval in writing from your agency on the your family guidelines. — Know agency procedures and issues from a legal point of view regarding allegations.
"We have completed your investigation and the allegations were unfounded."	The foster care providers are relieved that the experience is over, and angry that they had to go through this trauma. For those families who remain in foster care, there is joy that they can begin accepting children again. Unfortunately this declaration of innocence does not guarantee children. Some families experience a "quiet closing": they remain legally licensed, but they are given no new children. The family grows anxious, and then angry, when a new child never arrives.	In many cases the agency hesitates to return children to the family. If there is no intention of using the home again, the agency should inform the family. There is no logical reason to prolong the painful experience of an abuse allegation for the foster family or for the workers who still have faith in them. If the criminal investigation has been completed and an investigation for violation licensing is still needed, it is important to explain this to the foster care providers.	*What can a care provider do?* — Ask if the licensing investigation is also complete. — Ask if there is intention to use the home again and when to expect the next child or if there is any new stiplulation on their home as to the kind of children that the agency will place with them. — Get in writing date of next expected child and appointment for next home review. — If a child has not been placed in the time specified, meet with the assigned social worker.

Adapted and used with permission from material of Susan O'Neill, (1991) Observations of a Foster Parent and Trainer *published in* **Consequences of Child Abuse Allegations for Foster Families. A Report of a Symposium.** *Rosemarie Carbino, Editor.*

When trying to gather or provide information:

Act like a good listener—Lean forward, maintain eye contact, give feedback. Pay attention, set aside distractions, and make time to complete the conversation. Good listening shows you care. (Note: Not all cultures view eye contact as respectful.)

Ask open questions—Open questions take more than a yes or no answer. Open questions ask for explanation or discussion. They are both fact and feeling finding. Open questions begin with where, who, what, when, why and how. Ask questions you would like answered—*"What do you hope to accomplish today? What information are you going to need? How do other families you work with handle this? How many other allegations/investigations have you had against your homes? How often does this happen? What are the results as you've experienced them? Who would be helpful for me to talk to? Where can I go to get additional information? When will this process be over?"* The social worker may not be able to talk or share information about your specific situation, but may be able to speak in generalities. Open questions encourage information sharing.

Get more information—*"What questions will be helpful for me to ask? Tell me how it works. Can you tell me more about that?"*

Give feedback—*"Is this what you mean? Do I understand this correctly?"* Repeat back to the person what you have heard, and do not leave the issue until you have a clear understanding of what has been said. Don't listen only for the speaker's words, listen for meaning—clarify and prepare to dig. Try not to let your feelings interfere with your listening. The time to react is after you have truly understood what has been said.

Let the person know you are not informed about the subject—*"I don't know much about this. I've never been in this position before. Can you give me some ideas about what you or others would do? I haven't heard of that before—could you explain it more clearly?"*

Ask closed questions if you need to control the conversation and your time. Closed questions can be answered with one or two words and usually with a yes or no. A closed question helps to clarify understanding of a problem or request. Closed questions begin with did, can, do, is, will, have or would.

Good listening is not easy, but it is crucial if providers facing allegations are to understand what is being said to them. Allegations are painful, yet one of the best things a care provider can do is try to understand the perspective of social services. Without direct access or experience inside the system, it is difficult to understand the time required to perform a task. What plans or arrangements must be made? What paperwork must be completed? What projects must be set aside? Who else is involved and must be satisfied? What information do they need? Do they understand me? If individuals can begin to identify the wants and needs of each other, then cooperation and understanding can begin to replace defensiveness and negative reactions. Often, bad feelings emerge when social services and care providers are incapable of perceiving each other's situation.

The care provider need not set aside personal perspective in order to communicate better with social services. In fact, understanding personal motivation, position, and feelings is crucial in proper communication. Tone of voice communicates more than four times the words we use. Thus, *"I want an answer to my question"* can be interpreted as a statement or an objection. And, *"Why didn't I hear about this sooner?"* can be interpreted as a question or an objection. The interpretation of the words caused by voice inflection can be damaging to the outcome of a case.

We don't live in a perfect world, and we don't interact with perfect people. Negative experiences can bring out the worst in individuals. We have no power over the attitude and behavior of social services. We can gain control only of our own attitudes and behaviors. We have the power within ourselves to meet or exceed the expectations of social services with our attitudes and reactions. We can maintain courtesy, increase our knowledge of the system, and be responsive to social services' needs whether or not the same behavior is returned to us. We can be reliable, offer care and concern, and take the actions necessary to remain personally healthy.

Talking too much can lead to miscommunication during times of emotional upset. A sense of urgency along with feelings of anger, frustration, and pain normally accompany an allegation. Care providers often think a mistake has been made, and they sincerely want social services to know there is a problem. They feel an urgent need to communicate, be listened to, and find someone to understand and help. Yet, one of the most important things a provider can do is listen. Listening focuses attention on the other person and demonstrates that the provider cares about the situation. Negative thoughts and feelings need to be communicated to a support team, not social services or the investigator.

> *Anger, frustration, and defensiveness are not allies*
> *when providers communicate with social services.*
> *Listening is.*

Support for foster family —
With whom can they talk? Who do they tell?

Caring for other people's children requires maintaining confidentiality when discussing events and occurences pertaining to children in care. It is wise to use caution when discussing these sensitive issues. In general, other members of the treatment team, professional peers, legal counsel, and clergy are available. If a care provider is being interviewed by an investigator or social worker, the presence of another non-biased or supportive adult is very helpful and can be requested.

How does document confidentiality work?

Maintaining confidentiality is ethical in that it protects all affected persons. It is also a legal requirement that can have far reaching consequences. Confidentiality laws concerning agency records arise from the need to "protect the right of privacy of the subjects of the record." They are not intended to shield the agency from public scrutiny, but to prevent disclosure of information to third parties who seek information out of greed, vindictiveness, or even curiosity. As one court said, confidentiality restrictions *"were primarily concerned with disclosure which might result in a commercial or political use."* (American Bar Association 1989)

In the book, *Agency-based Social Worker, Neglected Aspects of Clinical Practice* by Weissman, Epstein and Savage (1983), the dilemma of "The Right of Access versus the Promise of Confidentiality" is addressed:

> *More than ever before there is concensus that a client has the right to access his records. Schools and social agencies and child care institutions, if challenged, may be required to permit the family and the child to read his record.*

More letters and more papers . . .

It didn't last long. Soon Brian was on his way home. Another sister volunteered to help.

Brian brutalized her smaller children, tried suicide, and was again sent home.

Frantic, Sharon called social services. She explained the situation and was told social services couldn't do anything unless Brian was taken by the police and admitted to a hospital. Then perhaps services could be provided.

Sharon called the police to have her son picked up and brought to the hospital. She was told not to follow the police car and that the hospital would call. She wrote a letter to the hospital explaining Brian's behavior.

Confused, the hospital called to find out why they had Brian and what they needed to do.

Sharon tried to explain what social services had told her.

On the other hand, we solicit all sorts of communications from professionals about their perceptions and assessments of our clients—communications previously assured confidentiality. The promise of confidentiality freed the professional to share not only his valid findings, but his hunches, intuitions and professionally educated guesses, often useful in alerting us to what we need to know to help the client. Abrogating the promise of confidentiality permits satisfying the client's rightful claim to assess; it also makes the less useful, less helpful communications as the professional becomes more circumspect in what he says. (Weissman et. al. 1983, p36)

I read the above paragraph almost ten years ago, and I wonder today how much personal opinion still remains in care provider files. During our investigation, my husband and I requested access to our records in writing. We wanted to review the information written about our parenting and our family. We were first told the information could not be released until all the names had been removed from the documentation. When reading our file it would be clear who belonged in the empty spaces because we would know who all the individuals were by just reading the information in context. A few days later we were called and told our request for access had been denied until the investigation was over. Our records had become *"confidential"* and no access would be granted to anyone but individuals directly involved in the investigation. I felt we were, or should be, directly involved, but I was feeling too discouraged to ask why. It would be two years before I finally had the confidence to ask that question.

What rights do providers have regarding private or confidential data about themselves?

The rights of access to child protective records and your own records is not absolute. The identities of persons who made the report or who cooperated with the subsequent investigation, including neighbors, babysitters, teachers, and other persons who are in regular contact with the parents are usually withheld if disclosure would endanger or adversely affect day-to-day interaction. In some situations, the danger to the person who is reported or is cooperating in the investigation may entail potential psychological or social harm, as opposed to physical injury. For example, the disclosure to a parent that a grandparent or spouse reported the alleged abuse or cooperated in the investigation could so disrupt family life as to be contrary to the interests of all concerned.

In addition, the agency may seek to withhold information that may be harmful to the subject of a record. Such information may involve statements of relatives, psychiatric reports or other information that, if known by the subject of the report, could cause mental anguish or harm. (Besharov 1991, p. 217)

Whenever a government agency asks you to provide **private** or **confidential** data about yourself, you must be told:

1. Why the data is being collected;

2. How the data will be used by the collecting agency;

3. If you can refuse or are legally required to provide the data being requested;

4. What the consequences are to you if you supply or refuse to supply the data; and

5. The identity of other persons or entities who are authorized by law to receive the data.

This notice is referred to as the **"Tennessen Warning."** (The provision of a license may waive the need for providing this warning to you.) Once it has been given to you, the agency cannot collect, store, use, or disseminate the data for any other purpose (except in limited circumstances). You have the right to know what data are maintained about you and how they are classified. You have the right to view, at no cost, all **public** and **private** data maintained about you and to have **public** and **private** data explained to you. You have the right to receive copies of **public** and **private** data about yourself, but you may be charged a copy fee.

You have the right to challenge the accuracy and completeness of any **public** or **private** data about yourself. In Minnesota, if you want to challenge results in an adverse decision, you may appeal the decision to the Commissioner of Administration.

You have the right to include in government data your own explanation of anything to which you object. That explanation must be included any time the disputed data is shared with another agency. You have the right to authorize other agencies or persons to see or use **private** data about yourself. (MN Dept. Admin. 1991)

How can providers access records regarding themselves and their family?

The Minnesota Government Data Practices Act requires all government agencies in Minnesota to:

1. Protect private information about individuals, and

2. Help citizens get public infomation.

It is the policy of the Minnesota Department of Human Services and the statewide welfare system to provide people data if the law says they can see it. The statewide welfare system is a group of agencies that provide services to people. The agencies include:

Minnesota Department of Human Services
County welfare boards and agencies
Human service center boards
Community mental health center boards
Regional treatment centers
State nursing homes
Ombudsman for mental health and mental retardation
People, agencies, institutions, and organizations under contract to any
    agency listed above.

You must know from which agency you need data. You have the right to ask any agency in the statewide welfare system whether they have information about you and how that information is classified.

You have the right to examine public and private data about you. You must generally have consent to see private data about someone else. Data about individuals contained in your file may need to be removed before you see it.

Data which is under investigation is classified *"confidential."* You *do not* have the right to look at confidential data even about yourself! Only people or agencies designated by a state or federal law can have access to confidential files. This makes it very difficult for persons facing allegations—especially when they are not sure what the allegation is—to prepare defense data, to know who to include in a support network, and to plan for the future.

If you wish to see your file, go to the keeper of the data during regular working hours, but not on weekends and holidays, and ask. You must show an identification and sign your name so that the agency can be sure you are who you say you are. It is a good idea to make an appointment with the office you plan to visit. An appointment will give the staff time to make sure your file is ready.

You may take any reasonable amount of time to read your file, take notes, and ask for copies to be made, but you must examine your file **with** agency staff. The agency may refuse to let you see your file again for six months, unless there is a law case pending or new data has been added. You may let other people see the data about you by signing a Consent for Release of Information.

All the information kept concerning you must be true and complete. If you disagree with information contained in data files, you have the right to challenge the keeper of the data on this information.

What about consent to review medical/psychological records?

Follow the law when authorizing provision of your medical/psychological data. No one can photocopy medical/psychological records without a court order or the consent of the subject of the records or the parents or legal guardian of the subject. It is the right of the patient to deny or authorize release of any medical records. If a provider family is already under investigation, *"Red Flags"* have already been flying. The following is a safe release policy which allows the provider to comply but also maintain some control:

> What specific information would you like to review?
> Who will be reviewing this information?
> When would you like access to this information?
> What will you be using this information for?

By signing a blanket release form for medical/psychological records, the provider authorizes immediate access to *any* person on *any* and *all* data. There is no guarantee that the records will be understood or read correctly by the reader. There is no disclaimer for who can discuss what or who can see the records. Your license may limit you from restricting information or access. The following are some restrictions which may be possible to request.

> What information will be provided.
> What psychologist's conclusion is.
> What the psychologist's recommendations are.
> Meaning of the diagnosis.
> Treatment plan proposal and assessment of
> compliance with plan.

Before any documentation is sent to anyone, you have the right to request to review it. You have a right to know the results of any summary or evaluation before it is released. Volunteer to go and pick up the information yourself, sit with the professional and have it explained to you. This will allow for an ongoing exchange of information between you and other professionals involved in your case. If you disagree with the interpretation or diagnosis, you have the right to a second opinion. Don't be afraid to ask investigators, social workers or the agency whom they recommend for a second opinion. The results of the initial assessment can be stalled while you obtain a second opinion. The county worker can go to the county attorney and a judge can force a release of any information if they need it. Then deliver the material to the person requesting it. Keep a copy for yourself and have them sign when they have received the information they requested.

Providing data without written simple interpretation
to an untrained professional may be dangerous.

The senator's staff was concerned, cooperative, and friendly. A relieved Sharon poured out her story.

Yes, their son was in voluntary foster care. Yes, they had received a paper stating that they had neglected their son. No, they had never neglected their son. No, they didn't have copies of their file in their possession. No, they didn't know how to get copies of their files.

The senator's staff person said she would get back to them, find out how they could get access to the files, and discuss the issue with the Senator. Within one day the Senator and his staff had kept their promises and returned a call to the family.

They explained how to obtain copies of their files, who to talk to in which department. They promised to check the status of the neglect charge and to stay in touch.

Sharon thanked them and set to work getting copies of her files.

How are data classified?

The Act classifies the data as follows:

Data on individuals	Data not on individuals	What is normally included and accessibility of data
Public *Anyone can ask for public data. Just walk into the pertinent government agency and ask to see. Looking is free. Copies and clerical search time may be billed.* *If you are denied access to see Public Data ask for the denial in writing and the specific statute to clarify refusal.*	Public	Most of the data maintained about a licensee is public. This includes the licensee's name, address, telephone number, licensed capacity, variances granted, type of dwelling, name and relationship of other family members, previous license history, class of license, and the nature and content of any past complaints if that information is not being maintained in anticipation of legal action, record of informal resolutions of licensing violations, orders of hearings, findings of fact, conclusions of law, and specifications of final disciplinary action. These data are retained as public so informed decision can be made. *(1993 Minnesota law made all applicant background information and 15 years of information on convictions public)*
Private *Is accessible by the data subject. Not accessible by the general public.* *Private and confidential data on deceased decendents becomes public data ten years after the death of the data subject and thirty years after the creation of the data.*	Nonpublic	Some data about licensees are classified as private or nonpublic, depending on whether the agency deems the care provider an individual or a vendor. These data include information about the care provider or other care provider family members which includes medical reports, reports from the Bureau of Criminal Apprehension, insurance information, social security numbers, social/home studies, and the identity and content of letters of reference. Information received by the care provider from the agency regarding the child and his family is considered confidential. Most data about clients maintained by the agency are private. Private data includes data that alone or in conjunction with other readily available public data can identify the subject of the data. *Can be given to:* • The person who is the subject of the data (the **data subject**). • Others who the law says can see the data. The individual **data subject** must be told at the time the data is asked for who else can see it. • Anyone the **data subject** says can see the data. The data subject may sign a "Consent for Release of Information," which says who can see or have copies of private or nonpublic data. • Minors who are the **data subject**, parent or guardian sign the release. However, minors need to be advised that they have a right to deny their parents access to private data. • If the court has granted custody of the minor to the welfare of placement agency, then the agency would make the determination of what information can be released to the care provider in order for adequate services to be provided.

I continued to read the file and listen to the tapes. The dynamics of the communications and miscommunications continued to haunt me. What was said and what was heard were different. The Smiths seemed to be very little fish swimming in a very big sea.

Knowing the rules, the reality, and the vocabulary, the social worker definitely held a one up position. It seemed he knew he held the power and could win. Sharon held her own in the conversaion, but was outmatched in knowledge and verbal skills. The whole thing seemed a cruel hoax. The social worker sounded like a despot.

I finished the file and let it settle in my brain. Then I called the family to discuss the issue of communication and to check on how they were doing.

Sharon answered the phone . . .

Confidential	Protected Nonpublic	Confidential data cannot be released without court order or statute specifically authorizing release. Data under investigation are often confidential. This poses a double bind for the agency and the provider home in that sometimes important information regarding the child and his background cannot legally be shared. Without data necessary to work with the child, providers can be placed in very vulnerable positions, yet social services is bound by law to not disclose this information.
This data is NOT accessible to the data subject unless data classification changes to PUBLIC or PRIVATE!		Active investigation files about the care provider cannot be seen by the care provider while the investigation is being conducted. However, once the investigation becomes inactive, most of the data becomes public, except for identity of reporter, persons who have been interviewed, and any clients involved.
		Cannot be given to the data subject. They can be given only to those people or agencies stipulated by state or federal law.
	Summary Data	These are statistics and come from private or confidential data. These data are publicly available, providing summary data presented cannot uniquely identify an individual.

Who is the data subject?

In any file containing your name, you are the data subject. This means for each child you care for and each license you hold there is a file containing data about you.

Examples of protected data:

Child Abuse and Neglect Reports	Information used to initiate an investigation of alleged child abuse or neglect.	
	• Initial report of alleged abuse or neglect of child.	**"Private"** can be seen by staff whose work assignment requires access, **data subject,** prosecuting authority, local welfare agency. (MS 626.556. Subd. 11)
	• Investigative data of law enforcement agency.	**"Confidential"** (MS 13.82. Subd. 5)
	• Name of reporter while report is under assessment or investigation.	**"Confidential"** (MS 626.556. Subd. 11)
	• Name of reporter after assessment or investigation is completed.	**"Confidential"** individual subject of record by court order.

Upon completion of the investigation, the classification of data may change from Confidential to Public.
Ask what the status of your data is before, during and after investigations. See sidebars pages 195-197.

Criminal Sexual Conduct with Minors Reports	Information used to initiate an investigation. Investigative data are used by the prosecuting authority to determine case disposition. • Reports and records on minors relating to complaints or indictments issued for criminal sexual conduct in the first through fourth degrees. • All other data, including the name of the defendant.	**"Nonpublic"** staff whose work assignment requires access, prosecuting authority, local welfare agency, **data subject**, court order[1] (MS 609.342-345, MS Ch387)
Sexual Abuse or Intrafamilial Sexual Abuse Record	Data collected during conduct of an investigation. • Identity of victims of criminal sexual conduct, intrafamilial sexual abuse, or the identity of a minor used in sexual performance.	**"Private"** staff whose work assignment requires access, prosecuting authority. (MS 13.82 Subd. 10)

1. Protection of identities. Public access to data on individuals when access to data would reveal the identity of (1) undercover law enforcement officer, (2) victim of criminal sexual conduct or intrafamilial sexual abuse, (3) an informant, or (4) victim or witness whose personal safety or property would be threatened. (MS 13.82. Subd. 10)

Investigative data

Active Investigations	Investigative data are gathered to prepare a case against a person and to determine if there is sufficient cause to prosecute. •Investigative data collected and created by law enforcement agency to prepare a case against a person, whether known or unknown, for the commission of a crime. • Inactive investigative data which has become active.	**"Confidential, Protected, Nonpublic"** staff whose work assignment requires access, prosecuting authority, crime victim with prosecuting authority authorization. (MS299C.065, MS CH387, MS 13.82, Subd. 5)
Inactive Investigations	Data collected and created by a law enforcement agency in order to prepare a case against a person, whether known or unknown, and the prosecuting authority or agency decides not to pursue the case or statute of limitations runs out or exhaustion or expiration of rights of appeal. Inactive investigative data becomes active.	These data are often destroyed. If a case is found unsubstantiated, the data subject should ask for complete copies of the file and the findings before the file is destroyed.

"Brian's most difficult relationship is with me, and yet we truly love each other. It is true, we cannot live together, but it does not mean it will always be so. We have not abandoned our son, but we feel that the system has abandoned us. By removing our family from the treatment process and focusing only on Brian, neither our family nor Brian is going to completely heal. We asked for help. We received help. But I question the kind of help we've received."

*"If Brian's issues are rooted in attachment, then additional separation is not going to help. But if the attachment disorder is rooted in our relationship, then unless it is healed we cannot live together. As a birth family we need training, support, and counseling **with Brian, not separate from** him. Brian is already twelve and waiting much longer will only continue to repress the reality."*

*Do not destroy unsubstantiated data files
without first making a complete copy for yourself.
Then authorize complete destruction of agency files.
An unsubstantiated allegation can return years later
and it is very costly to reconstruct old evidence.*

*It is understandable that you want to put this experience behind you,
but keep a copy in a safe place for future insurance.*

Do providers need to pay to see information about themselves?

There is no charge to see your files. However, you may have to pay for copies. Payment for copies of data must be made in advance. Talk to agency staff about the costs, how to request copies, and how payment should be made.

What happens when providers are told their files are lost?

Don't panic. Your files may be simply misplaced, located under a different spelling of your name, or filed by mistake with another person's file. It may also be out for temporary review and easily located when the correct person is asked. The file will most likely resurface. Document in your own records that it is presently unlocatable and offer other spellings of your name to the person you are speaking with. Let the person know you will be following up on date/time to see if the file has been located and then follow through.

How can providers see confidential data about themselves?

You cannot see your confidential data, but a judge can. Confidential data can only be given to persons or agencies stipulated by a state or federal law. A provider can file an injunction under the Data Privacy Act to challenge the accuracy of case findings and seek correction.

What if providers don't agree with the accuracy of the data?

If you believe the information is inaccurate or incomplete, you must inform the responsible authority in writing—preferably by certified mail—about the inaccuracy of the data. Send the letter to the agency that has your records. If data are confidential, you must get a court order to object to the data.

Within 30 days of the receipt of your letter the agency must inform you in writing of its decision. The responsible authority must either:

1. Correct the data that are not true or complete and try to tell others who got the data including those you asked that it be sent to;

2. Tell you the data are believed correct. These data can be given to others only if your statement of objection is included.

After the agency has replied in writing to your challenge you can appeal if you and the agency cannot agree about the truth or completeness of the data.

Appeals must be timely: a delay may remove your right to appeal the issue forever. Call your state's department of administration to learn about your rights to an appeal.

If you feel your data have been inappropriately handled, you may complain about it. Complaints about the handling of data in other agencies in the welfare system should be sent to the responsible authority of that agency. Call your agency to find out who the responsible authority is. Do not be surprised if your complaint falls into a black hole.

Is an independent family assessment a good idea? What is available?

Assessments done within the system may have biases. Therefore it is recommended you step outside the system for a second opinion. Qualified, honest, experienced psychologists and attorneys are expensive but may be worth the money. On the other hand, this expense may be to no avail if the investigating agency doesn't want or accept outside input. One care provider spent $2,500 on an attorney whom the county agency didn't want involved. Legal costs continued to mount as the family and the attorney jumped through hoops designed by the agency.

Parents accused of child maltreatment have relied on polygraph or lie detector tests, voice stress tests, hypnosis, psychological analysis, and other methods of assessment to prove their innocence. Some attorneys refuse to take a new client accused for child maltreatment unless a voice stress test and polygraph test are performed. These two tests can be done quickly and do not add delays to a crisis situation. These tests, along with client psychological evaluations done by a board certified psychologist, add credibility to a case. A board certified psychologist is recommended, especially in sexual misconduct allegations, because child psychology testing tools can be misused and misinterpreted. A board certified psychologist is more likely to search for a diagnosis instead of trying to find evidence to fit into the existing diagnosis. These evaluations should be videotaped. This allows for future analysis of the evaluation. Psychologists who refuse or respond defensively to videotaping an adult or child evaluation raise red flags. Parents can request that all interviews with their children be videotaped. If that is denied, a judge can order it. Video and audio tapes, however, can be edited—so use caution. The information in these videos, along with written summaries, can be very helpful in legal proceedings.

How can providers protect children from being removed from their home?

If rumors have started that an allegation has been made against your family, have your attorney file an injunction. An injunction is simply an order from a court prohibiting the agency from carrying out a given action or ordering a given action to be carried out. Injunctions can be obtained before you receive written information that an allegation has been made against you. This process can save unnecessary removal of a child, along with heartache, time, and money.

It may be appropriate to file an injunction which will provide temporary restraint from removing a child in care because of the psychological harm the child may suffer. This will temporarily place your case on hold, speed the proceedings, and put your case in front of a judge. An injunction can provide time to protect a child from an unneccessary move while you figure out the next step. It also will provide time to begin a thorough psychological evaluation of your family system and the child. If the child will be moving, it provides time for preparation, preplacement visits, and transition.

An injunction also can order action on possible inaccuracy of information alleged. This reverses the burden of proof from the family to the keeper of the data. Licensed providers do not need to wait until a license is revoked to take

The file lay on my desk and I pondered ...

Was Mrs. Smith an innocent citizen caught in a costly mistake with her son in limbo in the foster care system?

Or was Mrs. Smith confused, and was the system providing quality services to heal her son? Had Mrs. Smith baited the worker on the phone to become angry, knowing the conversation was being taped? Did she know what to say to encourage the negative response given?

I had no absolutes. Only questions without answers.

And I began to realize that one problem with the truth is not having all of it. Decisions made with only pieces of the facts are worse than guessing!

action. Care providers do not need to maintain a defensive position. Offensive action against a false allegation can occur immediately upon hearing that an allegation has been made.

How do providers appeal a decision?

If you receive written notice of a decision you do not agree with, call the person listed on the letter and ask to whom you should send a letter of appeal. An administrative law judge can throw a case out at any time without having reviewed the entire case. You may never go to court. Do not delay in submitting a letter of appeal. *If you do not respond within the designated time periods, you may never be able to.* If you do not know who the responsible authority is, ask a person employed by the agency that has the data. An appeal can be launched with or without an attorney.

The letter of appeal should include:

1. Your name, address, and phone number.

2. The responsible authority's name and address and what license or issue you represent.

3. A description of the nature of the dispute and why you feel the the data are untrue, misrepresented, or incomplete.

4. What you want done about it.

An allegation takes on a life of its own once the machinery of the system has been set in motion. Individual workers may easily get sucked into the process, regardless of whether or not they believe the allegation. It is in the best interest—financially and reputably—of the state and agency to prove their findings are correct and the individual or family is in the wrong. In some cases all stops are pulled out against the family to save face.

Families who move through the appeal process face additional personal financial costs. These families—on their own—must secure attorneys, child psychologists, medical professionals, character witnesses, etc. Each action costs time and money. Expenses can run into hundreds of thousands of dollars. Appeals are costly and both parties incur financial liabilities. Meanwhile the state has a whole army of people in place who are paid, trained, and available to help provide services, advice, and information for the benefit of the state or state's system.

Final costs incurred by the state are to be paid by the party who is the loser. The liability of having to pay double legal costs is perplexing to private individuals.

The end result can begin wars of litigation, with families suing the state and the state suing the family. Although states have lost in these cases, it is highly unusual for the settlement to be a lot of money.

If the state loses, a $500 settlement in damages may cover a couple of hours of legal fees, but hardly puts a dent in actual costs.

What happens to records once the case is closed or inactive?

Individuals have the right to include their own perspective of the situation within their data files and request in writing that their perspective be shared whenever the file is reviewed by another person. Individuals also can request in writing that inaccurate or misleading data be corrected. If an individual is unable to obtain files for review, an attorney can probably seek a court petition for file

It had been more than two years since Scott, age 15, had spoken to his mother. At 13, he had accused his stepfather of sexually abusing his sister. She denied the charges. Scott was placed in foster care.

Missing home, he called. Three months later he was advised he would be going home. His mother wanted him home again and the agency arranged for his return in less than two weeks.

Scott reacted destructively. His foster parents called the agency and said they thought he was asking for help.

Social services responded that the foster family was overreacting.

He went home as planned.

review. Then if the data still remain inaccurate or misleading, a "redress" (to set right) through a lawsuit may be necessary.

If a case is unfounded or unsubstantiated each state handles data retention differently. It is wise for the accused individual to keep a complete set of the original files in a safe place. If another allegation surfaces in the future, these files can be invaluable, and eliminate the need to reconstruct history.

Data can be corrected, destroyed, expunged, removed, or sealed.

Corrected means files are corrected as requested by the data subject.

Destroyed means the files are destroyed.

Expunging means erasing, deleting, or obliterating information. It generally refers to identifying information about the child and the parents and, under certain circumstances, the reporter or other persons who cooperated with the investigation.

Removing means the files are removed, but not necessarily destroyed.

Sealed data means that the records are not destroyed, but in accordance with legal procedures, can be reopened at a later time. The records are usually removed from the regular record-keeping area and placed in a locked file.

Some states require the entire record be destroyed. Some states retain records for the purpose of data gathering but expunge the names and other information identifying the subjects of the report. In other states, the data subject must request that their files be sealed, corrected or destroyed.

Contact your state elected representative
for a copy of individual state practices.

Summary

Proper communication is important to the outcome of the investigation. Cooperation is your best long-term strategy unless you feel the investigation is biased or prejudged. Information given to investigators needs to be concise and factual. Permitting your emotions to interfere with the facts is not helpful and in fact may hinder your case. Many times third party communicators—psychologists and attorneys—may be more effective in communicating than the individual accused of maltreatment.

If an allegation is made, an investigation must follow. If you are being investigated, the investigator's job is to conclude whether or not abuse or neglect occurred to this specific child and in this specific instance. The investigator's responsibility is not to judge the quality of care in your home. The investigator's job is not dealing with the emotions of the situation. The investigation itself should not be abusive to care providers, children, or the social services. If it is abusive, contact your care provider association, psychologist, or attorney to help you advocate your position.

— It is important that all factual information is available for the investigation process.

— Assertiveness is important to clear communication of your message. Being too aggressive or too passive can result in unfair labeling of you and your family.

Scott was returned home without preparation and reintroduction to his family system.

Within three months Scott was in a state residential treatment program.

Within a year the sexual abuse allegation against the stepfather was confirmed.

This letter was from the concerned foster family

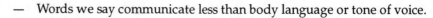

> *It is impossible for one to play God without being God. The system of child protection will never be able to be perfect.*

— Words we say communicate less than body language or tone of voice.

— Personality, cultural, and communication differences do occur. If this begins to happen, address the issue forthrightly. Get to know your own style of communication and understand your strong and weak areas. Seek additional training.

— Care providers need to be kept abreast of the investigation procedures. Investigations need to be timely and care providers must be notified upon their completion.

— Care providers need honesty regarding future placements and agency practices for child removal.

— Care providers can file an injunction to keep foster children in their home while an investigation is being conducted.

— Written policies regarding how allegations against care providers are to be handled must be made available immediately to families facing allegations.

— Access to your files will vary, depending on classification of data. During an investigation there will be some data about yourself and your family that you do not have access to.

— Additional outside assessments done by qualified and reputable professionals can be very helpful to the provider who is facing allegations.

— Care providers must be made aware from the outset of the fact the abuse allegation is a risk they may encounter.

— There is a need to eliminate the concept *"guilty until proven innocent"* for care providers.

Care providers and their families are not asking for a moratorium on abuse investigations. We acknowledge, with sorrow, that abuse does take place in some care provider homes. If the care provider system is to remain credible, investigations are a necessity. To deny any of this would defeat the very purpose for which we stand—the protection of children.

References

Besharov, Douglas. 1991. *Recognizing Child Abuse. A Guide for the Concerned.* New York: The Free Press.

Carbino, Rosemarie. 1989. *Child Welfare Issues in How Social Services Systems Respond to Allegations of Foster Home Abuse/Neglect. Putting Child Welfare Back into Child Protection.* in J. Sprouse (Ed.) *Allegations of Abuse in Family Foster Care: An Examination of the Impact on Foster Families.* King George, Va.: American Foster Care Resources, Inc.

Mattison, Scott. 1989. *Data Practices Refresher for Law Enforcement.* Minnesota: Chisago County Sheriff's Department, Sponsored by Minnesota State Sheriff's Association.

McFadden, Emily Jean. 1984. *Preventing Abuse in Foster Care.* Michigan: Eastern Michigan University

MN Department of Administration. 1991. *Your Rights as the Subject of Government Data.* Minnesota: Data Practices Division, MN Department of Administration, 320 Centennial Office Building, 658 Cedar Street, St. Paul, MN 55155. (612) 297-5888.

O'Neill, Susan. 1991. *Observations of a Foster Parent and Trainer.* in R. Carbino, Ed. *Consequences of Child Abuse Allegations for Foster Families.* Madison, Wisconsin: Health and Human Issues, University of Wisconsin-Madison, 21-23

Weissman, Harold, Epstein, Irwin, & Savage, Andrea. 1983. *Agency Based Social Work. Neglected Aspects of Clinical Practice.* Pennsylvania: Temple University Press

Chapter 7

Social Services: No Time for the Service?

*Care provider families need to understand
the requirements of the child welfare system.
Social services and the family
facing allegations of child abuse
are in very different positions.*

A service industry relies on client satisfaction. In my fantasy, I pictured social services serving clients the way my company serves customers. I found some important distinctions. First, my design company exists in a very competitive and progressive market. Second, my customers can choose what company they want to work with and how they want to work. Third, they can end the relationship when they want to.

Success depends on customer satisfaction. And customer satisfaction depends on whether or not expectations are met or exceeded and on whether or not budgets and deadlines are met. The checks and balances generated by customers keep businesses accountable. Administrative reviews, court reviews, and reports create some checks and balances in the social welfare system. But customer satisfaction checks and balances are limited. Clients of social services have little choice in whom they work with, for how long, or in what manner.

*People expect responsiveness to their problems.
Persons working in social services have the power
to make or break a relationship.*

Think of a time when you have been dissatisfied with a service company. Did you go back? If you returned, did you return willingly? Did you ask for advice or help? Was anything said or done to make you feel defensive or react negatively? Clients expect dependability, responsibility, and accountability. These are usually attainable when people skills are adequate and when time is taken to display empathy, care, and attention.

Not all clients or service providers are easy to work with. Each relationship demands time and attention. Each social service client and case is unique—needs and expectations vary. Some cases take considerable time and

Thirty-five cases... maybe if I could get through the paper work I could go see one of them.

emotional and financial resources. Other issues can be handled quickly. Social services must determine which issues are important, what services are available, and what needs to be done to stimulate positive growth.

People treated unfairly seek others to trust and stop communicating forthrightly with the very people who are in a position to help them.

Taxi drivers and bartenders are in unique positions to listen to people who are isolated and estranged from society. They have listened to devastating experiences that insecure and vulnerable people have had with social services. I bring this information to light here because I believe customer service training is often lacking in social services. Statements and actions that seem professionally appropriate may be easily misinterpreted at the client level. For example: conversations that avoid the personal name of the individual and refer to the person as "birth parent" or "client" evoke feelings of condescension and disrespect.

Budgets continue to be cut. Societal problems continue to escalate. Children and families continue to need support, intervention, and care. Agencies have little control over these circumstances. Decreased budgets and increased program needs do not warrant approval for depressed attitudes. In fact, negative attitudes will only compound this already complex issue.

Social workers frequently complain about lack of funding. But funding is not necessarily the only issue. There are many dedicated individuals in social services making do with very little. As in business, small, under-funded, and under-equipped entities can provide quality services and gain customer satisfaction. The difference lies not in the availability of money—it lies in the individuals who offer services.

Lack of time may prohibit even the best social workers from providing quality services. Workers who are overextended with complicated caseloads, court appearances, paperwork, and services may discover that even with the best plans and intentions, a day is too short. *Under these conditions, no amount of training will overcome sheer lack of time.* (McFadden, Ryan 1992)

Regardless of whether money and/or time is lacking, how we interact with each other is crucial to the outcome and satisfaction of those we serve. People work with people. The best program, operating with disgruntled employees, will perform inadequately regardless of the funding poured into it.

If you are a social worker, ask yourself: Would I like to be a foster family working for my agency? Would I like to be a client served by my agency? Why? Why not? Be as honest as possible. If you answer no, you have the opportunity to uncover areas in need of improvement. What would you change? What do you think clients and foster care providers need? At a minimum, they need a responsive social service and child welfare system.

Why is it so hard to be a social worker?

Child protection workers often witness the violent effects of child abuse and neglect. Seeing children injured or killed is difficult for people who have made a career of protecting young people. Many times child protection workers are the first on the scene after law enforcement or medical personnel have determined child maltreatment. These individuals have a difficult job, they must objectively assess a crisis situation and balance the protection of children with the hope of restoring the family.

Timing is very important . . .

People are not always ready to receive help. Change is not easy for many people.

The social worker cannot "rescue" people from their problems. The desire to change has to come from within the individual, but sometimes a supportive, caring, and helpful person can encourage a person to be willing to try again.

A social worker must accept people as they are, problems and all, and appreciate people for their differences in values, lifestyle, and personality.

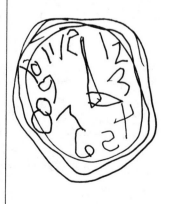

Protecting children and setting up reunification programs for abusive parents are difficult and opposing tasks. In some cases, one individual is called upon to both assess a family in crisis and provide preservation services. This places the worker in a complicated and conflicting position. The initial experience of being exposed to a battered child may weigh heavily on the heart of the very person required to develop and monitor a family treatment plan. It is difficult to experience a devastating event, interpret the event, and then act professionlly to *"help"* the very people who caused the devastation.

Two distinct temperaments are needed to manage both job responsibilities—reactive and reflective, thinking and feeling, sensing and intuitive. Few individuals can juggle this dichotomy for very long. Social workers who are placed in this difficult role must be self-caring and find support to keep from developing negative service attitudes and reactions.

What is a negative social service attitude or behavior?

Regardless of the event that triggers child protection response, social workers are required to maintain professionalism. Social workers may think they are acting professionally and yet harm the very relationship they are trying to establish. Some common behaviors which *"turn off"* clients and providers are:

Condescension—being treated with a patronizing attitude. Families are worked on—not with. Workers ignore the strengths and assets of the family. They point out limitations and problems and tell the family what needs to be done. The family's participation in solutions is limited or void. It is difficult for a person in crisis to cooperate with a worker who maintains a one-up position. Families in crisis want collaboration.

Unfriendliness/coldness—being treated with aloofness, indifference, inconsideration, or impatience. The family whose social worker maintains an air of coldness will distance itself from the worker and lose trust. Since it is in the best interest of the worker and the family to develop a relationship, this chain reaction becomes a roadblock to good social work practice. The family remains trapped in old issues and fears. Communication is limited, misinterpretation escalates, and real issues may be avoided or never uncovered.

I'm only following the rules—rules and procedures thwart children and families from getting necessary services. Agency rules and procedures must be respected and followed, yet they can be a barrier to relationships. Providing families with the rules in writing and explaining why they exist is a far better approach than simply saying, *"I'm just doing what I have to do."* Families are capable of respecting procedures and rules if they are made clear and described with warmth and caring instead of mechanically repeated.

Avoidance—a worker avoids dealing with the *"real"* concern and highlights issues of nonimportance. Questions can't be answered or an individual with a problem is handed off to others without assurance that someone will be able to help. The worker does not visit or return phone calls To the family, avoidance feels like rejection. For example, a foster family requests additional support for an acting out adolescent and instead of support hears, *"Well, yes, some children in the system do behave like this."* The comment is made without empathy, support, or ideas to offer help.

The bottom line is, "I'm responsible . . ."

Foster parents and social workers need to be accountable for children under their care.

Spontaneous and unannounced visits by the licensing worker provide a valuable evaluation tool in evaluating the foster home in providing normal day-to-day care.
Social worker

In any relationship, you need the good times to help you get through the bad.

If a care provider communicates with the social worker only when there is trouble and never reports positive results, the worker may discern that the provider relationship is difficult and is always troubled.
Social worker

Residential facility is a generic term used to identify group homes and residential treatment centers. Foster families offer a less restrictive environment and are the most normal settings available f or children in non-related, out-of-home care.

Foster families are versatile in providing services for a wide range of vulnerable individuals. Infants, children, adolescents, and adults can be served in the home family environment. The development of specialized foster families has especially widened this range.

Social worker

Any system will become unbalanced when the time spent doing administrative work outweighs the provision of services.

Supervisor

What do social workers do when working with foster care?

The illustration represents people and job functions social workers regularly work with for each child placed in foster care. Many social workers average 25 or more family systems. Each system may include 10 primary contacts. In addition, each system which places children in care—probation, child protection, clinical—has its own philosophies and program agendas. The social worker is often caught between the needs of the families being served and the requirements of the system.

TIME DISTRIBUTION

50% - 80%
ADMINISTRATIVE
(See Examples**)

TIME AVAILABLE FOR
CASE WORK

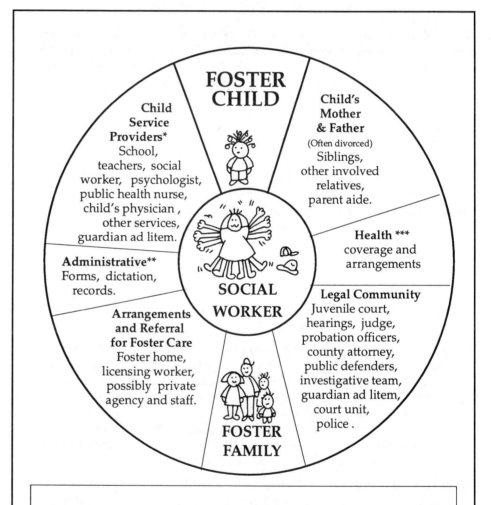

* Includes knowing which community services are available and how to access them for the child and family.

** Includes working with the unit supervisor, commissioner, and Department of Human Services, meetings, reports, documentation, dictation, summaries, analysis, recommendations.

*** Includes arrangements for medical assistance and counseling services for parent and/or child in dealing with mental health, physical or chemical dependency problems.

How do agency practices harm social worker, provider, and client relationships?

A social worker may perform exceptionally well and yet be thwarted by the practices of the agency. Agencies can impede success and influence failure. The leadership and administration of an agency dictate how the actual field work is carried out. When agency practices hinder good social work, the whole system is destined to fail and the social worker, child, and family are given a ticket to a roller coaster ride.

Answer is NO!—Instead of a "can do" attitude, this agency attitude is, "No, you can't." No is used more often than yes, and the workers spend time telling individuals they serve why they can't meet their needs instead of figuring out ways to solve issues of concern.

Buried in paperwork—Workers are required to fill out forms and special requests for every service provided and every action taken. The amount of paperwork required begins to hinder access to programs. This agency may also reject services requested because the paperwork wasn't completed properly. It is not uncommon for case files to be a foot thick. Such records, if the contents contain erroneous data, are as much a liability as an asset.

Clogged pipeline—Requests for services, information, and help get sent to the appropriate person and then disappear, never to be seen again. Eventually workers figure out ways to circumvent the individual who is clogging their actions or they quit asking for help.

No money!—Since funds are low, decisions revolve around available funding instead of seeking out alternative solutions.

Point the finger—This agency finds someone to blame for a problem. Workers avoid sharing issues or deny problems or responsibilities to avoid conflict. Foster parents are scapegoats as they provide direct services but are not in day-to-day agency contact. Social workers are caught in the middle when they stand behind a foster family or try a new idea or program.

Racism—Workers fear being labeled racist and the agency fears lawsuits. Poor decisions are excused because of following perceived cultural and ethnic requirements. Hiring practices may also contribute to dysfunction. Affirmative action objectives may be met, but the real needs of the population served may be missed. For example, if the general population minority ratio is twenty percent and the staff of the agency is twenty percent minority, the agency has fulfilled its mandated quota. If, however, the population served is eighty percent minority, the twenty percent quota falls short of the needs of clients. Yet if the agency advertised for minority employees to fill these spaces, it could be liable for an affirmative action lawsuit. A cross-cultural dilemna.

Stay out of my space—Instead of working as a team, the workers face difficulty when trying to work around or through various people or departments. Areas of responsibility are divided into each department's personal ego territory. These turf boundaries discourage cooperation, proper delegation, and a team spirit.

Your Eminence—"*You will do this or else.*" "*This is how it's going to be, take it or leave it.*" With this type of supervisor in authority, workers may be forced to follow dicta which may or may not be appropriate for a given situation. In addition, creative solutions, brainstorming, group decisions, and cooperation take a nosedive.

During an annual licensing visit in March 1992, the following conversation was overheard:

"Bobby touched my private parts!"
Eight-year-old foster girl

The social worker turns toward the voice to listen for additional conversation while the foster mother looks uneasy and embarrassed. Upon completion of the licensing review, the social worker goes to the supervisor to discuss the conversation. The decision is made to call law enforcement for suspected sexual abuse to a child.

Law enforcement is called in and a uniformed police officer knocks on the door of the foster home.

"Mrs. Smith, could we speak to your son Bobby?"
Officer

Social services had good intentions to protect the child. What additional assessment could this worker have done? Did the worker follow good social work practice?

Turn the page to learn the conclusion.

The relationship among the agency, social worker, and care provider needs to be like a healthy marriage. Healthy marriages require communication, honesty, support, trust, respect, and a sharing of responsibilities from both partners. Each partner works to understand and care about the other's needs. These marriages evolve over time and grow with shared positive and negative experience.

In March of 1993, 460,000 children were in foster care and 100,000 licensed families were available. Thirty percent of those families —from an already inadequate supply—leave fostering each year. Why do they come? What makes them leave? What makes them stay?

Information regarding something as important as families and their children must be carefully weighed. It is far too easy to enhance or detract from the reality.

The Child Welfare Institute (CWI) in Atlanta, Georgia, has developed a training and assessment program titled *Foster Family Recruitment and Retention: A Local Agency Assessment* (1993). This program describes why people choose to foster children and what relationship is needed between the care provider and the agency. The local agency assessment helps agency staff identify which foster care recruitment, preparation, and retention programs support or hinder services. Staff can use this information to make proactive decisions about intervention and improve the effectiveness of foster parent recruitment and retention. A sample of their general findings follows:

Individuals choose foster parenting to fill a need—does their need fit the agency need?

Ninety-nine percent accuracy is not good enough!

One hundred percent accuracy is the only acceptable result when we are dealing with the lives of children and families
. . . and those results may be impossible.

If we accept one percent inaccuracy, we can assume that it will be okay to . . .

. . . give twelve babies daily to the wrong parents.

. . . accept incorrect findings in twenty-seven thousand families accused of maltreating children.

Birth parent

> *For some, this need is to rescue, protect, and remove children from troubled situations. If this is the reason, the motivation to parent children in out-of-home care may wane when the real work begins. Foster care is no longer 24-hour-a-day child care for children who have been removed from families Today, children are removed when there is imminent danger, and foster parents are asked to become a part of the treatment team. This means interaction with the very people who perpetrated the maltreatment. Foster parents whose motivation is to rescue and protect children may not fit into the type of interdependent team needed. Often these families burn out on foster care within a few placements—hurt, dissatisfied, and misunderstanding the system. As in business, one dissatisfied customer will tell eleven others, who will tell five others. In essence the agency will have to overcome 66 negative public relations exposures.*

> *Others enjoy the role of parenting and wish to care for and nurture children. These individuals enjoy being challenged. They are secure in their present relationships and desire to parent, nurture, and raise children. They are willing to help children unlearn patterns of behavior and are willing to teach them how to have healthy relationships with parents. They also are willing to help birth parents develop healthy realtionships with their children. They teach children how to get their needs met and are not afraid to advocate to help a child in their care. These providers gain their satisfaction in caring for children by the growth they see in themselves and the small steps the children in their care make.*

CWI's research has revealed unsuspected care provider needs. Foster parents come to agencies primarily to improve children's lives. They leave agencies because they feel they are not being supported. *The Foster Family Recruitment and Retention: A Local Agency Assessment* helps to identify strengths and needs in relationships between agencies and foster parents. In the first component, it identifies how the absence or presence of concrete supports for foster families and children may affect foster parents. The second component measures practice emphasis. This component covers 13 aspects of an agency's relationship with foster parents. The variables include: clarity, partnership, support, commitment, responsiveness, preparation, openness, recognition, flexibility, stability, accountability, excellence, and leadership. Questionnaires are completed by administrators, child protection, foster care and adoption staff, foster care homefinding staff, and foster parents to avoid biases related to roles.

Some of the recent findings have concluded that foster parents:

NEED GROWTH AND COMPETENCE—Are foster parents given the information and skills they need to achieve goals and outcomes? What high standards are expected, maintained, and supported? Is the authority system in the agency responsive to the program's and individual's need for development and success? Do workers show an interest in the wisdom, experience, and knowledge of the provider? Foster parents need training opportunities that expand their knowledge. Experienced foster parents have been found to be excellent trainers for other foster parents, birth families, and professionals working in the system of child welfare. Social service staff training classes should be open to providers.

NEED SOCIAL INTERACTION—Are problems recognized and acknowledged? How much mutual participation and teamwork is there? How much sensitivity and empathy is there toward feelings of foster parents? Providing care for children is isolating. Issues that *need* discussion can be classified as confidential or private data. The social worker can offer safe social interaction when these discussion needs arise. Telephone calls need to be returned—voice mail and answering machines can help send and receive some messages.

NEED TO FEEL SECURE—To what extent do foster parents feel a sense of freedom to express thoughts, feelings, and needs without fear of reprisal or intimidation? Are roles, methods, and intended outcomes defined for foster families? Is there a sense of safety and security for foster parents? Foster parents will work to make themselves feel secure. How can the agency help?

NEED SELF-WORTH—Are foster parents' contributions positively valued and appropriately recognized? To what extent can foster parents feel responsible and accountable for the outcomes of the program and their own contributions? Caring for children in out-of-home care can be a thankless job. The birth parent may be wary, jealous, and angry. Society desires to keep kids out of the "horrors of foster care." Adoption agencies desire to save kids from foster care and find them permanent homes. Social services desires to get kids out of foster care and back home. Foster parents are locked in the middle. They care about the kids now.

NEED AUTONOMY TO PARENT CHILDREN—How much flexibility and openness to new ideas and change exist? To what extent are foster parents included in decision making and service processes? Foster care providers are with children in out-of-home care 24 hours a day. As the predominant service provider for children under their care, they ask for more active participation from the agency in developing and helping to carry out a child's and family's caseplan. They want to be able to testify in court proceedings and act as advocates for the needs of their children.

The Foster Family Recruitment and Retention: A Local Agency Assessment (1993) can be ordered for your agency by calling or writing: Child Welfare Institute, 1365 Peachtree Street, Suite 700, Atlanta, Georgia 30309. Phone (404) 876-1934. A full catalog of other excellent training programs and materials is available.

We've made it a family policy to have a two-week preplacement visit before accepting a high risk child in our home. During this time we meet the parents, get to know the child's caseworker, and assess and monitor the child.

After two weeks, my wife and I and the social worker are usually in agreement on what actions are best for the child and his family. We also have a clearer understanding on the issues needing to be addressed.
Foster father 20 years

Service requires . . .

. . . quick response

. . . on-time delivery

. . . timely resolution of disputes or errors.

If customers could come to social services under their own volition, would they make referrals to others in need of services?

Is there customer satisfaction?

What's the job of the caseworker?

Working with abusive or neglectful parents is extremely important to encourage change. When the parent and the child can be treated together as a unit in need of help—rather than as an abuser and a victim—positive results may occur within the family as parents recognize child abuse and resolve to do something about it. These parents may feel they are raising children properly. They may say, *"But, most of the time we parent well. This is an exception,"* or *"This was the way we were raised and we turned out OK."* If this is the case, understanding and training are much more appropriate and valuable than punishment for something they believed was correct.

When alleged maltreatment results in counseling and therapy for the family, and children remain in the home, child protection has succeeded. *Success is an improved family situation and prevention of future abuse or neglect.* This philosophy may be OK as a general principle, but for severe or repetitive abuse or neglect, it may be Pollyanna-ish and dangerous. In some cases, foster care is the best temporary solution for protecting the child and helping the family.

> *Starry-eyed and optimistic, Ellen graduated from college and began work in child protection. She immediately realized that four years of college and a degree didn't prepare her for the experience or responsibilities her job demanded. Eight complex family situations demanded every minute of her time. Financial resources were scarce and documentation seemed endless. It didn't take long for Ellen to realize that written policy and actual practice were not the same. What looked in perfect order on paper wasn't followed. On top of everything else, there appeared to be major issues within the agency, and Ellen hadn't yet discovered the players.*

Ellen jumped in and battled the system. She learned that the agency had unwritten rules and if they weren't followed, her job became very difficult. Services she needed weren't available when she needed them. She discovered that objective professionals also have biases—there were some things people wanted to know and some things they didn't. Some findings of investigations were accepted and other findings seemed to be ignored even though they held vital truthful pieces.

She uncovered the political players and the intricacies she needed to maneuver. She learned which individuals within the system had differing biases, when it was appropriate to be forceful and direct, and when it was time to be subtle. She worked hard at providing services for families and keeping children in their homes, taking the time necessary to listen to her troubled families and gathering the facts from all sides before making a decision. Some of her families grew and healed. In other cases, things didn't work out so well. Circumstances sometimes prevented success.

> *Erik Carson's family appeared in trouble. His first grade teacher had called child protection with concern after Erik came to school with a bruised cheek and sprained wrist. He said he had fallen off a chair.*
>
> *Erik had been physically abused before, and sexual abuse was suspected but not proved. Erik appeared to be the scapegoat when his father and mother were drinking. As the oldest child, Erik, age seven, protected his younger sisters, four-year-old Kati and three-year-old Tabatha. He also helped to care for his two-year-old brother, Sam.*
>
> *Erik's mother sometimes passed out before noon, and Erik would be left alone to care for the three young children. Erik's father would stop at the local tavern after work, enter the house angry, and interrogate Erik regarding why*

I've learned to have empathy for people in bad situations. I came from a sheltered, middle class background and the only poverty I had seen was on TV or making a wrong turn into a "bad" neighborhood. Now I go in that neighborhood a couple of times a week, and I understand these people are surviving, and there is beauty in their lives even though they live from circumstance to circumstance. The woman I'm an aide to has feelings and needs just like mine. She has wildflowers on her table in an orange soda bottle, broken tea cups for tea, and her five children sleep in one room on the same mattress. Yet in many ways we are more alike than different. I could be in her situation if my life had been different.

Volunteer parent aide, social worker in training

Both of the single moms I worked with had their parental rights terminated, and the kids went up for adoption. I was there to hold them and be a friend.

Parent aide

Pressures On Social Worker

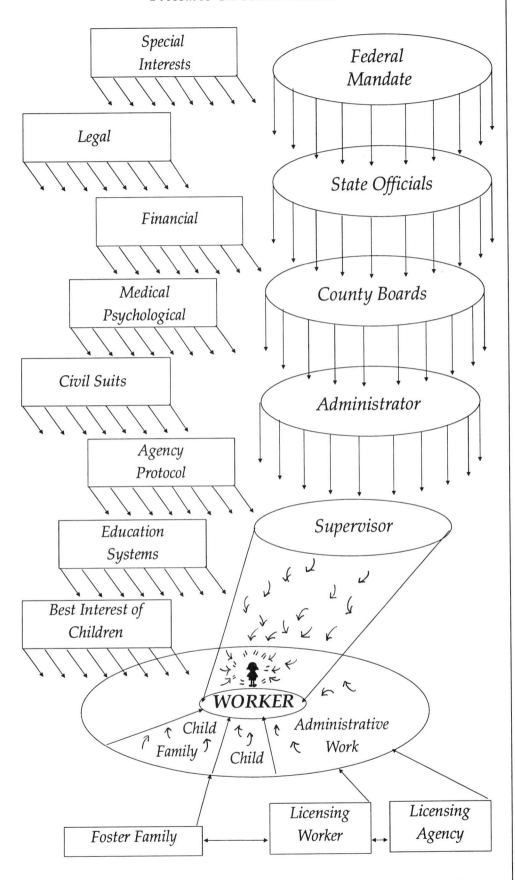

- Special Interests
- Legal
- Financial
- Medical Psychological
- Civil Suits
- Agency Protocol
- Education Systems
- Best Interest of Children

- Federal Mandate
- State Officials
- County Boards
- Administrator
- Supervisor

WORKER

- Child Family
- Child
- Administrative Work

- Foster Family
- Licensing Worker
- Licensing Agency

The social worker does not make a decision independently. Many disciplines weigh heavily on the choices and reactions a social worker can make.

he couldn't stop his mother's drinking. His father would rage at his mother, and Erik would sometimes intervene and receive the blows intended for his mother. His attendance record in first grade was poor, his personal appearance shoddy, and his behavior vacillated between complete withdrawal and aggressiveness.

Ellen was given the Carson family case. She thought it was similar to other cases as she looked through the file from the intake worker and the teacher's report. Two parent family. Father works up to sixty hours a week to stay financially even. Mother stays home. First child arrived while mother was in high school. Home is rented and in an older neighborhood. Father picked up once for DWI in last three years. No information on mother's drinking. From the file, the family appeared like many other families—some were abusive, some were not. Ellen's job was to determine the reality and the need for family services and support.

Ellen was required by law to assess the family and, if possible, keep the children in the home. To repair the family, she would have to compile documentation and order services she believed would enhance the family's potential for preservation. Ordering services was not as simple as telephoning to make an appointment. First, Ellen had to play "telephone tag" with prospective service providers. When contact was made, she checked to see if the provider would accept medical assistance. Then she could explain the situation and photocopy the background history of the case to be summarized and sent to the provider. Once the provider had offered to provide services, Ellen could tell the family, arrange for client transportation, and encourage the clients to attend. Finally, she had to follow up on the appointment, evaluate the outcome of services, and write up a report.

> Intially, Ellen offered parenting classes and a homemaker to help Erik's mother care for the four children. By removing some of the mother's personal stress, Ellen hoped to lower her frustration level. Erik's father reacted angrily toward this intrusion by child protection. He worked all day and believed his wife should be capable of managing the children and home while he supported them. Ellen arranged marriage counseling for the parents with free child care while they attended the program. Erik's father enrolled in an anger workshop. Erik's parents began working toward restoration. The drinking subsided, but didn't stop.

> One weekend, Erik's mother fell while intoxicated, sprained her ankle, and received a black eye. By this time, Ellen had a fledgling relationship with the family. After discussion with the parents and the medical doctor who treated the sprain, Ellen recommended an outpatient alcoholic treatment program for the father. Erik's mother appeared to need more intensive services and would benefit from an inpatient program for chemical dependency. In addition, Ellen wanted Erik to see a counselor and ordered an assessment of the other children. Ellen made contact with Erik's grandparents and they offered to take the four children while Erik's mother was in the chemical dependency program. The grandparents were aware of the drinking and abuse, but did not know how to intervene. They were relieved that someone was finally forcing change on the family.

If progress is not made by the family, out-of-home child care may be an option. Ellen can request referral to foster care by voluntary or involuntary placement of the children. Before a child enters foster care, Ellen must present her findings to a committee to get approval. When presenting her recommendation to the committee, Ellen may use reports from service providers familiar with the family situation. This includes reports from psychologists, school, medical personnel, law enforcement, and child protection. This internal committee then decides if out-of-home care is appropriate.

If out-of-home care does not appear to be necessary, additional service recommendations are made, and Ellen is required to offer services before placement. Ellen must be careful to present current documentation. If the information she provides is too old, she will need to get updated data from professionals involved in the case. Once all qualifications have been met and the committee has approved out-of-home care, Ellen may look for a family appropriate for the children. She is required by law to find the least restrictive out-of-home setting and, if possible, keep all of the children in the family together. Her first task is assessing all relatives to see if the children can be placed temporarily in their care. Relatives or kin are checked first, and often children can be taken care of without any additional financial obligation or intervention from the government. If a relative who can care for the children is found, Ellen will need to make sure the family and home meet appropriate standards. If a relative is not available or does not meet the qualifications of care, Ellen's job is to find a culturally similar family to care for the children.

Placing the four children with relatives seemed the perfect solution. The children adored their grandparents and appeared to have a delightful relationship. The grandparents owned their home, did not have any debts, and appeared stable and mature. They were retired and could spend time with the children. They did not drink, and from referrals, seemed to be just what every child needed. The grandparents liked both parents and were supportive of the programs social services offered. The father could visit anytime he wasn't working or in counseling, and the children could go home for weekends. The grandparents were willing to transport the children to visit their mother in the treatment center. The family would not need to be licensed, and Ellen could monitor from a distance. This seemed ideal.

Erik's grandparents are in their late sixties and even though their hearts were in the right place, caring for four young children was extremely difficult. Hazel, the grandmother, called Ellen and asked for help. The demands of a two-, three-, four-, and seven-year-old were physically, emotionally, and financially draining. Normally patient and caring, the grandparents had noticed they were becoming impatient. Things that hadn't irritated them in the beginning were becoming intolerable. The cost of caring for the children was more than the grandfather's pension and social security benefits could afford. Hazel and her husband had always gotten by. They had been financially hurting at times but had never asked for help. With their physical health failing and an inability to gain significant employment, they didn't know what to do.

When additional financial help is needed by relatives to care for children in out-of-home care, Ellen can recommend that the relative family become licensed. With the acceptance of the license, a relative home is required to abide by the same licensing regulations as other licensed families. Laws governing professional parents, however, may place excessive demands on relatives.

If options of relative and same race care fail, Ellen must document and seek out the least restrictive setting. Only then can she research alternatives, beginning in the less expensive county foster families. If none is available, she may proceed to the more specialized private agency homes or available treatment programs. Ellen called the licensing department to find out what foster family homes were available.

Annie, age 15, was another of Ellen's cases. Already the product of two failed adoptions, Annie wanted out again! There was no way she was going to stay

Like an emergency room, the shelter and its trained social workers work 24 hours a day, 365 days a year.

Determination is made if there is a history of child abuse or family violence. Connections with the county computer open the door to accessing social worker contacts already familiar with a family history.
Brandt, Star Tribune 3/8/93

I always wondered why medical professionals referred to patients as the gallbladder in 101. Then I became a child protection worker and heard myself say, "And I would like to hear what the birth mother has to say after the foster mother is finished speaking. Both women had names—I shivered—why hadn't I used them?"
Child protection worker

Least restrictive also means least expensive. Tight budgets may dictate appropriate care more than what's best for the child.

*with THAT adoptive family. She had tried. She had given everything she could but commitment to a family after six foster homes was too much. She had had enough! Ellen knew Annie required constant attention by someone Annie could begin to trust. Annie liked Ellen and wanted her to be available 24 hours a day. Ellen knew this wasn't possible. Her caseload had expanded from eight to twenty families. She also knew Annie was sexually active, **only** liked the city, and **only** liked living in a lower class environment where she felt more comfortable.*

A foster family from a private agency had previously worked with a child similar to Annie. They had raised older adopted children of their own and understood first hand the dynamics of caring for this type of child. After their own children had grown, they decided to care for children who had experienced disrupted adoption placements and help adopted children and their families work toward restoration. Ellen felt Annie would thrive there. The cost of this private agency licensed home, however, meant another county child would not receive services.

Public agencies may provide first class foster care programs and services for the majority of children needing care. However, private agency foster families more often specialize in children with special or complex needs. The family attends additional training classes, are provided support services, and receive higher payments to care for children. The social workers in these agencies carry smaller caseloads and can be more attentive to the families for whom they are responsible. A child under county care may be subcontracted to a private agency and placed in a private agency foster home if no other county licensed families are available or appropriate. Since these homes place a higher burden on county or state funds, they are often avoided until absolutely necessary.

Annie's adoptive parents were told to hang on by their fingernails as volatile and verbally abusive Annie waited for Ellen to find an approved home. Annie's adoptive relatives didn't want her. More importantly she didn't want them. The licensed families in the county homes were full or did not meet the criteria to handle Annie. Annie was going to need some special parents. Meanwhile, Annie's home situation continued to escalate. Annie accused her adoptive father of physically abusing her.

*Ellen secured **weekend respite care in a county foster family** group home for teen girls. Annie liked it there but the home was full and could not take another child. Ellen continued to document and search for a workable solution. **Another respite home** was tried. Annie hated it. Her adoptive parents tried to maintain. Annie alleged sexual abuse against her adoptive father. She was sure this would get her removed! Although the allegation was eventually unsubstantiated, Annie was right. Immediate removal did occur. Meanwhile her adoptive family went through an assessment and an investigation. The agency's time and money were thrown to the wind.*

*Two months later Ellen secured permission to try **a respite weekend in the private agency home** she would have chosen in the first place. Annie thrived and liked the foster parents who treated her like an adult and behaved as safe, yet firm grandparents. Funding was still not available for this home. **Two other homes** were tried. Both failed.*

Annie's behavior continued to deteriorate. A year later two options remained open—a residential treatment facility or Ellen's first selection. The committee agreed that the private agency home with the grandparent-style parents would be advisable. A long battle was won. Not a perfect ending, but a success. Annie's new foster home began to help her like herself and rebuild a relationship with her adoptive parents.

Besides advocating for children and families, fifty to eighty percent of Ellen's daily schedule was burdened with unit level meetings, supervision meetings, committee meetings, administrative reviews, hearing preparation, dictation, applications, forms, and filing all appropriate paperwork and support documentation. Ellen's work load was complicated, and priority was given to the children she was responsible for if an allegation was made against a provider home. Sometimes the best interest of the child was not served, and sometimes it was just easier to move children. Time was not always available to isolate what would be best for the child in the long-term, so Ellen sometimes did what appeared safest in the short-term.

For fifteen years, Ellen fought for children and families. *There were successes.* Families had healed, children had grown and graduated, and some had their own children. Foster families that had worked with "her" kids had been reasonably cooperative and did a good job of helping the children grow. There had been few instances of foster parent-instigated sabotage. Once in a while a former client would send a note or call and say hello. But they were few and far between. Ellen never knew the long-term story. Were her efforts effective? Did she make a positive difference?

Some were failures. Two children had died because the system moved too slowly. Ellen knew the truth, although agency records indicated the contrary. Children had been badly injured because abuse could never be proved and the case was dropped, only to be reopened later—there had been no time to properly investigate. Families had lost their parental rights, and allegations had been made against one of her "best" provider homes. Ellen had been forced to move children who were adjusted, attached, and progressing normally. The resulting changes in the families and the children still haunted her. Ellen's life had been threatened and her family placed in danger because of her career choice. Her caseload in those fifteen years had changed from eight to twenty-five families, and paperwork had begun to eat up most of the quality service time she had previously provided directly to families. Coordination of services had become an impossible task, and only the most demanding cases received attention. Her experience, contacts, and knowledge, now vast, were not enough to keep up with the mounting casework. Her energy and enthusiasm to do the job were gone. It was time to do something different with her life. The stars had left her eyes.

The role of the child protection social worker is not easy. Ellen's story provides just a glimpse at what it is like when social workers deal directly with families. There is always a new case, always documentation, and always loops of protocol to maintain, even if they are not in the best interest of the child or child's family. Rapid changes in policy occur without notification and cause miscommunication. The severity of client needs continues to escalate. Proactive services get left on the desk and are forgotten during a crisis.

The social worker often plays the dual role of case manager and direct service provider to the child and primary family. In small communities throughout the United States, one caseworker may be the child's case manager, direct service provider, and foster home licensing worker. If an allegation is made, the roles of these positions are different, and it is important that the care provider and the social worker *not* confuse them. In large counties and communities, complete child protection service and family service teams exist. In addition, citizen review boards, ombudsmen, minority councils, special interest groups, or internal committees may dictate or impose restrictions on services to be provided. These

Anyone can react inappropriately given a specific crisis or set of circumstances . . .

Providing care for children who are separated from their original families, are confused by a complex system, and have difficult histories is a breeding ground for unexpected crisis situations.

Immediate access to knowledgeable and experienced inviduals is crucial in preventing dangerous situations from occurring.

The best training classes I ever attended were given by foster parents who had worked with tough kids. It was fun to listen and get ideas on how they creatively solved their problems. I came away with many new ideas to help me with the kids I was working with.
Foster father

Foster parents
appreciate
caseworkers who:

additional individuals can be very supportive or very detrimental to good social work practice. The sample chart that follows pertains to the Minnesota system, but it is relevant to job role distinctions nationally.

The role of child protection is to protect children and to rehabilitate families.

State Department of Human Services	In Minnesota, the government agency that regulates and monitors human service programs.
Commissioner	In Minnesota, it is the commissioner of the Department of Human Services or the commissioner's designated representative. The commissioner, with reasonable cause, can deny, immediately suspend, suspend, or revoke the license of a foster care provider.
Child protection intake worker	This individual receives and investigates all reports of suspected child abuse and neglect, determines validity, and initiates the appropriate protective actions to be taken. Reports involving children in life-threatening and high-risk situations are investigated immediately. If conditions warrant, a case is opened and transferred to child protection field units.
Child protection field service units	These units assess or diagnose family dysfunction and develop case plans directed toward protection of children and rehabilitation of the family. Case plans and progress are evaluated for additional treatment, referral, juvenile court involvement, or case closure.
Child protection intensive services	Services which provide intensive intervention, including structured assessment, in-home services (Home Community Treatment), and Juvenile Court, in an attempt to expedite the legal and clinical treatment of families.
Child protection worker	Social worker employed by a local agency who is responsible for providing child protective services or who is responsible for supervising social workers. Child protective services are provided by the local agency to protect a child who reportedly has been maltreated by a person within the family unit or within a facility that is responsible for the child's care. These services include assessment or investigation; protective intervention; and the planning and provision of services.
Case manager	An individual employed by the county or other entity authorized by the county to provide case management services. A case manager in Minnesota must have a bachelor's degree in one of the behavioral sciences or related fields from an accredited college or university. For social workers to be effective as case managers they need to be attuned to the needs and motivations of all major players: child in placement, natural parents, foster parents, siblings, and significant extended family members. They must have a working knowledge of available community resources. Essentially, the case manager is an overseer of the caseplan. As case manager, the social worker mediates between the client and the service provider to ensure appropriate use and quality of services.

1. *Return phone calls promptly.*

2. *Follow through on promised services or information.*

3. *Show respect for the foster parents' knowledge and expertise.*

4. *Are honest.*

5. *Offer support when foster parents express a concern.*

6. *Seek appropriate— rather than merely expedient— placements.*

7. *Listen!*

(White 1992)

I spend so much time networking and referring clients to programs or services—I wish I had time to view some of the services I was recommending. I question sometimes whether actual services provided were the ones I would have chosen given more time.
Case manager

Some monitoring functions include:
— To "troubleshoot" when a family member is in conflict with another helper.
— To discover when services by various agencies are at cross purposes.
— To advocate when expected services are not delivered.
— To support other service efforts with encouragement, assessment, and accurate feedback.
— To provide each service provider with accurate information about the family and other service efforts.
— To assist the client in cutting back services when overloading has occurred.
— To collect data or testimony from providers, when necessary, for court actions and hearings.

Child's agency caseworker	The caseworker is the person responsible for making and carrying out the caseplan for the child and supervising the child's care. The caseworker is responsible for ensuring that the child's needs are met and that he or she is not abused or neglected while in substitute care. *Among the services to be considered and provided to the child are:* — Providing regular and preventive health services. — Arranging for psychiatric/psychological services. — Arranging for education services, including remedial and alternative school programs. — Preparing the older child for emancipation, including vocational and career counseling, higher education, or independent living. These services should be considered long before the child turns 18. — Providing opportunities for religious, spiritual, and ethnic development which does not conflict with the broad religious preference of his parents or his own religious faith. — Arranging for opportunities for leisure time activities and for the development of special abilities and interests. — Facilitating ongoing contact between the child and his natural family and significant others in the child's life.
Group work unit	Provides group services to families who maltreat their children and to victims within those families.

*The role of family services is
to strengthen and preserve families
and to assure permanency for children.*

Family support services	Services to families when the department is court-ordered to provide supervision. For example: — There is a child in care but the division's social worker is not the primary professional case manager. — A case is open in order to provide another service(s) such as special needs day care, day treatment, sheltered workshops, developmental achievement services, homemaker, representative protective payee, foster care payment to guardian or relative.

One of our licensed homes had a complaint, and I issued a letter stating that regulatory procedures had been determined and a letter would be forthcoming advising of the procedure we would be following.

In a hurry, I spell checked the letter and found "regulatory" spelled wrong. I immediately corrected it, hit the button, folded the letter, and sent it off.

Two days later my supervisor informed me that I had written "retaliatory procedures" and questioned what kind of war I was planning on starting.

Since that day, I don't use the spell checker without a double check on what it's changed.

Licensing worker

Home team services	A method of family-centered treatment which incorporates the following aspects: time limited; home-based services; intensive worker involvement with all family members and significant others; and utilization of a systems-oriented behavioral approach.
Reunification permanency services	Services that provide intensive family work with the goal of facilitating the prompt return of children in care to their homes. These services also include time-limited work with the entire family after the child's return to consolidate the progress made. For those children who cannot return to their biological family, placement services focus on the development of permanency.
Adolescent parent services	Arrangement for, or provision of, parenting education; health care/education for mother and child; vocational/educational/independent living planning for parents; counseling concerning family relationships and family planning.
Adoption services	Preparation and placement of children in adoptive homes; counseling for children; adults and families involved in the adoption and post adoption process; adoptive home studies; court-ordered petition studies; and genetic searches.
Special services	Arrangement for, or provision of, counseling, placement and reunification services, information and referral, community and county program assistance, independent living skills training, family support services, and cross-cultural socialization.

*The role of volunteer services is to
aid social services in helping children and families.*

Volunteer parent aide	A parent aide is a volunteer who works with abusive or neglectful parents to help foster nurturing of their children. A parent aide can act as a friend to an abusive or neglectful parent. The unique characteristic of this friendship is that it is one-sided. The parent aide will do all the listening, sympathizing, and initiating of contacts. The aide helps natural parents explore possible solutions to problems and helps the parent develop confidence and responsibility for his or her own decisions. Aides can point out community services which might be of help. Through guidance, modeling, and positive personal interaction, parent aides can help clients develop more effective and positive coping skills; form and maintain healthier relationships with others; make better decisions in everyday life; and establish beneficial goals for the future. Parent aides can play an important part in helping natural parents develop self-worth, which will enable them to be more successful in parenting, in caring for a home, and in making friends.
Guardian Ad Litem	A guardian ad litem represents children who are involved in juvenile court. A guardian ad litem is appointed to a case by the juvenile court judge and remains involved until court jurisdiction is dismissed. The guardian ad litem is expected to think independently and objectively about the

situation and may have an attorney assist. It is necessary for the guardian ad litem to make a separate investigation in order to develop first-hand knowledge about a situation. The guardian ad litem is not accountable to the social worker, foster care providers, or parents of the child. Guardians ad litem are appointed:

1. When the child has a legal claim against another party;
2. When the child has an interest in an existing legal action;
3. When an action has been instituted against the child by another; and
4. In all other instances when the best interest of the child requires legal counsel.

What is the reality of "family" for kids facing out-of-home care?

Social workers have a very difficult and complicated job. Decisions they make can change history for generations—for better or worse. Without adequate knowledge, time, or money they are expected to make decisions and choices amid conflicts. Serving the best interest of the child and family preservation may be incompatible goals.

Functioning families provide security, support, and continuity of care for family members. This includes basic shelter, food, clothing, health care, and hygiene for the children in care. For children facing out-of-home care, this initial crucial support system often has not existed.

Functioning families also provide empowerment. This empowerment is important to the development of the child and significant in terms of what individuals the child feels are family. The empowerment tools include:

Belonging	Identify with family and family's culture
Education	Learn to think, problem solve, develop attitudes about learning
Self-esteem	Confidence, feeling of value to self and surrounding environment
Nurturing	Emotional support, motivation, and encouragement
Social values	Basic values, personal discipline, beliefs, rules accepted by society, responsibility of members
Vision	Belief that future holds hope, promise, and opportunity

The system that empowers the child is
the system that supports the child and
may directly relate to whom the child calls family.

Social services must look at what the child's family provides versus who is "family" to the child. To the child, the family may be a gang, team members, friends, neighbors, or a congregation. Home may be the boxcar down the street or the garage on the corner as opposed to his mother's apartment. The 19-year-old-mechanic or softball coach may be his father figure.

When it does not appear to be in the best interest of the child to preserve the nuclear family, a social worker is faced with an extremely difficult decision— whether to remove the child or allow the child to remain in the family.

Life doesn't always work out as I would like. Some of the parents I work with want desparately to provide care for their children. Yet each time we develop a new plan, provide services, and offer help, their lives begin to crumble and we seem to go backwards.

I wish there was a perfect answer. This career just continues to break heart after heart—including my own.

My heart has been broken too often, along with the hearts of the children and adults I am pledged to help.

Social worker

"Family" is not a clearly defined term. What is a family? Who is family to the child? Is the person who is family to the child the same person/people who are related to the child? Is there a certain kind of family child protection should try to perserve? With lack of clarification of family, the preservation of the *"appropriate"* family for the child becomes impossible.

When does a child qualify for foster family care?

When the need for out-of-home residential care is determined, social services is mandated to provide the least restrictive placement available. If a relative is not available or appropriate the foster family provides the best opportunity for the child to experience family living in the least restrictive environment.

The following variables are sought in choosing to use foster homes:

1. The child has the ability to participate in and profit from family life within the community.

2. The school-age child has the ability to participate in a community-based program or an alternative educational program.

3. The child's age, developmental status, and behavior will mesh appropriately with other children in the home.

4. The child does not have a severe behavior problem.

5. The child is not a danger to self or others.

6. The child's family is able to accept this level of placement and is able to participate in a treatment plan.

7. A foster home is available which can assimilate the child.

8. The foster parents can support a child's cultural or religious participation.

9. The foster parents have experience in the type of care necessary and interest in the child.

Additional variables:

1. Therapeutic foster home for the emotionally disturbed.

    a. The ability to participate in treatment planning and to carry out sophisticated treatment interventions.

    b. The ability to constructively cope with the stress associated with this level of care.

2. Special service home for the developmentally disabled.

    a. The development of a sound knowledge base regarding needs of this population.

    b. The ability to meet children's special needs.

If a foster family home is not available a group home may be provided. There are two types of group homes—**agency-administered** and **group foster family homes.** A **group home** is used for populations of children with special needs. This home is a residential facility located within the community and usually indistinguishable from other family type residences. The agency-administered group home differs from a foster home in that services are provided to a group of unrelated youth who are experiencing socio-emotional problems and staff are agency employees. Group homes tend to specialize around such areas as sex, emotional disturbances, delinquency and/or mental retardation. Adolescents are often placed in this level of care because of their inability to tolerate family life.

In selecting a family for the high risk child, the social worker assesses the experience of the foster family in successfully handling this type of child. What training has the foster family had? What type of children are already in the foster home? Are there current stresses on the family and what is the availability of support and resources? Is the background of the foster family known? Has either parent experienced abuse or neglect as a child? If they have experienced abuse or neglect, have they come to a clear and healthy understanding of managing their own adult life? Can the family communicate clearly with the agency about their needs? How much time is available to prepare the family for the child? Will this placement be an open case? In other words, will the birth family know who the child is living with and where they live? Or will it be a closed case—supervised visitations only at the agency and the foster family information not disclosed?

Failure to place a child in an appropriate setting can be damaging to both the child and the foster family. In matching, the agency attempts to "fit" the stress producing variables of the child with the coping skills and style of the foster family. Foster care providers have the right to be thoroughly informed about the child before accepting him/her into their home. Without complete and accurate information about the child, care providers can inadvertently create a situation that could be damaging to both the child and the family. A child's strengths and capacities as well as problem areas need to be addressed honestly to prepare care providers for the challenge of placement. In the past, because of data privacy/confidentiality concerns, care providers were not given much information, especially about birth families.

Care providers need clear boundaries
regarding confidential information.
They also need the information.

Any child entering out-of-home care is a high risk child because of the separation process and the experiences which led up to the need for care in the first place. Specific high risk characteristics of a child can be found in Chapters 10-12. A number of additional factors consistently contribute to breakdown of foster care. These behaviors include violent, aggressive, or extremely passive behavior, and/or acting out involving abusive language, drinking, drugs, stealing, sexuality issues, or fire setting.

A high risk child requires monitoring and support by social services. The foster family needs clarity about the kind of support an individual social worker is willing to provide the family and a realistic idea of how long the child will remain in their home. A social worker can help care providers by going over potential problems and discussing when and how to ask for help. Emergency phone numbers, access to support services, and specialized training need to be provided to a family working with a special child. If the worker knows another foster family who works well with this type of child, the name and phone number of that family should also be provided. Mentor families are extremely helpful during difficult times.

It is the responsibility of the agency that delegates the responsibility to the social worker to protect children from harm in out-of-home care. The Vera Institute of Justice Study (1981) has identified social service practice issues and resource deficits which are correlated with abuse in foster care. Where these situations exist, awareness, support, and monitoring may prevent future negative experiences.

1. Child was placed on an emergency basis and does not match foster family's abilities or preferences.

2. Foster parent lacks training in handling child's behavior.

Bobbie was beautiful. She was sweet, and she tried hard to learn to be a mother. But at twenty-one, she herself was still a needy child. She had such a high mountain to climb, with five children and no education.

We didn't have a program that really fit Bobbie perfectly. I tried so many—homemaker services, educational support, occupational training. We offered counselors.

At one point she stumbled upon a church that reached out and offered help . . . a new apartment, transportation, day care, friends, food, time away from the four children, and older adults who seemed to care for her as a young daughter.

I remember hoping that this would be the success I couldn't provide.

3. Foster parent lacks information regarding child's life experiences and behavior patterns.

4. Training, written policy, and individual contracting about the needs of a specific child are lacking.

5. Care provider is unclear regarding acceptable discipline techniques.

6. Placement of too many children in a home or combination of children living in home creates conflict.

7. Foster family's levels of stress have increased because of circumstances not related to the child.

8. Foster care provider lacks formal or informal support system and mentor family is not available.

9. Social worker does not visit the home often enough.

10. Home study report concludes: rigidity, problems of foster care providers handling their own children, questionable motivation, inability to meet children's needs, and a negative attitude toward working cooperatively with the agency.

11. Social services fails to screen potential foster care providers through checks for criminal records and the Central Abuse Registry.

12. Social services fails to remove license from family known to be deficient.

What can social services do to help care providers?

Before licensing a home foster care providers need to be taught how to document incidents which may be construed as child maltreatment or licensing violation. They need to understand what types of situations could be misinterpreted. No matter how desperate the need, careful screening of prospective foster families must be done to protect the foster care providers the agency already has.

For the benefit of all, deficient foster homes need to be decertified. Interstate criminal and Central Abuse Registry checks need to be performed annually on licensees.

Respect foster care providers as professionals. These individuals handle the frontline parenting of complex children. The 24-hour-per-day care allows them a unique understanding and perspective of that child. Foster parents are daily advocates for children in care. They can be social services' best ally or worst nightmare.

Before placing a child in a foster home, social services must make sure that the provider understands that allegations are possible. The social worker needs to explain how allegations against a provider home are handled. Foster care providers must be informed—before placement—if the child has been in other homes, the reasons why the child was removed, and if there is a negative behavior pattern. Providers need encouragement to keep in touch with the placement agency. They need a strong support network with other care providers. This networking begins with the first orientation. Social workers should encourage and support foster families' interaction with care provider associations, and both workers and providers should take part in conferences and training programs.

After the allegation and during the investigation process foster care providers need someone to work with them, be their friend, understand what they are going through, and keep them informed about what is going on with the agency. The licensing worker cannot provide this support because of role- and agency-based conflict of interest. Provision of support does not imply or require taking sides on the issue under study. Agency inability or unwillingness to provide support does not negate the need. Alternative sources of support for foster families may be found through provider associations, a safe mentor family, or a professional.

Provide the care provider family accused of maltreatment with information on:
— State law on child abuse reports/investigations and implications.
— Agency policy/procedures followed when abuse is reported on foster family.
— Differences of child protection procedures from usual protections of the US Justice System.
— The legal and procedural rights they do and do not have and legal assistance that is/is not available to them.

Not pull children out of homes unless absolutely necessary. Value the child and foster parent relationship and use discretion in removing these fragile children from existing homes. Unnecessary movement of the child increases trauma for both the child and the family. If a child must be moved, allow for transistion time if at all possible to avoid compounded attachment, loss, and grief issues.

Offer support services to the care provider family accused of maltreatment:
— If appropriate, allow foster home services to continue without disruption on behalf of foster children in the house (e.g., relating to school functioning, natural parent visits).
— Provide family services for all provider family members relating to abuse report, investigation, and other agency procedures (e.g., removal of foster child). Whether or not substantiated abuse has occurred in the foster home, families need support throughout the process—community, other foster parents, extended family.
— Legal representation and information throughout the process, and particularly for appeals of child removals, revocations of license, and court hearings. Adequate representation is beyond financial means of many foster families.

Work on provision of legal information and resources:
Work needs to be done developing feasible means of obtaining legal information, legal assistance, and legal representation for foster care providers. This will underscore to foster care providers the intent of fairness and support in handling the situation.

In *Preventing Abuse in Foster Care*, Emily Jean McFadden (1984) has listed key foster care provider abuse prevention points. Her research is significant in protecting children, social services, and the families who care for children.

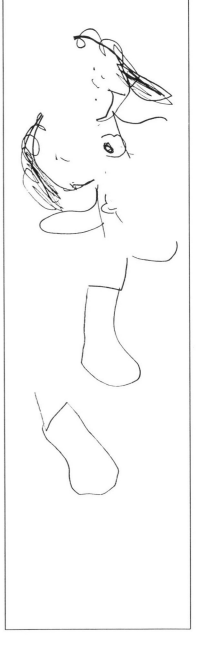

Historically, our approach in Minnesota has been to frame policy solutions in the context of specific "problems" facing children or families. While well meaning, that approach has created a fragmented and disjointed state bureacracy.
(Kids Can't Wait 1992)

ACTIVITY	WHAT CAN SOCIAL SERVICES DO TO PREVENT ABUSE IN FOSTER CARE? (McFadden 1984)
Recruitment	Develop needs statement specifying types of homes needed. Increase supply of homes. Clarify expectations of "professional" foster care providers (e.g., training) and encourage self-screening (*Chapter 3,*).
Licensing/ home study	Ensure compliance with licensing requirements. Gain initial understanding of the foster parents, especially how they relate to their own children. Use genogram or social history to pick up on intergenerational abuse. Examine attitudes toward discipline. Clarify expectations regarding discipline and explain complaint procedures. Use two workers on home study to have better observation of family process.
Pre-service training of foster care providers	Explain basic responsibilities. Clarify discipline policy and expectations. Provide basic understanding of foster children and the impact of separation. Give guidelines on when to ask for help. Explain about complaints and vulnerability of foster care providers. Clarify worker's role, especially the responsibility to monitor the child in the home.
Inservice training of foster care providers	Provide specialized skill and understanding of: the battered and abused child, the sexually abused child, the child with "special needs," developmental disabilities, emotional impairment, etc. Provide alternatives to physical discipline, appropriate management techniques, and understanding of behaviors such as lying, dishonesty, destructiveness, and provocative behaviors. Develop identified pool of parents trained to handle high risk children as support buddies. Develop professional support network for parents for handling these special children, i.e., counselors for parents.
Identification of high risk foster children	Know when to use extra care in selecting a home and how to develop supports for the foster family. Arrange for a physical exam of the child at start and end of placement, including blood and urine tests. Make results known to foster care provider.
Matching and selection of family for high risk child	Inform family of known characteristics of the child to encourage self-assessment. Assess the family for ability to handle the specific child. Utilize preplacement visit when possible. Contract around the needs of the child, discipline methods, and resources needed. Develop a placement plan including foster care provider and birth parent. Provide list of potential problems and a plan of action if and when they occur.
Monitor the child in placement. Work with the foster family.	Observe family dynamics and interactions. Develop and review plan for managing child behavior. Build communication, especially guidelines on when to ask for help. Go over behaviors and disciplines monthly and encourage documentation on child's behavior and progress.
Identify and respond to foster care provider "red flags"	Re-open communication to assess difficulty. Provide supports and reduce stressors to avoid high risk situation. Monitor safety and well-being of child.
Removal of child	Protect the child or other foster family members. Prevent liability issues. Collect data regarding problems.
Decertification of home known to be deficient	Protect childern needing care. Prevent liability issues. Collect data regarding problems. Inform Central Registry if abuse occurs.

What can caseworkers do to protect children in care from abuse or neglect?

The child's caseworker has the legal role of *"child advocate."* This is especially necessary when the natural parents do not exercise their responsibility to advocate for their child's needs or rights. This advocacy includes protecting the child from maltreatment while the child is in care.

It is crucial to establish a relationship with the child separate from the staff or foster parents in order to open communication and to ascertain if there are problems in the foster parent/child relationship. Without this relationship, the child will not trust the worker sufficiently to confide in him or her if abuse is occurring. From the child's point of view, the caseworker is closely aligned with the foster family. After all, this person originally made the placement.

Here are some ideas to develop a trusting relationship with the child in care:

1. Call the child to check on how things are going. Check in after school. Send a note saying hello.

2. Visit the child alone and away from the foster family. Children do not feel comfortable complaining about the home if they are on the premises. Time spent together builds a relationship. Offer to transport a child to appointments.

3. Ask specific questions to determine whether or not abuse is occurring. These questions can be non-leading. For example: *"What are the rules in your foster home?" "What happens if you break the rules?" "Do you share a bedroom?" "Who comes in your bedroom?"*

4. Make unannounced visits to the family foster home. This provides the opportunity to observe the function of the unprepared home.

5. Solicit comments and opinions from biological parents if they visit the child. *"Do you see any change in ---?"*

6. Be attuned to factors in the foster family which may create stress. Excess stress in the family can decrease tolerance on the part of the family to deal with a foster child's behavior. This, in turn, can lead to abuse.
   See potential red flags located in the appendix.

What's the difference between a private agency and a county agency?

The support provided to foster care providers is largely dependent on time available. County social workers serving foster parents have very large caseloads, so they are not always able to provide the support foster parents need. Private agency social workers have much smaller caseloads. As a result they are able to provide a much higher level of service and support to foster families and children in foster care. (CWL 1990)

The level of support provided by private agencies is dramatically felt when an allegation is made against a provider home. Private agency social workers tend to have more time available because they have smaller caseloads. These workers often know the families and the children they care for more intimately than county workers. They enjoy a higher level of trust with the families they serve and are better able to break through communication barriers and cultural issues to reveal the truth.

Private agency social workers, however, often are caught in the middle when an allegation is made against a care provider home served by their agency. The private agency worker is required to cooperate and assist in the investigation process, but the responsibility is often delegated to the county or state agency as the delegated representative of the child. The county or state agency acts on

"A ring of professional services and intervention services and treatment systems has too often taken over for the family and community rather than supporting and encouraging family and community roles."
(Terri Barreiro, Senior Director, United Way of Minneapolis, Kids Can't Wait, 1992)

behalf of the commissioner. Private agencies must be authorized by the commissioner (i.e., county or state) to perform functions for the commissioner. When an allegation is made against a private agency-licensed home, the county or state maintains the upper hand in the investigation, outcome, and authority.

Summary

Families in crisis demand time and resources. How social workers and agencies relate to families in crisis determines the trust and cooperation they receive from the families and providers who serve them. A social worker's job is difficult. The same person may view a maltreated child and then be required to serve the family. *Initial decisions about danger to children and questions of whether those who are in danger can be protected at home must be made quickly, under what can be viewed as crisis circumstances. Parental cooperation may be minimal, the child's response fearful, and the worker uninvited. (Rzepnicki, Stein 1983)*

It is difficult to set aside the emotions of initial experiences. Social work service involves many disciplines, and decisions are seldom made independently. The belief or recommendation of the primary family social worker may not be heeded when presented to a committee. Personalities, management styles, and previous agency history may play into the outcome of a case. The results are not always what the caseworker agrees with or would have chosen. On the other hand, the committee offers checks and balances in a paper-intensive but loosely regulated system.

Private and public agencies react differently when an allegation is made against a provider home. Private agencies are authorized to perform functions related to licensed family foster care. County or state agencies have child protection authority. This structure can place the private agency in the middle of a complex situation.

References

Action for Children Commission. 1992. *Kids Can't Wait. Action for Minnesota's Children. A Report to the Governor and People of Minnesota from The Action for Children Commission.* Copies of report can be ordered by writing or calling: MN Planning, Action for Children, 300 Centennial Building, 658 Cedar Street, St. Paul, MN 55155, (612) 296-4156.

Citizen League. 1990. *Does the System Maltreat Children. Public Affairs Research and Education in the Twin Cities Metropolitan Area.* Minnesota: Citizens League.

McFadden, Emily Jean and Ryan, Patricia. 1991. *Allegations of Maltreatment in Family Foster Homes. Maltreatment in Family Foster Homes: Dynamics and Dimensions.* Robin, Michael. (ed.) 1991. *Assessing Child Maltreatment Reports. The Problem of False Allegations.* New York: Haworth Press.

McFadden, Emily Jean. 1984. *Preventing Abuse in Foster Care.* Michigan: Eastern Michigan University.

MN Planning. 1992. *Kids Can't Wait. Action for Minnesota's Children. A Report to the Governor and People of Minnesota* from the Action for Children Commission.

Morton, Thomas D. 1993. *Foster Family Recruitment and Retention: A Local Agency Assessment.* Georgia: Atlanta: Child Welfare Institute.

Stein, Theodore and Rzepnicki, Tina. 1983. *Decision Making At Child Welfare Intake. A Handbook for Practitioners.* New York: Child Welfare League.

White, Ellen. Vol 13. No. 1. Aug/Sept. 1992. *Foster Parenting the Drug-Affected Baby.* Zero to Three, National Center for Clinical Infant Programs.

Just because a person appears to be listening and doesn't answer doesn't mean he or she agrees or understands.

Communication established on unequal ground sets up both persons for failure.

When a person is in a "superior" position and states, "It's agreed, we've talked it out," the underdog may be flailing with ,"I don't agree with a damn word you've said, but I feel defenseless to tell you."

The underdog's personal opinions —doubts, contempt, resentments—lie, shielded from the person in authority. The person who may be in a position to make a valuable contribution.

For temporary peace, the agreement is sealed. The future result, however, may be apathy, non-compliance, or repeated failure.

Chapter 8

The Amazing Legal System

*The dynamics of the legal system are complex.
A report against a care provider can
immerse the individual into administrative,
civil, and criminal legal repercussions.*

I have written this chapter for the lay person in hopes of offering some basic knowledge about how to access the legal system. Nothing in the following pages should be construed as legal guidance. My hope is to offer language clarification and help in determining whether to seek legal counsel and what type of legal counsel to seek.

On December 15, 1791, the Bill of Rights was added to the Constitution of the United States. These ten original amendments recognized the people's rights.

The first amendment—*"Congress shall make no law respecting an establishment of religion, or prohibiting the free exercise thereof; or abridging the freedom of speech, or the press; or the right of the people peaceably to assemble, and to petition the government for redress of grievances."*

The fourth amendment—*"The right of people to be secure in their persons, houses, papers and effects, against unreasonable searches and seizures, shall not be violated, and no warrants shall issue, but upon probable cause, supported by Oath or affirmation, and particularily describing the place to be searched and the persons or things to be searched."*

The fifth amendment—*"No person shall be held to answer for a capital or otherwise infamous crime, unless on a presentment or indictment of a Grand Jury, except in cases arising in the land or naval forces, or in the Militia, when in actual service in time of war or public danger; nor shall any person be subject for the same offence to be twice put in jeopardy of life or limb; nor shall be compelled in any criminal case to be a witness against himself, nor be deprived of life, liberty or property without due process of law; nor shall private property be taken for public use, without just compensation."*

The sixth amendment—*"In all criminal prosecutions, the accused shall enjoy the right to a speedy and public trial, by an impartial jury of the State and district wherein the crime shall have been committed, which district shall have been previously ascertained by law, and to be informed of the nature and cause of the accusation; to be confronted with the witnesses against him; to have compulsory process for obtaining witnesses in his favor, and to have the Assistance of Counsel for his defense."*

It is important for care providers to understand not only their agency and county procedures, but also their state and federal laws.

Unconstitutional policy can act as law at the agency level, without the agency or the care providers being aware of it.

Decisions can be made that directly affect the lives of many people without the public knowing. Policy can be made or changed at the agency level, with care providers being unaware of it and unable to challenge it.

The Bill of Rights was enacted by Congress and ratified by the states as the result of pressure from the citizens. These farmers and craftsmen believed that without such protections democracy and the new government's principles would never be realized. Dr. Martin Luther King, Jr. referred to the Bill of Rights and the Declaration of Independence as "promissory notes." Naive in legal matters, I had believed these basic constitutional rights were the bottom line of American government. It was true—I found—they were a beginning. Millions of pages of additional law and interpretation are built upon them, and wading through the maze of books and papers was impossible. Buildings exist just to hold this information, and my understanding was mediocre at best.

Legal expertise for licensed providers facing allegations of child maltreatment continues to be a difficult problem, both because of cost ($75 - $250 per hour) and because so few lawyers have expertise in this area of administrative law. State provider associations may be instrumental in acquiring data and names of qualified attorneys. This data would reduce costs and save time for families in crisis. Crisis line operators could share referrals with families in need. The route in the legal maze could then be more direct with fewer wrong turns and swifter results for families and agencies.

Most parents who are reported do not need a lawyer, and most reports are resolved without court action and without an attorney. But an attorney may be needed to:

— Defend you against a charge.

— Communicate for you.

— Gain protection for children in your care.

— Gain protection for you or your spouse.

— Gain access to your records

— Have your records corrected or destroyed.

— Supply advice and legal counsel.

Early representation by a lawyer can be crucial to preventing court action. It is much easier to convince investigators and prosecutors not to seek an indictment than to have them dismiss one. Many court actions are filed because of simple breakdowns in communications. A lawyer may be able to convince investigators that you are innocent or that the case is better resolved informally. (Besharov 1991-)

Families facing allegations must be aware, however, that merely stating they want to consult an attorney before answering any questions asked by social services or investigators may be misunderstood as being noncooperative.

The legal process today

Most child protection and licensing actions are handled under administrative law, not civil or criminal law which is why the usual due process guarantees which most people take for granted do not apply. Child protection procedures often are more informal and based on social considerations rather than on legal ones. It is important, however, that procedures—based on child protection practice or legal practice—include such basics as protecting the child from undue damage, allowing the provider to present evidence or testimony, setting a time limit on each investigation, and giving parents necessary information.

Parents faced with allegations may become involved with administrative, civil, and criminal law. Each type of law serves a distinct need and is handled in its own way.

Types of law:

Administrative: This is the law regulating public administration. It includes the organization, powers, duties, and functions of public authorities engaged in of all kinds of administration; their relationships with each other and with citizens and with nongovernmental bodies; legal methods of controlling public administration; and the rights and liabilities of officials. Administrative law may be further broken down into specialties—law of public health, law of taxation, law of public education, etc. Administrative law is the legal framework within which public administration is carried on. It is established to ensure efficient, economical, and just administration.

Today's American government is expected to maintain order and achieve progress. As government expands so does bureaucracy. Administrative law has a valuable contribution to make as an instrument for controlling bureaucracy. Citizens are aware of the impact of government in their daily lives—for good or evil. If administrative law denies justice to an individual, it fails. If administrative law hinders effective administration, it fails.

Well-considered procedure enables accountability to be fixed on a responsible body or individual at each stage of the administration process. It can safeguard the rights of citizens and protect the executive against the criticism of having acted in an arbitrary manner. It can insure regularity and consistency in handling individual cases. Much, however, depends on the quality and purpose of the procedural requirements.

Administrative due process does not include the Miranda warning since an individual's right to life and liberty is not at stake (imprisonment), unless a case moves into criminal law or an individual is found in contempt of court. Administrative due process includes the right to appeal and contest a decision made at any level.

Civil: This is the law regulating citizen-to-citizen issues. In some cases it may be referred to as common law. Civil law includes issues relating to marriage, divorce, succession, gifts, property, labor relations, and contracts. These are usually private controversies, as when two individuals or businesses are in dispute regarding contract, responsibility, or injury. The objective of civil court is to restore the parties so far as possible to the positions they would have occupied had no legal wrong been committed.

Civil due process includes notification and time to answer. Civil law does put a person's life and liberty at risk (imprisonment).

Criminal: The body of law which defines criminal offenses regulates the apprehension, charging, and trial of suspected persons and fixes penalties and modes of treatment applicable to convicted offenders. Criminal courts deal with persons accused of a crime, deciding whether they are guilty, and if so, determining the consequences they shall suffer. Courts in criminal law stand neutrally between the prosecution and the defense. Their objective is to decide between the two in accordance with the law.

Miranda warning is required since an individual's life and liberty is at stake, and imprisonment is a potential outcome.

"Parens parte" is a Latin term used in the law which describes the basis for intervention into the lives of families by the state. Parens parte simply means that a child belongs to the state if parents don't take proper care of the child.

One difficulty with parens parte is that proper care may be at the discretion of a small number of individuals.

Just because the police are investigating does not mean you are dealing with criminal law!
Attorney

You have the right to...

Common legal vocabulary:

Appeal: A request that a case be transferred to a higher court for rehearing or review. Appellate review is not automatic. It must be sought by some party aggrieved by the judgment of the court below. The appeal is usually time restricted, and the correct appeal procedures must be followed. Appellate courts review the record from the lower court provided by witnesses, the evidence, the findings of fact and conclusions of the law, and determine the outcome.

Defamation: False or defamatory statements that tend to harm or injure the reputation of another person or bring the person into disrepute in the community. Proving and measuring this harm is difficult. Some people have such good reputations that anything negative said will be disbelievd anyway—and some people have such poor reputations that any positive statement will be disbelieved.

1. *Libel* arises from defamatory statements made in writing, photographs, film or other relatively tangible or permanent mode.
2. *Slander* consists of verbal deprecation.

The statements must be false. For example:
If you have been accused of child maltreatment. Data that states you have been accused of child maltreatment is true—you have been accused— even if the allegation is proved false. The fact is that an accusation was made against you. The facts also may be that a screening, assessment or investigation was carried out. There is no defamation in the statement.

Due process: The course of legal proceedings established to protect individual citizens' legal rights. Children in the United States are citizens and so have the same rights to protection of life and liberty as adults. Children, however, do not have the capacity to access protection, and in some cases, the state (agency, agency representative, or appointed guardian ad litem) takes over watching out for the life and liberty of the child. In adult-child issues, the right of the child to life and liberty needs to be balanced against the rights of the adult. In some cases the rights of the adult may be deferred to protect the right of the child. Each of the different types of law has different procedures for due process. Any individual working within a law system needs to understand due process as influenced by type of law involved.

Guardian ad litem: An officer of the court appointed to be a legal advocate for a child who is under court jurisdiction or in out-of-home care. This individual will conduct an independent investigation on behalf of the child when maltreatment is suspected, watch out for the child's best interests when the child is placed in out-of-home care, and advocate for the child to the agency or court system when a child's needs or concerns are not being met. As a court appointed officer, the guardian ad litem has access to investigative data labeled "confidential."

Indictment: A formal accusation made on the basis of positive legal evidence — charging somebody with a crime.

Injunction: An order by a court prohibiting a person or group from carrying out a given action or ordering a given action to be taken. A parent, guardian, or person caring for a child can seek an injunction to keep a child within a specific environment to prevent undue psychological, emotional, or physical damage from occuring to that child.

License: Grants a formal or legal ability to do something. For example, a foster parent license grants the license holder the opportunity to care for other people's children. The same license may grant the state immediate 24-hour-a-day access to the family home and waive due process.

Ombudsman: The ombudsman is part of the administrative law system and is in a position to safeguard the rights of citizens by assuring administration according to law, discovering maladministrations, and eliminating various methods that include bringing pressure to bear on the responsible authority, publicizing a refusal to rectify injustice or a defective administrative practice, bringing the matter to the attention of the legislature, and instigating a criminal prosecution or disciplinary action. The ombudsman's concerns include error in the courts, procrastination, and improper conduct. The ombudsman has little political power, but can inspect and demand the fullest information. He can comment, criticize, and make recommendations as to the correct interpretation of the law. He can propose changes and expose maladministration.

Statute of limitations: All systems of law have statutes restricting the time within which legal proceedings may be brought.

Warrant: Enpowers a police office to arrest a suspected criminal, search premises, or seize property for the purpose of obtaining evidence. Licensed programs may not need a warrant for immediate access, as the license may waive the privilege.

Writ: A formal legal document ordering or prohibiting some action.

Roles of key legal players:

County attorney: Provides legal advice to county agency and agency staff. Decides when to prosecute and what not to prosecute and then proceeds to supervise charges. In larger counties, the county attorney's office consists of a number of attorneys and staff who specialize in various issues.

Defense counsel: Protects the individual against unfounded testimony, introduces evidence in the client's favor, employs various procedural devices for the client's benefit, and provides the client moral support. If the case goes to court, the accused has the right to be represented by an attorney. If the accused cannot afford one, one will be appointed. Normally, no lawyer is provided to assist a family undergoing investigations. The family must seek and hire their own legal counsel during this crucial time.

Judge: Types of judges vary enormously, from a rural justice of the peace, who is untrained, serves part time, and works in a makeshift courtroom, to a Supreme Court justice, who makes decisions of profound national importance at the highest appellate level. Yet, both are judges. Both determine whether or not the evidence presented is sufficient to justify further action. Both determine the outcome of a case.

Police: In criminal law, police play a primary role in pretrial procedures. They are responsible for arrest of suspects, execution of warrants, questioning of witnesses, and carrying out of searches and seizures.

Public defender: A court-appointed attorney paid by the state to defend citizens involved in criminal court cases. Public defenders are sometimes available in administrative law cases.

Prosecuting attorney: In criminal law, at the pretrial stage the prosecuting attorney's role is to decide whether or not he or she has a case that will stand up in court.

> *The best interest for the child is not always "for the child."*
>
> *It would be more beneficial if the best interest clause was addressed with forthright honesty.*
>
> *Instead of listing it as "best interest for the child," state "best interest of all parties involved" (social worker, social service agency, advocate, lawyer, foster care provider, birth parent, medical practitioner, grandparents, etc.) and then process ALL the best interests to discover the best interest for the child.*
> *(All Children's task force)*

Should I talk to an attorney?

If you talk to an attorney, you should talk to the *"right"* attorney. The attorney has the legal power to act for you, and the **right** attorney has the expertise you need. The wrong attorney can escalate a situation and create additional barriers to working relationships and communication. The outcome from hiring the wrong attorney can be financially and emotionally expensive.

Finding that attorney, however, may be like finding a needle in a haystack. If you are looking for an attorney to discuss your situation or represent your case, get appropriate referrals. Ask around and don't be shy. Ask about costs. If you are needing "pro bono" work, be clear that you have no money.

You must shop to find the **right** attorney. You wouldn't buy a refrigerator without checking a number of options. Finding the correct professional is more important than shopping for a refrigerator—yet most of us don't shop for the very people who are required to be intimately knowledgeable about our families. Accountants, doctors, psychologists, teachers, designers and attorneys all fall into this category. The rule of thumb is — buyer beware. There is a lot of selection: do proper research. Choosing an attorney who specializes in bankruptcy for a child protection issue is just as ridiculous as chosing an eye doctor for open heart surgery. Both individuals are good in their specialty, but neither has the competence needed to solve the other's cases. The future of your family may lie in the hands of this individual. Don't let a person *"learn"* on your case.

How can I find the right attorney?

Take the time to make the right choice. You will not regret it. If you are a licensed provider, you will need someone familiar with providers' licensing and legal issues. Get out your notebooks and telephone.

Ask your agency: Ask your agency for basic factual information regarding investigative procedures, statistics on negative licensing actions, or professional controversies concerning provider practices. Ask if they know of any professionals familiar with provider issues.

Call your provider association for names of people who have been through similar situations and ask what attorneys they know who have handled cases such as yours. Many cases are never publicized, and many individuals drop out of providing services once an allegation is made. An association may have access to information and these individuals. Parents Anonymous and VOCAL may also provide referrals. Don't be surprised if you call a previously accused provider and you hear, *"I've put that part of my life behind me. I won't talk about it."* Allegations are painful and the pain may never go away. Be considerate and don't push. The research you are needing is for legal counsel, not curiosity.

Call the American (or your state) Bar Association. This association will have access to names and specialties of various member attorneys. It also may be able to direct you to various state statutes and rules of interest.

Speak with attorneys. Once you connect with one attorney, ask for referrals. Professionals usually know others who specialize in specific fields. Don't be afraid to ask for other names. You don't need to make your choice based on one person.

Once you compile a number of attorneys' names, begin by calling those who appear multiple times on your list. Obviously, more than one person has been satisfied with this professional. Knowing that, it is a more comfortable place to start.

How do I interview an attorney?

Before you call any legal counsel to interview, take some time and write up an outline of points you want to cover.

Be clear about what you are asking the lawyer to do.

— *Do you want a short term commitment (witness a meeting, write some letters, file an injunction, or review a document)?*

— *Do you need a long-term commitment (defend you against serious charges)?*

You may be uncertain of your needs or you may need someone to negotiate on your behalf. If you don't know or have never used legal services, tell the lawyer the truth. This is no time to play games or lead a professional on with knowledge you don't really have. Let the professional know your level of knowledge. Then give *a brief, factual version of your problem.* Don't waste expensive time telling all the details. The attorney will ask the right questions. There are additional concerns besides specialization. As you compile your data, think about your personal needs and the needs of others in your family.

— *Do you prefer to work with a female or male attorney?*

— *Do you want to be under the umbrella of a law firm, or would you rather work with an independent?*

You need to know about the experience of the attorney.

— *What type of issues does he or she normally handle? Union issues, divorce, bankruptcy, business, abuse, employment issues?*

— *Does he or she work primarily in administrative, civil, or criminal law?*

— *How long will my case take to resolve? What are the likely results?*

— *Are there different approaches in handling this type of case?*

— *What background experience does the attorney have which will help?*

— *Has he or she handled any cases similar to mine? How many of them? How recently? How were those cases handled? What was the outcome? Be cautious. Winning or losing does not indicate how good an attorney is, but tells you of the experience he or she has had. Get references and call them.*

— *Is the attorney available to handle the case?*

— *Is there a potential conflict of interest?*

You need to know the fees and projected costs. Many attorneys give a free half hour of consultation to a new client. Ask if this applies and when. Most attorneys want to be paid ahead of time—a retainer may run from $500 to $5000. Ask for an estimate of the time and money involved in your case. This might change as circumstances change, but ask anyway.

— *How much money do you need immediately? Are there different hourly rates for different services?*

— *Does the time in court cost more? Letters, consultation, attending meetings with you, transportation costs, expenses?*

Relative searches need to begin immediately . . .

Parental and relative searches need to be done immediately upon out-of-home placement of children. Deciding to search for a child's birth father four years after out-of-home placement is unfair to the child, to the birth parent, and to the child's future permanancy plan.

To place notification of a parental search in a legal journal or other nonpublic paper is manipulation of a system and law that was designed to protect the rights of the child and birth parent.

Designation needs to be made to place search information in documents which possibly can and will be read by the parent or other adults who know the child.

— *What happens if you are late in paying or need to pay in installments?*

— *Do you have a letter of engagement or contract describing billing arrangements?*

— *When you receive a bill, what will it look like? The bill should detail exactly what was done and when. Save this paper, it is good documentation of deadlines that were met or of repeated attempts to reach someone. If you feel the fee is too high and you like the attorney, try to negotiate a fee acceptable to both parties.*

What is the attorney's attitude?

— *Can you work with this person? Is this someone you can work with, or regardless of the attitude or personality, are you willing to work with this person?*

— *Do you want an individual who is cautious, or one who is aggressive?*

— *Do you want the attorney to develop a friendly relationship with you or remain distant? How does this attorney work with children?*

— *Does the lawyer listen well? Does he or she ask probing questions?*

— *Do you like his or her approach and style?*

Engaging the services of an attorney is extremely personal. Only the individual(s) involved can determine if legal counsel is wise and who should be chosen. Douglas Besharov (1991) in *Recognizing Child Abuse, A Guide for the Concerned* lists six red flags to warn people seeking legal counsel that the attorney being interviewed may not be the best choice for them.

Avoid the attorney who:

— *Seems too busy to give your case time and attention.*

— *Guarantees a favorable outcome—even the strongest cases can go sour.*

— *Is vague on subject fees.*

— *Refuses to provide a contract or letter of engagement.*

— *Tries to impress you with legal jargon.*

— *Refuses to give you any references.*

What do I do after I hire an attorney?

Get down to business. Every minute is going to cost you money, so avoid talking about the weather or sports. Be efficient, organized, and creative. Keep all of your papers together. Get and keep copies of everything. Ask for reading materials about your issues and if there are any articles about other cases to help you educate yourself. Use the telephone and fax machine for simple communication. If you and your attorney are very busy, prearrange times for telephone calls and be prepared to efficiently and effectively cover details. Respect the other commitments your attorney has. You are not the only client. Be specific regarding your needs, but give advance notice. Avoid last minute demands.

Schedule ten minutes of private consultation prior to any meeting you and your attorney are attending together. Meet beforehand to discuss expectations and finalize last minute information.

There are times you may need to switch attorneys. Your attorney may be able to handle a certain portion of your case and then recommend further counsel from a more specialized lawyer. Changing lawyers to access better service is not detrimental. A patient with cancer would not be afraid of seeking additional advice. Neither should an individual accused of child maltreatment. More critical experience, available time, or even perhaps cheaper rates may all be legitimate reasons to move on to another legal counselor.

A poor working relationship, dislike, or mistrust are also good reasons to look elsewhere. If you are dissatisfied with legal work or if there is a lack of agreement on how to proceed, it may be wise to get a second opinion.

What do I need to know?

While children are in out-of-home care, the foster parent is acting as an arm of the state. This means foster parents do not have the same rights as birth parents and are not considered long-term commitment parents. In addition, a foster care provider is not considered a parent for purposes of liability under law. The legal relationship of the foster care provider to the foster child is limited. The authority and responsibility of the foster care provider are limited by statute and by contractual agreement. All licensed providers should have current copies of both in their possession and understand the meaning of their responsibilities. A foster parent is under licensed obligation to carry out responsibilities to the state for the child. If a foster care provider negligently fails to carry out the contractual obligations to provide adequate supervision or care for the child, legal action against the licensee may be taken.

What is the difference between a hearing and a trial?

A hearing is a court proceeding other than a trial, before a judge, or it may be a formal meeting of an official body for hearing or gathering testimony. A trial is a formal examination of the facts of a case by a court of law to decide the validity of a charge or claim. Trials are very expensive. Most work is done at the hearing or pretrial stage, and most cases never reach a trial stage.

Be sure to attend all legal procedings concerning you and your family. All court appearances are important, regardless of how painful or difficult to attend they may be. In some cases, notification may be served just hours prior to a hearing, leaving little time to prepare. Document the situation, drop everything, and go to court.

What types of court are there and how are they best used?

A number of different court systems may be involved in allegation issues.

Appellate court—A place to challenge a decision made by a court trial, hearing, or licensing department.

District court—First level of court to use. The district court handles only certain types of cases and only cases involving certain dollar amounts.

Family court—Domestic relations between family / related individuals.

Juvenile court—Children under eighteen.

What do I need to know at the agency level?

Private agency-licensed foster homes may experience allegations differently than families licensed through public state or county agencies. Legally,

---

Twenty years ago, at nineteen, I terminated rights on my two small children to allow them to be adopted. Once my life was in order, I reached out to other unwed mothers and offered support as a foster family.

Recent state legislation says no one whose parental rights have been terminated can be a foster parent. If this includes me, they will be losing a significant, supportive home for these young women."

Foster mother, fifteen years

I am always concerned about providing basic lay-legal information. The system of law is complex. As an attorney, I would choose to footnote each statement a number of times, due to variances.

Attorney

---

private agencies may be in a different position than county agencies in their responsibilites to investigate or support families facing allegations.

The foster care provider has a right to an administrative hearing concerning the removal of a child from his or her home even though the placement of the child may not be affected by the hearing outcome. An agency or foster parents can file an injunction to prevent removal of a child from the home, but the foster family's request may not carry as much weight as a birth family. Notification also may be made to the guardian ad litem—if a child has one—to request additional support in preventing removal of a child. If a child is removed from a licensed home, the foster family can request visitation and future contact privileges with the child.

In the event that there is an anticipated adoption, and the child has resided in a prospective adoptive home which has been licensed as a foster home, the prospective adoptive parent has the right to an administrative hearing concerning any removal of that child prior to the adoption.

Legally, the agency is ultimately responsible for protecting the safety and well-being of a child in care, not the foster care provider.

What do I need to know at the county level?

Birth parents are not agents of the county, but licensed care providers are. The county is responsible for children within its custody. Therefore, the county is required to make sure that children in foster home care are safe. The county is responsible for monitoring foster families. If an allegation against a provider family occurs, the burden to be smart enough to ask the right questions is on the county. The county is the delegated commissioner to represent the state in investigation of a family accused of maltreatment or a licensing violation.

What do I need to know at the state level?

The state delegates its initial investigation to the agency and county level. Once a determination has been made by the agency or county, the state will decide if a negative licensing action is warranted. The individuals at the state level do not usually have direct contact with families or individuals who have experienced allegations. The data are provided to the state department by the county or investigating agency. Provider families have a right to supply separate data to the state for review. Provider families also have the right to call or meet with the individuals who work in the state department to discuss a given issue.

What do I need to know at the federal level?

The Children's Bureau and the American Bar Association in Washington, D.C., can provide information on children in out-of-home care issues.

What are rights?

Rights are granted to an individual through law, nature, or tradition. Not all rights are provided by law, and those that aren't will not necessarily stand up in court. On the next three pages I have included rights for various individuals—children, children in out-of-home care, birth families, licensed families—written by concerned organizations. These are **not always** legal rights, but I have included them as illustrations of concern.

What rights should be available to children?

Children represent the future of the human race and how we choose to respect and care for them will determine the outcome of the next generation and those which follow. The following rights are not legally binding in any way but are a representation of rights children need:

1. The right to be loved by at least one individual.

2. The right to be recognized as a human being and treated with the fairness offered to other members of society.

3. The right to preservation of significant relationships based on the child's needs.

4. The right to food, safety, supervision, and protection.

5. Access to health care services and a basic education.

6. The right to independent legal representation in legal proceedings.

7. The right to have "the best interest" of the child truly mean something when decisions are made by adults for the child's benefit. When adults with power over children understand the trauma of separation and loss, a child's best interest is given precedence over the claims of interests of other parties, groups, or cultures who claim possession, ownership, or control of children.

8. The right to have decisions made regarding a child moving into out-of-home care handled by a variety of disciplines—medical, social welfare, psychological, primary parents, etc.

9. Access to all past and present medical, social, and mental health information regarding the child, biological parents, siblings, grandparents, and others related to the child so as to facilitate the best medical, psychological, and social care and minimize risk to the child.

What are the rights of young people in foster care?

Young people in Minnesota foster care have legal rights developed by the state Department of Human Services. Similar rights exist in many other states. The following information explains some of those rights, but it cannot provide complete solutions to individual legal problems.

1. You have the right to have what every person needs: enough food, clean clothes, a clean bed, adequate housing, and the attention of people who will listen to you.

2. You have the right to be safe from harm by foster care providers, caregivers, or other children. Foster care providers, caregivers, and other children may not physically, sexually, or verbally abuse you. Corporal punishment (hitting, slapping, spanking, pinching, shaking, kicking) may not be used to discipline you.

3. You have the right to medical and dental care. Your social worker should see to it that your medical and dental needs are met. Your foster care providers and caregivers should allow you to see a doctor or nurse if you are sick to ask them questions or to talk to them about how a medicine is making you feel. Confidential information and medical care for pregnancy, birth control, and drug problems should be available to you.

4. You have the right to go to school. You also have the right to join school activities. If you have special problems with learning, you have the right to receive special educational services.

Clinicians tinker with rules either by the kind of interpretations they apply to them or by using their discretion, as is permitted with an ambiguous or general rule.

Rules do not necessarily eliminate discretion, but they eliminate alternatives that might otherwise be considered.
(Weissman, Epstein, Savage 1983)

"I said it's in the Rules!"

5. You have special rights if you are placed in a hospital for treatment of a mental health or chemical dependency problem. You can seek assistance from the people designated by the Department of Human Services.

6. You have the right to have visitors and to make telephone calls during certain hours. You also have the right to send and receive mail. As a part of your caseplan, you should be allowed home visits with your family or friends. Contact with certain people may be restricted for your own safety.

7. You have the right to live in an unlocked place. This right is yours unless the court has ordered that you be kept in a locked place.

8. You have the right to apply for foster care benefits up to the age of 21. Six months before your 18th birthday you should talk with your social worker about getting foster care benefits between the ages of 18 and 21.

9. You have the right to preserve your heritage. You have the right to live in a home that will accept and be supportive of your religious, racial, cultural, and ethnic identity. If possible, placement should be with a family member or someone from your community.

10. You have the right to reasonable rules governing your behavior. If you are unable to control your behavior, discipline may be used to help you behave. For example, your right to watch television may be cut, or you can be *"grounded"* or given additional chores such as washing dishes or mowing the lawn. You also have the right not to be punished too severely. You should not be denied meals, sleep, mail, or family visits as a method of discipline. If time-out is used as a method of discipline, you may not be isolated in a locked room. You may not be isolated for longer than one hour.

11. You have the right to a social worker. Your social worker should talk with you regularly. If you cannot contact your social worker, call his or her supervisor.

12. You have the right to a caseplan. This is a plan written by you, your parents, and your social worker to meet your needs for your future. Your caseplan should explain why it was necessary for you to be placed in foster care, who will arrange your education, what days your parents may visit you, and when you are expected to return home. Your social worker should discuss the plan with you and ask you to sign it. You have the right to discuss this plan with your parents and ask for changes in it. You also have the right to ask for a lawyer to help prepare it. This plan should be reviewed every six months.

13. You have the right to ask for independent living. This results in both freedoms and responsibilities. There is no process of emancipation established by the courts in Minnesota. However, young people over age 15, in court as *"children in need of protection or services"* can ask to live in their own community. You can ask a lawyer about emancipation issues. If you are over 15 years old, your caseplan should include transitional services to help you move toward independent living.

14. You have the right to appeal any decision made by the local services agency concerning your services or plans for your future. If you disagree with your caseplan and cannot get it changed, you can ask for a state hearing to review the plan. Your social worker, guardian ad litem or a lawyer appointed to you are some of the people who can help you appeal. An appeal can be started by writing to your social worker or the Department of Human Services.

15. You have legal rights in court. You have the right to be in court and give your opinion when important decisions are being made about your future. You have the right to know about important Department of Human Services decisions regarding your case. You also have the right to be represented in court by a lawyer. You can call the lawyer who represents you.

What are the rights of a primary, birth, or custodial parents of children in out-of-home care?

Natural parents of foster children shall have the following rights:

1. To be treated as individuals who have all the rights guaranteed to them as citizens of the United States and their state.

2. To maintain custody of their child unless it has been demonstrated that this would jeopardize the child's health and welfare.

3. To be provided opportunities to demonstrate their capacity to provide a suitable home for their child and to regain custody of their child as quickly as possible when regaining custody is consistent with the health and welfare needs of the child.

4. To receive proper and adequate notice regarding any grievance or legal proceeding concerning their child.

5. To participate in planning for their child, to receive a copy of the caseplan, and to receive notice of any formal review of their child's case plan.

6. To receive a clear, written description of their rights and responsibilities and the agency's rights and responsibilities and to receive information about any recourse they have to contest actions taken by the agency.

7. To receive services, in accordance with the service plan, to assist them in overcoming the conditions which led to removal of their child, and if the return of their child to their custody is not feasible, to help them adjust to an alternative permanent plan for their child.

8. To visit and communicate with their child within reasonable guidelines as set by the service plan and by the court.

9. To have their cultural, religious, ethnic, or racial heritage respected as a plan for them and for their child is developed.

10. To receive an explicit, written description of the expectations they must meet in order to have their child returned home and of the services the agency will provide to help them meet those expectations.

11. To have informatiom maintained by the agency about them kept private/confidential.

12. To have access to information maintained by the agency within guidelines that take into consideration others' rights to privacy, and to correct errors contained in those files.

American Public Welfare Association. Standards for Foster Family Services Systems for Public Agencies. For Children's Bureau, Administration for Children, Youth and Families, Department of Health, Education, and Welfare. DHEW Publication No. (OHDS) 79-30231

Currently the following data classifications exist for Minnesota licensed care providers:

Public Data on licensed current and former care providers:
— Name, address, telephone number of all licensees
— License capacity
— Type of client preferred
— Variances granted
— Type of dwelling
— Name and relationship of other family members
— Previous license history
— Class of license
— Existence and status of complaints
— When disciplinary action has been taken against a licensee or the complaint is resolved
— The substance of the complaint
— The record of informal resolutions of licensing violations
— Orders of hearings
— Finding of fact
— Conclusions of law
— Specifications of the final disciplinary action contained in the record of disciplinary action.
— The nature of any disqualification set aside under 245.04 3b and the reasons for setting aside the disqualifications
— Reasons for granting any variance under section 245A.04

(MN Statute Sec. 13.46 1993)

What are the rights of primary, birth, or custodial parents facing allegations of child maltreatment?

1. Right to a confidential and discreet investigation.
2. Right to a courteous investigation—without harassment or threats.
3. Right to see any private or public data about you.
4. Right to authorize other agencies or persons to see data about you.
5. Right to receive copies of data about you.
6. Right to challenge accuracy or completeness of data. Right to include your own explanation in government data.
7. Right to have data about you explained to you.

What are the rights of the licensed care providers?

1. A clear understanding of their role as foster parents and the roles of the natural parents and the placement agency with respect to the child in care.
2. Respect, consideration, trust, and valuation as an agency employee or volunteer who is making an important contribution to the agency's objectives.
3. Involvement in all of the agency's crucial decisions regarding the foster child as team members who have pertinent information based on their day-to-day knowledge of the children in their care.
4. Freedom from built-in failure by not being asked to care for a child whose needs they cannot meet.
5. Continuation of their own family patterns and routines.
6. Support from the social worker in efforts to do a better day-to-day job in caring for the child and in working to achieve the agency's objectives for the child and his family through provision of:
   — Pertinent information about the child and his family.
   — Help in using appropriate resources to meet the child's needs.
   — Direct interviews between the social worker and the child, previously understood and discussed by the social worker.
   — Consultation regarding specific problems of the child.
   — Information regarding the child's progress after he leaves the foster family's home and opportunity—as indicated and desired—to have continued constructive contacts with the child.
7. Opportunity to develop confidence in making immediate and day-to-day decisions in regard to the child.
8. Consideration as possible permanent parents for the child who, after being in the home for some time, becomes free for adoption or permanent foster family care.
9. Opportunity to learn and grow in their vocation.
10. Opportunity to be listened to regarding agency practices they may question.
11. Full reimbursement for costs of the foster child's care.
12. Salary and all fringe benefits available to other agency staff members.
13. All rights accorded the agency's personnel, including procedure for fair hearing and liability coverage.

Reprinted from Children May-June 1970, Beatrice L. Garrett, Specialist on Foster Family Care, Children's Bureau.

What are the rights of a licensed provider facing allegations?

1. Right to a confidential and discreet investigation.

2. Right to a courteous investigation—without harassment or threats.

3. Right to see any private or public data about you.

4. Right to include in government data your own explanation.

5. Right to authorize other agencies or persons to see data about you.

6. Right to receive copies of data about you.

7. Right to challenge accuracy or completeness of data.

8. Right to supply separate data for the state to review.

9. Right to call or meet with individuals who work in state department to discuss issue.

What are your rights in securing government data?

Government data can have a positive or negative impact on peoples lives. Access and storage of this data becomes easier and easier as we continue to move into the information computer age. Files that previously needed large file cabinets can be now stored on tiny diskettes and sent electronically across the world for cross reference. The ease of storage and access presents its own inherent problems. The Data Privacy Acts enacted by federal and state governments hopes to avoid the *"big brother"* image by preventing misuse of information. The goals of Data Privacy Acts are:

1. The governments right to privacy regarding certain issues.

2. The public's right to get access to data.

3. The governments right to use the data.

Juggling the governments need for access and use and the public's need for independent and privacy is difficult. In child maltreatment issues this juggling act can get very complicated as the same file moves from Public—Private—Confidential—Private—Public status during various times of allegation, investigation, and closure.

The following rights are provided to Minnesotan's under the Data Privacy Act. Each state may have similar or very different rights. These rights are provided only as an example. All government data collected, created, received, maintained and disseminated by a government agency in Minnesota are **public** unless otherwise classified by law. *Public data is accessible by any member of the public for any reason.* The Minnesota Government Data Practices Act establishes the following rights and responsibilities for access to government data in general and to public government data in particular:

1. Records containing government data must be *easily accessible* for *convenient* use, and agencies must receive and comply with requests in an *appropriate* and *prompt* manner.

2. You have the right to *inspect* public and private government data about you at reasonable times and places *at no cost.* You may ask who else has requested to see this data.

3. You have the right to get *copies* of public and private government data about you upon request. You *may be charged* for the cost of copying public data.

---

*Data classified as private, confidential, nonpublic, or protected non public under this subdivision **become public data** if submitted to a court or administrative law judge as part of a disciplinary proceeding in which there is a public hearing concerning the disciplinary action.*

Data generated in the course of licensing investigations that relate to an alleged violation of law are investigative data.

Data that are not public data collected, maintained, used or disseminated that relate to or are derived from a report are subject to the destruction provision.

MN statutes 13.46 (1993)

All Minnesota licensed providers need to be aware of the provisions of this statute!

"I just wanted to help children. I guess I didn't understand the true weight of the law upon a license"

"People are so stupid. The statistics say seventy percent of American prisoners have been in foster homes. Does that say all foster homes are bad? My foster parents were the only people who really cared about me. I was just too pissed off and angry by then to let it sink in.

I spent my time in prison— apathetic public servants—name calling, poor food, lack of care. I learned a lot. I learned to get angrier. I got out on good behavior—parole—I was truly vicious. I went on a small reign of terror. I hated everybody and I hated myself. If a man can survive prison and get out on parole, his problems are not over. Most ex-cons return to prison two or three times. Luckily, I didn't. I looked up the only people I truly felt had cared for me— my foster ma and pa."

Ex-con, former foster son

4. You have the right to be informed of the *meaning* of public or private data about you.

5. If the data you ask to see are classified in a way that *prevents* you from seeing them, you have the right to be informed of that fact, and to be told *which state statute or federal law classifies the data.* You may request this be done in writing.

6. You have the right to know what data are maintained about you and how they are classified.

7. You have a right to challenge the accuracy and completeness of any public or private data about yourself. If your challenge results in an adverse decision, you may appeal the decision to the Commissioner of Administration.

8. You have the right to authorize other agencies or persons to see or use private data about you.

9. You have the right to include in government data your own explanation of anything to which you object. That explanation must be included any time the disputed data are shared with another agency.

Whenever a government agency asks you to provide private or confidential data about yourself, you must be told—*"Why the data is being collected. How the data will be used by the collecting agency. Whether you can refuse or are legally required to provide the data being requested. What the consequences are to you if you supply or refuse to supply data, and the identity of other persons that are authorized by law to receive data."* This is called the **Tennessen Warning.** Once it has been given to you, the agency cannot collect, store, use or disseminate the data for any other purpose (except in limited circumstances).

Summary

Daily living and public education do not prepare a person for entry into the legal or court system. The legal system is much more complicated than most people imagine. Care providers facing allegations of *"suspected"* child abuse may enter into three distinct areas of law—criminal, civil, and administrative. Each of these types of laws has different procedures and potential outcomes. In many cases legal counsel is recommended.

Hiring legal counsel takes care and investigative work by the care provider. References from associations, other families, and the agency may help direct a family to a number of appropriate individuals. At that point the family must interview and make a decision regarding who, if anyone, they would like to hire.

All citizens have rights. Sometimes, however, rights are not observed. Each individual is responsible to know his or her rights in the role he or she occupies.

References

Besharov, Douglas. 1991. *Recognizing Child Abuse. A Guide for the Concerned.* New York: The Free Press.

Horowitz, Robert, Hardin, Mark, Bulkley, Josephine. 1989. *The Rights of Foster Parents.* Washington, D.C.: American Bar Association.

Child Welfare League. 1991. *A Blueprint for Fostering Infants, Children and Youths in the 1990s.* Washington, D.C.: Child Welfare League.

SECTION IV

Sometimes Reality Hurts

*There is no turning back
the hands of time.
We can only remember, march forward,
and try not to repeat mistakes.*

I knew I couldn't live with either of my (adoptive) parents, but I never thought they'd give up on me completely. A lifeline still existed even though I fought against everything they did. I was afraid if they completely abandoned me, I couldn't bear it.
Adopted child in behavior treatment program

In my head I keep my bags packed. I'm always prepared for a move. I wonder when this family is going to tire of my stunts and get rid of me.
Child in foster care

"You have five minutes to get your things packed. Don't worry you'll be moved to a safe place."

Family Foods Store

"Five minutes... five minutes.... five minutes... five minutes... five minutes... five minutes... five..."

Chapter 9

Evacuation . . . for Safety or Protocol?

As abruptly as a hurricane moves inland, children can be uprooted from foster and preadoptive homes in response to allegations.

Julie was no stranger to moves. At fourteen she had lived with twenty families and in a variety of boarding schools or group homes. Prior to adoption she had lived with her birth mother and two foster families. Julie was a skilled mover and shaker, and any family containing Julie would be shaken.

Julie's initial adoption experience at age eight lasted three very eventful years. The healthier Julie got, the angrier she became. All the feelings she had stuffed inside began to pour out in uncontrolled and sometimes violent ways. Her anger at the injustices of her life flowed out freely against her adoptive mother and father. Eventually, after calling in a school bomb threat, setting a fire, and running away, Julie was removed from her adoptive family. Social services felt that Julie would thrive in a foster family with less structure and a closer cultural match. Julie innocently agreed.

During the three years away from her adoptive family, she disrupted fourteen different families. In January 1992, Julie, age 14, returned to her adoptive family. She was carrying her unborn baby. The new case plan for Julie stated that once the baby was born and Julie had spent some time with her child, she would return to her group treatment home to complete her behavior modification program. Her adoptive parents would care for her son.

By this time, Julie wanted to go home to her adoptive family. When her son Aaron was born, Julie allowed herself to become attached to another person, accepted help from her adoptive parents, and began developing responsible behavior. Yet, just as she began to reach out to her parents and love her son, Julie boarded the bus with empty arms and went back to treatment. On weekends she played mother, but without responsibility. It didn't take long to begin to lose the attachment she had begun to feel toward to her child.

John and Lisa recently moved their rainbow family of eleven to a beautiful seventeenth century house in a small New England village.

Everyone in the village knew who the new family was. Nine colorful and bright children, a dog, two cats, a herd of goats, a flock of sheep, and cages of cuddly Angora rabbits could hardly hide. There wasn't a chance for this family not to stand out! Julie was their adopted fifteen-year-old daughter; Aaron, their infant grandson.

Kidz Kare Welcoming kit
> toothbrush
> toothpaste
> hairbrush
> Kleenex
> paper
> pencils
> crayons
> Kidz Care notebook
> Stamped addressed envelopes to birth family
> Pictures of new foster family members with names and a little bio.

Mental Blueprint of the Maltreated Child

About himself:
I am WORTHLESS.
I am UNSAFE.
I am WEAK.

About caregivers:
They are UNRESPONSIVE.
They are UNRELIABLE.
They are DANGEROUS.

(Delaney, Kunstal 1993)

Adopting Julie brought challenges to her adoptive parents. As professional counselors, they were aware that as Julie got healthier, she would probably get angrier and that if they could deal with that anger before her teen years, they would have more influence in helping Julie learn to manage her adult life. Explaining to others that Julie's behavior was anticipated and acceptable was another matter, as was living with Julie. For Julie and her parents, a professional respite family may have been the connecting piece in keeping Julie in her adoptive home and helping her through this critical time in her life. Her adoptive parents had prepared for the anger. They even expected allegations of abuse. What they didn't expect was removal of Julie.

Adopted children normally fall into the category of nuclear family and are protected from unplanned moves. But their behavior can at times be so unusual that removal from the adoptive family appears warranted, even when additional support services or respite care may be a better choice. In *Trouble Transplants: Unconventional Strategies for Helping Disturbed Foster and Adoptive Children* (1993), Richard Delaney, Ph.D., and Frank Kunstal, Ed.D., write:

> *The behavior problems, signs, and symptoms of disturbed children in foster and adoptive homes are at times baffling, especially when taken out of context—the context being who the child is, how he has been raised, what he expects from others, and how he views his world. We will see next that the maltreated child's view of the world is skewed. Indeed, the maltreatment of the young child leaves more than physical wounds. There are invisible scars to the child's personality development and incalculable damage to his sense of trust, empathy, confidence, and security. Along with that comes the negative impact upon the child's view of the world, upon his "mental blueprint" of the way that people relate to each other . . . (p. 21)*

> *Unfortunately, even after the child is removed from the abusive, neglectful, exploitive environment and is placed in a nurturing, caring foster or adoptive home, his mental blueprint persists. Consequently, behavior problems—which reflect the underlying mental blueprint—continue or even worsen in the new home, much to the chagrin of the foster or adoptive family. Characteristically, the maltreated child views the surrogate family through distorted lenses. And, through a twisted metamorphosis, the unsuspecting, caring foster/adoptive caregivers are perceived and experienced by the child as the abusive, neglectful, exploitive parents from his past . . . (p. 22)*

> *A central goal of treatment of disturbed children is to elicit from them their underlying perceptions, beliefs, feelings about, and views of the world—their mental blueprint. This eliciting is crucial to understanding what lies behind the child's often inexplicable behavior problems. In many of these children, the invisible wounds from early maltreatment fester under the surface and later ooze out and contaminate later relationships. The mental blueprint functions as the receptacle of those unseen, festering wounds . . .*

> *Traditional family systems theory emphasizes how an individual's problems relate to larger problems within his family. For example, depression in a child may be seen as reflective of larger family issues, such as maternal depression. Or problems with anger in the child might be symptomatic of unspoken hostility between mother and father or between parent and grandparent. Understanding how marital and communcation problems in a family relate to puzzling emotional and behavioral problems in children has added immeasurably to our ability to treat children's difficulties by helping the family.*

> *Ironically, it is the strength of traditional family systems thinking which—applied to adoptive and foster care—is its great weakness. Typically the "power" of family work is that it suggests a larger, "systemic" explanation for problems in the child and removes that child from a harmful, "scapegoat" role.*

Once seen from the perspective of family, individual, marital, and other problems can be dealt with more productively. Unfortunately the traditional approach overlooks or underestimates the flip side—the effect of a dysfunctional individual upon the family as a whole. In the traditional view of the family system, the child is the thermometer which reflects family temperature; as things heat up the mercury rises in the child. In this view the child is a passive measure of the active family process. By contrast, in foster and adoptive families the disturbed child is more thermostat than thermometer. As the family thermostat, the problem child is "set" at a specific temperature; he controls the emotional climate in his new family.

Unfortunately, when looking for causes of the child's disturbance, traditional family theory often erroneously points the finger of blame at the foster or adoptive family. At the same time, the child gets off scot-free—the supposed blameless victim of a malfunctioning foster or adoptive family. But what about the child who is the victimizer rather than the victim? And furthermore, what of the child who was deeply disturbed long before placement with the family? . . . (p. 30)

While many families have welcomed children in with open arms, they did not count on the severity of the problems which are part of "the package." In effect, when a family takes on an adoptive or foster child, they often, as it were, "transplant" a diseased young shoot into their family garden. The planting, to continue the metaphor, often bears bitter fruit. Further, the whole garden is affected. Eventually family problems—predictable, dramatic and often fatal to the placement—unfold. (p. 31)

Understanding the complexities of foster and adoptive family relationships is crucial.
Good social work practice strives to keep children in their existing family homes.

Keeping children with their families eliminates many of the compounded losses experienced by children when they are moved to strangers. Consistency in caregiving is crucial for the child to develop personal safety and a sense of well-being. Every time feelings are discounted, overlooked, or viewed as unimportant, a child feels less lovable and self-worth is depreciated. A dependable, predictable environment must be established and maintained.

Social services' legal responsibilities to children in care is greater than to children in primary homes, and yet uprooting these children appears to be common practice. Children in care may be moved in circumstances like these:

- — Child is not adapting or does not like new foster family.
- — Child runs from foster home.
- — Foster family frustrated with child.
- — Foster family cannot handle child's behavior.
- — Foster family is not same race as child. Same race home has an opening.
- — Home with other sibling opens so children can be together.
- — Foster home under investigation for licensing violation. Children in foster and preadoptive care are more likely to face a move to a new home if an allegation is made against the family with whom they are living.
- — The foster home has no room for the child after he or she has been hospitalized because another foster child has been placed with the family.
- — The foster home provides interim or emergency shelter and does not accept children for longer than 30 days.
- — The foster parent needs a break and puts the child in respite care.

John called his wife, Lisa, after a 45-day review of their adopted daughter's progress at a residential treatment facility for behavior modification.

"You're not going to believe what the juvenile officer just requested. She asked if I would present a neglect and abuse charge against Julie in order to get funding and additional services for her child."

"I said I'd have no part of it and walked away. The officer continued to tell me it was all a formality and everyone knew it wasn't real. It was only procedure."

"Our daughter has been a good mother to that little boy. I'm not going to let her be set up and labeled before she's even given a chance."

They hoped it would end there.

Meanwhile at the Smith home . . .

As John and Lisa's family settled down for an evening meal, the doorbell rang.

"Mr. Smith, I'm police officer Jones and I have a petition of neglect filed by ___, which I need to serve against your daughter Julie.

A look of horror crossed Julie's face. This couldn't really be happening. Like a firecracker waiting for a match, Julie stayed stoic, ready to explode. It was only a matter of time before the explosion.

If all our talk of the need for permanency is real, our goal should be one foster home per child—just one. When a child is placed in out-of-home care, then only one of three things should happen for the child:

1. *The child returns to the birth family.*

2. *The child is adopted by the foster family.*

3. *The child is adopted by another family.*

A maximum of three total moves. One home is best for child stability and continuity of care. Most children seem to handle two all right. For some, three moves verges on too much. Four or more moves is more than most kids can handle. We will have done them in.

Thus we must all resolve to build a system which preserves the second family—until the final choice is made, until the final permanent choice becomes real.
Joanna O'Neill, president —Missouri Foster Care and Adoption Association

What qualifies as an absolute emergency to remove children?

Deciding whether to remove children from a home involves an element of risk. No one can predict the series of events which will keep a child in a home or move him or her to perceived safer care. Child protection, law enforcement, and licensing workers compile evidence to determine what action will be in the best interest of the child. This evidence includes:

Real evidence consisting of documents, photographs, x-rays showing child's injuries; certified school records showing patterns of attendance; return receipts of letters sent by certified mail.

Direct evidence from firsthand knowledge of events taken in the form of statements describing what an observer saw, heard, said, and did. This evidence should be obtained as quickly as possible to limit distortion.

Hearsay evidence, which is secondhand information. "Mr. Smith told me . . . "

Circumstantial evidence, which is indirect proof of facts. For example, if medical opinion holds that a child's injuries could not have been sustained by accident and social services knows who was taking care of the child at the time, it could be inferred that that person was responsible for the child's injuries. (Stein, Rzepnicki 1983)

In a birth/adoptive family home, out-of-home care is appropriate if:

1. There is no adult willing to care for the child, or the child refuses to stay in the home.

2. There is medical evidence that physical abuse or nutritional neglect is so severe as to be life threatening.

3. There was intent to kill the child, even if injury is not severe. Medical evidence should support a hypothesis of deliberate poisoning, or marks on the body should indicate assault with a deadly weapon or repeated beating with a heavy object.

4. There is medical or psychological evidence of abuse or neglect that, without intervention, may threaten the child's life *and* the parent refuses to help.

5. Medical evidence of repeated abuse exists. The reference is to previous untreated injuries, generally identified through x-rays where the location of the injury suggests prior maltreatment.

6. Severe abuse or neglect recurs after services are offered.

7. Major disturbance or withdrawal by the child *and* the parent rejects the child.

8. Medical or psychological evidence suggests that the parent is incompetent to provide minimum child care, and there are no resources (i.e., friends, family, community services) to help in the home during assessment.

9. A child has been raped by a related or non-related adult known to the parent, *and* the parent did not attempt to protect the child. (Stein, Rzepnicki 1983)

In a foster family home, moving a child is appropriate if any of the above conditions exists. In addition, licensed families are responsible for following current rules and regulations. Violations of rules and regulations must be carefully assessed prior to moving a child to another stranger's home.

What is full and adequate preparation in the mind of a child?

Moving a child to a new home must be approached with extreme care. All children are traumatized by being uprooted abruptly and moved. Children who have faced repeated moves may appear unaffected. In reality, these losses only add to the negatives in their lives. These fragile children have been traumatized previously, and another move revives past feelings of confusion, isolation, and loss. Children have all kinds of questions, but underneath they want to know if the removal is a personal rejection. They need reassurance that the separation is not caused by their behavior. If their behavior has been part of the reason for removal, tact and sensitivity are needed. Adults can answer questions more easily by putting themselves in the child's place and asking how they would feel if they heard the answers they are about to give.

> *The child needs to understand why the move is necessary.*
> *Children have real concerns about their future home.*
> *They deserve honest answers.*

Too often, children are not told what is happening to them when they are moved. Systems governing foster and adoptive parenting may seem logical to social workers, but they make no sense to children.

Children adjust more quickly when they know what to expect and when people of importance to them understand how they are feeling. Children don't have an adult command of the language and often relate nonverbally. The tone of voice, look in the eye, or actions over a period of time say more than words. Letting the child know that he or she is cared about does not place a burden on the child, but rather, teaches that relationships are important. Sometimes, sharing your own feelings helps the child understand his or her own feelings more clearly.

What can social services do to help prepare a child for a potential move?

Child welfare workers must analyze all the variables in making a decision to move a child. The child's developmental age and the situation play integral parts in deciding what can be done to ease the trauma of another move.

Social workers can be strategic in helping children cope with moving to another family. Multiple preplacement visits with the new family in the child's present home, at a neutral location (park, movies), and in the home of the new family allow for a much smoother transition. For children who have had repeated losses, these preplacement visits and meetings are crucial.

1. Provide prompt contact with the previous family so the child knows the

The filing of the neglect charge in itself was not unusual in child welfare practice. In order to secure protection and funding for baby Aaron separate from his mother, this procedure was necessary.

The resulting emotional trauma to Julie, however, was only beginning.

The Kidz Emergency Move Kit.

1. *A quarter in a little envelope, your address and phone number*

2. *Lifebook and/or Kids Kare Kit*

3. *Cassette tape of songs and stories*

4. *Stuffed animal, blanket, pillow*

5. *Recipes of child's favorite foods*

6. *Suitcase belonging to child*

family is still alive and cares.

    a.   *If the child is pulled from foster parents who have provided long term care and is never allowed contact again the child may feel abandoned, thrown out or very confused about what and why the loss has occurred.*

    b.   *If the child is kept apart from birth parents by agency policy, it is difficult to believe that the real goal of the agency is reuniting the child back with the birth parent(s).*

Julie held her anger in until she could not contain it. Her 15-year-old brother, Tom, bumped into her. Julie was ready for action. She chased Tom through the house, up and down the stairs. Finally having enough, Tom put his arm on Julie and told her to knock it off.

"Abuse!" Julie wailed. "You touched me! I'll get you! I'm going to tell everyone you touched me!"

Tom's mouth dropped. Two wide-eyed little children, ages seven and five, stood in the doorway watching.

"And you two, I'll get Mom and Dad taken away from you, too. Just like me. You wait and see. I'll get you removed for child abuse," Julie yelled.

Horrified, the two little ones ran out of the room. Could this really be happening?

2.   Introduce a new family to a foster/adoptive child through photos or videotape. Discuss who they are, what they are like, and what they like to do. Get questions from the kids to ask them and come back with answers. Some agencies require all of their foster families to create albums that are kept at the agency. The family album contains pictures of the house, parents, kids, and pets in the foster family. It also contains information about the family. These albums are on hand and available even for emergency placements.

3.   Help the child understand his or her role in foster care, what parents need to accomplish before the child can be returned home and how the caseworker can help. Even children as young as three or four deserve an explanation of what is happening to them and what the plan for their future is. Explain the role of various "parents" and their relationships to the child, as well as the role of the caseworker and the court.

4.   Provide information to the care providers regarding the agency communication, support, ongoing service, legal information, and advice. If the agency cannot provide these services, it does not mean foster care providers do not need them.

5.   Provide pictures of previous parents and siblings that the child can take to the new home. Such pictures give the child the message that the new home views birth or past parents as important people, and prevents the child from denying their existence.

6.   Encourage the foster family to work on the Lifebook, which can be a special gift symbolizing the foster family and foster child relationship. Take pictures of the current foster family to add to the book.

What can a provider do to help children prepare for a potential move?

If a care provider faces an allegation, he or she must prepare to have foster and preadoptive children moved. Foster care providers can utilize whatever time is remaining by being open and honest with children during the investigative process. Talk openly and tactfully about where children are going, why they are leaving, and what they can expect.

Care providers may choose to rush in with support when children express sadness. While it is important to provide support, it also is important to realize that children need to be able to express painful feelings openly without feeling that adults cannot tolerate their pain. They need someone who can empathize with them. Foster parents need to process their own feelings and let the child know they share some of the same feelings. It is an important step for children to accept their own feelings. If some children deny having any feelings about the separation, the care provider needs to initiate discussion. (Smith 1992)

Children need an explanation of what each professional's role is and what each person can do to help them. *Review the information in Chapter 2 regarding the different roles of parenting.* If the child is old enough, help him or her understand your role, legal responsibilities, and rights. Explain the role of the various parents in their lives and outline what each person's responsibilities are and how he or she fits in. Help the child understand personal rights. *(See Chapter 8.)*

A child leaving a short term placement may not exhibit much reaction. A child leaving a long term placement, however, may experience a sense of loss similar to the original removal from the natural parents. Children may feel sad, angry, anxious, rejected, helpless, hopeless, or hurt. They may feel as if they are being abandoned, regardless of the explanation offered to them. In an effort to feel in control, they may misbehave, as if they are giving people a reason to get rid of them. Problematic behaviors may recur or intensify. Some children may be happy to be returning home to parents, particularly if the situation has improved. Some may cling. Others may *"bargain"* or insist that they will be good. Some children act tough. Inside, their hearts are breaking. Others act tough and no longer know how to care. They buried their feelings long ago.

Generally, if the feelings are discussed and the child is given permission to talk, there will be less need for the child to express feelings through behavior. It is also important to talk about feelings of what they are leaving behind.

> *A care provider can bridge connections to the child's new home*
> *while securing a lifeline to the past.*
> *Foster parents can let the child know that he or she is*
> *cared about and loved, and will always be remembered.*

How can the care provider give the child a life preserver to the past?

When a child faces a move to a new family, his or her life is in turmoil, and any sense of stability has been lost. The Lifebook can be used to help prepare the child for the move, to get to know the new family, and to help the child understand what is important about the family he or she is leaving. It is useful for the next family, social worker, or therapist as they begin to develop a working relationship with the child. If a Lifebook has not yet been started for the child, start one now. This Lifebook can be as simple as a dimestore scrapbook or a stationery store journal. It does not have to be expensive or complex.

> *Most of all, have fun and do it today!*
> *Tomorrow may be too late.*
> *The child may be gone.*

Even if the foster child stays, the Lifebook is a memory maker and establishes bonds that will help the child in the future.

How to get started

Go to the stationery store with the child and purchase stickers, markers, or any other art materials to begin assembling pages. Make the book a family project and let each member of the family contribute. Let the dog or cat leave its paw print beside a picture. Get a couple of new rolls of film and shoot pictures. Don't worry about quality—at this point quantity makes the difference. Be spontaneous. Some care provider families make a set of photocopies for themselves of the Lifebook to remember the child. These photocopies can be very valuable in the future when a child returns years later and has nothing left from the past.

For the next ten hours Lisa held, counseled and cried with Julie.

John was away on business, and luckily an old friend had come to spend the weekend. She immediately stepped in to care for Julie's infant and the rest of the family.

Julie's rage was ignited and burned unmercifully.

John returned early to drive Julie back to her behavior modification program. Julie remained silent during the entire two hour drive.

"Julie, I know you're hurt and frustrated. You probably feel like life is out of control. I understand why you would feel that way, but you can't bring this behavior home with you the next time you come. Work with your counselors this week and we'll start over again next weekend," said John.

Julie remained silent.

On Monday, Lisa called social services to review the weekend and set up respite for Julie and the baby for the following weekend if Julie's behavior would not allow her to return home.

STEP ONE:
It's easy to begin!

Start with the child's name—look up the meaning in the dictionary or a baby name book. Let the child make the first page special or offer to make it special for the child as a gift.

STEP TWO:
Enjoy each other and have fun! Ideas to include in a Lifebook are:

1. Any information you have on the child's history—early pictures, cards, birthdate, birthplace, a piece of the old blanket if it's been set aside and is not in constant use.

2. Picture of the child and foster family. Think about what you like to do and say to one another. Catch one another in silly poses. Write favorite sayings on the page with these photos.

3. Pictures of the foster family and pets—handprints, thumbprints, and paw prints go great on these pages. If family members use a certain kind of perfume, cologne, or soap, write the name of it down and pour or rub it on the pages near the pictures of the person.

4. Make a list of words and what they mean if the child is preverbal. List favorite foods, eating times. Think about family smells. Get some scratch and sniff stickers of smells the child likes. Think about the family sounds. Make a tape of going-to-bed stories, songs, silliness, and bedtime rituals. Include other family members — the dog barking, Dad brushing his teeth, Mom blow drying her hair.

5. A page of favorite foods with recipes from the foster family kitchen. Magazines are great for cutting out food pictures. If the child needs to move, send a care package of some of her favorite nonperishable foods (crackers, cookies, Kool-Aid, etc.)

6. Take pictures of special extended foster family members. See if you can get them to write a note, send a card, or write a funny story about what makes this child special to them. Invite them for dinner/potluck or have a get-together to work on a page of the book.

7. Write stories about funny experiences. Let the child or other children draw pictures about what happened if you don't have photos.

8. Invite favorite friends over. Make sure names are available and take photos of the foster child and friends playing.

9. Go to school to get photos of teachers and things the child enjoys doing—scouting, clubs, teams. Collect memorabilia such as buttons, school colors, news articles, programs.

10. Go to a favorite restaurant. Include information about favorite foods and what the child likes best about the restaurant. Ask if you can have a menu to take home.

11. List any information about injuries, illnesses, or hospitalization.

12. Include church and Sunday school experiences. Tape a Sunday school class. Get the words to special songs and write them down, or sing them together and record the songs for the child.

13. Write stories and search for photos about special vacations or adventures the child has had with the foster family. If you haven't had an adventure lately, there's no better time to make one up than now.

14. Illustrate ways the child has celebrated special holidays, birthdays. Pieces of wrapping paper and ribbon are great things to glue on a page. Don't forget the glitter or lace from the sewing basket if the child wants to dress these pages up.

15. List favorite toys, games, and activities.

16. Make a "heart " page. Describe ways the child shows feeling and affection, what feels good.

17. Make a "bug" page. Let the child draw, write, or tell all the things that bug him or her. Cut out bug pictures or get bug stickers to place on the page. Do not judge this page — you may be one of the *"bugs."* Give the child an opportunity to express safely what the *"bugs"* are.

18. Write a letter about why you like/love/care for the child.

19. Make a videotape of family activities.

20. Keep a shoebox of photos to give to the child at later dates. During the Protest Stage, the Lifebook may be destroyed. Photos shared when the child comes back as an adult are especially welcome.

21. Add some ideas of your own!

STEP THREE:
Make sure there are lots of extra pages!
Remember, the child's life and yours do not end if you are separated.

The Lifebook may not appear beautiful, but to the child it becomes a warm patchwork quilt when life seems difficult and memories are needed. It's a comforter to curl up with when everything seems cold and unfamiliar. It's that far-reaching voice that continues to say, "I care, and you matter to me always."

The Lifebook can organize past events in a chronological order, even if it contributes only a small piece of the past. It can aid in ego development and increase self-esteem because the child has been important to someone. It remains constant when other things in life change. It builds trust in your foster home and provides a history of the child for a new family.

The University of Minnesota Early Childhood Studies Program has developed an excellent workbook set for providers greeting a new child. This workbook, *"Two Places Called Home: A Workbook For Foster Children And Youth,"* by Lane Fischer and Deb Jones, helps to build a new relationship and understand the needs and perceptions of a new child. Write: Early Childhood Studies, Continuing Education and Extension, University of Minnesota, 306 Wesbrook Hall, 77 Pleasant St. S.E., Minneapolis, MN 55455.

Why the relationship connection is so important to children

In *"Helping Children When They Must Move,"* Vera Fahlberg, M.D., (1979) writes:

> One of the functions of the family is to provide continuous contact with a small number of people over a lifetime. The long term relationships among family members allow each person an opportunity to clarify past events and reinterpret past events in terms of the present. Children in the child welfare system are frequently denied these opportunities. They change families, they change social workers; they may lose contact with birth family members.
>
> As a child moves into and through the child welfare system, pieces of information about life are lost. A child who loses track of these pieces of past events often faces stumbling blocks in psychological development. We have known adolescents who

Lisa found a family in the community to take Julie and her baby. Lisa packed Aaron, his clothes, and bottles and delivered them to Julie and the family.

Friday, Saturday, and Sunday, Julie mothered her baby son. Irritable and unhappy, Aaron cried and cried. On Sunday evening Aaron and the diaper bag arrived home. Julie headed back to behavior modification.

Lisa opened the diaper bag. Of the bottles of formula she had packed for three days only five had been used.

Aaron had hardly eaten.

grew up in care who didn't know whe
their birth parents, who do not know
who had few recollections of previous

It is difficult to grow up as a psycholc
one's past. The very fact that adults h
with the child implies that the past is
Whatever the past was, the child lived
live with the truth. The truth can be p
child's self-esteem or in a way that hel
thus raises her self esteem. Every indi
She has a greater right to this informa

Effects of separation on the care pr

The very essence of foster care is provid
care providers and their families live wi
foster child's stay. Both children and par
issues. Feelings of sadness over one chil
a new child is greeted. Foster care provi
acutely feel the loss of the foster child(ren). The grief process may become a way
of life. Foster care providers face these issues differently:

— In preparation for a future loss, some individuals and families begin feelings
  of loss even before a child departs.

— At other times, grief issues occur much later.

— Some foster care providers deal with this grief by not forming close
  attachments with children in care.

— Others displace their anger on the agency or the child's family. Some deny
  their emotions.

— Physical symptoms such as headaches or tiredness may be common.

*Different from birth families, foster parents provide services for children in
need. Separating this knowledge from practice can be difficult. Knowing
that this is not your child does not decrease the child's significance and
need for protection from further harm.*

When a provider faces an allegation, multiple children may leave at one time and
with very short notice. Neither the foster parents nor the child are able to
prepare. The immediate response is often disbelief. *(Further information can be found in
Chapter 5.)* If all foster children have been removed, the foster care providers
experience a loss of both child(ren) and personal identity.

When removal of a child seems unnecessary or abrupt, providers focus on the
resulting welfare of the child. *"How will this move affect the child's future? Will this
additional move increase attachment difficulties? Can we visit the child? Does the child
understand what has happened?"* If isolation is part of agency procedure during an
investigation, anxiety escalates. When an allegation is proved false and children
are not returned or granted visitation, the provider is more frustrated. The
uncertainties about where the child is, how the child is *"really"* doing, and what
actual harm the child has incurred complicate the provider's feelings.

Providing foster care is more than a profession, it is a way of family life. The very
presence of foster children is what defines a foster care parent. For an innocent

---

"*What is going to
happen to Aaron,
Lisa?*" I asked.

"*I would guess Aaron
will be a system kid.
We want to believe by
developing an initial
trusting relationship
with Aaron, we may be
able to provide the
foundation he'll need
to become a productive
adult, however, Julie
will move him in and
out of our home at her
or the state's
discretion. John and I
will be there for
Aaron.*"

"*That sounds so
difficult, Lisa.*"

"*We have to remember,
Aaron is not our baby,
he's Julie's. The court
has already provided
an attorney for him so
Julie will be able to
keep him, not us. It's
the way the system
works,*" said Lisa.
"*You know what?*"

"*What?*"

"*Sometimes you can
remove the kid from the
system, but you can't
always remove the
system from within the
kid. Julie is just one of
those kids.*"

---

family and the vulnerable children they care for, the damage caused to a child by unprepared moves may leave a family feeling that the child has been violated.

The desired outcome of reporting abuse and neglect is not to cause further child maltreatment by the unprepared moving of children. Yet, an agency may not be able to allow or want previous foster children to return to or make contact with a specific home.

Even when removal involves a difficult child, or when immediate action is warranted, a family may feel mixtures of relief, hurt, and anger——relief from the responsibility of care, hurt, or anger concerning how the situation was handled.

> *Care providers can give a going away gift of a shared specialness of their relationship with the foster child such as: a baseball glove or a soccer ball with the family autographs, a model rocket made with the foster parent, a quilt with patches of remembrances of the child, a baby blanket and pillow, a doll or stuffed animal, a piece of jewelry, or a letter of remembrance.*

Summary

Children in out-of-home care can be moved at the discretion of professionals who make the decision *"for the best interest of the child."* There are times when one can and should question whose best interest is really being served.

> *Aaron's social worker found him a new foster home, even though his grandparents (ages 42 and 43) were willing to care for him. He was nine months old, functioning beyond his developmental age, active, secure, and happy. He was oblivious to the politics. The neglect charge had been filed against his birth mother so that he could be placed in foster care. The county was proceeding to reunite Aaron with his 15-year-old mother, Julie, so that she could develop her relationship with her son. Three social workers and two attorneys had been involved in the case since Julie had become pregnant.*
>
> *Lisa and John drove Aaron to his weekend foster home. Tearful and agitated, Aaron was handed off to the strangers—Julie would arrive later. It was a quiet ride home for the grandparents. On Monday they repeated the two-hour drive to pick up Aaron. Aaron buried his head in Lisa's arms and whimpered. For the rest of the week Aaron would not let Lisa out of his sight. Lisa called social services and asked the worker to please provide transportation for Aaron so he didn't feel like they had abandoned him to strangers.*
>
> *Julie, who had been in a behavior treatment program since Aaron was three months old, was now going to be Aaron's full-time parent. She would be leaving her special education class with a six to one student-teacher ratio and joining a mainstream program in one of the largest high schools in Boston. As she preferred, she would be living in the city and would be completely responsible for the care of her small son. The foster family was to provide shelter and advice, but Aaron was to be Julie's total responsibility. This was the family's first foster daughter and they were anticipating the new relationship with excitement. The couple had been married three months. They were not aware of Julie's history.*
>
> *Aaron would join a day care program Monday through Friday, and Julie would be required to maintain her studies, accept full responsibility for Aaron, and learn to take care of herself as a responsible adult. Trial weekend visits would take place before the caseplan went into full swing.*

> *Reatha, an African American mother, had also chosen foster parenting as a way of contributing to the lives of complex children.*
>
> *Six years ago Danny, a caucasian, sickly and spindly little boy, had been placed under her care. Prior to placement in Reatha's home Danny, age four, had lived in six other homes. Reatha worked with Danny, loved him, and cared for him. He was a difficult child, but Reatha was a firm, loving, and experienced parent.*
>
> *Due to racial differences, Danny again was removed, this time from a home in which he had felt loved and wanted. This time Danny had not disrupted the placement, social services had.*
>
> *Needless placements later, Danny was available for adoption. Reatha applied and Danny came back to his heart home— regressed years from when he had left, the bonds of fragile trust now shattered.*

Rebuilding her relationship with Danny was difficult. Too many hopes had been shot down for this child. Too much anger remained repressed. Physically larger than Reatha, mentally handicapped and physically aggressive, Danny became dangerous to Reatha's preschoolers and jeopardized their lives. He did not understand why Reatha would have abandoned him. His years of surpressed anger were directed against the only home where he was loved.

In agony, Reatha called social services to have Danny moved to a safe facility.

Fully aware, John, Lisa, and Reatha had chosen adoptive parenting of complex children. They had chosen to import into their home the pathologies of these children.

Danny and Julie were family shakers, but these were experienced, firmly founded families.

Where else would they go?

Initially, Aaron moved between day care, the foster home, Julie, and his grandparents. Monday through Thursday at his grandparents' home, Aaron began to wake up in the middle of the night. Walking and rocking did not console him. He buried his little head deeply in Lisa's arms as she gently sang, soothing him to sleep. During the day he was fidgety and he jumped at every doorbell. He no longer liked to ride in the car. He screamed when Lisa was out of sight. He whimpered and remained agitated when placed in the arms of friends of the grandparents. Usually a good eater, he began to eat in fits and starts. His attitude became guarded and pensive.

The full case plan was activated, and Aaron's weekend visits ended. Initial reports from the foster home and Julie stated that Aaron was content and an easy baby. Within a short time, however, the foster family brought irritable and fussy Aaron into the hospital emergency room with bleeding stools—the diagnosis was colitis.

Once a well-adjusted, spirited, and happy baby—Aaron was now irritable and sullen. Aaron's journey into child protection began . . . the third generation.

Under the child welfare system, the last five years of Julie's life have cost taxpayers more than $_?_?_. Aaron, in less than two years, has added $_?_?_. Respite weekend care for Julie every two weeks in a professional mentor family would have cost taxpayers less than five thousand dollars for five years of support and provided John and Lisa support and needed breaks. Julie would have kept her family, and Aaron may never have been conceived. At least not when Julie was isolated and only fifteen.

Is Aaron's new arrangement in his best interest? Is it in his mother's best interest? Or is it a legal requirement of the system to prove her incompetence? The likelihood of success for Julie and Aaron seems questionable. Only time will tell what the next twist will be in his young life. Will Julie be able to raise Aaron on her own? Maybe, but it is highly unlikely. Will his grandparents remain standing guard for years with their revolving door always available for his needs? How long will Julie remain estranged from the only family who has truly loved her, the only family safe enough to be angry with? How many moves will Aaron face in his childhood—will his odds be any better than his mother's?

When a child in care is facing a move, the care provider needs to provide as much information as possible to help the child remain in touch with his past. The Lifebook is a tool the care provider can use to help a child remember his past. It also can help social workers and the new care provider or adoptive parent know more about the special needs and interests of the child.

Social workers who are responsible for children in care need to help the child and the care provider family prepare for and deal with the loss of separation. The more prepared a child and family are for a move, the less traumatic it will be.

References

Delaney, Richard and Kunstal, Frank. 1993. *Troubled Transplants: Unconventional Strategies for Helping Disturbed Foster and Adoptive Children*. Colorado: Wlater J. Corbett.

Falhberg, Vera. 1979. *Helping Children When They Must Move. Putting the Pieces Together Series*. Michigan: Michigan Department of Social Services.

Fischer, Lane & Jones, Deb. 1992. *Two Places Called Home. A Workbook for Foster Children and Youth*. Minnesota: University of Minnesota.

Chapter 10

Who's Kidding? It's OK for Our Kids to Be Different.

They say whatever doesn't kill you
strengthens you.
Children in out-of-home care
—adopted and foster—are strong.

In fantasy—perfect childhood from the beginning—the child feels secure, safe, and loved. Kids grow up in a stable, healthy family and share a common genetic and cultural disposition with their adult care providers. The pregnancy is filled with low stress, exercise, proper nutrition, and prenatal care. The child has a normal delivery and is healthy at birth. From the beginning the child is encouraged to grow and explore. The child is valued and respected as a human being. These dream children are the measure society uses to compare and judge adoptive and foster children, children whose lives are filled with at least one significant breakage from someone who matters. The differences in life experiences faced by children in out-of-home care are too great to compare to society's dream children.

Providers cannot change the past of a child in out-of-home care. It is difficult for the child to venture from preservation and survival to expression and freedom without the safety net of acceptance, love, and understanding. Ignoring a child's history will only encourage the child to bury the memories, assume blame for the experiences, or look for someone—usually another child—in whom to seek solace. These unhealthy preservation tools only perpetuate denial, confusion, and shame.

Even preverbal children are affected by traumatic life events. The feelings the child experiences are loud and clear, even if they are without word or form. These feelings become even more disjointed and misunderstood as the child is moved from caregiver to caregiver or is abused or neglected. The child may feel isolated because not even one human relationship can be trusted. A family can make an enormous difference in helping the child make sense of harmful past experiences by lending sympathetic, nonjudgmental support and consistent care.

Parenting a child like April is a challenge. Friends and relatives' children did not compare with the ball of fire we received— but then who's comparing?

This dynamic little person possessed traits potentially very valuable in an adult, but hard to cope with in a child.

April is a spirited child, and our hands have been full since she arrived.

April's spirit was complicated with significant separation and loss issues, projectile vomiting, and allergies. At five months she had already lived in five different homes.

Her real story was not written in the file—it was dramatized in her very being. When she arrived she had learned to shut off human contact. Her little body was rigid, and human touch brought fear and trauma. It took months of solitude, constant body contact, gentle touch, and soothing voices to bring her back into acceptance of relationships. At six months her first word was NO, and it's been an uphill climb ever since. Her temperament has become a strength as she has learned to work with it, and we have learned to laugh. We hired a nurse to help us and for the next six years the three of us parented as a team.

A child who is working through the past may not exhibit outrageous behaviors in the beginning of a relationship. Pathologies may remain hidden for years. Helping children who have barricaded their spirits to maintain psychological preservation is confusing and difficult. The barricade cannot begin to be dismantled unless the child feels safe enough to exhibit "core" and unusual behaviors. Once these behaviors begin, additional help can be offered.

It is not unusual to find the following behaviors exhibited by children in out-of-home care.

— **Delayed development** in hygiene, toileting, eating, dressing, and social interactions.

— **Immaturity and poor social skills**.

— **Problems with authority figures**—feelings of powerlessness and perceived need to act aggressively to gain attention, power, or authority.

— **Stress reactions**—violations of law, assaultive behavior, running away, suicide attempts, firesetting, animal abuse.

— **Self-destructive behaviors**—lying, stealing, cheating, self-mutilation, self-defeating behaviors, chemical abuse, suicide gestures.

— **Difficulty in relating to others**—passivity, withdrawing, dissociation, inappropriate touching, unclear personal boundaries, abnormal seeking of affection and attention.

— **Attachment and separation issues**—problems with separation from natural parents, difficulty with trust or attachment to current family or any human relationship.

— **Psychosomatic complaints**—night terrors, sleep walking, nightmares, stomachaches, body pains, twitches, nervous behaviors.

— **Impairments or handicaps**—physical, mental, or psychological. Presence of long-term untreated medical problems.

— **Cultural misunderstandings**—behaviors established in previous environment which are misunderstood in new home.

The world view of a child in out-of-home care is filtered through complex life experiences different from those of the family members with whom the child is presently living. The child brings no videotape of life experiences, and feelings and memories may be deeply buried. The child and the new parent are on their own discovery adventure. Luckily, children communicate by their behavior. It is the responsibility of the adult to catch the clues, process what the behavior may represent, and respond to the child in a safe way.

What do children in out-of-home care need in their new homes?

Children who require out-of-home care feel unsafe. Their most basic needs—safety and protection—have been disrupted. The connecting point to understanding the child's perception of safety is often unknown. Care providers become detectives, looking for subtle clues to understanding a child's real needs. Careful attention to detail is needed to find the pieces which spell safety to an insecure and wary child.

Children see what we do better than they hear or understand what we say. Every move a provider makes is watched by the child. Their senses—sight, touch, smell, taste, hearing—pick up nuances. Their very emotional, physical, and psychological preservation—personal safety—depends on tuning in carefully or turning off. The provider must offer unconditional acceptance and love in order for the child to feel safe. Consistency and predictability are a must to allow the child freedom to begin initial feelings of acceptance.

Dr. Cecil R. Benoit has authored the book, *When Love Is Not Enough, A Child's View of Parenting* (1989). He describes six needs that must be met to enhance a child's sense of well-being. His ideas are especially pertinent to nurturing the fragile egos of children in out-of-home care.

1. **Acceptance** for just being alive; this true acceptance always distinguishes the person from the behavior.

2. **Respect** that is a natural consequence of feeling accepted; that every person is unique and can be honored as a member of humanity.

3. **Recognition** that acknowledges with appreciation the mutuality of our experiences regardless of age.

4. **Approval** that who the child is, is more important than what the child does.

5. **Affirmation** that shows the child acceptance, even though the child makes mistakes or exhibits poor judgment.

6. **Consolation** when there is pain, fear, or uncertainty.

The child's original culture feels normal—
the new culture is strange.

To be assimilated into the new family, children in out-of-home care—both adoptive and foster—need their original culture understood and valued. The child must have the opportunity to grow into a healthy future while understanding, accepting, and cherishing the past.

How do individuals differ?

If we could shrink the earth's population in 1992 down to 100 people—and the human ratios remained the same—there would be 57 Asians, 21 Europeans, 14 people in the Americas, and 8 Africans. Fifty percent of the world's wealth would be in the hands of only six people and these six people would live in the United States. Seventy people would be unable to read; fifty would suffer malnutrition; eighty would live in sub-standard housing, and only one would have a university education. When we consider the world from this perspective, the need for understanding becomes glaringly apparent. (BPW 1992)

No human being is free of prejudice. Every day we make inappropriate judgments and statements. A child may be considered a space cadet, a boss, a nit-picker, a friend, a chatterbox, a bother, a slow learner. Labels without understanding or appreciation of differences put distance and distrust between people, cause misunderstandings, and can lead to unwanted self-fulfilling prophesies.

Let's start with our own differences . . . Our effectiveness in accepting and communicating with individuals who differ from us will depend on our life experiences, personality, and maturity. When you review the following potential differences, ask yourself if you are in a majority or minority position. If you are in a position of minority, is your difference valued or not valued by the majority? Do you value your difference and can you accept and communicate with others who are not like you? Compare your childhood with your adult life. Compare the life experiences of your children in out-of-home care with your own experiences. Then think of areas of sensitivity to explore so that you can promote healthier relationships.

When we chose the vocation of parenting, we made decisions, conscious or not, to defer some of our own needs and wants. We chose to limit our freedom to use time, energy, and money. Providing protective environments for our children during their vulnerable years is a great calling. Unfortunately, because of our own unfulfilled needs, few of us are prepared to live with the degree of selflessness that parenting requires.
Dr. Cecil Benoit
When Love is Not Enough
1989

Ability to communicate—Individuals who immigrate from other countries, have impaired hearing, speech impediments, developmental delays, physical or mental handicaps which prevent them from communicating like the majority. Individuals who have a literacy problem.

Socio-economic—Families who provide care for other people's children often face socio-economic differences. If the child has been raised in a family struggling for survival and is currently living in a middle class provider home, socio-economic cultural differences will exist.

Level of education, training, or intellectual capacity—Persons with average intellect who are working with low functioning individuals may not understand feelings, needs, or perceptions experienced by the other person. Individuals with differences in education may find it difficult to understand or appreciate the value of another person. A highly educated person may find it difficult to appreciate the value of a laborer. A laborer may feel inadequate to have a relationship with a highly educated person. Families who value education may not understand a child who has been raised with different values.

Personal influences—Each human being is unique. Our uniqueness makes us who we are. How we view ourselves and fit into our communities also contributes significantly. These differences also may cause additional barriers:

- Physically average/attractive
- Physically deformed
- Minority race
- Ethnic background
- Age

- Physically disabled
- Majority race
- Personality/temperament
- Mixed race
- Sex

Family dynamics— Interpersonal dynamics of each family vary. Some of the dynamics found in the homes of children in out-of-home care may have existed in our own families of origin, and others may be very different from what we are used to. How we have resolved our own history and life experiences will determine how we respond to children in our care. Conditions like these can cause confusion and communication difficulties.

- Chemically free
- Chemically co-dependent
- Emotionally neglectful
- Physically neglectful
- Sexually abusive
- Supportive family members
- Unsupportive family members
- Divorce of parents
- Death of parents
- Authoritarian parenting style
- Coaching parenting style
- Paternal authority figure
- Grandparents in home
- Adopted children in home
- Absent adult female influence

- Chemically abusive
- Chemically recovering
- Emotionally abusive
- Physically abusive
- Ritualistically abusive
- Estranged family members
- No family members
- Separation of parents
- Parent ill or injured
- Democratic parenting style
- Parenting abdicated
- Siblings in home
- Unrelated others in home
- Maternal authority figure
- Absent adult male influence

Community—Beyond each of our family systems is a community of others who interact with us. These individuals provide relationships which affect our lives and daily activities. Communities also provide services which support a family system.

EITHER	OR
• Community is supportive of family	• Community is not supportive of family
• Family has access to medical services	• Family cannot access medical services
• Family has access to education and training	• Family does not have access to education and training
• Telephone available	• Telephone not available
• Transportation services available	• Transportation services not available
• Plumbing/electricity available	• Plumbing/electricity not available
• Family has friends	• Family is isolated

Spirituality—Each individual experiences spirituality differently.

• Spiritually fulfilled	• Spiritually searching
• Spiritually satisfied	• Non-spiritual
• Challenging/growth producing	• Joyful and rewarding
• Shame or guilt based	• Oppressive/stifles growth

In our "enlightened" country, the predominant cultures tend to think wishfully that prejudice does not exist. It's easy to quote, *"different strokes for different folks."* It's another experience when the different strokes or different folks move next door or into your home.

> *In many neighborhoods, those different folks*
> *happen to be our foster or adoptive children.*
> *And the preconceived ideas of who they are*
> *and how they will act are only a beginning.*

How do we devalue differences?

Today's prejudice lies not in overt segregated actions, but in underlying covert practices. One must understand and be aware of words or behaviors—"cultural hot buttons"— which trigger miscommunication, and must also be attuned to nonverbal communication information and style differences. Stories and jokes need to be selected carefully. Open questions, feedback, and self-disclosure can help bridge difficulties in communication.

The language of differential treatment is important to understand when working with our differences:

Ageism: Preoccupation with youth in the American culture results in attitudes, behaviors, and policies that keep older people invisible and undervalued.

Bias: Expression of preference.

Bigotry: Intolerance of racial, cultural, physical, mental, ethnic, gender, personality, age, sexual, or religious differences. It may be very inappropriate, i.e., the belief that older people do not have new ideas or that high school students who are not slender are unattractive.

Discrimination: Exists when people's choices of and access to employment, education, housing, resources, and other public goods are limited by their race, sex, age, religion, disability, or national origin. (Some states are also beginning to recognize sexual preference discrimination.) It is the act of treating individuals or specific groups of people differently. In some cases it may be very appropriate, i.e., sidewalk ramps for persons in wheelchairs, braille elevator buttons for the visually impaired,

Infancy was a challenge.

At two and a half April finally slept through the night. The first holidays were spent in a bathroom keeping out the stimulation of lights and people. Shopping was banished. Too many people ignited an explosion. Grocery shopping carts were left full of groceries as we fled to the car. More than once I pulled off to the side of the road and held my flailing and wailing daughter. She refused to let my mother hold her until she was a year and a half—she would stiffen and shut down. There was nothing about this little girl that wasn't intense.

Ethnocentrism: The tendency to view one's own culture group as the center of everything—that one's own group is superior to other groups—the standard against which all others are judged.

Prejudice: Preconceived judgment; an opinion (favorable or unfavorable) formed in the absence of actual knowledge or reason.

Sexism: Both males and females are the object of sexual discrimination—in work atmospheres, education, clothing, income potential. For example: lifestyle—*"workwives" are a lot more socially acceptable than "househusbands,"* clothing—*"women can wear almost anything, but men aren't culturally approved for skirts, dresses, or most wormen's wear,"* and activity—*"girls can be 'tomboys', but boys better not be 'sissies.'"*

Stereotypes: Assignment of characteristics (mentally cataloging) to every member of a specific group. Stereotypes, "labeling or name calling," may create communication shortcuts and be convenient, but they hardly do justice to an individual. For the same reason they are often inaccurate—and racist, sexist, homophobic, ageist, handicappist, or ethnocentric.

The children we care for in foster care are in a very different family relationship than most children. Regardless of other difficulties— disabilities, minority status, disfiguration—these children face day-to-day peer pressure, community pressure, and **prejudice**.

Subtle, covert, or overt prejudice exists for children in out-of-home care. Following are some examples found in adult day-to-day life. These illustrations may prove helpful in understanding how foster children are denied access to opportunity.

Avoidance of contact: Unless each of us steps into the environment of the other, we will never begin to understand and appreciate differences. Using the excuse, *"I don't have the opportunity to understand,"* is not acceptable.

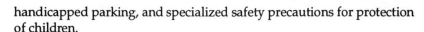

> *Sally is 35, she's my dear, childhood, birthday-party-attending friend—she also has MS with severe tremors and is confined to a wheelchair. Inside her trembling and crooked body, she is more similar to me than different. One warm fall day, she was in need of a package of incontinence support. Access to this product was not just a jump in the car and a drive to the drugstore. We decided it would be a drive through the park to the finest, most elaborate supermarket in the city. On Saturdays they had food demonstrations and we were hungry. Our appearance and behavior set us apart from the group as we wheeled into the store and as we giggled and shared and spill the goodies. People eyed us suspiciously. Why were we coming into this store on this day? We appeared to be embarrassing them. Luckily, we weren't embarrassed—we were together, and this was too beautiful a day to be spoiled by other people's opinions.*

It would be wrong for me not to notice Sally's handicap. It would remove a lot of the beauty and humor from our relationship. It would build a wall between us that would not allow either of us to share our pain when our differences get in the way or are misunderstood by society at large.

Denial of cultural differences: Minimizing the impact of individual differences can restrict access to services, ease of access to services, and mobility. It can block communication and raise the barrier of race. Denial places a person in a position of conformity in order to allow success—i.e., dress, walk, talk like the approved group.

At eleven months she played her first joke—eyes twinkling. By four she was competent at storytelling and teasing. She told her father that her grandma fed her snake and potatoes for supper. "Don't you mean steak?" he asked. "Oh no, Daddy, it really was a snake. It was long and skinny. We had snake." She confided later that her grandpa had called it sausage. Creative and dramatic, she never lets us know what is in store or what is a story.

"I don't even notice you're _____" *(black, white, mentally retarded, handicapped, etc.)* If people need to make such a statement, then it matters to them or they are noticing and feeling a need to express it. Differences are important and it is OK to notice them. I like being female. I also like white water kayaking, running a business, diverse friendships, and being a wife and mother. People who know me in one capacity of my life may not necessarily know me in another. If I am different, it's OK for you to notice.

Denial of political, social, or economic significance of difference: This kind of denial minimizes the influence of the difference on the lives of individuals—for example, not providing an American sign interpreter at a political rally or subtitles for movies.

> *Julie and Amy spent the day with their children visiting the zoo and then going out for hamburgers. Amy had six children, all under age ten. Julie had only one child, age five. They had had a really great day. At the restaurant, Amy ordered four large fries, two sodas, and seven small hamburgers and divided the pile of food among the troops. Julie ordered a "Happy Meal with toy" for her daughter and a large hamburger for herself, along with single orders of fries and sodas for each of them. Amy's children also wanted the Happy Meal, but held their tongues. Julie's daughter piped up as the food was passed around, "Didn't you guys want a Happy Meal, too?" The ambience in the room changed as Amy's children looked at each other knowing that with their family's resources, the special meal was out of the question.*

It is very easy to be oblivious to another person's financial difficulties. In this case, even a trip to a fast food restaurant was an exceptional experience for Amy's family.

Dysfunctional rescuing: Helping people with differences, based on a belief that they cannot help themselves. This help is often motivated out of guilt or not understanding a person's capabilities. Dysfunctional rescuing sets a person up to fail, if not now, in the future. This type of help often feels patronizing or condescending and limits the person's personal growth in the future.

Blaming the victim: Attributing results to the success or failure of a target group and not to the individual. Holding a whole culture accountable for the actions of a visible few. Not acknowledging or looking for the real cause of the problem. Blaming a person's problem on the difference versus lack of training or support.

> *The news reported another "gay bashing murder," that the latest victim was . . .* What?! I wanted to scream. What right do they have to say *only* that about . . . I've worked with this individual, I like this individual. This is a very special person you're talking about and in less than ten words you reveal very personal information about him, as though this murder could have been expected. *On television, to the world, you announce to his customers, friends, and unsuspecting parents this man's sexual preferences.*

How do people with differences devalue themselves?

Individuals oppress themselves subconsciously and unconsciously by regarding themselves as inferior because of their differences. They may displace true feelings and express feelings they feel are acceptable to the predominant culture. They may be unwilling to challenge authority or take a risk. They may refuse to trust others in their own or the predominant culture. This failure to trust may sometimes be appropriate. At other times it may lock an individual into complacency, which stifles healthy growth.

At fifteen months she decided she was a kitty and remained a kitty for six weeks. If we used her name she shrieked and wailed. It was unbelievable that a fifteen-month-old could be so persistent.

Avoidance of contact: Avoiding contact with the predominant culture. Distrusting and being overly concerned or suspicious. Being overly sensitive to rejection. Rejecting people within one's own cultural group who are learning to value the culture of others. Escaping through drugs, fantasy, dreams, sex, alcohol, food, withdrawal.

"I can't go to . . . because I am the wrong . . . (not good enough)"
"I don't trust any . . . person who spends time with . . ."

Blaming the system: Not taking responsibility for one's actions. Putting all the blame on someone else or the system for one's problems. Refusing to acknowledge mental, emotional, and stress-related issues as real.

"If I wasn't . . . this wouldn't have happened."
"The . . . makes me act like this. I have a right to . . . "

Denial of difference: Distrusting others within one's own culture. Rejecting or devaluing your own culture. Giving preference to people of the predominant culture. Valuing and overemphasizing the predominant culture as more attractive, powerful, superior, intelligent, or capable.

Lack of understanding of political significance of difference: Being passive and unassertive. Misdirecting anger to persons of less power. Avoiding conflict at all cost and turning anger inward. Ingroup fighting. Symbolic status striving through buying things. Taking advantage of other persons in the subculture because they lack information or power.

Refusing to seek help because it won't do any good.
Unwilling to participate in training because nothing will change.

System beating: Getting over, on, or around the system. Manipulating others or the system through guilt, games, or illicit activities; acting out anger, playing dumb, clowning, or being invisible.

Playing games with . . . to get undeserved support or benefits .
Violently demanding your own way because of your difference.

How does our temperament or personality affect our relationships?

We each need to increase self-awareness and gain insight in order to understand the attractiveness of individual differences. Some differences develop harmony, and others cause discord. We can develop patience to allow them to exist for the benefit of all when we begin to understand the value of difference.

According to Otto Kroeger and Janet Thuesen, who developed Typewatching Theory from the Myers-Briggs Type Indicator and the work of C.G. Jung, each of us develops a preference early in life and sticks to it. Many of our relationship and communication difficulties begin because we each react and relate differently to a given situation or the environment in which we live.

Each of us is born with preferences in the way we react to life experiences. These preferences emerge early in life and form the foundation of our personalities. Life experiences either enhance or diminish these preferences. Birth order, behavior of family members, and other environmental forces all affect how preferences develop.

Separation issues posed a real challenge.

Except for the daily nurse who cared for April, we could leave her with no one. It was as though all her past feelings would explode and she had no words or pictures to understand her intense feelings—just black memories. At four, when she began preschool, I sat in the nearby church sanctuary for two months until she felt secure enough to attend by herself.

Any change from a familiar routine—a walk to the park with her class— brought the fear of never being returned. We encouraged young friends to come to our home so there would be no separation problems. By five, she began to make friends and enjoy people—she even spent weekends at Grandpa and Grandma's all by herself!

The four pairs of preference alternatives used in the Myers-Briggs type indicator theory include:

Extroverted	or	Introverted
Sensing	or	Intuitive
Thinking	or	Feeling
Judging	or	Perceiving

Preferences grow and change over a lifetime. Though the preference will remain the same, the flavor of the preference may be very different. For example, if you are an extrovert in a family of introverts, you become a different type of extrovert than a child raised in a very extroverted family, where the loudest gets his or her way.

1. **Extroverts**

   Spend time actively involved with the people and things around them. Are energized by people and action. Gregarious, outgoing. Enjoy social interaction and multiple relationships. Tend to speak first—then think. Want to tell you all about experiences. Initiate conversations and talk easily. Need verbal approval. Talk through a problem in order to solve it. Interacting with people helps to maintain high energy level.

2. **Sensors**

   See the world in terms of the immediate, practical facts of experience and life.

3. **Thinkers**

   Make decisions based on an objective and non-personal analysis of the evidence. Do not let personal relationships affect decision.

4. **Judgers**

   Life is lived in a decisive, planned, and orderly way, aiming to regulate and control events. Tendency to draw conclusions, schedule, reach closure, and set deadlines.

1. **Introverts**

   Spend time thoughtfully, involved with concepts and ideas. Prefer to watch or listen before interacting. Are energized by spending time alone. Strong sense of personal space. Enjoy intensive, limited relationships. Tend to be reflective. Think first—then speak. Talk with close friends and family but distant from others. Grouchy if around people too long. Develop a few close, deep relationships.

2. **Intuitives**

   See the world in terms of possibilities and meaning of each situation.

3. **Feelers**

   Make decisions based on subjective judgment in which the effects it may have on others is considered.

4. **Perceivers**

   Life is lived in a spontaneous, flexible way, aiming to understand life and adapt to it. Tendency to collect and respond to new information.

From the eight brief descriptions above you get a glimpse of preference differences. Each of us falls into one or the other of the four paired categories. Communication between individuals can be easily misinterpreted when we mix these differences. We can utilize each of our unique characteristics in effective ways when we understand and value these differences.

The more we practice our preferences—intentionally and unintentionally—the more we rely on them with confidence and strength. It doesn't, however, mean that we are unable to use our nonpreferences. Just because we are right handed doesn't mean we never use our left hand. The following books are recommended if you are interested in learning more about personality preferences.

Type Talk or How to Determine Your Personality Type and Change Your Life by Otto Kroeger and Janet Thuesen. (1988)

Nap times were incredible.

Rocking and stories might fool her to sleep, but there was no fooling about waking up. We were guaranteed to experience forty minutes of disconnect.

"Earth to April . . ."

Meanwhile, April would wail, shriek, arch her back, refuse touch, and use her naughtiest language—luckily she only knew "poopy" and "yucky."

Eventually, April would gain control, focus, smile as though nothing had happened, jump out of our laps, and ask us to play with her.

We remained shell shocked.

Type Talk at Work or How the 16 Personality Types Determine Your Success on the Job by Otto Kroeger and Janet Thuesen. (1992)

Please Understand Me by Marilyn Bates and David Keirsey. (1978)

What effects can different temperaments have on child-parent relationships?

Children bring with them their own personal preferences of temperament. An introverted, intuitive, thinking, perceptive child living in a home with extroverted, sensing, feeling, judging parents is going to have conflicts. There is just no way around it. When differences in personality type erupt, it is important that the parent(s) learns how different personalities can work together to grow, enjoy, and respect one another. LaVonne Neff, in *One of a Kind—Making the Most of Your Child's Uniqueness* (1988), provides exceptional insight for parents working with children.

What about those kids with intense temperaments?

Some children are born spirited. They emerge from the womb marching boisterously to a different drummer. April's spirit was turned off, shut down, and squashed when she arrived in our home. When her spirit dared to emerge, we were faced with invincible determination. I believe spirit is what makes our children who they are. Once the child feels safe enough for attachment to begin, the new parents of an adoptive or foster child will probably get "more" than they bargained for. I share excerpts from *Raising Your Spirited Child, A Guide for Parents Whose Child is More—Intense, Sensitive, Perceptive, Persistent, Energetic* by Mary Sheedy Kurcinka, MA (1991).

Kurcinka takes parents and educators on a realistic journey of what it is like to live with and guide a very spirited young person. She uses gentle and "appropriate" language, which provides both children and adults with respectful coping tools in learning to manage temperaments.

The spirited child often embarrasses, confuses, frustrates, and humiliates parents. She stands out in a crowd. Her reactions are powerful whenever or however they are expressed. She drives you crazy one minute and endears you the next.

In her book, Kurcinka describes temperament as a preferred style of responding and states that there are positive and negative aspects in all temperament traits. There is no perfect temperament—parents of spirited children can make the difference by helping the child shape her particular qualities in the most advantageous way.

Nine categories which make kids spirited:

1. **Intensity:** How strong are your child's emotional reactions? Does he laugh or cry loudly and energetically or softly and mildly? Is she loud and dramatic or intently observant, planning a strategy for every move? There is rarely a middle road. Intense children don't whimper—they wail. They are easily frustrated, and every reaction is deep and powerful. One minute they can skip happily into a room, and the next minute leave screaming. Their tantrums are raw and enduring. *(April's non-stop wailing often lasted two or more hours!)* Intensity can be very positive when it is channeled positively—it is life's zest and exuberance. Look for clues that signal intensity is building—gestures, sounds, behaviors, sensations— before the screams begin. Keep track of the things that soothe and calm the child. Work with the child to help diffuse the intensity appropriately. Intense children need to learn how to express their strong feelings and

At six, April is secure and outgoing.

She attends kindergarten, goes on field trips, and can stand with her classmates in front of an audience. She is full of energy, alert, and bright. Her first report card scored high in respect for authority, cooperation, listening, memorizing, and sharing—only she and her family know what obstacles she had to overcome to meet such high standards. When she is healthy, nourished, and well-rested, she handles herself well and can begin to set her own limits. She alerts us when she has had enough and declares,"Mom, we better go. I just crossed the boundaries. I might take down some fences."

She's taken down her share of fences.

need the right words to do it. Talk with the child about feelings and share that you also experience these feelings and understand. Look for opportunities to short circuit a potentially intense situation with a humorous approach. Laugh more.

2. **Persistence:** They love debate and are not afraid to assert themselves. Getting them to change their minds is a major undertaking. They are committed to a task, unwilling to give up, and goal oriented. Conflict is an hourly occurrence. My husband and I focus on "yes" and limit the amount of "no" we use. When we reach a standoff, we work with April to help her "problem solve" and control her issues.

3. **Sensitivity:** These kids are keenly aware and respond to the slightest noises, smells, sounds, lights, textures, or changes in mood. They are easily overwhelmed in crowds. Many children react to little things that bother them—the difference is that these children re-eeee-act. They know when you've had a rotten day before you do. If your stress level is high, they open the throttle. Because she was easily overstimulated, we learned when to leave or quit before April launched into outer space. We limited our grocery trips to finding the necessities and paying for them. If April was still in control at the check out counter, we'd go back down another aisle and purchase the items we could have done without.

4. **Perceptiveness:** These kids see and hear things most people never notice. They are often accused of not listening, though they are usually listening very intently or noticing something else. The dew in the spiderweb. The squirrel at the top of the tree chewing an apple. The dead bug on the sidewalk. *(April senses life. She lies on the couch and eats music because her ears can only hear it, and that's not enough. She catches raindrops on her tongue because she needs to know if they taste the same way they feel. She licked the walls at the children's medical center because she wanted to know if the clinic tasted like it smelled—I almost died. April sees things I've never seen and experiences things I never will experience.* "Earth to April" means getting her attention and eye contact. A gentle touch often encourages her to face me. A puppet or song may have to relay the message.

5. **Adaptability:** Spirited kids are uncomfortable with change. They need to feel a sense of control. They need to feel successful. Cooperation is accomplished best when the child knows what the next step will be, what will happen, and how it may be experienced. Put these kids into foster care or adoption and you've got excitement. They hate surprises and have difficulty shifting from one event to another, let alone being bounced from home to home. In our home we pace our transitions to make life with April more pleasant. A trip out in public one day may mean we stay home the next day. We found a school which has full-day kindergarten every other day. We needed the day after to regroup.

In addition, Kurcinka states that these kids may come with some added bonuses that increase the challenge of parenting. She calls them "bonuses," but there are days I want to call 911.

6. **Regularity:** These kids are irregular. While most children are asleep these children are wide awake. When they eat may remain a puzzle for the parent. Luckily for April, my husband and I are both process time people—which means that we move from process to process instead of watching the clock. When we are tired we sleep, when we are hungry we eat. For us, April's irregularity meshed into our flexible lifestyle. If we scheduled our life, this kind of bonus would drive us nuts.

7. **Energy:** April has two speeds: overdrive and overdrawn. She needs to be moving constantly. Bottling up this energy is impossible, so we have

learned to engage it. April jumps up from the table to get everything we forgot. Guests compliment her on her helpfulness. When she is expected to remain quiet for a long period—over one half hour—I make sure she has a safe place to release. The bathroom, a long hallway, outdoors, or the car offer secure, let-loose, jumping, noisy, running space for her to unwind and regroup. Long drives in the car are interspersed with time-outs to "run around and shout."

8. **First reaction:** These kids need time to warm up before they are ready to participate. First reactions are not final responses, and most experiences need a second or third chance for the child to feel comfortable. Success may be a very small step—even a smile. Preplacement visits are mandatory for children with this trait if they are moving or in out-of-home care. Every excursion may need a careful explanation to diffuse anxiety. Bedtime is often a great time to discuss the next day and prepare for any new experiences. And morning affirmations recharge batteries that were beginning to run on worry.

9. **Mood:** The world is a serious place for some spirited kids. They are analytical. They pick apart experiences, find flaws, and make suggestions for change. Their smiles are few and far between, and they may be prone to whining. It is very easy to feel affronted by these kids. Luckily, for us, April forgot this trait—her disposition is sweet and positive. Some of the children who have lived with us, however, did have this bonus. *(One seventeen-year-old met the tax assessor at the door and proceeded to give him the grand tour of our home. Every flaw and negative detail was clearly pointed out. His eye for detail was sincerely appreciated when our property taxes were reduced.)*

Kurcinka's philosophy is "progress, not perfection." Her book doesn't give you all the answers, but it sure brings insight to the complications of living or working with a spirited child. Foster and adoptive children tend to have dynamic temperaments and intense feelings once they emerge. These children may challenge the most patient and experienced parents. Some of her sound advice includes:

Plan for success—learn to predict the child's reactions, organize the setting for success, work together, and enjoy the rewards—this gives the care provider power to face those typical tough times head on.

By planning for success you can
—avoid daily battles (bedtime, dressing, eating, bathing, sleeping, fighting).
—prevent tantrums.
—help your child handle frustration, anger, and other intense feelings.
—begin to enjoy travel, celebrations.

Get rid of lousy labels which often reflect a character strength being overused by the child. For example, with guidance, aggression can become assertiveness. The possibilities are endless. One wise sixth grade teacher who had made exceptional progress with a complex child wrote a year end report for the next year's teacher and then asked the parent to review all the child's school records from previous years. Together, the teacher and the parents separated out the pertinent facts and rewrote the data which had previously labeled the child as delinquent and incorrigible. The child changed schools and graduated with honors.

Old	New
Demanding, fussy	Holds high standards, exacting
Unpredictable	Flexible, creative problem solver, progressive
Loud, noisy	Enthusiastic, zestful, zeal, gusto
Argumentative	Opinionated, strongly committed to goals
Stubborn	Assertive, determined, a willingness to persist in the face of strong difficulties, perserverance, tenacity
Nosy, snoopy	Curious, inquisitive, interested
Wild	Energetic, boisterous, exuberant, industrious, vigorous, lively
Extreme	Tenderhearted, extravagant, thorough
Inflexible, rigid	Traditional, rooted, established
Manipulative	Charismatic, charming, enchanting
Impatient, restless	Compelling
Anxious, nervous	Cautious, careful, discrete, watchful
Explosive	Dramatic, high-powered, stimulating
Picky	Selective, discriminating, particular,
Whiny	Persistent, analytical, discerning
Distractible, spacy	Perceptive, musing, ruminative
Reckless, careless	Adventurous, courageous, exploring, gallant

Compound spirited temperaments with allergies
and you've got more than a handful.

What effect can allergies have on children?

Children who are in out-of-home care or who have been adopted may be under stress other children in the family are not feeling. This stress can trigger allergic reactions.

A significant study has been made by Dr. Doris Rapp concerning behavior exhibited by children who have allergic reactions to food, chemicals, or their environment. For children exhibiting bizarre or unusual behaviors, changes in diet or environment, and avoidance of chemicals may make an incredible difference. Dr. Rapp has a full range of videos and books, and I highly recommend them if you are making little progress with a complicated or difficult child.

Some excerpts from her books, *The Impossible Child* and *Is This Your Child?* include:

Stresses put additional burdens on the body's ability to maintain normal balance. Unusual sensitivities to ordinary exposures can develop suddenly after serious stresses occur in a child's life.

The emotional stress of one child who won't mind, bites, kicks, screams, pinches, hits, swears, and destroys is enough to place parents in emotional turmoil. The child may keep the entire household in a constant state of turmoil by fighting, bickering, crying and by their negative responses to ordinary suggestions related to normal everyday living. These children often have irritability, depression, headaches, muscle aches, and abdominal complaints in addition to typical hay fever, asthma or eczema. They often cannot sleep, have nightmares and wet the bed. Some children or adults manifest depression or write suicidal notes after eating certain foods or being exposed

This event in the snow actually proved very helpful in April's development. For the first time, we isolated the feelings she had felt in her infancy and she had words to describe them.

Finally her intense feelings began to make sense . . .

She had lived with us for more than six years.

to pollens, dusts, molds or chemicals. Other children may develop asthma, hay fever, cry easily or crouch in a remote area due to these same items.

Many of these children appear to be angelic until they eat the wrong food or are exposed to dust, pollen, molds or chemicals. This only compounds the parental guilt because they burden themselves with being inadequate parents.

All in all few families can withstand the stress created by one child who has severe undiagnosed allergies affecting the brain. It is always surprising and most gratifying to observe how a family's tensions diminish after the true cause of the child's problems are recognized and resolved. (Rapp 1986)

The influence of diet on behavior and development needs more critical evaluation. Missed essential nutrients in children's early years plays a role in development, intelligence, and behavior. Improper nutrition at any point in life affects behavior and coping skills.

Building cooperation from our differences

Caring for other people's children requires extreme sensitivity. Compassion and consideration for children and their families are needed to build trust and a partnering relationship. Care providers have the opportunity to begin to build bridges between differences—both with the children and with the children's primary families.

Following are some of the insensitive things people say without understanding alternative statements which are more helpful.

Common statements made to children with disabilities:

Mommy, what's wrong with him? Is he/she like that because he/she was bad? How come you ---(walk, talk, look, wear, can't do)--- like that? Innocent questions from children. These questions handled properly by adults build the bridges of understanding and acceptance between people with differences. Encourage your child to make contact with challenged children. Parents can facilitate friendships by asking challenged children to special activities, parties, and outings. Challenged children want to be regarded as children first, not someone with a disability. Movies and television shows that may be helpful to open conversation are—*Children of a Lesser God and Reasonable Doubts,* with Marlee Matlin and *Life Goes On* wih Chris Burke. Joni Eareckson Tada also has many fine published materials and videos dealing with disabilities. Ask yourself—How would I want others to react if this were my child? Would I want a passerby to stare, look horrified, or turn away and whisper? Or would I appreciate a smiling mother holding her child's hand, approaching, and saying, *"Would you mind if my child asks you a question about your disability?"* Some other responses may be. *"Even though his legs don't work, he has wheels to get around." "She wears her wheelchair, like mommy wears her glasses. Mommy's glasses help me see. Her wheelchair helps her get around." "She's a child just like you, she likes to play and have friends, let's go over and get to know her." "We all come in different packages, but we all need people who like and care about us."*

Common statements made to foster children:

How come you don't live with your mom and dad? This question places the child in the difficult position of explaining something she or he may not understand or betraying private and sensitive family information. Often children still want to live with their biological parents and really miss them. A statement which would show compassion is, *"I'm here if you need me. I'd like to be your friend. Please ask if you need something."*

Common statements made to foster parents:

Are you just in this for the money? How much do you make? Why do you take these kids? Foster parents work twenty-four hours a day with complex children. In some states, monthly payments are less than $200 per child. This may seem like a fair amount of money to care for one child, but in reality a month contains an average of 720 hours—an hourly wage of twenty-eight cents. From this twenty-eight cents per hour comes clothing, food, entertainment, transportation, allowance, and shelter for a child in care. Even at double or triple monthly rates, a foster home provides inexpensive family care for a child in need of a home. Foster parents are not special: they are ordinary individuals who love children and provide homes for children who need them. A better statement to a foster family would be, *"I have a bicycle, inline skates, etc., my kids have grown out of. Could you use them? If you need someone to talk to when you're frustrated, you can call me and I'll listen."*

Common statements made to birth parents:

What did you do to get your kids removed? Didn't you love them? Some parents love their children so much, they realize they cannot care for them the way they desire. Not all children in foster or adoptive homes have been placed in out-of-home care because of inappropriate parenting. Children may be difficult to care for, or family circumstances such as age, finances, or health may place a parent in a position of not being able to properly care for a child. A temporary family crisis may have erupted. In other cases, a family situation may have been misinterpreted, and a child has slipped through the cracks. A better statement would be, *"If you ever feel lonely and need someone to listen to you, I'd be happy to offer a hug or an ear."*

Common statements made to adopted children:

How come your mom gave you away? Why are you adopted? When are you going to go and look for your "real" mom and dad? Why don't you look like your family? Children who are adopted often ask these questions to themselves and are unable to answer them. To confront a child directly with this question is emotionally abusive. Many times a birth mother or father is too young, or is physically, financially, or emotionally unable to care for the child. The parent loves the child, and by giving the child up, is doing what she or he believe is in the child's best interest. In other cases the child's parents may be deceased. Sometimes children have been removed because of abuse or neglect, and parental rights have been terminated. Whatever the case, many adopted children have not resolved the issue within themselves enough to discuss it with another adult or child. A better statement would be, *"I'm glad you're part of the . . . family. You are a special person and I like getting to know you."*

Common statements made to adopted parents:

Couldn't you have your own kids? There are a variety of reasons children are adopted. Some couples have medical problems and cannot biologically have children. *The Miracle Seekers, An Anthology of Infertility* by Mary Martin Mason provides sensitive insight into the world of infertility and adoption. The inability to have a child is very disheartening for many, and adoption fills their parenting desire. To ask a question as personal as *"Couldn't you have your own children?"* may touch a very emotionally difficult subject. Whatever the reason, adoptive parents need to be accepted as parents to the children they care for by their extended family, the community, and their adopted children.

The people of Uganda quote a proverb that says . . .

"The one who has not traveled widely thinks his mother is the only cook." Human nature seems to push us toward uniformity. We like the familiar, the tried and true, and shy away from what is different. We are often skeptical of new ideas and unusual combinations, convinced that what works for us should surely work for others as well."
Joetta Handrich Schlabach (1991)

From the book Extending the Table. . . A World Community Cookbook— *an eye opener to world cultures and daily life.*

Our children need balance.

In a system skewed in ifs . . .

. . . could we make it happen.

If our plans
could be
actions

If our thoughts
could reflect
feelings

If our policies
could be
practice

If our education
could be
experience

If
we could value . . .

The differences between planning, thinking, policies, education . . .

. . . And actions, feelings, practices, experiences.

Our children would have the balance they deserve.

A better statement for an adoptive or foster parent would be, "Congratulations on your new family member. If you need anything, please call me." Then drop off a frozen casserole, offer to pick up some groceries, run an errand or take a couple of the kids for an hour or two!

Summary

Children whose lives have been disconnected from their families of origin will exhibit behaviors different from biological children raised in one loving and nurturing home. Children in out-of-home care bring into their new homes cultural differences which may be misunderstood by the new family.

— Individuals who work with children in out-of-home care or adopted children need to be sensitive to unusual behaviors these children may display. These children carry within their beings a history of loss many children never experience.

— Children in out-of-home care have the same physical needs as other children. Children in out-of-home care need more emotional supports.

— Children in out-of-home or adoptive care should not be compared developmentally with stable, biological children. To compare an adopted or foster child with a biological child is unfair.

— Personality and temperament play a significant part in a child's behavior. Allergies can affect behavior in unusual ways.

References:

Benoit, Cecil R. 1989. *When Love Is Not Enough, A Child's View of Parenting.* Tennesee: JM Productions.

Keirsey, David and Bates, Marilyn. 1978. *Please Understand Me. Character Types and Temperaments.* Del Mar, California: Prometheus Nemesis Book Company.

Kroeger, Otto and Thuesen, Janet. 1988. *Type Talk or How to Determine Your Personality Type and Change Your Life.* New York: Delacorte Press.

Kroeger, Otto and Thuesen, Janet. 1992. *Type Talk at Work. How the 16 Personality Types Determine Your Success on the Job.* New York: Delacorte Press.

Kurcinka, Mary Sheedy. 1991. *Raising Your Spirited Child. A Guide For Parents Whose Child Is More Intense, Sensitive, Perceptive, Persistent, Energetic.* New York: Harper Perennial.

Neff, LaVonne. 1988. *One of a Kind—Making the Most of Your Child's Differences.* Portland, Oregon: Multnomah Press.

Rapp, Doris. 1989. *The Impossible Child.* Practical Allergy Research Foundation, PO Box 60, Buffalo, New York 14223-0060.

Rapp, Doris. 1991, *Is This Your Child? Discovering and Treating Unrecognized Allergies in Children and Adults.* New York: William Morrow and Company.

FOR MORE INFORMATION ON ALLERGIES WRITE:
Practical Allergy Research Foundation, PO Box 60, Buffalo, New York 14223-0060.

FOR MORE INFORMATION ON DISABILITIES
Organizations, children's books, and resources. Send a self addresssed, stamped envelope to:
Disabilities Resource List, c/o CPT, PO Box 850, Sisters, OR 97759-0850

The Fine Line. . .
Discipline,
Punishment,
Maltreatment, or
Abuse

*Clarification of the fine line between
discipline and maltreatment
of children.*

*Discipline is a
thoughtful process . . .*

*. . . It does not
hinder the
relationship
between two
individuals . . .*

It encourages it.

*. . . It does not
threaten the dignity
of an individual . . .*

*It accomplishes the
goal of changing an
undesirable behavior.*

DYNAMICS OF A PARENTING SYSTEM

Transmit values by doing rather than telling.

What you do speaks louder than your words. Be the kind of person you want the children in your care to become.

A seeing eye guide dog for the blind is trained to be loyal and obedient.

This animal is completely trustworthy caring for the life of a vulnerable human being.

The training for this dog is accomplished without physical pain, mistreatment, or punishment.

If a seeing eye dog is not in need of hitting . . .

. . . why is a child?

DISCIPLINE
Development and Guidance of Internal Control
Includes respect, communication, acceptance, mutual understanding, truthfulness, and growth

PUNISHMENT
Exertion of External Control
Includes less communication, viewed by recipient as negative

CORPORAL PUNISHMENT
Exertion of External Control
Includes hitting, confinement

CHILD ABUSE
Exertion of Extreme Control
Includes extreme levels of control causing damage

Force or intervention by parent, adult, social services, or law enforcement which causes trauma or damage to the child in order to protect the child's life or liberty may be abusive to the child, but not be considered child abuse.

Chapter 11

Discipline
or
Punishment

*The word **discipline** comes from the word disciple,*
a follower of a teacher. A disciple follows a teacher
out of inner conviction, not out of fear.
Thus, the teacher guides the disciple until
the disciple is mature enough to also become a teacher.

*The word **punishment** means to control by force,*
is often administered by a person in power,
and is viewed negatively by the recipient.

Discipline and punishment are different. Discipline can be viewed as the long-term, positive approach to guiding behavior. It is patient and focuses on the future development of character, self-control, self-esteem, and orderly conduct. Punishment, on the other hand, enforces penalties and may be a quick fix solution to an immediate problem. It is often used to gain control when a child goes outside of approved social behaviors. Punishment may have an unwanted negative effect, frighten children, or make them angry. The definitions of discipline, punishment, maltreatment, and abuse are often confused. What a parent thinks of as discipline, a child may view as punishment. What social services perceives as abuse, parents may view as discipline or necessary intervention. Each parenting system and professional discipline has a slightly different perception of what constitutes discipline, punishment, maltreatment, and abuse. In many cases the distinctions are not clear.

The diagram on the left illustrates a parenting system containing areas of discipline, punishment, corporal punishment, and child abuse. The size of the circles and the amount they overlap will vary with each parent-child and family relationship. It would be unusual for any parenting system to never use punishment in raising a child. Every parent-child relationship will have different amounts of discipline and specific times punishment is used. Highly evolved parenting systems in some cultures, however, never use methods beyond helping children develop internal controls. Exertion of external control or the use of punishment is used sparingly, if ever. These systems may never use corporal punishment, and except in the case of emergency intervention, would never

Children can't develop healthy self-esteem (good feelings about themselves) if they cannot control their own desires and respect limits.

If they are allowed to assume that happiness and satisfaction come only from getting their own way, they will grow up frustrated and bitter because many times they will not achieve their desires.

Guiding children in self-discipline does not mean "going easy" on the child or ignoring mistaken, difficult, inappropriate, or damaging behavior.

It does mean having respect for the child.

*Stay calm. Think
before acting. The
parent needs to remain
in control of the
situation and guide the
child in dignity and
strength while
maintaining authority
and respect.*

*ASK what happened
before the behavior.*

*ASSESS what exactly
the behavior is.*

*ACT, don't react. Take
a deep breath, close
your eyes if you dare,
and /or count to ten,
then . . .*
— *Stop the behavior.*
— *Acknowledge the
behavior, tell the child
what you see him
doing and how you feel
about it.*
— *If the child is out of
control—hold him.
Avoid kicks and hits.
Try not to take it
personally.*
— *If you are unable to
hold the child, direct
him to some safe area
to gain control. Stay
by the child until the
child runs out of
energy.*
— *Once the child is
settled, sit close and
hold; acknowledge
his feelings. Actively
listen.*
— *Get the child's ideas
on how to solve the
problem. Then work
together to make it
happen. Talk about
appropriate ways
to let out anger.*

harm a child psychologically or physically. In other parenting systems punishment may be the only method of rearing a child. Not knowing other alternatives, these parents may predominantly punish but never use corporal punishment or abuse their children. In other cases, maltreatment may exist, but be extremely rare and occur only when other alternatives seem useless or impossible or are unavailable.

It would be unreasonable to say human beings do not learn by negative consequences or pain. There are times in adult lives when punitive action is warranted. A drunk driver should not continue driving while intoxicated, a serial killer should not be allowed to remain free, or an abusive parent should not continue abusing a child. Society has begun to question all violence against children. What is included presently in definitions of violence is vague and subject to personal interpretation.

> *I remember our first foster child. He was a volatile and frenetic bundle of mis-directed behavior. A "well-behaved" day was enough to put his mother into a fit of depression, trigger a reaction of abuse, or at least prompt her to pour down a drink to soften reality. His behavior put him in a foster home—ours. We were told by social services that we would be experiencing a quiet, shy child coming out of his shell. Under the shell was a child who ran away from the children's home because he needed a smoke. (They didn't know he smoked—we found out the first day.) At twelve, he still ate by shoving hand-fuls of food in his mouth, voiced stomach-turning vulgarities in public and private (we're not talking the "F" word—believe me!), smoked a pack of stolen cigarettes a day (liberated from Tom Thumb stores), lied continuously, ripped living small animals in pieces, played with matches, and refused to use toilet paper. He sniffed glue and toxic substances when he could find them and had no understanding of caring for property or people. He would attack his peers with what he called weapons to get a reaction and once attacked our twelve-year-old son with a toilet plunger. The ensuing fight, which lasted less than two minutes, put a four-foot hole in our shower wall. When his defenses were down, he had sleep disturbances and nightly wet the bed. Under-standing appropriate levels of discipline became mandatory if we were to reach him and help him grow.*

Our normal parenting system would not work with this child. We had no previous relationship to build upon and very little knowledge of the child's past life experiences. My husband and I spent hours researching books, working with the child protection worker and therapist, talking with more experienced foster parents, and attending training classes to come up with effective and appropriate methods of discipline and potential behavior modification. With the help of the child protection worker and therapist, we developed a number of discipline strategies as we worked through the maze of behavior this child exhibited. We learned as we changed our parenting system that . . .

— There is a fine line between discipline and punishment.

— A child with such extremes in behavior can provoke even the most patient of parents, social workers, and therapists.

— Written records and constant contact must be maintained with the child's social worker to keep a clear understanding of the day-to-day impact this child's behavior has on the school, neighborhood, and foster home.

It became acutely important to establish appropriate family definitions and guidelines for discipline and punishment. In redeveloping our parenting system we chose to set up criteria we hoped to meet for each child we were to parent.

— *We wanted each individual in our family to retain dignity and be confident that we, as parents, valued his or her contribution to our family. We wanted children to know they mattered and were important to us; to show them they were valuable, lovable, and worthwhile; and to give them a sense of acceptance and belonging.*

— *We wanted children in our care to know we would set limits, keep them safe, and teach them how to do better next time if they made a mistake. We would guide them in developing self-discipline, understanding, cooperation, and accepting responsibilities.*

— *We acknowledged that every child makes mistakes and behaves poorly at times. If a child's behavior is difficult, the purpose of it may be to see how safe a situation is and establish boundaries. Sometimes it is for attention or power. A hurting child's behavior may arise from feelings of frustration or inadequacy. An angry child may feel a need to get even or take revenge. We would discover the triggers of the difficult behavior.*

— *We understood that children go through developmental stages which are important yet can be difficult to handle, and that children in care will not be at normal developmental levels. We would lower our expectations for children in care until we could assess their capabilities.*

— *We also accepted that these developmental stages would be altered by loss, separation, grief, and a child's life experience.*

— *When problems occurred, we would try to isolate responsibility for the problem—the parent or the child—and respond accordingly.*

— *We established realistic boundaries which were understandable to all family members and enforceable. We set up reasonable disciplines and positive and negative consequences for working within the family boundaries.*

— *We resolved that discipline would never harm a child's self-esteem or body. We would focus on communication, cooperation, and commitment in our relationships with children in our care.*

— *We would parent as a team, drawing on each other's strengths and supporting each other in weak areas. We knew we would be on the front lines in dealing with a child's past experiences.*

— *We understood that parenting was a challenge and would be frustrating at times. We would work to maintain flexibility and our sense of humor.*

— *We would give ourselves permission to be human and make mistakes.*

Once these definitions had been established, we set up procedures for maintaining personal boundaries and support systems. My husband and I realized that nothing was going to be accomplished for the good of the child or our family unless we were unified as parents, therapist, and social worker. The complete treatment team needed to agree on procedures and methods of discipline, and as the daily parents, we needed to be prepared to carry them out. Establishing approved guidelines was crucial for parenting a child whose behavior deviated so far from the norm.

Normal behavior for fragile or emotionally disturbed children can be confusing to people who are not used to working with these children every day. Discipline methods are subject to personal interpretation and can be misjudged. Both the child's behaviors and parental management of behaviors are subject to personal interpretation. Licensed care providers are especially vulnerable to judgment from primary families, the agency, and the community at large. The expectations of parenting performance, combined with the types of children being parented, yields the need for clear and concise guidelines. Yet these guidelines vary from state to state, agency to agency, and even from social worker to social worker.

Conflicts arise between children and parents because they have different needs.

Adults need some semblance of order, cleanliness, routine, and courtesy.

Children, often, could not care less.

How many children would, of their own volition, take a bath, say "please" and "thank you," or even change their underwear?

How many children would wear underwear?
(Doyne 1988)

"It was an accident, I'm sorry," Jerry shouted at his little brother.

Huh? This was the tenth accident with an unreal sorry today. I instigated a new family program—accidental consequences—sorry Jerry.
Foster parent

I hope the strategies our family has found effective can serve as guidelines for establishing consistent disciplinary practices in other homes.

Why is communication the connecting link?

Establishing trust in the parent-child relationship is the basis for control and discipline. Mutual respect between the adult and the child is crucial in working with a child's behavior. Effective communication is the connecting link to accomplishing this. Parent-child talks don't have to be just about problems. Talk about things of interest, ask for the child's opinion, have fun. Encourage your child to talk with you. Mix affection and humor in your communication. More than all the words you can say, the most important communication skills you have to offer a fragile child are listening, attention, follow-through, and consistency. These tools lay the foundation for trust.

PAY ATTENTION to the child. Children require attention and will seek it regardless of whether the result is positive or negative. For many children even negative attention is better than no attention at all. Parents can use attention to their benefit in working with children. Dr. Kenneth Kaye in *Family Rules* (1984) provides an excellent illustration about paying attention to children. When a child behaves the way you want and wants more or less attention, respond accordingly. However, when a child behaves the way you do not want, you can use attention to help make adjustments in behavior. An introverted child tends to want less attention. An extroverted child will demand more attention.

For example. . .
. . . A teenager usually wishes for less attention and parenting. As the behavior improves, the parent can back off and give the child more freedom from parental attention.
. . . A young child who behaves appropriately would receive more attention because that's the reaction the child desires.

	CHILD WANTS	
	More	**Less**
	ATTENTION	
Behavior **Good**	Give More	Give Less
Behavior **Not Good**	Give Less	Give More

Our family babysat a Dalmation puppy when April was three. The puppy was frisky and knocked April to the floor. Exasperated, I said, "That dog needs some forceful parenting." April's little ears perked up. We had three other dogs, and inquisitively she asked, "What does Abraham need?"

"Abraham needs jail, he's a criminal. There's nothing we can do to help him behave," my husband answered.
"What does Izy need?" she continued.
"Izy needs consistent parenting. He forgets to listen and he doesn't always behave," my husband said.
"What does Joey need?" she pushed.
"Joey just needs love because he is so obedient. What kind of parenting do you need April?" my husband asked.
"I need attention parenting!" she proclaimed. She was right. We couldn't have said it better ourselves.

Discipline is like tools in a toolbox. You never use a sledgehammer when a tap hammer will do. The wrench, screwdriver, and pliers all have different functions. Using only one method of discipline is as inappropriate as using a crowbar for every job requiring carpentry tools. Neither will be very effective and the more destructive and massive the tool, the less refined and detailed work it can do.
(Author)

Young children need clear guidelines and limits. In many cases, environmental controls will provide the security and safe liberty they need to grow, explore, and play.

As children grow, they need personal liberty and freedoms to develop a sense of positive personal power.

LISTEN AND RESPOND with understanding, reflection, and caring. Children often give up talking if they believe that they are not being heard or that what they are saying does not matter. Children find it difficult to see things from another person's viewpoint; their perspective is hindered by their lack of life experiences. Their knowledge of feelings and the words for feelings are often limited. Listening to a child signals acceptance and allows a child to begin to trust and value his or her own ideas and feelings. Responsive listening lets children know they are understood. By listening and teaching a feeling vocabulary, adults help children learn the language of feelings and gain the ability to express themselves more clearly. As they gain knowledge, they gradually understand their own feelings, the feelings of others, and the value of listening.

Your attitude is important when you listen to children. Partial listening is perceived by children as not listening at all, even though you may have heard what was being said. Your attitude needs to convey that you are open to what they say and feel, you are interested in the meaning behind what is being said, and you value the speaker. Using attentive listening with children in out-of-home care is the cornerstone for building a foundation of trust.

1. Establish eye contact and listen carefully to what the child is saying. Check your attitude.

2. In your own mind, put together what the child is expressing.

3. Feed back what the child has said in your own words and acknowledge the feeling you believe the child is feeling.

Listening acknowledged	**Response to feelings**
It sounds like you're saying Johnny is being favored in our home and getting more consideration.	*Boy, I bet that feels unfair.*
It sounds like Sally is really messing around with your stuff.	*It must really bug you when she does that.*
It sounds like you think you deserved a better grade on that paper since you worked so hard.	*I can hear you are disappointed and feel cheated.*
It sounds like your teacher really scolded you in class today.	*You must have felt embarrassed.*
It sounds like your friend said awful things about your family.	*I'll bet that hurt you and you felt sad.*

Do not add your own feelings. Let the child retain ownership and develop better recognition of these feelings. Show you understand the child's feelings by putting them into your own words; do not parrot words back to the child. Do not ask the child why she is feeling a certain way; she most likely will not know. Accept the feelings of the child and speak only in response to her. If the child is silent, remain silent. Sometimes listening is joint solitude.

"I" MESSAGES communicate how you as the parent see, feel, hear, and experience things that happen around you. "I" messages do not point fingers or ownership to other people—they truthfully acknowledge to the other person your position on a given situation.

> Parent upon arrival of a child who is two hours late:
> *"I" feel worried and upset when "I" don't know where my children are. "I" was concerned for your safety. "I" thought something bad might have happened to you.*
> *"I" love you and "I" think about you often.*

Whispering in a child's ear when the child is involved in group pressure situations is often a great help in dissipating the negative energy.

Get the child's attention before giving direction. Then be clear and concise.

Do not talk down to a child, talk too much, or repeat unnecessarily.

The right words at the right time can plant the seeds needed for healthy growth.

Parent do not need to subject themselves to bickering and fighting among children. Emotionally falling into the fighting of children by yelling to break up the ruckus does not model positive methods of conflict resolution.

Children watch our every move and seem to hone in on our weakest attributes. Cleaning up our own act is crucial if we want to avoid those behaviors from children.

Parent unsure of foster child shoplifting scarf from store:
"I" saw you pick up the blue scarf from the store and put it in your coat pocket and "I" felt hurt and frustrated. "I" need to look in your pocket.

BE DIRECT. Don't beat around the bush. Say what you mean by providing simple direct instructions. Don't "ask" to have something done when you need it done. Asking provides options that include saying no when you "ask for help." If you need cooperation, say so. Don't allow for options.

Direct Statement	Indirect Question
Parent needing help with trash (or anything parent may need help with):	
Jesse, in ten minutes I need you to take out the trash.	*Could you tear yourself away from the (TV, book, etc.)? I need help.*
Parent carrying in groceries, needing door to be opened:	
Julie, open the door so I can bring in the groceries.	*Julie, could you catch the door for me?*

BE POSITIVE. Expect the best. Let the child know the sort of behavior you expect and explain family rules and limits. The more positive expectations you have of children, the better cooperation you get. Positive expectations build self-esteem. Find opportunities to say yes. There are usually plenty of times you can say no. Provide choices as an alternative to saying no.

One day Helen stopped by to play with April. Having heard the horror stories about this child, I gathered my composure and greeted her warmly at the door. "Helen, that dress is a pretty color. Are you here to play with April?" Finger in her nose, looking at her shoes, she mumbled, "Uh huh." I knelt down and put my hands softly on her shoulders. I looked into her big blue eyes and with sincerity I said, "Helen, I like when you come over because I know how much you like to play with April's toys. I know how careful you can be and how nice you can play with April." A small smile crossed her face, and for three years Helen hasn't let me down. Although there have been moments she needed guidance, she has never lived up to her reputation in our home.

Positive communication uses language in positive terms to describe what you want, rather than what you don't want.

Positive	Negative
Parent holding bath towel with defiant preschool child wanting to stay in tub:	
The drying machine is ready to dry you, you better get out.	*I'm tired of asking. Get out of that tub, now!*
Parent looking into a very messy bedroom:	
What should be organized first? Got any ideas on how to get started?	*Clean up this mess, now!*
Child running around swimming pool:	
Walk around the pool.	*Stop that running.*
Child hitting another child:	
If you're angry, let's find another way to deal with your feelings.	*Don't hit. Stop that fighting now!*
Child biting another child:	
Food is for biting.	*Don't bite!*
Child hugging smaller child very hard:	
We hug gently in our home. Try it like this.	*Don't hug so hard.*

COMPLIMENTS. It feels good to receive honest compliments. A quick *"I like your hair today," "That's a nice shirt," "I like your smile"* can be very rewarding. Compliments should be straightforward, sincere, and specific. Don't say it unless you mean it. Compliments about the child in front of others can be very helpful in building the child's self-esteem. Relaying kind messages others have expressed about the child are also great perks. The esteem a parent or adult has for a child is directly linked to the child's self-esteem.

ENCOURAGEMENT is an internal motivator. Encouragement means one person has faith and provides hope to another. It acknowledges specific behaviors or strengths and helps the child believe in herself. We accomplish this by setting reasonable and attainable goals with the child which she is capable of achieving, accepting efforts, and appreciating improvements. The slightest improvement can be recognized and the contribution appreciated. Acceptance and value are placed unconditionally on the child for who the child is and where she is developmentally. Children learn to focus on the effort rather than on the result. When an adult has faith in a child, the child has the opportunity to reach out and begin to have faith. Encouragement helps the child be part of a functioning unit and participate in solving problems and new experiences. It accepts mistakes and promotes solutions. Encouragement points out the positive aspects of behavior and does not dwell on the negatives. You accept the child, even though you may not accept the behavior. Encouragement is not always verbal—a smile, a wink, thumbs up, OK sign, a touch—all add support to the child. The benefits of encouragement and appropriate praise are lasting—a belief in self and abilities and an excitement for life.

ENCOURAGEMENT focuses on the effort and enjoying the process	APPROPRIATE PRAISE focuses on the accomplishment	MISUSED PRAISE moves praise ownership to another person
I can see you're really trying. Those are pretty colors you chose.	*This looks like it needs to go on the refrigerator. Eye contact, hug, and smile.*	*I am so happy you can color in the lines. You make me so proud. (Child thinks—what happens if I don't?)*
That's a good idea to put the bear on that shelf. He looks nice there.	*Great job. Your room looks so much neater with the toys put away. It's so nice you're big enough to help.*	*Aren't you wonderful to be able to do this? (Child hears— I'm wonderful because you think so. To be wonderful I must do things to please you.)*
We all enjoy being together at ____. I like being with you.	*Let's go out together again soon. I had a really good time. Thank you for being so well behaved.*	*I'm so proud of you for behaving at ____. (They own my good behavior. I make them feel proud because I behave well.)*
I can hear you playing piano so much more smoothly. I can tell you've been practicing.	*You sure worked hard to do such a good job at the recital. I had fun listening. It looked like you really enjoy playing the piano.*	*I'm awfully proud of your performance at the recital. Child feels, I need to be perfect to please my parents. My performance makes them like me.*

PRAISE is an external motivator—a verbal reward. It is most valuable when given at the completion of a task or accomplishment or when a child has pleased a parent. Praising a child to another person and letting that information get back to the child is very rewarding. It shows the child you cared enough to risk sharing specialness with another. Praise recognizes the individual. Praise makes a child feel special. Let the praise stand on its own. Don't send a mixed message to the child by saying, *"This is a great ----. Why can't you do this well all the time?"* *--or -- "Wow! What a great ---! Good job! You should learn to do that all the time."* That

---

When a parenting team initiates a set of family rules or procedures, the parents must decide:

1. *Rules must*
   — *Be clear and specific.*
   — *Be observable by the parenting team.*
   — *Have a valid and logical reason.*
   — *Offer a choice of responsibility or consequence.*

2. *What the consequence is for violation.*

3. *How to amend a rule if necessary.*

Write down, explain, and post rules.

The parent must be consistent and firm. In two-parent families, both parents must agree on limits and consequences. Children will try to appeal a consequence when they feel they have the opportunity.

When parents disagree or vacillate on methods of discipline, they undermine their own authority.

type of statement discounts the original praise. If improvement encouragement is needed, make a mental note to discuss it later.

Misused praise can be terribly discouraging and is often concerned with superior-inferior relationships. The child receiving *"misused"* praise becomes frustrated and confused and may be provoked to anger. Immediate praise with no recognition of the effort often leaves the child wanting more praise with no guarantee that additional praise will come. It can set up competition, jealousy, and rivalry. Pleasing others may become the child's focus instead of self- motivation. A child who has set extremely high personal standards may see the praise as a mockery if the results are not as good as she had imagined. If the child's efforts fail to bring the expected praise, she may feel inadequate and give up trying. In addition, the child who sees a sibling praised while being ignored may feel jealous, angry, inadequate, or competitive. Sometimes praise is skewed so that the person giving the praise to the child is actually taking the credit for the accomplishment.

> *Our dining table is a safe place to vent problems or bring up difficult issues. It is also the safe place where we offer praise and thanksgiving. Before dinner, everyone holds hands and offers a thank you to another person or higher power. There is no pressure on who is given the thank you or the praise. As parents, we never see all the good things our children do. The dining table has been an excellent place to reveal good deeds and accomplishments and allows us to discuss, praise, and encourage all the people who are in our home. Questions to encourage discussion include: What was the hardest thing you did today? What was the funniest thing that happened today? Did anyone come up with a new idea?*

INCENTIVES are internal motivators. Positive consequences (incentives/ motivations) help the child focus on desired behavior. When an action is followed by a positive consequence, that action is likely to be repeated. Catch the child being good. It's easy to ignore children when they play cooperatively, read quietly, experience joy, or try a new activity. Noticing when a child displays a positive behavior or attempts to display a positive behavior helps the child learn what is expected. It reinforces the positive behavior. It also helps the child feel able to please adults. Positive consequences come in three forms: *"care," "time,"* or *"thing"* incentives.

1. Most incentives will be *"care"* or *"time"* rewards. *"Thing"* incentives only need to be used for special situations. "Thing" incentives are often referred to as rewards. Rewards are external motivators. They are most valuable when given at the completion of a task on which a child has excelled or been challenged. They are a material statement that says the job was well done.

    Care incentives
    Appropriate touch, hugs, or kisses.
    Paying attention to child.
    Encouragement, praise, or direct compliments.
    Relayed compliments: When someone says something positive about the child, pass the comment on to the child.
    Third person positives: Letting children overhear you tell another person something positive about them.
    Indirect positives: Demonstrating by your actions you love and respect the child.
    —Kneel down to the child's level to talk.
    —Make eye contact and devote full attention to discussion.
    Ask the child's opinion or preference and then accept it.

    Special time incentives
    Going with Dad on Saturday for the doughnut run.
    Playing a game with Mom or Dad alone.
    Going with Mom or Dad alone without other children.

Going on a walk or bike ride with a parent.
One jump rope twirl for every word read.

Thing incentives

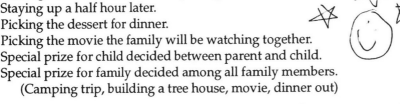

Visiting the ice cream store and picking out the ice cream.
Staying up a half hour later.
Picking the dessert for dinner.
Picking the movie the family will be watching together.
Special prize for child decided between parent and child.
Special prize for family decided among all family members.
(Camping trip, building a tree house, movie, dinner out)

2. An incentive comes after a promised behavior, not before. The incentive payoff should be as immediate as possible, especially for younger children. The parent, not the child, must be in control of when the incentive is given. An incentive given prior to the designated behavior is a bribe.

The attitude trade: I have always had a bad attitude about playing with Barbies and April knows it. It's the one thing I avoid playing with her and when I do the lack of joy in play shows through compared with the fun we share with other toys. April hates reading! She has a bad attitude. So I offered a trade. A good attitude for one half hour of reading in trade for a good attitude for one half hour of playing with Barbies. We enjoyed the whole hour together — the phone went on the answering machine. No calls or interruptions allowed!

In our entryway is a family growth chart. Each day before bed or at the dinner table we review the day. Points are given in six areas:

   1. *Did I have a good attitude?*
   2. *Did I do something nice for someone else without being asked?*
   3. *Did I contribute to my family? How?*
   4. *Did I take care of my own things?*
   5. *Did I take care of myself?*
   6. *Did I learn something new?*

Mom and Dad are also included in this program. There are days none of us gets all six—and that's OK. But for each day all six areas are checked off we gain one point per person. Five points equals one wrapped present in Mom's special bowl. Mom and Dad are contributing points to the family prize—a new treehouse!

3. Keep your program based on positive behaviors. If a point system is used, award points only for positive behaviors; do not remove points for negative behaviors unless a child can quickly gain back points. Foster children often develop a *"what's the use"* attitude. Taking away points discourages a child and builds resentment toward the adults monitoring the system, since points can be lost continuously and can outweigh the points gained. It can build competition and one-upmanship when a comparison is being made between biological children and children in care. The reaction from the foster child is often give up or try to sabotage the system.

April was entering kindergarten and was compulsive—every five or ten minutes— going to the bathroom. She would run into the bathroom every fifteen minutes, and this was not going to be acceptable to the kindergarten teacher. April and I drew and colored eight pretty potty coupons and negotiated a deal. If April had to go in less than one half hour she turned in a coupon. If she held her urine for one hour she could get the potty coupon back. If she had eight coupons at dinnertime, she got chocolate chip ice cream. Within two months, April could manage waiting two hours without running in to check out the plumbing.

WIN-WIN SOLUTIONS search for solutions that satisfy both the adult and the child—nobody has to lose. A win-win solution feels warm and not hostile. It allows parents to get beyond the *"presenting"* issue and seek out the *"real"*

Praise recognizes the actor. Praise of a child rewards the individual and tends to focus his attention upon himself.

Encouragement acknowledges the act. It stimulates the effort and places attention on capabilities and capacities to cope.

How to say "Good for you!"

— *I'm glad you enjoy learning.*
— *I enjoy being with you.*
— *Your room looks nice.*
— *It's so nice that you're big enough to help.*
— *You really worked hard. Thank you.*
— *Thank you for sitting down.*
— *I like the way you're working.*
   — *That's a good point.*
   — *What neat work.*
   — *You did it yourself.*
— *It looks like you've put a lot of work into this.*
   — *Keep it up.*
   — *What beautiful colors.*
   — *What an interesting design.*

problem. It meets the needs of both parties. It strengthens the child's problem-solving abilities, and the child is motivated to carry out the solution because he has been a part of it. Win-win solutions get positive results. (Farmer 1989)

Child arguing with parent about not wanting to wear mittens in cold weather.
"Sounds like you really don't want to wear your mittens." (Address issue)

"No way!" (Acknowledged by child)

"You and I don't agree. We have a conflict. (Addresses a conflict) *I want you to wear your mittens, since I think it's really cold outside and I'm worried you'll get frostbitten fingers.* (Mother's position) *You say it's not cold and you don't need them.* (Child's position) *Can you suggest a solution that would make us both happy?"* (Request for solution)

"The guys will think I'm a baby if I wear mittens. (Real problem) *How about if I carry them, but just put them on if I get cold?"* (Solution offered)

"You'll be happy with the solution and the guys will understand?"
(Clarify, acknowledge real problem)

"Yeah, it's OK."

COLLABORATION means working together with an opposing force. Children lack power and control in their lives. They also lack experience in knowing what they can and cannot handle. *"Power plays"* are to be expected and can be exhibited by manipulation, tantrums, or smarting off. Often children use power plays to grab some control over their lives. Not all parent-child issues can be resolved as a win-win. Sometimes, it's best to just walk away or disengage in the battle. Other times it may be effective to advance additional responsibility and freedom to the child. Perhaps a child has reached a maturity level to begin to handle more responsibility or believes he or she is capable of something he or she is really not. There are times the parents may need to give in to the child in order to allow the child room to make a mistake and grow. Giving in does not, however, mean accepting disgruntled behavior—that also needs addressing.

At fourteen, Anna proclaimed that she had kissed Jonathan until her lips hurt. Although her parents felt the urge to jump in and save their daughter from the lips and hands of fifteen-year-old Jonathan, they handled the problem in a slightly different and respectful way.

"Anna, what do you think happens after kissing someone until your lips hurt?" her mother asked.

"Probably touching," Anna answered shyly.

"What do you think happens after touching, Anna?" asked her mother.

"Probably more touching," answered Anna.

"What do you think happens after more touching?" her mother continued.

"Maybe going all the way, I don't know," said Anna.

"Anna, where would you like to stop?" asked her mother.

"I'm just ready for the kissing part, Mom," said Anna.

Anna and her mother discussed ways Anna could establish boundaries and prevent herself from getting into a situation she had difficulty controlling. Anna left the discussion with acceptance, ideas, and understanding that her parents would be available when she needed more advice or support. A similar approach can be adapted in working with other dating issues, alcohol, driving, or drugs.

There are many other times, however, when children will be required to give in to a request from a parent. When an issue arises that requires a relinquishing or change from a standard position, the child needs to understand why the agreement has been made and to know if this is a new and extended boundary or if this is a one time special occurrence.

Children need to be clear on how to communicate their needs. They also need clairification on the future process expected from a decision.

Reactions to win-lose solutions:

Parent Wins-Child Loses
Child appears to comply with parent's request, but performs task begrudgingly or just barely goes through the motions. Job completed may or may not be adequate. Resents parental authority. Child does not increase self-discipline.

Parent Loses-Child Wins
Child becomes unmanageable, self-centered, and demanding. Has difficulty with other children. Lacks inner control of impulses. Child has difficulty with authority and following rules. Loses respect for parental or other authority.

PROVIDE PERMISSION TO CHANGE. Children in general may become involved in behaviors—drugs, alcohol, vandalism, sex, shoplifting, etc.—that carry great prices they are not even aware of. Let me illustrate shoplifting, an illegal and negative behavior most parents are willing to enforce abstinence on. A parent does not tell a child shoplifting is wrong and then take the child to the store and say, *"But if you are going to shoplift, I'd rather you don't get caught or in any trouble. I would be embarrassed and it could hurt your reputation and our standing in the community. So I will show you how to shoplift in a safe way. When you become an adult you may need some help getting over this, but then you will be older and can handle the difficulties yourself."* A parent more likely would tell a child, *"Shoplifting is wrong. It is against the law* (describe factually society's rules regarding it). *What is taken belongs to someone else. When people take things from stores that do not belong to them, the store must raise its prices to everyone to help pay for what has been stolen. If you are caught, you will face dealing with the legal system and that means ----."*

All young people have the power to make choices. A young person who says no to drugs, sex, alcohol, vandalism, and shoplifting is showing independent and personal power to his or her friends. This young person has strength and courage. Greatness shines through. Every young person has the capacity to become great—even a young person who has experimented. Stopping is much harder than starting. Adults can help young people by saying—*"Let's talk about it and you can start over again on a clean slate. I will help you gain the power to say NO."*

BECOME KNOWLEDGEABLE IN REALITY. Children don't need to be handed a line of what you think is true. Study the realities of issues that affect your child—drugs, alcohol, pregnancy, abortion, sexual activity, AIDS. *Basic health education should start as early as possible, in keeping with parental and community standards. Children must be taught values and responsibility as well as skills to help them resist peer pressure that might lead to risky behavior. AIDS is one of the most serious health problems that has ever faced the American public. It is important that we all, regardless of who we are, understand this disease. Many people feel that only certain "high risk groups" of people are infected by the AIDS virus. This is untrue. Who you are has nothing to do with whether you are in danger of being infected with the AIDS virus. What matters is what you do.* (Former Surgeon General C. Everett Koop 1992)

Often the young person wishes an adult they respect would talk frankly and provide the courage to say no or stop a risky behavior the young person is already involved in. A truthful conversation with a child can go like this:

Behaviorally, does your child . . .

— *Have allergic reactions or allergic relatives?*

— *Act like a Dr. Jekyll=Mr. Hyde?*

— *Get an"A" one day and an"F" the next?*

— *Show an inability to write, draw, or do math at various times?*

— *Earn poor grades compared to IQ?*

— *Crave certain foods or odors?*

— *Act too tired, hyper, irritable, depressed, or vulgar?*

— *Never seem to feel well?*

Physically, does your child have. . .

— *Red earlobes or cheeks?*

— *Dark eye circles?*

— *Puffy bags under eyes?*

— *Eye wrinkles?*

— *Glassy, glazed eyes?*

— *Nose rubbing or nose wrinkles?*

The Impossible Child, Dr. Doris Rapp, 1986

"What's the worst thing that can happen to you if you choose to have sex?"

Usually the young person answers—pregnancy.

"That's the best thing that happen. A pregnancy lasts nine months. What about all the other things that can happen?"

At present rates fifty percent of sexually active teenagers could be dead of AIDS before they are thirty. In addition, the venereal disease epidemic in the United States results in ten to fifen million new cases of gonorrhea, syphilis, herpes, and chlamydia each year. Translated that means one in every twenty sexually active adults (and children) contracts venereal disease. The odds of contraction are high. Teens can die or become sterile from sexually transmitted infections. Some of the infections, like herpes, last a lifetime and affect a person's life forever. Presently AIDS is an early death sentence. Sex is no joke.

Teenagers believe that they are immortal—that nothing bad can happen to them, that they will not die of anything, much less AIDS. They have a limited ability to conceive of the remote consequences of their behavior. Health researchers have concluded that many young people contract the AIDS virus in their teens, but do not become symptomatic until their twenties. (Koop 1992)

You can't tell by looking at a person if he or she is infected. It is possible to be infected for years, feel fine, look fine, and have no way of knowing you are infected unless you have a test for the AIDS virus. During this period, however, people infected with the AIDS virus can pass the virus to sexual partners, to people with whom drug needles are shared, and to children before and during birth. This is one of the most disturbing things about AIDS.

Dating and getting to know other people is a normal part of life. Dating doesn't mean the same thing as having sex. Sexual intercourse as a part of dating can be risky. Any person involved in risky behaviors can become infected. The most effective way to prevent AIDS is by avoiding exposure to the virus, which you can control by your own behavior, to some extent. Choosing to become *"blood brothers or sisters,"* partaking in consenual intercourse or sexual activity or using needles of others are choices young adults, teens and preadolescents make. Rape on the other hand would not.

You need to be careful about the person you become sexually involved with, making your own decisions, based on your own best judgment. That can be difficult. Think of it this way. If you know someone well enough to have sex, then you should be able to talk and ask these questions.

> *— Has he/she ever had a sexually transmitted disease?*

> *— How many people has he/she been to bed with?*

> *— Has he/she experimented with intravenous drugs?*

If someone is unwilling to talk, you shouldn't have sex. You have a personal responsibility to ask. It's your life—or your death.

The following are risky behaviors when performed with an infected person.

> *— Sharing drug needles and syringes.*

> *— Anal sex, with or without a condom.*

> *— Vaginal or oral sex with someone who injects drugs or engages in anal sex.*

> *— Sex with someone you don't know well (a pickup or prostitute) or with someone you know who has had several sex partners.*

— Unprotected sex (without a condom) with an infected person.

Condoms are the best preventive measure against AIDS and other venereal diseases besides not having sex, having only one lifetime partner, and practicing safe behavior (not sharing drug needles/syringes). But encouraging condom use is a bit like telling children you'll show them how to shoplift so they won't get caught. Condoms are 96% effective against pregnancy if used properly *every time, from the beginning of the foreplay to washing afterwards*. Most passionate, young people are not prepared to take that amount of responsibility. The AIDS virus is much smaller than a sperm—there is no current research to tell how much protection a condom actually provides.

If you use a condom, you should remember these guidelines recommended by former Surgeon General Koop:

1. Use condoms made of latex rubber. Latex serves as a barrier to the virus. "Lambskin" or "natural membrane" condoms are not as good because of the pores in the material. Look for the word "latex" on the package.

2. A condom with a spermicide may provide additional protection. Spermicides have been shown in laboratory tests to kill the virus. Use the spermicide in the tip and on the outside.

3. Condom use is safer with a lubricant. Check the list of ingredients on the back of the lubricant package to make sure the lubricant is water-based. Do not use petroleum-based jelly, cold cream, baby oil, or cooking shortening. These can weaken the condom and cause it to break.

AIDS is a sexually transmitted disease. A person becomes infected with the AIDS virus through the exchange of body fluids—the virus is present in semen or vaginal fluids, or the virus is present in the person's blood.

No matter what you have heard, the AIDS virus is hard to get and is avoidable. You won't "catch" AIDS like a cold or flu because the virus is a different type. The AIDS virus is transmitted through sexual intercourse, the sharing of needles, or to babies of infected mothers before or during birth. Some people receiving blood tranfusions between 1978-1985 also have been infected from blood containing the virus. Presently all blood used in the United States is tested for the AIDS antibody. Medical and dental professionals currently use latex gloves to protect patients and themselves from either contact or transmission. Call your local blood bank or the AIDS lines if you have questions.

You won't get AIDS from:

Everyday contact with people in school, child care centers, at parties, or in stores. You won't get it by swimming in a pool, even if someone with AIDS has also swum in the pool. Students attending school with a student infected with the AIDS virus are not in danger from casual contact. You won't get the virus by being on a bus, train, or crowded elevator with an infected person.

Saliva, sweat, tears, urine, or a feces.

A kiss.

Clothes, a telephone, or a toilet seat. It can't be passed by using a glass or eating utensils that someone else has used.

A mosquito. The AIDS virus is not transmitted through a mosquito's salivary glands like other diseases such as malaria or yellow fever. You won't get it from bed bugs, lice, flies, or other insects.

Technique to resolve conflict and solve problems:

1. *STOP! What is the problem?*

2. *Whose problem is it? Assess your own needs. Ask "What do I need? Why?"*

3. *Separate the process from the content. Often a conflict feels personal, but it's not. The anger is not necessarily directed at you.*

4. *Brainstorm some alternative solutions.*

5. *Pick the best solution for you.*

6. *Discuss the solution.*

7. *Use the solution.*

8. *Evaluate how the solution worked.*

Will not work with anyone under the age of seven.

The best way to prevent AIDS is:

— Not having sex.

— Sex with one mutually faithful, uninfected partner.

— Not using intravenous drugs.

Anyone—male, female, adult, child, heterosexual, homosexual, bisexual, white, black, Hispanic, Asian and native American—can get AIDS.
It's not who you are, it's what you do.
If you need answers to this tough issue
call 1-800-342-AIDS.

What is positive discipline?

At every developmental stage children behave in various ways which are difficult for adults. Babies cry to be fed, toddlers are demanding, preschoolers are curious, elementary students are challenging, and adolescents are striving for separation and independence. All of these behaviors, although frustrating, are a normal part of healthy growth. Children may be difficult to handle because they are tired, sick, or hungry. They may *"mis—takenly—behave"* because they are too small, curious, or clumsy or because they simply don't know the rules or danger. These mistaken behaviors need parental understanding and patience.

On the other hand, *"misbehavior"* occurs when the child knows how to cooperate, understands what is expected, and is able to cooperate but refuses or fails to do so. Under these circumstances children need to know their behavior is not appropriate, but they still are loved and valued.

Discerning mistaken behavior from misbehavior
is not always easy.

Positive discipline demands that parents stop before they act and ask:
1. *Is this mistaken behavior due to the development of the child or misbehavior?*
2. *Whose problem is this—the child's or my own?*
3. *How will this discipline show the child I care?*
4. *How will it encourage our relationship and build self-awareness and self-respect?"*

Positive discipline is educational rather than punitive. It looks toward future changes rather than dwelling on the past. It is a process of motivating a person to internalize principles of self-discipline that will equip the individual to reach his or her own potential.

Discipline is not easy! Following are some guidelines:

1. **Isolate the owner of the problem.** Does the adult or the child own the problem? If the answer is yes to any of the following questions, the adult owns the problem. Does it involve the safety of the child or others? Does it involve the protection of property? Does it interfere with the adult's rights as a person? Is the child developmentally incapable of owning or solving the problem? If the answer is no to all of these questions, this problem may be the child's. If the problem is the child's, the parent's job is to help the child learn how to take responsibility and to solve the

problem on her own. The person who owns the problem is the one who is responsible for handling it. Babies own no problems, toddlers may help fix problems, and as children grow older, they begin to take more responsibility for their problems.

Problem	Owner
Hungry baby crying	**Parent**. Parent feeds infant.
Toddler writes on walls	**Parent** problem, but may let toddler help clean the wall. Parent owns responsibility of supervision.
Preschooler writes on wall	**Parent/child** problem. Parent shows child how to clean wall if it can be cleaned safely by child and supports child's work.
Elementary age child writes on wall	**Child** problem. Parent shows child how to clean wall and take care of tools.

For four and a half years, April had difficulty with overstimulation in her surroundings. Initially she feared contact with everyone. Visits to any public place were a nightmare. Shopping, April would withdraw inside herself and explode emotionally. Knowing what was coming, I would leave and head for quiet or open space. I knew who still owned this problem—I did. Both of us were going to need space to survive two or more hours of screaming. Holding this small traumatized bundle, I rocked and sang as others stared. Interspersed in the lullabies and caresses, I softly said, "Control, April, control." By two, April could recognize when her emotional outbursts would come, and I'd hear a small, shaky voice say, "Control, me, control." As she worked on control, I moved to the word "focus," and she learned to focus on smaller details, to see one thing at a time. At three, we would hear, "I control, I focus." By four and a half, April was still incapable of separation from our house or her family, but we enrolled her in a very small and loving preschool. For two months we sat in the room next to her classroom, followed the school bus to the outings, and allowed her time for separation. By five, she began to own her emotions and manage her environment. We began to work on attention—what it was and how to try to achieve it. Five and a half years later, April is outgoing, friendly, and an extrovert. She goes to school on the bus just like other kids. She owns her behavior and can control, focus, and work on paying attention. She can laugh and joke and make friends. Today her behavior is mostly her problem.

2. **Identify your response feelings.** How do you feel about the misbehavior? What is your mirror reflection of the child's feelings? What are you telling yourself? Children trying to get attention may be annoying. Children trying to test limits or attain power may make you angry as they challenge your authority. You may feel like fighting back or giving in to avoid a battle. Children in pain who seek revenge may leave you feeling vulnerable and financially, emotionally, or physically injured. Despondent children may reflect feelings of despair in others. Adults may feel like ignoring the child simply because they do not know how to deal adequately with the behavior.

3. **Rank the priority of the behaviors.** If you try to change every behavior that displeases you, you are destined to fail. In addition, you are likely to make the child feel inadequate. Behaviors that are dangerous to the child or others and behaviors that are illegal or destructive need to take top priority. When there are more than two or three behaviors needing adjustment, rank them and work on only a few at a time. Concentrating on only one behavior may be all the child and the parent can handle. Set small goals and be patient. Notice the tiny improvements.

An approach to using natural consequences:

1. *Point out a way to be helpful.*

2. *Express strong disapproval without attacking character.*

3. *State your expectations.*

4. *Show youngster how to make amends.*

5. *Give a choice.*

6. *Take action that allows natural consequences of your choices with firmness, dignity, and respect.*

7. *Allow youngster to experience natural consequences.*

Tell a child what behavior is expected and ask for feedback. Let the child tell you what she will do in the future and ask for some examples so she can have a ready reserve of ideas when a future crisis occurs.

4. **Assess the behavior.** Pay attention. Why is the child behaving this way? Is the child choosing this behavior or does it appear the child cannot control the behavior? Are you reinforcing the behavior in any way? What happened just before the behavior? Just after? What time of day does this behavior occur? How often does it occur? Does it occur in specific places such as home, school, church, indoors, outdoors, in the car? Do specific situations trigger this behavior? Does it happen after the child has eaten a specific food? Does it happen only when waking from sleep or when the child is tired? How does this behavior fit into the child's developmental level? What are the long-range consequences of the behavior?

5. **Provide environmental controls.** Determine the reasons for the child's behavior and in what situations the behavior is likely to occur. If it is a physical reaction to food or environment, make appropriate adjustments. Difficult behaviors with organic foundations are symptoms, not causes. A child experiencing allergies to food, environment, or chemicals will not be able to adjust behavior unless the cause is eliminated. Try altering routines to eliminate some of the problem. Adjustments in family schedules and eating can sometimes make incredible differences in helping a child manage his life. With the proper rest, exercise, nutrition, and guidance, a child may be happy and well behaved, however, one chocolate bar or orange soda can create an uncontrollable and impossible child. Dr. Doris Rapp has written *The Impossible Child, A Guide for Caring Teachers and Parents in School and at Home* (1986). This book provides easy-to-read information about the reaction between behavior and the child's environment.

Examples of environmental control are:
Child becomes aggressive whenever he's eaten a chocolate bar.
   Remove chocolate from child's diet.
Older sibling angry at younger brother for always getting into his things
   Provide a lock with key for area child wants to protect from little one. Give older child responsibility to keep area locked and off limits to little one. Make an extra set of keys in case first set is lost.
Toys and children's belongings always a mess.
   Provide simple ways for a child to organize personal belongings. Baskets under the bed, bookshelves, a hammock for stuffed toys, or a basketball hoop above the clothes basket make picking up easier, faster, and completed more often.
Children getting edgy on long car trip.
   Pull over at a park or rest area and play "run around." This is really a very loud game of tag, but it gets all the energy directed outside instead of inside. Do this when they are not hungry. Hungry children are hard to handle and need to be fed.
Siblings fighting and camping trip is planned.
   Let each sibling invite one friend. Everyone usually stays happy in this situation. The parents have each other while the kids focus on their friend and not rivalry.

6. **Redirect the behavior.** Substitute an acceptable behavior for an unacceptable one. This works very well for preschoolers. Older children need to come up with ideas for their own redirection.

For older children:
"You cannot ride your bike to ——. What are some other alternatives you can think of?"
"You cannot buy ——. What else are you saving your money for that you could buy instead?"
"You cannot attend ——. Can you think of some other things you would like to do instead?"
"You cannot be with ——name——. Can you think of some other kids you would like to be with, and come up with some fun things to do with them?"

For younger children:

"You cannot play with your brother's stereo. Let's get the Playdough and you can make pretend cookies."

"You cannot pull the kitty's tail. Let's go read a book."

7. **Provide choices.** Parents can choose two options which will both yield acceptable results. Be prepared to find a third option available for an innovative child who can put the two options together.

    Dinner was being served as April jumped off the chair, ran and got her tape recorder, turned it up full blast, and proclaimed she was providing the dinner music. Her choice of music was not what we had expected.

    "April, you can listen to your tape in your room or after dinner, but not during dinner at the table."

    Eyes sparkling, April took the tape recorder and ran to her room. The music didn't get any softer, in fact, she turned it up. Running back to the table and sitting at her place, she looked at my husband and she said, "I made my choice—I'm listening to my tape in my room."

8. **Teach choice-making.** Children need to learn to think for themselves. They need to find out how the world works. Give children the opportunity to discover alternative behaviors or reactions to difficult situations on their own. Dr. Foster Cline has excellent reference materials to teach children problem-solving techniques to dissipate negative situations.

    My husband and I had been studying Dr. Cline's research and behavior modification techniques. His techniques had been effective with the teenagers we had cared for, but we questioned whether they would work with very young children.

    April had just turned three and understood the power of choice and making her own decisions. One day, I heard a loud crash in the living room. Listening for the next loud wail, I heard silence and then an emphatic, "Bummer. I wonder what other kids do? (Pause) I get my suitcase and fly to Grandma's!" I waited until it was cleaned up and put away before I joined her in the living room. To this day, I still am not sure what exactly the crash was. She didn't fly to Grandma's, but she knew who was responsible for the problem and she did clean up the mess.

9. **Explain the behavior needing work.** Children may not be able to tell what it is about their behavior that is not good. Clearly and simply explain the behavior needing work and what about the behavior is not good. Give the child choices to make in dealing with behavior. Explain why the behavior needs to change. Set a rule. Let the child own the behavior by being responsible for the results and learning to manage it. The parent will monitor the behavior and provide positive consequences for learning to control the behavior and natural, logical, or artificial consequences if inappropriate behavior is displayed. A parent must be sure the child understands the expected behavior, the rules, and consequences of positive or negative performance. For older children, a written note may take the edge off of the explanation.

10. **Encourage honest questions**. Solve problems together. We can help our children understand what we are trying to teach them by allowing them to raise questions and providing honest answers to those questions. Children who are allowed to question and receive answers begin to understand why certain boundaries exist. Clear understanding of reasons for boundaries gives children the internal encouragement necessary to monitor their responses in difficult situations. Care must be taken to not avoid the issue at hand while answering hundreds of

---

Four-year-old Susan had always been a handful in the car for Karen. She would kick and scream and carry on until Karen was so frustrated that she would start to yell. This would only escalate Susan's behavior.

Upon advice from a noted child behavior therapist, Karen told Susan that from now on that type of behavior would no longer be tolerated while the car was moving. If Susan decided she needed to behave in such a manner, Karen would stop the car in a safe place and let Susan stand outside to get rid of all that energy. Susan could stay outside until she had finished her tantrum.

One night after a pizza party, Susan did not want to leave. She began her performance. Karen sat in the car, doors unlocked, windows up, and said, "When you are finished, just open the door and put your seat belt on." Susan kicked the tires, she banged on the windows, she screamed louder and louder. Karen asked, "Are you done yet, Susan?" Susan opened the door and quietly put on her seat belt.

---

questions. In these cases, parents may have to set limits on the number of questions they will answer.

Two miles later, Susan began screaming again and kicking the back seat. Karen pulled into a parking lot and asked Susan to get out of the car while she finished her temper tantrum.

Susan got out of the car and within two minutes was settled in her seat belt.

"I love you, Honey. That was a really good decision," said Karen. "You really did a good job of pulling yourself together."

A mile down the road Karen stopped for gas. Turning to pump gas, she came face-to-face with a uniformed officer. "Ma'am, I've had a complaint against you for child abuse. Your daughter was really carrying on, and people are concerned. Can we talk about it?"

Karen felt in control of the situation. "Susan, would you sit in the car while I talk to the officer?"

"Officer, that behavior is usually in the car. It is much safer in the parking lot."

The officer agreed.

11. **Offer a safe place to bring a problem.** The family council in our home is always available and any issue can be brought to the table. The wrongdoer has permission to decide a new pattern of behavior and stick by it without consequences determined by the parents by simply bringing an issue honestly to the table. By admitting the problem, the child is not given negative consequences and the people at the table work toward a win-win resolution. Any problem brought to the table is handled with fairness and maturity. Anyone at the council table can offer advice or ideas—even the littlest person's idea is valued. We use the table for rulemaking, planning, or problem-solving. For every member of our family, the dining table is the safest and best place to bring the worst problem. Everyone working through the issue is required to maintain a proper tone of voice and respect for all family members. When outbursts occur, the person responsible is given a time-out. Even Mom has been known to go to her room momentarily to compose her feelings. If conflict arises, the conflict must be resolved and completed before the issue leaves the table. This encourages children to be forthright and courageous in letting parents know of problems and helps them understand that conflict can be healthy, providing it is resolved and managed respectfully.

One day five-year-old April announced that she needed a family council. Crawling up and standing on the chair behind my back for protection, she peeked over my shoulder and stated her case.

"Well, you see, Dad, I've been leaving poop in my panties and I don't want to wear a diaper, because I'm not a baby."

"So, April, how do you want to handle it?"

"I guess I'm just gonna stop doing it, be more careful, and wipe better."

April stopped. She committed herself and was pleased to find her own solution and take responsibility for solving the problem. She would now make 100 trips to the bathroom a day, a problem which we dealt with a couple of months later using potty coupons and ice cream. *(See page 239)*

12. **Set aside individual time for loving and learning.** Choose something in which both you and the child will be interested. Set aside time to enjoy the child and build a special relationship.

13. **Show parental leadership in role modeling.** Children watch adults very carefully and they instinctively imitate behaviors used by adults. Parental leadership shows by example the behavior desired from the child. By role modeling, you can discuss your actions with the child and explain why you chose to do things a certain way.

Parents need to clean up their own act if they expect their kids to. This means simple things like: keeping commitments, not breaking promises made to a child, not cheating on traffic laws (seat belts, speeding, not yielding to traffic), and not taking things that belong to you without asking (pens, matches, etc.).

— Parents show **respect** for the child's ideas, feelings, privacy, and property. Child learns what it feels like to have ideas, feelings, property, and privacy respected and begins to understand the need to respect others.

— Parents keep **commitments and promises** to children. Follow-through on commitments builds trust between parent and child. Children learn to value and keep commitments.

— Parents tell the **truth** even when it's difficult. Child sees parents risk telling the truth and begins to understand why it is important.

— Parent behaves in a way that brings difficulty to another person and asks the person for **forgiveness**. Child sees that the parent is not perfect but can handle tough issues in a caring manner. Child will also learn it is OK to make mistakes and ask forgiveness.

— Parents show respect for **authority** (i.e., employer, law enforcement, social worker, clergy). The child will also learn to show respect for authority.

— Parents utilize **empowerment** in training children. The child begins to understand that power can be positive and used to encourage and strengthen people.

— Parent **asks for help** when needs arise in respectful manner and gets help from family and friends. Child learns to ask for help.

— Parents don't always agree on every issue and **conflict** arises on an issue. Parents work through their differences in a respectful manner. Children learn it's OK to have differences of opinion and work through conflict.

14. **Be creative.** Sometimes nothing is going right, and as the parent, you may simply be too tired or not ready to handle a difficult child. This is a good time to be creative. Turn the problem around. Sometimes the opposite reaction a child expects gets the best results. Children in pain who behave with intent to inflict pain or injury need love, firmness, and kindness. Despairing children need encouragement and interaction. Children misbehaving out of a need for power need independence and a sense of personal positive power. Children needing attention need attention, whether it is positive or negative.

Once when April had been striving to attain more personal power in our home and was behaving in an exceptionally bossy manner I said, "Boy, I bet you feel like people are always telling you what to do and you never get to do that to others. How about if you be the mom and I'll be the kid for the rest of the night?" April and I ended the evening delightfully. The only disappointing part was that she had to put herself to bed and I got the tuck-me-in and good night kisses.

15. **Expect failures.** It is important to avoid implying that making a mistake is a catastrophe. All people make mistakes and behave in ways that get them into trouble. Let the child understand that a mistake is an opportunity to make changes and does not need to be feared. Failure builds strength, courage, and ingenuity if handled in an appropriate way. Positive parenting and healthy discipline do not assume perfection on the part of the parent or the child. Parents who practice healthy ways to discipline children come to appreciate and value the courage it takes to admit a mistake and work to change it. The child's willingness to change is rooted in reason, honesty, consistency, love, and open communication. Have children help figure out what's a fair thing to do if they break the rules. Prepare Plans B through Z to deal with the failures.

Motivation to change comes from within. You cannot make a person change or fix a life. But you can plant the seeds.

Be clear to label the behavior, NEVER the child.

Desired behavior can be labeled:
— *responsible,*
— *strong,*
— *great,*
— *courageous,*
— *intelligent,*
— *creative,*
— *attractive,*
— *compassionate,*
— *self-disciplined,*
— *independent,*
— *mature,*
— *honest,*
— *accountable.*

Undesireable behavior can be labeled:
— *immature,*
— *damaging,*
— *cowardly,*
— *foolish,*
— *giving away personal power*
— *sneaky.*

People cannot claim to
understand a situation
when they see only a
small segment of it and
experience even a
smaller part.

Assuming that we
understand the
problem in the life of a
person is dangerous.
The problem may only
be a symptom and not
the cause.

If the problem is only a
symptom, then it is
likely we will follow
the wrong treatment
path and do more harm
than good.

Adult child of alcoholics

Each of us listens to
words through our
own screen of
attitudes, histories,
values, beliefs,
preconceived notions,
and judgments. We try
to add ourselves into
what others say, thus
distorting their very
truth. Listen to what
people say, but find out
how they feel. The
meaning is not in the
words, it is in what the
person means when he
uses the words.

Two family rules: (1) April cannot be outside alone with a dog, and (2) April is not allowed near the street. The rules are clear and with purpose. The dogs are 60 to 80 pounds, and she is not able to maintain control of them near our busy street. See how April both "misbehaves" and "mis-taken-ly" behaves at the same time.

One night at the table, April said, "Dad, Izy ran across the street today." "How did he get out, April?" "Well, he snuck out when I went outside and then he ran to the neighbor's and I ran after him and then he ran into the street and a lady helped bring him back and he ran right back into the house." "So you left the door open and let him out." "No, I didn't want him to get out. He just did." "Who was holding the door?" "Me, but I didn't let him out. He went out." "April, you need to be more careful with the doors." April was now yelling—"I said I didn't do it. Do you think I told him to go out? I was just standing there. He's the one with bad behavior, not me!" My husband wrapped April in his arms, understanding that April didn't know why she should be responsible for Izy running out the door. "April, Izy doesn't know about cars and he isn't as smart as you, so he just runs in the street. Izy could get run over flat as a pancake. I know Izy went out by himself, but you are the one who can think. That means it's your job to protect Izy from his own behavior, just like we protect you because we love you."

"I can protect Izy, Dad. I love him like you love me."

16. **Be consistent.** Use self-control in choosing your reactions to the child's behavior. When you discipline children consistently, you set an example of what you expect from them and what they can expect from you. If 10:30 is curfew, don't put up with 10:45 one Friday night and come down harshly on a child for coming in at 10:40 the following Friday.

17. **Enforce restrictions.** Children want limits and guidelines. Restricting a child does not imply a lack of trust in the relationship—it simply recognizes that you can also "trust" in the fact that human emotions, logic, and will are vulnerable to certain temptations. Restrictions are dependent on the child's age, development level, and personality. Restrictions and liberty will be changing constantly as a child grows. Restrictions need to be made by establishing clear expectations and consequences. Restrictions should not ignore personal liberty and responsibility. They should not deny children the learning experience of how to cope in the world.

18. **Follow through**. The simple rule of trust states that threats as well as promises must be carried through. Before implementing a plan, check it through carefully to make sure that you are both willing and able to carry it out. Start with as few rules as possible, then enforce them no matter what happens. When adults make a rule and don't enforce it, they teach children that rules are unimportant. The most frequent reasons for not carrying through are either because it is difficult to monitor behavior consistently or because the consequences are too large. Frequent use of small consequences may be more effective than one huge consequence. For example, instead of extending time restrictions by hours, start with minutes. The child will probably wear down before you do, and you will be able to work through the conflict efficiently and with care.

See how my mother followed through with her unique privilege removal system.

Once when I was fourteen I stayed out two hours beyond my curfew. I was having a good time playing Monopoly with my friends and didn't look at the clock. I knew that being unaware of the time was no excuse for being late and

I expected a good talking to when I arrived home. Although she must have been worried about me, my mother simply said, "It's two hours past your curfew, I'm going to say no to the next three things you want to do."

Thinking fast, I came up with three things so I could extricate myself quickly from the mess I was in. Mom said, "I love you, Sweetie. I'm glad you're home. Now, get to bed."

The next day I asked her if I could go fishing after school. Mom said OK. (Maybe she forgot!) Later, I asked her if I could watch the eight o'clock movie. Mom said sure. (So far, so good!) Friday night was the school dance. Mom said I could go. (She really didn't mean it after all!)

Saturday afternoon, I wanted to go roller skating with my best friend. Mom said, "No. That's one of the things you really want to do. You have two left."

It took me two months to meet the terms of her discipline. I was able to do plenty of things I enjoyed, but Mom always seemed to know what I most wanted to do. Mom won. For the rest of the time I lived at home, I arrived home when I said I would, and twenty years later, I still have respect for her ingenuity.

My mother established her authority but did not abuse it. She used her power to say no, set limits on the behavior she expected from me, and established consequences for behavior. After that one incident I did not question that my mother was a woman of her word. I expected her to follow through on what she promised.

My father and my mother ran our family as a team. There was never any debate about who was in charge; when the final or big decisions were made, the kids had input, but the parents made the final choices. Children were respected as family members and were given responsibility as they grew. They were given additional authority over their own lives and some authority over the smaller siblings. It was always clear who had the control—the parental leadership team—not the kids. And because they had control, we had control.

Why consequences make sense in parenting.

Children need help to stay within reasonable limits of behavior. One of the daily struggles of parents is helping children behave in ways that are acceptable to the parents and society. The challenge is to turn over to the maturing individual the power from without to the power from within. You can teach children self-control by allowing them choices. This not only gives them the responsibility for the behavior, but also the responsibility for reaction to their behavior.

Consequences are not always appropriate, depending on the circumstances and age of the child. Sometimes natural consequences may take too long to have an effect, or the child may not care about the results. Parents must then find creative ways to teach the child why a certain rule exists. In some cases the natural consequence may be dangerous, too mild, or delayed for too long of a time; a logical consequence which correlates with the behavior may be better.

Everything is not worth a struggle, sometimes it is better to let go or wait until the appropriate time.

A secure person can afford to be patient and gentle, even when dealing with difficult situations and individuals.

When your needs are not being met, you can choose to:

—Express your need

—Leave

—Maintain

—Adapt

—Ignore

Being in authority is a conscious choice a parent makes for the child. As the child grows the expression of authority changes to meet the child's needs. Eventually, the child attains full authority for herself.

*INSTEAD OF —Oh no, here she
goes again.*

*TRY—She wants my
attention. I'll ignore
the behavior and
redirect her.*

*INSTEAD OF —He can't get away
with that. He will do what I say.*

*TRY—He wants to fight
and gain **power**. I will
remain calm and refuse
to fight.*

*INSTEAD OF —This child is
beyond help, I've failed. There is
nothing I can do.*

*TRY—This child is
discouraged. I will
not buy into that, too. I
will look for the slight
improvement.*

*INSTEAD OF —How dare she say
that to me? I'm hurt and angry.*

*TRY—This child is **hurt**
and wants to hurt
back. I'll show
compassion.*

Consequences are Assertive:	Punishment is Aggressive:
Tells other person where you stand. "This is how I am going to take care of myself."	Tells other person where to go. "This is what I am going to do to you."
Difficult and time-consuming for adults.	Easy or expedient for adults.
Come from reactions of real world to actions of child.	Adult imposes actions on child, often revengeful.
Can be administered in a friendly manner, as you would with a neighbor.	Usually delivered with open or concealed anger.
Teaches a child what to do. Teaches choices, alternatives, and opportunities for actions.	Tells a child what not to do. Closes options to individuals—choices are made for person.
Encourages child to reach out to adult for ideas to solve problems.	Teaches child to avoid adults so won't be scolded, yelled at, shamed, etc.
Results in more successful outcomes and increased problem-solving capabilities for the child.	Focuses on negative attention and power struggles. Can actually encourage repeated behavior.
Comes from within—assumed by person doing—builds inner control.	Is done to someone—responsibility is outside of the control of the person.
Can focus on what will happen now and what will come next.	Focus is on past behavior compounded with present behaviors.
Long-term knowledge is acquired.	Long-term punishment may develop covert aggression.

Consequences allow the individual to increase self-esteem and responsibility, whereas punishment may stop the behavior immediately but not enhance the individual's development. In most cases, logical or natural consequences will be the bridge parents need to help children learn to develop inner control in managing their own behavior.

NATURAL CONSEQUENCES allow the child to experience the results of his or her choice or behavior without any action by the parent. The child assumes the risk and responsibility of choice or behavior. The parent does not protect the child from reaction to behavior. Natural consequences must be age appropriate. Babies and toddlers need complete parental protection, and environmental controls are mandatory in caring for very small children.

— *April chose to wear outgrown shoes to a party because she thought
they were pretty. April got a blister.*
— *Johnny chose not to wear his jacket. Johnny got cold.*
— *Sam forgot his lunch on the kitchen counter. Sam didn't eat lunch.*
— *Sara missed the bus. Sara walked to school.*
— *Ellen puts her clothes inside out in the clothes hamper.
Parent washes and folds her clothes and returns them inside out.*

LOGICAL CONSEQUENCES are imposed when a natural consequence is not appropriate or when behavior goes against the rules of social cooperation. Logical consequences separate the deed from the doer. They are related to the misbehavior.

Repair or responsibility—*for broken objects the consequences should be appropriate to the development of the child.*

> — *Sam, age 10, broke the window. Sam can research how much the window will cost to repair, arrange for the repair of the window, and do extra chores to help pay for it. If a parent is repairing the window, Sam can help with the repair.*
> — *Andy and Jeff, teenagers, fight and put a hole in the wall. The boys help repair the wall and do additional chores to earn money to help pay for it.*
> — *Eric, age five, spills his milk. Parent hands him the sponge to clean it up.*

Denial of use of objects—*for taking things from other children or handling an object inappropriately.*

> — *Alice and Mike argue about which program to watch. Parent turns off the television until a mutual decision is made on the program.*
> — *Amy, age nine, leaves her bike outside. Amy cannot ride her bike next day.*

Denial of privilege or object—*for not being responsible when capable of handling the responsibility. Parent may temporarily remove privilege or object.*

> — *Sally, age seven, refuses to brush her teeth. Sally does not get any sweets and parent brushes her teeth on evenings she has not brushed.*

Denial of access to places—*for causing disturbances (throwing things, fighting, temper tantrums, etc.).*

> — *Two teenagers argue in the back of the car while Mom is driving. Mom pulls over, lets them out, and says, "Meet you at home, I won't drive you anywhere if you are fighting."*
> — *Susan, age three, throws sand in the sandbox. Susan cannot play in the sandbox if she is throwing sand.*

Denial of cooperation—*for interruptions, demanding, whining, being disrespectful.*

> — *Sarah, age six, constantly interrupts her parents when they are talking. Parents ignore Sarah's interruptions and give her the choice of leaving the room or remaining silent.*
> — *Tommy demands that his mother help him. He is disrespectful, whines, and raises his voice. Mother tells Tommy she will gladly help him when she is asked with respect.*
> — *On summer nights, April loves to say good night from her bedroom window after she is tucked in. If I delay getting to my bedroom to say good night, she causes a scene. April has the option of waiting patiently and quietly or not having the final good nights.*

Loss of involvement—*disrupting activity, demanding attention.*

> — *Andy, age four, constantly disrupts the games, stories, and activities of his friends. Andy can gain control or be removed for time-out.*

Denial or delay in activity—*not cooperative, fails to perform tasks required.*

> — *Helen, age 14, forgets to feed and walk the dog. Father feeds and walks the dog. Since it takes 20 minutes to take care of the dog, Father does not drive Helen to dance classes that day. She must take the bus with her own money.*

INDIRECT CONSEQUENCES are imposed by the parent and have no direct connection to the behavior. *They often cross the boundary between discipline and punishment because there is no direct logical correlation between the two events.* Sometimes indirect consequences are the only thing a parent can think of

Positive power means being responsible for your own behavior and choices.

Children seeking power need guidance in order to establish a positive sense of independence and capabilities.

When children learn true discipline, they learn controls from within, and the result is respect and value for self and others. They can be authoritative and accept authority. They do not need authoritarian or coercive demands for obedience.

Values replace rules and respect replaces obedience.

Society focuses on the negative. Isn't a proactive neighborhood safety program better than a reactive crime prevention program?

immediately. Sometimes they are linked to the child's favorite thing to do. Indirect consequences are best used when natural consequences are inappropriate or logical consequences have had no impact.

In our parenting system, indirect consequences are established as family policy in advance so there are no surprises. Often we don't even know we need a consequence until a given behavior arises or continues to resurface with no change in a child's behavior. We bring the irritating behavior to the family table, discuss it, and agree upon what indirect consequence will be applied when the child does not follow through.

When using indirect consequences, it is best to explain why you have chosen a specific reaction. At this stage, especially if it is a repetitive and annoying behavior, contracting may be more appropriate.

> — *Abraham left his bike out. Abraham cannot watch TV tonight.*
> — *Sylvia forgets to feed the dog. Sylvia cannot have her friend over.*

The more immediate the consequence, the more effect it will have on an individual. The younger the child, however, the more important an immediate response is to connect the behavior to the consequence. A two-year-old, for example, may forget what he did five minutes ago. A five minute delay could be enough to make him feel that the parent has attacked him for no reason. The child must connect the consequence with the behavior.

Start with the smallest consequence possible when trying to manage a behavior. Often a small consequence will work just as well as a larger one. It is in the best interest of the parents and the child to keep consequences small. Smaller consequences are easier to carry through for parents and provide them with a significant buffer zone in which to escalate consequences.

Foster parents need to work with their social workers to develop a multiple-level consequence strategy when working with complicated children. Escalating consequences in small steps can be strategic in helping to guide a child to compliance.

> *Once a child has complied with a requested behavior,*
> *it is in the parent's best interest to de-escalate consequences*
> *as quickly as possible.*

What is the difference between discipline and punishment?

An important distinction must be made between discipline and punishment. A fine line exists between them and in a healthy parenting system both will be used in raising a child. The difficulty arises in interpretation. Many people equate the term discipline with punishment. This is inappropriate because most discipline is not punishment. Since discipline and punishment are not exclusive, there is always some overlap. Unfortunately, most foster children need a lot of discipline in their lives and may have received a lot of punishment instead.

Many children in out-of-home care have already been overpunished, abused, or neglected. It is of utmost importance that the previous cycle of abuse or neglect is not continued in out-of home care. Care providers need to develop a workable balance between accepting the child and not accepting a particular unwanted behavior. As adult role models, we must not respond to provocative behaviors with inappropriate reactions.

Often a child in out-of-home care has been raised with a combination of rewards for "*good*" behavior and punishment for "*bad*" behavior. This approach is easier than using consequences, takes a lot less thinking, and does not place high demands on parental self-control. The drawback to this approach is seen in the American culture. A materialistic and manipulative society reinforces the idea that the goal in life is to grab all the rewards you can.

Some of the possible disadvantages of using only reward and punishment as a system of developing self-discipline are:

1. Punishment indicates children are insignificant and inferior. It lowers the dignity and worth of every member of the family.

2. Punishment diminishes respect for authority and leadership. Children respect authority when they can gain advice, counsel, guidance, and support.

3. Punishment and rewards focus on control as the basis of family togetherness. Harassing the child to conform and please the parent can precipitate both self-hate and a desire for revenge.

4. Punishment is often administered to hurt the child rather than to solve the problem. It is hard to break a cycle of covert aggression for inflicted hurt.

5. Reward and punishment, used selfishly by parents to get their own way, reinforces selfishness in children.

6. Children often use punishment to get angry and thus convince themselves that future misbehavior is justified.

7. Rewards and punishments can lead children to believe that acceptance in the family depends solely on performance; this in turn can cause frustration and feelings of inadequacy and rejection.

8. Children may deliberately seek out punishment as a way of getting attention or they may welcome it as a means of relieving guilt and avoiding responsibility to change. When this happens punishment fails to accomplish its purpose of discouraging misbehavior.

9. Rewards for good behavior may teach children to behave properly only when they receive pleasure.

10. Punishment teaches children that power is the only way to gain desires.

In a well-disciplined family, punishment may never be needed, but in some circumstances, with some children, punishment is necessary. In parenting systems where punishment is seldom used, it accomplishes compliance with the rule and gets an immediate reaction. Punishment in these families is done with respect for the individual and the responsible adult does not harm either the emotional or physical health of the child.

In parenting systems where adult authority is abdicated and little discipline is provided, children may lack boundaries and self-control. Parents who avoid teaching self-discipline and responsibility may find themselves overpunishing a child whose behavior has become too difficult to manage. They avoid confrontation for so long by being *"nice"* that they eventually overreact. They thought they were doing their parenting job by providing freedom and loving their children.

In parenting systems where punishment is used predominantly instead of self-discipline training, the child may develop a need for external control in order to function. These parents often use punishment to get back at the pain, worry, or inconvenience caused by the children. It attacks the person and not the problem. It can injure the body and the spirit and falls short of genuine caring.

The social worker asked a long-term foster family, "What kind of discipline do you use with your own children? Do you ever spank?"

"We mostly use shock therapy when things get out of hand," said the father.

"Shock therapy on children?" gasped the social worker.

"It's something I learned from my father. It worked on me, so I figured it would work on them. So far, it's been very effective," the father answered.

The social worker's eyes opened wide and she swallowed hard. What didn't she know about this family?

"Yes," continued the father, "the procedure is very simple . . ."

The differences between discipline and punishment are significant.
In a crisis situation, distinctions may become blurred.

"When our children are really out-of-control I get down to their level, hold both their wrists, look them straight in the eye, lower my voice, and speak slowly and directly. They understand clearly what I mean."

Here are some comparative statements that show why discipline is appropriate when working with children in out-of-home care, and why punishment is not.

Discipline	Punishment
Proactive focus on preventing problems.	Reactive intervention after problem occurs.
Builds relationships by correcting the behavior while accepting the child.	Rejects the child who has behaved undesirably. The result is alienation
Is designed to encourage children toward responsibility.	Seeks retribution for misbehavior.
Is a learned and self-disciplined process that adults model for children.	Often attempts to secure obedience by sheer force, without care and understanding.
Focuses on present learning experience without harshness.	Focuses on the misbehavior causing hurt.
Displays anger appropriately—against the deed and not the doer.	Displays anger against the doer and uses power to gain the punisher's way.
Allows for cooperation and mutual respect to develop.	Sets up power struggles and cycles of revenge and counter-revenge.
Control by inner values expected.	Control by external rule enforcement.
Motivates by natural consequences, firm kindness, and consistency.	Motivates by arbitrary consequences, fear, and inconsistency.

Demanding greatness in children instead of obedience calls forth the great potential of young people.

Greatness demands mature, responsible behavior.

Greatness does not allow you to run over the rights of others.

Greatness holds the child accountable for his behavior and challenges inappropriate actions.

(Brendtro, Brokenleg, Van Bockern 1990)

Children who have lived under a reward and punishment system will expect misbehavior to come with punishments and good behavior to come with rewards. To the child, the punishment and reward system is understood and comfortable. The new system of discipline and consequences may induce tirades in the child.

In a parenting system of mutual respect, a job is done because it needs doing, and the satisfaction comes from the harmony of the people doing the job together. Satisfaction comes from contribution and participation. When children are rewarded for participation and contribution, their internal sense of satisfaction is destroyed.

It's easy to think of punishment as what other people do to kids, and yet punishment is inherent in the American culture. The problem with punishment is that the end results are hostility, resentment, and the desire for retaliation. It's interesting that these same results are produced in children, teenagers, and adults. Dodson (1978) gives some excellent examples of how well punishment works on adults. It is helpful to think about employment-related incidents when a person in authority reprimands you. How do you react? How do you feel?

Scolding: You wore your new jeans while changing the oil in your wife's car. The jeans have grease all over them and most likely will be stained even after presoaking and washing. *"John, how many times have I told you not to wear your new clothes out in the garage? What do* you think we are made of anyway? Money? I'm sick and tired of cleaning up after you." OK, John, who's going to change your wife's oil next time? Not you, right? I'll bet you feel really appreciated right now. Could this conversation make you think twice before you change her oil the next time?

Lecturing: You back the car out of the driveway and hit the corner of your husband's car. You've come in to tell him and he says, *"Now Dear, how many times have I told you just how to back the car up? You turn around and look behind you—you do not look forward. Sometimes, I don't know what I am going to do with you. You act like a ten-year-old. How could you possibly do something as stupid as back into my new car? I just don't understand you."* Did you like the lecture? Ready to be more careful next time?

Taking away privileges: You have already used up your food budget for the month, and it is only the eighteenth. *"I'm sorry, Dear, but I'm going to have to take away your care privileges since you can't maintain the food budget. You will need to learn to be more responsible with our money. You can have the car back in six months."* How does that make you feel? Are you motivated to manage the food budget better next month? Or are you seething with fury and planning to mess up next month's budget also?

Sending you to your room: After working in the garden, you come in the house and tramp mud all over the recently waxed floor. Your wife sends you to clean the garage for the rest of the day and says you will fix your own dinner and eat alone. Are you motivated to be more careful the next time? Did you offer to mop up your footprints? Or did you think—she can just clean it herself for treating me that way? How do you feel while cleaning the garage? Enthusiastic?

Spanking: You have not kept a running balance of your checkbook, and checks are bouncing right and left. Your husband grabs you by the arm, marches you into your room, and proceeds to turn you over his knee and spank you to teach you a lesson. Does this make you feel like being extra careful with the checkbook?

The absurdity of punishment for adults is obvious, but the effect it has on children is not. Yet children have opinions and feelings, too. Evoking negative feelings in children to accomplish responsible behaviors doesn't add up. What can adults do that will provide the positive discipline, increased self-esteem, and behavior they desire from their children?

What if nothing is working?

Professional parenting is not an easy job. While potentially beneficial, separation from the primary family is very stressful and lonely for the child. It is helpful to remember that even mature adults struggle when they are grieving or in new and different surroundings. Viewing the child in your care as immature and younger than the child's actual age will help you lower your expectations and allow the child to gradually readjust and grow again. Behavior expected in your home will most likely not be the same behavior that was accepted in the child's previous living environment. Children in care need the same love, patience, and parenting you use with your biological children, but they often need more time and understanding to grow in managing their own behaviors. If specific behaviors arouse concern, contact your social worker for advice and an approved program for handling the behavior.

The moral beliefs of man are always greater than the behavior of man.

What one says and what one does may be two very different things.

A child's perception of discipline is far different from the perception of the person administering it.

Avoid the Pawn Game

"Go ask Dad."

"What did your Mother say?"

"Wait 'til Dad gets home."

Teaches a child to manipulate and increases confrontation rather than avoids it.

Take responsibility. Say "yes," "no," or keep the child out of the triangle by saying: "I'll talk to your father/mother and let you know the answer in fifteen minutes." If the child bugs you, keep your fifteen minute rule, but begin timing again.

— Learning and behavioral problems in school.
— Lying, stealing, endlessly argumentative.
— Chronic whining or complaining.
— Non-assertive, passive, overly submissive, inert, lifeless behaviors.
— Hyperactivity.
— Disturbances in sleeping, toileting, and eating.
— Frequent complaints of headache, stomachache.
— Fecal smearing or urinating in places other than bathroom.
— Difficulty in getting along with others.
— Hostile or violent behaviors toward self or others.
— Feelings of sadness, depression, anger, rage.
— Fear of separation, insatiable neediness, regressed, helpless.
— Withdrawal from others.
— Low self-esteem.
— Provocative behaviors, negative attention getting.
— Over-friendliness to strangers.

(Refer to Chapter 3 — Potential Stresses of Foster Care Providers, or read the books:
Children on Consignment *by Philip Michael Stahl*
Troubled Transplants *by Richard Delaney and Frank Kunstal*
Reclaiming Youth at Risk *by Larry Brendtro, Martin Brokenleg,*
and Steve Van Bockern

TIME-OUT removes the child from the situation just as a coach removes a player from the playing field. As a coaching tool, time-out allows a child to refocus, regroup, and go back into the game to play again. The role of the coach is to train, mentor, and guide. As a coach, a parent does not need to burn out by engaging in the battle. A skilled coach will know when to apply just the right amount of pressure to motivate or settle down the team player.

Time-out used for a child to gain self control (open ended) is a logical consequence and a useful discipline tool. Time-out used to punish (closed ended) can create resentment, anger, and revenge. Time-out should be open ended. Sending a child to his room for the whole afternoon is close ended and results in hostility and resentment or in the child forgetting why he is confined to his room. Close ended time-out does little for future behavior adjustments. On the other hand, a shorter time-out on a "stop and think about it" chair in full view of the parent can open the opportunity for additional communication once the time-out is over. A specific chair or place in the room can be identified as the child's time-out place. Time-out should not be for an indefinite or lengthy period of time, usually one to two minutes per year of the child's age. It helps to set the kitchen timer so the child knows you are being fair. Keep an egg timer handy and give it to the child to watch while on the time-out chair. Smaller consequences give parents space and time to escalate discipline if needed without harming the child.

REVERSE TIME-OUT by removing yourself from the child and the situation. Go to your room. Put on the headset and sit in the time-out chair yourself. Take a break in the bathroom with a magazine. Go for a walk. Review the stress management ideas in Chapter 3. *(Remove yourself only as far from the situation as is developmentally safe to leave the child.)*

CONTRACTING is negotiating with the child to create a written mutual agreement that provides incentives for the child to focus on a desired behavior. The child promises to do something, and the parent promises to do something in return. Or the child changes his behavior and the parent changes his behavior in return. Contracting allows for mutual benefit for both parent and child. (Dodson 1978)

Restoration of damaged development is difficult for children who have been raised in abusive or neglectful environments.

The length of time spent under oppression, the level of maltreatment experienced, the personality of the child, and the age of that child during the experiences all directly affect whether this child can be reached and begin to move toward stable mental health.

The intensity of the child's experiences will directly influence the quality and type of parenting system needed for the child. The more intense the experience, the more direct one-on-one supportive parenting services are needed.

Important steps in contracting include:

1. The contract must be a mutual agreement. It cannot be, *"I won't let you —— if you don't——."* That cannot be a contract since there is no negotiating. It is simply a unilateral statement coming from the parent.

2. The negotiation process results in a commitment from both sides. Child commits to do — every ——. Parent commits to — in return.

3. The commitment is written, and there is a copy for each person.

4. The contract must be concrete and specific. All actions specified in the contract need to be observable and countable. Include specific ways a child will cooperate, behave, or complete a task. Include measurable progress points.

5. The contract should be positive in nature. The child should agree to *do* something rather than agree *not to do* something. It is easier to get motivation and cooperation if the child has something positive to do to earn a payoff.

6. The contract must be fair. Both parent and child must end up feeling they got a good deal.

7. The contract must be designed to be successful.

8. The art of negotiating is not instinctive. The parents have to be willing to relinquish some of their power and develop the art of compromise. Almost all negotiations involve compromise between the parent and the child.

You may want to take a trial run at the contract that is short term and attainable. This allows for an evaluation process within a short period of time and renegotiation if needed. If the child fulfills the contract as written, the parent must come through.

Every day Sally, age 10, would wake up in a bad mood. She would complain about getting dressed, scowl at breakfast, and the whole family would be miserable by the time Sally reached the school bus. Sally loved ballet. The contract between Sally and her mother read:

Sally Smith, May 1, 1992
Johnny Johnson, May 1, 1992 (witness)
I, Sally Smith, will wake up in the morning and put a smile on my face. If I cannot find my smile when I get dressed, I will not share my bad mood with the rest of the family.
I, Mother, will provide two tickets to Swan Lake *and go to the ballet on May 15, 1992 when Sally has been able to have a good morning attitude for 12 of the 15 days.*
Signed — Mother, May 1, 1992   Signed — Sally, May 1, 1992

Give a child the freedom to grumble and gripe, as long as she does what the contract specifies. As long as the behavior or task is accomplished, feelings and actions need to be kept separate. Even if the child performs the contract in his own creative way, the parents must fulfill their side of the obligation. The parental payoff may include a fishing or camping trip, tickets to a concert or ballgame, a visit to a museum or park, or swimming or dance lessons.

CONFRONTATION AND INTERVENTION requires sensitivity since there is a fine line between confrontation and harassment, without embarrassing the child in front of friends. If a parent can succeed in pulling it off forthrightly it can be very effective. (Kaye 1984)

Ten years ago, Rebecca, an experienced counselor and special education teacher, and single African American mother of a fourteen year old son, chose to reach out to a special needs child—Eric.

Eric, age four, had disrupted six other placements, including a facility for Down Syndrome children. Eric's next step was another institution or — you guessed it — Rebecca's home.

Rebecca felt confident. She had the education and counseling background and had already raised a very wonderful son of her own. Together she and Jonathan, her fourteen year old, would DO ERIC.

Eric arrived a silent, pathetic little bundle of energy. He was unable to talk, was not toilet trained, and could not feed himself. He was diagnosed mentally retarded—Rebecca felt the diagnosis was wrong.

Eric had never had a long-term relationship with anyone. She and Jonathan would give Eric that relationship.

Parent upon overhearing teenage boy boasting to his friends about "making it" with his girlfriend.

> *"It doesn't seem like Alice is a human to you. I don't know whether you're telling the truth or not about the encounter, but if you are, I wonder if she cares as little for you as you seem to care for her."*

The parent leaves the room.

REMOVING PRIVILEGES relating to the unacceptable behavior. The loss should be of short term duration. A parent must be careful not to remove privileges or deprive a child of something over such a long time that it becomes meaningless. The younger the child, the less time is needed because time is less understood. Long term removal of privileges can result in covert aggressive actions by children against the parent. Use of the phone, time with friends, bike, car, or TV are potential privileges which can be removed.

FIND THE "REAL" NEED OF THE CHILD. Sometimes the "real" need of the child is hidden in such difficult behavior it is hard to discover. Maybe you've missed the subtle clues through the myraid of actions. For example, a child who has been neglected may be hoarding food and storing it in unwanted and unusual places. Filling the child's need by providing unlimited food until the child trusts that food will always be available in your home may by far more effective than trying to stop the child from filling his or her emptiness. The book *Troubled Transplants* (1993) offers a variety of unconventional strategies in working effectively with troubled children.

CHANGE THE VOCABULARY. The words we use often express emotions. If a young person describes hurting or destructive behavior as "cool" or fashionable, adults should relabel the behavior in a way that will convey that it is unacceptable.

In order to be effective, the adult must convey the genuine message—*"This is very irresponsible behavior for such a great young person as you."* (Brendtro, Brokenleg, Van Bockern 1991)

"Rip off" sounds macho, but "being sneaky" sounds like something little kids do.

"Truancy" sounds romantic, but "playing hide and seek" doesn't sound adventurous to an adolescent.

Tough Love—What is it?

Tough Love is a program designed by Phyllis and David York, whose lives were torn apart by their teenager's wild and irresponsible behaviors. It must be noted here that the Yorks took back their parental authority, which they had been allowing their children to abuse. Their methods and techniques have proved very successful in working with children who are secure in the love and trust of their parents. For children who have been neglected or overpunished by adults and who are in out-of-home care, a tough love program may be more damaging than effective.

Children in out-of-home care need to develop trust and begin to attach to the families responsible for their care before a program such as tough love can be truly effective. Even though their behavior is out-of-control and the adult response seems warranted, some of the techniques used in the tough love program may be misinterpreted by children in care. Before deciding to implement a tough love program with out-of-home teens or late elementary school age children, get written approval and work with the child's therapist, school counselor, and social worker.

The ten basic principles developed by the Yorks are helpful guidelines in many parenting situations. Since there have been times we have used tough love in working with long-term placement teens, I add these principles here.

To protect Eric from being institutionalized or moved into another foster home, Rebecca, applied to adopt Eric—a normal looking, blond child—into her African American home. Racial bias never entered the picture. Rebecca and Jonathan were offering their love and nurturing to a needy, broken child.

Within six months, Eric was toilet trained. His first words were in anger—Jesus Christ and Fuck. He no longer ate off his plate like a puppy. He was able to dress himself. This confirmed to Rebecca—Eric was not severely retarded.

By eight years old, Eric had finally quit eating trash out of people's garbage cans. It had taken four years of professional parenting to squelch the desire once the need was removed.

He still acted out sexually—fondling other children, exposing himself in public, masturbating to relieve tension. The acting out seemed to be rooted in lack of personal boundaries. Eric wasn't aroused by this behavior.

1. **Family problems have roots and support in the culture.** Violence, crime, unemployment, drugs, alcohol, divorce, world change, chaos, poverty, education, illness, inattentiveness of parents, neglect, abuse, sexuality, etc.

2. **Parents are people, too.** Kids want parents who are people. Children do not want parents who are pushovers. They want parents who stand up for themselves, assert themselves, and get their needs met. When parents helps themselves they also help their kids. Parents do not need to let their children walk on them.

3. **Parents' material and emotional resources are limited.** Parents have the right and need to say, *"I need something from you. . ."* or *"This is it, I've had enough."*

4. **Parents and kids are not equal.** Parents have responsibility for the needs and care of kids. Because they have these responsibilities, they also have the authority to carry out their responsibilities.

5. **Blaming keeps people helpless.** As long as everyone in the family dances around pointing fingers at each other and dwelling on past wrongs, nothing is going to change. One must stop blaming and start planning.

6. **Kids' behavior affects parents, and parents' behavior affects kids.** When a family is in crisis, everyone's behavior affects everyone else's. The important question is not *"Who brought us to this point?"* but *"Who is going to lead us out of here?"*

7. **Taking a stand precipitates a change.** The reaction can be crisis or peace.

8. **A controlled crisis may bring about the necessary change.** Often parents resist taking a stand because the distress they have grown used to is less frightening than the unknown results of a crisis.

9. **Families need to give and get support within their own community in order to change.** Peer families who have experienced similar situations in their own lives can offer support and understanding that counseling cannot provide.

10. **The essence of family life is cooperation, not togetherness.** The direction of family life is toward autonomy. The agenda of the child is to acquire more freedom, along with the skills and confidence to enjoy that freedom. The agenda of the parents is to relinquish controls over the child's actions one step at a time until the child has independence and begins living apart from the family. Togetherness runs counter to real life.

Tough love has helped many families work through difficult parenting issues by providing education and support groups for families and children. It takes courage to change and take a stand. Tough love gives parents the tools to begin to change. If nothing else is working, reading Phyllis and David York's books or attending a support group may be helpful.

How can parental authority be abused?

Depending on past experiences, children in care will be extremely sensitive to discipline by the new parents. Previous care providers may have responded in the following ways in addition to abusing or neglecting them:

— Failing to listen to the child's feelings.
— Allowing behavior one time, then giving an excessive punishment on the same behavior.
— Giving a big punishment for a small offense or a little punishment for for a large offense.

Eric may not have been aroused, but his behavior sure got the attention of the rest of the world.

Rebecca knew she needed additional professional support when Eric was ten. Eric was stealing, running away, and vandalizing the neighborhood.

Rebecca hired a professional therapist and felt the sting of the double-edge sword— blame.

"Obviously, your parenting could use some improvement, Rebecca. What do you think you are doing to cause this type of acting out? Are you having other family problems?"

Rebecca began to question her parenting, her knowledge as an educator, her other relationshipships. What had she done wrong to make Eric act like this? She felt rejected. Defeated.

"Eric, why don't you work with your family? Your mother loves you." Eric's denial, anger, and resistance escalated. His behavior began to escalate.

A giant rift was beginning to grow.

— Belittling the child with sarcasm and contempt.
— Punishing the child in front of others.
— Being unfair and unreasonable in the kind and amount of discipline.
— Preventing the child from learning to make decisions and consequently learning personal motivation for change.
— Controlling the child by fear and guilt rather than by encouraging the child to become discerning in making choices.
— Giving the child the impression that acceptable behavior is necessary only when the authority figure is present.
— Disrespectfully forcing children to conform, creating a power struggle, causing resistance or even retaliation.

And, sometimes nothing you do will work.
The mountain is too high to climb.

There is no guarantee with a damaged and fragile child that even the best professional parenting, counseling, and support services will produce the desired results. Sometimes the mountain is too high to climb.

This is the foundation Rebecca began with.

Isolated and locked in a room alone at two, with no toys, Eric learned to keep himself busy and quiet by masturbating. His normal two year old temper tantrums had been beaten out of him. **Rebecca had worked with children like this before.**

Living with four different families after he was removed from his birth family, he learned anger was a powerful feeling and there were ways of using it to get your needs met. **Rebecca had fostered a number of children prior to Eric and seen dramatic results in the children and helped birth families heal.**

Living in an institution for mentally retarded children, Eric learned what types of behaviors got the kind of attention he desired. This institution provided a library of disabilities to choose from. **Rebecca teaches special education, she also holds a degree in psychology. Daily, her classroom of students is filled with learning disabled and mentally challenged children.**

Eric learned you couldn't trust white people, caucasian caregivers always gave you away. **Rebecca was the right color for the job. Eric could identify safely with her as a caregiver who would not give him away.**

Eric's files from birth to four have vanished, they begin when Eric arrived at Rebecca's. Due to confidentiality, Rebecca was never allowed to see them. She has gathered information about these four lost years of Eric's life by finding, befriending, and interviewing his street person birth father, visiting the foster families he lived with and disrupted, and offering her services to the institution for mentally challenged children. Investigation and living with Eric for ten years have provided her practical knowledge. Fourteen years as a special education teacher and counselor for hundreds of children and their families has provided her tools to work with. But nothing she equipped herself with prepared her for the reality of living 24 hours a day with Eric.

By age twelve, Eric was no longer safe at home. Nightly he would escape to go on a rampage. Anger that had been repressed began to surface and at times even the strength of a sturdy police officer could not contain him. He was a danger to himself, his family, and the community—no one was safe.

Eric was removed from Rebecca's home and placed in residential care for observation and assessment. It has taken two years to make that assessment—he has now also disrupted that placement. The facility can no longer help fourteen-year-old Eric. Rebecca believes he is culturally retarded, not mentally retarded.

His IQ score maintains 40 points, Rebecca thinks it's closer to 80.

The two year separation for Rebecca has been good. She married the father of two of her foster children after their mother died, and together they have decided to welcome Eric home. Her marriage is strong and with the support of another adult, especially a strong male figure, they feel confident in beginning again with Eric.

Eric is no longer Rebecca's mountain and will not become the family's mountain. In the last two years, Rebecca has gained a different perspective on her survivor son. She no longer expects perfection of herself or success with Eric. Her concepts of discipline and behavior modification have been refined to allow Eric room to express himself. (*Presently he has a haircut that is shaved on one side and four inches long on the other. Rebecca styled it for Eric and Eric is proud to show off this new free spirited look.*)

Eric looks to Rebecca as a nurturing adult. He gives her hugs and kisses—a new phenomenon. He trusts her more than any other person in the world, though he is not attached to her. He would not offer her help if she was hurt. He would not feel sorry if he hurt her or one of the young children. His sorrow would be from getting caught or not being smart enough to manipulate his way out of it. His manipulation skills have increased from the knowledge he has gained in psychiatric wards and his last facility. He will continue to use them to his advantage. He has no conscience. He has no logic of cause and effect from his behavior. He may never gain those skills.

Rebecca and her husband have determined to work on Eric's intensity level, instead of his individual strange behaviors. They will not allow him to control the behavior thermostat in their home. Aware that Eric's homecoming brings his pathologies back into their home, Rebecca has developed a program to avoid becoming enmeshed in Eric's behavior.

1. A parent aide (*college student studying social work/special education*) is available from 6:30 am - 8:30 am, helping and encouraging Eric to dress, eat and transporting him to school.

2. Another parent aide (*college student studying social work/special education*) is available from 3:00 pm - 6:00 pm, helping Eric with studies, occupying him with games, discussion, and local field trips; essentially a supportive young adult friend.

3. A professionally trained respite family who can befriend Eric and take him every other weekend from Friday night to Sunday night has become available.

Rebecca's family will offer Eric the love, support, and nurturing of a family environment. Eric may never be able to even accept that offering. With Rebecca, he has a "*real*" advocate, someone who will search for the support programs he needs and be there to advocate when no one else will. The four years of empty parenting that began Eric's journey into child welfare cannot be filled. Rebecca is leaving that job to God. Eric can be God's mountain to climb.

*God gave Eric his survival skills, because a world
that can't understand couldn't meet his needs.*

Summary

Discipline is a vital part of human existence. It begins with building a trusting relationship. Children as well as adults need discipline in their lives. In order to accept guidance in discipline training, there must be mutual respect between teacher and disciple. Positive discipline training guides a child to growth without

When you first meet Eric, there is no clue that this child has problems. He looks like any other fourteen-year-old young man.

Within an hour, however, you begin to see other behaviors. The reaction depends on what he perceives is necessary to get his needs met. If something is said to his disliking, he may migrate to the middle of the floor and remain in a fetal position. Or he may break out in an uncontrollable tantrum. Or Down Syndrome behaviors begin to be exhibited.

Later Eric easily communicates what happened and what he thought about it.

He is extremely uncooperative with strangers. He has been diagnosed as blind by eye doctors, only to make a miraculous recovery at the next appointment. He has never cooperated on any testing. All of his IQ scores have tested 40 points.

Eric is a survivor. He has learned many behaviors that are effective to model.

sacrificing the child's self-esteem. It builds acceptance, a sense of belonging, and an understanding of responsibility. Children need the external controls provided by parents or adult leadership while they are developing their own internal controls for self-discipline. Parents must not abdicate their responsibilities of authority over their children's lives. They need to maintain consistency and be willing to follow through both on their promises and on their threats. In dual parenting families, the parents need cohesiveness in parenting their children.

Children whose behavior is out-of-bounds need control. Before deciding on the appropriate discipline for a specific behavior, a parent must take careful inventory of what is causing the behavior. If the behavior could be caused by a physical ailment, the environment, or food allergies, the cause must be isolated first. If the behavior is a symptom, then the cause of the behavior needs to be removed before a parent can expect a child to learn to manage a specific behavior.

There is a fine line between discipline and punishment. Most parenting systems use both discipline and punishment in guiding children to adulthood. The percentage of parenting time used in the training of discipline or the administration of punishment varies from family to family. Families rooted in training children in self-discipline and responsibility tend to use punishment very seldom. Families who punish immediately without working through discipline training can overpunish a child when their immediate reaction does not get their desired response. Families who abdicate the training of their children can overpunish when a child's behavior get out of bounds and the parent is frustrated.

Children in care have complex and varied backgrounds needing consistent and respectful discipline by sensitive, caring, and understanding adults. The behavior exhibited may be peculiar or unrealeated to what is happening. Care providers must be a united team in developing discipline practices that are beneficial for children in their care and approved in writing by social services.

References

Brendtro, Larry; Brokenleg, Martin; and Van Bockern, Steve. 1991. *Reclaming Youth at Risk.* Indiana: National Education Services.

Delaney, Richard and Kunstal, Frank. 1993. *Troubled Transplants.* Colorado: Walter J. Corbett

Dodson, Fitzhugh. 1978. *How To Father.* New York: Signet.

Dodson, Fitzhugh. 1977. *How To Discipline with Love; From Crib to College.* New York: Signet.

Dreikers, Rudolf. 1974. *Discipline Without Tears.* New York: Dutton.

Farmer, Steven. 1989. *Adult Children of Abusive Parents. A Healing Program for Those Who Have Been Physically, Sexually or Emotionally Abused.* New York: Ballantine.

Kaye, Kenneth. 1984. *Family Rules, Raising Responsible Children Without Yelling or Nagging.* New York: Walker & Co.

Koop, C. Everett. 1992. *The Memoirs of America's Family Doctor Koop. The Former Surgeon General.* Michigan: Zondervan Publishing House

Rapp, Doris J. 1986. *The Impossible Child. A Guide for Caring Teachers and Parents in School, at Home.* Washington: Life Sciences Press.
In addition, Dr. Rapp has produced a number of other books, videos and cassettes to help teachers and parents understand children's behavior caused by allergies. When diet and environmental modification can make such a difference in a child's behavior, it cannot be overlooked as a safe and powerful behavior management tool. For more information on Dr. Rapp's work, write: Practical Allergy Research Foundation, PO Box 60, Buffalo, NY 14223-0060.

Stahl, Philip Michael. 1991. *Children on Consignment. A Handbook for Parenting Foster Children and Their Special Needs.* Massachusetts: Lexington Press.

York, Phyllis and York, David. 1982. *Tough Love.* New York: Doubleday.

Chapter 12

Defining Child Maltreatment

*Child **abuse** is any act of commission that endangers or impairs a child's physical or emotional health and development.*

*Child **neglect** is any act of omission which negatively affects the general welfare of the child.*

The terms neglect and abuse of children are used freely in our society with little clarification about what actually may be involved. When guidelines vary or are unclear, misunderstandings and misjudgments occur. In this chapter, I hope to expose the damage to children who are exposed to overpunishment, neglect, or abuse, and the vulnerability of adults who may or may not abuse children. Maltreatment of children is wrong regardless of who does it. *Adults have the capacity of choice. Children deserve adult protection.*

> *I met Tom and Linda through professionals I had been working with while writing* Families at Risk. *Two years previously, Tom had been accused of sexually abusing his eight-year-old stepdaughter. Sheila had been placed in foster care and then sent to New York to live with her birth father for protection. Tom had been asked to leave his family's home to provide Linda the opportunity to allow Sheila to return. Separated, isolated, and alone, Tom and Linda tried to make sense of their situation. Social services told the foster family Sheila had been removed because of sexual abuse and that her birth parents were sick people and in a deranged state. Tom appeared volatile. He did not have permission to see Sheila. Linda, on the other hand, could communicate with her daughter one hour a week under supervision at child protection. She seemed compliant.*

Foster parents need concise information about maltreatment and what has truthfully occurred in a child's life. They need to be prepared for behaviors that differ from the behavior of their own children. Potential crisis situations need to be discussed within their family and with their social worker to develop correct responses. Caring for children who have been maltreated and repairing maltreating families are difficult tasks. As the family begins to build a trusting relationship with a child in care, they may be placed in a very vulnerable position. Professionals in contact with these children need awareness that as the child gains a sense of security, the very people who are providing the daily relationship may become the target of attack. Children in out-of-home care may

In assessing abusive and neglectful situations, a professional must always ask:

Did the abuse or neglect actually occur?

Is the abuse or neglect likely to occur in the future?

Is this an isolated case?

What responsibility has the adult taken regarding the abuse or neglect?

Is the family situation chronic or extreme? To what degree?

What is the level of seriousness?

Can this family be moved from crisis to restoration?

What services need to be provided?

determine that foster or adoptive families are safe repositories for the anger they have repressed. They may display provocative behavior to encourage reunification with their primary family or to show the social services system that these *"new parents"* are no better then the parents they *"really love."*

> *Sheila's foster parents comforted her and tried to make her feel safe. They explained that her parents were sick and needed help. No additional harm would come to her while she remained in their care. Sheila wrote a letter to her parents:* **Dear Mom and Dad, I know now that you are sick. I still love you and hope you get well soon so I can come home. Love, Sheila**

> *Finally some help was available to Sheila and her parents. Social services and the new foster parents were determined to protect and provide help for her.*

Care provider families, social workers, and therapists must work as a team to provide the love, sweat, and tears it takes to unwind the tangle of maltreatment and grief present in out-of-home care. Professionals who decide to remove children from their homes need clear guidelines. Failure to remove a child in need of protection is as tragic as mistakenly removing a child from a safe home.

Children who are emotionally, physically, or sexually maltreated often feel abandoned by their parents when a parent cannot or will not take care of their needs. How much additional abandonment do children feel when they are removed from the only home they have ever known? They do not have a comparison scale. Adults caring for children who have been maltreated need a clear understanding of what constitutes neglect or abuse and leads to placing children in out-of-home care.

> *Sheila's stepfather, Tom, worked in crisis intervention and with chemically dependent adults. He was called in during national disasters to manage major crises. He was extroverted, spontaneous, and used to taking charge in difficult situations. Sheila's mother, Linda, was a thoughtful person, very organized and stable. She shared her feelings cautiously after she had completely thought through an issue. The immediate removal of Sheila caught the family off guard, and each parent reacted according to personality, experience, and behavior patterns.*

> *The story is long and drawn out over a two-year period. Tom was eventually found not guilty, not because evidence was lacking, but because a mistake had been made and he actually was innocent. During the five months Sheila was away, she had lived in two foster homes and with her biological father. She came home a damaged little girl—confused and fearful of adults, police, and medical professionals. She will be in psychological counseling for the foreseeable future. Tom was proclaimed safe and allowed to return to his family after a period of ten months. He lost his business, two apartment buildings, and his self-esteem during the ordeal. The legal and psychiatric fees for his family have totalled $160,000. Linda is quiet and bitter. Her stability and thoughtfulness maintained the family home. Inside she is shattered and needs support. They are again a family—piece by painful piece putting life together.*

> *I asked Linda what she wanted foster families to know based on her experience. She answered quietly, "Please don't assume anything about the birth family until you know the truth. Tom and I were not sick people. A mistake was made and we were caught in the middle of it. Regardless if we had been guilty or innocent, my husband, our daughter, and I needed compassion and support. The foster family treated our daughter with love and compassion—we appreciate their time and care of Sheila while she felt isolated, confused, and alone. The foster family treated us as though we were rags—we did not deserve their reactions—yet we understand they did not know the truth. We needed a support team. Each of us was traumatized by the experience. As child advocates, we believe in child welfare and the protection of children. We have also become dedicated to the welfare of families. Both my hus-*

band and I are interested in moving forward, not just for our family, but for future families and children. What happened to Sheila can be prevented."

Families are often stronger and more resourceful than many people believe. Day-to-day existence may be from crisis to crisis. The family's strength may already have been proved by their very survival.

The family situation must be carefully assessed to determine services needed. These assessments take time and require trained individuals who have a solid understanding of cultural differences, individual and family dynamics, and legal responsibilities. Initial contact with children and their families can be heartbreaking. Yet, regardless of how disastrous or damaging the family may appear upon initial contact, professionals working with these families must not automatically assume the family situation has always been this way or that it cannot change.

Regardless of the quality of care or intensity of punishment administered, children love what they know best, sometimes without question. They believe the people who love them and whom they love. Often they place the blame for the parent's behavior on themselves.

Maltreatment of children has probably existed as long as there have been children. Not until the mid-1800's did the Animal Humane Society begin political and social efforts to protect children. It is interesting that previous laws existed to protect animals, but did not protect humans. Recognition of maltreatment of human beings has come a long way since the 1800's.

Changing parenting systems is difficult. Families pass on methods of child rearing from generation to generation. In the past thirty years much has been written regarding abuse and neglect and some progress has been made. Child-rearing practices that were once perceived as acceptable and normal within the family may be viewed as unacceptable and abusive by present social standards. Some of today's parents are caught off guard without adequate training of how to parent within accepted discipline practices. These individuals are shocked when child protection officials knock at their door with a complaint. They believe they are "just doing their job." Doing a quality job is based on the only performance scale they know—their own childhood and their parents' style of parenting. Their knowledge of approved child-rearing techniques is limited, and these limitations can place even loving and caring parents into complications with child protection authorities.

There may be reasons for the maltreatment. There are NO excuses!

*Children who are overpunished, abused, or neglected
are in crisis regardless of whether or not the parent is in crisis.*

It is the parent's or adult's role to care for, protect, and teach children. Children can be annoying, embarrassing, confusing, disruptive, and difficult to handle. Their behavior can be damaging to themselves or to others. The difficulties caused by a child are real and some forms of behaviors cannot be allowed to continue, but how adults respond or react to these feelings is up to them. *Adults can choose their own behavior, regardless of the behavior of the child.*

A question often asked is, *"Do parents who maltreat their children love them?"* Most often the answer is yes. Parents who overpunish or abuse their children may believe they are disciplining a child for the child's good, to remove the badness, or to build a strong character. They believe it is their responsibility to force proper behavior from the child.

Abusive parents need:

— *To feel good about themselves.*

— *Someone to help them feel valuable.*

— *Someone who will help them understand their children.*

— *Someone who understands how hard it is to have children when they may never have been allowed to be a child themselves.*

— *Someone who is available in times of crisis to provide support, but who will not remove their independence and responsibilities — leading them to resources or teaching coping skills.*

— *Someone who can empathize with them.*

Adults who abuse may have a history of overpunishment or maltreatment in their childhood and have no alternative discipline tools from which to draw. Their understanding of love and nurturing may not include caring for or valuing the child. They may lack child development knowledge, have unrealistic expectations, or misinterpret mistaken behavior as defiant or bad. The child may simply be showing age appropriate behavior. Compassionate intervention and training may be all these parents need to begin to understand normal child development and gain ideas to work through difficult child-parent conflicts.

Given the right help at the right time, many families can change and raise their children in safer and more productive ways. Training, support, counseling, and education may be the perfect solution to instigate reform when parents lack positive discipline tools, are frustrated, or come from childhoods of maltreatment themselves. In other cases, parents may not be qualified to parent, and the best action is to allow the child to begin a new life with another permanent family.

Does it mean all parents who were raised in difficult childhoods will continue the pattern in the next generation?

Emphatically, no. Many individuals raised in troubled homes do not continue the pattern of abuse or neglect they experienced. These individuals, through their own determination, counseling, or life experiences, have consciously made a choice to parent the next generation of children differently from their own childhood. In many cases it takes only the loving model of another significant adult to make a difference.

These adults make a personal commitment to use new parenting techniques and strategies to prevent regression during a time of crisis. New discipline methods must be understood, accepted, and appreciated before they are integrated into a new parenting system. Many adults raised in difficult childhoods find adult children programs helpful in learning to love and to reparent the child they once were. By reparenting and loving themselves, they are released to find patience, understanding, and love. Adults who have worked through childhood issues have found forgiveness, joy, and inner peace, which becomes a lasting gift to future generations of children. Opening that closed door from childhood, however, is a very scary process.

What types of families allow the maltreatment of children?

No one is a perfect parent, and all individuals, given the right circumstance and stress components, have some potential for abuse or neglect. Enough life complications can make anyone *"lose their cool"* or ignore parenting responsibilities for a period of time. It's a matter of degree.

Families from all socio-economic levels, educational levels, races, nationalities, and spiritual groups maltreat children. Child maltreatment does not choose a specific area of the country to manifest itself— families who abuse live in cities, the suburbs, and the country. They may have two parents or one parent. Education does not necessarily stop a parent from abusing if that parent has been raised in an abusive or neglectful situation, is under the influence of a chemical substance, or is under extreme pressure.

Parents who maltreat may lack personal support services. They may find it difficult to love and care for children or develop friends. Families may lack resources and live from situation to situation. Adults may be employed under difficult conditions and work long hours for very little income or for an abusive employer. Families may move frequently because of availability of jobs or housing. Child care may be unavailable, and children may be home alone for long periods of time. Expectations of parenting may not meet the realities. The parents may have conflicting or inconsistent styles of discipline. The child-parent relationship may be reversed with the child appearing in control. The parent may be developmentally immature—a young adolescent or a low-functioning adult. In some cases too many children have arrived too soon, or a child has arrived after the parents thought the family was raised. They may be physically or mentally ill. They may be chemically dependent. There are many reasons.

Does that mean any parent can potentially maltreat a child?

At any given time any family may experience one or more of the situations listed below. Each family is unique in its ability to cope with stress and life's problems. Just because one of the following situations is present in a family does not mean that the family is abusive or neglectful.

— A parent may forcibly intervene to protect a child or save a child's life, yet the child may sustain injury from the effort. For example, one father lifted his eighteen-month-old out of the bathtub. The child wiggled loose and was crashing head first toward the ceramic floor. The father grabbed the child's leg and jerked the child upward. The child suffered a spiral fracture normally suspected as abuse. Yet, this father saved the child from severe head and neck injuries.

— A child may suffer accidental burns, lacerations, bruises, or fractures.

— A frustrated parent may scream at a child on a particularly stressful day, or be too fatigued to offer a consistent reply.

— The heat, water, telephone, or electricity may be disconnected temporarily because a parent could not pay the bill; the next paycheck may alleviate the problem.

— A parent may have a medical problem and be temporarily unable to care for the house or children.

— The refrigerator may contain spoiled food or be empty because of a lack of money or time.

— A child may have an undiagnosed physical disability (cerebral palsy, hearing difficulty).

— A person significant to the family may be chronically ill and require specialized and intense caretaking.

— A parent may be intoxicated on a particular day as a result of a crisis.

— There may be a *"last straw"* equipment failure such as the car, washer, vacuum cleaner, plumbing.

— A parent may be experiencing the loss of a significant relationship to death, illness, accident, or divorce.

— A parent may be under economic hardship due to fire, theft, accident, unemployment.

— A child may be difficult to manage due to allergies or other organic reaction.

— A child may be abandoned by a parent in order to protect the child from further injury. This may happen in the case of mental illness relapses, seizures, or persons who are prone to violence. If the parent has no support system, the child may be safer temporarily abandoned.

Expose the "secret?" Who would dare? Everyone in the family may have felt scared, unhappy, and sad, but nobody would talk about it. We just continued living each day as it came.

The keeping of the "secret" protected the abuser and allowed the abuse to continue. Even as an adult, "the secret," still undercover, kept me locked in its silent, choking hold. As a child, I was always afraid to tell because I thought there would be more abuse, or worse yet, no one would believe me. I felt responsible for the abuse. Guilty and inadequate. Hopeless and without power. Even as an adult, I still felt dirty and "bad."

At 30, I finally risked telling a safe other adult who I knew wouldn't judge me. It was as if bread yeast was finally allowed to grow and expand. I felt such relief. I started to feel love and goodness.
Adult child of alcoholics

What about the children?

The Minnesota Mother Project has studied high risk, lower income, young urban mothers and the results of their parenting styles on their children. These parenting styles were divided into five groups: physically abusive, verbally abusive, neglectful or uncaring, psychologically unavailable (withdrawn, unemotional or unresponsive), and normal. The 200 children in the study were chosen at random without prior knowledge of whether they were abused.

At 12 months, the physically abused infants were less than half as likely as the normal infants to be securely attached emotionally to their mothers. These abused children were more prone to express anger and frustration, placing additional stress on their mothers. The children with psychologically unavailable mothers formed even weaker attachments than the abused children. By 18 months, none of the children with unresponsive mothers had formed attachments, while nearly seventy-five percent of the children of normal mothers had. These unattached children often become future maltreatment statistics.

An abuse survivor experiencing trauma is totally absorbed in surviving that trauma and lacks the option of exploring the different avenues life offers. Survival may mean blocking the pain of harsh words, avoiding the physical trauma of a blow to the face or other body parts, or numbing the shame of being sexually touched or even penetrated by a caregiver. Children repress feelings they feel are unsafe, such as anger, hurt, fear, and humiliation. These feelings are often hidden until circumstances allow them to resurface.

Children feel powerless when they are being abused. They often doubt their own feelings and believe that the abuser's behavior is correct. Childhood is the time a person is most vulnerable to emotional and psychological scarring due to trauma or maltreatment. When one's body or mind is assaulted or neglected, the heart and spirit also are wounded. Bodily

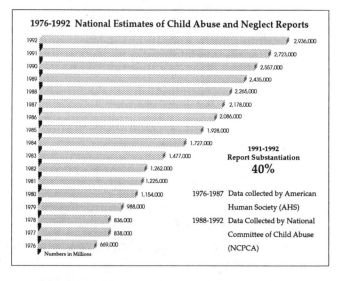

injuries heal relatively quickly and may leave visible scarring. Emotional injuries leave scars inside. These scars are less obvious and more difficult to uncover. They may never heal. James Garbarino and Anne C. Garbarino in *Emotional Maltreatment of Children* (1990) state, "*Unless emotional maltreatment is considered an essential piece of the puzzle, efforts to protect and nurture children are incomplete and doomed to failure at worst.*" As surely as one can break a child's bones, one can break a child's spirit. Society is coming to grips with the physical abuse and neglect of children, and that is a major accomplishment. But physical assault is not the only form of abuse; nor is malnourishment the only form of neglect. Emotional assault and starvation are of equal, if not greater, importance as social problems.

Maltreated children often become the go-between for significant adults so that the adults do not need to directly confront each other. The child may feel important, needed, and loved and possess an important family position, but in reality, the child is being used, confused, and abused. Fear of abandonment motivates the child and the payoff is acceptance and feeling needed. The cost to the child, however, is high—emotional abandonment. Managing the details of adult lives is not the responsibility of children. It is the parent's job to protect the child. The needs of the adults are being served at the expense of the child. The child learns to get needs met by becoming involved in the problems of others. This message sets up children for inadequate conflict resolution as adults. They become the buffers for those individuals who have difficulty facing confrontation. They absorb pain, anger, and other feelings which aren't theirs. Their friendships are based on their positions as buffers.   (Wills-Brandon 1990)

Children who have lost empowerment as a consequence of abuse have difficulty setting limits in adulthood for fear of being abandoned, rejected, or abused by those with whom they set limits. They find it very difficult to say no to others. They often continue to be used, abused, and victimized until the pain becomes intense enough to move toward exploring the origins of their roles as victims.

Can maltreatment be prevented?

Raising children can be extremely frustrating. Specific children may be more difficult to handle than a family is physically, emotionally, or financially able. The child may have an emotional, physical, or mental disability. Circumstances may have led to poor attachment to parents. Adolescents may be openly rebellious or sexually active, or may be gang members or drug users. Children may have been exposed to drugs before birth. Physical and learning disabilities may enter the picture. The child may be perceived differently by a parent or may remind a parent of a relative he or she dislikes. The parent may feel out of control and the child may be abused or neglected. Following are some dangerous feelings and signs which can lead to maltreatment. *A plea for help needs to be respected and seen as a sign of caring.*

Dangerous feelings which elevate frustration levels:

- Out-of-control.
- Troubled, anxious, nervous, or depressed.
- Frightened about what she/he might do to a child.
- Isolated with no one to turn to for help.
- Doesn't feel he/she can talk to child.
- Feels child doesn't listen.

- Inadequate or unable to cope.
- Overwhelmed and cannot find way out.
- Confused about sexual feeling toward a child.
- Feels child misbehaves on purpose.
- Feels child rarely does what is asked.

Danger signs for parents:

- Chemical dependency problem that interferes with daily functioning.
- Physical or mental illness is causing complications in parenting.
- Strikes out physically or verbally at child when angry.
- Takes frustrations out on child.

- Does not like child or feels relationship is extremely negative.
- Physically hurts child when angry or frustrated with self.
- Mistreated as a child and is repeating the past.
- Picks on one particular child.

It's not easy to reach out for help, but those who do often find caring individuals who will listen and provide assistance. If frustration levels are reaching a dangerous level, parents can contact their church, synagogue, United Way, Parents Anonymous, local crisis lines or nursery, mental health center, family or social services. *Help is often free.*

Love-Intimacy touches occur between close family members and friends and are expressions of deeper affection and caring. Included in this are hand-holding and hugs of all types. All of the touches up to and including this one are nonsexual.

Sexual-Arousal touches are ones that occur in erotic sexual contacts.

Of these five types of touch, only one is sexual. The rest indicate differing degrees of friendship and intimacy. It's sad but true that in American culture, gentle, loving touch among friends occurs at a strikingly low rate. Perhaps this is why we have bumper stickers to remind us: "Have you hugged your child today?"

(Farmer 1989, p 139-140)

What can be done?

There is no simple cure because there is no simple cause. Maltreatment of children will not decrease unless adults in society focus on families and the children for whom they care. Successful family support programs are diverse in approach, but share in prevention and empowerment of families by promoting their strengths. Lisbeth Schorr (1989) has identified certain guiding principles that are common to these programs:

— See the child in the context of the family and the family in the context of the community.

— Offer a wide range of learning opportunities in an accepting and culturally sensitive atmosphere.

— Promotes strengths and capabilities, personal growth, and empowerment in an individualized fashion.

— Remain available to families over an extended period of time.

— Take a comprehensive view of families and offer a broad spectrum of services, crossing traditional and bureaucratic boundaries.

— Be flexible in meeting individual needs.

— Provide services which are coherent and easy to use.

— Invest substantial resources in outreach.

Americans need to take a serious look at the conditions of and attitudes toward our families. Families need assurance that they will receive understanding, support, and help when they reach out and ask. They need compassion instead of criticism. Parents need to be encouraged to ask for help when they begin to question how they are dealing with their children. A plea for help must to be viewed by professionals as strength, and if help is requested, safe programs must be available for parents and children. Nonsexual touching which is gentle and caring needs to be encouraged. Sexually explicit and violent materials available to a child through literature and television need to be discouraged as they convey harmful values. Cultural diversity and ethnic heritage need to be valued and appreciated.

There's a big difference between family and child saver.

Schools can begin equipping children with independent living skills they will need as adults. Training in child development, nurturing children, communication between partners, cultural diversity, and adult job skills can be taught beginning in early elementary curriculum. Nursery and preschool programs free to low income or high risk families can be provided at public schools with parent training and curriculum offered to all students.

Resource parents and mentor families located near or within the family's community can be trained and matched to offer assistance, recreational opportunities, support, and friendship. Introduction to a resource or mentor family could begin as early as a pregnancy is discovered in a teen or young parenting couple.

Agencies and professionals need to work together instead of competing. This means combining programs, eliminating repetitive paperwork, and communicating with each other. Services need to be developed that can be implemented under time and budget limitations.

I remember so many nights, I'd lie in bed awake and pray that no one in our family would be hurt. My stomach would be tied in knots and my ears would strain to hear each word that was being said. I was always afraid. Afraid roughhousing and tickling was going to go too far. Afraid an obscene phone call would be made to a friend. Afraid someone would go to jail. Afraid the neighbors would hear. Afraid the police would come and we'd go into foster care. Afraid they would drink so much they would die. What a paradox. Five minutes later I'd wish they were dead!

All the yelling, screaming, and drinking—I never knew when I'd be pulled out of sleep by the hair to wash the supper dishes. It could be three o'clock in the morning. Once they passed out, it was safe to get up and check for burning cigarettes, dump the leftover booze down the sink, and check on the little kids. When it was safe, maybe then I'd do the dishes.

Adult child of alcoholics

What constitutes maltreatment?

There are many different opinions on what constitutes child maltreatment. Adults parenting, protecting, and treating children each carry within their own backgrounds a variety of beliefs and experiences that determine their individual perception of what abuse or neglect is and when they will intervene.

— If professionals have had no personal life experiences with overpunishment, neglect, or abuse, these individuals may misread subtle clues that could alert them to a family's cry for help. Children may remain in a home too long while help is provided over and over again to a nonresponsive family.

— If a professional's upbringing included overpunishment, or abusive or neglectful conditions, he or she may have difficulty providing a balanced assessment or adequate treatment program for families and their children. Personal agendas to save children from experiences similar to their own can lead to assumptions and unnecessary removal of a child without an adequate and complete investigation.

Regardless of the professional's background, his or her reaction may be inappropriate—leading to children who are injured or killed or families who are misinterpreted and lose their children. Destruction of families because of improper system management is tragic. Improper removal of children may be more abusive than the original maltreatment. Both children and their families need protection from system abuses.

Some basic guidelines used to determine whether an injury to a child is accidental and when it was caused by neglect:

ACCIDENT: An incident that is not likely to recur given the circumstances, AND if occurring in a licensed program, where all requirements or procedures of the program and licensing were being followed.

NEGLECT: When an event was foreseeable or likely to occur given the circumstances AND/OR proper and reasonable procedures were not followed or precautions/actions taken.

INTENTIONAL: When an event is planned that intentionally causes injury or damage to a child or other vulnerable person.

UNINTENTIONAL: When an event is unplanned and unintentionally causes injury or damage to a child or other vulnerable person. It occurs during the process of preventing further harm, i.e., catching a wet, recently bathed, slippery child and causing a leg injury, but saving the child's life or preventing worse damage by nonintervention.

THREATENED HARM: Repeated threats or harassment against a child's well-being. The child is unsure when or if an act will be carried out and maintains a state of fear.

*What constitutes abuse or neglect
in a licensed professional home is not necessarily
abuse or neglect in a primary family.*

A child picks up both sets of family rules —spoken and unspoken.

It's OK to "talk" about your feelings.

Unspoken: It's not OK to cry, get angry, or be sad. Keep your mouth shut if you are hurting emotionally or physically. Good feelings can be shown. Therefore, only good feelings are OK. The other feelings must be hidden.

Parents love and protect children.

Unspoken: Mom and Dad don't take care of themselves. Dad lets Mom emotionally abuse him. Mom lets Dad physically abuse her. Mom takes care of everyone but herself. Dad works himself to death.

You are an important individual.

Unspoken: Privacy violations in bathing or dressing are allowed. Physical or sexual abuse. Parents reading diaries, combing through drawers or closets. Listening in on phone conversations. Opening child's mail.

Children don't need written rules—they read clues.

Children who are victims may not be able to express their feelings about victimization in their families of origin until they are adults and have their own families or a sense of safety or power.

"Poor Me Victim" looks helpless, pitiful, and powerless. They whine, they complain, and they feel they just can't go on. They may become suicidal or depressed. Paradoxically, these people wield a lot of manipulative power and control in getting their needs met.

"I'll Get You Victim" looks very angry and powerful. They know they are right, that the world owes them a fair deal, and that they'll get even. They waste time, money, and energy proving people wrong or getting even. They often abuse, sue, and lose the very battles they set out to win.

Healthy adults may not always get their desires or needs met. Things may not always work out as they planned. But they communicate their needs respectfully and clearly.

Definitions and interpretations of definitions of abuse and neglect vary from individual to individual. Child abuse and neglect are typically found in a combination of two or more of the following:

NEGLECT:	An act of omission which endangers or negatively affects the general welfare of the child.
EMOTIONAL NEGLECT:	Failure to provide the nurturance or stimulation necessary for developing the child's social, intellectual, and emotional capacities.
PHYSCIAL NEGLECT:	Failure to provide for a child's adequate care and protection in the areas of food, clothing, shelter, school, and medical attention, or to reasonably provide for a child's safety.
ABUSE:	An act of commission which negatively affects the general welfare of a child.
EMOTIONAL ABUSE:	A pattern of verbal assaults or coercive measures against a child which is destructive to a child's sense of self-worth. Consistently ignoring the child's cries, needs for physical or verbal affection, or treating the child as "invisible."
PHYSICAL ABUSE:	Intentional physical injury to a child by a caretaker. This includes hitting, shaking, slapping, shoving, kicking, burning, twisting, pulling, choking, confinement with ropes, locking in small confined spaces, or any other cruel or unusual punishment.
SEXUAL ABUSE:	The exposure of a child to sexual stimulation inappropriate for a child's age, level of psychological development, and role in the family.
RITUAL ABUSE:	The exposure of children to bizarre and physically unsafe ritual practices which may include combinations of sexual, physical, and emotional abuse.

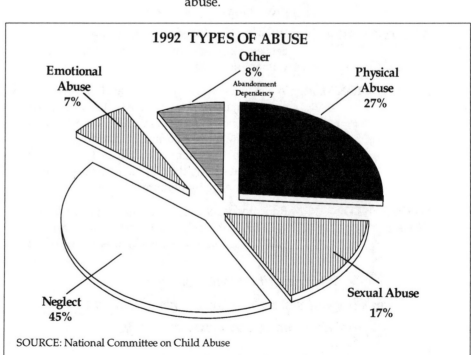

1992 TYPES OF ABUSE

Emotional Abuse 7%

Other 8% Abandonment Dependency

Physical Abuse 27%

Neglect 45%

Sexual Abuse 17%

SOURCE: National Committee on Child Abuse

The Minnesota Department of Human Services Social Services Manual lists the following as definitions of child maltreatment severity.

FATAL:	The child has died. Allegations where the death of a child is subsequently ruled as due to intended, natural, or accidental cause. A fatality can be the result of neglect, abuse, or both or neither.
LIFE THREATENING OR SERIOUS INJURY:	Injury that may not have lasting serious consequences, but that would be life threatening at the time of or immediately following injury or injuries, including limb or rib fractures that may result in long-term disability or deformity.
MODERATE OR NON-SERIOUS INJURY:	Injuries which may or may not require medical attention but would not have the apparent serious affects of cases (above).
POSSIBLE INJURY:	Pain has been inflicted or there are symptoms of an injury, but the injury itself is not yet identified.
EXPOSURE TO THREATENING OR DANGEROUS CONDITIONS:	Parents or caretakers fail to protect a child from dangerous conditions either through neglect or willfully, whether or not harm is incurred and whether or not such exposure induces stress.
APPARENT HEALTH IMPAIRMENT: (PHYSICAL, MENTAL, or EMOTIONAL)	The child appears to have a physical, mental, or emotional impairment which might reasonably be attributed to abuse or neglect in the judgment of the child protection worker.

What must be evaluated is whether the maltreatment is accidental, unintentional, intentional, or caused by neglect; whether the situation is an isolated case, situational, repetitive, or chronic; whether the level of abuse or neglect is inappropriate, borderline, extreme, or criminal.

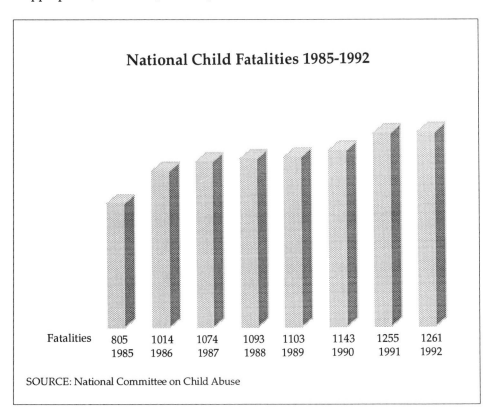

National Child Fatalities 1985-1992

Fatalities	805	1014	1074	1093	1103	1143	1255	1261
	1985	1986	1987	1988	1989	1990	1991	1992

SOURCE: National Committee on Child Abuse

Medical professionals and child protection workers ask the following questions regarding potential physical abuse injuries:

Are injuries inconsistent with the explanation offered?

Are injuries inconsistent with the age of the child?

Are the patterns of the injuries consistent with abuse?

What is the reaction of parents during questioning?

Does parent's explanation remain consistent?

Some basic guidelines to determine whether a situation is an isolated case, situational, repetitive, or chronic, and what type of services could be provided:

ISOLATED CASE:	Adult in authority mishandles an unusual crisis situation which perpetuates emotional or physical trauma to the child. One time occurrence. Adult in authority seeks help to alleviate any future problems, or help may be suggested by others involved.	Additional parent training or counseling may be needed. This may be provided in family or individual support groups, reference materials, or classes.
SITUATIONAL:	Initial crisis reaction with no or limited knowledge of other ways to manage the situation. Individual may also have misinterpreted information from previous parenting program or counselors and need clarification. Adult may or may not seek help on own, but usually understands the need to change and willingly does so.	Additional parent training and/or counseling needed. This may be provided in support group, reference materials, or classes. Personal one-on-one services may be necessary to develop a trusting and supportive relationship to help the family.
REPETITIVE:	Reaction with no or limited knowledge of other ways to manage the situation. Adult does not initiate help, and even with additional knowledge, the individual is unable or unwilling to change response. Adults in repetitive abuse or neglect roles may feel righteous, resentful, hostile, or harassed when services are offered or provided. Or they may become further withdrawn or depressed.	Additional parent training and counseling needed. Support services and programs provided for children. Personal one-on-one services, supportive relationships, and additional help to the family. Children or specific child may need out-of-home care to protect child and/or establish need for change in the family.
CHRONIC:	A situation of abuse or neglect which does not improve even with additional training or services. These adults may be involved in substance abuse, have attachment disorders, be mentally ill, low functioning, or exhibit fetal alcohol effects. Parent-child conflict may be unable to be resolved. The child may remain outside of parental controls or the child may be delinquent and unable to provide care or controls.	Reassessment of all services provided and failed or rejected. Little or no progress in family situation is made even after a significant period of time. Children are often in out-of-home care. Additional parent training may be provided or parental rights may be terminated and children become a ward of the state and available for adoption.

Some basic guidelines to determine the level of reaction by parent, and what type of services should be provided:

INAPPROPRIATE: A response that is inappropriate but is unlikely to occur again. The child is well taken care of by the adult and the adult is genuinely concerned for the child's well-being.

Parent questions and responses and initiates help or support for self, the child, and/or the family system.

BORDERLINE: A pattern of established discipline which is inappropriate given the age or development of the child. These discipline patterns may have been culturally established and handed down from generation to generation. Parents may believe they are doing it for the child's own good and are committed to their parenting style.

Parent does not question discipline methods used on children, but does not have other tools to use and is reacting from generational or cultural discipline responses.

EXTREME: A pattern of established child maltreatment which is inappropriate given the age or development of the child. Parent may say, "It's for child's own good." Parent exerts coercive power and cruelty.

Parent does not question discipline methods used on children. Additional training and discipline tools have been provided, yet parent continues to use inappropriate techniques.

CRIMINAL: Each state has different statutes and interpretations of what constitutes criminal abuse. Included in many state statutes are:
— Sexual misconduct by an adult with a child under age 16. Or willful neglect to protect a child from sexual maltreatment when they are aware it is occurring.
— Physical injury inflicted intentionally by an adult upon a child.
— Willful deprivation of food, clothing, shelter, and health care when provision is available, and deprivation substantially harms child.
— Intentionally causing or permitting a child to be placed in a situation likely to substantially harm the child's physical or mental health.

Parent has demonstrated behavior dangerous to the life, health, and/or safety of a child. This behavior assessment is handled by specialized child abuse teams and law enforcement departments and is prosecuted by the criminal courts according to the penalities imposed by written law. Counseling, treatment, probation, fines, community service, termination of parental rights, or imprisonment may be sanctioned.

I used to close my eyes and grow very, very small so no one could find me . . . or hurt me. It was safe being so small. I could set aside any abuse I was experiencing and let my other self experience it. When I grew bigger and put myself together again, I could walk out the door with a smile on my face. No one ever had to know the truth that way . . .

Not even me!
Adult child of
sexual abuse

Disassociation in children is not "crazy" behavior when they live in abnormal or abusive situations. It is a normal and healthy survival response.

In adults, this means there are most likely periods of time not remembered or blocked in childhood. Adult Children of Abusive Parents Programs can help heal adults who have grown up in abusive or neglectful childhoods.

What does a care provider need to know?

One of the first steps in helping maltreated out-of-home children is learning to separate the symptoms of grieving from the symptoms of child abuse and neglect. Foster and adoptive children have loss, separation, grief, and attachment issues which may affect behavior. Abusive or neglectful behavior indicator conditions may actually be only a mask of grief. Untangling this web of experiences and emotions is difficult. Skill, intuition, and compassion are taxed when working through these issues. Children in out-of-home care may have very complex histories—a physically abused child could also have been emotionally mistreated, and a sexually abused child may have been neglected. Knowing what experiences these children actually lived through and their perception of those experiences is a journey into uncharted territory.

What is emotional abuse and neglect?

MINNESOTA STATUTE 626.556 Subd. 2
*(k) **Mental injury** means an injury to the psychological capacity or emotional stability of a child as evidenced by an observable and substantial impairment in the child's ability to function within a normal range of performance and behavior with due regard to the child's culture.*
*(l) **Threatened injury** means a statement, overt act, condition, or status that represents a substantial risk of physical or sexual abuse or mental injury.*

Emotional abuse or neglect is damaging. A child may never be injured physically or neglected by parents, yet may be emotionally abused or neglected. Much cruelty and power can be wielded with words or the absence of words. The lack of consistent nurturing, protection, and guidance leaves a child feeling isolated, abandoned, fearful, and in pain. The child enters adulthood feeling inadequate and of little value.

Adults who emotionally abuse children are unable to attend to the child's emotional needs. Parents may have poor self-esteem and a history of emotional abuse in childhood. If adults have not been touched or loved as children, how do they learn to touch and love their own child? If emotional pain was never allowed expression, can they allow expression from their own children? The child they thought would provide the love and care they did not receive now demands care which they are incapable of providing. The expression of feelings from their own children may awaken their own repressed feelings. They perpetuate emotional abuse into the next generation by ignoring their own needs.

Many adults were not allowed to be children. They may have grown up in damaging role reversal situations and provided emotional support to their parents. Adults are more powerful than children and to include them in personal problems invites children to share power they are not emotionally equipped to handle. It is the parent's job to handle adult pain and problems. Adults need to seek empathy from other adults and not expect children to care for their emotional needs or responsibilities.

A pattern of verbal assaults or coercive measures against a child destroys a child's sense of self-worth. Belittling, blaming, or sarcasm breaks down a child's belief in self. Unpredictable responses bring discord to a child's life, leaving the child confused and on constant guard. Disassociation occurs in children who are emotionally abused, just as with children who are physically, ritualistically, or sexually abused.

Keep Child Abuse Out of Children's Sports

Three out of four young children will not be playing team sports when they are teenagers.

Too often, bad experiences outweigh good ones.

— *Not enough playing time.*

— *Criticism from parents and coaches.*

— *Playing sports was no longer fun.*

— *Too much emphasis on winning.*

For more information write or call:
PACS
1-800-748-4843
3160 Pinebrook Road
Park City, Utah 84060

Emotional abuse is common
in children's sports.

Child abuse in sports can be defined as any action taken by an adult which results in direct or indirect physical and/or emotional harm to children. Child abuse can be either active or passive.

ACTIVE CHILD ABUSE *occurs when a child (or children) directly experiences harsh or abusive actions from parents or coaches which result in feelings toward lowered self-worth, worthlessness, fear, and/or failure.*

PASSIVE CHILD ABUSE *occurs when a child (or children) observes another child (or children) being the recipient of harsh or abrasive actions by parents or coaches.*

How an adult can emotionally abuse or neglect a child:

VERBAL ABUSE is the most commonly occurring abuse in children's sports (and families). Verbal abuse includes any ridicule or put downs such as: name-calling, harmful comments regarding performance, swearing at players or game officials, and comments to demean a child's integrity.

> *Inappropriate or shaming statements* devalue a child's sense of self. Shame is a painful feeling of having lost the respect of others. Many children coming into foster care have existed with shaming statements being a part of their daily lives.

> *Samples of shaming blame or comparison statements:*

- *You're . . . always doing that . . . slow. . . clumsy.*
- *Why can't you be more like . . .*
- *You're going to (wear, do, eat, say, buy, bring)* **that***?*
- *Can't you do anything right?*
- *You can't feel that way! or Don't even think that!*
- *I love you, leave me alone.*
- *Don't think you can come back here if it doesn't work out.*
- *That's really a stupid thing . . . (to do! to think!)*
- ***SHAME ON YOU!***

- *You're so . . . (fat, skinny, stupid!)*
- *Get going, you slowpoke!*
- *Do I have to do everything for you?*
- *Can't you use your brain?*
- *Look at you. You are always such a mess.*
- *Shut up you little . . !*
- *C'mon now. You can't be that (angry, sad, scared, etc.)*
- *Why should I tell you? You didn't ask me right away.*

> *Humiliation of a Child.* Hurts the dignity of a child by causing him or her to appear foolish, unacceptable, or inadequate. Embarrassment in front of peers is devastating to a child. Calling a child names, belittling, or persistent teasing can leave scars of insecurity, apathy, and low self-worth. Public humiliation of a child can avalanche into untold difficulties for the child.

EMOTIONAL ABUSE of children in sports means having unrealistic goals and expectations for children. Examples include: winning every game, scoring the most points, being the best player on the team, playing without errors. Emotional abuse also includes keeping children from participating in activities due to limits or undeveloped skills.

> *Extreme inconsistency.* Child never gets a clear sense of how things work between people because the parent changes behavior so dramatically that the child never knows what to expect — anger or warmth. The child learns to remain constantly on guard with chameleon-like responses as a parent's mood changes.

At thirty five, I still shook whenever I was alone with my father. While he never physically or sexually abused me, his voice humiliated and scared me to death.
Adult child of emotional abuse

In loving families, a child grows up protected and validated as a worthwhile individual.

In abusive families, the very protector of the child may also be the perpetrator or the ally of the perpetrator. The validation of worth is left up to the child.

For parents who grew up emotionally neglected or abused, no one wiped the tears or supported them when they faced emotional pain, yet they may have been expected to provide that type of support to the very people who were not supporting and protecting them. Their lives were touched not with loving words and caresses, but with yelling or withdrawal.

Rejection is when a parent denies a child love, attention, or affection. The child is discarded and seen as worthless. The child feels isolated and abandoned.

Chronic coldness. Demonstration of warmth, understanding, or support is void or limited. The child cannot learn what emotions are and how to live with them without models. The parent is unable or unwilling to acknowledge the existence of the child and care for the child's emotional needs.

Lack of empathy. Empathy is the ability to be sensitive and responsive to another's feelings and needs. It is the ability to walk in another's shoes and feel what the other feels. Empathy allows a person to share in another's feelings without becoming enmeshed in them or giving pity. Parents who lack empathy may view children as objects to exert control over, without concern for the child's spiritual or emotional needs.

Expecting more of a child than the child is capable of giving. Placing unreasonable demands on a child. A five-year-old cannot be expected to responsibly care for a two-year-old sibling. A teenager does not have the maturity to handle details of Mom's or Dad's new romance. A child does not need to become the go-between in parent conflicts or take care of an adult's emotional needs.

Children who are emotionally maltreated may exhibit the following behaviors:

Physically

- Speech disorders (stuttering, failure to speak)
- Delayed physical development
- Failure to thrive
- Asthma, severe allergies
- Colitis, ulcers, stomach problems
- Disassociation

Behaviorally

- Habit disorders (sucking, rocking, picking, banging)
- Anti-social, destructive
- Pre- or adolescent delinquency
- Behavior extremes
- Self-destructive—substance abuse, suicide attempts

Children who exhibit these behaviors are not necessarily emotionally maltreated. There may be other organic or situational causes. If a child in your care does demonstrate these behaviors, maintain careful documentation and seek professional advice if a pattern emerges or a behavior is displayed over a long period of time.

What is neglect or endangerment of a child?

MINNESOTA STATUTE 609.378 Subd. 1. Persons guilty of neglect or endangerment. The following people are guilty of neglect or endangerment of a child and may be sentenced to imprisonment for not more than one year or to payment of a fine of not more than $3,000 or both.

(a) *Neglect.*

(1) *A parent, legal guardian, or caretaker who willfully deprives a child of necessary food, clothing, shelter, health care, or supervision appropriate to the child's age, when the parent, guardian, or caretaker is reasonably able to make the necessary provisions and the deprivation substantially harms the child. If a parent, guardian, or caretaker responsible for the child's care in good faith selects and depends upon spiritual means or prayer for treatment or care of disease or remedial care of the child, this treatment or care is "health care" for purposes of this clause.*

(2) *A parent, legal guardian, or caretaker who knowingly permits the continuing physical or sexual abuse of a child is guilty of neglect of a child.*

(b) ***Endangerment.***
*A parent, legal guardian or caretaker who endangers the child's person or health
by intentionally causing or permitting a child to be placed in a situation likely to
substantially harm the child's physical or mental health or cause the child's death
is guilty of child endangerment. This paragraph does not prevent a parent,
legal guardian, or caretaker from causing or permitting a child to engage in activities
that are appropriate to the child's age, stage of development, and experience, or from
selecting health care as defined in Subdivision 1, paragraph (a).*

The neglected child is the child whose basic needs for health and survival are not
being met by parents or caretakers. Neglectful conditions may be the cause of
some of the most harm to children and represent the primary cause of death in
almost half of the child fatalities reported. (Daro & Mitchell, 1989) Neglect can
permanently damage every aspect of a child's physical and emotional
development.

Neglect is more prevalent, but less disclosed, than abuse. People are more
reluctant to report it because it is harder to define and easier to ignore. When
neglect is reported it is often reported against low income families because the
family situation may be visible to the community. Yet, educated and professional
families may also be neglectful of their children through their lack of availability,
nurturing, or providing.

Low income families may be observed as having characteristics of neglect
without actual neglect occurring. If a family lives in poverty the judgment of
neglect versus inability to provide must be heavily weighed. Amidst abysmal
conditions—broken windows, leaking roofs, non-functioning bathrooms,
rodents, insects, holes in the walls exposing wiring—poor families may be
providing unconditional love, nurturing, and care to their children. The children
are secure and feel safe, cared for, and loved. Removal of their children—the only
valuable possession they have—would be devastating.

*Joan became pregnant as a teenager. Her young husband, Homer, found
employment, and the couple began to manage their life. Neither grandparent
approved of the early marriage—they were on their own. In the seventh month
of Joan's pregnancy, Emily was born. Medical bills soared. The young family
reached out for medical assistance and a home nurse was provided. Emily
struggled and thrived, but maintained a very small stature. Joan, reserved and
quiet, had always been willing to accept help. She didn't venture out to make
friends or try new things because she was unsure of her abilities. As a small
girl she had been placed in special education classes for children with learning
disabilities. Homer, on the other hand, was a self-starter, a wheeler-dealer when
things got tough. He didn't want to have to ask for help and didn't appreciate
help when it was offered. He wanted to make a success of himself and care for
his family. Within the next five years three more children were born. Joan loved
and cared for her children, and although she and Homer had little money, they
loved and enjoyed their children.*

*Emily began kindergarten; she was still small and frail. Her kindergarten
teacher was concerned. Emily appeared withdrawn and did not interact with
other children. Social services became involved. Joan was compliant with social
services, maintained a quiet demeanor, and appeared to accept help. Homer was
agitated. He had become a manager of 60 men, had a company car, and was finally
making enough income to consider relocating his family in the spring into their
own home. Homer did not like the social worker and was not afraid to vent his
feelings against intervention in his family. There was nothing there for them to
find; he insisted he was providing for the family.*

*In February, four armed policemen removed the four children to emergency shelter
and then distributed them to four different foster homes. The social worker was con-*

*Sometimes growing
up means doing
something for
yourself that breaks
someone's heart.*

Including your own.

*Confronting abusers
directly usually
results in anger and
defensiveness. The
viewpoint of the abuser
is very different from
the viewpoint of the
victim or the witness.*

*Acknowledgement of
abusive actions is the
beginning of healing
for the abuser.*

*Admittance of wrong
doing and sincere
apology play a
significant role
in the healing
of the victim.*

cerned about Homer's ill temper and worried the children could be harmed. Joan, in distress, went into labor early and gave birth to a tiny little boy. Homer, devastated at losing his children, lost his job, too. With no money, they lost their rented duplex. The new baby was moved into a foster home. Joan and Homer lived on the street and in church basements. Crumbled and broken, neither Joan nor Homer has been able to pick up the pieces and start over. There weren't any pieces left.

On the other hand, a well appointed house located in the wealthier part of a city may appear to be a beacon of health and quality care. Television sets, stereos, TV dinners, and junk food, however, may take the place of parental nurturing. The parents may be absent to nurture their child—work long hours, entertain friends, or are frequently traveling.

Alcohol or substance abuse often is involved when neglect is present. Other factors, however, also may come into play. Parents may have chemical imbalances or limited intelligence, which interfere with their ability to parent. Some parents may be mentally ill and exhibit irrational or bizarre behaviors during changes in medication or because of allergic reactions. Other parents may leave a child unattended because of ignorance or depression and forget to tend to the children's physical needs. Some parents may simply not have the resources to meet the living standard expected by the American majority.

Caution must be used in judging neglect
versus inability to provide.
Love, nurturing, and adequate parenting
can flourish admidst poverty.

An adult who physically neglects children may:

- Be inattentive to physical needs such as food, shelter, safety, health, medical attention.
- Have limited knowledge of how to care for children's physical needs.
- Have poor self-esteem.
- Appear indifferent to child.
- Have limited intelligence.

- Abuse alcohol or other substances to the point of interfering with daily functioning.
- Leave child unattended because of ignorance or depression.
- Seem apathetic or depressed.
- Have experienced physical neglect in childhood.
- Exhibit irrational or bizarre behavior.

Neglect (or lack of resources) in children can be suspected when:

PHYSICAL INDICATORS

- Poor skin hygiene, consistently dirty, severe body odor.
- Severe insect infestation—lice, pinworms, fleas, etc.
- Failure of child to thrive physically, mentally, emotionally, or socially.
- Always tired, falls asleep in class, listless.
- Lack of medical attention.
- Children who need prosthetics such as eyeglasses, hearing aids, or corrective shoes who, after the need is established, don't receive proper help.
- Lack of medical attention for obvious infections or skin rashes.

BEHAVIORAL INDICATORS

- Begs or steals food or money from classmates/friends.
- States there is no one at home to provide care.
- Is frequently absent from school.
- Reluctance to go home or leave after school.
- Lacks adult supervision.
- Excessively seeks out and "pesters" adults for attention and affection. Clinging, extreme dependence on teacher, counselor, or other adults.
- Child refuses to eat or eats little and is very frail.

- Chronically inadequate dental care or the lack of necessary immunizations.
- Prolonged pain, diarrhea, vomiting, or respiratory disease not taken care of.
- Abandonment, lack of living quarters.
- Distended stomach or emaciated body, graying skin color, sunken face.
- Anti-social behavior such as aggression-disruption, bossiness, bully behavior.
- Child gorges when food is available and hides or pockets food for future use. Hoards food.
- Consistently has inappropriate clothing for the weather.
- Sudden, unexplained behavior changes or drops in performance.

Neglect in a home can be suspected if the following conditions in the home exist:

LIVING CONDITIONS

- Unsanitary conditions in child's residence (garbage, excrement).
- Sleeping arrangements cold, dirty, otherwise inadequate.
- Exposure to unhealthy or dangerous conditions.
- Lack of heating in residence.
- Fire or building hazards.
- Infestation of insects or rodents.

NUTRITIONAL CONDITIONS

- Meals not prepared, children snack when hungry.
- Poor nutritional quality of food.
- Spoiled food.

SUPERVISION

- Supervision by other children and adults not available.
- Child left alone in house or unsupervised (left in car, street) for any period of time in which injuries occur or when the child's health or person is endangered. *Most police officials consider unattended children under twelve at risk.* However, the maturity of the child and child's access to the parent is always an issue. There is significant difference between a twelve-year-old who is left alone infrequently, who can reach his parents by phone, has food and shelter, has neighbors or caring others close by, and who feels confident about being able to care for himself and a twelve-year-old who is left alone for extended periods of time and is without emotional or physical resources to cope, who does not know where his parents are, can't sleep, loses his appetite and is afraid and anxious. If either of these children is caring for a smaller child, additional supervision issues surface.

Infant medical neglect is another serious type of neglect. It can be alleged when a child is prenatally exposed to a controlled substance used by the mother for nonmedical purposes, as evidenced by withdrawal symptoms in the child at birth, results of toxicology tests performed on the mother at delivery or the child at birth, or medical effects of developmental delays during a child's first year of life that medically indicate prenatal exposure to a controlled substance. Neglect can also be alleged when parents withhold medical treatment from a disabled infant with a life-threatening condition.

Children learn how to be parents from their parents, and the legacy of neglect is passed from generation to generation in the same way abuse often is transferred. Neglected children have poor self-esteem. They grow up believing that they must be worth very little or their parents would care more about them. Their self-esteem is eroded further by their belief that, since their own parents did not love them, then no one else could possible love them either. Neglected children may be in trouble in the community at an early age because their parents do not teach standards of behavior or provide supervision.

All maltreatment of children is damaging to the well-being of the children and society. Child neglect is as serious as child abuse, and it must receive the same concern and attention. Caution must be exercised, however, in discerning between inability to provide and neglect.

Children in out-of-home care may try to reproduce the conflict which brought them into the foster care system in the first place. By reproducing the situation, they can prove to themselves that they are bad, and it is not their parents who are bad.

If my parents got rid of me and they love me, then these "new" parents will probably do the same thing. My parents must hate me and these parents will, too.

The more placements a child has experienced, the higher the risk that he or she will expect or provoke maltreatment.

The child may feel . . .

"Since I know they won't want me sooner or later, I might as well get it over with before I start liking this place."

or . . .
"I'll reject you before you reject me!"

(McFadden & Ryan 1991)

What is physical abuse?

MINNESOTA STATUTE 626.556 Subd. 2
(d) Physical Abuse means any physical or mental injury, or threatened injury inflicted by a person responsible for the child's care on a child other than by accidental means, or any physical or mental injury that cannot reasonably be explained by the child's history of injuries, or any aversive or deprivation procedures that have not been authorized under section 245.825.

Some behaviors are difficult to manage, and given the right amount of stress or a difficult situation, all parents have the potential to react in ways they regret later. Abuse is a matter of degree. The problem with defining abuse is clarifying exactly what is abusive and what is acceptable in disciplining a child. Parenting techniques such as hair pulling, yanking, screaming, pinching, or public humiliation may be hard to tolerate, but are considered by many to be justifiable forms of parent-child interactions. These behaviors may or may not qualify as abusive depending on the level of intensity, situation, or frequency of actions.

> ## Abusive parents make promises to themselves they cannot keep.

Donna was unable to keep her promise. This was her third visit to the emergency room this month with her two year old son. As he sat quietly beside her, his eye was swelling shut and a large, ugly, bright red, swollen bruised area appeared. Donna told the nurse that he fell, hitting the edge of the coffee table. She remembered her mother saying the same about her.

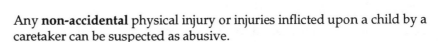

Mary was also unable to keep her promise. She called the doctor, frantically explaining that her son had poured a pan of hot soup from the stove all over his stomach. "They won't suspect I did it," she thought. When she was a child, her mother scalded her by pouring hot water down her legs. (Magid 1989)

Any **non-accidental** physical injury or injuries inflicted upon a child by a caretaker can be suspected as abusive.

John rushed eight-month-old Adam into the emergency room with a head injury. Adam's forehead was bleeding; he was hardly breathing. The injury appeared to be the result of a blow to the head with a blunt object.

John told the doctor he had slipped and fallen on Adam. The injury and the story did not match.

Areas of injury to skin suspected to be non-accidental injury:

INFLICTED	ACCIDENTAL
Buttocks	Forehead
Ears and neck	Hips (iliac crests)
Genitalia	Lower arms
Sides of face	Prominences of spine
Trunk	Shins
Upper arms	Under chin
Upper anterior legs	

Potential child abuse physical indicators:

BRUISES AND WELTS

FACIAL BRUISES ON AN INFANT

BRUISES IN AN UNUSUAL PATTERN that might reflect the pattern of the instrument used or human bite marks. Common instruments include, but are not limited to:

Belts	Electrical cords	Hot burners	Golf clubs
Kitchen utensils	Garden hose	Hot water	Hands/feet
Hairbrush	Teeth	Ropes	Broom
Flyswatter	Paddle	Board	Pipe
Coat hanger	Belt buckle	Shoe	Switch/stick

BRUISES ON THE POSTERIOR SIDE OF THE CHILD'S BODY. Lower back bruises need to be considered more severe because of the potential damage to the kidneys. (Birth marks on all children, or Mongolian or sport marks on children of color, are not to be considered bruises.)

CLUSTERED BRUISES indicating repeated contact with the hand or an instrument.

EXTENSIVE BRUISES covering a large area of the body.

BRUISES AT VARIOUS STAGES OF HEALING The appearance of bruises differs at various stages of healing and the look of a bruise will vary depending on the injury, depth, and location. Bruises show more color and appear more quickly on loose, soft tissue such as around the face versus on the shin area.

0-2 days	—	Area swollen, bright red, tender
1-5 days	—	Blue, red, purple
5-7 days	—	Green
7-10 days	—	Yellow
10-14 days	—	Brown and fading
14 days +	—	Clear

BURNS: *Any burn on a child under one year should be questioned, along with burns on the inside of the arms or legs, on the soles of the feet, or on the back.*

IMMERSION BURNS indicate dunking or forced immersion in a hot liquid. These are sometimes called "stocking burns" because of the distinct boundary where the burn stops on the hands, feet, or buttocks. "Doughnut" burns get their name from the doughnut shaped pattern on the buttocks resulting from focibly holding a child's buttocks in a tub of hot liquid.

ROPE BURNS indicate confinement.

DRY BURNS indicate that a child has been forced to sit upon a hot surface or had a hot surface applied to skin.

PATTERN BURNS come from instruments such as a cigarette, or a household implement such as an electric iron, grate of an electric heater, curling iron.

SPLATTERING OF HOT LIQUIDS indicates intentional pouring or splattering of hot liquid on a child.

LACERATIONS AND ABRASIONS

ON THE LIP, EYE ,OR ANY PORTION OF AN INFANT'S FACE.

TEARS IN THE GUM TISSUE from forced feeding.

ANY LACERATION OR ABRASION TO EXTERNAL GENITALIA.

Once violence starts, it generally doesn't stop without intervention.

Violence begets violence.
It is a vicious circle.

"I lie in bed at night, thinking of how I can get even. How I can hurt back. I go over and over the letter I'll write. The act I'll carry out. I've tried making deals with God—take away my feelings of being trapped, out-of-control, and defeated."
Teen in care

HEAD INJURIES

HEMORRHAGING BENEATH THE SCALP from vigorous hair pulling.

ABSENCE OF HAIR from hair pulling.

HEMORRHAGING BENEATH THE OUTER COVERING OF THE BRAIN from shaking or hitting.

RETINAL HEMORRHAGE OR DETACHMENT from shaking.

JAW AND NASAL FRACTURES from hitting or squeezing of face.

SHATTERED EGG SHELL PATTERN OF SKULL from being thrown against wall.

There was no doubt in the doctor's mind that this was a case of abuse. John appeared guilty, though he denied the abuse and stuck to his story regarding Adam's injury. Adam died—child abuse homicide.

The investigation discovered the real story . . .
John had arrived home from his third shift job to a very wide awake Adam. Tired and needing sleep, he put the portable television on a shelf above Adam's crib, turned on Sesame Street, and handed Adam a bottle. John fell asleep, only to wake up to the television on top of Adam, the cord in Adam's hand, and blood covering the crib. He rushed Adam to the hospital, making up a story he thought the hospital would believe. John was found negligent, not physically abusive.

INTERNAL INJURIES

BLOOD CLOTS IN THE SMALL INTESTINE from hitting or kicking in the middle of the abdomen.

RUPTURE OF THE VEIN CARRYING BLOOD FROM THE ABDOMEN AND THE LOWER EXTREMITIES from hitting or kicking.

INFLAMMATION OF THE LINING OF THE ABDOMINAL CAVITY from a ruptured organ from kicking or hitting.

SKELETAL INJURIES to bones caused by twisting or pulling. *Any fracture on a child under two years should be questioned.*

SPIRAL FRACTURES that wrap or twist around the bone shaft.

CORNER FRACTURES OF LONG BONE (METAPHYSEAL) a kind of splintering at the end of the bone.

EPIPHYSEAL SEPARATION a separation of the growth center at the end of the bone from the rest of the shaft.

PERIOSTEAL ELEVATION a detachment of the periostium from the shaft of the bone with associated hemorrhaging between the periostium and the shaft.

(Material adapted from Module 1, Child Abuse and Neglect an Overview, by the San Francisco Child Abuse Council, 4093 24th Street, San Francisco, California 94114)

I remember being very small, and a hand so large that it covered my whole head swooped down and cuffed me and I flew against the wall. I had only opened my mouth to state my opinion.

For the next twenty years I could not open my mouth when conflict arose. Each time I went to open my mouth I got dizzy and sick to my stomach.

After a year in counseling I finally was able to accept the truth and begin to deal with anger and conflict in healthy and assertive ways.
Adult child of physical abuse

Physical abuse behavioral indicators in children:

- Has learning problems that cannot be attributed to specific physical or psychological causes.
- Shows sudden changes in behavior or school performance. Comes to school early, stays late, and does not want to go home.
- Lying and stealing which gets worse as the child grows.
- Inability to distinguish between reality and fantasy.
- Severe depression or anxiety, discontent.
- Self-mutilation, suicide attempts.
- Fearful of new experiences or people.
- Inability to make friends, inordinate shyness, poor self-esteem.
- Lack of reasonable concern for own safety, well-being, inability to recognize danger.
- Excessive masturbation in small children.
- School failure, phobia, trauma.
- Complains of soreness, moves uncomfortably.
- Alcohol or drug abuse.
- Has not received help for physical or medical problems brought to the parent's attention.
- Is always watchful, as though preparing for something bad to happen. Cowers when adult raises hand.
- Is overly compliant, an over-achiever, or overly responsible.
- Excessive fear of failure or making a mistake.
- Excessive fear of being touched, of males, or of going home.
- Adolescent pregnancy.
- Abnormal fear of getting hurt.
- Unwillingness to do things for self or make own decisions.
- Encopresis, enuresis, persistent bedwetting beyond age four or five.
- Night terrors, excessive fears, anxiety.
- Repeated running away.
- Wears clothing inappropriate of weather to cover areas of body.
- Sexual acting out, prostitution.

These behaviors are possible indicators of abuse. Children who are not abused may also exhibit these behaviors from time to time.

Child abuse laws are meant to protect children and stop abusive parents from continuing to abuse. Medical personnel are on alert and mandated to discover abusive situations. Not all injuries to children are a result of abuse by or neglect from the parent: many are accidental or unintentional. Injured children need immediate care.

If an injury occurs to a child, medical attention must be sought immediately, and caretakers should be truthful in telling how the injury happened. The laws are meant to protect children not to prosecute innocent or caring parents.

What is adult-child sexual abuse and exploitation?

There are two types of sexual abuse—direct and indirect. Direct sexual abuse, as opposed to indirect sexual abuse, is intentional. Its purpose fulfills the sexual needs of the adult, not the nurturing and affectional needs of the child. Both types of abuse affect the lives of the individuals involved. Many people have a number of misconceptions about what exactly constitutes sexual abuse.

Sexual abuse is any sexual contact, ranging from exposure, fondling, and oral sex, to sexual intercourse, incest, and rape between an adult and child aged 16 and under, or a vulnerable adult (victim) by a person in authority. Direct sexual abuse takes on many forms and in some cases, disguises.

The following are examples of direct sexual abuse:

- Exposure to pornographic movies or magazines by an older person.
- Inappropriate touching, hugging, kissing, or dancing with an older person which feels wrong, bad, scary, or icky.

A child growing up with sexual abuse may learn . . .

. . . *Sexual abuse is an acceptable way families interrelate.*

. . . *Protectors are also abusers.*

. . . *You must always please people to win their approval.*

. . . *In order to be close to someone, you need to be sexual.*

. . . *Maybe if you are very good you can avoid abuse.*

. . . *Self-worth comes from sexual worth.*

. . . *Individuals have no rights to their bodies and they cannot say "no."*

. . . *"Bad" children are sexual. "Good" children are not, so they must be bad.*

. . . *The child must fulfill the needs of the adult.*

. . . *They are incapable of fixing, stopping, or controlling the abuse, so it is better to go along with it.*

These are distorted, harmful, and not true! The children live with the lie.

- Exposure by an older person to adult sexual activities, such as acts of sex, sexual games, bars, strip joints, adult book stores, prostitution.
- Being masturbated or being used for masturbation.
- Being penetrated vaginally or anally with fingers or other implements.
- Being forced or seduced into performing oral sex, anal sex, or intercourse.
- Rape as an adult or a child is abusive.
- Using sex acts as a way of nurturing a child.
- Setting children up to believe since the act of sex was pleasurable, the offenders involved were not in the wrong.
- Being told not to tell.
- Being fondled or touched inappropriately under the guise of bathing, lap sitting, having clothes tucked in, while being put to bed.
- Being fondled or touched sexually while being tickled or roughhousing.
- Being forced or encouraged to act out sexually with other children.

(Wills-Brandon 1990)

Sexual abuse often begins with violation of emotional and personal boundaries. In an emotionally violated relationship, the child's association with the adult reaches an intimacy level normally reserved for adults. Sometimes adults turn to abusing children to fulfill a need for closeness, personal sexual gratification, exerting power over another, or control. In order to abuse children they must have both access and space for the opportunity. Most sexual abuse is a planned event by the abuser. Children are talked into the *"secret"* or *"game"* with special attention, favors, or bribes. Under the guise of support, friendliness, and kindness, the child is violated. The assailant rarely has to use force. There is often a progression of sexual abuse, beginning with attention and affection and becoming more sexual and intrusive. Offenders are male or female. Boys and girls of all ages are sexually abused.

Many sexual abusers are people known and trusted by children or are in positions of authority or otherwise respected by the family. There are often very few clues to suspect an individual of sexual misconduct. Some of the following adult behavioral indicators may be present but are not necessarily exhibited in adult perpetrators.

- Are very overly protective of their children. May severely limit a child's contact with other children, especially children of the other sex.
- Are secretive and isolated—intrafamilial and social.
- Paranoid—sensitive, suspicious, mistrustful, hostile regarding outside world.
- Have family difficulties involving power struggles and sexual relations.
- Sexually deviant adult, marital sexual dysfunction.
- Poorly defined boundaries or roles.

Not every accusation of sexual abuse is true
even though each accusation must to be taken seriously.

If a child says something indicating sexual abuse, look the child straight in the eye and believe him or her. If the disclosure is true, the child is already feeling guilty and exerting extreme courage to reveal the secret. If the child is not telling the truth, this type of misstatement needs to be handled carefully and nonjudgmentally. If you overreact, the child may refrain from providing any additional information. It's hard to remain calm, but it is important if you want the child to communicate with you and trust you for support. Keep a clear head, gather information, and obtain additional support. Assure the child the right thing to do was to tell and you are glad you are the person available. Concern for the welfare of the child is the best gift you have to give. A reaction of revulsion, anger, or blame will not help the situation.

Sometimes, someone may want to touch you on your penis or your breasts or your butt or between your legs, or they might want you to touch them there, and if that happens you get to say no, get away, and tell someone if you can. If you can't, and something happens, it is never your fault. And we want to know about it. If you can't tell us for some reason, tell someone else, someone you trust, a teacher or a policeman.

The abuser may be a parent, so it's also very important to tell kids that the person may be someone the family knows, but that the touching is still not OK.
Program Director, Sexual Offence Services

Children learn how to behave. They do not arrive knowing what is expected.

Simply state:
"I believe you and I will help you get help."

Children need support and reassurance that their bodies are their own and they can feel safe and good about their bodies. If someone touches them in a way they don't like, it's OK to say no. The feeling of being special to someone or being loved does not mean being touched sexually to get affection and attention. If someone is touching them in a way that makes them feel uncomfortable, it is OK to tell. Each child needs a safe person to confide in. No secrets.

Children may or may not show outward signs of abuse. Children will experience different levels of trauma and reactions depending on the level of seriousness and type of sexual abuse they encounter. The stability and mental health of the primary family and their reaction to the abuse will play a key role in the affect on the child in the long term. The development, age, security level, and personality of the child will also play a part in whether feelings are repressed or expressed.

Sexual abuse of children can be suspected when:

PHYSICAL INDICATORS

- There is venereal disease.
- A girl is pregnant, under 14, and very evasive in naming her partner.
- May show no outward physical signs of sexual abuse.
- Any genital injury or bleeding not explained by accidental cause.
- There is tearing or specific inflammation of the mouth, anus, or genitals, or evidence of semen in oral, rectal, or vaginal areas.
- May have trouble sitting or walking or partaking in physical activities with other children.
- Pain or itching genital area, frequent bladder, yeast infections.
- Massive weight change.

BEHAVIORAL INDICATORS

- The child reports sexual activity.
- The child shows an over-awareness of sex at an early age.
- A child is known to be the victim of other forms of abuse.
- Simulating intercourse with peers with clothing off.
- Forces others to touch their genitals or coerces, bribes, or fools other children into sexual play. Manipulative and secretive.
- Suddenly refuse to change for gym or participate in physical activities.
- Oral, vaginal, anal penetration of dolls, animals, children.
- Fear of touching or being touched.
- Fears, guilt, anxiety, depression, sadness, social withdrawal.
- Overly concerned for safety of siblings.

These physical and behavioral indicators do not necessarily mean sexual abuse is occurring. Jumping to conclusions without careful evaluation can lead to additional damage to a child and trauma or destruction for an innocent family. Complete medical examinations and history need to be addressed. If there is pain, bleeding, or discharge determination needs to be made where it is coming from—rectum, urethra, vagina. All potential accidental and medical causes need to be reviewed. If the child has a specific medical problem—that needs to be addressed medically. If the child was sexually abused—that needs to be addressed separately. The two do not necessarily correlate. A child who gives a clear history of being sexually molested has probably been sexually molested and most likely this child will have a completely normal examination. A child who has bleeding from the vagina may have actually fallen straddle legged on a hard object and never been touched sexually. Both children need compassion; both need different types of professional attention.

Not all allegations of sexual abuse are true. Mike Robin has edited the book *Assessing Child Maltreatment Reports—The Problem of False Allegations* (1991). This book is exceptional in helping professionals understand the dilemma posed in

Seductive behavior in a child is learned behavior, and it is the responsibility of the adult to teach the child acceptable behavior and not take advantage of the child.
(Stovall 1981)

Children who have been sexually abused have learned complex and subtle interaction patterns with adults. These include touching, stroking, gazing, appearing partially undressed, intrusive eye contact, hugging, and clinging. These are often referred to as "seductive" behaviors, which is a misnomer. The child who exhibits such behaviors is neither seducing nor asking to be seduced. Such a child is asking for attention or affection, and trying to please adults. Unfortunately many adults misread such signs.
(McFadden & Ryan 1991)

assessing sexual abuse allegations, uncovering the truth, and avoiding unnecessary disruption of children from families who have not abused their children, but are suspected of sexual abuse.

Evaluations of sexual abuse allegations require meticulous investigation and analysis of the data gathered (Sgroi, 1982; Mrazek, 1981; White, Santilli, & Quinn, 1988), knowledge of the development of memory, and current data on children's vulnerability to suggestion (Goodman, 1984; King & Yulllie, 1987). Included in the differential diagnosis of each allegation should be consideration of factors within the child, the person bringing the complaint, the family, or the professional systems which lead to false positive or false negative conclusions concerning the allegation. A false positive assessment of a complaint may needlessly sever family relationships and ruin reputations; a false negative may cause the child and others to be reexposed to victimization (Quinn, 1991, Robin, 1991).

Children who have been sexually abused or exploited may demonstrate bizarre, sophisticated, or unusual sexual knowledge or behavior. They may engage in excessive fantasy behavior. They may have touching problems and intimacy difficulties. They may use bedwetting or feces retention as a protective coping maneuver to ward off penetration. Children may intentionally self-mutilate as a call for help. In teenagers, sexual promiscuity, drugs, or alcohol may be used to cope. Eating disorders, depression, running, and suicide are also *"red flags."* All too often these disguised and nonverbal messages go unheard.

Children may begin to question what is real, or separate life into safe areas and unsafe areas. They may learn to disassociate or choose to live two distinct lives—one involved in the *"secret"* and one exposed to the public. Nightmares and sleep disturbances are common. They may have difficulty trusting and developing lasting peer relations. Children are caught in a double bind. They feel anxious, fearful, and alone, yet, if they tell they may be ignored, disbelieved, punished, or blamed for the abuse.

Sexually abused children feel guilt, shame, humiliation, violation, and rage. As adults these children may not remember the experiences, yet have a gnawing feeling of discontent, insecurity, and unhappiness and that something is wrong. Sexually abused children may become adults who are sexually promiscuous or uninterested in sex. They may believe the only way to receive love is to be sexual or that being sexual is dirty, hurtful, or degrading. They may have a distorted viewpoint of roles for men and women. They may feel a certain pride in their body because it gets them attention, or they may feel ashamed of their body, that it is ugly and dirty.

Children experiencing sexual abuse have been forced into experiences and responsibilities they are not capable of handling at their developmental level. If the situation is incest, the parents have not protected them, nor taught them to protect themselves. The adults they trust and love have used them, and attention has moved from caring and support to sexual experiences. Children may believe they have to perform sexually in order to maintain the adult's love or to please the parent. Or they may have been threatened with, *"If you tell . . . I'll go to jail, "* or *"I'll hurt you,"* or *"I'll say it never happened and no one will believe you."*

According to Emily Jean McFadden, in *The Sexually Abused Child in Specialized Foster Care* , what is *not clear and needs to be spotlighted for foster parents is the manner in which the child's previous experience affects his or her adjustments to the foster home and colors perceptions of the foster family. The intimacy and touching of normal family life are confusing and appear to involve sexual content to a child whose only physical nurturing came through sexual contact. Such a child is aware of the progression of activities which led up to an actual sexual contact and does not know how to differentiate that which is sexual from that which was part of seduction.*
(McFadden 1989)

Tom, a nine-year-old in foster care, had been involved with a pedophile who had taken pornographic pictures. His "friend" had first engaged Tom by hiring him to sweep out the front of his shop. Tom was pleased to earn the extra money. The perpetrator then gained Tom's confidence by spending a lot of time talking to Tom about his family and his concerns about school. He had taught Tom to wrestle and how to swing a baseball bat. When Tom became comfortable with the perpetrator's touch, he allowed his friend to hug and fondle him. Then Tom was photographed nude in athletic poses. Finally the perpetrator made manual/genital contact and ultimately took pornographic photos. In foster care, Tom's foster parents were perplexed about the anxiety and acting out Tom displayed when they tried such routine activities to enhance Tom's self-esteem as teaching him sports, giving him small jobs, hugging him, or telling him he looked nice. They finally began to appreciate the complexity of Tom's situation when they were photographing him, and Tom asked if he was supposed to take his clothes off. With horror, they realized that each of their innocent attempts to build self-esteem had been perceived by Tom as a prolonged seduction attempt, replicating his earlier experience.

Foster (and adoptive) *parents need full information about sexual abuse incidents and the progression of events which were part of the seduction, including nonsexual ways in which the perpetrator gained the child's trust or cooperation, to avoid inadvertent replication of the child's earlier experiences. It is important for foster* (or adoptive) *parents to be aware of the context of the incidents. Where did the sexual abuse take place? What time of day was it? If the location of the episodes is not known, the three most common places for the sexual abuse to have occurred are bathroom, bedroom, and car. With this understanding, foster* (and adoptive) *parents can be careful not to be alone with children in these settings.*

The agency has the legal responsibility to provide foster (and adoptive) *parents with the information relevant to the care of the child* (Hardin & Tazzara, 1983). *Failure to do so can result in situations which jeopardize the safety of both parents and child. Many of the false allegations of sexual abuse lodged against foster* (and adoptive) *parents involve the child's misinterpretation of foster or adoptive parents' behavior, because the child perceives the situation to be similar to a former experience* (McFadden & Stovall, 1984). *Many substantiated allegations involve younger children who had been sexually abused prior to placement and acted out with sexualized behaviors which were misperceived as sexual cues* (McFadden & Ryan, 1986). *An agency which avoids fully informing foster* (and adoptive) *parents in order to protect them from the reality of the child's past risks setting up the foster* (or adoptive) *parents with an ultimate liability situation.* (McFadden 1989)

Sexual maltreatment of children by adults is a serious offense.

Sexual abuse is a violation of the life and liberty of a child. Sexual abuse is a criminal violation and so it incorporates very stiff penalties. These penalities are life changing for the alleged perpetrator. In Minnesota, charges of criminal sexual conduct carry the following penalties:

First Degree	Second Degree	Third Degree	Fourth Degree
Imprisonment up to 40 years	*Imprisonment up to 35 years*	*Imprisonment up to 15 years*	*Imprisonment up to 10 years*
Fines to $40,000	*Fines to $35,000*	*Fines to $30,000*	*Fines to $20,000*

Fifth Degree	Incest	Subsequent Offense
Imprisonment up to 1 year	*Imprisonment up to 10 years*	*Imprisonment up to 37 years*
Fines to $3000		

Accusations of child sexual misconduct are **not** taken lightly by child protection, law enforcement, or professionals in the medical, educational, or psychological field. Although accusations may not be true, they are handled with due care as if

Document and communicate:
— *Keep open communication with spouse and social worker.*
— *Keep good documentation about child and changes.*

Protecting the child:
— *Provide enough privacy for child.*
— *Instruct and encourage child to practice proper hygiene.*
— *Give children permission to talk about experiences and feelings.*
— *Avoid games or play with children that involves a lot of physical contact.*
— *At first, avoid leaving the child alone with another person.*
— *Involve the child in age appropriate activities.*
— *Attempt to help child clarify values around sexual issues.*
— *Involve child in specialized therapy to help overcome the effects of sexual mistreatment.*

they were true. Immediate assessments or investigations are often mandated and children are placed in protective custody until an assessment can be completed.

Sexual abuse occurs not just between children and adults, but also between children and children. Child-child sexual behavior can be normal and inquisitive or very degrading and damaging.

What is child-child sexual abuse and exploitation?

In *Understanding and Responding to the Sexual Behavior of Children* (Ryan et al. 1989), the full range of behaviors is placed along a continuum from normal to abusive. Within the normal range, adults need to recognize the behavior, and responses may be educational, redirecting, or limiting.

> *Born five years after her three brothers, Jennie was an active, alert child. At five years old she was determined, strong willed, and capable of standing up for herself. If she didn't like something everyone knew about it. Lynnette, Jennie's mother, worked and Jennie spent Monday through Friday in day care. The day care home was well-run and clean and Lynnette felt comfortable leaving Jennie there.*

> *For Jennie it was another story. The home cared for toddlers and infants, and at times diapers were left in the bathroom. Jennie vehemently refused to go to the bathroom for the whole day she was in provider care. This concerned the day care mother. Her behavior also concerned Lynnette, who had not yet figured out how to tell the day care provider her daughter didn't like the condition of the bathroom.*

Many of the behaviors in the middle of this continuum may be exhibited by many children occasionally as they experiment and imitate things seen or heard. Adults responsible for the care of children need to pay attention and not ignore these behaviors.

> *Jennie liked playing doctor and would pester her older brothers into playing with her. Lynnette had monitored the play and was confident there was no inappropriate sexual play between the children. One day Jennie was giving shots with her doctor's kit. Her eleven-year-old brother pulled down her pants to give her a pretend shot. Off went Jennie to tell her mother.*

> *Lynnette discussed with all three boys why it was not proper to pull down the pants of a little girl—including their sister! She explained it was embarrassing and that it would not be allowed. The boys apologized and agreed not to do it again. Together they discussed restitution, and the children decided Jennie could be their boss for the next day and they would do everything she asked.*

> *Jennie assured her mother she would let her know if it happened again and proceeded to take full advantage of being a "boss for the day."*

It is helpful to understand the ranges of child sexual behaviors. Normal childhood sexual behavior is exhibited when children of the same age group play with peers in inquisitive or innocent ways. This play includes *"show me yours and I'll show you mine,"* imitating seduction by kissing or flirting, or playing doctor. Conversations include talking about genitals or reproduction or telling dirty jokes within their cultural or peer group. Children also masturbate from very early ages, and this is done externally and without penetration.

As the behaviors move away from the norm, parents should be alert and consider seeking evaluation and advice from professionals trained in child sexuality. Sibling to sibling and neighborhood child sexual abuse does occur.

Each child who has been sexually abused, first and foremost, is a child with all the normal needs of children.

— *All children need attention, affection, and feelings of being loved and special to someone.*

— *All children need to feel safe and good in their bodies.*

— *All children need a degree of freedom to explore their world*

— *All children need to have some limits set for them.*

Children who have been sexually abused are more like other children than different. Foster parents of sexually abused children require an education grounding in the normal development of children. They especially need to know about the normal sexual development of children so they do not mistake normal behaviors such as masturbation and self-exploration as signs of sexual abuse.
(Chiaro, Marden et al., 1982)

Exploration Child-Child	Sexually Explicit Child-Child	Perpetrator Child-Child
Normal child sex play occurs between children of similar ages and is done on a voluntary basis. It usually occurs only a few times and in a few specific periods in a child's life. If the children are discovered and asked to stop, the sexual behavior diminishes and then stops. The reaction of children is usually silly, embarrassed, and giggly.	Many of these children may have been exposed to pornography or sexually stimulating movies, or sexual abuse. These children do not force other children into sexual play with them but may expose their private parts, simulate intercourse, touch inappropriately, self-stimulate, and talk about sex. They may be involved in sexually explicit words verbally and in writing to tease others. They do not display the level of anger about sexuality that the child perpetrator does. Feelings of guilt, shame, or confusion are common.	Child perpetrators, on the other hand, seek out children whom they can coerce, fool, bribe, or force into sexual play. They are secretive and manipulative. The victim child is not involved mutually in the decisions. When asked to stop, their behaviors may increase. There is an aggressive, impulsive, or compulsive nature to their sexual behaviors.

It is not helpful to overreact to a child who may be imitating language or behavior seen on television, talked about by others, or even experienced by the child. Children look to adults in their lives for verification and validation. They expect adults to correct negative behavior. A parent's failure to respond to sexually exploitive behavior may covertly support it. When a non-specific response occurs, the child may be confused. When no response occurs, the child's perception may be that the adult condones the behavior.

Warning signals for parents

Parents need to become aware when their children's sexual behaviors move into *"warning"* or *"yellow flag"* areas. It is at this time that guidance and support can be most helpful to children in understanding what is appropriate for their developmental age. Family counseling may be warranted depending on the severity or repetitiveness of the behavior. At certain ages some children have a preoccupation with sexual themes, especially sexually aggressive themes. It may be typical behavior to pull down another child's pants or lift up another child's skirt, but the victim child does not see the humor in the issue. To the victim child, it is embarrasing, and the child who does it needs an adult to explain why it is not appropriate.

Depending on the age of the child and the culture of the family, sexuality needs to be addressed to fit within the family boundaries. The old adage *"boys will be boys"* does not excuse harmful behavior. Teasing and harassment which is detrimental to others is never appropriate. Sexually explicit conversations, sexual grafitti, and sexual teasing need to be addressed as hurtful and inappropriate. Many children experiment at least once with peeping, exposing, obscenities, or pornography—these need immediate attention.

Masturbation issues need sensitivity. Private masturbation may be a normal functioning of the developmental age of the child, but preoccupation with masturbation or public masturbation needs to be addressed.

Flashing lights and sirens for parents

Children who exhibit child perpetrator traits or other *"red flags"* need immediate professional support. These children may carry on sexually explicit conversations with children signficantly younger in age, sexually degrade or

---

Mistaken allegations of sexual abuse can happen.

"Do you all know what French kissing is?" asked the teacher.

My twelve-year-old sister raised her hand and said, "Oh yes, my daddy always French kisses us girls and Dutch rubs my brothers."

Alarmed, the teacher sought help and reported suspected sexual abuse . . .

Adult woman

"The one thing a child learns from sexual abuse is how to be abused. Sexually abused children teach themselves to endure assault. Instead of learning to protect themselves, they learn they can't protect themselves.

"Someone who has never been abused can say "No", walk or run away, can scream and fight. The incest victim often doesn't know what to do except wait for it to be over."
(Somers 1992)

humiliate others or themselves. They may force others by fear to engage in sexual play, write sexually explicit notes, proposals, or threats. They may repeatedly be involved in peeping, obscenities, or pornography. They may compulsively masturbate or expose themselves to others. If these traits are present in a child in your care, carefully document the behaviors and seek professional support from a person trained in child development and sexuality.

What is indirect sexual abuse of children?

Indirect sexual abuse of children occurs unintentionally in families and in the medical profession. This type of abuse violates personal sexual boundaries and can create shame, guilt, humiliation, and powerlessness for the child.

Possible experiences which can be considered indirect sexual abuse are:
(Wills-Brandon 1990)

Families

Emotional incest: Being put in the position of surrogate parent or spouse. Hearing about adult problems. Being *"Daddy's little princess"* or *"Mommy's little man."* Being expected to side with one parent during a parental disagreement. Being set up to protect one parent against another. Being told to relay messages from one parent to another. The child is the surrogate spouse, playmate, protector, or in some cases, lover of the parent.

Face slapping. Our face is a part of our identity in that it shows others who we are as sexual beings. It is sexually shaming to be slapped in the face.

Inappropriate sexual information. Each culture varies in its disclosure of sexual information to children. Based on cultural norms, parents provide too little information about sexual development or too much information about sexual development too soon.

Lack of personal privacy. As children grow older they need areas of privacy for dressing and bathing. Family cultures vary on the degree of privacy accepted, however, if children are showing a need for privacy, that need should be respected. School age children in out-of-home care especially need privacy in dressing and bathing.

Living with parents who are sexually inappropriate. Living with a parent who is having extramarital affairs, who is sexually addicted, or is involved in casual sex. Exposure to adult's pornographic literature or movie collection.

Living with parents who have difficulty with their own sexuality. Living with parents who have sex-role confusion. Living with parents who appear to be repressed sexually, never touching, never kissing, sleeping in separate rooms. Living with parents who have unresolved sexual abuse issues.

Shamed for being male or female. Being told you should have been the opposite sex. Being told all females are whores, bitches, etc. Being told all males are pimps, abusive. Being shamed for having sexual feelings. Shaming comments made about pubescent development, breast size, genital size, etc. Overcontrolling or undercontrolling of opposite sex relationships.

Medical Profession

Breast examinations with sexual overtones. Professional does not explain procedure, continues to fondle after examination is completed. Hugs or kisses patient.

Enemas may be humiliating and shaming if the child does not understand why or what is happening.

Immunizations on the buttocks.

Medical procedures involving genital areas. These procedures may be necessary but may still be misunderstood and invasive to the child.

Social Services

"Suspected" sexually abused children must be worked with cautiously and with consideration. In the case of false allegations, the medical procedures may be the most sexually invasive procedure the child has ever encountered. Pelvic and digital rectal examination on a child who has been removed from his parents for suspected sexual abuse can be psychologically damaging. The child is already isolated from his most significant relationships and usually is dealing with adult strangers.

Jennie's story continues. . .

Two days after the incident, Jennie proclaimed to a friend in day care, "My brothers pull my pants down and I make them kiss my butt." Alerted to potential sexual abuse, the day care provider called child protection. She discussed Jennie's unusual behavior in toileting. She discussed her generally intense behavior. Social services was concerned and sent out the police to pick up Jennie on a 72-hour protective hold.

Jennie was met at the children's shelter by a smiling lady who gave her a teddy bear. She and the strange, smiling lady went off to a doctor for an examination. Everyone seemed pleasant enough, but Jennie was exasperated. Her mommy had told her never to go anywhere with strangers and she was getting farther and farther away from her mommy all the time. At the doctor's office another lady gave her a little gown and told her to take her clothes off. The strange, smiling lady helped her take her clothes off—her mommy had told her never to let strangers take her clothes off—she was getting worried. The strange, smiling lady also took off her panties—not even her brothers were allowed to do that! Jennie had never been to a male doctor before, her own pediatrician was a lady, and she was surprised when the door opened and a man bigger than her daddy came in. He seemed nice and was smiling, too—but now she was with more strangers and still her mommy hadn't come. "Let's just take a look at you," he said. "Let's see how you're doing. You seem like a very nice little girl. Can you climb up on this?" Jennie climbed up on the table—she was scared, the smiling, strange lady stroked her head and helped her lie down. The smiling doctor lifted her gown and Jennie knew he was looking right at her privates. Her mommy would be really mad. Jennie closed her eyes and pretended her mommy was with her, she could feel the strange smiling doctor poking her bottom. Not even her mommy had touched her that way when she had messes. It felt very naughty. Finally, she heard the strange, smiling man say, "I don't see any trauma. You can help her get dressed." Jennie wondered what trauma was. It must be good not to have because the poking had stopped, and the strange, big man had left the room. She wished her mommy was with her.

Jennie's examination found no trauma because no trauma ever existed. The result of the examination and the manner in which Jennie was removed were harmful to her. To Jennie, the experience felt like a kidnapping. Jennie's family was assessed, and social services determined Jennie could return home. A damaged little girl came home. But at least she came home, home to her mother's

---

Even as an adult, I felt GOD was watching over my shoulder ready to pounce on me for the slightest offense.

Not only did I fear GOD, but I harbored incredible bitterness that any GOD would allow such injustice to exist in the world.

It wasn't until I made my own spiritual journey that I discovered the joy and peace found in Truth.
Adult child of religious manipulation

My anger always brought everyone out-of-control back in line. When I slapped up the wife or kids I'd get the release and power I felt I needed, then I'd drown my denial in the booze.
Recovering alcoholic father

arms. Jennie was lucky. As a spirited, extroverted child, she was able to express her feelings, and her parents had visible issues to work through. Introverted children are not so lucky. Thoughtful and introspective, they keep the experience and their jumbled feelings locked inside. Jennie screams and covers her head when she sees a police car. She refuses to go to day care. A visit to her own pediatrician is a battle. She is afraid of men bigger than her daddy. The kitty has been found with a pencil in his rectum. The family has sought counseling and Jennie's mother quit work to give Jennie increased attention. I asked Lynnette why Jennie had said, *"My brothers pull my pants down and I make them kiss my butt."* *"We wondered about that ourselves,"* she said, *"and then my husband and I remembered a conversation we had doing dishes the night Jennie had been the designated boss. John had made the statement 'Jennie's got those boys running around in circles, I wouldn't be surprised if she's asked them to kiss her butt.' We had laughed at the statement, thinking we were alone. Obviously, we weren't, Jennie overhead it and brought it with her the next day to day care."*

"What about social services? Did anything happen to help you pull your daughter and family through this crisis?" I asked.

"The case was closed and designated that no further action was needed. If Jennie's case had initiated change for other children, maybe my husband and I would not feel so violated. It's unreasonable to expect any system to be perfect—mistakes will happen. I believe it is also unreasonable for any system not to attempt to correct itself when a mistake has been made. In this case the child was harmed. Child protection harmed the very child they had pledged to protect. Is it enough for CPS to walk away from the situation, shake their head and continue on as before? I think not," said Lynnette.

What is religious manipulation?

If an adult speaks of love and then incorporates cruel and unusual punishment in parenting, the child is confused and often spiritually rebels in adolescence. It is not appropriate to use the Bible or religion as a weapon or an excuse for inappropriately shaming or disciplining children. A child's first concept of a higher power has the characteristics of the adults living in the child's environment and their relationship with their higher power.

When parents use religious principles to shame, threaten, or punish their children, spirituality becomes a scary, fearful, and an authoritarian institution. Statements such as *"God is watching and doesn't like you"* set the child up to believe that God is an ogre who looks over your shoulder and capriciously removes His like for you if you do something naughty. These children may also believe that God is punishing them when something tragic happens in their life, such as death of a parent or terrible accident. They may blame God or themselves when ever any tragedy occurs.

> *Non-religious parents may shame their children based on parental authority. When Christian (or other spiritually observed doctrines) parents use God's Word or teachings to back up shaming the child, the effect is devastating. Not only are the parents shaming the child, but God, Himself appears to be in on it too! When we view ourselves as bad in God's eyes, it becomes extremely difficult to believe that God truly loves and forgives. We tend to view Him as an insatiable, harsh judge who considers us to be bad no matter what.* (Henslin 1991)

The Bible does endorse discipline and says, *"Spare the rod and spoil the child."* The rod of discipline is mentioned in Proverbs 13:24, 22:15, 23:13-14, and 29:15. The word *"rod"* is translated from the Hebrew word *she'vet.* To the Hebrews, *she'vet* meant a stick or a staff, such as that used by a shepherd. The rod was used for guidance, as in Psalms 23:4, not brutality. It is also used to represent authority as found in 2 Samuel and Isaiah. One must not take a single passage and build a parenting system. Ephesians 6:15 states, *"Fathers do not exasperate your children; instead bring them up in the training and instruction of the Lord."* Colossians 3:21 states, *"Fathers, do not embitter your children, or they will become discouraged."* Overpunishment and abuse exasperates and discourages—I don't believe the Bible endorses it.

Colossians 3:12 states clearly the expectations of *God's chosen people, holy and dearly loved—clothe yourself with compassion, kindness, humility, gentleness, and patience. Bear with each other and forgive whatever grievances you may have against one another. Forgive as the Lord forgave you. And over all these virtues put on love, which binds them together in perfect unity.* The Bible says in Proverbs 22:6, *"Train up a child as he shall go and when he is old he shall not depart from it."*

If the virtues of God are love, compassion, kindness, humility, gentleness, and patience—child abuse has no place in biblical parenting principles. [NIV references]

What is ritualistic abuse?

Ritual abuse occurs infrequently and is very secretive. Professionals and surrogate parents agree that it is more difficult to deal with than sexual abuse, for a number of reasons. Ritualistic abuse leaves deep scars on people. Nothing in our experience prepares us to hear about ritualistic abuse, much less believe that it could occur and deal with it. Little information is available. There are few peers to turn to for consultation and support. Perhaps even more problematic is the fact that few therapists know how to treat survivors. (McNamara 1990)

Children in ritual abusive situations who are discovered are immediately removed and placed in out-of-home care. Many times social service workers fear telling the new care providers the details of what has happened to the children. Without knowledge of ritual abuse and the damage it can cause to children, these care providers are extremely vulnerable to misinterpret unusual behaviors or react to the child in unhelpful ways. It is important for foster parents caring for these children to understand more about the dynamics of ritual abuse.

Adults who ritualistically abuse children may be found in any section of the population. They do not necessarily exhibit any strong characteristics which differentiate them from people you interact with every day. Adults involved in ritualistic abuse are often alienated from their families or have a hatred toward their families and religion. They may or may not display obnoxious anti-social behavior, use drugs or alcohol, and have an undue fascination with death, torture, self-mutilation, suicide, or animal sacrifice. They may be very secretive in their behavior surrounding satanic *"holy days."*

It should not be assumed that all persons who worship Satan or consider themselves Satanists are perpetrators of ritualistic abuse.

Satanism is not the nonbelief in God, but rather the antithesis of standard Christianity, and the majority of satanic practices revolve around defamation of Christian practices. In reversing the credo of love toward others, it becomes a selfish cult, centered on what individuals can get for themselves. This emphasis on personal power is what gives Satanism much of its appeal, particularly to weak and unsuccessful personalities. Its further appeal comes from its creative side. There are no rules and no restrictions governing the practices of Satanism. One of black magic's most flamboyant exponents, Alistair Crowley, had great influence on the development of modern Satanism, and his *" 'do what thou wilt' shall be the whole law"* has provided the justification for fulfilling many abnormal sexual or violent urges.

When the foster parents, worker, and therapist mutually understand the child and share common treatment goals, the child's emotional needs will be met, and he or she will be ready to learn new and positive messages about family living.
(McFadden 1989)

Many foster children have not learned the difference between guilt and shame:

Guilt is what we feel about our behaviors and guides us in making good choices. When we feel guilty we feel bad about some behavior we have engaged in.

Shame, on the other hand, is feeling bad about who we are as a person.

Many youths have received the message that they are stupid or no good. Anger may be a mechanism for youth to hide their shame.
(Jones, 1991)

"The victim of an angry person is usually not the cause of the initial anger."

Many Satanists see themselves as simply practicing a chosen religion and no more, a right everyone is guaranteed under the United States Constitution. They eschew the darker images of animal mutilations, bloodletting, and human sacrifice and say that most of what is reported about them by the press is the work of practical jokers, horror-fiction writers, and propagandists from the fundamental religious groups.

Common characteristics of children who have been ritualistically abused:

- Interference with important early developmental processes such as object consistency; promotion of constant fear of abandonment; and inability to form attachments.
- Confused value system in which good is bad and bad is good.
- Loss of self-esteem with a feeling of being unworthy of anyone's love or respect.
- Constant fear of harm and extreme fear of being alone.
- View of self as not just bad, but evil.
- Repression and dissociation in order to cope and survive, possibly leading to multiple personality disorder.
- Extreme fear of harm or death. Fears ghosts, monsters, bad people taking the child away.
- Writes numbers or letters backwards (devil's alphabet), speaks or may recite backwards.
- Talks about drugs, pills, candy, mushrooms, or injections. Injections may also create loss of memory.
- Sings songs or chants that are sexual or bizarre or that have a threatening theme of "you better not tell."
- Is preoccupied with urine and feces.
- Is aggressive or sadistic in play.

- Elimination of spontaneous emotions. The goal is to make the child robotlike, to be brainwashed or programmed by the cult.
- View of self as perpetrator rather than the victim.
- Belief that evil is more powerful than good and that good is powerless.
- Periods of amnesia or "black spaces" in recall.
- Loss of innocence and childhood.
- Belief that adults, including parents, are not protective so there is no safety.
- Feelings of powerlessness, helplessness, and belief there is no love, no safety, no hope.
- Is preoccupied with the devil, magic potions, supernatural powers, crucifixions.
- Refers to television characters as real people (perpetrators will often assume other names so child will not be believed).
- Has marks on back, unusual bruising, especially in patterns.
- Is preoccupied with death.

Ritualistic child abuse and human sacrifice still linger in the netherworld between fact and fiction, as police investigators have virtually never been able to turn up sufficient evidence that rumors of homicide have occurred. On the other hand, a considerable number of children over the past ten years have reported startlingly similar experiences.

Common traits in the disclosure of ritualistic abuse:

- Use of satanic paraphernalia or imagery, such as a goat's head, inverted cross or pentagram, candles, altar, and ongoing references to death.
- Use of feces and urine, descriptions of eating and drinking of the waste or smearing it on the child's body.
- Killing of adults or children, with some children recounting participation in the killings.
- Forced sexual activity between perpetrators and children, the children themselves, or children and animals.
- Repeated berating of the child as bad or stupid.

- Isolation of the child in dark place, such as a basement, cage, casket, or grave, for what the child descibes as a long period of time.
- Killing and mutilation of animals, and use of the blood and body parts in ceremonies.
- Desecration of the Bible or cross, making fun of God, particularly Jesus.
- Threats of injury to the children, families, or the person they tell, if they disclose.
- Use of what the children describe as magic, spells, or drugs.

Chapter 12 - Defining Child Maltreatment

- Taking pictures of the children nude or in sexual acts.
- Kidnapping.
- Eating the flesh of those who were killed.
- Multiple perpetrators of both sexes and multiple victims.
- Binding or gagging of children.
- Being confirmed in the belief and commitment to Satan.

These reports are not only quite consistent among very young children, but they are widespread, occurring in vastly separated parts of the United States, as well as Canada, Great Britain, and continental Europe. (Hayden 1991)

Satanists and other occult groups share certain holidays when there is a marked increase in ceremonial activities. During this time children in care who have experienced ritualistic abuse may exhibit anniversary reactions which can be misunderstood by care providers. Satanists often perform matching ceremonies opposite Christian *"holy times,"* such as particular saints' days, Easter, Christmas, and Halloween (the day before All Saints Day). There is also reportedly increased cult activity around full moon nights and Friday the thirteenth. Additional special ceremonial/ritual dates are:

BLOOD RITUALS

- St. Wineblad Day - Jan. 7
- St. Walpurgis Day- Feb. 25
- St. Eichatadt Day - Mar. 1
- Preparation for Sacrifice-April 21-26 Grand Climax-April 26-May 1
- Demon Revels-July 1
- Midnight Host-Sept. 20
- All Hallow Eve-Oct. 29
- High Grand Climax-Dec. 24

SEXUAL RITUALS

- Satanic Revels-Jan. 17, Feb. 2, Aug. 3, Nov. 4
- Spring Equinox Feast Day- Mar. 20
- Summer Solstice-June 21
- Marriage to the Beast Satan- September 7
- Equinox Feast Day-Sept. 22
- Halloween-Nov. 1
- Winter Solstice-December 22

Occult and Satanism - A Rising Fad for America's Teens

Teenagers are buying into the occult and satanism regardless if we adults choose to recognize it. Regardless if we believe these practices hold any power. Regardless if we believe this is hocus pocus and fantasy—a little dabbling never hurt. Teen groups are springing up. The problem is often these practices lead an unsuspecting teen into deeper and deeper practices, drugs, sexual behavior, depression, violent actions and suicide. Teens and pre-teens in out-of-home care, regardless if they've experienced ritualistic abuse in the past may seek out the occult on their own. Why? Curiousity, control, power, knowledge, excitement, surprise and fun.

Kids who need satanism are kids who need help. They're looking for something , not finding it in their lives, and striking out for Hell to find it. A teenager who finds encouragement, love, understanding, responsibility, relationships to emulate, spiritual substance, consistent loving discipline, training in critical thinking, openness to discuss tough issues such as sex, social training, wisdom, integrity and attention at home, won't risk all that just to gut chickens and beg for demon possession. Think of the opposites of those qualities. If those things characterize the Hell your teenager is already living in or has recently been removed from, there's little you can do as a quick fix to prevent such a kid from being lured into the forbidden pleasures and thrills of evil.

Teenagers lives are in transit. They are always going through something. And transition is the key period when teenagers are especially susceptible to the lure of cultlike groups—satanic or otherwise. Betty Naysmith, the volunteer researcher for the Cult Awareness Network in Chicago, suggests there are critical times when teenagers are especially open to the lures of cultlike groups.

Feelings alone are neither good nor bad, they are simply feelings and may feel comfortable or uncomfortable. The behavior that goes with any feeling can be positive or negative.

My counselor in treatment was a gold digger. He dug right into my heart and connected it to my brain.

What are you really feeling? Get real.

I ain't felt nothin' for so long, how do I know? Okay, okay, I guess I'm scared.

I'll bet you are scared.

Then he would pause, and like reeling in a big fish, he pulled my feelings into his boat real slow, one at a time.
Recovering alcoholic father

— After graduation from school, during the first year away from home

— When going through stress of getting a new job

— Anytime the teenager is new to a school or group

— During period of trauma—accidents, sickness, loss of a good friend, etc.

— Whenever a family is undergoing a crisis—divorce, a death, etc.

Many new books are available discussing the current fad of occult and satanism with America's teenagers. In researching many of these books I would highly recommend—*"The Edge of Evil, The Rise of Satanism in North America"* (1989) by Jerry Johnston. Johnston's practical research and non-sensational approach complete with many references for additional reading is an excellent beginning place and reference for a concerned parent.

Kids do climb out of the worst cesspools of life to lead healthy, productive lives if they want to.
They have a choice about what they do and who they become—no matter how much they want to foist the blame on others.

How can care providers react to help the child?

Children need to be supported, protected, and feel safe. Even if the care provider has good reason to believe the child is not telling the truth, abuse confidences or unusual behaviors need to be documented. See Chapter 14, *"Document. How to Put it in Writing."*

An atmosphere of acceptance and trust needs to be established for the child to have the confidence to stand in the truth as he or she believes it or to have the freedom to change the story and admit to the truth if it is an illusion or lie. If the child is not telling the truth, the child still needs to be supported so that whatever is causing the dramatics can be dealt with. If the child is telling the truth, the child needs immediate support and help.

Some of the most sensitive statements I have read have been written by Torey Hayden, a special education teacher. The conversations she has had with children who have reacted in a bizarre or unusual manner are not judgmental, believing, or disbelieving, only supportive. If I were an untrusting and fearful child they would be comforting to me.

"I'm not angry. And I'm not going to get angry, so you don't have to worry about that. I am concerned though, ***. When little girls/boys do something like you were doing, it's usually because they've seen it done before. Sometimes, someone older shows them or does it to them and so they know." — pause for child response or reaction—

"It's not your fault, ***. I'm not angry. But if someone is making you touch the private places on his or her body or is touching you like that, it's important to tell me. Or if not me, some other adult you can trust." —pause—

"If something like this is going on, chances are, someone has told you not to tell. Chances are they've said something like, if you do tell, you'll get in trouble. Or that people will think it's your fault it happened. Or that no one will believe you. Or that you'll get taken away from your parents or some other horrible thing. When a grown-up is doing something wrong, that is the sort of thing they will say to you, because they know they shouldn't be doing what they are doing. They're lying to keep you from getting help. But if some-

one is touching you or making you touch them, you need help. You're just a little girl/boy and these are grown-up matters. You need a grown-up to help you sort it out." —pause—

"I'm here if you need me."

Summary

Children need safety and protection to grow into healthy adults. Care providers and professionals need to have a clear understanding of maltreatment of children. Determination that abuse occurred is complex. Both under-reporting and over-reporting lead to devastating results for children and families.

Victims of abuse or neglect do not have to hesitate to seek help. The old adage that a child who lives with love learns to love, and a child who lives with criticism learns to criticize holds true. Family violence is found in every level of society. A child who grows up in an abusive or neglectful home may continue patterns of abuse or neglect into the next generation of children. These adults need encouragement and support in reworking their own childhood issues.

Adult children programs can be very helpful in reparenting and learning to love the child who once was. Other treatment programs also may be helpful. The inner peace achieved by adults who have successfully completed reparenting programs bridges the chasm between loss and violation as children and love and volition as adults. Opening the closed doors of childhood is painful, but very cleansing.

Repairing damaged families is not as effective as preventing abuse or neglect in the first place. A high value needs to be placed on our most precious resource—our children, and the environment they come from—the family. By strengthening families today, we can improve family life for future generations.

The job of restoring emotional health to a fragile and damaged child can take years of blood, sweat, and tears. Providing parental care to children who have been overpunished, abused, or neglected can be confusing and difficult. Children who are in out-of-home care begin to express themselves as they get healthier and feel safer. Foster parents may become very vulnerable to allegations of the same abuse which occured in the child's past, even though the foster parents never abused or neglected the child.

It takes time to provide services necessary to help families and children in crisis situations. Out-of-home care may be the best choice for children in need of healing, nurturing, and protection while their family system is being repaired. Educational programs can help to prepare people to become parents and foster development of loving relationships and healthy attachments between parents and children.

"The proper time to influence the character of a child is about a hundred years before he is born."
Dean Page

References

Doris, Michael. 1989. *Broken Cord.* New York: Harper Collins

Garbino James and Garbino Anne. 1990. *Emotional Maltreatment of Children.*

Hayden, Torey L. 1991. *Ghost Girl. A True Story of a Child in Peril and the Teacher who Saved Her.* New York: Avon Books

Hennepin County. 1990. *Decision Point Policies Child Protection Services.* Hennepin County Minnesota.

Henslin, Earl R. 1991. *The Way Out of the Wilderness. Learn How Bible Heroes with Feet of Clay Are Models for Your Recovery.* Tennesee: Thomas Nelson.

Johnston, Jerry. 1989. *The Edge of Evil. The Rise of Satanism in North America.* Dallas, TX: Word.

Jones, Deb. 1991. *Working with Abused and Neglected Adolescents in a Foster Care Home.* Minnesota: University of Minnesota Press.

Magid, Ken and McKelvey, Carole. 1989. *High Risk Children Without a Conscience.* New York: Bantam Books

Material adapted from: Prevention of Abuse and Neglect of Children in Out-of-Home Care. Module 1, "Child Abuse and Neglect: An Overview, San Francisco Child Abuse Council, 4093 24th St., San Francisco, CA 94114

McFadden E. J. & Ryan P. 1991. Allegations of Maltreatment in Family Foster Homes: Dynamics and Dimensions. In Robin, Michael *Assessing Child Maltreatment Reports, The Problem of False Allegations.* (1991) Ypsilanti, Michigan: Eastern Michigan University.

McFadden E. J. 1989. *Part II: Program Issues. The Sexually Abused Child in Specialized Foster Care: A Normalizing Experience.* New York: Haworth Press.

McFadden E. J. & Ryan P. 1986. *Preventing Abuse is Foster Care, Final Report.* National Foster Care Education Project. Ypsilanti, Michigan: Eastern Michigan University.

McNamara, Bernard and McNamara, Joan. 1990. *Adoption and the Sexually Abused Child.* Maine: Human Services Development Institute, University of Southern Maine.

Minnesota Committee for Prevention of Child Abuse, A Chapter of the National Committee for Prevention of Child Abuse, Suite S-191, 1821 University Ave., St. Paul, MN (612) 641-1568.

Pride, Mary. 1989. *The Child Abuse Industry. Outrageous Facts About Child Abuse and Everyday Rebellion Against a System that Threatens Every American Family.* Illinois: Crossway Books.

Robin, Michael. 1991. *Assessing Child Maltreatment Reports, The Problem of False Allegations.* New York: Haworth Press.

Schorr, Lisbeth. 1988. *Within our Reach.* Minnesota:

Schorr, Lisbeth. Vol 8:1, 1989. The Family Resource Coalition.

Somers, Suzanne. 1992. *Wednesday Children, Adult Survivors of Abuse Speak Out.* New York: Jove.

Stovall, Bennie. 1981. *Child Sexual Abuse.* Michigan: Ypsilanti Eastern Michigan University.

Wills-Brandon, Carla. 1990. *Learning to Say No. Establishing Healthy Boundaries.* Florida: Health Communications.

EARLY CHILDHOOD STUDIES—UNIVERSITY OF MINNESOTA

> Materials developed for working effectively with abused and neglected children in out-of-home care can be purchased by writing: Early Childhood Studies Program, University of Minnesota, 306 Wesbrook Hall, 77 Pleasant Street SE, Minnesota, MN 55455. Or calling (612) 625-1088.

THE HAWORTH PRESS

> A number of excellent professional reference books are available through this publisher. To obtain a catalog write: The Haworth Press, Inc. 10 Alice Street, Binghamton, New York 13904-1580.

A good foster parent is someone who:

— *Cares.*
— *Can be trusted.*
— *Knows how to listen.*
— *Is encouraging.*
— *Has confidence in the child.*
— *Withholds judgment.*
— *Points out strengths of child.*
— *Promotes independence.*

Chapter 13

Guidelines for Care Providers

Borderline discipline methods
are not appropriate for children
in out-of-home care and
can result in negative licensing actions.

On April 27, 1989, the National Foster Parent Association adopted, by unanimous vote, the following resolution:

Whereas, numerous studies have overwhelmingly confirmed that hitting, spanking, slapping, and other forms of physical punishment are harmful methods of changing children's behavior and alternative forms of discipline are more effective, and

Whereas, a workshop on violence and public health convened by Surgeon General Koop recommended that "a major campaign should be carried out with the help of the media to reduce the public's acceptance of violence in general and violence against children in particular, including physical punishment, and further, that the American people come to understand that corporal punishment should be abolished," and

Whereas, the use of physical punishment is deeply engrained in American society and will be difficult to eliminate, but the detrimental effect of physical punishment indicates that the time for action is immediate and urgent, and

Whereas, the National Foster Parent Association would be remiss if it did not join the groundswell of public and professional protest against corporal punishment of children, in the home and in the school, as well as the stated opposition to corporal punishment by the American Academy of Pediatrics, Child Welfare League of America, American Bar Association, and others,

Now therefore be it resolved, that the National Foster Parent Association adds its voice to those urging the abolition of corporal punishment of children and those efforts to heighten public awareness of other forms of discipline more effective and less damaging to the bodies and spirits of children.

Licensed foster care providers are expected to maintain self-control, creativity, and discipline at higher standards than primary families. Selected and screened as capable and mature parents, they are expected to take on challenging and complex children who are in crisis and grieving, accept and integrate them into their home, and maintain supervision. In addition, they are to guide them and help them adjust behaviors that may have been established for several years.

A good foster parent is someone who:

— *Cares.*
— *Can be trusted.*
— *Knows how to listen.*
— *Is encouraging.*
— *Has confidence in the child.*
— *Withholds judgment.*
— *Points out strengths of child.*
— *Promotes independence.*

"I looked dismayed at all that needed to be done . . . the yard, the garage, the car. I saw the small brown eyes and my heart knew without my attention the grass would keep growing, the garage situation wouldn't change, and the car would still be in the driveway. The small brown eyes without my attention would grow away." **Father**

Foster parents are often caught in conflicting expectations:

"Treat them just like your own . . ."
   BUT
"Restrict discipline to what is allowed by agency standards."

"Give them all the love you can . . ."
   BUT
"Be careful how you touch them."
(Carbino 1991)

Being a foster child stigmatizes the child in care.

— If the child is in care due to a parent's antisocial, scandalous, or abusive behavior, the child may feel ashamed to be connected to such a parent.
— If the child believes he is to blame for being removed from his family home or believes he has damaged the family the child may feel shame.
— Just being a foster child places a child in an outcast situation and creates shame.

To reach into the heart of a troubled child, the adult must create an atmosphere of total trust to allow for open communication and healing—confessions of past actions, feelings, secrets, doubts and forgiveness. Truth must be allowed expression and be respected as truth to allow the door for attachment to begin to open.

Children respect people who tell the truth. They need facts. Children feel respected when they are told the truth.

Continual support services and training are necessary to equip care providers to help children constructively in out-of-home care. Foster and adoptive parents also need information about any child who is proposed for placement in their home. Agencies have an obligation to provide this information prior to placement. Getting answers to the following questions is helpful when working with a child in care.

Fears. Children in out-of-home care have fears. Some are visible. Some are invisible. Compounded losses, unresolved grief issues, and living with strangers in a new environment would scare anyone. The expression or repression of fear, however, is different for each child.
— Does the child have any known specific fear?
— How does the child handle this fear?
— What is the child's experience and relationship with adults? Animals? Older children? Younger children?

Sex. Each family handles this subject differently. Some children have been exposed to sexual activity very early, others have no knowledge. What a child knows and how that knowledge was attained will have a direct effect on behavior, thoughts, and feelings.
— How much does the child know?
— What words are familiar to the child?
— Does the child act out sexually? How? When? Why?
— What amount of privacy is the child used to?
— What boundaries have been set for the child in the past?

Relationships. Connections to others are important for all people. Another human connection to the child's past is very helpful. This person can provide information about the child's behaviors, thoughts, and feeling patterns.
— What types of relationships has the child experienced?
— With whom does the child have the healthiest relationship? Is this person accessible?
— What kind of response does the child make to a reasonable request?
— Does every issue escalate into a battle? Is there an escalation pattern?
— How does the child handle routine chores and expectations? Are there any specific issues with which the child has problems? Why?
— How does the child react to people in authority?

Personal. Caring for another human being is very personal. In order to respect the child, a provider needs clues to maintain the child's personal boundaries and yet project acceptance.
— How does the child handle anger? Psychological pain? Failure? Stress? Disappointment? Anxiety?
— How do you know when the child is happy?
— How does the child feel about expressions of affection? Touching?
— Does the child like adults to initiate affection, or does the child prefer to do it?
— How does the child like to receive approval?
— Does the child prefer men or women?
— Does the child lie? About what? Steal? Hoard food? Wet the bed, soil, or smear feces?

Eating. Family dining experiences vary from home to home. Table manners and behavior have a direct impact on family relationships.
— Is the child used to scheduled meals? Table prayers?
— Does the child have table problems? Can the child sit still at the table?
— Does the child pick at food? Does the child gorge food?
— Is the child talkative at the table? Silent?

Speech. What we say and how we say it have a direct impact on what the other person hears and responds to. Knowing communication clues about the child can help eliminate misunderstandings early on.

— Can the child communicate needs? Does the child say special things which may have different meanings? Does the child have body language that signals something?

— Does the child know what feelings are? Is the child expressing feelings or stuffing them? Can the child talk about feelings?

Sleep. Nighttime is an especially lonely and fearful time for children in out-of-home care. Knowledge of a child's past sleeping program can help new care providers respond in reassuring ways.

— Does the child sleep with a special object? What kind of pillow, sheets does the child like?

— Is the child used to a bedtime ritual? Prayers? Hugs? Stories?

— Does the child sleepwalk, wander, or wake at night? Does the child have night terrors?

— What soothes the child?

— Does the child get up and go to the bathroom, get a drink at night?

— How hard is the child to get to bed? To get up?

— Has the child been traumatized while sleeping? Age? By whom?

School. School-age children spend almost as many waking hours with teachers and educational professionals as they do at home. Knowledge of the child's school behavior and abilities is helpful in keeping surprises to a minimum.

— Can the child read? How well? What subjects does the child like?

— How well does the child get along with teachers? With other students?

— How does the child react to reprimand at school?

— How well does the child get along on the bus?

History of maltreatment. Knowledge of maltreatment is important to prevent misinterpretations or recurrences. Children who have been maltreated may react strongly to words, body language, or behaviors of adults.

— How was the child abused/neglected?

— When was the child abused (time of day or night)? Frequency of the abuse (once a day, week, month)?

— Who abused the child (male, female, relationship to child)?

— Where did the abuse occur (what room, indoors, outdoors)?

— Does the child exhibit any special behaviors, particularly behaviors toward adults, which resulted from the child's abusive experience?

— Does the child have any medical condition attributed to the abuse?

— Does the child exhibit behaviors which could have contributed to the child's abuse?

— Has the child made allegations against an adult? What? Relationship?

— Has the child's family made allegations previously against a provider? What? Why?

It is the responsibility of adults who know the child to provide this data for the social worker, therapist, primary parents, and new parents. This information helps them to resolve issues and respond constructively to the needs of the child. Information often is lacking because the people who know the child well are unable to share it. In other cases, someone may choose not to disclose information under the guise of data privacy and client confidentiality. The right to data privacy is important, but it should not supersede the child's right to attain the best possible care.

If possible, a medical examination of the child before placement is valuable both for the health of the child and for developing a baseline standard of the child's physical condition prior to placement. If a medical examination is not possible,

A case in point . . .

Johnny, age ten, was "forced" into foster care by that stranger who always tried to seem so nice. Sure, he said he wanted to go, what could he say? It didn't sound like no was an option.

Johnny didn't really care how "bad" his family was. At least at home he knew what to expect and how to react to it. He could always hide out in his own messy space with his own stuff. Even when his dad got trashed and smacked him around, it was better than living with these smiling strangers.

Johnny had often wished his dad would die or go away. He never figured he would be the one who would have to go away.

Johnny wanted to cry, but he was too big. He hadn't cried since he was little and he wasn't going to show anyone how he really felt. He'd hang tough. If he cried, he might let his guard down and he'd have to deal with how he really felt. He'd been pushing his bad feelings down for so long he feared they would come out unleashed like dragons and he might kill someone.

the care provider should document any signs of previous injury (scars, bruises, scratches, etc.). If such conditions are found, the care provider needs to document this information and share it with the child's social worker and licensing worker.

Each child in care poses new and different challenges to a family. What one child enjoys may trigger rage in the next child. Guessing a child's reactions is perplexing at best. Many times the outcome is unlike the reactions of healthy, secure children. Preparation and knowledge are necessary for the care provider to help newly placed children move through the maze of buried feelings, controlled responses, and sideways expressions they have developed to survive.

Training in a child's special issues is vital prior to, or very early in, placement. If no specialized training sessions are available the family needs access to competent counselors, support families, and reference materials to help develop proper response. With care and a little assistance, reasonable rules can be established which provide children in care with healthy and familylike relationships while protecting surrogate families from allegations of abuse.

Eventually, pieces of the child's behavior, thoughts, feelings, and life experiences can be filled in. Documentation of data can serve as a road map for the child, therapists, social workers, and families (birth, foster, and adoptive) in bridging safe and healthy relationships to the child.

What are borderline disciplines?

Borderline disciplines are adult behavior responses that are not accepted by social services for care providers to administer to children in care. They are usually personal boundary violations of a child in out-of-home care and are disrespectul and impulsive.

Borderline disciplines may include, but are not limited to, locking a child out of the house, unreasonable time-outs, withholding mail, and negative remarks against the primary family. For children in care, these procedures can be psychologically very damaging. Care providers cannot be sure of what life experiences a child has had.

Most states prohibit all corporal (physical) punishment administered against children in care, spanking included. These rules also govern aversive or deprivation procedures that restrict a person's normal access to nutritious diet, drinking water, adequate ventilation, necessary medical care, ordinary hygiene facilities, normal sleeping conditions, and necessary clothing.

Why borderline discipline is not appropriate for children in care.

The child joining a surrogate family brings his or her own pathology and pain. Only within the child is the true history known. The devastation, grief, and isolation felt by the child can be enormous. A child who has been removed from a primary home may appear to be grieving just as he or she would grieve after a death. Inside the child, it is worse. A death is final and because of its finality, it allows for a passage into a new beginning. After a death, a child is often surrounded by a caring community. Removal to foster care is more intense than the grief a child feels after a divorce. After a divorce a parent still is physically, if not emotionally, present for the child. After a divorce the child's belongings and community often remain intact. Feelings such as those attributed to abandonment and kidnapping are more common for children in out-of-home care. The child in out-of-home care is in crisis in the midst of strangers. Consistency, support, and reassurance will begin to repair the damage, but will not remove the scars.

What are abuse and neglect classifications in licensed family homes?

Licensed families are subject to significant rules for what can constitute maltreatment to a child in care. The following classifications come from the state of Michigan; not all states have these policies.

CLASS I ABUSE: Non-accidental act which causes or is meant to cause serious physical injury. Sexual molestation is included.
Examples:
— Throwing a large, heavy, or pointed object at a child in care.
— Choking or biting a child in care.
— Using a weapon against a child in care.
— Sexually molesting a child in care in any way; penetration is not necessary for molestation to occur.
— Providing a child in care with alcoholic beverages or street drugs.

CLASS II ABUSE: Non-accidental act which causes or is meant to cause nonserious physical injury. Unreasonable, disproportionate use of force is included, with or without apparent injury.
Examples:
— Hitting, punching, slapping, pinching, kicking, scratching, or hair pulling. This includes slapping a small child's hand for reaching for something he or she shouldn't have. Children in foster care are not allowed to be hit, and this means slapping—even if only on the hand. *A child who cannot understand what the adult is saying needs additional supervision, environmental control, removal, or distraction from the situation. A firm "no" in the right tone of voice often will get the same reaction as a slap on the hand.*
— Discipline of children in out-of-home care is not to be connected to living functions. This means care providers are not allowed to deliberately withhold food or water or deprive a child from sleep as a means of discipline.
— Washing out a child's mouth with soap, applying Tabasco sauce, or a similar noxious substance. *Washing a child's mouth out with soap is a forceful and invasive procedure. A child who has been sexually abused may be reminded of forced oral sex. It may cause gagging, nausea, and severe gastrointestinal distress. A child may be allergic to soap and have a reaction. A child who feels ashamed or dirty may be reinforced in believing it is true.*
— Forcing a child to run, stand, sit, or kneel outside of part of a planned intervention strategy. Child runs 50 laps. Child made to write *"I will be good"* 250 times. Child confined to room all weekend. Having child stand in corner or with nose on the wall.
— Using excessive force (pushing, shoving, restraining) handling a child.

CLASS III ABUSE: Use of language or other means of communication to degrade or threaten a child in care.
Examples:
— Derogatory gestures.
— Shaking a child in care.
— Swearing at a child in care.
— Spitting at a child in care.
— Teasing or making fun in a way that is vulgar, degrading, sexist, or otherwise offensive to the child in care.

CLASS I NEGLECT: Deliberate non-compliance with accepted standards of care and treatment which causes serious physical injury to a child in care.
Examples:
— Permitting a child in care to wield a weapon.
— Allowing a child in care to engage in self-injurious behaviors.
— Failing to intervene when a child in care is being assaulted.

After school, Johnny couldn't wait to sneak into his new room. If he didn't hurry, his new foster mom would be asking him what happened in school, how was lunch, what happened that was fun today. Why couldn't she just leave him alone. All he wanted to do was "veg out" in his room like he used to, put on the tube, and get a soda—but no o o! Here he could have an orange juice and do his homework. There was no soda before dinner and that alone was irritating.

His new foster father would come home and start the interrogation again. "How did your day go, Johnny?" he'd ask. Then he would rub the top of Johnny's head and tell him he was glad he was living with them. Johnny thought it was disgusting. After all, a self-respecting, grown man didn't act like this.

Johnny liked the way his foster father looked him straight in the eyes when he was talking, at least that was what a man should do.

He always knew his real dad loved him because they would box and fight. Sometimes it got out of hand, but most of the time it felt good. Besides, a dad's job is to make you tough, make you into a man.

Johnny wondered what this new foster father was made of. He tried every trick he could think of to get this boring dude to rough him up a bit. It seemed like very little upset this crazed man. Maybe he would need to work a bit harder.

Finally, Johnny's real dad got to visit him. Johnny ached to be home. Home with his real family.

Johnny's real dad smiled and punched him on the shoulder. Johnny punched him back. The contact felt great. His dad wrapped him in his big arms and gave him a good strong wrestler's hold. A real man's kind of hug. None of that wimpy stuff.

Johnny's dad asked him how it was going. Johnny looked at his feet and quietly said, "Oh, OK." Then his dad asked, "How do you like the foster dad?"

— Permitting a child in care to attempt suicide.
— Allowing a child to go outside without seasonally appropriate clothing.
— Depriving a child in care of foods and fluids.
— Not providing adequate shelter, sleeping space, or safety resulting in serious physical injury or illness

CLASS II NEGLECT: Non-compliance with accepted standards of care and treatment which directly results in nonserious physical injury or illness. *Examples:*
— Ignoring a reasonable request, resulting in injury or discomfort.
— Failure to change dressings, diapers, soiled clothing.
— Permitting a behavior which will elicit retaliation from others.
— Allowing a child in care to eat inedible objects.
— Permitting a child in care to starve him/herself.
— Allowing self-injurious behavior to continue.
— Not seeking medical help when needed for a child in care.

CLASS III NEGLECT: Non-compliance with accepted standards of care and treatment which puts a child in care at risk of serious/non-serious injury. *Examples:*
— Leaving medicine cabinets unlocked.
— Not buckling seat belts.
— Leaving a child in care at home unattended. Young child left unattended. Child with special needs left with unskilled adolescent. Child care workers who are caring for children when care providers are away must be additionally approved by social services.
— Leaving household cleaning supplies out.
— Not providing blankets and pillows.
— Depriving a child of his or her personal allowance. *(Small payments for reimbursements of damages or loss may be established in consultation with the worker and the child.)*

Other actions by foster parents which may be deemed inappropriate and lead to licensing sanctions in various states include:

— Failure to supervise a child in care and . . .
 — Child lights a fire.
 — Child victimizes another child.
 — Child does property damage to another's property.
— Instruments which can do bodily harm, such as firearms and ammunition, are accessible to a child.
— Inappropriate use of time-out. Depriving an individual of access to water or restroom every thirty minutes. Confinement area is smaller than six by six feet. Area used for time-out is dirty, not lighted, or not ventilated. Child is not supervised or checked on while in time-out.
— Misuse of funds designated to meet needs of the child.
— Failure to allow a child to visit primary family.
— Mail is censored or not given to a child.
— Food is not handled, contained, or stored properly.
— Home is dirty, contains peeling paint, vermin, rubbish, or insects.
— Chemicals, detergents, or other toxic substances are stored with food.
— Child is not provided with clean linens and towels.
— Pet health is not maintained. Immunizations are not current.
— Failure to get a child in care necessary medical attention.

In trying to protect children, adults may avoid providing discipline when it is needed. By the time action is taken, the redirection process necessary may be out of the realm of administering in a foster family.

What is corporal punishment?

Corporal (physical) punishment includes but is not limited to hitting, slapping, spanking, striking, pinching, shaking, yanking, poking, kicking, hair-pulling, biting, washing mouth out with soap. Children in care shall not be subjected to cruel, severe, unusual, or corporal punishment inflicted in any manner upon the body of the child with a hand or instrument—paddles, belts, cords, rulers, sticks, etc.

> *Spanking is a prohibited practice in most states for children in out-of-home care.* Care providers need to be aware of exact licensing laws. One swat on the buttocks of a diapered two-year-old may not be abusive in a primary family—*it is abusive in a foster home* to children in care. One slap on the hand of a child reaching for a hot stove is abusive in a foster home. *It is a matter of law.* Children in care have not developed a trusting and attached relationship with their caregivers. Spanking reinforces the child's feelings of being powerless and worthless. In addition, care providers do not initially have the same attachment to children in care as they do to their permanent children.

> *To avoid argument, let's begin with the same definition:* Spanking is the administration of an open hand on the child's buttocks and is never more than one or two slaps. It is not done out of anger. Neither the child nor the parent is tired, sick, or hungry. It occurs infrequently. The parent understands that the best amount of punishment is the least amount of punishment. The parent accepts and respects the child, and the spanking is administered out of love and concern. The parent is not under stress, and the spanking is developed as a part of the parenting system. The child is aware of what a spanking is. The child knows how and why it is being done. The child is consoled after the administration of the spanking. Both the parent and the child reach a mutual agreement regarding future behaviors and set up a plan with some solutions to help the child not need a future spanking. The child is not humiliated publicly or physically harmed. *Even at this level, thirty-seven states prohibit the spanking of children in out-of-home care.*

> Care providers need to teach children personal boundaries. Most of that guidance is achieved through modeling. Neither adults nor children like to be hit. Hitting breeds resentment instead of positive alternative behaviors. Many children who are hit say they would like to hit back, but can't, so they bury their resentment and anger. In some cases, the child's behavior in the home improves—but the behavior may instead move out against the community. In addition, spanking involves the buttocks, which are private. Sexually abused children need to learn not to touch another's private parts. Spanking a sexually abused child may sexually arouse him or her.

Physical punishment does not include temporary physical restraint to prevent a child from harming himself or herself, to protect others or property, nor does it include self-defense by an adult. If restraint or self-defense becomes necessary with a child who is in out-of-home care, the licensing agency and the child's worker must be contacted immediately. Methods of self-protection and child restraint authorized for use by licensed care providers differ in each state.

> *Locked Up:* Children who are in foster care have been assessed by social services as safe for living in an unrestricted home. Under normal conditions a care provider cannot lock a child in a room or the basement as deterrent or punishment. However, as a child begins to experience a sense of safety and works through life experiences, rageful behavior does erupt, and the surrogate parent may become the scapegoat and be in the direct line of fire. Temporarily restraining a child for protection

A foster parent is a model of parenting behavior, both to the children cared for and the primary families of those children.

Condoning even the lightest and most occasional physical punishment sustains the notion that physical punishment is a child rearing norm for all children, and parents who cannot control their anger will use this justification to physically abuse their children.

Sweden pioneered a law prohibiting physical punishment of children in 1979. Finland, Denmark, Norway, and Austria soon followed. Foster parents in the United States can be the same type of examples for children in out-of-home care. The challenge is not an easy one, but the modeling impact on one child may prevent harm to another child in a future generation.
(Haeuser 1992)

of child, parent, or other family member may be required. If a care provider believes a child is dangerous, he or she should call the community's emergency number, the child's social worker, or the police. Care providers should get immediate assistance. They should not wait until the child calms down to seek help. They should immediately document the incident and its potential causes.

Locked Out: Foster parents are not allowed to lock a child out of the house. If a child is out-of-control or violent, foster parents should call their community's emergency number, the child's social worker, or the police. Leaving the child alone in a home may set a family up for thousands of dollars in unrecoverable damages. Locking a child out of the home may set up a neighborhood or community for vandalism.

What is emotional abuse of children in care?

Beyond their tough exteriors, many children in out-of-home care are sensitive and fragile. They are the most vulnerable when they are pushing the hardest away from a relationship with the care provider. Risking the trust and honesty that forms a relationship means risking feeling. And feeling means accepting or remembering events forgotten. The potential for breakthrough in relationships and healing comes when children are at their very worst behavior. The care provider is faced with a difficult task—to avoid responding emotionally in a very emotionally charged and stressed environment.

It is not easy to choose a response which will be appropriate for a specific child. Sometimes the child can push the right of buttons, pull the right strings, and off the provider goes. It is possible for a care provider to emotionally abuse a young person in care without meaning to. The lack of emotional bonding between the care provider and the child, and the temporary loss of the child's family helps to set the stage for conflict. Without existing emotional bridges to the new caregivers, the child sets up a protective screen of defenses—anger or retreat.

Statements made harmlessly may penetrate deeply into buried hurt feelings without the provider being aware that harm has occurred. Name-calling, labeling, threats of removal, or other forms of emotional abuse can be very damaging. Care providers must not show criticism of birth parents, attack the child as being *"bad"* like his family, or make such statements as, *"Oh, your mother is always doing that."* Providers need to focus on the feelings of the child, control their responses to their own feelings, and lend support and care to the child.

Communication triangles in social services: As in divorce, the very nature of foster care sets up children to run messages directly or indirectly to adults. Children do not belong in the middle of adult communication. Birth parent communication through children or social workers to care providers is not appropriate. If communication from a birth parent needs to come through social services, it is safest when it is in writing and the birth parent understands and acknowledges what is being shared. If a care provider needs to communicate with social services, the information must be communicated by the adults involved, not through the child. Adult-to-adult communication needs to be handled by the individuals responsible for sending and receiving the data. Problems may need meetings and mediators— they do not need child messengers.

Communication triangles in the surrogate family: Children who have difficult life histories are ususually superb manipulators. Instead of asking directly to get their needs met, they may set up parents (social workers and birth parents) for a game of *permission ping pong.* The skill and endurance level of the child often surpasses the adults involved and emotional erosion occurs. It is easy to pass the ball to the other adult involved in the game by stating, *"Go ask your mother/father/social worker,"* or *"What did your father/mother/social worker say?"* This appears to remove initial confrontation and place the responsibility on another adult. The problem with this type of interaction is that the child can work to play one adult against the other by filtering the message to his or her advantage. If the answer is not a clear yes or no and additional adult consultation is needed say so. Don't set the child up to be in control by manipulating. Simply say, *"That's a good question. I can't decide this by myself. Give me (--time--) and then I will speak to (--other adult--) and we will decide together."*

Contact with family: The child needs to be supported to maintain contact with agency-approved family and friends—writing letters, sending school papers, and making phone calls. Depriving a child of visits, phone calls, or mail as a form of discipline, when these contacts have been identified as appropriate, is abusive to the child. If a care provider has a problem with visitation, phone calls, or mail from significant others to the child, this issue needs to be discussed between social services and the provider. Correspondence and contact between the child and his family or friends can magnify behavior problems or cause other difficulties for providers and the children for whom they care. Providers need to use caution in keeping a child out of the middle when these difficulties arise.

Discouragement finds fault, humiliates, and demands—often in very subtle ways—it nags and prods. In a healthy, established parent-child relationship, the child can discern the parent being helpful, even though the words may be critical. Some people call this constructive criticism. For children in out-of-home care, words of discouragement can be devastating. All children need feedback, but it seems that children in care have a bottomless pit of need. Even the lack of encouragement may be perceived as disapproval, criticism, condemnation, or discouragement. Children in care may have such a negative image of themselves that even statements of encouragement can be taken as critical and provoke rebellion instead of comfort or a change. Quality care providers learn the special needs of each child so that encouragement is appreciated instead of devalued. It helps to ask yourself— *"Would I make this comment to an adult friend? Am I being patronizing or respectful? What is the point of view of the child? Is it different from my own?"*

About face praise provides the child with a compliment and then turns around and immediately criticizes. Causing a child to feel inadequate in order to gain improvement makes little sense. Some examples of simple critical statements which can create devastating results are: *"Your room looks fine. It would have been helpful if you had also picked up your shoes."*

    (Child thinks, "Even when I try, I'm not good enough. They don't think I'm helpful.") *"I noticed your behavior. It sure was an improvement over the last time. Maybe we can go again someday."*

    (Child hears, "Even if I behave well, there's no guarantee I'll get to go again.") *"Your music is getting better, but you missed a few notes at the end. I don't know what it was, but something wasn't just right."*

"This is a good report card. Why can't you always do this well?"

    (Child hears, "I'm not perfect, I'm not good enough," devalues the accomplishment.)

As of October 15, 1992, thirty-seven states prohibited physical punishment of children in licensed foster care programs. Local county agencies may prohibit physical punishment of children even though there is no state law prohibiting it.

All states prohibit except:

Alabama—permits except for some types of punishment.
Colorado
District of Columbia
Georgia
Indiana
Iowa
Massachusetts
Mississippi—permits except in agency licensed homes
Nevada—permits if social worker approves
North Carolina
South Carolina
South Dakota
Tennessee
Texas—permits except for special needs children.

Jake Terpstra, Licensing Specialist, Children's Bureau, U.S. Department of Health and Human Services

As of October 15, 1992, twenty-two states prohibited physical punishment in public schools.

What can a care provider do to help a maltreated child?

Children who are maltreated have little self-worth. Feelings often have been buried under the guise of control and colored by misunderstood or forgotten experiences. The child's interpretation of an event may be unclear and behavior may be exhibited in ways that shock even experienced families.

Children need to love themselves. Enormous amounts of compassion and concern may be necessary to fill the cracks in the broken self-worth of a child. This takes time and energy. Sometimes more time and energy than one person is capable of giving.

In working with children in care, our family has found when children are given time, respect, joy, creativity, intimacy, power, generosity, assurance, understanding of paradox, and forgiveness the child begins to attach his or her self-worth to a framework and begins to risk an honest adult-child relationship.

Children in out-of-home care need time. Relationships take time. They do not happen in hours or minutes, quality or quantity—but in actual relationship to another person. Our family calls this process time, and it is how we manage our personal relationships with children and significant others—one process at a time. Children need assurance that they are significant, that who they are and what they think and believe have relevance in your family. A clock cannot tell this kind of time, only the process of being and doing.

In process time, we finish what we start, or we reach a transition point with child interaction before we move on to the next process. We don't judge a child by developmental norms, but by single steps. We don't plan a lot of time outside scheduled activities, and when we do, we provide plenty of transition space to make appropriate adjustments or meet schedules. We observe daily expected patterns of actions, but they remain on a process time versus clock time.

Children in out-of-home care need respect. The key to letting go of emotional pain is honor. Like genuine love, honor or respect is a gift we give to someone. It involves the decision we make before we put love into action—that a person is of high value. In fact, love for someone often begins to flow once we have decided to honor him. Children in care need the compassion of one person who cares enough to share their pain. Listening and being sensitive to the child's needs is only a beginning. They need someone to be genuinely interested in their life. Gary Smalley and John Trent in *The Gift of Honor* (1987) take readers on a journey to combat low self-worth by treasuring those we care for and love. They guide the reader in how to communicate honor to individuals we esteem. This highly recommended book provides insight and a path to guide children out of darkness and rejection into believing in themselves.

Children in out-of-home care need joy. Childhood, for some children, can be a time of joy—a time of spontaneity, living in the present, being totally interested in and thrilled with life. For other children—especially children in out-of-home care—even the spark of joy has been snuffed.

Linda and Richard Eyre's book *Teaching Children Joy—Bring Lasting Joy into Your Child's World* is exceptional. For care providers it is priceless. The Eyres's book is written to help adults preserve and teach thirteen different joys to children. They have provided stories, ideas, and guides to help parents encourage all the different types of joy in life for children and their families.

Johnny's story continues

"He's OK, Dad," Johnny answered, trying not to sound too enthusiastic. He didn't want his real dad to think he would be disloyal.

Johnny's father squinted his eyes and a tear fell. Johnny felt awful—that new foster dad made his dad cry. That ****! Johnny felt violated and mean. He would get back at that stupid foster dad. His real dad needed him. Somehow he would get home. He would make that foster dad do something really bad—then he could go home to his real dad.

Kids just know when you've hit a core button, Johnny thought. Dad thinks I've betrayed him. Why did I have say he's OK?

Johnny was furious. All the anger he had ever felt against his dad got placed on that *** foster father. Johnny would get home—one way or another—and that foster father was not going to stand in his way!

Chapter 13 - Guidelines for Care Providers

Physical joys	Mental joys
Spontaneous delight	Interest and curiosity
The body	Imagination and creativity
The earth	Obedience and decisions

Emotional joys	Social joys
Order, priorities, and goal striving	Realness, honesty, and candor
Trust and the confidence to try	Communication and relationships
Family, security, identity, and pride	Sharing and service
Individual confidence and uniqueness	

Most children in out-of-home care have significant *"joy damage."* The Eyres's book gives care providers ideas to help a child find and practice real joy.

Children in out-of-home care need creativity. Along with joy damage, the hopes, dreams, and visions of children in care have been damaged. The ability to think creatively is a crucial life skill. Creative thinking allows a person to solve problems, adapt to change, and build a happy future. It provides choices when the opportunity to make decisions arises. Creative thinking empowers children. Creativity is not limited to fine arts: it is hidden in everything we do in our daily life from how we pick our clothes to what we eat.

— *Creativity in children is messy*. Creativity mixes recipes and scatters flour on the floor. It brings in a dishpan of snow or sand when it is too cold to play outside. It finger paints with shaving cream on the shower walls. It sprays food coloring on the snow for a winter garden. It stomps in puddles while looking at the rainbow. It enjoys all five senses.

— *Creativity takes adult patience and time*. Adults step back and do not rescue children from life's problems when non-dangerous problems occur. Creativity supports natural consequences and promotes problem solving. Support, coaching, and adult supervision are necessary. Adults help children by providing the cheerleading necessary for perseverance and determination.

— *Creativity provides opportunity, not direction*. Creativity is adult silence when a child is thinking up possibilities. Adults encourage creativity when they offer provision of supplies, guidance, and support when the child asks for help, but in their provision they do not accomplish the task the child can do alone.

— *Creativity enjoys the process*. A person with a creative, inventive mind may see new ideas or possibilities which others feel annoyed at or see as problems. Problems offer opportunity. Westinghouse, a temper-tantrum-throwing, scheming, problem child directed his energies and invented more than 400 patents, founded Westinghouse Electric, and put safe electricity into the homes of millions of Americans. Enjoying the process more than the results, people like Westinghouse turn lights on in the darkness, create jobs for many, and make life more enjoyable for future generations. Many of the world's greatest men and women have been difficult children with positive direction.

Children in out-of-home care need intimacy. Real, personal intimacy is a rarity today. Children in out-of-home care have relationship problems that need healing. Chances are that they have been confused and violated in relationships. Normal relationships with others may feel very dangerous, and the child may have no idea what a healthy and intimate relationship feels like. Dr. Archibald D. Hart's book, *Healing Adult Children of Divorce, Taking Care of Unfinished Business So You Can Be Whole Again* (1991), gives excellent insight into real, personal intimacy:

"Feelings are not good or bad . . . they simply are!"

Pleasant feeling states feel better than the unpleasant emotions. They provide a sense of empowerment and security to those feeling them.

Pleasant feeling states include:

Adequacy: able, active, adequate, bold, brave, capable, competent, confident, courageous, effective, fearless, healthy, important, nervy, peerless, powerful, robust, secure, self-assured, stable, strong, sure, together.

Happiness: aglow, calm, content, elated, ethusiastic, excited, fantastic, gay, glad, good, great, happy, joyous, overjoyed, pleased, proud, relaxed, satisfied, thrilled, wonderful.

Love, caring: affable, affectionate, altruistic, amiable, caring, close, concerned, considerate, cooperative, devoted, empathetic, forgiving, friendly, fulfilled, genuine, giving, humane, intimate, kind, loved, lovable, peaceful, sensitive, sympathy, tender, warmth, whole.

Uncomfortable feeling states are:

Anger: aggravated, angry, annoyed, belligerent, bothered, bitter, bugged, cool, cruel, unnerved, enraged, furious, hateful, hostile, intolerant, irritated, mad, mean, peeved, perturbed, resentful, spiteful, vengeful, vindictive.

Distress: ambivalent, anxious, baffled, bewildered, bothered, caught, confused, conflicted, disgusted, dissatisfied, distressed, disturbed, doubtful, exposed, frustrated, futile, helpless, hopeless, nervous, overwhelmed, perplexed, puzzled, skeptical, trapped, unbearable, uncomfortable, unsure, upset, vulnerable.

— *Intimacy demands commitment.* A foster care provider cannot promise permanency as a basis for commitment. The essence of foster care is temporary—the possibility of a move always exists. Instead, a foster care provider can commit to openness, honesty, and integrity in the relationship with the child. Inherent in the idea of commitment is the decision to give. *Intimacy is never self-serving.*

— *Intimacy demands truthfulness.* The child needs to be sure that nothing in life is so bad that it cannot be shared. Intimate honesty provides security that the other person (friend, parent, foster or adoptive parent, or spouse) will not abandon the relationship even after the truth is shared.

— *Intimacy takes time to develop.* There is no such thing as instant closeness. It grows between two people when both understand that there is a commitment: *"I'm with you through thick and thin, good and bad, acceptable and unacceptable. Whatever happens while you're in our home, I'll be here for you."*

— *Intimacy is essentially warm and affirming.* The child needs to feel the warmth and care of the provider family. Love is first a behavior, not a feeling. The expression of affirmation and warmth is repeated over and over again and may never be reflected back by the child.

— *Intimacy is a shared memory.* All truly intimate relationships have a history. Children need continuity in relationships to build memories. Lifestory books, videotapes of life in their foster family, and correspondence after they move on provides children with the knowledge that the foster family cared and is committed to a relationship.

— *Intimacy always involves accountability.* One holds oneself accountable for keeping confidences and never using the intimate knowledge of another to hurt or betray. The act of commitment opens the way for trust. (Hart 1991)

Children in out-of-home care need assurance. All children are in a continuous process of learning, growing, and changing and need to be assured that they are doing OK. When children don't believe in themselves, they need someone who is willing to believe in them and their abilities. Like respect, assurance elevates a child's sense of self-worth. Children in out-of-home care seem to have so many holes in their self-esteem that much of what you put in runs out through deaf ears or is filtered as a negative when it was meant as a positive or an offer of help. Assurance encourages to the point of a lost voice, parental tears, sleepless nights, or exhaustion. It points out what the child does right, compliments the child on trying, and catches the child being good. It focuses on the child's strengths instead of weaknesses. It places reasonable expectations on the child and gradually increases those expectations as the child grows. Assurance builds one tiny step at a time until the child can stand psychologically and emotionally independent. It gives children permission to value and own their actions, thoughts, and feelings and encourages children to judge their own growth honestly and positively. Assurance can help to fill the holes (voids) children in out-of-home care feel when they think of who they are, where they belong, what they can try, and how to accomplish something.

Children in care may have unrealistic expectations for themselves and others. These expectations vary from assuming nothing will work out well to demanding perfection in everything. Both of these beliefs set the child up for failure. Children need to know that life is not always fair, and that bad things do happen to good people. For children in care, your home is temporary, and they are not safe from removal. But you can teach them how to find safe people wherever they are who will help them if they are alone. That they are not the only people in the world who are vulnerable and who get hurt. They need to know everyone experiences pain and upset, and it's OK to find someone to share feelings with. Children need to know that everyone is different and will act differently or say things without understanding all sides. They need hope that even if problems arise, every day is new and it's OK to pick yourself up, dust yourself off, cry if needed, and start over again—or change directions.

Children in out-of-home care need power. Children who have been maltreated have a sense of powerlessness. They have valid reasons to believe bad things happen to them. They feel vulnerable and frightened. Their concept of power is often distorted. They feel they have lost control of their lives. People they hardly know and seldom see make decisions for them. Unpleasant behaviors can be expected as the children seek to take back power they have never had, or which has been stolen from them. It is common for a powerless child to try to control and bully others or repress feelings and neglect personal issues. A care provider can help a child move from a sense of vulnerability and powerlessness to a sense of empowerment. Empowered children can reach out, ask for, and achieve their needs without constantly stomping on the needs of others or themselves. Healthy power feels whole. It feels respectful of self and others. People who are truly powerful do not need to "use" other people. They can say no and still care. They can say yes and feel safe. (Friel and Friel 1990)

— A child needs to feel dignity and respect as a legitimate human being. A child needs personal ***rights to thoughts, feelings, and physical space.*** Often the child's needs have been neglected, and he or she needs encouragement and guidance in ***learning to ask and get personal needs*** met or establish boundaries.

— ***Choices and decision making*** build healthy power. A child can learn how to decide what he or she really wants and then be taught to solve a problem or make a wish happen by breaking the issue into manageable steps. Learning to solve problems gives children power. Although a child may not be capable of making major decisions, small decisions within the context of the bigger decision may be available to the child. For example, the child must go to bed, but the choice of pajamas can be up to the child.

— Care providers have the opportunity to help children understand that ***conflict can offer opportunity and that it can be respectfully resolved.*** Working respectfully through conflict takes courage. It accomplishes knowledge and growth. Children who are caught in the position of *"I win and you lose"* often have the perception that all conflict is negative.

— All childen need to feel safe. Vulnerable children in out-of-home care especially need this security. ***They need to be able to rely on adults to provide levels of safety which provide protection but also promote growth.*** *As frightened children, they may rather lie than admit a mistake, wet the bed rather than face getting up in the darkness, go along with the group rather than risk losing friends, or run away rather than face being sent away.* (Ryan 1975) ***Healthy limits*** give children external boundaries (protection) they can work within. These limits also give the child a space to say "no" when confronted by peers. Children need to know how and when to say no in respectful and effective ways. Provide children with ***the power of "no."***

Additional uncomfortable feeling states include:

Fear: *afraid, alarmed, anxious, apprehensive, desperate, embarrassed, fearful, frightened, horrified, insecure, intimidated, nervous, overwhelmed, panicky, restless, scared, shy, tense, threatened, timid, uneasy, worried.*

Inadequacy: *broken, cowardly, crippled, deficient, demoralized, disabled, feeble, helpless, impotent, inadequate, incapable, incompetent, ineffective, inferior, paralyzed, poor, powerless, small, unsuited, useless, vulnerable, weak.*

Sadness: *abandoned, alienated, alone, ashamed, awful, blue, crushed, defeated, depressed, despondent, disappointed, down, forlorn, foresaken, grief stricken, hopeless, humiliated, hurt, isolated, lonely, low, neglected, rejected, sad, small, sorrowful, unhappy, unlovable, unloved, worthless.*

"Being patient or tolerant doesn't include discounting your own feelings along the way."

— **Responsibilities** give children an opportunity to build self-worth. A careful balance needs to be kept between the child's capabilities and need for responsibility.

Children in out-of-home care need to feel and give generosity. Learning to give to others and accept giving is an important piece of our family system. We find areas of need in our neighborhoods and offer our family as a resource. Children deliver flowers to a neighbor, carry leaves to the compost pile, or ride in the snowplow. Together we mow a lawn or secretly weed a flower bed. Together we may cook a meal and serve food in a low income area, wrap and distribute small gifts, or offer possessions we have to a person in need. There has always been enough food to share with another and time can be found for someone who reaches out in need even when we are busy with day-to-day life. Direct people-to-people service is a daily way of life. Care is given without an expectation for return.

Children in out-of-home care need to begin to understand paradoxes. A paradox is something that seems like a contradiction, but in fact it is not. *In the Native American culture it is to seek harmony among seemingly antagonistic elements. It means looking beneath the surface to understand the deeper relationships and explain them with clarity and simplicity. It means not just seeing a behavior but learning to decode it. With children in care it means looking at a behavior such as aggression and anger and understanding the reality. Is this revenge by a child who feels rejection? Is this frustration in response to failure? Is this rebellion to counter powerlessness? Is this exploitation in pursuit of selfish goals?* (Brendtro, Brokenleg, Bocken. 1990)

In addition, a child needs to understand that you can love and hate someone at the same time. You can be more powerful by yielding and you can be weak by continuing to fight. You can be surrounded by people and still feel very lonely. People who think they are helping you may be hurting you and people who you think are hurting you may be helping you. Your behavior may be out of line sometimes, but you are still a good person. Life is a constant change, and it's OK to change and grow and still remain who you are. Children need to know it is all right to say goodbye to yesterday and be sad—and still say hello to today and be glad. To learn to forgive pain, sadness, and hurt and also to remember the experiences and not forget. (Friel & Friel 1990)

Children in out-of-home care need forgiveness. Children in out-of-home care often don't know what is healthy, normal, or appropriate. *"The way life is"*—which is the way the home life they have come from was—is their reference point. Inconsistency, trauma, and suffering may feel safe and normal to the child. The child may have a high tolerance for inappropriate behavior from others and himself. Hiding food may ensure there will be something later. Stealing may be the way to get nice things. Swearing or bad language may feel powerful. The child may expect and even seek unusual treatment from others for attention, affirmation, or affection. Being hit is better than being ignored. Sexual affection is better than no affection at all.

As a child learns, grows, and changes, old behavior patterns or actions which once felt very normal may evoke shame. The child may blame himself for family troubles. *"If only I'd been better."* Children need to know that they have a right not to be abused, neglected, or exploited—that abuse from previous caregivers does not need to continue in the future. That alternative methods to express needs are available and it is not necessary to provoke others to feel temporarily better. Children in out-of-home care need to discover and understand more than acceptance of their history to let go and move forward. They need to forgive themselves and others who have hurt them. Forgiveness gives a child permission to give up the right for bitterness, revenge, and continued provocation of others. This forgiveness is much easier said than done and may take years to accomplish or never happen.

How can a care provider learn to respond instead of react to a child's behaviors?

A child's behavior may threaten the way we believe people are supposed to act and challenge how we have been taught to behave or what we think is right. These behaviors evoke emotional feelings — care providers are not saints, they are human. The difficulties created by the child are real and some forms of behavior cannot be allowed to continue, but how we react or respond to these feelings is up to us.

Adults can choose their own behavior
regardless of the behavior of the child.

Adults cannot expect to live unprovoked or void of the anger of others. As human beings, we cannot avoid angry feelings. We can, however, avoid acting irresponsibly when we are angry or when a child is angry with us. As parents, we can express our true feelings and model for the child responsible behavior, even when we feel like performing an adult temper tantrum.

The care provider's role is to
care, protect, teach, and model healthy behavior
for children in out-of-home care.

It is impossible to anticipate all of the kinds of behavior a care provider will come in contact with in caring for an out-of-home child. These behaviors can range from annoying or embarrassing to serious and damaging to the child, others, or property.

Behaviors may be confusing and difficult to handle.
   —*A child using bath towels for toilet paper*
   —*A ten-year-old smearing feces on the tiled walls*
   —*A child masturbating in public*
   —*A child spitting on another child's dinner plate*
   —*Chronic lying, bedwetting, nose picking, gas passing or belching*

They can be disruptive to family life.
   —*A child who does not respect rights or property of others*
   —*An aggressive or withdrawn child*
   —*A child pounding on the neighbor's door yelling abuse*
   —*A child abusing or killing animals*
   —*A child sexually or physically abusing another child*
   —*Sexual acting out in provocative or seductive ways to other family members*
   —*A child chasing a sibling around the house with a knife—just to tease.*

The battle lines have been drawn.
The child's behavior has finally pushed your last button.
Your emotional sirens are flashing. What can you do?

What would you do?

Jeremy, age twelve, was adopted at thirty months. He had lived in three homes previous to his adoption. Biracial, he was placed in a rainbow family, in a small, quiet, rural New England community.

"I'm not a part of this family. You hate me. I hate you. You adopted me to be a slave. Don't hit me! Don't hit me!"

Jeremy's mother's mouth dropped. Where had this come from? She was standing ten feet away, no one had appeared to cause the child a problem.

Out the door Jeremy ran, "They're going to beat me, they're going to kill me!"

His mother ran after him, "Jeremy, come back. What's wrong?" Jeremy continued yelling and running. He ran up the driveway of a neighbor and began banging on the door.

"Jeremy, you stop that right now. What do you think you are doing?" Confused, embarassed, and frightened, Jeremy's mother didn't know what to do. A flashback had captured her son.

David sat on the couch reading to one of his foster daughters.

"Dad, can I talk to you?" Shannon softly said.

David looked up. Startled he found his 16-year-old other foster daughter is a short, black, see-through negligee.

"So, what do you think? Do you like it?" Shannon coyly asked.

David stared, not out of sexual perversion, but in shock, gathering his composure on what to say next.

"Get that thing off and put on something decent," piped the child sitting next to him.

David sighed.

The report got back to social services that Shannon wore a see-through negligee and David stared at her and didn't say anything.

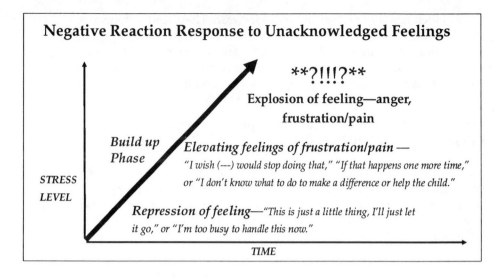

Negative Reaction Response to Unacknowledged Feelings

?!!!?

Explosion of feeling—anger, frustration/pain

Build up Phase

Elevating feelings of frustration/pain — "I wish (---) would stop doing that," "If that happens one more time," or "I don't know what to do to make a difference or help the child."

STRESS LEVEL

Repression of feeling—"This is just a little thing, I'll just let it go," or "I'm too busy to handle this now."

TIME

When confronted with a difficult behavior—stop!
Ask yourself, is this behavior purposeful
(manipulative with premeditated thought)
or out of control (a reaction without understanding)?

Take a deep breath. *Are you overreacting? Is this a small detail that has finally tipped the scales? Be honest, this is not the time to conveniently rationalize your behavior. Get real! What is the "real" problem here? What is the purpose of the child's behavior? Should you have reacted earlier? Are your feelings escalating because you have put off dealing with an issue?*

Tell yourself. *"I am a good person. I take care of myself in healthy ways. I am of value and so is the other person. The way I am feeling is real and I can choose how I respond to these feelings."*

Do you need to take control *of the situation that is getting out of hand or do you need to supply reassurance and support? Remaining calm while the child is upset is very powerful for both the adult and the child. Is it best to leave the situation and set a time to get back together?*

Our own life experiences and stress levels will trigger accelerated reactions. Adult behavior can fall short of expectations when we don't take time to evaluate and regulate our initial reflex feeling. Adults may read more into a behavior than is necessary or may be having a difficult day and not have the capacity to stop and think.

Our perception of the child's behavior will have an impact on our reactions or responses to the behavior. All parents—foster, birth, and adoptive—have feelings of anger, frustration, and embarrassment more often than we would like to admit. These feelings are normal and should not be denied. However, our responses to those feelings are up to us. To blame ourselves for the child's behavior—*these things wouldn't happen if only I was a better parent*—is not helpful. Or to blame the child for our own feelings and reactions to those feelings is unjustifiable. As adults, we are accountable for our feelings and responsible for our actions.

Once we begin to explore our own feelings we often discover we are complicating the problem. Understanding our own feelings and reactions to those feelings is critical in working effectively with complex children. By acknowledging our feelings and the intensity level of those feelings, we can become less reactive and more responsible in response to children in our care.

Explore your own childhood. Have you dealt with your own past? Do you remember how you felt toward your parents' reactions to behaviors they did not like? Is there a particular part of your childhood that you do not remember, or leaves you feeling uncomfortable—family chemical abuse, illness, abandonment, divorce, insecurity, violence, sexual abuse, emotional abuse, or neglect? Could your own repressed feelings interfere with responding safely and appropriately to a child in out-of-home care? Caring and concerned adults may enter foster care with a sincere desire to help and protect children from future abuse and then find themselves faced with similar abusive or neglectful issues in their own homes. A well-functioning, healthy family, combined with the imported pathologies of a child in out-of-home care, can begin exhibiting the same reactions as the child's original family.

Anger on its own is a healthy emotion and vented properly releases tension. Stuffing the anger, deciding to think about it later, delaying the feeling and/or expression of anger are not healthy. Layer upon layer of hostility may become stored.

Our feelings about sexuality, honesty, substance use, anger, selfishness, and self-control are directly reflected in our responses when behaviors occur contrary to our beliefs. Often we do not like to face some of our feelings regarding certain behaviors. We may fear that we cannot cope with a certain behavior or that the child's behavior will escalate. We may be shocked and embarrased if a child masturbates in public. We may feel resentful and defenseless when a child shouts, *"I hate you, you're not my parent,"* or *"Don't touch me, you're hurting me,"* when we are standing ten feet away. We may feel hurt and confused when a child continually lies or manipulates to get a perceived need met. The feelings of fear, shock, embarrassment, anger, resentment, and confusion are normal—we must give ourselves permission to feel them. We can address these feelings then by name, evaluate the situation, and regulate our response accordingly. *(See pages 18-19 for ideas.)*

Honestly look at a child's (and your) methods of hiding unpleasant feelings—especially anger.

Life's pleasant feelings are easy to deal with. Unpleasant feelings are quite a different story, and unpleasant feelings often predominate the life of the child in out-of-home care. These unpleasant feelings are often hidden, compounding the problem of interpretation for the parent and the child. Appropriate expression of unpleasant feelings for these children is difficult. Past appropriate expressions may have caused additional pain or suffering. The child, a survivor, has learned to harbor the true feeling deep inside, deny the existence of these feelings, or has developed alternative coping mechanisms to express the hidden feelings. These alternative coping mechanisms can be very frustrating to new care providers and uncovering the true feelings behind the child's masks can be very difficult. Sometimes the anger is released on *"safe"* people, animals, or things that will not challenge the anger. Other times it perverts the day-to-day personality of the child.

Children with hidden anger may demonstrate the following behaviors:

— *Violent expressions* over little things.

— *Mutilation* of self, others, or possessions.

— *Manipulating* people and circumstances to the child's advantage.

— *Displace anger* to other people or causes that the child does not agree with.

— *Sugar coat* the anger or other feelings and no longer feel them.

— *Feigning loyalty* while plotting revenge.

— *Disassociation* or taking on alternate personalities.

— *Pessimistic, complaining* attitude about everything.

What would you do?

Steve put on the head-phones, took his shoes off, put his feet up on the ottoman, and closed his eyes. It had been a hard day. Sandy had just run down to the corner store to pick up milk and bread. Sally, their foster daughter splashed in the tub.

Feeling someone had tickled the bottom of his feet, Steve opened his eyes. There on the floor in front of him lay seven-year-old Sally, naked, masturbating. "Sally, go in your room and get dressed, now," Steve said. He got no response but a wry smile. "I said, go to your room now." Sally laughed.

Steve got up and stood over Sally. "Young lady, do as I say, go to your room."

"Make me," came the taunt back. Reaching down under Sally's armpits, Steve lifted Sally to her feet just as Sandy came in the door.

Sally was still rubbing her bottom and immediately said, "He made me do it, you weren't here and he made me."

— *Provocation* of others to continue abuse.

— *Rumors and gossip* to undermine others.

— *Taking risks* by placing self in danger.

Removing the *"safe"* mask that hides the real feeling may take months or years to uncover. Deb Jones describes these masks like peeling an apple or an onion. For some children you peel the first layer and you find healthy, wonderful fruit like an apple with a solid core and seeds that are ready for planting and new growth. For other children, you peel off layer after layer, each layer revealing another layer, a little smaller, but made of the same stuff. A tearful, heartbreaking discovery.

Turning the child's behavior intensity level down in stages is easier than trying to turn it off.

It is typical that an out-of-home child's behavior will not be not age appropriate or at a normal intensity level. A ten-year-old, for example, may behave more like an eight- or six-year-old. Parenting the child with expectations for a ten-year-old will not transport the child into age appropriate behavior. Successful care providers work from developmental stage to developmental stage, rather than judging a child on biological age.

Providers must use care in not taking ownership of the child's behavior. In most cases, the child's difficulties are neither a cause nor a reflection of the provider's care. Providers may become concerned that if children do not behave properly and if they don't stop them, the children will only get worse. Sometimes this is true. At other times, children in out-of-home care may be exhibiting normal developmental behaviors at a much higher intensity. Turning the child's energy level down a notch is often much more effective than turning it off. Movement from intense to subdued feelings occurs often before you see movement from unpleasant to pleasant feelings in a child. It may be easier to work to change the intensity of the feelings than it is to move the child from unpleasant or negative states into more pleasant or positive emotional states. Once the energy level of the child is manageable, you may find the behavior is not so distressing and is easier to work with.

Humor or surprise often work to move a child from negative feelings to more positive feelings. Laughter is one of the best ways to reduce stress and feel good. The chemicals released in the body through laughter reduce pain and tension. There is no better way to move a child's intensity level than by finding ways to have fun with each other respectfully. Deb Jones gives an example:

> Hearing her son growling under his breath in frustration, knowing that the next behavior would be a dangerous, violent temper tantrum, one mother of a fourteen-year-old challenging child grabbed him by the arm and ran out the door screaming, "There's a bear in here! There's a bear in here! Run!" Quickly shutting the door and out of breath, the boy asked, "Where's the bear? Mom, you're crazy!" "Well," said the mother, "I heard you growling and I knew the next thing that would happen was you'd turn into a mauling bear, and I wanted both of us out of there and in safety." They looked at each other laughing. A memory had been made. From that point on—the family was put on "bear alert."

If the adult shares a common goal or connection with the child, it also will be easier to move a child from a negative feeling state to a positive feeling state. The adult may need to break the issue into small pieces to find a point of mutual agreement and a place to begin redirecting.

— *What do the child and I share in this issue? Are we both feeling similar feelings?*

— *Is there some part of this issue where I can make an emotional connection?*

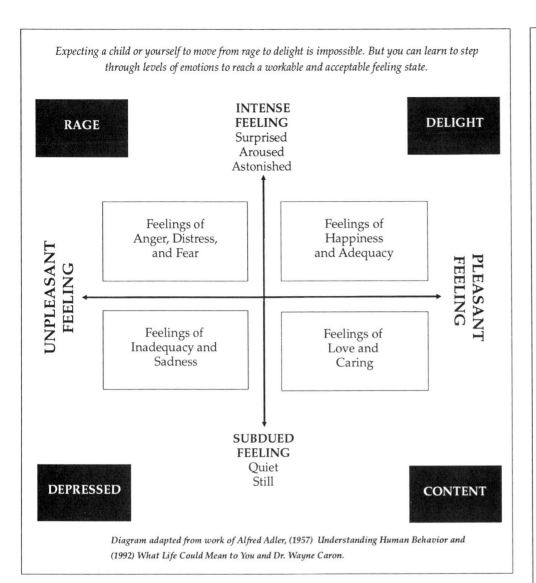

Expecting a child or yourself to move from rage to delight is impossible. But you can learn to step through levels of emotions to reach a workable and acceptable feeling state.

RAGE

INTENSE FEELING
Surprised
Aroused
Astonished

DELIGHT

UNPLEASANT FEELING

Feelings of Anger, Distress, and Fear

Feelings of Happiness and Adequacy

PLEASANT FEELING

Feelings of Inadequacy and Sadness

Feelings of Love and Caring

SUBDUED FEELING
Quiet
Still

DEPRESSED

CONTENT

Diagram adapted from work of Alfred Adler, (1957) Understanding Human Behavior and (1992) What Life Could Mean to You and Dr. Wayne Caron.

— *Are these feelings immediate or are they coming from hidden feelings?*

— *Is there a statement or action I can take to move the child into another feeling state?*

— *What will this child respond to?*

Parents responsible for difficult children need to help them learn to direct intense reactions. Redirection, however, may be a guessing game. Depending on a child's temperament, he or she will respond uniquely to various stimulation. Additional energy may quiet one child while it escalates the behavior of another. A quiet space may encourage rambunctious behavior instead of producing peace. Finding a common thread and taking care of one piece can begin to direct feelings into a manageable direction.

Parents of difficult children need
other caring adult supports.

Robert G. Wilhite has been treating individuals and families who are dealing with anger. Starting from the teachings of Alfred Adler, Wilhite has created therapeutic systems that help clients uncover the roots of their rage in their family backgrounds and develop healthier ways of expressing their emotions. In his recently released book, *The Family Game of Anger* (1993), Wilhite provides case histories to illustrate cycles of rage and to show us how to break them. ***This is absolutely recommended reading for any family dealing with children in out-of-home care.***

Expecting a child or yourself to move from rage to delight is impossible.

But you can learn to step through levels of emotions to reach a workable and acceptable feeling state.

Children who Hurt become master manipulators. When they misrepresent what goes on—exaggerate, distort, or minimize—they manage to keep adults in turmoil. . . They seem to thrive on this disharmony and derive some sort of satisfaction from the disharmony between adults and systems involved in their lives. They do not realize that such disharmony increases their own feelings of anxiety and insecurity and often results in further inappropriate behavior. They observe the adults involved become uncertain how to relate to each other or that they become openly hostile and confronting. Such repercussions appear to reaffirm for some children that adults are not to be trusted.
Arent 1993

Here are some examples from Wilhite's wisdom:

. . . Anger never exists by itself. It always attaches itself to another feeling or set of feelings. However, in most cases, the anger becomes the overriding emotion and the one we choose to express. We are so focused on the anger, we overlook the other feeling(s) and never resolve the real issue that's troubling us.

Take frustration for example.

1. *Instead of owning the frustration, **we might burst out in an expression of anger.** That's one step on the anger path.*

That's not the only possible response to being frustrated, just one choice among many. But we usually don't see a range of choices. We just blow our tops and say the reaction was inevitable. Just the same, there are other possibilities.

2. *Recognize the frustration; own it and deal with it.*

3. *Give the anger power; intimidate others to get our way.*

4. ***Stuff the feelings of anger and frustration and pretend there is no problem.** Appear virtuous because we've handled the situation so well (which we obviously haven't). Go home and kick the cat or scream at the garbage disposal unit, since we haven't dealt with the original frustration hours ago.*

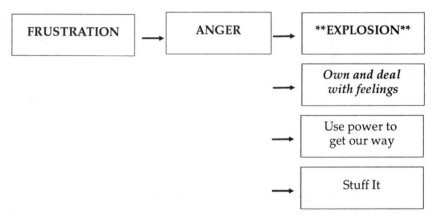

It seems logical to most of us that resolving the frustration is the sensible route. So why don't we do that? Because our private logic (read the rest of Wilhite's book The Family Game of Anger to understand) gets into the process and overrides our good sense. It's like being on autopilot.

So what happens when we don't stop ourselves, when we let our emotions run away? The illustration on the next page traces unmanaged anger through several informal stages:

Wilhite explains his diagram of the Pathological Progression of Rage:

As though our behavior had a life of its own, our intellect stands outside our body watching an emotional explosion we feel powerless to stop. We're not interested in stopping it; we're interested in seeing what unfolds.

1. *Perceiving emotions as anger.*
2. *Feeling agitated.*
3-5. *Losing more and more control.*
6-8. *Feeling remorse for resulting actions.*   **Start the cycle again.**

THE PATHOLOGICAL PROGRESSION OF RAGE

Robert Wilhite (1993)

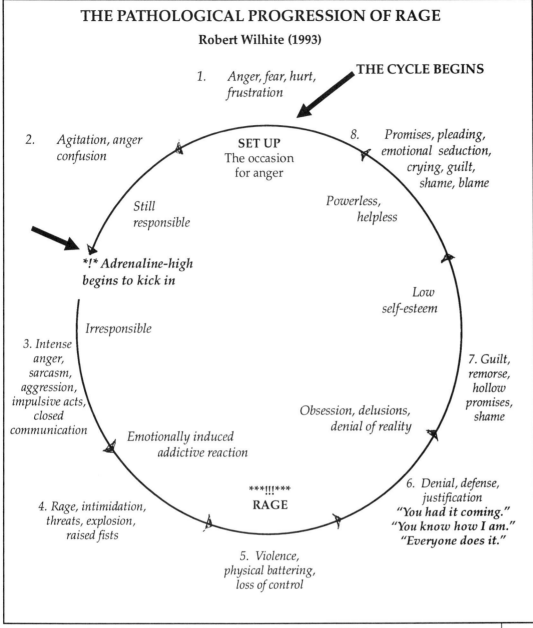

THE CYCLE BEGINS

1. *Anger, fear, hurt, frustration*

2. *Agitation, anger confusion*

SET UP
The occasion for anger

8. *Promises, pleading, emotional seduction, crying, guilt, shame, blame*

Still responsible

Powerless, helpless

! Adrenaline-high begins to kick in

Low self-esteem

Irresponsible

3. Intense anger, sarcasm, aggression, impulsive acts, closed communication

7. Guilt, remorse, hollow promises, shame

Obsession, delusions, denial of reality

Emotionally induced addictive reaction

!!!
RAGE

6. Denial, defense, justification
"You had it coming."
"You know how I am."
"Everyone does it."

4. Rage, intimidation, threats, explosion, raised fists

5. Violence, physical battering, loss of control

Diagram adapted from The Family Game of Anger (1993), *Robert Wilhite. See also* Anger during Protest Stage —Chapter 1

We begin the cycle with an anger reaction based on fear, hurt, frustration, or whatever. Our desires may have been denied, our rights violated, someone may have been victimized—you may have been victimized. At the next stage, moving counterclockwise, we feel upset and confused but maintain a reasonable state. Beyond this point in the circle (marked with an *!*), we cross into the realm of irresponsibility. (A person may be stuck in any of these areas for a significant period of time before moving on to the next stage or may simply deal with the reality of anger and rage and begin a healthier emotional pattern.) From this point our emotions inevitably carry the activity all the way around the circuit until we are ready to begin again.

Irresponsible behavior takes many forms. *It may be aggression (either passive or active). It may be a more subtle, controlling technique such as sarcasm, which is used to garner greater power. Or it may be impulsive actions designed to keep the other party off-guard. All these irresponsible behaviors have the same function: they cut off communication. And then, **BINGO!***

We don't lose our temper; we use our temper.

We realize that we get mad because we want to get mad, because our private logic tells us that's the appropriate way to respond.

The blame doesn't belong to anyone or anything but ourselves.
Wilhite 1993

Children Who Hurt often manage to manipulate adults into a pattern of misunderstanding, misrepresentation, and mutual mistrust. As an adult, you do not have be be victimized by the manipulations of a child who has never learned to trust. You must establish a clear feedback system to other adults involved in the child's life, even though you may be greeted with disdain, hostility or indifference.
Arent, 1993

Cheri, twenty seven, was a licensed foster parent to emotionally disturbed teenage boys. She was also the stepmother to a sixteen-year-old son.

Intelligent, warm, and charming, she and her husband enjoyed the active lifestyle and surprises these young men offered.

Her stepson, James, had entered her life eight years earlier. Shifting between two homes is never easy, and it was no different for James. His mother and father's estranged relationship placed him right in the middle of message carrying and emotional tug-of-war.

When James was ten, Cheri noticed a significant change in his mood. He was no longer joyful, but on guard and worried whenever his weekend with his father arrived. He seemed very introspective.

Having come from an alcoholic childhood, Cheri took James aside and shared what it was like living with abuse. Tears flooded to the child's eyes as he shared how worried he was for his mother and the abuse that was happening at home.

We're on our way!

Continuing along the anger path, we get into what I call an emotionally in-duced, addictive reaction. Our inappropriate behavior is fueled by run-away emotions. We become addicted to the crazy high that anger produces, just as the alcoholic is addicted to delusions resulting from booze. We're excited by the power of our anger, and as we act out our rage, we add more fuel to the emotional blast furnace inside.

Physical violence may erupt at this point; the perpetrator batters his victom and seems to career further out of control. **(Except we never truly lose control. We simply relinquish responsibility for our behavior. It's a cop out. We choose our actions.)** At the next point in the circle we feel we must justify what's happened. Rather than admit to acting inappropriately, we use excuses and shift the blame.

Guilt is a feeling we substitute for the good intentions we never really had in the first place. If we actually wanted to be different, we'd change. We'd think, **"I didn't like what just happened; I learned from that experience."** But guilt buys more time to continue our inappropriate behavior. We internalize the following: **"I always feel bad when I do this, but I'm going to do it again, folks, and I'm going to keep on doing it. I'm not going to change what I do, but I'm going to feel rotten doing it."**

Therefore, we deny the reality, frequently defending our position by stating (or at least feeling), **"You had it coming!"** or **"Everybody does that!"** Sometimes the other person believes us, especially if the relationship is dys-functional (or when the victim is a child). But even when justifications work, we ultimately come face-to-face with our low self-esteem—the insecurity needed for the cycle to generate itself. We feel ashamed of our behavior and sorry we acted in so lousy a fashion.

Finally, we feel powerless and helpless, fear abandonment, and often apologize, promising never to repeat what's occurred. We stay "good" for a while, try to retain a calmer attitude, and hope the other person doesn't really walk out. But when no real consequences happen, when the other party doesn't say, **"Knock it off. I'm not putting up with this,"** we're ready to fall into the same old pattern of behavior. Soon somthing ticks us off, and here we go again.

Getting angry doesn't just happen. Nobody forces us to act in a certain way. We choose to get mad, choose to get hostile, choose to get violent. Why? Because in our mind, in our private logic, that's what works best for us. But it's so much easier to blame others for our irresponsibility than to take a look at ourselves. (Wilhite 1993)

The four diagrams represented on pages 308-313 are important for caregivers and professionals to understand. Adults need to understand anger in both themselves and the children they care for to help manage their responses.

When a crisis arises, it often comes down to who overpowers whom. There are times when the child may have more power because of life experiences and abilities in areas the caregiver does not understand—sexual abuse, violence, and verbal manipulation. The child may be physically stronger than the adult provider or the child may be enraged and exhibiting extreme force. In other instances, the child's behavior or crisis can trigger an anniversary experience in the adult, confounding the adult on what the next appropriate response should be. The adult's mouth is left gaping for an appropriate response to a *"very inappropriate"* action.

As a child begins to feel safe and comes into connection with him or herself, a feeling of freedom and wonderful excitement occurs. Along with the good feelings, however, the unpleasant feelings of the past begin to stir. This can be a very sad and painful time. An emotional rollercoaster. As the child begins healing, it is normal and common for the child to feel:

— *The need to be defensive over past relationships.*

— *A knot in the stomach that doesn't go away.*

— *Crying or sadness for no apparent reason.*

— *Headaches during certain situations.*

— *Inadequate and unworthy.*

— *Rage when frustration or anger would be more appropriate.*

— *Apathic about doing things.*

— *Intense fear or sudden panic when nothing appears to have happened.*

— *Apprehensive about sleep because of nightmares or disturbing dreams.*

— *Detached from situations—numbing, tingling, dizziness when under stress.*

— *Like she or he is watching from a dream, even though it is really happening.*

— *The need to control relationships and situations.*

— *Like avoiding intimacy or any emotioanl closeness.*

These feelings MUST NOT be silenced. They need to be talked about and identified in a caring safe environment. Without acknowledgement, understanding, and expression they can lead to more intense feelings of depression, rage, suicide, or violence.

At this time a supportive therapist and family is vital for the child. Together the adult and the child can handle the weight of the past. Together they can understand deep feelings and begin to heal old wounds. Together they can set new protective boundaries and discover new ways to live. (Henslin 1991)

Chapter 11, "Discipline or Punishment," provides ideas for helping care providers work in a healthy way with children in out-of-home care. Please review that chapter for additional ideas in working with these children.

Helping a child get in touch with the self.

Children who are dealing with backgrounds of abuse, neglect, or exploitation often have very little concept of "owning" their body or personal space. These children are little space invaders—talking in your face, stepping on your toes, or sitting so close you cannot move your arm. What's so interesting above their space invasion tactics is that they do not usually accept the normal, appropriate, caregiving affection that goes along with space interference.

Helping a child understand boundaries and personal space issues is important in healing the child. But how? Where do you start? Start with the basics and don't move too quickly through these lessons. Take the time the child needs to grow and feel safe.

Cheri offered James her friendship and confidentiality and made herself available when he needed to talk.

One night, Cheri was bent over filing bills in the family room and James, now sixteen, came up behind her and put his hands on her breasts. Startled, she removed them, told him to let go, and advised both his birth mother and father of the incident. They did not confront the child, but laughed it off as probably a mistake in hugging. Cheri wasn't so sure.

A month later, James repeated his actions. This time all three adults agreed that if it happened again the family would seek a counselor.

Cheri woke up startled to see James sitting on the edge of her bed. Her husband was out of town on business and the seventeen-year-old in out-of-home care was asleep downstairs. "Can I help you? Is something wrong, James? Did you have a bad dream?"

James put his hand over his stepmother's mouth. He had thought about this for a long time. He would have her.

Jessica had busily cleaned the flat for the arrival of her daughter with her social worker. Just prior to their arrival she let the dog out the front door and in the back door.

Although she was poor, Jessica had always felt she had done a good job with Jenny. Social services felt otherwise, and Jessica had reacted poorly to intervention into her private life. It had been five months since Jenny had been able to spend a day at home. Finally the day had come.

Jenny's social worker had transported Jenny to her mother's house, stepping in dog feces just prior to entering the flat. The little yapping mut came rushing up to the door, knocking the trash can over just as Jessica opened the door to greet her daughter and the child protection worker. Trash was now strewn accross the kitchen floor.

"Oh, shit, you little varmint," Jessica said as she opened the door to face the rather serious face of a social worker wiping dog feces off her shoe.

1. **Breathing.** One of the safest and most basic places to start is *"breathing."* Have the child take deep, conscious breaths to relax. As the child inhales, explain how the air she is breathing is available for her, to keep her alive and healthy. She can feel it in her nose, going down her throat, into her lungs and chest cavity. Each of those body parts is special. Let the child tell you about them and how they feel. Encourage the child to make statements containing *"My . . . . feels like."* Ask the child to try to breathe with her stomach, through her nose, with her mouth. Try different kinds of breathing patterns and sounds. Make up some silly ones. Have the child show you how she breathes when she is scared, confused or angry. Let the child own the smells, sounds and breath. Have the child pick an unpleasant feeling and breath it out of her body or blow the feeling into a balloon until the balloon pops. This exercise lays the foundation for future relaxation when a child is feeling unpleasant feelings. Document what you have learned for future references.

2. **Muscles and relaxation.** Have the child squeeze his toes tightly together and then slowly open them. Talk about the strength of the child's wonderful body. Have the child close his eyes tightly and then very slowly open them. Talk about the darkness and the pressure, the slow release of peaking out and then the relaxation of opening the eyes fully and seeing light. Do the same, tightly closing and slowing opening other body parts—hands, knees, stomach, mouth. Talk about how hard it is to keep the muscles tight and how much better it feels when the muscles are relaxed. Talk about how holding onto feelings is like muscles that are tight. See if there are any old feelings that need to get released and relaxed.

3. **Personal space.** Find out from the child how close other people can get to her before she feels uncomfortable. Give the child a piece of string to make a border. Show the child your border. Explain how your border changes with different relationships. Discuss privacy—drawers, bedrooms, bathrooms, etc. Help the child visually understand personal space and boundaries.

4. **Personal hygiene.** Encourage children to take care of the wonderful bodies given to them. We encourage compliance with house rules and getting to know their own bodies in private and personal space with soaps, shampoos, bubbles, kid flavored toothpaste, glow-in-the dark toothbrushes, and favorite cartoon character towels. Beta the siamese fighting fish guards the bathroom from nighttime bathroom fears—his lighted fishtank and swishing tail greet children in their lonely night bathroom runs.

5. **Nutrition.** Whenever we discover healthy food a child likes—especially in the fruit and vegetable category—we make that food readily available for snacks and meals. Strawberries, melon, and popcorn have always been a big hit. Celery, carrots, apples, oranges, and bananas are usually readily available. Peanut butter and sour cream stand by as dips. Homemade bread—frozen loaves, by scratch, or bread machine—smells wonderful and children enjoy eating what they've helped make. The checkout counter has always been a burden to get through. Candy counters line both sides of the aisle. Finally, after years of frustration, I've given up. Whoever goes to the store with me and behaves appropriately gets sugar-free gum (they must keep in their mouths) at the checkout. No calories, no cavities, and no tears! Some stores are finally wising up and making a candy-free checkout line available. Look for it and use it!

As children get to know, respect, and love their bodies, they begin to recognize how their bodies respond when they are nervous, stressed, or angry. This body awareness becomes an important key to unlocking the hidden anger and pain inside. As caregivers, our healthy and respectful awareness of the child's body and personal boundaries begins to build trust with the child. Slowly, one day at a time, the little space invader or evader learns to trust, love, and hug.

How can a family help a youth who has anxiety, is depressed or suicidal?

Disappointment in relationships, educational or vocational set backs, feelings of guilt, or financial worries all can trigger feelings of apathy, dissatisfaction, or unhappiness. Children in out-of-home care face many disappointments. Everything is new, different and very confusing. The new adult authority is untested and unproven. Friends have been left behind and many new relationships must be developed.

Common anxiety signs in children include:

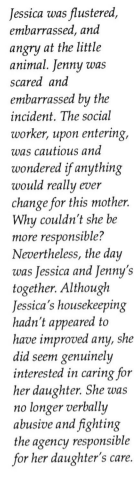

— *Social and/or school avoidance*

— *Panic attacks with an overwhelming sense of doom*

— *Staying in bed, extensive sleeping, not eating*

— *Fear of separation from parents*

— *Persistent worry, nervous habits, and/or restlessness*

— *Unreasonable fear of heights, animals, or closed spaces*

— *Recurrent stomachaches or headaches*

— *Exaggerated need for reinforcement or approval*

— *Tendencies toward perfection*

Feeling stress and anxiety when living away from your familiar environment is normal and to be expected. Stress and anxiety can lead to growth for secure and attached children living in their own home with their own families. These children learn to face their fears and develop new skills. The result is a sense of accomplishment and self-confidence.

The results may be much different for the vulnerable child in out-of-home care. Children who find it difficult to communicate with new *"strangers"* —care providers or social workers—are at risk for moving into depression. The expected anxiety and stress the child feels can race into the silent agony of depression and sink the child to the depths of suicide. Adults responsible for these children need awareness to the signs of stress and anxiety in children.

Most people suffering from depression are not able to explain their overwhelming emotions. They simply feel sad, discouraged, and dejected. These feelings are often accompanied with a loss of initiative and a reduction in activities. The person's self confidence is lowered and he or she may feel a sense of overwhelming anxiety or apprehension. It is normal to suffer from the *"blues"* during some time in life. When these feelings persist it can lead to clinical depression, marked by a chemical imbalance in the brain.

Clinical depression may last for weeks or months. Diets, talking with supportive friends or relatives, professional therapy, antidepressant drugs, and active participation in hobbies have all been effective in helping treat clinical depression. As the responsible care provider it is essential to:

Jessica was flustered, embarrassed, and angry at the little animal. Jenny was scared and embarrassed by the incident. The social worker, upon entering, was cautious and wondered if anything would really ever change for this mother. Why couldn't she be more responsible? Nevertheless, the day was Jessica and Jenny's together. Although Jessica's housekeeping hadn't appeared to have improved any, she did seem genuinely interested in caring for her daughter. She was no longer verbally abusive and fighting the agency responsible for her daughter's care.

It was Jessica's responsibility to get Jenny home to her foster provider. Jessica had planned this weekend for a long time. She knew the bus routes to get Jenny back to the provider's home. She had saved her money and planned spending Sunday night in the downtown area so she could access the right transfers to get Jenny home without any trouble.

The day was delightful. Both mother and daughter wished it would never end.

Time flew by as they walked the shopping streets looking at windows. Late in the afternoon they stopped in a little cafe and ate.

Looking at the clock on the wall, Jessica realized they had better leave if they were to make the next bus. Jenny had to go to the bathroom. Jessica flagged the waitress for the bill. Neither Jenny nor the waitress was very prompt. Jessica was getting worried. If they missed the bus they wouldn't be able to get back on time. Jessica called the provider family to let them know she may be late. There was no answer.

Jenny came slowly out of the bathroom. She had been crying. "I don't want to go back, Mom, I want to stay with you." Jessica hugged Jenny and told her she had to go back, but someday they would be together again.

Two buses later, Jessica and Jenny arrived at the home of the very worried provider. "Where have you been? We were worried sick."

A somber, sad Jenny said goodbye to her mom.

1. Seek professionals trained in working with severely depressed and suicidal youth.

2. Get a complete physical to determine if there is a chemical imbalance, allergies, or other physical ailments influencing the child.

3. Determine if the child is safe. Does the child need to be protected from self-harm? Will the child agree to no self-harm?

4. Seek a supportive adult for yourself.

Those items are the easy part. The difficult piece is day-to-day, 24-hour living with a depressed and/or suicidal person. Suicide is now the second leading cause of death among young people ages 15 to 24. Therefore, it is important to recognize those teens at risk and know the warning signs of suicide and how to help.

The hopelessness that leads to suicide may result from:

— *Traumatic relationship events—loss of loved one, separation or divorce of parents.*

— *Recent major losses, humiliation, or disappointments.*

— *Increased exposures to violence, death, and loss.*

— *Emotional, physical, sexual, or ritualistic abuse.*

— *Recent suicide of relative or friend.*

— *Alcohol or drug abuse (including prescribed antidepressants, illegal drugs, and steroids).*

— *Academic, social, athletic, or spiritual pressures to succeed.*

Depression and suicide are often attempts at making things that seem out of control more manageable. It is common to hear, *"I can't handle it,"* (you'll need to discover what "it" is) or *"I'm not good enough."* Withdrawal is often a silent scream for attention. How a caregiver can provide the *"right"* kind of attention varies with each child.

In an attempt to gain control, the young person pulls his or her universe into a smaller space—sometimes that space is withdrawal, sometimes it's death. There is no single reason why teenagers commit suicide, but most suicides and suicide attempts are reactions to intense feelings of loneliness, worthlessness, helplessness, and depression.

The key to preventing suicide lies in the ability to recognize and respond to the child's cry for help. Most individuals give signals in advance of what they are thinking about.

Suicide warning signals:

— ***Giving away prized possessions*** *to close friend or family.*

— ***Heavy use of drugs or alcohol*** *(the downer after the high or the hangover.)*

— ***Sudden changes in attitude or personality.*** *The extrovert who suddenly becomes isolated, or the shy child who suddenly becomes a risk taker.*

— ***Sudden change in appearance.*** *The child who no longer cares what he or she looks like.*

— **Sudden changes in school behavior.** *Lack of interest and increased irritability. Abrupt changes in attendance, failure to complete assignments and overall change in performance.*

— **Suicide threats.** *"I might as well be dead." "My family would be better off if I were dead."*

Always take a suicide threat seriously.
Never dare the person to actually do it.

Suicide is the depth of personal discouragement.

The book, *The Family Game of Anger,* has excellent case histories of individuals in depression and/or contemplating suicide.

Some basic rules from Robert Wilhite for caregivers living with suicidal or depressed children:

1. **Don't argue with a depressed or suicidal person.** Arguing adds to the destructive cycle, creates more hostility and frustration, and thwarts flexibility. There's little to be gained by telling the person, *"you're wrong."* We may feel better having vented our frustrations, but the individual's problems haven't abated.

2. **Don't minimize the problem.** Be a good listener. Listen carefully to what the person says and be sensitive to what is left unsaid. Often what is unsaid is as or more important than the statements. Show that you care and that you are willing to talk about it. Be direct, talk openly about the problem. *"Are you considering suicide?" "Do you have a plan?" "Will you talk to someone who can help?"*

3. **Keep cool.** Afraid of change, feeling safer in their small designed world, the young person will likely criticize our attempts to help. Do not react with anger. This feeds the destructive cycle and creates frustration.

4. **Ask the therapist** (document your discussion), *"Am I helping (child) by (doing, saying)?" "If I think (child) is in trouble, what should I do?" "What's the best way to work through a situation like this?"*

Depression and suicidal thoughts are bigger than either the individual or the family. Even with the help of mental health professionals the family can get sucked into the individual's destructive behavior. Provide space for yourself to retreat, relax, and regroup. Maintain accurate, up-to-date documentation.

How can a family safely live in the community and work with sexually abused children?

There are a number of preventive steps a care provider can take while working with sexually abused children. Information can be shared if handled in an ethical and respectful way.

1. Inform your immediate family that you are caring for sexually abused youth (caution them about confidentiality), but prepare them with specific guidelines such as:
   a. No family member should compromise himself or herself by being alone with the child in a room with the door closed. Whenever possible, have a third party present.

Safe and appropriate touches:

Gentle clothed neck and shoulder massages.

Lightly touching the shoulder of a child while talking.

Rubbing a charley horse out of a child's sore leg or arm.

Bandaging and cleaning a child's injury.

Gently rubbing the temples of a tired child's forehead.

Gently washing the hands before dinner.

Brushing the teeth of a small child.

Shampooing the child's hair at the kitchen sink.

Brushing the child's hair at bedtime.

Washing the dirty feet at the end of a busy play day.

---

b.   No male or female should enter a foster youth's bedroom because of same sex or opposite sex experiences foster youths may have experienced in the past.

2.   Give relatives and regular guests in your home only the information they need to know to protect their own children from possible abuse. (i.e., no bathing of small children with small foster children and/or sleeping in the same bedroom).

3.   If unable to supervise, use an intercom or monitor.

4.   No touching until the youth feels confident or safe enough to approach you, the foster/adoptive parent.

5.   If a new foster/adoptive child touches you excessively—establish definite guidelines which are comfortable and appropriate for you the foster/adoptive parent.

6.   Advise school and medical personnel working with the child that the child's behavior may be unusual at times because of his or her history. If an unusual behavior occurs, you need to have it documented and immediately shared with you so that the treatment team can help the child. (McFadden)

What are some old and new assumptions about living with children who have been sexually abused?

Increasingly, waiting children moving into adoptive and foster homes have backgrounds that include chronically dysfunctional families, often with substance abuse, and high impact sexual abuse. These children have also often face many moves in relative, kinship and foster care. Typical professional parenting—foster and adoptive issues—of separation and loss, identity, and attachment are combined with these traumas for a volatile mix within the new adoptive or foster family.

The SAFE-TEAM Curriculum: *Preparation and Support for Families Adopting Sexually Abused Children*, is an excellent curriculum for helping families grow, love and enjoy a challenging and damaged child. *(***Highly recommended***)* This curriculum proposes some new assumptions upon which to build effective strategies for healing and growth of these children and their new families. The following list is a sampling of some of the old assumptions and the new working assumptions being proposed in their stead.

Old Assumption	New Assumption
Your love will make all the difference to change this child.	*Your family is a healing place, a secure place that offers tools and love.* a. *The child needs more specific structure and guidance than most.* b. *The child will need additional services beyond the family.* c. *The family needs supports because of these challenges.*
The child needs just what any other child needs; all children behave this way.	*This child was hurt in ways that have left deficits and scars. Some needs will be developmentally delayed; others will be expressed inappropriately or be considered deviant. Behaviors sometimes express disturbed emotions rather than typical stages of development.*

A child who has suffered physical or sexual abuse and demonstrated provocative behaviors should not be left alone for extended periods of time with a foster parent's teenage child as the only babysitter.

A sexually abused female should not initially be left alone with the foster father or other male family members.

A teen male sexual perpetrator should not be left alone with the foster mother or other young women.

Your child will be pleased to trade the negative past for the emotional and material benefits of your family.

Many negatives are not given up willingly; some are defended. The child views some as positives, or a reinforcement of his view of himself and the world. Some behaviors have become compulsive.

Children never lie about abuse

Children, especially adolescents, do manipulate abuse complaints for revenge, power, attention and validation. Also, children often are confused about these emotionally charged subjects.
   a.   They may point to a "safe" person instead of the abuser.
   b.   They may remember and/or release information in segments and over time.
   c.   They may blank out certain events (often permanently)
   d.   They may confuse time, place, event, and person.

Summary

Children in out-of-home care are vulnerable, regardless of their tough exteriors. At their worst, these children loudly request safety, compassion, and care—while they push the very people who care away. Wading through the mire of complex behavior is often a tiring and difficult task. Providers, parents, social workers, and specialists need to work together as a team to maintain continuity. The child's behavior may elude and frustrate even the best of professionals.

Successful providers honor and believe in the child. They allow the child to make choices and provide assurance and encouragement to keep the child trying. They set realistic standards, focusing on the child's strengths. They encourage mutual respect, promote responsibility and expect the child to contribute. They avoid making the child feel guilty and they promote independence. For the child in out-of-home care, the road to self-worth and self-esteem is long.

The behavior of these children is complex because their lives have been complex. Much of the history of the child remains buried in silent spaces within the child. Care providers often have inadequate knowledge of where and how to begin, let alone why a specific situation or statement triggers an unusual reaction. Charting a course that is without twists and turns is impossible. Neither the provider nor the child knows enough to predict every response to every event.

Reactions which are not considered abusive in primary family care may be considered abusive in a licensed foster family home and result in immediate removal of a child, negative licensing action, and provider program investigation. Guidelines and legal regulations have been developed to protect children in out-of-home care. Given the children being cared for, following these guidelines may be difficult. Care providers are human beings and it is normal to feel frustrated, angry, and confused when parenting.

Support services, training, and alternative ideas for parenting help licensed care providers deal with complex situations and crises without reacting to their initial emotional responses. Understanding and acknowledging anger is crucial in parenting out-of-home children.

Personal space issues are not a two way street. The child who talks in your face, steps on your toes, and almost sits on you when asking for something, stiffens like a board and runs from a safe hug when faced with appropriate affection.

Boundaries are areas set aside for protection.

Inside the protective boundary is the whole person, both the conscious and the unconscious selves. The conscious self is where we operate today. The unconscious self is where the feelings and memories of the inner child are stored. The unconscious self still remembers.
(Henslin 1991)

A parent can affect eternity. You never know where the influence will end.

Trust and believe in your ability to change the future of a child. Dare to make a difference.

When in doubt—reach out for support!
Caring for other people's children
is a high risk profession indeed!

References

Arent, Ruth P. 1993. *Trust Building with Children Who Hurt*. New York: Nyack, The Center for Applied Research.

Adler, Alfred. 1957. *Understanding Human Behavior*. Faucett: Premier.

Adler, Alfred. 1992. *What Life Could Mean to You*. One World Publications, Ltd.

Brendtro, Larry K. Brokenleg, Martin, Van Bockern, Steve. 1990. *Reclaiming Youth at Risk. Our Hope for the Future*. Indiana: National Education Services.

Carbino, Rosemarie. 1991.

Eyre, Richard & Eyre Linda. 1984. *Teaching Children Joy. Bring Lasting Joy To Your Child's World*. New York: Ballantine.

Friel, John and Friel, Linda. 1990. *An Adult Child's Guide To What's Normal*. Florida: Health Communications.

Hart, Archibald. 1991. *Healing Adult Children of Divorce. Taking Care of Unfinished Business So You Can Be Whole Again*. Michigan: Servant Publications.

Haeuser, Adrienne. 1991. *Reaffirming Physical Punishment in Childrearing as One Root of Physical Abuse*. Wisconsin: University of Wisconsin-Madison

Henslin, Earl. 1991. *The Way Out of The Wilderness*. Tennesee: Thomas Nelson.

McFadden, Emily Jean. 1984. *Preventing Abuse in Family Foster Care*. Michigan: Eastern Michigan University.

Ryan, Patricia. 1981, 1975. *Discipline and Behavior Management*. In *Preventing Abuse in Foster Care*. McFadden, Emily Jean. (1984) Michigan: Eastern Michigan University.

Smalley, Gary & Trent, John. 1989. *The Gift of Honor*. New York: Simon and Schuster.

Wilhite, Robert., Cole, Merrilee. 1993. *The Family Game of Anger*. Arizona: Keyes Publishing.

THE FAMILY GAME OF ANGER can be purchased by sending $9.95 plus $3.00 shipping and handling to: Self Care Books, PO Box 1348, Mountain Home, Arizona, 72653. Please add appropriate tax if you live in Arizona. Training classes are available by faxing Robert G. Wilhite, MSW at (501) 424-2413.

He trains nationally in the areas of: anger, suicide and depression, family systems, sleeping disturbances and stress reduction.

TRUST BUILDING FOR CHILDREN WHO HURT is a one-to-one trust building program designed to help children make a connection to one adult who they can trust. This exceptional program is perfect for teachers, coaches, social workers, neighbors, group leaders and churches who outreach to Children Who Hurt. An excellent support program for providers and parents who care for out of home children. Write to: The Center for Applied Research in Education Business Information and Publishing Division, West Nyack, NY 10995 and request the book TRUST BUILDING WITH CHILDREN WHO HURT by Ruth Arent. *(See also review in Resource section at the back of the book.)*

Growing Up Again, Parenting Ourselves, Parenting Our Children *by Jean Illsley Clarke and Connie Dawson provides wonderful, respectful insight into ideas to reparent vulnerable children in out-of-home care.*

They recommend—

Stay underwhelmed!

When you feel impatient, repeat to yourself:

— *One hole at a time.*

— *One task at a time.*

— *One experience at a time.*

— *One new decision at a time.*

— *One new behavior at a time.*

— *One day at a time.*

Clarke, Dawson 1989

Excellent reparenting learning materials can be obtained by writing to :

> *Daisy Press*
> *16535 9th Ave. N.*
> *Plymouth, MN 55447*

SECTION V

Reference Tools for Preservation

Reach out to others—parenting children in out-of-home care requires safe support services for both adults and children.

Don't forget to be good to yourself! Allegations can be very painful.

Make a list of all the things you do well.

Practice asking others to help you with your needs.

Listen and don't interrupt when others are talking.

Practice debate or disengage in an argument.

Give yourself permission to feel the way you feel and don't ridicule yourself.

Do a project that can be completed.

Take a self-care break (walk, talk to a friend, play with a pet).

Set priorities and make a list so you can see the things you are accomplishing.

Recognize even small accomplishments—"I made it through the last half hour" to "I made it through this task/visit/job."

Reach out to someone who needs help more than you do.

Take a five minute vacation—stop and smell the roses.

Kidz
POCKET FOLDER
Different Color for each
child – Store all Social
Service Papers

PARENTS CARE
NOTE BOOK
Log information
pertinent to parenting
each child

Kidz
CARE
A safe place to
share ooo

Chapter 14

Document— How to Put It in Writing

In the system of child welfare - if it's not written down, it never happened or it happened the way someone else documented it.

There is only one way to keep information current, concise, and immediately available to all necessary people— **keep good records and document!**

The value of the written word cannot be overestimated. Care providers should not risk their family's or the child's well-being to their own memory, the social worker, or any of the other individuals involved. Keeping track of the details while parenting difficult children is often a trying or forgotten task. Yet, accurate and proper documentation can be life saving. Documentation can serve as evidence in advocating for a child or family with the agency or a judge.

Experienced surrogate parents recognize that some children can provoke very strong feelings in adults. When this happens it is very disconcerting and the provider may want to verbally or physically strike out at the child. How the provider controls these feelings and how he or she recognizes them is important to social services. Communicating such incidents to the social worker in writing is crucial. Together the social worker and the care provider can develop an approved and accepted plan for future incidents. A written and approved plan for managing the behavior of the child and the responses of the provider is valuable in working as an interdependent team member.

In addition to normal stress, surrogate care provider families deal with the additional pressures of the social service agency, child protection workers, licensing workers, psychologists, doctors, special school programs, the birth family, and a host of other people and systems.

Before you are up to your neck in "allegators" and allegations be prepared—document.

How can a care provider document properly?

Blank pages—I hate them. When I sat down to write the first page of this book, the tears streamed down my face. I'm not a friend to lots of writing, but sometimes there is no choice. I had had enough, and if I felt this way others must too. And those who have not experienced allegations deserve the information of how to maintain personal and family health.

Care providers need a pocket folder and notebook for each child in their care. An additional notebook should be kept for themselves documenting overall daily or parenting issues.

How can the care provider start a family notebook?

A journal allows for immediate review of a situation. It is an excellent resource for discovering repetitive behaviors in the family, the child, or the social services system. This notebook may be more like a journal or diary than a business document. Within these pages the care provider can list accomplishments and bring up questions needing answers. Explain the children being parented and the parenting responses to each of these children. This journal can be used as a private account of the provider's journey through the foster care system. Under normal circumstances, the care provider does not need to share this document with others. Under allegation, this document can be requested for use in the investigation.

How can the care provider document for children in care?

Each child in out-of-home care needs a Kidz Kit. A Kidz Kit consists of a stenographer's notebook, a 3"x5" notepad, and a pocket folder. The pocket folder contains forms, agreements, and letters from the agency. A duplicate copy of these forms and agreements may be kept in the care provider's personal files. The stenographer's notebook, or "Parents Care Notebook," logs the events in the child's life. It is also the place a care provider can document the information social services shares about the child prior to placement and the findings of reality as the child lives in the foster home. Documenting expectations and outcomes can be very helpful to both social services and other professionals working with fragile children. For an older school-age or adolescent child, the Kidz Care 3" x 5" notebook can be used as a communication device between the care provider and the child. The notebook is a safe place for a fragile child to express feelings, test ideas, and share information too scary to verbalize. For the older child, this notebook can serve as the vehicle to check on feelings and ask questions too hard to say out loud. For the younger child, it can be used as an opportunity to draw pictures of experiences and feelings.

The Parents Care and Kidz Care notebooks can and should be copied and sent with the children and/or social worker when the children leave your home. These two notebooks can be used as reference tools for social services and new foster or adoptive parents when dealing with surrogate children. These notebooks highlight day-to-day information about the child and allow a continuum of care to be established for the next caregiver. Keeping a copy in the care provider home is wise, as a copy of these documents may be a crucial piece in investigative work needed if a later allegation does occur.

The Kidz Kit pocket folder should have the following information:

— The Placement Agreement

— Copies of contracts with child, agency, or natural parents

Make yourself a Kidz Kit for each child in your care.

Include in the Kidz Kit:

A pocket folder to store all data from social services about the child.

A stenographer's notebook for you to log information pertinent to parenting the child.

A 3"x5" notebook to write daily messages and get feedback from children in your care.

- House Procedure Agreement

- School, medical, and psychiatric reports

- Personal correspondence between agency and care providers regarding child in care

- Copies of any documentation received from social services about child

- Notes from parents regarding child in care

The Parents Care Notebook should have the following information:

- Documentation of dates and times of parental and significant other visitations and phone calls

- School progress reports or significant school experiences

- Medical needs of child and what has or has not happened

- Behavioral patterns, changes in behavior, and what your personal parenting efforts have been in working with the child

- Documentation of lying behaviors, what the lies are, what the truth was, and how the truth was discovered

- Conflicts that arise with child, parents, social worker, teacher, licensor (include documentation of threats or angry outbursts)

The Kidz Care Notebook should have the following information:

- Write a question regarding the child's day.
  "You looked sad when you came home from school. Can you tell me about it?"

- Make a positive statement about the child.

- Answer the child's questions.

- Let little children draw pictures and then tell you about them. You can write their story on the back side of the picture.

Whereas the Lifebook allows children access to their past on a personal level, the Kidz Kit allows the next set of parents the tools to begin parenting where the foster parent left off. For birth parents, the Kidz Kit can provide insight they may need for parenting their child when reunification occurs. For adoptive parents, the Kidz Kit bridges the gap between past and present in understanding responses and behaviors in their adopted child.

How can care providers establish personal specifications of caring for children?

Surrogate parents need clear specifications of the types of children they can handle and enjoy raising. If parents disagree about the types children who are compatible with their family, it is important that these differences be discussed openly *before* accepting a child into the home. Children's behavior problems will magnify if the adults in authority are not in agreement about accepting and caring for such children.

Agencies work hard to match out-of-home children with families that will blend well. Matching children to appropriate families is often difficult. What the agency and new care provider don't know can cause problems. Care providers have the right to be well-informed concerning the child before accepting him or her into their home. Strengths, potentials, and capabilities of the child should be

All neatly contained between the pages of a manila file folder sitting in a black metal file cabinet lies the life history of the child, written and well documented as required by the protocol of the agency.

The child is neatly labeled into appropriate categories and proper action is taken by the system to "help" the child.

In most of these manila folders there is no day-to-day documentation by the parenting parent. The actual three-dimensional life of the child is written in two-dimensional perspective.

It is the job of the professional public parent to provide the third dimension of that child's life in written form. The spirit of the child comes forth in the words of the parenting parent.

Family Child Preferences

Adults need to agree on the types of children they like to parent. If preferences differ greatly, an agreement must be made before accepting children with these differences into the family for surrogate care. As you become more experienced with the types of available children, your skill, energy level, and tolerance preferences may change.

	PARENT												PARENT									
	Do not want									Prefer			Do not want									Prefer
	1	2	3	4	5	6	7	8	9	10			1	2	3	4	5	6	7	8	9	10
Age Infant																							
Toddler																							
Preschool																							
Elementary Age																							
Junior High																							
Senior High																							
Gender Female																							
Male																							
Number of Children in Care																							
Ages can be mixed																							
Sibling groups																							
Ancestry African																							
Asian																							
European																							
Hispanic																							
Native American																							
Other																							
Previous Neglect Emotional																							
Physical																							
Previous Abuse Emotional																							
Physical																							
Sexual																							
Ritualistic																							
Sexually active Heterosexual																							
Bisexual																							
Homosexual																							

discussed as well as problems and histories. In selecting an appropriate care provider family, social services carefully assesses the experience of the family in dealing with this type of child in addition to available support services and training requirements that will be necessary to help the child. Expectations of care providers and procedures followed in the family must be clear between the provider family and social services.

How can foster care providers set up foster home guidelines or procedures?

Deb Jones from PACER (Parents' Advocacy Coalition for Educational Rights) and author of *Working with the Abused and Neglected Adolescent in a Foster Care Home* (1991) encourages foster parents to establish written guidelines by analyzing their personal and family needs prior to accepting any foster children in a home. I have used her experience, knowledge, and in some cases forms, to provide the reader with documentation tools.

Each family has different rules and ways of handling situations. Care providers need to think about how they deal with many specific issues in their families. If care provider family members are involved in developing the guidelines, family consensus and follow-through will be established. Children in a family often know more about the silent family rules than the parents do. By assessing these areas of conflict before accepting a child, the provider family will be able to lessen misunderstandings between themselves and the foster children and social services. After the family has discussed and agreed on policies it may be helpful to fill out the "Family Child Preferences" on the previous page. This form should be shared and discussed with the licensing worker.

Personal hygiene and bathroom: Everyone in a family should develop and practice good hygiene habits. Children coming into out-of-home care may not have been previously required to keep clean. Each family has different expectations involving personal hygiene. Teaching children in out-of-home care your requirements is important. However, little things can become irritants. Many family rules are silent, the kind no one talks about, but everyone just follows. Knowing what your family does and how they do it is important in being able to teach children what you expect. One person may like the roll of toilet paper installed a certain way. A pet peeve may be toothpaste tubes squeezed at the top. Do you have specific rules regarding lifting the toilet seat for males? Cleaning up after oneself? Toothpaste in the tube? Flushing the toilet at night? Shutting the door of the bathroom when you use it? Replacing the toilet paper? Does the toilet paper have a special direction? Usage of towels? Bathtub? Giving the dog a bath? How many people are allowed in the bathroom at one time?

> *What does your family do?*
>
> Clothing storage _____
>
> Care of clothing _____
>
> Laundry/sheets_____
>
> Bath towels_____
>
> Toilet training_____
>
> Toilet seat _____
>
> Teeth _____
>
> Toothpaste _____

A care provider family must have a clear understanding of how their own family system operates.

Children in the home are an excellent resource in checking how the system truly operates versus how the parent(s) believes it operates.

Children living in the family home usually have a realistic idea of what the rules are and what procedures need to be followed.

A variety of excellent foster parenting books are available through the University of Minnesota Early Childhood Studies Program. Information can be obtained by writing to:

Early Childhood Studies Program U of M
306 Wesbrook Hall
77 Pleasant Street SE
Minneapolis, MN
55455
or calling
(612) 625-1088

Resource titles available include:

Working with the Abused and Neglected Adolescent in a Foster Care Home
by Deb Jones

For Foster Parents Working with Older School Age Children Who Have Been Abused
by Sandra Heidemann and Beth Koskie

Working with Abused Preschool and Early Elementary Children in a Foster Care Home
by Sandra Heidemann and Beth Koskie

Caring for the At-Risk Infant and Toddler in a Foster Care Home
by Sandra Heidemann

Personal body care (razors/shaving) _____

Deodorant_____

Baths/showers_____

Personal menstrual products_____

Positive behavior: Healthy families encourage positive behavior. Children raised in your family will know what positive behaviors are expected of them. They will know how to express their feelings appropriately and talk about their problems. Usually, they will respect each other's property.

Some family rules we have regarding positive behavior are:

Expected manners _____

_____

What do we consider a good job_____

_____

How do we respect other people's property_____

_____

How do we express our feelings_____

How do we talk about problems_____

_____

Respecting people and property: Generally, families have similar rules regarding property and respect for others. Most familes require asking permission to do things and insist that family members don't demand things. Family members are expected to treat people and property with consideration; to treat animals with respect and never be cruel to them; to treat the foster home and furnishings with respect; not to mar walls or drive nails without permission. Family members usually need to ask how to operate equipment before using it. Your family may have specific procedures for property that require special knowledge of care. Do family members walk into rooms freely? Do they knock before coming into rooms? Who knocks? Do kids have their own rooms? How much can they personalize their rooms? Who shares rooms? Are there sharing rules? What about the closets? Do people borrow things? What can be borrowed? How are things borrowed? What can't be borrowed? Think about what these specific procedures may be:

_____

_____

_____

_____

Room and personal belongings: Each person in a family has a right to space which is private. What are the rules your family has?

Bedroom _____

Drawers/closets _____

Dresser/shelves_____

Personal belongings _____

Floor _____

Walls _____

Bed/naps _____

_____

Privacy: All family members should know and respect family rules regarding
privacy. Foster families must be aware of the need for privacy for
children in care and respect those boundaries. Bedroom doors open
unless alone or dressing? What are your rules for privacy? Adequate and
age appropriate privacy for dressing, bathing, and sexual matters needs
to be understood and addressed by all family members. Who should be
allowed in whose bedroom and during what times? What special
consideration is needed for individuals who share bedrooms? Making
forts? Being under blankets? In tents? Sleepovers?

_____

_____

_____

Sexuality and affection: All children need affection for healthy development,
but many children who are in out-of-home care have been sexually
abused. What types of nonsexual hugging and touching does your
family commonly use? How do you show affection? What do your
children know about the facts of life? Are you a touching family?
Tickling? What do your children know about touching? What kinds of
things have you told your children to protect them from molestation?
What are your rules regarding privacy and modesty? Masturbation?
Sexually active teenagers? Preteens? Birth control? Abortion? Pregnancy?

_____

_____

_____

Physical contact: Similar to affection, foster families need to establish
guidelines to respect the type and extent of physical contact acceptable
between family members. See Chapter 13, "Guidelines for Care
Providers," for more information about working with sexually abused
children. Rules for sports contact.

_____

_____

_____

Verbal communications: Families providing care for children living away
from home need some guidelines for verbal communication. It is
important to establish that secrets between foster family members and
children in care are not allowed. Secrets involve collusion and do not
build healthy family unity. Avoid sexual innuendos or sexual teasing:
this form of communication is inappropriate and can lead to allegations
against a provider family. Does your family have a safe place to bring a
problem? Is there a family counsel? What kind of humor or joking does
your family enjoy? Do you have endearing words? What are they?

_____

_____

_____

_____

*The more you
understand your
family from each
member's perspective,
you will be better able
to handle surprises and
crisis with responses
that are healing and
helpful to a
challenging and
damaged child.*

Job responsibilities: In a family, all members contribute to the well-being of the family. Job responsibilities and expectations vary with each family. Ages and physical capabilities of family members often determine what each member will contribute. Some questions our family asks:

What is expected of each person _____

Quality and time expectation _____

General attitude _____

How do we try to help people _____

If you are having a bad day _____

Accepting "no" or criticism _____

School: Maintaining school work is important. How does your family handle school responsibilities? What can students expect from parents for help? How do they ask for help? Do you have a special time set aside for schoolwork? What after-school activities and transportation are available?

Homework _____

School rules _____

Trouble in school _____

_____

_____

_____

Projects and studies: Families vary in hobbies and available activities for children. What activities are available for children to participate in? Where do they get their supplies? What are the rules for using the supplies?

Positive actions using spare time _____

What things do you like to do _____

What supplies are available _____

How do you get permission to use supplies _____

How do you handle supplies _____

How are they stored _____

Where can you do project _____

Additional contracts and response forms that may be helpful to surrogate care providers.

Children in surrogate care work with many people outside of the provider home, including social services, natural parents, schools, and medical and psychiatric professionals. A number of forms are included to keep in the child's files regarding information important to the child's life. These include:

- House Procedures
- Teacher Evaluation Form
- Behavior Contract
- Placement Agreement

- Home Visit Report
- Self Harm Contract
- Professional Evaluation Form
- Behavior Documentation Form

HOUSE PROCEDURES

As a member of this family you are expected to follow house procedures. Here are the procedures we follow in this family. If you disagree or do not understand a rule please come to one of the parents to discuss the procedure in question.

Personalized for _____

1. Describe your average household routine. Do you have a daily schedule?

    a. Bedtimes _____

    b. Mealtimes _____

    Eating _____

    Refrigerator_____

    Snacks _____

2. Special days for doing special tasks? Expectations for Saturday, Sunday, or holidays?

    a. _____

    b. _____

3. What are job responsibilities/chore expectations?

    a. _____

    b. _____

    c. _____

4. What is general family policy on:

    a. Going for walks _____

    b. Running away _____

    c. Swearing _____

    d. Fighting_____

    e. Problems _____

    f. Damage to property _____

    g. Ironing, curling irons _____

    h. Pets_____

    i. Shutting doors _____

    j. _____

    k. _____

    l. _____

Family Policy for these specifics on:

1. Physical Affection/contact

    a. Hugging/kissing_____

    b. Sleeping arrangements _____

    c. Other _____

As your new foster family, we will be providing your day-to-day care. We want your time with our family to be enjoyable and as hassle-free as possible.

As your foster parents, we will provide you with food, clothing, and a living environment.

Foster father's name

_____

Foster mother's name

_____

Our phone number is:

_____

Our address is:

_____
_____
_____

The other members of our family are: (name/age)

_____
_____
_____
_____
_____
_____

2. Verbal communication

    a. "Secrets" policy _____

    b. Teasing, joking, innuendos _____

    c. Lying _____

3. Dress code, who wears what, when, where?

    a. Afterschool _____

    b. Nightwear _____

    c. School _____

    d. Church _____

    e. Other _____

4. Privacy

    a. Bath/shower _____

    b. Drapes/windows _____

    c. Respect for the privacy of others _____

    d. Feelings book _____

    e. Parents' bedroom _____

5. Child's room/personal belongings

    a. Stereo/radios _____

    b. Friends, dates _____

    c. Telephone _____

    d. Smoking, drugs, alcohol _____

    e. Money _____

    f. Mail _____

    g. Clothes _____

    h. Sports equipment _____

    i. _____

    j. _____

6. Child's personal time

    a. Homework/school _____

    b. Visits with parents _____

    c. Visits with social services _____

    d. Outside activities _____

    e. Sick days _____

    f. _____

7. Child/family time

    a. Family council _____

    b. Foster family activities _____

    c Other family members _____

    d. _____

BEHAVIOR OR INCIDENT REPORT

Child's name _____

Date _____

Describe the behavior or incident: _____

_____

_____

_____

Why is the child behaving this way? _____

_____

Is the child choosing the behavior or unable to control it? _____

_____

What happened just before the behavior? _____

_____

_____

What time of day? _____

What has the child eaten? _____

Where did the behavior occur? ___Home ___School ___School bus ___Car

____Outdoors ____Indoors Other _____

Is the child tired, hungry, sick? _____

_____

How does this fit into child's developmental level of behavior? _____

_____

_____

What are long range consequences of this behavior? _____

_____

Plan of action? _____

_____

Adapted from *Working with the Abused and Neglected Adolescent in a Foster Care Home* by Deb Jones (1991)

Behavior of children outside of the home is important. As surrogate parents, we are interested in monitoring our child's progress and knowing when and how we can help the child and the school system work with the child.

A behavior contract should promote positive behavior. It should be mutually agreed upon between child and parent. Both parents should sign the agreement with a handshake and a smile, looking forward to producing the results.

Refer to Dr. Fitzhugh Dodson's book How to Discipline with Love *(1978) and Chapter 11, "Discipline or Punishment," in this book for more information about contracting.*

BEHAVIOR CONTRACT

Youth name: ______________________________

Date: ______________________________

Witness: ______________________________

Date: ______________________________

I, ______________________, will

____

____

____

____

____

____

and I, ______________________________

will provide ______________________________

____

when ______________________________

____

____

____

____

is completed.

Signed ______________________________

Date ______________________________

Signed ______________________________

Date ______________________________

Adapted from *Working with the Abused and Neglected Adolescent in a Foster Care Home* by Deb Jones (1991)

HOME VISIT REPORT

Please fill out and return after each home visit.

Name: _____

Date: _____

How did you feel the visit went?

_____

_____

_____

What was the most special thing about the visit?

_____

_____

_____

What was the hardest thing about the visit?

_____

_____

_____

Is there anything you would like to see changed?

_____

_____

_____

Were the house rules followed?

_____

_____

_____

Any other information you would like to share with us?

_____

_____

_____

Adapted from *Working with the Abused and Neglected Adolescent in a Foster Care Home* by Deb Jones (1991)

Your visits with your parent(s) are extremely important. We want to be able to provide the help your family needs in making your experience in foster care as short-term as possible.

SELF-HARM
CONTRACT

In order to provide safe care for a child, the child must agree not to inflict harm on himself or herself. Setting up a plan of action will allow the child an immediate place to go and come up with ideas in maintaining self-care.

Youth name: _____

Date: _____

Witness: _____

Date: _____

I, _____, will not attempt to harm myself in any way. If I feel like hurting myself I will follow this plan:

_____

_____

_____

_____

I am willing to keep this contract from _____

to _____

Other people who will be notified of this contract include:

_____

_____

_____

Youth signature:

_____

Adapted from *Working with the Abused and Neglected Adolescent in a Foster Care Home* by Deb Jones (1991)

TEACHER
EVALUATION FORM

As surrogate parents, it is our day-to-day responsibility to help the child in our care in his or her education endeavors. Please help support our efforts by completing this form.

Student:_____

Date:_____

Teacher:_____

Is the student following the rules set down for the classroom?

_____

_____

What attitude has the student had since last report?

_____

_____

Is the student completing assignments on time and turning them in on time?

_____

_____

What improvements have you seen since the last report?

_____

_____

Any other information you would like to share?

_____

_____

Any special areas that the student needs extra help with?

_____

_____

Do you need a meeting with the foster care providers?

_____

_____

Adapted from *Working with the Abused and Neglected Adolescent in a Foster Care Home* by Deb Jones (1991)

Proper understanding of the needs of the child we care for is pertinent to maintaining the level of care expected by professionals working with our children. Please complete this form and return to the care provider upon end of psychiatric or medical visit.

If information requested here violates the Data Privacy Act, please provide as much information as you are allowed to share.

PROFESSIONAL EVALUATION FORM

Child:_____

Date:_____

Professional: _____

I have spent _____

working with this child and have found the following results:

_____

_____

_____

_____

_____

I recommend the following follow-up care:

_____

_____

_____

_____

_____

_____

Signed:_____

Date:_____

Adapted from *Working with the Abused and Neglected Adolescent in a Foster Care Home* by Deb Jones (1991)

PLACEMENT AGREEMENT

This placement agreement will describe type of placement and clearly define responsibilities of foster parent to child placed and to the agency.

Today's date	Individuals present (list all)	
Foster parents		Phone
Address		
Social worker		Phone
Agency	Address	
Social worker's supervisor		Phone
Agency	Address	

CHILD DATA

Name of child		Nickname
Birthdate	Present chronological age	Other
Type of placement	Legal status of child	Expected duration of placement
Religion	Level of commitment	

Siblings (names/age/birthdate/status)			

Reason child is in foster care

Previous history of ___Abuse ___Neglect ___Maltreatment explain (includes approximate age of child at time):

Permanency goal for child

EATING Appetite	Favorite foods		
Used to three meals a day	Can use eating utensils		
SLEEPING Usual bedtime hours	Bedtime ritual		Crib or bed
Enuresis	Sound or restless	Mood when awakening	
SELF-CARE Can dress and undress	Toileting	Teeth brushing/combing/shampooing	Bathing

BIRTH PARENT DATA

Birth parent(s)	Phone	Visitation
Address		
Approved visitation policy (where, when, how)		
How will natural family be involved in foster care program?		
Rules on correspondence or phone calls		

Can parent drive __Y __N Needs public transportation __Y __N	Do parents work?	Work Phones
Policy for child to accompany on vacation	Policy on substitute care	

Significant others important to child/type of relationship	Phone	Visitation

PREVIOUS CAREGIVERS

Previous foster home parents	Phone	Visitation
Previous social worker	Phone	

Number of other previous homes	Total years in foster care	Number of social workers
Name/phone 1st caregiver	Reason moved	
Name /phone 2nd caregiver	Reason moved	
Name /phone 3rd caregiver	Reason moved	
Name /phone 4th caregiver	Reason moved	
Residential Treatment or Group Home		

Has child even been involved in allegation against caregivers?	Why?	
Has child previously had significant male relationship?	Who?	Visitation
Can child still be in contact with this person?		

CHILD'S GUARDIAN AD LITEM
Name/address/phone

Responsibilities

MEDICAL DATA

Main physician name/clinic		Phone	Seen since
Address of clinic			
Date of last physical	Medical card number	Current health	
If no physical just prior to placement — date, time, and place of scheduled physical			
Currently does child have lice?	Worms?	Infection/open sores?	
Medication taken by child		Immunizations current	
Has child been previously hospitalized? Why?			
Previous broken bones/sprains?			
Previous abuse substantiated?	What?		
Allergies Hayfever	Drugs	Food	
What physical limitations does child have?			
Eyes/sight has been checked	Ears/hearing has been checked		
Medical specialist name/clinic/specialty		Phone	Seen since
Address			
Medical specialist name/clinic/specialty		Phone	Seen since
Address			

PSYCHOLOGICAL DATA

Physchologist/therapist/clinic	Phone	
Address		Seen since
Present therapy schedule		
Therapy dealing with these issues		

DENTAL DATA

Dentist/office		Phone	Seen since
Address			
Last check-up	Needed follow-up care		

EMERGENCIES

Who to contact

EDUCATIONAL DATA

Last grade attended	Academic level	Name of school
School to attend	Counselor's name	Favorite teacher's name

What subjects does the child like best?	What subjects does the child like least?
Difficult school behaviors	Truancy

How has child received special help in the past?
What special services will the school provide?

Social worker has met with or talked to school personnel	Who?	When?

School contact knows these details

Special academic needs	Driver's education	Athletic insurance
Sports/school activities		

RECREATIONAL DATA

Child's hobbies	
Sports child likes	Child can ____Swim ____Ride bike ____Skate
Prefers indoor/outdoor play	Prefers to play alone/with others	Television—which programs

What activities does child like to do with adults?
What activities does child like to do with families?
What activities does child like to do with friends?

Child's friend's name	Phone	Visitation

ATITUDINAL DATA

Attitudes of child relating to foster care placement	
Present attitude toward parents	Towards authority
Problem areas presently needing work	Temper tantrums—when/type
Has child behaved violently or destructively? Describe:	Behavior when tired/hungry
Does child experience mood swings? What leads to these mood swings?	Has child run away?/When?
Any known history of drugs? **Has child ever taken drugs/narcotics?	Does child smoke?

**Does child drink alcohol?	When was the last time?	What and how much?
Has child engaged in stealing?	Lying (what does he lie about/how to recognize lies)?	
Other		

Known high risk characteristics of child

- _____Premature or low birth weight
- _____Peculiar looking
- _____Sexually provocative behaviors
- _____Sexually acts out (describe below)
- _____Night roaming
- _____Hyperactive
- _____Excessive lying
- _____Has been physically abused
- _____Violence toward other children
- _____Has had more than one placement or separation
- _____Has been sexually exploited or abused
- _____Delays in attaining early development milestones
- _____Problems with hoarding, gorging, or stealing food

- _____Fetal Alcohol Syndrome
- _____Non-attached
- _____Drug Use
- _____Sleep disorders
- _____Rocking, head banging
- _____ADD diagnosed
- _____Previously alleged abuse against care providers
- _____Is known to have hit, kicked, or attacked caregiver
- _____Violence toward animals

- _____Failure to thrive infant
- _____Health problems
- _____Wetting, soiling, smearing
- _____Self destructive behavior
- _____Physical handicaps
- _____Tunes out, withdraws, won't listen
- _____Damaged or destroyed property
- _____Stealing
- _____Displays masturbation or other sexual behaviors
- _____Has attempted suicide
- _____Alcohol use

List known behavior	Approved methods of handling behavior
Call social worker immediately if	Non-permissible disciplines

Additional training requirements	
Books and reference materials available	
Social worker availability for support and resources	Best time to reach
Social worker to provide	Social worker will phone Social worker will visit family

In accepting the placement of this child, we understand the licensing laws we have promised to abide by and the special needs of the child we are accepting in our care.

Signature of foster parents_____

I have clearly explained the special needs of this child to the foster care providers and will provide support outlined.

Signature of social worker

_____ Date_____

Other information needing notation on placement agreement:

_____

_____

_____

_____

_____

_____

_____

_____

_____

_____

_____

HUMAN SERVICE RESOURCES of MINNESOTA offers national training for FOSTER PARENT PEER-to-PEER trainers. Mary Lou Gilstad developer of the University of Minnesota program is available to develop training programs nationally to help foster and other out-of-home care providers develop safe practices for the prevention of additional abuse to children. The following materials are available from HSR.
(1) So You Want To Be A Trainer
(2) Child Abuse Issues for Foster Care Providers
(3) Understanding Psychological Abuse: A guide for foster parents
(4) Let's Vote! All in Favor
(5) A Quality Care Checklist for Foster Care Homes
(6) When Love is not Enough.
Call Mary Lou or Dick Gilstad at (612) 698-0562 or write Human Service Resources of Minnesota 288 Macalester Street, St. Paul, MN 55105.

Why is the placement agreement so important to the care provider?

A placement agreement should spell out expectations clearly. It specifically focuses on the foster family and the child and not on the natural family. It clarifies resources available for the child and the foster family. It should provide the care providers with history about the child that will allow continuity of care. It details appropriate disciplines, additional training requirements, and resources available for help. It spells out expectations and guidelines for visitation — frequency of visits, length, phone contact, holiday plans, and special conditions, and lists others who can or cannot visit children in care.

The placement agreement should define clearly responsibilities and expectations of social services to the foster family. It sets up worker accountability by requiring the social worker to document how he or she will assist the family in behavior management and how treatment will be arranged; how often the family can expect a call and if there is a special time the social worker is available.

The placement agreement needs to be updated as more knowledge is acquired regarding the needs of the child. The placement agreement should be reviewed and updated at each quarterly review with social worker and care provider.

Summary

Documentation is vital to care providers in maintaining up-to-date written information concerning their families and the children for whom they care.

References

Jones, Deb. 1991. *Working With the Abused and Neglected Adolescent in a Foster Care Home.* Minnesota: University of Minnesota, Minneapolis

TRAINING PROGRAMS AVAILABLE:
    The University of Minnesota Early Childhood Development Program offers a wide range of speakers and trainers for children in out-of-home care, child care issues, and working with at risk children. Contact the Early Childhood Studies Program, UofM, 306 Wesbrook Hall, 77 Pleasant Street, SE, Minneapolis, MN 55455 or call (612) 625-1088.

Chapter 15

Staying Healthy as a Family

Being suspected of maltreatment to children and the object of an investigation is extremely stressful. Maintaining physical, emotional, and pyschological wellness for you and your family system is crucial.

Caring for previously abused and neglected children can be physically and emotionally stressful. Compound that stress with the normal day to day stresses of American family living. Add a measure of social system stress and heap on an allegation for suspected maltreatment of a child. Mix well with an investigation and beat all ingredients at high speed. There you have it—the recipe for an extremely stressful experience.

Emotions rise and fall like the waves in an ocean. Depending on the situation and the complexities of any given day, emotions change. The pain of any given situation may seem unbearable and it's easy then to let our emotions overpower us. At other times, even through great storms, we can float on top of the waves and ride them out, choosing our own course.

Each person has the opportunity to choose behavior and reactions to the pain involved in reports of maltreatment of children and investigation procedures. Care providers often become bitter and angry. They give up and quit the system, leaving their knowledge and wisdom in a heap, without clues for the next family to pick up. In other cases, the stress and stigma of the allegation have actually triggered heart or asthma attacks and killed care providers. *The initial support materials for the Minnesota Foster Parent SOS for PEA (Services of Support for Persons Experiencing Allegations) were made possible by a memorial fund set up for Jan Carlson of Anoka, Minnesota, whose allegation triggered a fatal asthma attack.*

It is hard to focus on the contribution care providers make to the children they care for in the midst of an investigation.

Some care providers have chosen to experience the pain and share knowledge with others. They have laid down past experiences, ended unsubstantiated or substantiated allegations, and opened their hearts to other families who are just beginning this incredible journey. Looking back, it is easier for us—the

Healthy, nurturing relationships share some common characteristics:

— *tenderness and warmth*
— *calmness and serenity*
— *kindness and courtesy*
— *truth even when it hurts*
— *balance of giving and receiving*
— *respect for differences and gifts of each person*
  – *roles*
  – *talents*
  – *culture*
  – *personalities*

survivors—to analyze and set up preventive and supportive systems for families in need of care. The commitment to be involved in a child's life can give a child hope that his or her life can change. And that hope can be a springboard to a better future, not just for that child, but for his or her children and grandchildren. Because one significant individual cares, an important stepping stone may be laid for a brighter future for many generations of children.

A care provider in the midst of an investigation needs:

— To seek support from friends, family, and other providers. Isolating yourself or keeping the crisis a *"secret"* from everyone places additional stresses on an already stressful situation.

— To maintain a healthy lifestyle. Eat well and avoid unhealthy foods and drinks. Exercise. Get plenty of sleep.

— To realize that perfection is impossible. No individual can do it all. You may need to give up some things that occupy time, but don't give you satisfaction, in order to make time for relaxation.

— To attend workshops or classes that will give you more information about abused children in foster care. By finding constructive ways to interact with peers, you can fill time, share experiences, and begin growing from what is happening to you.

— To seek out resource centers, child protection workers, or other professionals to get support and information concerning the allegation and investigation.

— To separate personal worth from quality of care of children issues. Caring for foster children may seem like your whole life. Search for other important areas of interest.

Within the loss, compassion and empathy for families facing allegations can be born. A previously accused family can offer a warm hand, a quiet hug, and shared tears. They can offer a listening silence that is understanding without condemning or demanding.

How care providers can take time out—rest and find a neutral zone.

In her book, *How To Take Care of Yourself...So You Can Take Care of Others,* (1988) Sue Vineyard writes about two related paradoxes. The first is *"Every change begins with an ending,"* and the second is, *"For something new to begin, something old must end."* These related paradoxes, if unacknowledged, can cause great feelings of uneasiness, imbalance, and confusion. When we realize their existence, we can begin to cope with their ambiguity and incongruency. (Vineyard 1988)

Care providers need to take a deep breath, gather perspective, and say goodbye to what was. Saying goodbye enables the care provider to handle the confusion and subsequent new beginnings demanded by this unique and difficult change.

*Change is a fact of life.
It is the process of evolving and becoming,
and it will not be denied.
Setting oneself up with an expectation that
today's change will "flatten out" to produce
permanency is to set oneself up for disappointment.*

Care providers need time to rest. Rest is very productive even though it may not be marked by "works" or "doing." During extremely difficult times temporary breaks and shifting into neutral instead of trying to assess the situation allows the care provider space to work through and accept devastating changes. Care providers will increase stress if they spend all their time trying to figure out how it all came about or work on making decisions for their future. This does not mean they should draw away from life completely or send out red flags saying "rescue me, I need help." It means taking out the time necessary to begin adapting, healing, and most importantly renewing and refilling.

Resting is different for everyone. For some people, a large gala event can be relaxing. For others, renewal can only be accomplished in solitude. Individuals need to pursue opportunities that bring peaceful reflection and renewal.

Possible rest opportunities:

- Going to and from work
- Alone time at work
- Listening to music
- Sports activities
- Getting up an hour early or staying up after everyone else has gone to bed
- Alone time at home
- Walking, jogging, etc.
- Doing handwork (crafts)
- Walking the dog
- Pursuing a hobby
  –photography
  –gardening
  –woodworking, etc.

Creative relaxation opportunities:

- Taking a day off from work
- Going to a retreat
- Staying home alone while the family goes off to an event
- Giving yourself permission not to react to a situation for a given length of time
- Communicating with your children. Use the time you spend riding in the car, eating, and putting to bed
- Schedule consistent, special time for togetherness with your children
- Taking a vacation
- Taking a fun class
- Going off by yourself—to a resort, cabin, hotel
- Finding an activity that does not let you think about your concerns
- Planning an in-home activity to share with children—projects, cooking, art
- Taking an hour break from everyone's time but your own

I don't know about your family, but in mine—unless it's four o'clock in the morning—our house is not quiet. I have the needs of our daughter to tend to. Sometimes I think one active, alert child is much more difficult than a number of kids. I have a husband with whom I share an important personal and business relationship. As a business owner, I have three shifts of people who may need my time. Finding a bit of space for rest and quiet time is not easy. The contemplative and research time needed to write this book was not available unless I disciplined myself to find it.

This morning as I write, I look out our living room window, listening to the birds and watching the sunrise. Everyone is asleep. The house is quiet. The sky is pink and blue and white. The air smells like spring. Today, this is a place and time of rest. This isn't always my resting place—five o'clock in the morning listening to the birds—I'm not nuts. Some days, I prefer to throw my pillow over my head, burrow deep under my covers, and try hard not to hear the buzz of family life. On those days, my rest is a shower and a cup of hot coffee. On an especially bad day, I might pull weeds in the garden to release the tension or go out to the garage and crush aluminum cans. I've found recycling can provide a great relief for stress. Rest cannot be forced. It needs to be experienced. In today's busy world, it needs to be respected in order to be achieved.

Help each other not boil over. Take turns to let off steam. Don't create fights when your partner needs to let off steam. The steam is not meant for you. Don't take it personally. Take turns lifting the lid.

Don't try to solve problems when you are tired, hungry, feeling poorly, or sleepy.

Don't try to solve problems if you are drinking.

Mistakes can be painful or embarrassing. Give each other permission to admit mistakes and encourage new growth.

Places to find rest

- Near water
- The theater
- Retreat center
- A hotel
- Home of a friend
- Garden
- Mountains
- A museum
- Campus
- Parent's home
- Home of family
- Couch for nap
- Woods
- Church/temple
- A farm
- Golf course
- Library
- Park

Activities which refresh

- Fishing
- Reading
- Sewing
- Dancing
- Praying
- Writing
- Sailing
- Painting
- Building
- Snowmobiling
- Bird watching
- Weeding/yardwork
- Riding horses
- Golfing
- Walking
- Knitting/handwork
- Hunting
- Attending church
- Talking with friends
- Cooking
- Working on car
- Woodworking
- Camping
- Visiting zoo/park
- Flying models
- Computers
- Skiing
- Gardening
- Exercising
- Singing
- Bible study
- Giving a party
- Eating out
- Cutting wood
- Shooting (skeet/trap)
- Hiking
- Visiting arboretum
- Skating
- Floral arrangements

Places for rest exist where an individual can find them. The list above is only a beginning to offer ideas.

*Care providers need to take care of themselves in
order to decrease the effects of stress.*

> *Nutrition:* A moderate diet high in carbohydrates and including a variety of plant foods, such as fruits, vegetables, whole grain breads and cereals, nuts and seeds, is best suited for health and digestion. Today's processed foods can take a heavy toll on health. During the stressful time of allegation, the body needs all the help it can get.

> *Exercise*: Not only does exercise keep the body physically healthy, it also allows individuals to relieve stress and enjoy activities alone or together as a family. Biking or walking are inexpensive and healthy.

> *Sleep:* Staying well rested helps an individual cope when dealing with periods of extreme stress.

> *Get a check-up:* If you haven't had a physical or dental check-up lately and are overdue, do it now. If something is wrong, it is not going to get any better with increased stress.

Care providers need to take time to celebrate.

Life is wonderful. Life is unfair. Both are true statements, especially when faced with reports of maltreating a child. Accused families need to take time out to celebrate life. Although it may be unfair, it doesn't need to be depressing. Special events and changes from normal routines can help families get their minds off the investigation. Some celebration or just-for-fun ideas include:

1. Have each person in the house **make a list of 50 things** they would like to do. Fifty is long enough to add little things, such as eat spaghetti alone

with Dad, along with big things like going to Disney World with the whole family. Share lists and find out what each person desires and who those activities can be shared with. Focusing on positive interactions helps a family enjoy life while living through the stress of allegation.

2. **Pack up an adventurer's picnic.** Eat in a crazy place—the middle of the garden, the family tree fort, or the attic. Take pictures. If neighbors think you're crazy, invite them over.

3. **Trade houses for the weekend** with some close friends in another city. This is an inexpensive way to get out of town, relax, and enjoy a mini vacation.

4. **Plan a trick picnic.** Plan a messy, unconventional menu for a picnic, such as spaghetti eaten without forks or a "grab-cake" eaten by the handful. Be prepared for memorable silliness that helps you forget the investigation. Don't forget the camera.

5. **Date your significant other**. Care providers need quiet and private time with the significant people in their lives. Write a list of easy-to-forget items and plan to work through some problems without the children around. If you forget to work on the problems, just enjoy each other. It's OK!

6. **Start a family collection.** Our family of preschool age children started collecting the alphabet. We got 26 clear plastic take-out containers with lids from the paper warehouse and a package of stick-on letters from the stationery store. Everyone in the family joined in filling the 26 letter boxes with little items we found around the house. For example, our "N" box contains a nut, a nail, a nest, etc.

   Other collecting ideas could include collecting experiences:
   — How many city parks, rivers, or lakes can we visit?
   — If the kids are into a special sport or hobby—
     How many different teams can we watch play or how many hobby shows can we attend?
   — How many animals can we see and draw pictures of them?
   — How many different cars, tractors, trains, or trucks?

7. **Feeding friends.** Feed fish, birds, or ducks at your local parks. Put up some bird feeders and watch birds in your yard. Get a bag of peanuts and watch the squirrels have a picnic. Better yet, volunteer as a family for a night at a food distribution center for the poor and feed some new friends.

8. **Note night.** Get out the pens, pencils, stickers, plus a list of people who need notes, cards, or letters. Everyone can write something as each person is mentioned. Or make up a special note for each person and pass them around the table for each person to write a silly or fun thing they have done. Or write a family letter about the good things happening. I know it's hard, but it's really a good exercise. Let each person add a line, and send to friends and relatives.

9. **Family awards night.** All family members can dream up a gag or silly award. No hurtful ones. Also, a series of special awards, such as helpfulness, thoughtfulness, promptness, growth, good idea, attitude, achievement. Make sure there's something for everyone!

10. **Pack a lunch for fun.** Send lunch along with the kids or your spouse with little notes, jokes, or other tidbits that let them know you are thinking about them. A new eraser, stickers, pencil sharpener, or baseball card are great surprises at lunchtime. Let the kids decorate their own bags at the beginning of the week with sticker, markers, glitter, and glue.

Child protection had stressed that our daughter should not see John, as it may cause emotional trauma and compound the problem. This was difficult, as the three of us were always together—riding bikes, hiking, cross-country skiing.

Once the initial shock was over, John and I made the decision that the truth would eventually be discovered— we just had to wait it out. On Sundays, we attended different services in our family church—John, the early morning service, and I, the later service. We really weren't physically together as a family, but we felt close to each other whenever we attended those services.

Birth mother

Traits Of A Healthy Family

How close is your family? Delores Curran, author of *Traits of a Healthy Family* (1991), evaluates 15 traits that go together to make healthy families. The following questions are adapted from her research. I have added this questionnaire to help families in crisis focus on healthy family traits and visualize their strengths.

How to take this test. Rate the intimacy quotient of your family by responding to the questions. Award yourself points for each answer as follows:

> 1 pt We're definitely not there yet
>
> 2 pts This is sometimes true in our family
>
> 3 pts This is usually true in our family

Circle number closest to your family

1. In our marriage, my spouse and I share power equally, complementing each other's strengths and weaknesses 1 2 3

2. At the dinner table, our family shares more than food. We also share ideas, feelings, disappointments, dreams 1 2 3

3. If there is a conflict between a family tradition and an outside responsibility, the family tradition usually wins 1 2 3

4. As parents, we allow our children freedom to make decisions in certain areas, and expect them to accept the consequences of those decisions 1 2 3

5. Our family shares together in at least one leisure activity a week 1 2 3

6. As parents, we are aware of our children's facial expressions, body language, and physical gestures, and from these pick up clues that lead use to ask appropriate questions and initiate discussion 1 2 3

7. The basic, underlying mood in our family is hopeful and forward looking; we have our sources of stress, but we consider them temporary and manageable 1 2 3

8. When we are alone together, my spouse and I are vulnerable to each other and risk exposure of our deepest feelings 1 2 3

9. We allow our children to make choices between various activities outside the family but do not allow these activities to interfere routinely with our leisure time together 1 2 3

10. We have different rules for children of different ages 1 2 3

11. We know what we believe and find strength in our faith 1 2 3

12. We have a vision as a family, and seek to be involved in something bigger than the quality of our relationships 1 2 3

13. We have our share of problems, but we usually see the positive side of things no matter how bad the situation 1 2 3

14. No matter how busy we are, our entire family eats a meal together at least once a day 1 2 3

15. My spouse and I agree on what is right and wrong 1 2 3

16. We make an effort to gather regularly with those in our extended family 1 2 3

17. We refuse to remove obstacles from our children's lives that will
potentially foster their growth and responsibility 1 2 3

18. As parents, we occasionally spend time alone with each of our children 1 2 3

19. We keep our work commitments under control and do not routinely allow
them to crowd out family time 1 2 3

20. Although we go through rough periods, we stick together and try
to make things right 1 2 3

21. In our family, we make each other feel important by supporting
each other in our failures as well as our successes 1 2 3

22. As parents, we allow our children to be exposed to situations in
which they can gradually earn more trust or rebuild trustworthiness 1 2 3

23. When conflicts arise, we give everyone a chance to speak and
we work at negotiating solutions before the conflicts become volatile. 1 2 3

24. Different personality styles and preferences are accepted within our family life 1 2 3

25. Our definition of success is not based on promotions, possessions, or power,
but on the quality of our service to others 1 2 3

26. We laugh at ourselves and with each other, as we use humor to defuse
potentially stressful situations 1 2 3

27. As adults, we provide for our kids a value system out of which certain
rules and accepted behaviors arise 1 2 3

28. We present opportunities in our home for our children to prove
their capabilities 1 2 3

29. The underlying religious attitude of our family is one of moving
closer to a shared core of spirituality 1 2 3

30. We allow our children to change as they move from age to age.
We respect their fads, friends, confidences, privacy, and time—
their right to be alone and their right to be different—
as long as these things are not destructive 1 2 3

Now add up your total points (there are two questions representing each trait — in random order). If your total score is:

1-30: Your family has the potential to become an intimate family if you are willing to apply energy and determination to the process.

30-60: Your family has a strong foundation upon which to build further intimacy.

60-90: You are maintaining strong momentum in the direction of intimacy.

Christian Parenting Today, May/June 1991

I am...   I know   this about   myself

\+

I could be...   I think   of myself   as

\+

I should be...   Other people   think of   me as

↓

**SELF
 CONCEPT**

11. **Ride your bike or walk** if possible, instead of using the car for all the errands. Our family built a wagon train. We harnessed our large dogs to a red wagon, bundled up the kids, and away we went to the grocery store, one-and-a-half miles away. There were lots of giggles and memories. Two years later, Joseph asks for the dogs, the wagon, and our yellow truck when we get to visit. As the kids say — *"Let's pack 'em up and head 'em out!"*

12. **Celebrate life.** Go to the library and research international celebrations. Ideas include: the maypole on May Day, corned beef and cabbage on St. Patrick's, etc. Let the kids decorate. Go to the library and borrow tapes, books, and music. Experience, learn, and enjoy! Look up recipes, costumes, and history. Plan a family party!

Roll out a good round of laughter.

My sister-in-law is a joy. She is an experienced adoptive mother with a rainbow of children of all sizes and varieties. When life gets too unbearable for either of us, the phone is our immediate access tool for relief. Having a peer to relate to is important for both of us. We widen the perspective of the situation and allow freedom to laugh at the absurdity of the situations we get into with our children and the system. When things seem bad, we bring out the best in each other.

> *Laughter is the sunshine that <br> peeks through clouds on a stormy day.*

Laughter promotes a love for life, reduces stress, and smooths interpersonal relationships. A ready smile and a sense of wit employed at the right moment can be just the medicine you and/or your family needs. Confrontation can be defused and tempers soothed with a bit of wit. Promote laughter and a good sense of humor. Just because life hands out a bowl of cherries doesn't mean you have to eat the pits!

1. When life gets really discouraging, make connections with people who put the sunshine back into life. Step through your experience with someone you can laugh with. The new perspective that comes from laughter allows situations or problems to be viewed differently. Stepping outside of the problem briefly with someone else through laughter lets us laugh at ourselves and our mistakes.

2. When everyone's tired or the weather's lousy, laugh together. Find some funny stories to read aloud, or go through a book of world records for some chucklers such as the world's longest fingernails. Talk about how these records may have been achieved. Brainstorm about their silliness. Rent a good family comedy for the VCR.

3. Buy some joke books and lighten up tedious family chores with some good jokes or riddles. Make regular drudgeries like dish washing or yard raking a time for sharing funny stories and jokes. Our five-year-old started knock-knock jokes. We now have a grand collection and they are always funny, especially to the five-year-old. And, of course, a five-year-old with a deep belly laugh is very funny to parents. So here's a sampling of April's collection:
   Knock. Knock....Who's there?
   Pencil. Pencil Who? Pants will fall down if you don't wear a belt!
   Lettuce. Lettuce Who? Lettuce run over and tickle Daddy!
   Boo. Boo Who? Mommy, why are you crying?

4. Keep your spirit young through healthy practical joking. When family members think enough of each other to play good, clean pranks, it says a lot about their mutual love and appreciation.

5. Keep an eye out for spontaneous, funny family moments that can be recorded and cherished for years to come. You may even find a standard "line" that can be used again and again to break tension or elicit chuckles. April had a six month dental check up. Just before her teeth clearning she was busily coloring with markers at the children's table in the dental office. She climbed up into the chair and opened her mouth for her check up. The dentist gasped. There were hundreds of little brown spots all over her enamels. *"This child has a mouthful of cavities,"* he said. Having just examined her brushing job before we left the house, I knew it couldn't be true. I said, *"That's impossible."* Looking into April's mouth, I saw that the dentist was right— her mouth was full of little brown specks on every tooth. *"April, how did you get the brown on your teeth?"* I asked. *"Ah, Mom, the dentist has chocolate-smelling markers, and I had to taste them!"* Now we always brush to keep the browns off.

6. Be careful to distinguish between healthy laughter and ridicule, sarcasm, or excessive teasing. Laughter heals. Ridicule, sarcasm, and improper teasing can wound.

7. Clip cartoons to share with family members or tape to the refrigerator or family bulletin board.

8. Collect funny stories or incidents through the day and make a habit to tell them at dinnertime. Spice up the meal with jokes and funny riddles. Laughter aids digestion. (Lewis 1991)

How can care providers maintain a good self-concept?

Self-esteem is the result of a comparison among our knowledge of ourselves, the expectations and standards we have for ourselves, and the perceived expectations others have of us.

SELF-IMAGE	SELF-ESTEEM	SELF-IDENTITY
The Image Aspect of Self	**The Evaluative Aspect of Self**	**The Identity Aspect of Self**
How I see myself	My judgment of myself	How I am unique
How I imagine myself to be or to look like	My evaluation of self-worth	Who or what I identify with (positive or negative)
Role images I perceive	What I think others' judgment of me might be	How others identify with me

(Wakefield, Norma, *Building Self-Esteem*)

For example: Only the people directly involved in the reported incident know exactly what happened. Yet each individual involved will have a different perception of the event. Once the investigation takes place, completely new ideas and ways of viewing the event are developed by the investigative team. It is a balancing act for the foster care provider to maintain good self-esteem while others are investigating, making judgments, and determining life changing reactions over which the foster parent has no control.

After our daughter was shipped out of state to relatives, and my investigation continued, Jessica and I would meet in our work parking lot each afternoon with a cold lunch. Many times neither of us would talk, we would simply hold each other. Sometimes Jessica would cry as I stroked her hair. Other times she would silently listen while I ranted and raged about the injustice of the system.
Accused stepfather

Time after time, care providers express feelings of lost self-esteem after being reported for suspected maltreatment of a child. Many reasons contribute to these feelings, among them:

1. **Loss of worth.** Foster care providers do not feel valuable any longer to the foster care system. Because the system has lost respect for the family, the foster parent no longer feels appreciated or needed.

2. **Loss of competence.** Parenting competence and quality of care provided to children has been questioned. The social system may feel the foster parent is no longer able to handle the job of parenting foster children.

3. **Loss of belonging.** The family has lost an important part of their support system—social services. The foster parenting role may appear to be ended with the removal of foster children. The foster parent is no longer allowed to identify with social services or being a foster parent.

Reports of child maltreatment come unexpectedly; reactions from social services often happen quickly and without notice. Foster care providers are caught in the middle with a new need for reestablishing their role in providing care for children.

During an investigation process the disparity between what we know and what others may think can cause insecurity and lower our self-esteem and self-image. It can also render us ineffective as we work through the issues of investigation.

The foster care provider needs to assess his or her own feelings of self-esteem and then work with a support team to make adjustments. In *How To Take Care of You*, Sue Vineyard provides a self-esteem evaluator:

1. When do you feel good about yourself?

2. How can you perpetuate such opportunities?

3. Who makes you feel good about yourself?

4. How often are you with them? How can you increase time with them?

5. What activities make you feel good about yourself?

6. How often do you get to do these things? How can you do them regularly?

7. Where do you feel most valued? How often can you be there?

If there is too much difference between what we know about ourselves and what we expect of ourselves, our self-esteem will be low and we will have feelings of failure. If what we know about ourselves and what we expect of ourselves is fairly close, our self-esteem will be high and we will have more feelings of success.

Reach out to others and be ready to accept help.

Independent people often have difficulty asking for help. Once they have found the courage to ask for help, they also need to find the humbleness to graciously accept it. Care providers can keep a better perspective on asking and receiving help if they remember how good they feel when they help others. By asking for help they are allowing others to also experience these good feelings, in addition to attaining personal support when they are in need.

How a care provider can build a support team when faced with an allegation:

— Assess the present network of friends, advocates, and supporters. Who do you know from training classes or conferences?

— Choose two to six people whose friendship is valuable. Choose people who understand themselves well in addition to understanding you. People who are mature, knowledgeable, and experienced will be the most helpful when facing allegations.

— Get rid of draining relationships.

— Keep relationships balanced. Care providers may not be emotionally capable of expressing the gratitude they feel. A simple thank you may be the only expression of appreciation to supporters they are capable of giving during very difficult times.

Care providers should not be fearful of asking for help. By being assertive with the support team, the care provider will find help in meeting personal self-concept needs. The support system can help influence self-concept, offer feedback, provide a shoulder to cry on, and listen to the care provider. Care providers need a healthy self-concept to work through the demanding issues of abuse/neglect allegations.

Support team members can provide:

— Time to listen so that care providers can express needs and feelings.

— Constructive feedback regarding care provider's behavior (positive or negative).

— Ideas to help resolve problems and deal with present conflicts.

— Challenges to begin positive steps in dealing with allegations.

— Practice in communicating with social services and investigators.

— Reading documentation or letters to social services to make sure that the information written is clear and understandable.

— Help in getting needed information, support, and resources.

— Accompaniment during interview processes to bear witness to statements and situations.

Feedback and support are necessary elements in getting through the process. Care providers should not attempt to do this alone. If you are a care provider and feel isolated or know someone in that situation, call your local, state, or national association for names of people who can help you. (Lewis 1991)

What does the care provider need from support team members?

A care provider facing allegations cannot expect crisis support team members to take a position of guilty or innocent. They will work with the individual to resolve the initial impact of the crisis so the individual can resume responsibility of his or her emotions and life. This means the individual will begin to understand the reality of the situation and become aware of the real dangers and not perceptions of danger. Once the social function of the person is restored the support team member will exit the relationship. They may remain available as individual needs arise, but they continuously encourage and help the individuals work to handle the crisis independently.

After six months, my daughter was returned home. She had spent the first two nights in the children's shelter, two weeks in an emergency foster home, and the remaining time with relatives. During that time, my husband remained under investigation and was unable to visit her. While she was in the state, I was allowed three visits under supervision at the child protection agency.

It was such an isolating, humiliating, and humbling experience.
Birth mother

Quality team support members are:

Honest	*They don't play games.*
Real	*They don't play roles.*
Sharp	*They don't get taken in.*
Moral	*They maintain a high standard.*
Open	*They keep the door of communication open.*
Accessible	*They provide for flexibility.*
Vulnerable	*They recognize the need for additional support and get help.*

Care providers facing allegations have seven essential needs. Each of these needs is based on a principle which can be supplied from peer counselors trained in crisis support services.

Principle	**NEED**	**RESULT**
Confidentiality	To feel safe from gossip	Builds trust
Acceptance	To be recognized as a person of worth	Restores dignity to person
Non-judgmental feedback	Not to be judged	Restores hope
Empathy	To get a sympathetic response to problems	Affirms person has value and concerns
Individualization	To be treated as an individual	Restores independence
Expression	Purposeful expression of feelings	Restores self-esteem
Self-determination	To make their own decisions	Restores self-worth

The goal of the peer support counselor is to restore an individual in crisis to a self-help position. A typical peer counselor role would be to establish a constructive relationship quickly and help the care provider evaluate the situation. Peer counselors assure the individual that others have gone through the same situation and survived; they provide hope. They listen and do not judge while the provider vents his or her feelings. This allows the provider to explore options for self-preservation. They discuss the event, equip the person to move forward, and restore pre-crisis functioning. Peer counselors then terminate their roles to allow the person in crisis to become self-sustaining. They also check in periodically in the future.

What are common parent group dynamics?

Parent groups organize because of a basic concern for kids. All groups share this common concern, but the level of intensity and focus of groups varies somewhat. The North American Council on Adoptable Children has developed a publication called *"The Parent Group Manual, Resources and Ideas for Adoptive Parent Support Groups."* This manual contains excellent information for understanding and developing quality parent organizations. If you are seeking a parent support group, it is important to understand what type of group focus you want. Your own personality, experience, and present situation will influence what group focus is best for you.

How groups mature and what focus each level of maturity has.

Group Level	SPIRIT OF GROUP	PURPOSE OF GROUP
ONE: *VENTILATION OR FRUSTRATION GROUP*	Typically, anger appears at this level. Parents experience frustration when their personal needs are not met, and they come together to more effectively achieve their personal objectives. Members of the group focus primarily on self, and most members leave once their needs are met. These groups offer an informal structure and service to parents.	Parents gather to help each other through the system, knowing they cannot confront it directly because it controls access to kids. ***If you are still venting and need individuals to listen to you, this is a good place to start.***
TWO: *SUPPORT GROUP*	Provides a shoulder to lean on and sharing of information between individuals with similar interests or situations.	Helps parents realize their experiences are not unusual. They exchange valuable information and insight about parenting. These groups serve both parents and the children they care for.
THREE: *SERVICE GROUP*	The group's attitude is "we believe we can do it better," and the group members work together to provide services to and for other people.	Service groups bridge the gap between their needs and the limitations of the existing system. These groups are action oriented and develop projects to instigate change.
FOUR: *ADVOCACY GROUP*	Want to see the system change and are willing to challenge the way in which services are delivered to kids and families. They are often formally organized, but tend to have limited resources and react to crises rather than anticipate them.	Parents at this level see children not being served and want to hold the system accountable. They lobby for new laws, advocate policy changes, and hold the system accountable for services to children. They may work on citizen review boards or develop programs to improve exisiting services.
FIVE : *POLITICAL FORCE GROUP*	Proactive and operate with a base of support and political influence that requires the bureaucracy and legislature to check with them.	Introduce legislation, recommend budgets in the interest of children. These groups are advocacy groups which are so effective they become a political force.

Each group serves a very distinct purpose and is valuable to individuals at different times. Initially, individuals may need only to let their experience and emotions flow out, and a group level one may be a perfect connection. The problem with a group level one, however, is that members get stuck on a single

One of the hardest things I had to fight against was negative self talk.

It was easy to tell myself that . . .

I must be a bad mother or this wouldn't have happened to our family.

The social worker is an idiot or she would know immediately this was a mistake.

The system is corrupt and steals children.

Foster parents are liars and try to take children from people.

My husband is a bad person and got us into this mess.

My daughter is a liar and got us into this mess.

Maybe it's easier to give up than to keep on searching for the truth.

. . . and many others.

None of them very realistic or appropriate, but alone and isolated, they constantly filled my mind.
Birth mother

issue and continue to rant, rave, and ventilate without moving on. If this is your group, you may want to look for another group with additional focus. Healthy level one groups operate respectfully and have decision makers. These groups often then develop into level two groups. They maintain high visibility and they don't disappear after a battle. They develop written literature such as brochures, flyers, and newsletters. They provide services and actions which keep their profiles high. Eventually this group has gathered realistic numbers and facts and the facts show that their issues are pertinent. As advocates in group level four they begin to stand up for their principles. And finally they begin to WIN—reversing legislation, developing programs, and changing the system.

Members of advocacy or political force groups have also been significantly influenced by the system. Their case histories may be much more devastating than your own. The difference is that they have worked hard and challenged themselves to do something proactive. If you are new in the system and join a more mature group, hold back from discussing your personal experiences within the group. Listen to the experienced group members to gain insight and focus on individuals whom you can connect with later to direct, support, or listen to your situation. Even the most mature group leader has been in a rant and rave mode at least once—he or she will understand your need, but also help you focus. (NACAC 1989)

What if the media arrive during the heat of a crisis?

A crisis has occurred and the media have arrived quickly on the scene. The *"Holy shit"* factor of this story is right at the top. This story holds just the twist that makes it stand out from the rest. This is the kind of news you call the kids in to listen to, talk about at the office, and discuss with your neighbors. This is a scoop, a story that's going to make headlines and the headline is YOU. Personal and dramatic stories sell—this story has both. What do you do?

Before someone sticks a microphone in your face and starts shooting questions, take a deep breath and say, *"Just a moment, I need fifteen minutes to compose myself and I'll be ready for your questions"* or *"Folks, I'd like to answer your questions, but I need to regroup. I'll be back at ----time---."* Then go someplace quiet and prepare for the interview ahead. Plan for the unexpected, pull reference information you may need. Remember, the media have a responsibility to us. The media work to cover us. You can remain in control. By choosing to interview, you have the opportunity to communicate your understanding of a situation.

Be positive and selective on what you say. Before the interview, take time to write down four main points you want covered. Keep coming back to these four points. Keep the main point up front. Don't lose track of your issue.

How you look and sound on the air is your responsibility.

Attire: Dress simply if you have a choice and remove any costume jewelry. White tends to be reflective. Plaid patterns can create some problems. Stick to primary colors, pastels, blacks, or greys.

Body language: Think of an interview as sitting at a kitchen table talking to one of your friends. Looking down, twitching, or blinking a lot gives the appearance to the audience that you are hiding something. Excessive gestures of the hands can be very distracting, hold your hands together. Every movement you make will be greatly exaggerated on videotape, so try to remain fairly still.

Eye contact: In direct one-to-one interviews look at the person who is interviewing you. The job of the cameraperson is to capture the right angle. Don't surprise your audience by looking suddenly straight at the camera and getting into a viewer's face. In a live audience interview, as a panelist, look at the camera and pretend there is a bird sitting on top of it. This will keep your eyes open and raised, instead of looking down. NOTE: When women make a strong or powerful statement they often immediately look down. Keep your eyes up.

Voice: Be firm, mildly-passionate, but not animated. Be confident, but not self-important or arrogant. Know your topic. Tell only the truth. If you can't tell the truth, don't talk. Do not be abusive. Keep your answers short, concise. Don't speak too fast, slow down.

How do the various media differ?

On television, image sticks more than the message. Nonverbal communication counts for more than 50 percent of the impression. One of the shortcomings of television is that impressions are more important than faces. Act pleasant, look pleasant. The audience is the viewer watching the show. All viewers will decide if they like or agree with you, but few viewers remember your name. Viewers do remember your issue. The reporter is only the channel to get the message out. Time is of the essence, an interview of four or five minutes will be cut to a 30-45 second spot.

On radio, the medium is sound. Your visual appearance is not important, but the sound of your voice is very important. Speak clearly. State your goals and mission. Get on and get off.

Newspaper and printed media listen for what you say, rewrite it, and then additionally edit the copy. Headlines are written by someone other than the reporter and are created to attract the attention of the reader. Headlines are also written under space limitations.

There is no "off the record." Once the statement is made the potential for seeing it in print is possible. Your worst statement may be the media's best statement.

Who are reporters? What do they expect?

Reporters are people. They are all unique with different personalities. Their interests and desires are not identical to yours. Some will be easy to talk to, others will be offensive.

The reporter is just trying to perform his or her job for the day. A good reporter will not be pro or con on an issue, he or she will remain objective. Don't get upset with a controversial question. If questions become critical the reporter may be playing the devil's advocate to get another side of the story. Reporters need access to stories and their job is to dig out the pieces of interest to the public. These questions do not mean the reporter doesn't like you or is picking on you. The reporter is simply fulfilling his or her assignment.

If difficult questions are posed, admit your mistakes and correct any wrong assumptions. If you cannot comment, simply state, *"I'm sorry I cannot comment"* and leave it at that. Bridge a reporter's question back to your answer. For example, *"Yes, I understand how you feel about that, but here's the real story --"* or *"Yes, that is what is being circulated, but here's the other side of the issue."*

The goal of a quality reporter is to scoop out a *"real"* story and communicate it with clarity, grace, persuasion, and passion.

"If we cannot make mistakes we will always go backwards. If we cannot learn from our mistakes we cannot go forward."
Friel 1990

What if I am taken "out of context"?

Before you make your complaint, know what your complaint is. How you looked or sounded is your responsibility. If you are taken "out of context" call the reporter and explain factually what was wrong with the story. The media need to maintain credibility.

Summary

Families can forgive, heal, and work to create an atmosphere of unconditional acceptance. If the care provider family is willing put all their issues out on the table, most situations can be worked through and dealt with. Grievances can be aired truthfully, lovingly, and straightforwardly. Each individual family member will be given the respect needed to state opinions, issues, and grievances. The family members do not need to deny the unpleasant feelings they have. By exposing unpleasant feelings, the family can stop the cycles of hostility, bitterness, and distrust. The road of straightforwardness and truth takes courage, but the family that can remove the masks of denial and self protection has the opportunity for true healing, whether from the trauma of false allegations or from the necessity to change a behavior.

A well-informed support team can be the connecting link for the care provider family to maintain healthy during allegation procedures. Look for a support group, join, and participate.

If your crisis precipitates action from the media, remain calm and be prepared.

The investigation does not last forever. Each family will need to slog through the process and come out on the other side. The experience can leave the provider family more mature, knowledgeable, and understanding, or it can leave the family desolate and devastated.

References

Kroll, Joe and Frank, Roberta. 1989. *Parent Group Manual. Resources and Ideas for Adoptive Parent Support Groups.* Minnesota: North American Council on Adoptable Children.

Lewis, Paul, San Diego, Calif, Pres. of Family University. May/June 1991 He publishes *Dads Only* and *Dads and Moms Newsletters* and has written *40 Ways to Teach Your Child Values* (Tyndale), Christian Parenting Today.

Vineyard, Sue. 1988. *How To Take Care Of You...So You Can Take Care of Others.* Illinois: Heritage Arts.

FUN BOOKS TO GAIN INSIGHT AND RELIEVE TENSION:

Do Plastic Surgeons Take Visa and Other Confessions of a Desperate Woman by Kathy Peel.(1992) Dallas: Word Publishing.

Splashes of Joy in the Cesspools of Life by Barbara Johnson. (1992) Dallas: Word Publishing.

So, Stick a Geranium in Your Hat and Be Happy. by Barbara Johnson. (1990) Dallas: Word Publishing.

CHAPTER 16

The Future— Creative Reform for Children and their Families

Children's and their families' issues are unique.
There are no simple answers.

As I finish writing this guide for families and professionals, I pass the baton to you to carry on where I have left off. I wish in this research process of two years that more changes had taken place to serve the best interests of children. Perhaps in the future that dream will be realized. Finally, we are beginning to see an outcry and public awareness.

On my journey, I have determined six goals of reform that could change a complex and expensive system. Most of all, I believe these goals, if attained, would help protect the life, liberty, and psychological safety of children.

1.   **DESIGNATED PARENTING PROGRAM:** Based on the successful driver's license organ donor card system already in place, parents would have the option to legally designate individuals who will immediately provide surrogate care for their children in the event of injury, accident, illness, seizure, mental incapacity, incarceration, or death of the parents—avoiding delays while relatives are contacted, wills are found, and kids are stranded in terrifying custody limbo. The names of the individuals would be printed on the parents' driver's licenses or identification cards. The person(s) would be chosen by the parents as legally designated parents and would not need to be related or of the same race.

     a.   Designated parents could help connect the disconnected high-risk families by serving as mentor or co-parents for parents faced with terminal, chronic, or mental illness during their times of crisis.

     b.   Designated parents could serve as co-parents for low-functioning parents or parents with executive disabilities.

     c.   Designated parents could serve as co-parents in the case of young teen parenthood.

2. **PROFESSIONALIZE THE FOSTER PARENTING PROGRAM:** With the goal of establishing a closer partnership between social service agencies, birth families, and foster families, establish a two-year nationally accredited training program for prospective care providers.

   a. **First year training program:** The goal of the initial year of training would be to learn to respect the needs of children and their birth families by providing friendship, mentorship, and support to high risk families. Contact with these families would be on neutral ground and would provide recreation and education for both families—sporting events, museums, zoos, parks, etc. During this first year a curriculum of personal growth work, professional parenting, and cultural diversity classes would be developed. Complete investigations of these families would be completed in order to qualify for the second year training program. Classes and recreational activities could be government sponsored.

   b. **Second year training program:** The second year's goal would be to develop respect for and understanding of social services. This year's practical experience would be providing emergency placement or respite care for children needing care. The curriculum would include child development, attachment, separatation, loss, grief, discipline and creative problem solving in a crisis. It also would include an internship in child protection so the foster family will understand the dynamics of the system and its workers. Upon completion of the two-year program, approved families would be licensed for longer term care of children. Meanwhile, social services would work on sensitivity training to assure that foster parents and birth parents receive the respect and professional services they need and deserve.

3. **INVESTIGATION OF FOSTER FAMILIES:** Since foster families are part of social services, when the social service system investigates an abuse allegation, it essentially investigates itself. To prevent conflict of interest, agencies independent of social services should be established to carry out immediate, complete, and fair investigations of all abuse allegations. Investigators must receive sensitivity training in child development, grief, loss, attachment, abuse, neglect, and licensing issues. Anyone facing a child maltreatment allegation or investigation must receive a standard set of published investigation procedures along with a list of personal rights.

4. **SOCIAL SERVICE PROFESSIONALS ANNUAL PRACTICAL EXPERIENCE IN FOSTER CARE:** Each professional given the responsibility of working with children in out-of-home care would provide two weekends of respite annually for professional foster parents or high risk clients.

5. **A CITIZEN REVIEW BOARD** and a foster parent ombudsman would be appointed in every state to review individual child protection cases.

6. **A NATIONAL PUBLIC RELATIONS CAMPAIGN** would be initiated which casts light upon the vital and positive role designated co-parents and foster parents can play in the lives of children, their families, and our communities.

As Dr. Martin Luther King, Jr., so solidly proclaimed on August 28, 1963 in Washington, D.C., for the African American community—

"We cannot walk alone.
And as we walk, we must make the pledge that we shall always march ahead.
We cannot turn back."

Epilogue

As this book goes to press, inquiries have been made about the stories of families used as illustrations. For many of them, an additional three years has been added to their lives.

Julie and Lee's children are still living in their home. They are not yet adopted, it's been three years.

Lisa, age nine, is growing healthy with her adoptive family. She has recently met her little birth sister, age seven, who was adopted into another family. The families have become friends and the two girls are sharing camping trips, family reunions, and sleepovers. Watching the two girls play, the mothers shared, *"These children need each other and we parents need each other, too. They are wonderful and challenging. I don't know how anyone could parent the two of them together, but separately and with supports it's a joy. Their intensity gives you excess in delight, surprises, and trauma."* Jesse and Jerry are reunited with their birth father.

Gretchen's immigrant parents still grieve the loss of their daughter and do not understand how the *Land of the Free and Home of the Brave* failed them.

Joan and Homer are living apart because of state intervention. Joan is living in a foster home as a low functioning adult, but has been reunited with one of their four children. Tubal ligation after the birth of their fourth son appears to have failed, Joan is again pregnant by Homer. Homer is required to stay away. He is working and trying to save money to re-establish his family. He is attending law school.

The taxi driver is still comforting people and transporting the disconnected from the county courthouse to their residences. During the last three years a number of his customers have committed suicide soon after termination of parental rights. These people have lost the little they had and reached the ultimate in discouragement. Others have moved into homeless shelters. His life has been threatened as he has offered help. He also is attending law school.

Johnny hangs out with his buddies and is back with his birth father.

Jennie is still a handful. Her parents have enrolled her in a structured private school, and she is under the watchful eyes of both parents and teachers. They continue counseling. There have been no additional pulling-down-pants incidents in that household.

Amy and Abby still live in the same house. Except for the accidental meeting in the park, they have not seen or heard from or about Kris. Amy still has her foster parent license, but appears to be under a quiet closing. Since Kris left three years ago, no other children have been placed in her home. *"You know I don't worry about Kris. She's one of those kids who won't be stopped. She's got the attitude, personality, and intelligence to be successful, regardless of circumstances,"* Amy shared.

The court has awarded custody of Aaron to his grandparents. Aaron is happy and free spirited, running in the place his heart calls home. Julie's parents are saddened that Julie is now in a locked juvenile facility and preparing for an independent living program. The courts had enough and let Julie know it. It took five years and thousands of taxpayer dollars. Her adoptive parents wish the courts would have believed their real needs five years ago when a professional support family would have provided the additional structure the family needed to reach Julie.

Sheila, Tom, and Linda have worked hard to rebuild their family. The allegation, therapy, and court costs have totaled more than $160,000—but they are united.

I wish these stories all had happy endings. It would be easier to close the pages of this book and walk away.

Any of these people, however, could have been you or me—given the right, or better said "wrong," circumstances.

Bobby and her four children have found another church to support them. The family still collects AFDC, and Bobby, at 22, is slowing working toward her GED.

The angry young man still will kill his birth father if he finds him.

Eric is enjoying being home again and Rebecca's program is working. Last Sunday at church her seven-year-old came running—*"Mom, Eric's locked himself in the bathroom and not letting anyone in. I know he's in there, but he won't answer."* Another power play for Eric—the community knows he's home. But Rebecca and her new husband are ready to play the game with new rules without entanglement. *They are unbelievably, thinking of adopting again!*

The curiousity seekers have asked for more data on "Our Story." Most of it can be found within the pages of this book—a piece here, a piece there— whenever the application was appropriate. As with the other stories, the names have been changed to protect the innocent. The child welfare system has taught me over and over—do no harm to a child, and it is not my intent to hurt anyone with this writing—children, professionals, or other caring adults. In 1995, we will be able to reapply for our foster care license. Knowing the risks and having a better understanding of the system, I question even more whether this would be a wise choice for our family. To date we still have not been allowed to read our file.

My beloved Joseph is now four and a half years old. He is still in foster care. His mother's rights are projected to be terminated. She is feeling very vulnerable in the midst of the mass of professionals. Her marriage is stable and she is rebuilding her life. Joseph just recently was told who his birth mother is. It was a surprise, his four and a half year old mind had thought his foster mother was his mother and my husband was his daddy. I remain just Jodee. Joseph's birth father has never come forward. Joseph's recent psychological evaluations diagnosed attachment disorder due to multiple placements. He hides in his own world when he is discouraged and rages when he is frustrated. Whoever takes on the challenge of permanently parenting him will have mental health work to do.

Joseph's baby sister is almost three. She has been diagnosed with Fetal Alcohol Syndrome and Attention Deficit Disorder. Her foster mother would like to adopt her, but may not be able to if the siblings must remain as a unit. His older two sisters are now seven, they are a handful. Adolescence with the twins will be an adventure. Joseph's five-year-old brother also diagnosed with Fetal Alcohol Syndrome, will be permanently placed with his birth father. His father loves him unconditionally. The little boy who left with his birth mother just prior to Joseph's arrival has returned to Joseph's foster mother as a newly adopted son.

The county discovered, in a file after four years, a relative in another state who is interested in offering a home for all four children. The relative, a retired aunt, will be getting her hands full if four grieving, emotionally damaged children arrive on the doorstep of another stranger. The reality and the fantasy will collide. In the near future, Joseph and his sisters face another move.

Upon hearing the latest news, April announced . . .

*"Don't worry about Joseph, Mom.
Me and him are in each other's hearts,
and no one can get us out of there . . .
I think I'll marry him. Then no one can divorce us
unless we decide that's what we want."*

The wisdom of the children has always amazed me. ——Jodee——

APPENDIX I

Ideas from the
Minnesota Foster Parent Association

Join a care provider association and work to change the legal and social system.

1. Define policies as to how abuse allegations will be handled. The foster care provider must understand these policies fully before accepting children for placement.

2. Employ someone who will work with foster care providers during investigations of abuse allegations, being their friend, knowing what they are going through, and keeping them informed as to what is going on with the agency.

3. Mandate that foster care providers must be informed, before placement, if the child has been in other homes, the reasons why the child was removed, and whether or not this is a pattern of behavior

4. Encourage investigation of potential foster care providers thoroughly before placement of any child in a home. No matter how desperate the need, screening must be done to protect the foster care providers the agency already has.

5. Educate foster care providers in correct and accurate systems to document constantly all incidents that may be construed as child abuse or neglect.

6. Push foster care providers to continually keep in touch with the placement agency, even though many of us do not see a worker for months, sometimes for the whole year.

7. Find sources of support for foster families during allegation proceedings. Provision of support does not imply or require taking sides on the issue under study. Agency inability or unwillingness to provide support does not negate the need for support.

8. Help work on provision of legal information and resources.
   Work needs to be done toward developing feasible means of obtaining legal information, legal assistance, and legal representation for foster care providers. This will help ensure agency fairness with foster families and will underscore to foster care providers the intent of fairness and support.

9. Promote foster care provider networking beginning with the first orientations to develop strong support networks for foster families.

10. Encourage and support foster families' interaction with foster care provider associations because some foster families still look to the agency for guidance and direction.

I looked all around at all the children suffering in the world. I saw the abuse, the neglect, the pain.

I looked up to heaven and said, Why? Why don't you do something to help these children?

The reply came back: I did do something. I created YOU!
(Unknown)

APPENDIX —II

*Position Statement:
Child Abuse/Neglect Allegations
in Foster/Adoptive Families from
Nebraska and New York*

Initial paragraphs for Nebraska and New York:

The Nebraska Foster and Adoptive Parents Association, herein referred to as
NFAPA is an organization of foster and adoptive parents. We are extremely
concerned about the increasing number of allegations of child
abuse/neglect among foster/adoptive parents. This problem is apparent in
Nebraska and throughout the country.

OR

The New York State Citizen's Coalition for Children, Inc., is an organization of
over 70 adoptive and foster parent support and advocacy groups
throughout New York State. We are extremely concerned about the
increasing number of allegations of child abuse/neglect in adoptive and
foster families. This problem exists in New York State and throughout the
country.

Main body of position statement:

Under no circumstances do we condone child abuse/neglect in *any* family.
However, we recognize there are circumstances which make some adoptive
and foster families especially vulnerable to reports of abuse/neglect and
susceptable to misjudgement. These circumstances are as follows:

Children who have experienced the uncertainties and insecurities of years
of foster care, often with multiple moves, have been damaged in ways
which affect their behavior for years. Many children who have suffered
such damage have learned maladaptive or anti-social coping behaviors,
thus are manipulative, unable to trust, lack a sense of honesty and respon-
sibiity, and are deficient in many areas of their development.

Such children, due to their histories, typically behave in ways which jeopardize the security and stability of the families diligently striving to undo
some of the damage of the past and to help the children develop more appropriate and socially acceptable behaviors. These children often lie and
play on the responses of other adults who do not view their behaviors in
the context of the children's prior experiences. Some children deliberately
hurt those who offer help and try to destroy close relationships. After a sequence of adult rejections, they cannot accept that others care about or love
them. It is not uncommon for the children themselves to make false reports
of abuse/neglect in an effort to control adult behavior and to deal with
fears of close relationships.

Adoptive and foster parents of difficult or emotionally disturbed children
are often subjected to community scrutiny and suspicion that biological

families do not experience. Adoptive and foster families are sometimes highly visible in their communities due to their size or composition. Many people do not understand why someone would choose to parent older children, large numbers of children, children with handicapping conditions or negative histories. Hence, they are suspicious of adoptive and foster parents' motives.

This lack of understanding can also apply to the agencies responsible for investigations of alleged abuse/neglect. In addition, agency standards for investigations are not uniform in practice nor necessarily of high quality. Protective service workers may be untrained and inexperienced. Workers may not be familiar with the complexities of the pathologies displayed by the children and the stresses they bring to family living.

The child's psychological, medical, and educational records may not be considered in an investigation. Appropriate child management techniques and therapeutic interventions may be viewed out of context by those not familiar with their purposes. Unsubstantiated charges can go unchallenged, and the New York State evidentiary standard in child abuse/neglect investigations of "some credible evidence" can result in overly subjective decisions.

Due to these factors, adoptive and foster parents can be unfairly targeted and unduly stressed. Instead of receiving support and assistance from the community, they may be forced to expend their energies on defending themselves rather than getting on with their parenting job.

Adoptive and foster parents join with all parents in seeking acceptance and support from their communities. We share a commitment to our children and a belief in the value of family life. Above all, we seek the health and well-being of all our children. Therefore, we support the following:

1. Continued efforts to identify child abusers/neglectors to assure that all children are safe and that their parents provide nurturing environments.

2. Increased preventive, corrective, and rehabilitative services. All parents must have continuous opportunities to learn about and improve parenting skills. Community agencies must provide on-going and widely publicized programs. Young people must have instruction in the area of children's psychological and physical needs in order to prepare themselves for responsible parenting.

3. Provision of ongoing support and educational services to parents adopting or providing foster care for children with special needs. We encourage Social Services Departments to use Preventive Services monies and resources in order to prevent the disruption of families with special needs children.

4. Higher standards for the selection of protective services workers and increased training requirements. Continuing education must be provided concerning adoptive and foster families and the behaviors presented by some adoptive and foster children. Workers must be required to include in their investigations all historical information on the child, as well as testimony from knowledgeable therapists, educators, and medical resources.

5. Appropriate legislation and/or regulation to assure the above. (1989)

I had made the assumption that the worker was a peer in an open relationship. The reality is that the worker-family relationship is one-sided. The family is required to share all confidences, yet the family knows nothing of the worker's private life. The worker can use these confidences (told without witnesses) against you whenever he or she chooses.

It is wrong to assume the worker is a peer or a supporter or an advocate or anything other than a person acting in the job role to which he or she has been assigned.

In a peer-friendship relationship, confidences and support are shared. From that type of relationship—true advocacy can emerge.

Appendix III: Examples of Red Flags Experienced By Social Workers

The first column of the chart *"Possible Red Flags,"* has been compiled from the book *Preventing Abuse in Foster Care* by Emily Jean McFadden. The second and third columns have been provided by the dedicated efforts of the Minnesota Foster Care Provider Association, experienced social workers, and professionals in developing the potential for abuse and neglect and other possibilities. It is important to remember when one is dealing with Red Flags that there may be many explanations.

Possible Red Flag	Potential Abuse or Neglect	Other Possibilities
CHANGES IN HEALTH IN FAMILY		
A dramatic gain or loss of weight by foster care provider.	Bulimia, anorexia, depression, stress, self-destruction.	Thyroid, diabetes, pregnancy, toxemia, taking dessert classes, working out, dieting, health program, quit smoking.
Frequent illness of foster child.	Child depressed. Poor diet. Lack of medical attention.	Child depressed. New placement, child came like that. Medical misdiagnosis. Previous way child got attention was by getting sick.
Medical appointments for child postponed or not kept.	Child being medically neglected by care provider.	Medical assistance card has not arrived. Physician will not accept any additional medicare patients. Family emergency and needed to reschedule.
Foster care provider usually fatigued.	Increases likelihood of inappropriate reaction to child.	Family member may have been sick. Job or project may be temporarily very demanding. May be hayfever, flu, or cold season. Allergies.

- **OTHER POSSIBLE RED FLAGS:** Frequent chronic illness of another family member. Pregnancy, false or real, in parent or child.

Possible Red Flag	Potential Abuse or Neglect	Other Possibilities
REVIEW OF FAMILY INTERACTIONS AND PROCESS:		
A pet or younger child appears fearful when an adult speaks.	Physical abuse present. Ritualistic abuse present. Potential psychopathic behaviors present.	Puppy placed in home at eight weeks of age and never recovered from loss of mother. Animal adopted from Humane Society. Animal previously injured. Animal has ear infection or other physical problem. Female animal displaying normal passive personality. Child abused prior to placement.
One of the foster care providers is usually withdrawn when interacting with spouse or worker. One person talks for the whole family. Other family members seek nonverbal "permission" before speaking.	Care provider feeling guilty or hiding something from worker. Breakdown in worker-care provider relationship.	Providers may work as a team and have designated one spokesperson for family to social services. Personality may be introverted. Care provider may not trust worker. Language barrier. Care provider hard of hearing and missed details but afraid to say anything. Culturally appropriate response. Knowledgeable care provider being cautious is opening up with worker.
One of the foster care providers' "own" children is acting out.	Children usually are barometer to family stress and family may be having problems.	Natural consequences of maturing in culture. Foster family is normal. Natural reaction of a child when faced with integrating new family members and redefining roles of family members.
Denial of conflict, no communication of feelings.	Care provider hiding information and not being truthful.	Conflict may not have happened and person is telling the truth. Person may be afraid to communicate feelings to investigator or social worker, fearing misunderstanding.
Parents don't set limits on child's behavior.	Neglectful home situation. Care providers not trained or inadequate to handle child.	Child may have had no previous boundaries and refuses to accept any form of discipline. Care provider may have had an allegation in the past and is afraid to set boundaries. Child may be holding care provider hostage with allegation threats.

- **OTHER POSSIBLE RED FLAGS:** One parent excessively authoritarian and other very permissive.

FOSTER PARENT COMMUNICATION WITH WORKER:

Poor eye contact, other nonverbal behavior such as agitation—finger drumming, leg shaking—over control—clutched fists, rigid posture.	Parent is tense, guilty, nervous. Parent is concealing anger and could become uncontrollable.	Parents may be angry at what social worker is saying or the situation and are afraid to say what they really feel for fear of being misunderstood. Nervous habit established in childhood and not broken. Eye contact may not be culturally appropriate. Muscular problem, arthritis, or other physical pain.
Suggests the child should be returned home or placed elsewhere.	Something may have happened that parent is not willing to talk about.	Care provider may have more information on situation than social services. Child and birth parent may actually be ready to reunite. Parent may know personal parenting limits and is afraid to continue parenting this child.
Increases complaining about child's behavior.	Parents being stretched. Potential for abuse.	Child may be done with honeymoon and beginning to protest. Child may finally be getting healthy. Parents need additional support while child is going through protest stage.
Seems to be avoiding or changing the subject.	Provider hiding information.	Subject may bring up painful past experience or current out-of-family situation and care provider does not want to discuss details. Social worker may be asking about something provider is not allowed to discuss under the Data Privacy Act. Parent may be trying to bridge conversation to *"real"* issues.

CHANGE IN FAMILY ECONOMICS:

Sudden or unusual concern for reimbursement. Complaints about expense of the child.	Care provider complaining and not appreciative of social services.	Agency and previous workers have not responded to care provider's financial requests in the past. Child in their care has just done major damage to the home and additional financial support is needed to fix damage. Additional physical or educational support needed for the child. Very appropriate question.
Foster father takes an extra job.	Financial difficulty. Additional stress on family.	Advancement to new and better career. Educational opportunity. Friend of family needs temporary help. Temporary need for additional funds.
Mother begins working.	Financial stress on family.	Mother may need a break to refocus. Mother may have opportunity to do something she has always wanted to do. Family may need additional monies temporarily.

FAMILY BEGINS ISOLATION:

Drops out of training or other foster care provider activities.	Isolation. Not interested in educational advancement.	Training available is too basic and care provider does not want to waste time. Children in care need personal attention and time away is not appropriate.
Can't transport child to appointments.	Care provider not performing requirements of job.	Appointment beyond 10 mile radius allowed to transport child. Car is not working or is unreliable. Other duties needed to be taken care of for other children. Child is volatile in care and places provider family in danger.
Changes in patterns of church attendance.		Child in care has difficulty with church of foster care providers. Care providers have additional project to help church. Problems with church they are attending. Life in America—things change.
Won't come to foster care provider activities.	Isolation. Inactive. Not a team player.	Busy with other activities which include foster children. Social worker who they have had difficulty with is part of the activity.

FROM DIRECT OBSERVATION BY THE WORKER IN THE FOSTER HOME:

Fights between children in the home.	Volatile situation needs monitoring.	Child finally feels secure enough to let out true feelings. Child in protest stage. Normal rivalry.
Housekeeping has deteriorated.	Inattentive, non-caring, neglectful.	Just back from vacation. Company over the night before. All neighbor kids over. Major family project. Illness in family. Focus not on homemaking but on interaction with kids. School just started.
Conflict between foster care providers regarding the child.	Trouble in relationship.	Care provider sharing differences of opinion with social worker to help gain perspective and opinion of differences in parenting.
Child unfavorably compared to other children in home.	Child under attack and vulnerable.	Child may be extremely difficult and care providers are asking for help in dealing with difficulties. Comparisons may be used to highlight variances from normal or typical child's reaction or behavior. Child is really like care provider says.

- **OTHER POSSIBLE RED FLAGS:** Discipline "threats." Overfocus on one child as "favorite." One family member (father/mother) involved. One family member overinvolved with child.

FROM COLLATERAL CONTACTS:

Teachers, doctors, therapists, etc. may sound concerned but don't articulate reason.	Suspected maltreatment.	Professional is inexperienced in working with foster children and their special behaviors and needs.
Neighbors, babysitters are concerned about difficulties with the child.	Suspected maltreatment.	Individual is inexperienced in working with foster children and their special behaviors and needs.
Other workers using the home.	Suspected maltreatment.	Personality conflict with worker.
Natural or birth parents.	Suspected maltreament.	Natural jealously of foster parent role.

- **OTHER POSSIBLE RED FLAGS:** Police reports. Other foster care providers express concern. Media items (arrests, sentencing, etc.).

FROM TELEPHONE CALLS TO SOCIAL SERVICES:

No calls.	Avoidance. Isolation.	No reason to call.
Frequent calls with nothing to say.	Withholding information.	Following requested agency procedures.
Foster care provider hesitant to set up appointment for home visit.	Avoidance of social service requirements. Non-compliant.	Calendar is busy. Has not had previous positive experiences with worker showing up on time or attending appointments.
Slurred, disjointed speech.	Alcohol or drug problem possible.	M.S. or other disability is acting up. Stutter when under stress. Novocaine from dentist. Just woke up from deep sleep.
Never home.	Avoidance of social services. Potential non-compliance	Out having fun with kids. Running errands. Visiting sick friend or family.
Questions about limits of policy.	Non-cooperative with procedures.	Asking good questions that need to be asked. Care provider recognizes there is a potential difficult situation and wants clarification to properly handle.
"Yes, but . . ."	Making excuses for problem. Denial.	Information is not being interpreted properly and needs clarification. Bad habit established in childhood.

All care providers need a call answering machine that is working. This prevents "I tried to reach you, but you were not home." Social service workers need voice mail for messages from care providers.

FOSTER CHILD APPEARANCE OR BEHAVIOR:

Poorly dressed.	Neglect. Care provider not taking proper care of child. Child depressed.	Child likes to be poorly dressed. The poorly dressed look is the new fad at school. Child depressed. Child came with no clothing. Child has outgrown all clothes and clothing allowance or first care payment has not come.
Doesn't eat well or always ravenous.	Care provider not taking proper care of child.	Child going through growing spurt. Child selling lunch tickets for cigarettes. Child concerned about weight but won't say anything. Child stressed. Undiagnosed physical ailment.
Child fearful of foster parents: too good, too quiet.	Suspected maltreatment.	Child has learned in past if she opens her mouth she may lose her new home. Child is working through loss issues. New placement. Maybe this was the overachiever and the kid likes to be good.
"Accident prone" bruises and bumps.	Suspected maltreatment.	Child learning to walk. Child has undiagnosed cerebral palsy or other physical disability. Going through growing spurt. Child is hyperactive. Child is FAS or FAE. Child working through new experiences—roller skating, riding bike, etc. Child has hearing or visual impairment.
Child appears in discomfort when sitting down.	Suspected maltreatment.	Child fell down rollerkating, sliding and hurt tailbone. Child is hyperactive. Child has hemorrhoids. Child has worms. Child has yeast infection. Child has to go to the bathroom. Child has menses.
Child fearful of worker.	Child may be hiding something from social worker.	Some social workers are pretty scary. *How would you feel if your kidnapper came to your house?* Abandonment issues. Afraid worker is going to take them.
Child clings to worker.	Child may be hiding something from social worker.	Pervasive attachment disorder. Non-attached child.
Child withdrawn or aggressive.	Child may be hiding something from social worker.	Child has undiagnosed allergies. Personality disorder from previous history. Child working through grieving.

- OTHER POSSIBLE RED FLAGS: Child develops allergies.

FROM CONTACT WITH THE FOSTER CHILD:

Child seems to have secret and won't discuss foster family.	Child may be hiding something.	Last time child shared information, she was removed and does not want to risk losing this family, too. Last time child said something, everything got all mixed up.
Child shows extremes of depression or aggression.	Child not adjusting properly to family.	Child is adjusting very well to family and is finally able to show true feelings. Child has learned that by displaying these specific behaviors—aggression or depression—he or she can get needs met. Children who have been in institutional settings may also display mental illness, retardation or disabilities to meet needs.
Runaways.	Child unhappy and this is not appropriate placement.	Placement is very appropriate and child is beginning to establish a real relationship and is fearful of it. Child has pattern of running away when certain situations happen.
Child wants to move, but won't say why.	Child unhappy and this is not appropriate placement.	Relationship is healthy, but child is fearful of healthy relationships or long-term continuity of care. Self-fulfilling prophesy. Therapist or other professional may have made statement to child about moving.
Child doesn't want to return from respite or camp.	Child unhappy and this is not appropriate placement.	Having fun! Child does not want to go back to structured lifestyle of care provider. Child has fallen in love with camp counselor.

FROM INFORMATION GIVEN TO LICENSING WORKER REGARDING CHANGE IN THE FOSTER FAMILY SITUATION:

Move to a new home is not a "step up."	Financial difficulty.	New home is closer to school, medical facilities. They like the neighborhood because of the type of foster child they have. They like the new house. What is a "step up" anyway and why is it important?
Loss of employment and/or foster mother seeking employment.	Financial difficulty.	Company may have laid off because of change in economy. Family may be reestablishing roles and foster father would like to spend more time at home with children for a while. Foster mother may need a break or would like to re-enter work field to keep her professional credentials current.
Request to be licensed for fewer children.	Care providers having problems with children they have.	Care providers have honestly assessed their situation and decided to take a break or cut down on number of children. Type of children family has are getting more difficult as they are gaining more experience. Limiting the number of children will allow more attention to children they have. Why is more better?
Father doing shift work, mother working.	Family having financial problems.	Company has begun new shift and asked mature and trusted worker to establish it. Mother needs a break. Mother has always worked and likes working outside of home. Parent prefers shift work and enjoys days free. Shift work offers better compensation. Family saving for something special or to get out of debt.
Change in appearance of home.		Family beginning remodeling project. Foster child is destructive and family cannot keep up repairs. Foster child is destructive and family refuses to make repairs until child leaves or his behavior changes.
Foster care provider motivation for fostering is infertility due to sexual dysfunction.		Social services needs clear understanding of what sexual dysfunction and infertility means to care provider. What is the cause of infertility and how has the family dealt with it?

- **OTHER POSSIBLE RED FLAGS:** Marital separation. Retirement.

FROM OBSERVATION OUTSIDE THE FOSTER HOME (AT TRAINING, MEETINGS, ETC.):

Foster care provider complaining about lack of agency support.	Uncooperative, complaining. Non-compliant.	Inconsistency of support is typical in large agencies. Different workers provide different levels of support. Care provider may not be complaining but voicing a truth.
Foster care provider feels need to escalate discipline.	Potential for abuse.	New placement causing safety concerns so family procedures and restrictions need review and updating.
Foster care provider angry with worker.	Potential for abuse.	Personality or cultural differences. Social worker may have made a mistake and done harm to child or family.
Foster care provider sleeps in training.	Care provider under stress and exhausted.	Worked late night before. Child up all night. New baby. Training session is boring. Listening with eyes closed (no snoring allowed).
Foster care provider in training says ,"I have a friend who . . ."	Care provider hiding something.	Appropriate way to state something because of confidentiality of situations.

Often the only calls social services receive from care providers is when they have trouble.
Providers need to call on good days too for balance.
Social workers need to hear the successes and the troubles.

Helpful Resources

The author does not endorse personally any of the following references, nor do these organizations or persons endorse this book. These references are provided to you as a service. As adults responsible for children, you must make the ultimate decision if any of these resources can work for you.

ABUSE

SUPPORT SERVICES:

Adults Molested as Children United, PO Box 952, San Jose, California 95108

Incest Resources, Women's Center, 46 Pleasant Street, Cambridge, MA 02139

Incest Survivors Anonymous (ISA), PO Box 5613, Long Beach, California 90805-0613, (213) 422-1632

Incest Survivor Information Exchange, PO Box 3399, New Haven, CT 06515

Parents United. (Daughters United/Sons United) PO Box 952., San Jose, CA 95108. (408) 280-5055. Provides long term and crisis support for families in which incest has occurred.

Survivors of Incest Anonymous, PO Box 21817, Baltimore, MD 21222

BOOKS WORTH READING:

The Battered Child, 4th Ed., by Ray E. Helfer and Ruth S. Kempe, Eds. The University of Chicago Press, (1988) Clear writing and photographs help in understanding of child abuse and neglect, its identification, assessment, intervention, treatment and prevention.

Breaking the Cycle of Child Abuse; Herbruck, Christin Comstock; Winston Press, Inc., 430 Oak Grove, Minneapolis, MN 55403, 1979

Child Abuse and Neglect: A Professional's Guide to Identification, Reporting, Investigation and Treatment by the New Jerseys Governor's Task Force on Child Abuse and Neglect. (1988) Addresses the roles of medical, social worker and law enforcement professionals in responding to child abuse and neglect. Medical examination and hospital management sections, model law enforcement/child protection services joint investigations sections are particularly useful. Write: State of New Jersey, Governors Task Force on Child Abuse and Neglect, CN700, Trenton, New Jersey, 08625 or call 609-292-0888.

The Child That Never Was, Grieving Your Past To Grow Into Your Future, Kaye, PhD, Yvonne, 1991, Health Communications (Recovery journey for adults from dysfunctional families.)

Wednesday Child by Suzanne Somers

ADOPTION

SUPPORT SERVICES:

Adoptive Families of America, 3333 Hwy 100 North, Minneapolis, MN 55422. (612) 535-4829. Publishes OURS MAGAZINE, has catalog of books, tapes, culurally diverse toys and dolls. Parent support groups and training.

C Kempe National Center for Prevention and Treatment of Child Abuse and Neglect, 1205 Oneida Street, Denver, CO 80220. (303) 321-3963

Child Welfare League of America, 440 First Street NW Suite 310, Washington, DC 20001. (201) 638-2952. Catalog of books and publication. Professionals available for training.

North American Council on Adoptable Children, 970 Raymond Ave. #106, St. Paul, MN 55114. (612) 644-3036. Publishing numerous manuals and training programs. Also publish ADOPTALK newsletter. NACAC works closely with a wide spectrum of local and national groups and individuals serving children and families. It is a nonprofit, broad-based coalition of volunteer adoptive parent support and citizen advocacy groups, caring individuals, and agencies committed to meeting the needs of waiting children.

Spaulding Center for Children. National Resource Center for Special Needs Adoption, PO Box 337, Chelsea, Michigan 48118 (313) 475-8693. Source for After Adoption book. Curriculum, books, newsletter, training, videos available.

University Of Southern Maine, Human Services Development Institute, Research Librarian, 96 Falmouth Street, Portland, Maine 04103. (207) 780-4430. Books, videos, consultation, etc.

BOOKS WORTH READING:

Adopting the Older Child. Claudia Jewett, adoptive parent and nationally known family counselor invites readers into the journey or parenting older adoptive children.

Adoption and the Sexually Abused Child. Joan McNamara and Bernard McNamara. A practical and realistic journey into parenting children who have been sexually abused. If you cannot find this book, please contact Family Resources Adoption Program, 226 North Highland Avenue, Ossining, New York 10562. (914) 762-6550.

The longer I live, the more I realize the impact of attitude on life.

Attitude to me, is more important than facts.

It is more important than the past,

than education,

than money,

than circumstances,

than failures,

than successes,

than what other people say or do.

continued

*It is more important
than appearance,*

giftedness,

or skill.

*It will make or break a
company . . .*

a church . . .

a home . . .

continued

The Miracle Seekers: An Anthology of Infertility. Mary Martin Mason authored *The Miracle Seekers* to shed light on the realities of living with infertility. Her forthcoming book *With This Child: The Renaissance Guide to Adoption* will open the eyes of many into the world of adoption through the eyes of the birth parents, children, and adoptive parents. Mary writes from her heart—as an adoption advocate, adopted child herself, and as an adoptive mother who shares respect and friendship with her son's tummy mother. Mary speaks nationally on issues surrounding adoption. She has also developed a series of excellent videotapes called ADOPTAPES. Contact Mary Martin Mason, 4012 Lynn Avenue, Edina, MN 55416 (612) 922-1136.

IMPORTANT REFERENCE MATERIAL

PUBLIC LAW 96-272, The Child Welfare and Adoption Assistance Act of 1980 and its amendments, codified at 42 UCS 620 et seq. Those interested in improving their understanding of or compliance with the law should also be familiar with the U.S. Department of Health and Human Services issuances interpreting the law. These issuances can be found in Policy Interpretation Questions (PIQs), Policy Issuances (PIs) and Policy Announcements (PAs) They are available through Policy and Review Operations, U.S. Children's Bureau, PO Box 1182, Washington, DC 20013 or call 202-205-8820.

The Adoption Assistance and Child Welfare Act of 1980 (Public Law 96-272): The First Ten Years produced by the North American Council on Adoptable Children (1990) A Collection of articles covering outcomes, implementation by the courts and federal regulation. To order write: North American Council on Adoptable Children, 970 Raymond Ave. #106, St. Paul, MN 55114. (612) 644-3036. Cost is $7.00.

Children Can't Wait: Reducing Delays for Children in Family Foster Care by Katherine Cahn and Paul Johnson, editors and published by the Child Welfare League reviews five sites which received grants from the US Department of Health and Human Services to study and try to eliminate barriers to timely termination of parental rights. Order: Child Welfare League, 440 First Street, NW, Washington, DC 20001 or call 202-638-2952.

TRAINING PROGRAM:

AUDIOVISUAL MATERIALS LIST: Contact National Adoption Center, 1218 Chestnut Street, Philadelphia, PA 19107. (215) 925-0200.

The SAFE-TEAM Curriculum: Preparation and Support for Families Adopting Sexuaqlly Abused Children. Contact: SAFE-TEAM Project on Child Sexual Abuse and Adoption, Family Resources, 226 North Highland Avenue, Ossining, NY 10562. (914) 762-6550.

FAMILY PRESERVATION: The Second Time Around (post-legal adoption services based on peer counseling principles) Contact: NACAC, 970 Raymond Ave. #106, St. Paul, MN 55114. (612) 644-3036.

SPECIAL NEEDS ADOPTION CURRICULUM: Contact: Drenda Lakin, National Resource for Special Needs Adoption, Spaulding for Children, PO Box 337, Chelsea, MI 48118. (313) 475-8693.

AIDS

SUPPORT SERVICES:

National Aids Hotline: 1-800-342-AIDS.

ALCOHOLISM

SUPPORT SERVICES:

Al-Anon, Family Group World Service Headquarters, PO Box 862, Midtown Station, New York, NY 10018

Alcoholics Anonymous-World Service Office (AA), PO Box 459 Grand Central Station, New York, NY 10163. (212) 686-1100.

Children of Alcoholics Foundation, Inc. , 200 Park Avenue, 31st Floor, New York, NY 10010

National Association of Children of Alcoholics, 31706 Coast Highway, Suite 201 South Laguna, California 92677. (714) 499-3889.

BOOKS WORTH READING:

Adult Children, The Secrets of Dysfunctional Families and An Adult Child's Guide To What's Normal. John Friel and Linda Friel are nationally known writers, speakers, and consultants in the areas of dysfunctional families. Whether you are a child of a dysfunctional family or the care provider to a child from a troubled family, this book is an eye opener.

Children of Trauma, Rediscovering Your Discarded Self. Jane Middleton-Moz helps readers come face-to-face with emotional fears that may be the result of childhood trauma. Opens the opportunity to heal unresolved grief and unrecognized loss.

Healing the Child Within, Discovery and Recovery for Adult Children of Dysfunctional Families. Charles Whitfield describes the journey of discovery and healing fears, confusion and unhappiness of children of alcoholics. Useful for adult recovery work or helping children who are in out-of-home care.

Learning to Say No. Establishing Healthy Boundaries. Carla Wills-Brandon presents examples and self-evaluation exercises to help the reader identify, realize, evaluate, and then proceed to develop healthy boundaries.

ALLEGATIONS

F.A.S.T.

Minnesota Coalition for Provider Vulnerability, Greater Minneapolis Day Care Association, 1628 Elliott Ave. S., Minneapolis, (612) 341-1177.

S.O.S. for Persons Experiencing Allegations.

ARTICLES AND BOOKS WORTH READING:

****Assessing Child Maltreatment Reports. The Problem of False Allegations.* Michael Robin and a nationally recognized team of professionals evaluate current child abuse risk assessment systems, clinical methods for assessing the accuracy of sexual abuse allegations, false sexual abuse allegations in custody/visitation disputes, and reports of maltreatment in foster homes. Write for complete catalog of titles: The Haworth Press, Inc. 10 Alice Street, Binghamton, NY 13904-1580.

A Conceptual Model for Judging the Truthfulness of a Young Child's Allegation of Sexual Abuse, Mary de Young, October 1986, American Orthopsychiatric Association, Inc. For reprints: Mary de Young, 2226 Saginaw Road. S.E., Grand Rapids, MIC 49506

Accusations of Child Sexual Abuse, Hollida Wakefield, MA and Ralph Underwager, M.Div., Ph.D., Charles C. Thomas Publisher, 1988.

Clarifying Erroneous Child Sexual Abuse Allegations, David M. Mantell, Ph.D., October 1988, American Orthopsychiatric Association, Inc. For reprints: David M. Mantell, PhD., 16 Russell St., New Britain, CT. 06052.

Consequences of Child Abuse Allegations for Foster Families, A Report of a Symposium. Cosponsored by Health and Human Issues, University of Wisconsin-Madison, School of Social Work, University of Wisconsin-Madison, Rosemarie Carbino, Editor, 1991

False Allegations of Sexual Abuse in Divorced Families, Children and Teens Today, June 1988.

False Sexual Abuse Allegations: Causes and Concerns, Kathleen M. Dillon, National Association of Social Workers, Nov.-Dec. 1987

How To Differentiate True from False Allegations of Sexual Abuse, September 1986, Dr. Arthur H. Green, M.D., Presbyterian Hospital, BH616, 622 West 168th St., New York, NY 10032.

Preschool Children's Erroneous Allegations of Sexual Molestation, Alayne Yates, M.D. and Tim Musty, SCSW., American Journal Psychiatry, August 1988.

Psychology's Responsibility in False Allegations of Child Abuse, Robert L. Emans, University of South Dakota, November 1988, Journal of Clinical Psychology

Spiders and Flies - Help for Parents and Teachers of Sexually Abused Children. Donald Hillman and Janice Solek-Tefft, 1988, Lexington MA, Lexington Books

When Sex Abuse Is Falsely Charged, February 1986, Children and Teens Today, Domeena C. Renshaw, Professor, Dept. of Psychiatry, and Director, Sexual Dysfunction Clinic, Loyola University, Chicago, IL 60611.

Validation of Child Sexual Abuse: The Psychologist's Role, Leslie I. Risin and J. Regis McNamara, Ohio University. Journal of Clinical Psychology. For Letters to the Editor, April 1989. American Journal Psychiatry.

ALLERGIES

SUPPORT SERVICES:

Pan American Allergy Society, PO Box 947, Fredericksburg, Texas 78624

Practical Allergy Research Foundation, PO Box 60, Buffalo, New York 14223-0060 (716) 875-0398. Research, pamphlets, books, speakers, audio, and videotapes
Videotapes:
Allergies Do Alter Activities and Behavior (3 tape series)
Audiotapes:
 —*Environmental Aspects of Allergy*
—*Infant Food Allergy*
—*Allergy Diets*
—*General Aspects of Environmental Illness*

Allergy Product Directory, PO Box 640, Menlo Park, California 94026-0640 (415) 322-1663. *Non-allergen products*

ANGER

The Family Game of Anger. Breaking the Cycle. Robert G. Wilhite and Marrilee Cole provide assistance to those who have been affected by anger and want to help themselves or loved ones. It comforts those who are angry or who have lived with anger and bridges understanding. It holds the personality of Bob Wilhite—the energy, the enthusiasm, the charm and wit that allow us to learn about anger. Workshops are availble on: Anger, Stress, Family Systems, Suicide and Depression. Books and workshops are available by contacting: Self Care Books, PO Box 1348, Mountain Home, AR 72653. (501) 424-2433. Fax (501) 424-2313.

The Anger Workbook. Lorraine Bilodeau. An excellent workbook to use in training sessions for care providers of children in out-of-home care. CompCare.

The remarkable thing is we have a choice every day regarding the attitude we will embrace for that day.

continued

We cannot change our past . . . we cannot change the inevitable.

The only thing we can do is play on the one string we have and that is our attitude . . .

continued

ATTENTION DEFICIT DISORDER

BOOKS WORTH READING

How to Reach and Teach ADD/ADHD Children by Sandra Rief. Can be ordered through The Center for Applied Research and Education, Professional Publishing, West Nyack, New York, 10995. This center has a number of other exceptional materials for teaching children in need of special services.

SUPPORT GROUPS

Co-ADD (Coalition for the Education and Support of Attention Deficit Disorder), "Attention Deficit Disorder" address: Co-ADD, PO Box 242, Osseo, MN 55369-0242.

CHILD BEHAVIOR

BOOKS WORTH READING:

Have You Hugged a Monster Today by Alan Cohen explains to a child how the people around us can seem like monsters. And challenges us to think of how tough it would be to be a monster. (1982) Alan Cohen Publications, Haiku, Hawaii 96708.

Teaching Children Self-Control by Stanley A. Fagen, Nicholas J. Long, and Donald J. Stevens offers adults who work with children ideas for personal growth that in positive behave from internal self-control versus external controls. (1975) Columbus, Ohio: Charles E. Merrill.

CHILD DEVELOPMENT

BOOKS WORTH READING:

Infant and Child in the Culture of Today
The Child from Five to Ten
Youth: The Years from Ten to Sixteen, Arnold Gesell, Frances Ilg, and Louis Ames, Harper-Row. These books cover the development of the child at various ages. Typical days in the life of specific age youngsters are described including eating, playing, sleeping, past times, self-activity, and sociality.
Also available from Louis Bates Ames, Frances L. Illg, and Carol Chase Harber are the excellent resources:
—*Your One-Year-Old, The Fun-Loving, Fussy*
—*Your Two-Year-Old, Terrible or Tender*
—*Your Three-Year-Old, Friend or Enemy*
—*Your Four-Year-Old, Wild and Wonderful*
—*Your Five-Year-Old, Sunny and Serene*

Improving Your Child's Behavior, Madeline C. Hunter and Paul V. Carlson, Bowman Books. A small, very practical book with advice on how to discipline a child and improve behavior. Order from Bowmar Books, 4563 Colorado Blvd. Los Angeles, California 90039.

Learning In Their Own Way. Discovering and Encouraging Your Child's Personal Learning Style by Thomas Armstrong, Ph.D. Dr. Armstrong takes a solid look a children who experience less than desireable success in school. He doesn't write these kids off as *"unmotivated"* or *"underachievers."* He shows that in most cases these children are individuals with distinct personal learning styles—linguistic, spacial, interpersonal, intrapersonal, musical, kinesthetic, logical-mathematical—and explains how to help them acquire knowledge according to these sometimes extraordinary aptitudes. Chapters are included on attitude, imagination, attention, self-esteem, nuitrition, exercise and more. An inspiration for working with children in out-of-home care. (1987) Published by The Putnam Publishing Group, Jeremy P. Tarcher/Perigee Books, 200 Madison Avenue, New York, NY 10016.

MegaSkills--In School and in Life--The Best Gift You Can Give Your Child, by Dorothy Rich. This book offers practical and creative day-to-day learning activities to do with children. This book helps you put across the essential values of education, the pleasure of hard work, the delight of accomplishment, the joy of working together. Builds confidence, motivation, effort, responsibility, initiative, perserverance, caring, teamwork, common sense and problem solving. (1988, 1992 Revised)

Success With the Reluctant Learner by Jim Fay. School Consultant Services, Inc. 2207 Jackson St. Golden, CO 80401.

Teaching Children Joy and Teaching Children Responsibility, Linda and Richard Eyre. In addition to these insightful books, the Eyres have developed a program that regularly brings parents together with other parents, provides objectives, incentives and a road map to drive on. Write: TCJ, Lamplighter Square, 1615 Foothill Drive, Salt Lake City, Utah 84108 or call (801) 581-0112.

When Love is Not Enough. A Child's View of Parenting. Cecil R. Benoit, Phd. is available for seminars and workshops based on the *When Love is Not Enough* workbook. Three, six, and twelve hour sessions have been developed. Additional presentations of one-half hour to forty-five minutes are available on:
—*When Your Child Is Afraid*
—*The Angry Child*
—*Discipline vs. Punishment*
—*"Good Enough" Parenting*
—*How Did I Get to Be the Parent I Am?*

Books, workbooks and contracting seminars are available by writing or calling Cecil R. Benoit PhD, 325-3 East Park Avenue, Charlotte, NC 28203, (704) 332-7599.

TRAINING PROGRAMS AND SUPPORT MATERIALS:

Early Childhood Studies Program, University of Minnesota, 306 Wesbrook Hall, 77 Pleasant Street SE, Minneapolis, MN 55455. (612) 625-1088.
> —*A Foster Care Training Program for the 1990's*
> —*Training for Trainers (Foster Parenting)*
> —*Child Abuse Prevention Program*
> —*Culturally Sensitive Training Programs*

CHILD WELFARE

SUPPORT SERVICES:

Child Welfare League of America, Inc., 440 First Street, NW, Suite 310., Washington, DC 20001-2085. Publishes a variety of books and publications on child welfare issues.

CULT AWARENESS:

SUPPORT SERVICES:

Believe the Children; Leslie Floberg, PO Box 1358, Manhatten Beach, CA 90266

Cult Awareness Network, 2421 W Pratt Blvd., Suite 1173, Chicago, IL 60645. (312) 267-7777

BOOKS WORTH READING:

The Edge of Evil. The Rise of Satanism in North America. Jerry Johnston. 1989. Word Publishing. Johnson takes a careful look into the current fad of Stanism facing America's teens. Well researched and written with personal non-sensational interview from many perspectives. Provides parents and professionals with a better understanding of why and how teens are attracted into these ancient practices.

DIVORCE

BOOKS WORTH READING:

Healing Adult Children of Divorce. Taking Care of Unfinished Business So You Can Be Whole Again, Dr. Archibald D. Hart. Dr. Hart is dean of the Graduate School of Psychology and professor of psychology at Fuller Theological Seminary in Pasadena, California. His books include *Overcoming Anxiety, The Hidden Link between Adrenline and Stress, Depression, Coping and Caring, Children and Divorce, and Healing Life's Hidden Addictions.*

The World of the Formerly Married, Morton M. Hunt, McGraw-Hili. A valuable resource in helping to understand life as a divorced person and single parent.

DRUGS

SUPPORT SERVICES:

Cocaine Anonymous, PO Box 1367, Culver City, CA 90232.

Drugs Anonymous, PO Box 473, Ansonia Station, New York, NY 10023.

EAR SPECIALISTS

SUPPORT SERVICES:

American Academy of Otalarygic Allergy, Suite 302, 1101 Vermont Avenue NW Washington, DC 20005

ENVIRONMENTAL MEDICINE OR CLINICAL ECOLOGY

American Academy of Environmental Medicine, PO Box 16106, Denver, Colorado 80216

FAMILY VIOLENCE

Batterers Anonymous, PO Box 29, Redlands, California 92373

Survivors Network, 18653 Ventura Blvd. #143, Tarzana, California 91356.

FEELINGS

SUPPORT IDEAS:

Ups and Downs With Feelings Game, by Carole Gesme helps children and adults recognize, name, and be responsible for their feelings. Available through Daisy Press, 16535 9th Avenue North, Plymouth, MN 55447.

I am convinced that life is ten percent what happens to me and ninety percent how I react to it.

And so it is with you . . .

continued

FETAL ALCOHOL SYNDROME

SUPPORT SERVICES:

Fetal Alcohol Syndrome, c/o The Seattle Foundation, Washington Federal Building, Suite 510, 425 Pike Street, Seattle, Washington 98101. (206) 622-2294.

BOOKS WORTH READING:

The Broken Cord. Micheal Dorris's deeply moving story of parenting his adopted fetal alcohol syndrome child.

FOSTER CARE

SUPPORT SERVICES:

National Foster Parent Association, Information and Services, Gordon Evans, 226 Kilts Drive, Houston, TX 77024 (713) 467-1850.

BOOKS WORTH READING:

A Child's Journey Through Placement by Vera Fahlberg. An excellent book by an internationally respected and recognized trainer, consultant, pediatrician and psychotherapist who has worked extensively with disturbed children and their families since 1964. Much of Dr. Falhberg's work has been focused on attachment and separation problems with special empahsis on children in out-of-home placement.

Foster Parenting Abused Children. Eliana Gil. National Committee for the Prevention of Child Abuse, 332 South Michigan Avenue, Suite 950, Chicago, IL 60604.

Fostering the Child Who Has Been Sexually Abused. Emily Jean McFadden.

Preventing Abuse in Foster Care. Emily Jean McFadden. Training and materials available by writing: Institute for the Study of Children and Families, Eastern Michigan University, Ypsilanti, Michigan 48107. (313) 487-0372.

Screening Tool For Selecting Foster Parents To Care For Sexually Abused Children A 100 item questionnaire dealing with child development, issues of sexuality, disciple. family relationships, etc. is available from Child Protection Team, 22 West Lake Beauty Street, Suite 208, Orlando, FL 32806.

Sex Education for Foster Families Project. American Foster Care Resources, PO Box 271, King George, Virginia 22485

REFERENCE MATERIALS

Child Protection and the Law, by Lynn Lewis Rhodes, ACSW, Social Work Studies Department of Spaulding University (1986) Training caseworkers in *"effective use of the legal system"* to protect the best interests of the child, creating a closer working relationship between caseworkers and their attorneys, and minimizing potential liability are goals in this training curriculum. Topics include: legal and statuatory systems, interdisciplinary collaboration, the juvenile court, termination of parental rights, testifying and liability. Forms and checklists are included. Order: ABA Center on Children and the Law, attn: Annotated Bibliography, 1800 M Street, NW, Washington, DC 20036 or call 202-331-2250. Cost $10.00 plus $3.95 shipping.

Foster Children in the Courts by Mark Hardin, ed, Butterworth Legal Publishers (1983) A comprehensive guide to the legal response towards children in foster care or children likely to be placed in foster care. This book is out of print but may be available at social work and law libraries. Most of the book still remains timely and valuable, though some information is obsolete.

Placement from the Child's Viewpoint by Dr. Leontine Young in Social Casework Vol 31, pp250-255 written in 1950. As timely todays as when it was written in 1950, Dr. Young explains the child's view of placement.

Steps for Preserving Families, Guidelines for Practice for Courts, for Child Welfare Professionals, for Attorneys and for Advocates by Kent County Juvenile Court Reasonable Efforts Project Staff developed this manual to provide information and training on the Child Welfare and Adoption Assistance Act of 1980, Public Law 96-272, and on similar Michigan legislation. The manual addresses the juvenile court process from initial hearing through termination of parental rights and other permanency plans. Forms and checklists are included. Order: Children's Charter of the Courts of Michigan, 115 West Allegan, Suite 500, Lansing, Michigan 48933 or call 517-482-7533. Price: $26.50 plus shipping.

Working with Courts in Child Protection, Jane Nusbaum Feller with Howard A. Davidson, Mark Hardin, and Robert M. Horowitz, U.S. Department of Health and Human Services (1992) Staff from ABA Center on Children and the Law write this manual to help nonlawyers through the process. Topics include the court system, recent legal developments and practical examples and tips to enhance court performance; a selected bibliography is also included. To order: Clearinghouse on Child Abuse and Neglect Information, PO Box 1182, Washington, DC 20036 or call 703-385-7565. There is no charge for this publication.

Your Child In Foster Care: What Happens and Where Do You Go From Here, Becky Pryor, Ed., Law and Child Protection Project (1983) Parents of origin will find this booklet an easily understandable description of how and why children are placed in foster care, and the rights and responsibilites of the parents of such a child. Some language is Indiana specific but it could be adapted to fit into your jurisdiction. Write: ABA Center on Children and the Law, Attn: Annotated Bibliography, 1800 M. Street NW, Washington, DC 20036.

LEGAL RESOURCES AVAILABLE FOR CHILDREN IN OUT-OF-HOME CARE:

We are in charge of our Attitudes.

Charles Swindoll

The American Bar Association has a number of publications available concerning the needs of children in out-of-home care. Call 312-988-5555 or write: American Bar Association Order Fulfillment, 750 Lake Shore Drive, Chicago, IL 60611 and ask for a listing of titles and information available.

Legal Courtwise by Linda Katz, ACSW, addresses the roles and responsibilities of the legal and social work profession and how these different roles cause misunderstandings and strains. Discusses legal principles, social work beliefs, different approaches of the two professions, and the expertise each profession brings to case planning for children. Sample court contract and written agreements are included. An excellent resource for lawyers and caseworkers. To order: Lutheran Social Services of Washington and Idaho, 6920 220th Street, SW, Mountlake Terrace, Washington, 98043 or call 206-672-6009. Price $10 plus $3 shipping and handling.

Collaborative Court Education Project Training Manual, Alice Bussiere, National Center for Youth Law, 114 Sansome Street, Suite 900, San Francisco, CA 94104; Charlotte Vick, Joe Kroll, North American Council on Adoptable Children, 970 Raymond Ave. #106, St. Paul, MN 55114.

PARENTING

SUPPORT SERVICES:

Caregivers Support Groups—Community Care Resources. Wilder Foundation. (612) 643-4046.

Childhelp USA, 6463 Independence Ave., Woodland Hills, CA 91367. (818) 347-7280 or **800-4-A-CHILD. Immediate assistance** is available by a counselor to provide immediate assistance and refer parents needing help to groups or organizations in your area. .

Parental Stress Service, Inc., 154 Santa Clara Ave., Oakland, CA 95610

Parents Anonymous, 22330 Hawthorne Blvd, Suite 208., Torrance, CA 90503. **800-352-0386 provides 24-hour hotline!**

BOOKS WORTH READING:

The Black Child: A Parent's Guide, by Phyllis Harrison Ross and Barbara Wyden, Wyden Books. Written for African American parents as well as Caucasian parents. It deals with the special problems of the African American parent, but it also offers specific guidance to help white parents raise children with a total awareness and acceptance of both racial differences and similarities. Excellent.

High Risk Children Without a Conscience, Ken De Magid (1987) Bantam

Living With the Actice Alert Child. Linda Budd. (1991) New York, Prentice Hall.

Raising Your Spirited Child, A Guide for Parents Whose Child is More, Intense, Sensitive, Perceptive, Persistent, Energetic. Mary Sheedy Kurcinka offers a new and refreshing positive approach to parenting spirited children, offering parents the kind of emotional support and proven strategies they crave. Founder of Spirited Child workshops.

Stop Struggling with Your Child. Evonne Weinhaus and Karen Friedman.

Troubled Transplants. Frank Kunstal and Rick Delaney specialize in the treatment of disturbed children and their families. Troubled Transplants takes a realistic look at children in out-of-home foster or adoptive care and provides redirection strategies that work. Books, articles, and workshops are available by contacting: PO Box 271036, Fort Collins, CO 80527.

Who's Raising Whom? Strategies for Saving Your Sanity by Michael M. Thompson, Ph.D. Dr. Thomson provides parents with a new set of lenses to view our role as parents. To order : Productive Thinking Skills, PO Box 751, Dublin, OH 43017-0851 1-800-290-2482. $17.95

PERSONALITIES

BOOKS WORTH READING:

One of a Kind. Making the Most of Your Child's Uniqueness. LaVonne Neff explains how understanding personality type can bring enormous improvement to family happiness and harmony.

Please Understand Me: Character and Temperament Types. David Keirsey and Marilyn Bates explain how the four Myers-Briggs Type Indicator temperaments affect our leadership styles, learning patterns, and childhood development.

Type Talk, The Sixteen Personality Types that Determine How We Live, Love, and Work. Otto Kroeger and Janet Thuesen. An excellent book that encourages respect for individual differences. Training seminars and workshops available for families as well as social services. Contact: Otto Kroeger Associates, 3605 Chain Bridge Road, Fairfax, VA 22030 (703) 591-MBTI.

SELF-ESTEEM

BOOKS WORTH READING:

Growing Up Again, Parenting Ourselves, Parenting Our Children, Jean Illsley Clarke and Connie Dawson, is for people who inherited unsatisfying parenting and don't want to pass it on to their children.

Self-Esteem a Family Affair, Jean Illsley Clarke, helps people become better parents by putting into practice beliefs and principals about self-esteem. Ms. Clarke is available for workshops and lectures by writing: Daisy Press, 16535 9th Avenue North, Plymouth, MN 55447.

> *The parent is the family manager and will need to make decisions children like and some they don't like. Parenting is not a popularity contest.*
>
> *Children do best when parents act self-assured, follow-through, do what they say they will do, are consistent, and model self-discipline and good self-esteem.*
> *Arent 1993*

WHAT CAN YOU DO TO HELP?

Ideas of things to say to Children Who Hurt from the book Trust Building with Children Who Hurt.

GET INVOLVED WITH THE CHILDREN
"Trust Building with Children Who Hurt" Program

by Ruth P. Arent, M.A., M.S.W.

Helping Children Who Hurt takes a community. As our society continues to produce more and more troubled children, the demand for adults to help them grows. Ms. Arent has developed a successful and vital program for concerned adults—teachers, coaches, surrogate parents, group leaders—to work one-to-one with Children Who Hurt ages five to fourteen. Recommended reading for all adults who work or live currently with Children Who Hurt. An exceptional training and outreach program, in an area that can affect a child's future. This is a Child-Adult program. It is child-focused, and does not expand to parent problem-solving. The adult is the key. The relationship with the child is pivotal. Working with Children Who Hurt is the ultimate test of your professionalism, you may feel punctured by a child's defensive sarcasm or rudeness. Nevertheless, you know the child cannot learn to trust alone. The adult must decide to be the leader in this relationship and anticipate that the work will be both frustrating and rewarding.

"If you run away, you are not taking care of yourself. You may need a break to be away for a short while, let's explore some other ways for you to get the break you need."

> *Following are excerpts from her book:*

> *Children Who Hurt are wonderful kids but something sad or bad has happened in their lives. They are anxious and frightened—some neglected, others abused. They have lost trust in adults; perhaps they have never experienced trust. Without a trusting relationship, they lose faith in themselves and become locked in self-defeating attitudes. They are damaged children who may become angry, antagonistic, withdrawn, or defensive. They can become a real pain in the neck. They are predictably immature. Their inappropriate behaviors are pleas for unqualified acceptance as human beings—as children. Children will rarely ask for help; it is not to be expected. Their inappropriate actions are their pleas for help. Most will respond to overtures of a caring adult. It is an aspect of their strength—their wellness.*

"I know some other ways to manage your behavior to help you cope. You have learned to—freeze, hide, attack—and this helped you survive or face the reality of the trauma you were in. I have some ideas of how to help you gain control and be in charge of yourself! Want to hear about it?"

> *A Trust Building Program is designed to build on a child's strengths to create a powerful trust experience. Children Who Hurt can benefit from help to become more stable and self-accepting. They need vivid encouragement— wrapped in hope. Trust goes beyond reassurance. It is a bond, substantiated by honesty, consistency, dependability, and caring. Trust is a "bundle of attitudes" that denotes unconditional acceptance. It allows for good days and bad days. It permits kids to be kids. Children who trust feel protected and respected. They become willing to improve in many ways . . . Trust must be built. It doesn't just happen. Adults engineer the program.*

"It's easy to remember— STOP, THINK, CHOOSE! You are in control of what you do or say. You can choose to smile or frown. To stop from saying something nasty and say something nice. I can help you learn to get into the habit of asking—What else can I say or do? What options do I have?"

> *Children Who Hurt may be locked into angry, nonproductive relationships with other adults. The children themselves are solely responsible to their own behavior. They are are responsible for all changes. They can learn to manage their behavior—even with someone they do not like. Most children can learn to tolerate unresponsive adults, sarcasm, or other unpleasant attitudes or difficulties without being destroyed—when they have a significant other adult they are able to trust.*

"What can you say or do that you will not be sorry for later?"

A Trust Building Program:

- *Provides enough consistent, positive acceptance to convince the Child Who Hurts that an adult can be trusted.*

- *Helps a child become more self-accepting.*

- *Helps a child acquire a positive attitude toward self, school, and others—to feel respected.*

- *Helps a child manage what he or she says or does.*

- *Helps a child internalize that he or she can be special to one adult.*

- *Reminds a child that improvements can be permanent—can grow and grow—even if there are still problems at home.*

- *Magnifies the importance of trustworthiness as a way of life—as basic to respect and communication in all relationships.*

A Trust Building Program has limitations:

- *It is not designed to change a child's personality.*

- *It is not designed to fix or repair problems at home.*

- *It is not designed to correct any difficulties the child may have with other adults.*

The child must witness your strength on his or her behalf. It can override other messages. The child can witness that the adults in his or her world do care.

The Trust Building program is founded on the conviction that facts, plans, expectations, and goals should be explained to children fully. Children can deal with almost anything if they are told the truth. They can handle facts, although they may need repeated explanations. They respect people who tell the truth. Children Who Hurt have had trauma in their lives. It cannot be denied. As a Trust Builder, you may be the first person who can help the child confront old and current feelings and experiences. Children can learn that all families have problems to solve that children cannot repair. Children can learn that their responsibility is to manage their own feelings and behaviors. Learning to trust is a healing process. For Children Who Hurt it is a struggle.

A Trust Building Program is a challenge. It is not an overwhelming task. It can be enormously satisfying. Learning to trust is a process—an experience. It cannot be read in a book it must be given, shared, and nurtured from one human being to another. This program can be used by social services, schools, child-centered programs, and churches. Wherever adults exist who want to supply outreach to Children Who Hurt.

For more information write to
The Center for Applied Research in Education Business Information and Publishing Division, West Nyack, NY 10995.

"Looks like your smiler is broken, can we talk about it. I promise to be straight with you. If I don't know the answer, we'll go find out the facts together."

"I know it's a struggle to learn to stop saying mean things and say nice things instead. Sounds like you're a bit snappy today. Got any ideas how we can tame that alligator?"

"Everyone has a way of showing that they are mad, but there are limits and one is hitting. Hitting is not okay. That's a rule. That's a limit. Calling someone a -- is better than slamming someone around."

"The word hate is a strong word and it tells me a lot about you. Lots of people use that word when they don't mean it at all. Did you think our relationship would end if you told me you hate me? No, that won't happen."

"Sorry, you are angry. Do you want to talk about it?"

WHAT CAN YOU DO TO HELP?

GET INVOLVED
Count the costs—to the children, to society—to yourself

Children need adults who care and are willing to take the risk to care!

- **ASK YOUR DOCTOR OR MEDICAL FACILITY IF A FAMILY OR CHILD NEEDS A SUPPORTIVE ADULT OR FAMILY.**
  Children who live with terminally, chronically, or debilitating physically ill—AIDS, cancer, MS—*or chronically or debilitating mentally ill*—psychosis, schizophrenia, borderline personality disorder, sociopathy—*parents need caring adults to provide trusting, consistent adult-child relationships. In addition, these parent often appreciate another caring friend. **Ill parents can care for children with support services, community efforts are needed to help these children and their families during their times of struggle.***

- **ASK YOUR LOCAL SCHOOL OR CRISIS PREGNANCY CENTER IF THERE IS A TEEN MOTHER OR YOUNG COUPLE WHO COULD USE A MENTOR FAMILY.**
  *Teenagers choosing to raise babies need guidance and friendship not always available within their extended families. **Adults are needed who can teach skills necessary to raise children and maintain a home and provide mentorship to young parents.***

- **ASK AT YOUR LOCAL SOCIAL SERVICE AGENCY, HOMELESS SHELTER, CHURCH, OR FOOD SHELF IF THERE IS A FAMILY WHO COULD USE SOME HELP.**
  *Children in high risk families facing the possibility of separation need mentors and families who are willing to outreach to another family—preventing foster care and separation from ever needing to occur. **Many children are in the foster care system today due to parental neglect— removed from parents who don't know how** (raised within the foster care system, raised in generationally abusive or neglectful homes, or in group care) **or are not able to care for their children** (family poverty level significant, parents are intellectually impaired and have significant trouble even with self-care and no extended family support systems). **These parents need parents—extended families who can model and teach family living and parenting skills.***

- **CALL YOUR LOCAL SOCIAL WELFARE OFFICE AND VOLUNTEER TO BE A CHILD ADVOCATE OR BUDDY.**
  *Children already in out-of-home care need "one" consistent adult advocate in a system where the "best interest of the child" is often quoted, but so often misjudged, procrastinated, misplaced, or forgotten. **Many children are misplaced temporarily on a desk or file folder while social workers change positions, court dates get rearranged, or determination is made concerning "reasonable efforts" for reunification.***

- **REACH OUT TO ADOPT OR FOSTER A CHILD or REACH OUT TO A FOSTER OR ADOPTIVE FAMILY and GET TO KNOW THEIR REAL NEEDS BEFORE MAKING JUDGMENTS.**
  Children who cannot be reunited with parents or no longer have parents—except for the government—need immediate permanent adult caregivers and families to belong to. And these adults and families need community support, understanding, and respect! *Many children today (13% of children in foster care) are locked in foster care even though adoption has been determined as the child's best option.*

Timeframes and continuances that seem reasonable to adults and appropriate in other circumstances are unacceptable when a child's right to permanance is at stake.

Six months is 25% of a 2-year-old's life.

Six years is a lifetime of care in a 7-year-old's life.

A childhood is relatively short— 18 years or 216 months— and a chance of permanance is easily missed while those in charge meet, debate, wait, and write reports. (Bussiere, Vick 1993)

Decisions to remove children from their homes—whether temporarily or permanently—are among the most important decisions that child welfare workers and judges make. According to child development experts, a judge determining the placement of a child should take into account the child's need for continuity with a primary caretaker, and the reality that children experience the passage of time very differently than do adults. When courts overlook these basic principles, human tragedy results.

Federal legislation and policy clearly favor reunification of families as the preferred foster care outcome. A significant number of children, however, cannot return to biological parents because child welfare professionals judge that, even with the provision of social services and other assistance, their homes cannot be made safe within a reasonable amount of time.

These children's families may have documented patterns of domestic violence between parents for one year or longer and yet parents refuse to get help or separate. The parents may be addicted to debilitating illegal drugs or alcohol and unable to quit and/or refuse treatment. The child or other children in the home has suffered more than one form of abuse, neglect, or sexual abuse. The parent has killed or seriously harmed another child in the past and no significant change in parent has occurred. Other children in the family have been abandoned with friends, relatives, the hospital, or foster care. The parent has repeatedly and with premeditation harmed or tortured the child. The child has experienced physical and/or sexual abuse in infancy and treatment of parents may be so lengthy that child would spend years in foster care. The parents have not visited or made contact with the child once the child is in foster care. The parent's only visible means of financial support continues to be in illegal drugs, prostitution, and street life. The parents may be in prison or jail due to serious criminal activity.

*Children can wait in limbo for years as adults meet, debate,
and determine what actions should be taken.*

Why do children stay in foster care limbo so long?

The social welfare and court system is set up to respond to adult needs and requests. The children are not the ones who get listened to—there is no squeaky wheel for them. Children cannot often acceptably and professionally express their very *"real pain."* Once the child is in the foster care system, time seems to often stand still. Children grow up waiting for permanency, while decisions are made for and about them by people who don't often know who the child really is or what the child's real desires and needs are. Some of the common adult reasons for foster care limbo or drift are:

Don't rock the boat. Child comfortable in foster care home and no need to disrupt placement. Foster care provider (for whatever reason) not interested in adoption. Foster care may be the only way to continue necessary services to child and payments to the foster care provider.

Lost in the shuffle. High turnover of social service staff leads to transfer of cases or long periods of service dormancy, cases may be unassigned during a lengthy transition. During these transitions, treatment and permanency goals become unclear and valuable information is lost.

Conflict avoidance. Avoidance of termination of parental rights by attorneys and social services even if *"reasonable efforts"* have been made. Guidelines to *"reasonable efforts"* vary and may be unclear. Social services risk liability in making a mistake. Parent's rights come before child's rights and best

Judges who are trained in child development needs and child welfare issues, who serve a specialized term in child welfare cases provide decisions that result in the best interest of the children they serve.

Sadly, this wisdom of specialization is sorely lacking in our judicial system.

No one ever asked me what I thought or what I really wanted. Decisions kept on being made without anyone listening to me.
Grown foster child

Participation[1] in Title IV-E Foster Care Assistance and Adoption Assistance

Year	Foster Care[2] Assistance Payments	Adoption[2]
1981	104,851	165
1982	93,309	2,402
1983	97,370	5,309
1984	102,051	11,581
1985	109,122	16,009
1986	110,749	21,989
1987	118,549	27,588
1988	132,757	34,698
1989	156,871	40,666
1990	167,981	44,024
1991	202,687	54,818
1992	222,315	66,300
Estimated 1993-1998		
1993	232,995	81,378
1994	246,271	90,609
1995	259,400	99,200
1996	273,100	106,600
1997	287,600	112,599
1998	302,800	117,000

1. Participation defined as the average monthly number of recipients

2. Number of children
SOURCE: U.S. Dept. Health & Human Services (1993) Green Book

interest. Litigation is time-consuming and stressful for careworker, and painful and difficult for the child. Court and welfare systems do not always agree on what is needed to help the child or the family.

Scheduling delays. Scheduling professional schedules may be very difficult. Current crisis in a social service agency may preempt hearing of child in long term care. Even for the most basic hearing, a judge must schedule hearings to ensure the presence of one or two biological parents, three or more attorneys, a social worker, and one or more volunteer child advocates. If professional witnesses are required or the foster parents and their representatives wish to play a role, the number of parties can grow to a dozen people. Continuances (interruptions and rescheduling of hearings) can further delay proceedings. Most child custody proceedings, once on the court docket, will be heard and decided in one day. Court dockets are crowded and judges are overwhelmed with cases, are often uninformed about community resources and options for families, and as a result frequently provide no more than a cursory review of the child's situation.

Inexperience in child welfare needs. Counsel for the government are also frequently overwhelmed. In one state 6 judges were responsible for 3,600 cases. Judges may rotate into child protection duty and they are the least wanted cases. To save money, law students may be used to represent children. Their lack of experience, training, and child development knowledge provides little justice for a child. Judges are reluctant to grant termination of parental rights unless adoptive family is waiting and child in care may be considered unadoptable by social services.

In such cases, other long-term options become a child's permanent plan. These long-term placement options, however are not without risk—to the child, the caregivers, and to the original family. No longer are the rights of any of the people involved clear. *See pages 397-398 for more information.*

What cost savings can be achieved by releasing children determined for adoption earlier?

If we could eliminate just one year of foster care in the 13% of children determined to be adopted, the federal tax savings is incredible. The emotional trauma saved for the child is non-measureable. (BASED ON 1988 FIGURES)

FEDERAL MAINTENANCE COSTS PER CHILD

FOSTER CARE	DESCRIPTION
120,000	Children in foster care receiving Child Maintenance Payments 1988 Title IV-E (1992 figures were est. 236,333; 1993 est. 257,603)
$4,500	1988 annual Federal maintenance costs per child in Foster Care
13%	Percent of children in foster care who are eventually adopted
15,600	Total number of children in foster care who may be adopted
$70.2 million	**TOTAL ANNUAL FOSTER CARE MAINTENANCE COSTS FOR CHILDREN WITH ADOPTION PLANS** ($4,500 x 15,600)

ADOPTION	
$2,100	Federal adoption Title IV-E assistance payments per child Annual Federal costs per child in subsidized Adoptive Care
$32.8 million	Total adoption subsidy assistance costs.
$37.4 million	**TOTAL FEDERAL MAINTENANCE SAVINGS**

FEDERAL ADMINISTRATIVE COSTS PER CHILD

FOSTER CARE	DESCRIPTION
120,000	Children in foster care receiving Child Maintenance Payments 1988 Title IV-E (1992 figures were est. 236,333 and 1993 est. 257,603)
$3,300	Staff Administrative Costs Annual per child Federal foster Care administrative costs
13%	15,600 children in care with permanency plans of adoption
$51.5 million	Total administrative costs for children with adoption plans ($3,300 x 15,600)
ADOPTION	
$629	Federal subsidized adoption administration costs per child
$9.9 million	Total Federal costs for subsidized adoption administration
$41.6 million	**TOTAL FEDERAL ADMINSTRATIVE SAVINGS**
$79 million	**1988 TOTAL AVAILABLE FEDERAL SAVINGS**

How long does it take a child whose best option is adoption to be adopted?

MONTHS WAITING	PROCESS BEING ACCOMPLISHED TO BENEFIT CHILD
6 to 54	Time spent in foster care—providing family reunification services and determining what to do with the child. The national average in foster care prior to adoption decision is 30 to 42 months (2.5-3.5 years).
3 to 12	Adoption determined to be the best permanent placement plan for the child.
3 to 12	Petition for Termination of Parental Rights is filed.
3 to 12	Court grants petition. Adoption offered into immediately available home—relative or current foster parent.
12 to 18	Homefinding if home is other than relative or current foster parent. The child is placed with potential adoptive parents once an approved family is selected.
3 to 12	An official waiting period to protect the final adoption from threat of appeals and to allow agency staff to observe and evaluate the placement.
Then ...	Adoptive parents must petition the court to adopt the child in their care.
Then ...	The court grants these petitions and proper notification is provided to State's vital records.
Finally ...	The children belong to families again.
24 to 108	Time children spend in child welfare pending final adoption. (2-9 years)
42 and 66	The national average for children who are adopted leave the foster care system after they enter. (3.5-5.5 years)

Source: United States Department of Health and Human Services, Robert Kusserow, Inspector General, February 1991

FEDERAL FUNDING FOR CHILD WELFARE— FOSTER CARE AND ADOPTION—TITLE IV-E
Under current law— differences due to rounding

Title IV-E
FOSTER CARE
State Claims
(In Millions of Dollars)

Total[1] $	Maintenance payments	Administration, training
1989 1,153.1	646.0	507.1
1990 1,473.2	835.0	638.2
1991 1,819.2	1030.4	788.8
1992 2,209.8	1,192.1	1,017.7
1993 *(Estimate)* 2,546.0	1,481.0	1,065.0
1994 *(Estimate)* 2,649.5	1,482.1	1,167.4
1995 *(Estimate)* 2,953.5	1,648.1	1,305.4
1996 *(Estimate)* 3,288.7	1,834.5	1,454.2
1997 *(Estimate)* 3,647.6	2040.7	1,606.9
1998 *(Estimate)* 4,052.9	2,270.0	1,782.9

Title IV-E
ADOPTION ASSISTANCE
State Claims
(In Millions of Dollars)

Total[2] $	Maintenance payments	Administration, training
1989 110.5	86.2	24.3
1990 135.7	104.9	30.8
1991 175.3	130.3	45.0
1992 *(Estimate)* 219.6	161.4	58.2
1993 *(Estimate)* 279.8	205.6	74.2
1994 *(Estimate)* 321.3	236.8	84.5
1995 *(Estimate)* 363.7	268.6	95.1
1996 *(Estimate)* 404.8	299.4	105.4
1997 *(Estimate)* 442.0	327.3	114.7
1998 *(Estimate)* 475.4	352.3	123.1

1. Total includes administrative and training expenditures, as well as maintenance payments, but does not include transfers to Title IV-8 child welfare service program.
2. Total includes administrative and training expenditures, maintenance payments, and nonrecurring payments.
SOURCE U.S. Dept. Health and Human Services (1993) Green Book

Current Long-Term Permanency Options for Children
Legal status of substitute parents providing day-to-day care

	Foster Parent	Foster Parent (with long-term foster care agreement not ratified by the court)	Foster Parent (specific foster placement ratified by the court)	Legal Custodian and/or Guardian under Juvenile Court Jurisdiction	Guardian through Probate Court Proceedings	Legal Custodian through Post-Divorce or Equity Proceedings	Adoptive Parent
Control of child without welfare agency supervision	**NO** Under supervision from licensing and child protection agency	**NO** Under supervision from licensing and child protection agency	**NO** Under supervision from licensing and child protection agency	**YES** No supervision	**YES** No supervision	**YES** No supervision	**YES** Post adoptive agency services, training, and support may be available, but no legal supervision
Major decisions regarding education and medical care of child	**NO** Complete responsibility for day-to-day care, but little or no authority for major decisions	**NO** Complete responsibility for day-to-day care, but little or no authority for major decisions	**POSSIBLY** Complete responsibility for day-to-day care. May have court ordered authority for major decisions	**YES**	**YES**	**YES**	**YES**
Freedom from court or citizen review	**NO** Both agency and federally mandated reviews	**PROBABLY** Subject to periodic review	**PROBABLY** Subject to periodic review	**PROBABLY NOT** Subject to periodic review	**YES**	**YES**	**YES**
Right to a hearing prior to removal of child	**MAYBE** Foster parent or social services can have child removed. Allegation, change in legislation, or licensing violation can mean immediate removal of child	**MAYBE** Foster parent or social services can have child removed. Allegation, change in legislation, or licensing violation can mean immediate removal of child	**PROBABLY** Foster parent or social services can have child removed. Allegation, change in legislation, or licensing violation can mean immediate removal of child	**YES**	**YES**	**YES**	**YES**
Types of cash assistance generally available to pay for child care	**FOSTER CARE PAYMENTS** Plus services as: medical care, counseling, special therapy, transportation	**FOSTER CARE PAYMENTS** Plus services as: medical care, counseling, special therapy, transportation	**FOSTER CARE PAYMENTS** Plus services as: medical care, counseling, special therapy, transportation	**GENERALLY NONE** except possible child support from biological parents	**PROBABLY NONE** except possible child support from biological parents	**PROBABLY NONE** except possible child support from biological parents	**POSSIBLY** Adoption subsidy for special needs children, AFDC, Social Security, Veteran's Assistance, Inheritance rights will be affected, Medical Assistance for special needs may be available

Legal rights of biological parents while child is in substitute care

	Foster Care	Foster Care (with long-term foster care agreement not ratified by the court)	Foster Care (specific foster placement ratified by the court)	Third Party Legal Custodian and/or Guardian under Juvenile Court Jurisdiction	Third Person is Guardian through Probate Court Proceedings	Third Party have Legal Custodian through Post-Divorce or Equity Proceedings	Adoption
Visitation and communication with child	SUBJECT TO RESTRICTION BY COURT AND AGENCY	SUBJECT TO RESTRICTION BY COURT AND AGENCY	SUBJECT TO RESTRICTION BY COURT AND AGENCY	SUBJECT TO RESTRICTION BY COURT	SUBJECT TO RESTRICTION BY COURT	SUBJECT TO RESTRICTION BY COURT	POSSIBLY Some states allow court ordered and/or supervised visitation
Right to initiate legal action for return of child	YES	YES	YES	YES	YES	YES	PROBABLY NOT
Biological parents given preference in litigation for the return of the child.	YES	YES	YES	PROBABLY	MAYBE	MAYBE	NO

* *Juvenile court refers to the court that hears non-criminal neglect, abuse, and dependency cases.*

** *Probate Court refers to the state court that hears cases involving probate of estates, conservatorships, as well as guardianships of person and estate.*

Common circumstances where this permanent arrangement is appropriate

FOSTER CARE	THIRD PARTY LEGAL CUSTODIAN AND/OR GUARDIAN	ADOPTION
— Changing the placement would clearly harm the child. — The foster parents are willing to keep the child. — Maintaining payments to foster parents is a strong financial necessity. — Adequate cash assistance is not available under any other option. *Long-term foster care should be secured by written agreement or court order if permitted by state law or policy.*	— Termination of parental rights is inappropriate. — Adoption is not appropriate. — Custodian does not require government assistance. — Parental visits not likely to create serious difficulties. — There is low risk of further litigation concerning care and control of child. **CUSTODY**—*the right to physical custody of the child; the right and duty to protect, train and discipline him; the duty to provide him with food, clothing, shelter, education, and ordinary medical care; the right to determine where and with whom he shall live, and the right, in an emergency, to authorize surgery or extraordinary care.* **GUARDIANSHIP**—*the authority to consent to marriage, to enlistment in the armed forces, and to consent to major medical, surgical, or psychiatric treatment.*	— Security for child — Adult commitment to child — Stability for parent/child **Types of adoption:** — **Open adoption** (*biological parents have visitation rights*) — **Adoption without visitation rights, but visitation is expected** — **Adoption without visitation by biological parents**

Source: *Foster Children in the Courts*, Hardin (1983)

Index

Order Forms

ORDER FORM — FAMILIES AT RISK

Name _____

Title _____

Agency Name _____

Address _____

City/State/Zip _____

Phone ( ) _____

Pricing:
1-5 copies	$29.95 each
6-12 copies	$24.95 each
13 or more copies	$19.95 each

Additional discounts available for group purchase/wholesale.

Families at Risk   QTY_____ x $_____ = _____
  (Canada Add 25%)
Shipping and Handling ($2.90 copy)   _____
Minnesota residents add 6.5% tax   _____
Add applicable MNcity taxes .5%   _____
                              TOTAL _____

___Payment enclosed or
___Bill my _____VISA ___Master Card
Card #_____Exp. Date_____

Signature_____

Mail check or money order to:
  Better Endings New Beginnings
  119 N. 4th St, #401, Minneapolis, MN 55401
  612-341-9870   Fax: 612-337-5104
1993-2   Softcover   408 pages   ISBN 0-9637072-0-5

ORDER FORM — FAMILIES AT RISK

Name _____

Title _____

Agency Name _____

Address _____

City/State/Zip _____

Phone ( ) _____

Pricing:
1-5 copies	$29.95 each
6-12 copies	$24.95 each
13 or more copies	$19.95 each

Additional discounts available for group purchase/wholesale.

Families at Risk   QTY_____ x $_____ = _____
  (Canada Add 25%)
Shipping and Handling ($2.90 copy)   _____
Minnesota residents add 6.5% tax   _____
Add applicable MNcity taxes .5%   _____
                              TOTAL _____

___Payment enclosed or
___Bill my _____VISA ___Master Card
Card #_____Exp. Date_____

Signature_____

Mail check or money order to:
  Better Endings New Beginnings
  119 N. 4th St, #401, Minneapolis, MN 55401
  612-341-9870   Fax: 612-337-5104
1993-2   Softcover   408 pages   ISBN 0-9637072-0-5

ORDER FORM — FAMILIES AT RISK

Name _____

Title _____

Agency Name _____

Address _____

City/State/Zip _____

Phone ( ) _____

Pricing:
1-5 copies	$29.95 each
6-12 copies	$24.95 each
13 or more copies	$19.95 each

Additional discounts available for group purchase/wholesale.

Families at Risk   QTY_____ x $_____ = _____
  (Canada Add 25%)
Shipping and Handling ($2.90 copy)   _____
Minnesota residents add 6.5% tax   _____
Add applicable MNcity taxes .5%   _____
                              TOTAL _____

___Payment enclosed or
___Bill my _____VISA ___Master Card
Card #_____Exp. Date_____

Signature_____

Mail check or money order to:
  Better Endings New Beginnings
  119 N. 4th St, #401, Minneapolis, MN 55401
  612-341-9870   Fax: 612-337-5104
1993-2   Softcover   408 pages   ISBN 0-9637072-0-5